TAX BY DESIGN

'Like the Meade Report, the *Mirrlees Review* is an impressive study and will be a standard reference for years to come. . . . The two volumes produced by the *Mirrlees Review* provide valuable policy analysis and demonstrate the vitality of modern public economics. They are worthy successors to the Meade Report and represent a new landmark in the field.'

Prof Sir Tony Atkinson

'A major study of utmost political relevance.'

David Walker, *Prospect Magazine*

'*The Mirrlees Review* offers a blueprint for simpler, fairer, and more efficient taxation. Taking up its proposals is a better use of government time than trying to alter the past.'

Editorial, *Financial Times*

'The outlines of what . . . a reforming chancellor might do were recently set out in an extraordinary review of the tax system led by Sir James Mirrlees of Cambridge University for the Institute for Fiscal Studies. . . . It is the most comprehensive and devastating indictment of the current situation. . . . For the main part it is hard to disagree with Mirrlees.'

Will Hutton, *Observer*

TAX BY DESIGN

The Mirrlees Review

Chair

SIR JAMES MIRRLEES

Authors

Stuart Adam, Timothy Besley, Sir Richard Blundell, Stephen Bond,
Robert Chote, Malcolm Gammie, Paul Johnson, Gareth Myles,
and James Poterba

for the

Institute for Fiscal Studies

OXFORD
UNIVERSITY PRESS

OXFORD
UNIVERSITY PRESS

Great Clarendon Street, Oxford, OX2 6DP,
United Kingdom

Oxford University Press is a department of the University of Oxford.
It furthers the University's objective of excellence in research, scholarship,
and education by publishing worldwide. Oxford is a registered trade mark of
Oxford University Press in the UK and in certain other countries

© Institute for Fiscal Studies 2011

The moral rights of the authors have been asserted

First published 2011
First published in paperback 2018

Published in the United States of America by Oxford University Press
198 Madison Avenue, New York, NY 10016, United States of America

British Library Cataloguing in Publication Data
Data available

Library of Congress Cataloging in Publication Data
Data available

ISBN 978–0–19–955374–7 (Hbk.)
ISBN 978–0–19–881638–6 (Pbk.)

Links to third party websites are provided by Oxford in good faith and
for information only. Oxford disclaims any responsibility for the materials
contained in any third party website referenced in this work.

Preface to the Paperback Edition

It is more than ten years since we came up with the original idea for *The Mirrlees Review*. As we put together the arguments for tax reform the financial crisis unfolded changing the entire economic landscape. At first we wondered whether the conclusions of the *Review* would survive such a tumultuous period in the economic lives of the majority of developed countries and their peoples. In fact they have done more than survive, they have become more pressing. The pressures on tax revenues and the strains on the tax system resulting from the crisis underlined the need for a tax system that redistributes effectively and taxes efficiently.

The Mirrlees Review has become a blueprint for reform. It is read on the screens (and sits on the shelves) of policy makers and policy researchers around the world. It has been the foundation reference for many tax proposals and continues to be so. Taking a holistic approach to reform and recognizing the complexity of interactions between the different parts of the tax system, the *Review* presented a comprehensive reform agenda. By separating the reform of personal income taxation, value added taxation, capital taxation, the taxation of housing etc., into a sequence of related but bite-sized analyses, the *Review* provided an attractive and accessible framework for coherent reform.

Steeped in the empirical tradition of the research at the Institute for Fiscal Studies, the analysis in the *Review* was based on solid evidence. It used the Mirrlees approach to the trade-off between equity and efficiency as a framework for organizing thinking. With increasing focus on inequality together with the clear requirement for efficient design, this approach could not be more relevant to today's needs. The empirical underpinning of the analysis places it firmly in the real world, recognizing the differences across individuals and firms in the way they interact with the tax system.

Since we wrote the review concerns about the boundary between incorporation, self-employment, and employment have grown, as have concerns about increasing returns to capital and the growing role of artificial intelligence. Our proposals, which bring together tax rates on different forms of income while avoiding the taxation of the 'normal' returns to investment, look to us more appropriate and more urgent than ever as these changes sweep the world.

While there has been some piecemeal progress, tax systems around the world remain in serious need of reform. Much needs to be done to rationalize them and make them ready for new challenges ahead. There continue to be many (far too many) examples from around the world of poorly designed reforms to tax systems. While important new evidence and new theory has emerged since the *Review*, the underlying ideas laid out there still stand. Arguing the case for coherent tax reform is never ending. The *Review* remains the best evidenced and most comprehensive statement of that case.

Professor Sir Richard Blundell
Director
ESRC Centre of the Microeconomic Analysis of Public Policy
Institute for Fiscal Studies

Paul Johnson
Director
Institute for Fiscal Studies

Preface

Thirty years ago, the Institute for Fiscal Studies (IFS) published a seminal review of the UK tax system, the fruits of a commission chaired by the Nobel Laureate Professor James Meade. Explaining the motivation for the review, Dick Taverne, then Director of IFS, lamented: 'For too long, ... tax reforms have been approached *ad hoc*, without regard to their effects on the evolution of the tax structure as a whole. As a result many parts of our system seem to lack a rational base. Conflicting objectives are pursued at random; and even particular objectives are pursued in contradictory ways'.

Unfortunately, this critique still holds true today. In some important respects, the tax system has evolved in the way that the Meade Report recommended, but it remains the product of often incoherent piecemeal changes rather than strategic design. The tax system has also struggled to adapt to profound changes in the economic, social, and institutional environment in which it operates. And tax design has not benefited as much as it could from advances in theoretical and empirical understanding of the way features of the system influence people's behaviour.

For all of these reasons, we felt that the time was ripe once again to ask an expert commission to take a hard look at the tax system: to try to identify the characteristics that would make for a good tax system in an open economy in the 21st century; and to suggest how the British tax system in particular might be reformed to move closer to that ideal. In doing this, we have been, if anything, even more ambitious than our esteemed predecessors on the Meade Report.

Whilst Meade focused largely on direct taxes, we set out to look across the whole tax system. Indeed, the insight that the tax system needs to be seen as a whole underlies our entire approach. And whilst we retain a clear focus on the UK, we have also tried to ensure that our conclusions are relevant internationally—we have taken more than just a UK-centred approach.

In addition, this volume is not the only output of the review. In a companion volume, *Dimensions of Tax Design*, published in 2010, small teams of experts from IFS and around the world addressed a number of key themes in tax design. That volume contains an immensely rich and varied set of analyses. The papers there provide comprehensive and state-of-the-art surveys of the economic thinking in the main areas of tax design. They also provided invaluable inspiration for this, the final report.

From the outset, the intention of the review was to take a 'big picture' view of tax design, asking what society wants the tax system to achieve and how best it might be structured to accomplish that. In this final report, we have tried both to set out an overarching vision for the tax system and to suggest some desirable incremental reforms. The starting point has been to look at the economics of the tax system, although we have received a great deal of useful input from tax lawyers, advisers, and practitioners, as well as those involved currently and in the past with the practicalities of tax design and implementation. Inevitably, some of those who spend most of their time thinking about tax design and implementation from these perspectives might have identified different priorities and have taken different approaches if they were to have undertaken this review themselves. Economists cannot claim to have all the answers to good tax design—and some of our answers will pose new questions. But thinking hard about the economics of the tax system is essential if it is to work effectively.

In addition to administrative practicality and the difficulty of turning economic intentions into robust legislative language, proposals for tax reform are, of course, constrained by politics—not least the unfortunate observation that those who lose from tax reforms tend to be vengeful while those who gain from them tend to be ungrateful. But there is no point in a review of this sort confining itself only to recommendations that we could confidently expect to receive immediate and enthusiastic support across the political spectrum—this would be a very short report if it did. Whilst we have tried to take explicit account of the political economy of tax reform in setting out a possible path to a better system, there will always be a tension to some extent between what is economically desirable and what is politically practical.

In thinking of a worthy successor to James Meade to chair a review of this ambition, there was one obvious choice: the Nobel Laureate and founder of the modern theory of optimal taxation, Professor Sir James Mirrlees. This volume is very much the joint work of Sir James and a distinguished team of eight other economists and one lawyer, who have been working together on the review for four years. In addition to myself, this team contains some of the most pre-eminent public economists in the UK, and indeed the world. It has been both a pleasure and a privilege working with them.

Even a team such as this is dependent on others. Our thoughts and views have been influenced over the period of this review by discussions at conferences, seminars, meetings, and presentations far too numerous to list. All of the 63 authors who contributed to *Dimensions* have played an important part in forming and developing the ideas that underlie our conclusions, both through the contributions they wrote and through the many discussions we had with them. We are incredibly grateful to them all. Many staff at IFS with expertise in modelling and analysing tax policy have also played a vital role. And we have relied on them to keep everything else going at IFS whilst we have spent far longer than we ever intended on this endeavour.

So I am going to resist the invidious temptation to single out any individuals who have contributed to the content for thanks. The many dozens on whose wisdom, patience, and insights we have drawn know who they are and can be assured of our deep gratitude.

There are others who have made this volume possible, though, and they do deserve special thanks. Judith Payne has once again shown her extraordinary abilities as a copy-editor, and more than ever before has had to display equally extraordinary patience. Our publishers at OUP have also shown a degree of patience, for which we thank them. At IFS, Bonnie Brimstone and Emma Hyman have both provided the highest-quality support.

Finally, one of the most important and well-known lessons from economics is that there is no such thing as a free lunch. We must therefore express our heartfelt thanks to those who have paid for this one: the Nuffield Foundation and the Economic and Social Research Council. Both have long been much-valued supporters of IFS and we hope that they will think their investment in this project worthwhile. It just remains for me to echo Dick Taverne's words on the launch of the Meade Report: 'We hope and believe that this Report will be a rich quarry for tax reformers and a valuable reference point for students of taxation for decades to come'.

Paul Johnson
Director
Institute for Fiscal Studies

The Nuffield Foundation is a charitable trust with the aim of advancing social well-being. It funds research and innovation, predominantly in social policy and education. It has supported this project, but the views expressed are those of the authors and not necessarily those of the Foundation. More information is available at http://www.nuffieldfoundation.org.

The Economic and Social Research Council (ESRC) funds research and training in social and economic issues. It is an independent organization, established by Royal Charter, receiving most of its funding through the Department for Business, Energy and Industrial Strategy.

Contents

Figures

Tax by Design

Tables

About the Authors

Sir James Mirrlees is a Fellow of Trinity College and Emeritus Professor of Political Economy at the University of Cambridge, Laureate Professor at the University of Melbourne, and Distinguished Professor-at-Large at the Chinese University of Hong Kong. He is a Fellow of the British Academy and past President of the Econometric Society, the Royal Economic Society, and the European Economic Association, and has been awarded numerous honorary degrees. Working primarily on the economics of incentives and asymmetric information, he founded the modern theory of optimal taxation, and was the joint winner of the Nobel Prize for Economics in 1996. He was knighted in 1997 for contributions to economic science. In 2009, he was appointed Founding Master of the Morningside College of the Chinese University of Hong Kong.

Stuart Adam is a Senior Research Economist at IFS. His research focuses on the design of the tax and benefit system, and he has written about many aspects of UK tax and benefit policy, including income tax and National Insurance, capital gains tax, tax credits, Incapacity Benefit, work incentives and redistribution, support for families with children, and local government finance.

Timothy Besley CBE is School Professor of Economics and Political Science at LSE and a Research Fellow at IFS. From 2006 to 2009, he was an external member of the Bank of England Monetary Policy Committee. His work is mainly in the fields of development economics, public economics, and political economy. He is a former co-editor of the *American Economic Review*, Fellow of the Econometric Society and of the British Academy, and a past President of the European Economic Association. He was a 2005 recipient of the Yrjö Jahnsson Prize, and was awarded the CBE in 2010 for services to social sciences.

Sir Richard Blundell is Director of the ESRC Centre for the Microeconomic Analysis of Public Policy at IFS. He holds the David Ricardo Chair of Political Economy at UCL. His research has been mainly in the fields of microeconometrics, household behaviour, and tax policy evaluation. He is a Fellow of the British Academy, honorary Fellow of the Institute of Actuaries, President of the Royal Economic Society, past President of the European Economic Association and of the Econometric Society, and former co-editor of *Econometrica*. A winner of the Yrjö Jahnsson Prize and the Frisch Medal, he was awarded a Knighthood in 2014 for services to *Economics and Social Science*, as well as the the Nemmers Prize in Economics in 2017.

Stephen Bond is a Senior Research Fellow at Nuffield College, Oxford, a Programme Director at the Oxford University Centre for Business Taxation, and a Research Fellow at IFS. His main interests are in corporate tax policy and the effects of corporate taxation on the behaviour of firms. Other interests include empirical research on company investment and financial behaviour, and the development of econometric methods for the analysis of panel data.

Robert Chote has been Chairman of the Office for Budget Responsibility since 2010, having been reappointed for a second five-year term in 2015. He was Director of IFS from 2002 to 2010. He was formerly an adviser and speechwriter to the First Deputy Managing Director of IMF. He was Economics Editor of the *Financial Times* between 1995 and 1999, and previously served as Economics Correspondent of *The Independent* and a columnist on the *Independent on Sunday*, where he was named Young Financial Journalist of the Year by the Wincott Foundation. He is chair of the Royal Statistical Society's advisory group on public data literacy, a governor of the National Institute of Economic and Social Research and a member of the Advisory Board of the UK Centre for the Measurement of Government Activity at the Office for National Statistics.

Malcolm Gammie CBE QC is a barrister at One Essex Court. He has been associated with IFS for almost thirty years, and is currently Research Director of its Tax Law Review Committee. He was a Senior Tax Partner at the City law firm of Linklaters until moving to the Bar in 1997, becoming a QC in 2002. He was named Tax Lawyer of the Year 2008 at the LexisNexis Taxation Awards. A past President of the Chartered Institute of Taxation, he teaches at universities in Australia, the Netherlands, and the UK. He has advised governments of several countries, the European Commission, and the OECD on tax policy issues and was awarded the CBE in 2005 for services to taxation policy.

Paul Johnson is Director of IFS. He started his career at IFS working on tax, welfare, and distributional issues. He went on to spend periods as Head of Economics at the Financial Services Authority, as Chief Economist at the Department for Education, and as a Director in HM Treasury. From 2004 to 2007, he was Deputy Head of the Government Economic Service. He has worked extensively in many areas of public economics and policy, both as a researcher and within government. Paul is currently also a member of the committee on climate change, the Banking Standards Board and of the executive committee of the Royal Economic Society and is a visiting professor at University College London.

Gareth Myles has been Professor of Economics and Head of the School of Economics at the University of Adelaide since January 2017 and a Research Fellow at the Institute for Fiscal Studies in London since 1998. He was previously a lecturer at the University of Warwick, and Professor of Economics and Director of the Tax Administration Research Centre at the University of Exeter. He is a Managing Editor of the *Journal of Public Economic Theory* and was managing editor of *Fiscal Studies* from 1998 to 2013. His major research interest is in public economics and his publications include *Public Economics* (1995), *Intermediate Public Economics* (2006), and numerous papers in *International Tax and Public Finance*, the *Journal of Public Economic Theory*, and the *Journal of Public Economics*. Gareth has been an Academic Adviser to HM Treasury and HM Revenue and Customs.

James Poterba is Mitsui Professor of Economics at MIT, President of the National Bureau of Economic Research, and past President of the National Tax Association. He is also a Fellow of the American Academy of Arts and Sciences and of the Econometric Society. His research focuses on how taxation affects the economic decisions of households and firms. He served as a member of the US President's bipartisan Advisory Panel on Federal Tax Reform in 2005, and is a past editor of the *Journal of Public Economics*. He studied economics as an undergraduate at Harvard University and received his doctorate in economics from the University of Oxford.

1

Introduction

Modern states could not exist without tax systems which raise large amounts of revenue to pay for public services. Most take in excess of 30% of national income in tax. Some take nearly half. The way in which these systems are designed matters enormously to economic welfare. Yet policymakers rarely step back to consider the design of their national tax systems as a whole. Public understanding of taxation is limited. And the political and public discussion of tax design is woefully inadequate.

Tax by Design is both an imperative and a description of our approach in this review. Our aim is to set out the principles on which a 21st century tax system should be based and then to apply them in suggesting concrete policy recommendations to improve the UK tax system. To that end, we use insights from economic theory and empirical research to discuss the impact that the tax system has on people's behaviour, and the resulting trade-offs that policymakers have to make between the various and often conflicting objectives that they might wish the tax system to achieve.

In doing so, we follow in the footsteps of the Nobel laureate James Meade, who chaired a previous review of the tax system for the Institute for Fiscal Studies three decades ago. The Meade Report[1] focused on the structure and reform of direct taxation and has been influential in debates over tax policy ever since. Dauntingly, our canvas is wider than that, covering the whole tax system and some areas of interaction with the social security and tax credit systems.

[1] Meade, 1978.

Recognizing the importance of law, accountancy, politics, psychology, and other approaches, we nevertheless approach these issues through the prism of economics. This provides us with a framework that allows us to ask, for example: What are we trying to achieve? How does the structure of the tax system influence people's behaviour? What are the economic costs and benefits of particular policy choices? And who gains and loses from them?

The tax system is, of course, both enormous and fearsomely complex. Tax legislation in the UK runs to over 8,000 pages, and the books that lawyers and accountants use to interpret it run to millions of words. Confronted with that size and complexity, we try to be as detailed in our analysis and recommendations as is necessary to guide real policy decisions, without getting tangled in the undergrowth that is comprehensible only to specialists. This means that there will always be further avenues to explore and difficult special cases to consider. But these difficult cases should not drive the overall design of the system, even if they need to be accommodated by it.

The primary task we have set ourselves is to identify reforms that would make the tax system more efficient, while raising roughly the same amount of revenue as the current system and while redistributing resources to those with high needs or low incomes to roughly the same degree. Our motivation is not to achieve textbook tidiness for its own sake, but to unlock significant potential welfare gains. To the extent that these gains show up as higher national income, they would also allow the government that achieves them to loosen the constraints under which the tax system operates—in other words, to spend more on public services or to redistribute more without lowering post-tax incomes in aggregate.

Reforming the tax system may not be easy or popular in the short term, but it holds out the prospect of significant economic gains and hence the promise of higher living standards in the long term.

Our conclusions on reform are guided by three key considerations. First is the importance of taking account of the actual economy and population on which the tax system operates. Taxes apply to people and businesses in the world as it is, not as we might wish it to be. A tax system that might have been ideal in the middle of the 20th century will not be ideal for the second decade of the 21st century. Second is the crucial insight that the tax system needs to be seen as just that—a system. While we will often address the impact of each tax separately for simplicity of exposition, we focus throughout on the impact of the system as a whole—how taxes fit together and how the system as a whole achieves government's goals. Third, we base our analysis on the modern economics of taxation. This allows us to develop a systematic conceptual approach that joins together our thinking across the whole range of taxes. What we do is rooted in economic theory that models the constraints people face and the way they behave when taxes change. Our approach is also determinedly empirical, drawing upon the best available evidence on the effects taxes have in practice.

While we have a very broad canvas, there are some important issues on which we deliberately do not take a stance. For example, we do not recommend what the overall level of taxation should be. The economic issues involved in this decision are huge, and in many ways fundamentally different from those involved in designing a tax system. The choice also involves political judgements about the appropriate role and scope of the state. Similarly, we do not take a view on the extent to which the state should seek to redistribute income and wealth from rich to poor. That again is a primarily political choice, although it does of course have economic consequences. But we do try to suggest how the state might best use the tax system to raise more or less revenue—or to redistribute more or less income and wealth—if the government of the day wished to do so.

We go about this by looking, chapter by chapter, at how to tax earnings, spending, savings, wealth, housing, and companies. In the next chapter, though, we consider the economic approach to tax reform and, specifically, some of the issues in designing the tax system as a whole. And we conclude by putting forward a long-term strategy and package of reform in Chapter 20.

In this introductory chapter, we provide just a little context which it is important to understand before we get on to the economic arguments and the analysis of each type of tax. First, there is a very high-level overview of the UK tax system and how it has evolved. Second is a quick look at some of the key changes to the economic environment in which the tax system has to operate. And third, because tax policy is made in a deeply political environment, we briefly address some of the political context and constraints on policymaking.

1.1. THE EVOLUTION AND STRUCTURE OF THE UK TAX SYSTEM

Many features of the UK tax system today would be familiar to a visitor from the late 1970s. The government still raises the bulk of its revenue from taxes on income, spending, and corporate profits and from local property taxes. At this level of generality, there are important similarities across most industrial countries.

Nevertheless, there have been some dramatic changes. Value added tax (VAT) has gained in importance relative to excise duties, the main rate having more than doubled. The income tax system has moved from joint assessment of married couples to independent assessment of individuals. Income tax rates have come down dramatically. The infamous top levels of 83% on earned income and 98% on unearned income have fallen to 50%— and in fact stood at 40% for most of the period. The basic rate of income tax has fallen from 33% to 20%. Rates of National Insurance (NI) contributions have risen, the ceiling for employer contributions has been abolished, and the structure of NI has become more closely aligned with the income tax system. Tax credits have been introduced and expanded on a grand scale. Taxation of savings has been reformed and somewhat improved. The structure of corporation tax has been overhauled: the main rate has been cut from 52% to 26% in 2011 with further cuts to 23% due by 2014; tax credits have been introduced for research and development (R&D) spending. Capital transfer tax has been replaced by inheritance tax. Domestic rates have been replaced by council tax, via the brief and disastrous experiment with the poll tax (or community charge).

Table 1.1 summarizes UK revenue forecasts for 2011–12. Nearly two-thirds of all tax receipts come from just three taxes—income tax, NI contributions and VAT. Corporation tax accounts for nearly another 9%. Fuel duties, council tax, and business rates raise just under another 5%

Notes and Source for Table 1.1:

[a] Most of the cost of tax credits is counted as government spending rather than a reduction in income tax revenue and so is not included in this table.

[b] Consists of Carbon Reduction Commitment, social tariffs, feed-in tariffs, and Renewables Obligation.

Note: Figures may not sum exactly to totals because of rounding.

Source: Office for Budget Responsibility, 2011, table 4.7 and supplementary tables 2.1 and 2.7 (available at http://budgetresponsibility.independent.gov.uk/category/topics/economic-forecasts/).

Table 1.1. Sources of UK tax revenue, 2011–12 forecasts

Source of revenue	Revenue (£bn)	Percentage of taxes (%)
Income tax (gross of tax credits)	157.6	28.0
Tax credits counted as negative income tax[a]	−4.7	−0.8
National Insurance contributions	100.7	17.9
Value added tax	100.3	17.8
Other indirect taxes		
Fuel duties	26.9	4.8
Tobacco duties	9.3	1.7
Alcohol duties	9.7	1.7
Vehicle excise duties	5.9	1.0
Air passenger duty	2.5	0.4
Insurance premium tax	2.9	0.5
Betting and gaming taxes	1.6	0.3
Climate change levy	0.7	0.1
Landfill tax	1.2	0.2
Aggregates levy	0.3	0.1
Environmental levies[b]	1.8	0.3
Customs duties	3.3	0.6
Capital taxes		
Capital gains tax	3.4	0.6
Inheritance tax	2.7	0.5
Stamp duty land tax	5.8	1.0
Stamp duty on shares	3.3	0.6
Company taxes		
Corporation tax (net of tax credits)	48.1	8.6
Petroleum revenue tax	2.0	0.4
Business rates	25.5	4.5
Bank levy	1.9	0.3
Council tax (net of Council Tax Benefit)	26.1	4.6
Licence fee receipts	3.1	0.6
VAT refunds to public sector bodies	15.0	2.7
Other taxes	5.6	1.0
National Accounts taxes	562.4	100.0

apiece, with a range of other taxes accounting for the remainder. These include indirect taxes on cars, alcohol, tobacco, betting, and various polluting activities, which between them raise around 6% of government revenues.

These shares have not changed a great deal over time. For example, at just under 30%, income tax raises much the same proportion of total tax revenue now as in the late 1970s, despite the cuts in rates. The most significant changes have been in the composition of indirect taxes, with VAT raising a larger proportion and excise duties a smaller proportion of total revenue.[2] Similar trends can be observed internationally. Between 1975 and 2008, the proportion of OECD tax revenues coming from 'general' consumption taxes rose from 13% to 20% while the proportion coming from 'specific' consumption taxes fell from 18% to 10%.[3]

By international standards, the UK raises more than most countries from income taxes—30% against an OECD average of 25%—and less than average from social security contributions—19% in 2008 against an OECD average of 25%.[4] One feature of the UK system that is unusual by international standards is its degree of centralization. In the UK, only council tax, which accounts for less than 5% of total revenue, is collected locally. Only Ireland has a smaller proportion of taxes administered below the national level. Local government in the UK is, therefore, funded to an unusually large degree by central government grants, with local taxes playing a comparatively limited role.

So, at the macro level, tax systems have many similarities in terms of how they evolve over time and between countries. But structures differ a great deal, especially in their details. It is with these structures and design features that we are concerned—what is the measure of income on which income or corporate taxes are levied; how are savings treated; how do personal and corporate tax systems fit together; how progressive is the system; what is the base for indirect taxes and how are they designed?

By getting these design features right, all countries can reap very valuable dividends in terms of both increased economic efficiency and greater

---

[2] Details of changes over time can be found at http://www.ifs.org.uk/fiscalFacts/taxTables.
[3] OECD tax revenue statistics, table C, http://www.oecd.org/document/60/0,3746,en_2649_34533_1942460_1_1_1_1,00.html#A_RevenueStatistics.
[4] OECD comparative tables, http://stats.oecd.org/Index.aspx?DataSetCode=REV.

fairness. And, to be fair, within the UK there has been progress towards a better system over the 30 years since the Meade Report was published. Tax administration has improved with the use of technology. We no longer have wholly ineffective tax rates of 98% on unearned income. The taxation of savings has been much improved. Taxation of owner-occupied housing has been rationalized. National Insurance contributions and corporation tax are now more broadly based. And, for all their unnecessary administrative problems, the introduction and extension of tax credits have helped improve work incentives, at least for some groups.

By international standards, the UK system has relatively few loopholes and opportunities for avoidance. For most people, for most of the time, the tax system works: it is not overly intrusive and it does not require vast effort to comply with—although some people on tax credits, in self-employment, or with complex financial affairs may disagree. We would certainly not characterize the British system as brutally as some characterized elements of its US counterpart back in 1995: 'The federal income tax is a complete mess. It's not efficient. It's not fair. It's not simple. It's not comprehensible. It fosters tax avoidance and cheating. It costs billions of dollars to administer. ... It can't find ten serious economists to defend it. It is not worth saving.'[5]

But the UK system is still unnecessarily complex and distorting. Tax policy has for a long time been driven more by short-term expedience than by any long-term strategy. Policymakers seem continually to underestimate the extent to which individuals and companies will respond to the financial opportunities presented to them by the tax system. They seem unable to comprehend the importance of dealing with the system as a whole. And real and effective reform remains politically extremely difficult.

The litany of poor (and expensive) tax policy decisions is a long one. It includes successive changes to the structure of capital gains tax, the introduction and abolition of a 10p starting rate of income tax, the introduction and abolition of a 0% rate of corporation tax for small companies, tax breaks for film-making (which were estimated by HM Treasury to have cost an astonishing £480 million in 2006–07), and the introduction and abolition of the 'poll tax'. Moreover, the failure of political

---

[5] Hall and Rabushka, 1995, 2.

will means that council tax bills in England and Scotland in 2011 still depend on estimates of the relative values of different properties in 1991.

These are the issues on which the rest of this book concentrates. But before focusing down on tax design, it is important also to raise our sights towards the economic context in which tax design must occur.

1.2. THE CHANGING ECONOMIC CONTEXT

Tax systems need to be designed for the economies in which they are to operate. Developing economies often need to put a very heavy weight on collectability of taxes. Economies rich in natural resources need a tax system designed to reflect that. Highly federalized countries will have tax systems in which the setting of taxes at the sub-national level is a major concern. In the UK context, two changes have been so profound over the past three decades that they really do deserve some special attention. The first is the great increase in inequality and associated changes to the labour market. The second is the change in the structure of the economy—the move from manufacturing to services and the changing international context.

1.2.1. Inequality and Labour Market Change

Income and wealth are much less equally distributed across the population than they were 30 years ago. It is rarely understood quite how dramatic that change has been, nor how important it is for the formulation of public policy in general and tax policy in particular. The increase in income inequality over the past 30 years—concentrated in the 1980s—has been without historical precedent.

In 1978, when the Meade Report was published, someone at the 90th percentile of the (household) income distribution (in other words, richer than 90% of the population) had an income three times that of his or her contemporary at the 10th percentile of the distribution. Now, he or she has five times as much as that person. In 1978, 7.1 million people had incomes

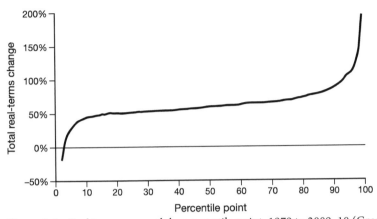

Figure 1.1. Real income growth by percentile point, 1979 to 2009–10 (Great Britain)

Notes: The change in income at the 1st percentile is not shown on this graph. Incomes have been measured before housing costs have been deducted.

Source: Authors' calculations using 1979 Family Expenditure Survey and 2009–10 Family Resources Survey.

below 60% of the contemporary median—the person in the middle of the income distribution from rich to poor. By 2009–10, that figure stood at 13.5 million.[6]

The change is perhaps best illustrated by a chart such as Figure 1.1, which shows how real income levels changed at each percentile (i.e. in each successive 1%) of the overall income distribution between 1979 and 2009–10. The continuous upward slope of the graph shows that the higher up the income distribution we go, the higher was the rate of income growth. The real income of someone at the 5th percentile of the distribution (poorer than 95% of people) was about 30% higher in 2009–10 than that of the equivalent individual in 1979. Increases were around 50% at the 25th percentile, 70% at the 75th percentile, and more than 100% at the 95th percentile.

The incomes of the very richest have risen very fast indeed and well away from those of the rest of the population. Of the 30 million or so people who pay income tax, about 200,000 are expected to record incomes of over £200,000 a year in 2011–12, with a further 160,000 having incomes between £150,000 and £200,000.[7] And the richest taxpayers pay a large portion of

---

[6] All figures are measured *after* housing costs and *net* of tax payments and benefit receipts, and are drawn from IFS analysis available at http://www.ifs.org.uk/fiscalfacts.php.

[7] HM Revenue and Customs income tax statistics, table 2.5, http://www.hmrc.gov.uk/stats/income_tax/table2-5.pdf.

Tax by Design

total tax revenues: in 2011–12, the top 1% of income tax payers are expected to pay nearly 28% of all the income tax revenue received by the government,[8] more than double the 11% contributed by the richest 1% back in the late 1970s. The poorer half of income tax payers pay just 10% of all income tax. This extraordinary level of, and increase in, the contribution of the richest is not down to a more progressive income tax structure—quite the reverse, as higher rates of income tax are much reduced. Rather, it is down to the very high levels of income enjoyed by the richest relative to those received by everyone else.

Table 1.2. Weekly net household incomes in the UK, 2009–10

	Mean	10%	25%	50%	75%	90%	Percentage in the UK
Families with children							
Lone parent, working	£471	£269	£325	£410	£520	£723	4.2%
Lone parent, not working	£318	£179	£230	£287	£375	£497	3.9%
Couple, both working	£867	£409	£531	£703	£954	£1,356	21.7%
Couple, one working	£737	£299	£380	£496	£683	£1,010	11.0%
Couple, not working	£390	£130	£256	£347	£465	£610	2.9%
Families without children							
Single, working	£653	£215	£328	£520	£826	£1,205	11.1%
Single, not working	£437	£97	£166	£316	£562	£898	6.4%
Couple, both working	£840	£393	£523	£700	£941	£1,312	13.4%
Couple, one working	£578	£225	£322	£459	£689	£988	5.4%
Couple, not working	£372	£111	£221	£310	£470	£698	2.5%
Pensioners							
Single	£294	£134	£175	£237	£335	£507	7.2%
Couple	£487	£225	£293	£388	£563	£818	10.4%
All	£637	£207	£320	£500	£755	£1,098	100.0%

Source: Authors' calculations based on 2009–10 Family Resources Survey.

[8] HM Revenue and Customs income tax statistics, table 2.4, http://www.hmrc.gov.uk/stats/income_tax/table2-4.pdf.

To provide a better understanding of the overall distribution of income, Table 1.2 provides a detailed snapshot of how *net* household incomes vary by family type. It also provides a picture of the distribution of different family types and of how incomes vary within family types. It illustrates, for example, the preponderance of two-earner couples, both with and without children.

Of course, one cannot directly compare the incomes of different family types to understand relative living standards—couples with children need more money to live on than the single childless. As one would expect, couples where both are in work have higher average incomes than any other group, and single pensioners have lower incomes. But there are big overlaps between all the groups—no group is universally poor, none is universally rich. Differences within family types are generally greater than differences between family types. The tax and welfare systems need to be designed with all these aspects of the shape of the population and their incomes in mind.

Returning to the question of how the income distribution has become more dispersed over time, much of this change has resulted from a more dispersed distribution of wages. In large part, this reflected a rise in the financial pay-off people received from achieving higher levels of skills and education, though inequality has also increased dramatically within groups of people with similar skills. Changes in labour market institutions—for example, falls in trade union membership—have also played a part. Levels of unemployment and non-employment also rose rapidly, and whilst official measures of unemployment fell back from the early 1990s, levels of labour market participation for men are still well down, reflecting greater numbers giving illness or disability as the main reason for not working. Over 90% of working-age men were in employment or self-employment in the mid-1970s; only 76% were in 2009.[9]

As we shall see in Chapter 3, and as illustrated in Table 1.3, most of the reduction in the proportion of men in work occurred among younger and older age groups. This fact matters enormously in thinking about tax design.

Nobody should argue that the tax and benefit system alone *created* these extraordinary changes in participation. Recessions in the early 1980s and

---

[9] Office for National Statistics, *Social Trends 2010*, figure 4.4, http://www.statistics.gov.uk/downloads/theme_social/Social-Trends40/ST40_2010_FINAL.pdf.

Tax by Design

Table 1.3. Percentages of men and
women in work by age, 1979 and 2008

Age group	Men (% in work)		Women (% in work)	
	1979	2008	1979	2008
16–24	75	58	60	56
25–54	93	88	60	75
55–64	80	67	38	49
All, 16–64	87	78	56	67

Source: Calculations from Labour Force Survey
(with thanks to Antoine Bozio).

early 1990s changed the labour market beyond recognition. But the incentives in the tax and benefit system can prolong or ameliorate the impact of such shocks. The recovery after recession in the employment rates of older workers in the UK is very different, for example, from that in France, where responses to the recession of the 1980s included generous pension and layoff arrangements that have not been unwound. Only 19% of men aged 60–64 in France were in work in 2009 compared with 57% of such men in the UK.[10]

Another profound change has been in the role of women in the labour market. Their employment rates have risen—with particularly big increases among married women with children. As more families with children have, and aspire to have, both parents working, the impact of tax rates and benefit withdrawal rates on the potential second earner becomes more important. A tax system that encourages a primary earner to work by providing tax credits, which are then withdrawn as *family* income rises, may discourage a second earner from working. There is powerful evidence that it is women with children whose work patterns tend to be most sensitive to the structure of the tax and benefit system. Making working a bit less attractive relative to not working tends to have little impact on whether men (at least those aged 25–50) work, but rather more impact on the behaviour of women.[11]

But there has also been a divergence in the experience of different types of women in the labour market. While employment rates have increased for

---

[10] Blundell, Bozio, and Laroque, 2011.

[11] See Meghir and Phillips (2010) and Brewer, Saez, and Shephard (2010).

women in general, they fell to a very low level for the rapidly growing group of single mothers, recovering somewhat after 1997. The tax and benefit system has responded to, and also helped to shape, these social changes, with the introduction and subsequent extension of tax credits doing much to increase the incentives for single parents to move into work. These sorts of issues were much less salient on the policy agenda at the time of the Meade Report in the 1970s. Tax system design needs to be robust to social and labour market changes. A system that provided generous benefits to non-working lone parents has, perhaps unsurprisingly, helped facilitate a great increase in their numbers when economic opportunities for the low-skilled dried up and social norms changed.

Overall levels of inequality in incomes are also important. In the first place, of course, we might want to design the tax system to do more work to ameliorate the underlying growth in inequality. Second, with relatively high levels of non-employment and low-wage employment, the impact of the tax and benefit system on both incentives to work and the incomes of low earners will matter a lot. We come back to this issue in some detail in Chapter 4. Third, and more generally, a given tax system will have very different effects depending upon the distribution of incomes among the population on which it is imposed—the effects of a higher rate of income tax on earnings over £100,000 are likely to matter more if there are more people earning over £100,000.

Similarly, the distribution of wealth naturally has consequences for our views about taxing wealth. If, for example, the distribution of inheritances were reasonably equal, then the argument put by many for taxing inheritance on equity grounds would fall away. If, as has indeed happened, the distribution of wealth and inheritances becomes more unequal, then the case for a progressive inheritance tax becomes stronger.

1.2.2. Structural Change and Globalization

Changes to incomes and in the labour market themselves, in part, reflect structural changes in the economy. These have, of course, been considerable over the period since the publication of the Meade Report. Financial and business services accounted for 32% of national income in 2008 compared with just 15% in the late 1970s.[12]

One very salient example of a change that has mattered enormously to the tax system has been the increased role of financial services. Their share in gross value added increased by more than half between 1980 and 2007. This makes their exemption from VAT an increasingly important tax design issue—one to which we devote Chapter 8. It also increased the government's reliance upon them for corporate and income tax revenues—a fact that has been painfully underlined in the subsequent financial crisis. The banking, finance, and insurance sector was responsible for £12.3 billion of corporation tax in 2007–08—27% of all corporate tax revenues and nearly three times what might be expected on the basis of its share in the economy. That total fell to £7.5 billion in 2008–09, just 17% of that year's corporation tax.[13] The Treasury's own analysis confirms that the 'increased importance of the financial sector' is one of the factors responsible for 'increased sensitivity of receipts to the cycle'.[14] It estimates that fully half of the total increase in tax receipts enjoyed by the government in the five years running up to 2007–08 was due to taxes raised on the housing and financial sectors.[15] Unfortunately, the sensitivity of these sectors to the economic cycle meant that annual tax receipts from them fell by a full 1½% of GDP[16] (over £20 billion) in the two years from 2007–08 to 2009–10.

The shape of the economy affects the appropriate tax policy. Tax structures may also help shape the economy, possibly in unwelcome ways. The public finances suffered as a result of the financial crisis. But the tax system may itself have played at least some, albeit minor, role in creating or facilitating the crisis. The tax treatment of housing and financial services, the very low taxes on capital gains, and the incentives in the corporate tax system for debt

[12] Measure refers to gross value added at current basic prices. Data from *The Blue Book*, ONS. For the most recent statistics, see table 8.3, *The Blue Book*, 2010 edition. Time series available in OECD STAN database (variable id 'VALU').

[13] Source: HM Revenue and Customs corporation tax statistics, tables 11.4 and 11.5, http://www.hmrc.gov.uk/stats/corporate_tax/menu.htm.

[14] HM Treasury, 2008, 17.

[15] Including corporate taxes, stamp duties, and income tax and National Insurance raised from earnings from financial sector employees.

[16] Source: HM Treasury, 2010a, box C3.

funding over equity funding are all possible culprits. We address all these issues in the relevant chapters.

Meanwhile, technological advances have transformed the productive economy from which taxes are raised, while at the same time making it easier to administer the tax system and easier to structure activities to avoid tax. The role of technology in cross-border transactions and the implications of this for the tax system are touched on in Chapters 7 and 18. This and other aspects of globalization mean that cross-border issues more generally are now much more important than they were 30 years ago, and this has undoubtedly placed new constraints on what is possible within the tax system. Real complexities are also created by increased globalization—for example, regarding the appropriate treatment of companies by national tax systems. How does one think of taxing a Swiss company that develops a drug in a research facility in the UK, manufactures it in Belgium, and mainly sells it in the US?[17]

But despite some predictions to the contrary, countries are not being forced inexorably to tax less in an increasingly globalized and competitive world economy. Between 1975 and 2008, taxes rose as a proportion of national income in virtually every OECD country. On average, the tax take rose from 29.4% to 34.8% of national income. In no OECD country was there a significant fall in the tax take over this period. And the variation between countries is striking. Denmark, Sweden, the US, and Japan are all rich countries. In Denmark and Sweden, taxes accounted for 48% and 46% of GDP respectively in 2008. In the US and Japan, they accounted for only 26% and 28%.[18] There is no straightforward relationship between the total tax burden and economic performance.

It clearly remains possible for a successful economy to raise 40% or more of national income in tax despite the pressures of globalization. But, within the total tax take, we might expect that governments would find it more difficult to raise taxes from internationally mobile companies and people. In fact, revenue from corporation taxes has more than held up over the past 40 years—corporate income taxes accounted for 9% of tax revenues across the

---

[17] Example used by John Kay at a conference at the London School of Economics in May 2011.
[18] All figures from OECD tax revenue statistics, table A, http://www.oecd.org/document/60/ 0,3746,en_2649_34533_1942460_1_1_1_1,00.html#A_RevenueStatistics.

OECD in 1965, 8% in 1985, and 10% in 2008.[19] As we have already seen, the richest—and probably most mobile—1% of taxpayers in the UK are expected to contribute 28% of income tax revenue in 2011–12, compared with just 11% in 1979.

This is not to imply that there are no problems. The fact that some people and companies may be able to avoid taxes because of their international mobility might mean that the burden is in some respects now borne more unequally, and inefficiently, than before. In addition, if there is a sense that some individuals or companies can avoid paying tax because of their domicile or ability to shift profits around, then acceptance of the system and belief in its equity may be damaged.

However, the resilience of these revenues highlights the fact that while it has certainly become easier and cheaper to cross national borders—and it may well continue to become so—it is far from costless. Policymakers must therefore decide whether to design the tax system in readiness for the day when globalization does indeed make it much harder to raise revenue from mobile individuals and businesses, or whether to collect the revenue while they can and reform the system once these pressures have materialized. Either way, for the time being, as we discuss in Chapters 4 and 18, globalization certainly affects the rates at which we can reasonably hope to tax high incomes and the feasible structure of corporate taxes.

1.3. THE POLITICS OF TAX REFORM

Of course, it is not just the economic context that matters for tax policy. Politics matters too. It is not possible to understand the structure or development of the tax system outside of a political context—not least because making people obviously, or apparently, worse off is rarely good politics, at least in the short term. And almost all tax reforms make some people worse off.

This makes much reform rather harder to put into practice than to design. Worse, when governments need money they tend to look to raise revenue in

---

[19] Source: OECD tax revenue statistics, table C, http://www.oecd.org/document/60/0,3746,en_ 2649_34533_1942460_1_1_1_1,00.html#A_RevenueStatistics.

ways that make the losers relatively hard to identify. This results in complexity and poor policy. A classic example is the way in which governments have often used *fiscal drag* to increase income tax revenues whilst cutting the basic rate of income tax. Fiscal drag occurs where tax bands and allowances are raised more slowly than the incomes on which the tax is levied. Fiscal drag was largely responsible for an increase in the number of income tax payers from fewer than 26 million in 1996–97 to a peak of 32.5 million in 2007–08.[20] The number paying the higher (40%) rate of income tax roughly doubled from 2 million to nearly 4 million over the same period. These are big changes that mean that some people have gained less from higher wages and salaries than they would otherwise have done—a fact that appears to get little play in the policy debate.

For similar reasons, rates of National Insurance contributions have risen while income tax rates have fallen. Compared with income tax, NI taxes a narrower range of income, does less to redistribute resources from rich to poor, and is less transparent to the citizen, especially that part which is levied formally on employers. As we will see in Chapter 4, its original function as a payment for rights to contributory benefits such as the state pension has been almost entirely eroded, although governments exploit the lingering belief that the link is still a strong one. Indeed, a remarkable number of people believe that NI in some way pays for the National Health Service—a misapprehension played upon in 2002 when an increase in NI rates was announced purportedly to pay for higher spending on the NHS.

Raising revenue through more radical reform has proved difficult. The attempt in the early 1990s to impose VAT at the full rate on domestic energy consumption created a political backlash strong enough to see the policy partially abandoned, and then further reversed by the next government. This reform was to have been accompanied by measures that left most poorer people better off, while still raising revenue overall. But people who spend unusually large proportions of their income on energy would still have been left worse off. That makes the change difficult to achieve in political terms. But suppose we started, as some countries do, in a world where VAT was already levied on fuel. To abolish it would not look like an attractive policy. The rich spend more in absolute terms on fuel than do the poor. Hence,

---

[20] HM Revenue and Customs income tax statistics, table 2.1, http://www.hmrc.gov.uk/stats/ income_tax/table2-1.pdf.

abolishing an existing tax would look like subsidizing the well-off to increase their consumption of a polluting good. But we rarely think of the fact that failing to tax something is, in effect, subsidizing its usage. This thought experiment is also valuable in demonstrating the extent to which tax is one area of public policy where the 'tyranny of the status quo' is strongest. Changing it substantively is difficult. We hope to challenge some of that tyranny here.

Whilst the attempt to place full VAT on domestic energy consumption was unsuccessful, weakness in the public finances can sometimes facilitate beneficial tax reform. If people accept that there is a need to raise money, then there is no escaping the need to leave some people worse off. The period after 1992—the last significant episode of fiscal consolidation—saw the final phasing-out of mortgage interest relief and the married couple's allowance as well as big increases in petrol and tobacco duty, policies that might have been hard to implement in the absence of a widely recognized need for fiscal policy to be tightened. The recent crisis has seen less reform—increases to rates of NI, to higher rates of income tax, and to the VAT rate have been used to raise money. That is something of a shame. As Rahm Emanuel observed when he was President Obama's Chief of Staff, one should never let a crisis go to waste.

Some poor policymaking can be understood, if not excused, by reference to straightforward political pressures. The complexity of the tax system and lack of public understanding make poor policy, and indeed explicit misrepresentation by government, much too easy. They can lead to an undesirable narrowing of public debate and a fixation on a few easy-to-understand elements, such as the basic rate of income tax. This then drives out wider considerations. Governments have also been accused of relying on so-called 'stealth taxes', taxes where the incidence on individuals is unclear. The use of such taxes can itself undermine trust in the tax system.

The significant and growing complexity of business taxation makes public debate in this area very limited indeed. Corporation tax and business rates between them raise almost as much as VAT, nearly half as much as income tax, and nearly three times as much as fuel duties. And, of course, they must all be paid by individuals in the end. Their lack of salience and the lack of debate are regrettable. The increasing complexity of corporate taxes also leaves room for a great deal of corporate lobbying to introduce and extend special treatments and allowances. The story of the R&D tax credit is a good example, as commented on by Alt, Preston, and Sibieta (2010, 1205):

Enacting tax policy can create interest groups and constituencies in favour of that policy. Even when they did not lobby for the policy in the first place, ... they will lobby both for persistence and extensions that allow policy to drift from its original motivation. Therefore, any potential tax reformer should remember that any new allowances enacted or favourable tax treatments provided to particular groups could prove difficult to remove and may be distorted into something different over time.

Good tax policy requires an open, transparent, and well-informed public debate based on credible data. Poor public understanding is a constraint on good tax policy. It allows poor-quality analyses of policy reforms to gain prominence.

Good tax policy also requires effective processes within government. At present in the UK, there is arguably a more limited level of discussion and debate about tax policy within government, and as part of the legislative process, than in other areas of policy. The Treasury is a remarkably powerful institution and, as far as tax policymaking is concerned, has become more powerful in recent years, as it has taken on much of the policymaking capability of HMRC. There are no checks and balances within the executive. The Chancellor effectively takes sole responsibility for his Budget.[21] The legislature—parliament—also effectively has a rather weak oversight role, particularly when it comes to some of the more complex areas of tax policy.

Finally, we should not forget one very important change to the political and institutional environment for tax reform over the past 30 years: the growing integration of the European economies and the increased influence of the European Union (EU). Thirty years ago, the main role of the European Union (then the European Economic Community, EEC) was to bring down trade barriers. Since then, it has grown in importance and it now exerts an important influence on UK tax policy, both directly and indirectly. Member states of the EU retain sovereignty over direct taxation, but are nevertheless required to exercise it in accordance with EU law. In recent years, there have been a number of successful legal challenges to elements of national corporate income taxes at the European Court of Justice (ECJ). This has prompted a variety of reforms—for example, changes to anti-avoidance

---

[21] In the UK, it has always been *his* Budget. We have had women Foreign Secretaries and Home Secretaries and most famously a woman Prime Minister, but never a female Chancellor.

rules designed to limit the ability of multinational firms to shift their taxable income between countries with different tax rates.

The EU has greater formal influence over indirect tax policy, including explicit limits on the ability of countries to alter their VAT rates. This reflects the fact that an open market in goods requires some kind of system for dealing with differential tax treatment of goods across country borders. Issues of dealing with VAT and excises within the EU are central to our discussion in Chapter 7.

1.4. CONCLUSIONS

Taxes, like death, are unavoidable. But we can design our taxes. We are not bound to have a tax system as inefficient, complex, and unfair as our current one. To improve things, we need to see the system as a whole, we need to design the system with a clear understanding of the population and economy on which it operates, and we need to apply economic insights and evidence to the design. We also need a much more informed public debate and a much better set of political processes than the ones we currently have.

Our purpose in this book is to create a framework and directions for reform. In the next chapter, we explain in more depth what we mean by an economic approach. We then look in turn at taxes on earnings, taxes on consumption, environmental taxes, taxes on savings, taxes on wealth, taxes on land and property, and taxes on companies. In the final chapter, we draw all this together to propose an overall set of reforms to the tax system which, we believe, has the potential to make us all better off and free us from at least some of the shackles created by the complexities and inefficiencies of the current system.

2

———

The Economic Approach to Tax Design

This is not a book about how much public spending or how much redistribution there should be. Nor are we addressing the question of what is the right total level of taxation. But if we are to have public spending, we must also have taxation. And taxes are certainly not costless. It is impossible to take 40% or more of national income in tax—as most advanced economies do—and not have major economic impacts. Most taxes influence people's behaviour in unhelpful ways and all reduce the welfare of those who bear their economic burden. The challenge for tax design is to achieve social and economic objectives while limiting these welfare-reducing side effects.

Most of this book looks at particular aspects of the tax system—how it treats earnings, savings, consumption, companies, housing—and asks how taxes can be designed to minimize their negative effects on welfare. To understand these particular effects, we need a framework for thinking about how to judge a tax system and how to think about its effects on welfare, distribution, and efficiency. These are the subjects of this chapter.

We begin by looking at how we might evaluate a tax system, in particular with respect to its impact on distribution and on economic efficiency. Starting with a clear understanding of what our objectives might be is crucial, and the issues are not altogether straightforward. We then move on to the really important insights of the economic approach to tax design and ask how we achieve and trade off different objectives. That is the focus of Section 2.2, where we introduce the optimal tax approach to tax design and also introduce some important 'rules of thumb', one of which—a presumption in favour of neutrality—plays a very important role throughout this book.

2.1. ASSESSING TAX SYSTEMS

How do we identify a good tax system when we see one? One way is to see how it stacks up against a 'checklist' of desirable properties. The most famous is the four canons of taxation set out by Adam Smith in *The Wealth of Nations*:

(i) The subjects of every state ought to contribute towards the support of the government, as nearly as possible, in proportion to their respective abilities ...

(ii) The tax which the individual is bound to pay ought to be certain and not arbitrary ...

(iii) Every tax ought to be levied at the time, or in the manner, in which it is most likely to be convenient for the contributor to pay it.

(iv) Every tax ought to be so contrived as to take out of the pockets as little as possible, over and above that which it brings into the public treasury of the state.

These recommendations may command near-universal support but they are not comprehensive, and they do not help with the really difficult questions which arise when one objective is traded off against another. The way we formulate the objectives of a tax system is to say that *for a given distributional outcome*, what matters are:

- the negative effects of the tax system on welfare and economic efficiency—they should be minimized;
- administration and compliance costs—all things equal, a system that costs less to operate is preferable;
- fairness other than in the distributional sense—for example, fairness of procedure, avoidance of discrimination, and fairness with respect to legitimate expectations;
- transparency—a tax system that people can understand is preferable to one that taxes by 'stealth'.

As we will see below, simple, neutral, and stable tax systems are more likely to achieve these outcomes than are complex, non-neutral, and frequently changing systems. But simplicity, neutrality, and stability are desirable because they promote these ultimate outcomes, not in their own right.

A good tax system will not just limit negative effects on efficiency. It will also promote economic welfare by dealing with externalities which arise when one person or organization does not take account of the effects of their actions on others. Taxes can affect this behaviour by altering the incentives for certain sorts of behaviour, most notably when polluting activity is taxed to reduce the total amount of pollution.

We have formulated the question of the assessment of a tax system by suggesting what to take into account *given* a desired distributional outcome. So understanding how to think about the impact of the tax and benefit system on the distribution of income (or welfare) is clearly central. We look at that first. We then focus on the effects of the system on economic efficiency. This is the most important constraint on tax system design. We then turn to issues of fairness and transparency, and the other positive effects a tax system can have on correcting market failures such as externalities.

2.1.1. The Impact of the Tax and Benefit System on the Distribution of Income

People differ, of course, in the extent to which they value redistribution. But assessing the degree to which redistribution is achieved by any given tax system is by no means easy.

The redistributive impact, or progressivity,[1] of a tax system is often judged by looking at how much tax individuals or households pay relative to their income over a relatively short time period—rarely more than a year. But people's incomes tend to change over their lives, which means that this approach can be a poor guide to how progressive the tax system is relative to a person's lifetime income. This is important in practice.

Focusing on snapshots of current income can paint a misleading picture. A tax change that hits someone who is earning a lot this year will seem progressive. But if this is an unusually good year for the person in question,

---

[1] Progressivity has a particular meaning for economists, set out in Box 2.1.

Box 2.1. Progressivity

There is a strict economic definition of progressivity. A tax is said to be progressive when the average tax rate rises as the tax base rises. So an income tax is progressive when the average tax rate rises as income rises. (We usually think in terms of annual income, though lifetime income may be the better base against which to assess progressivity.) This is the case when the marginal tax rate (the proportion of an additional pound of income paid in tax) is higher than the average tax rate (the proportion of total income paid in tax). In effect, the higher marginal tax rate pulls the average rate up towards it.

The simplest way to achieve progressivity in an income tax is to have a tax-free allowance before tax starts being payable. To see this, suppose the first £10,000 of income is free of tax and all further income is taxed at 20%. Someone earning £20,000 has a marginal tax rate of 20%. Their average tax rate is 10%.[a] Someone earning £100,000 would still face a marginal rate of 20%, but their average rate would be 18%. Thus a *flat tax*—an income tax charged at a single constant rate above a tax-free allowance—is progressive, as long as there is a tax-free allowance. This income tax can be made more progressive by (i) increasing the tax-free allowance, (ii) increasing the single rate of tax, or (iii) introducing one or more higher marginal tax rates on higher incomes. Progressivity does not, however, require that the marginal tax rate keeps on increasing as incomes rise.

[a] The tax payment is £2,000, which is 20% of £20,000 – £10,000. This gives the average tax rate as $(2,000 / 20,000) \times 100 = 10\%$.

then the lifetime effect may be quite different. Variation in earnings across years is not uncommon. Over a lifetime, earnings tend to start low when young, rise for a period of time, and then flatten off or fall in later years until retirement. However, this pattern is highly variable among people, depending on the nature of their occupation and skills. Ideally, we should judge the distributional impact of the tax system over a lifetime rather than at a point in time.

To illustrate this variation, consider a policy aimed at increasing taxes on the 1% of the population with the highest incomes. Generally, around 4% of 45- to 54-year-olds are in this group at any time, which suggests that *at least*

Table 2.1. Position of individuals in the income distribution by quintile in 2008 in relation to 1991

	Position in 1991				
	Bottom quintile	Second quintile	Third quintile	Fourth quintile	Top quintile
Bottom quintile	34	23	18	15	10
Second quintile	25	26	21	18	11
Third quintile	18	22	21	20	18
Fourth quintile	16	17	21	23	23
Top quintile	8	12	18	25	38

(Position in 2008)

Source: Department for Work and Pensions, 2010e, table 4.1 (BHC).

4% of people are in the highest-income 1% at some point in their lives.[2] Table 2.1 illustrates the point further by showing how people moved around the income distribution between 1991 and 2008. The population is divided into quintiles (fifths) from poorest to richest and the table shows how position in the distribution changed over the 17-year period. For example, whilst 34% of those in the poorest quintile in 1991 were also in the poorest group in 2008, 8% of them had made it into the top quintile by 2008 and a further 16% were in the second-richest group. Conversely, while 38% of those in the richest group in 1991 were still there in 2008, 10% were in the poorest quintile by then and 11% in the second-poorest.

These lifetime variations help to explain why the treatment of savings is so important when deciding how to tax—and why such attention is paid to the issue in this volume. People accumulate and run down savings and debts to smooth their spending over time and, as we shall see in Chapter 13, it is in principle possible to treat savings so as to approximate taxing people on their lifetime income.

While we might ideally like to know how people's lifetime tax payments vary according to their lifetime resources, we cannot usually observe either lifetime tax payments or lifetime resources. However, the use of current expenditure alongside current income can help in assessing the degree of redistribution achieved by the system. If people borrow and save to maintain

[2] Source: Our calculations based on Brewer, Saez, and Shephard (2010).

a stable level of consumption in the face of varying income, then current expenditure may be a better guide to lifetime resources than current income. Of course, consumption needs also vary over the life cycle. Often, current income and current expenditure provide complementary indicators; much can be gained by looking at both and considering what each measure reveals. As well as the use of income or expenditure to assess whether a household is 'rich' or 'poor', we must also consider whether to assess the household's tax payments as a proportion of its income or its expenditure. It can be misleading to look at current payments of all taxes as a percentage of current income: in general, a better guide to the lifetime distributional impact is to look at income taxes as a percentage of current income and expenditure taxes as a percentage of current expenditure. In the absence of data on whole lifetimes, snapshots of current income and expenditure must be used judiciously to give a rounded impression of the distributional impact of taxes.

In assessing progressivity, we should also look at the impact of the system as a whole rather than at its individual components. This assessment should include welfare benefits and tax credits because it is the overall effect of the tax and benefit system that matters. Making the system as a whole progressive does not require every individual tax to be progressive. Different taxes are designed to achieve different ends. Some current taxes are quite regressive—taxes on tobacco, for example—because they are intended to achieve a different purpose, not progressivity. This is an issue we return to in Chapters 6 and 9, where we consider the structure of VAT and argue that zero-rating goods consumed disproportionately by poorer households is not a good way to achieve progressivity in the tax system as a whole.

A further issue concerns the need to think about whether to judge the redistributive effect (and other effects) of taxes on an individual or a household basis. Economics has developed a comprehensive theory of individual behaviour. But most people live in households—with spouses, partners, children, or parents. Over time, the structure of households is fluid because of birth, death, and break-up. This poses difficulties for tax design. Current UK practice is not consistent: income tax and National Insurance contributions are levied on individuals, while benefits and tax credits are paid to households. Economic theory has similar difficulties in reaching a consensus on the right approach.[3] The issues that are raised by the individual/household distinction cannot be easily resolved. We consider them a little more in the context of direct taxes and benefits in Chapters 3 and 5.

The Burden of Taxation

An even more fundamental question regarding the redistributive effect of taxes relates to how we assess who is actually bearing the economic burden of the tax. That need not be the person or organization that makes payment to the tax authority. Nor need it fall on the *statutory bearer*—the person or organization legally responsible for the tax. To illustrate the difference between these two concepts, note that under the Pay-As-You-Earn (PAYE) system in the UK, the worker is the statutory bearer of income tax, but the firm remits the tax. The allocation of the statutory burden of taxation among taxpayers is called the *legal incidence*. The legal incidence of a tax can be very different from the *economic incidence* or who *bears the burden*. An individual bears the burden of a tax to the extent it makes him or her worse off (that is, causes a loss of welfare).

The fact that income tax is remitted by employers does not alter the fact that at least part of the economic incidence falls upon employees. Similarly, although employers and employees formally pay separate National Insurance contributions on the employees' earnings, the eventual economic incidence of the contributions is likely to be the same. Employers make decisions based on the total cost of each employee, and employees are interested in their salary after tax. In the long run at least, the allocation of National Insurance contributions between employee and employer should make no difference to the number of people the employer chooses to employ or the after-tax wage of the employee.

In many cases, the economic incidence of a tax can be hard to identify. For example, when the excise duty on alcohol is increased, the price of drinks in the shops need not rise by the amount of the tax increase. Firms that produce and supply alcohol may choose to absorb part of the tax increase and only pass a fraction of it on to consumers. Or consider stamp duty on the sale of a house. It is natural to assume that, since stamp duty is paid by the purchaser,

---

[3] The literature is surveyed by Apps and Rees (2009).

it does not make the seller any worse off. But this is wrong. Suppose there is a completely fixed supply of houses. The price of a house will then be determined by demand—the willingness of buyers to pay a certain amount. Imposing stamp duty will not change the total (price plus stamp duty) that buyers are willing to pay, so the price must fall: the economic incidence falls on the seller of the property, not the purchaser.

Allocating the economic incidence between firms and consumers is only the first step of the analysis. The second step follows from observing that firms are just legal entities and enjoy no economic well-being beyond that of their customers, employees, and shareholders. The impact of any tax paid by a business—either in the sense that the tax is remitted by the business or in the sense that it is the statutory bearer of the tax—can be traced ultimately to a reduction in the economic welfare of the owners of the business, the suppliers of capital and other inputs to the business, and/or the employees. So, even though the first step allocates part of the incidence to firms, the burden must ultimately be borne by some combination of customers, employees, and shareholders. The final distribution of the burden is nearly always unclear to the individuals concerned, and often difficult for economists to determine. This no doubt helps explain why, in virtually all countries, the statutory liability of employer social insurance contributions is much greater than that of employee contributions, and why taxes on firms are often seen as 'victimless'. They are not. They are in the end paid by customers, employees, and shareholders. We cannot emphasize this point too much.

2.1.2. The Effect of Taxes on Economic Output and Efficiency

Prices play a central role in the modern market economy, as signals that reflect and guide the decisions of consumers and producers. Taxes disrupt these signals by driving a wedge between the price paid by the buyer and the price received by the seller. For example, income tax means that an employer pays more for an hour of work than the employee receives for it, while VAT means that a retailer receives less for a product she sells than her customer pays for it.

By increasing prices and reducing quantities bought and sold, taxes impose losses on consumers and producers alike. The sum of these costs almost always exceeds the revenue that the taxes raise—and the extent to which they do so is the *deadweight loss* or social cost of the tax. A key goal for tax design is to reduce the deadweight loss of the system as a whole as far as possible.

The size of the deadweight loss is related to the *elasticities* of demand and supply for the item being taxed—in other words, the extent to which demand and supply respond to changes in price.[4] The more elastic is the demand for a product with respect to its price, the more a given tax increase will reduce demand for it. High elasticities therefore mean large deadweight losses for a given change in tax.

There are generally two channels through which tax changes influence behaviour: the income effect and the substitution effect. Consider the impact of an increase in a tax on earnings on people's work decisions. The tax will reduce the income that people receive for a given number of hours of work, encouraging them to work more to limit any decline in living standards. This is the *income effect*. But the tax will also make an hour of work less attractive relative to an hour of leisure than it had been previously, encouraging people to work less. This is the *substitution effect*. The two effects work in opposite directions. For any individual tax change, it is impossible to say a priori which will dominate. But for revenue-neutral changes to taxes, income effects will tend to roughly balance out on average: money given away to some people must be matched by money taken from others, so a positive income effect for one group will be offset by a negative income effect for another (though it is possible that one group might be more responsive than the other). Substitution effects will not necessarily balance out in this way.

In addition, most empirical work[5] suggests that it is the substitution effect that dominates. So additional taxes on labour earnings typically reduce hours of work. But the strength of these effects differs between different types of worker. Often they affect behaviour less at the *intensive margin*—whether to

---

[4] If an increase in price prompts no change in behaviour, then the elasticity of that behaviour with respect to price is 0. If a price change leads to a behavioural change of the same magnitude—e.g. a 10% increase in the price leads to a 10% fall in demand—then the elasticity has value –1. An elasticity of –0.1 means that a 10% increase in price reduces demand by only 1%.

[5] See e.g. Blundell and MaCurdy (1999) and Meghir and Phillips (2010).

work slightly more or less—than at the *extensive margin*—whether to undertake paid work at all. This is an important insight which we dwell on in the next chapter.

It is not just income taxes that have income and substitution effects on decisions about working. The introduction of a uniform VAT means that less can be purchased with any given income (giving rise to an income effect) and that each hour of work can purchase fewer goods (leading to a substitution effect). What matters in deciding whether and how long to work is what can be purchased with the earnings received. So increasing taxes on goods and services reduces the pay-off to working more in the same way that increasing direct taxes does—a fact sometimes overlooked by those who argue we should move away from income tax and towards indirect taxes to preserve work incentives.

Measuring these effects is crucial if we are to assess the impact of tax changes. In general, we would want to levy taxes at higher rates where they will have less effect on behaviour. If there are groups of people who respond to high tax rates more than others, then we might want to shape the tax system accordingly. A 'one size fits all' tax system is economically costly when people respond differently to tax changes. The question is whether the benefit of designing the tax system in a more tailored way outweighs the operational and compliance costs of a more complicated system. One needs to be sure that all the possible behavioural effects are well measured and then trade off the gains from differentiation against the costs. In many circumstances, there is sense in demanding a high standard of proof that divergences from uniform treatment are worthwhile.

Importantly, taxes can have long-term or *dynamic* effects as well as immediate effects on behaviour. We know, for example, that higher petrol taxes have more effect on petrol consumption and less effect on miles driven in the long run than they do in the short run, because people respond by demanding more fuel-efficient cars and manufacturers respond by supplying them. We know rather less about the dynamic effects of some other important policies. For example, benefits supporting low earners, such as the Working Tax Credit in the UK, are effective at getting more people into work in the short run. But what effect do they have in the long run, perhaps by influencing the decisions people make about education or training? We know little about these effects and they may be more significant than many of those that we do understand much better.

That there are major effects of taxes on behaviour is undeniable. This fact has led economists to think about the potential for two sorts of taxes that should not have these effects—lump-sum taxes and taxes on economic rents:

- Lump-sum taxes are taxes liability to which cannot be altered by any change in behaviour. In principle, the liability to a lump-sum tax can be linked to any unalterable individual characteristic (such as a taxpayer's age or some measure of inherent ability). In practice, such characteristics tend to be either undesirable as the sole basis for determining someone's liability or impossible to define or measure. Levying the same lump-sum tax on everyone is, in principle, feasible, but the lack of any link between the tax and ability to pay renders it politically unattractive, to say the least (even though we should care about the redistributive consequences of the tax system as a whole rather than of any individual component of it). Public reaction to the UK community charge, to give the poll tax its official title, is a graphic illustration of this point.

- Taxing pure economic rents does not create a distortion. An economic rent arises when a resource generates a high return relative to its next-best use. When a rent arises, taxing it should not alter behaviour, since only the excess income over the next-best use is taxed. Rent is most often associated with the return to land. Land derives its value from its location and this makes the return to owning land attractive to tax, because the owner cannot move it elsewhere. We address the issue of the taxation of land value in Chapter 16. Rents may also arise from the right to extract scarce and valuable natural resources and among innovators, artists, sports stars, and firms with recognizable brands.

Neither lump-sum taxation nor the taxation of rents is a terribly helpful guide to most policymaking. The fact is that most taxes will alter behaviour and reduce both welfare and economic output.

2.1.3. Taxes Designed to Change Behaviour

In general, taxes reduce welfare. But there are situations in which taxes are deliberately used to change behaviour in order to promote welfare. Environmental taxes designed to tackle spillovers, or externalities, are the most obvious examples. Where one economic agent imposes costs (or indeed benefits) on others and does not take account of those effects when deciding on his actions, the tax system can be used to ensure that he 'internalizes' the costs he imposes. In other words, one can use a tax to provide a price signal which would otherwise be absent. It is because the tax can stand directly in place of a market price signal that taxation can be a particularly efficient way of dealing with externalities. We discuss these issues in some detail in Chapter 10 and with specific reference to climate change and to motoring in Chapters 11 and 12 respectively.

It is not just with respect to reducing environmental damage that taxes are used to alter behaviour. Excessive drinking can cause costs to society, and most countries impose taxes on alcohol well above the usual rates of consumption tax. High taxes are also imposed on tobacco. In fact, particularly in the case of tobacco, these taxes are not wholly, or perhaps even largely, designed to reduce harm to others. They are imposed in recognition of the harm that individuals can do to themselves, particularly in the face of addictive substances.

There is also likely to be a large dose of straightforward paternalism in such taxes. Governments (rightly or wrongly) do take a view as to how they would like their citizens to behave and adjust tax systems accordingly. This may be the best explanation for the zero-rating of books for VAT purposes in the UK.

Some actions by individuals or companies can also create benefits for the wider economy that are not recognized in the price signals they face. Again the tax system can help to compensate for the absence of such price signals. A good example is the R&D tax credit, which is found in a number of countries and provides a subsidy to companies investing in research and development (R&D). Any one company's R&D is likely to create positive spillovers for the rest of the economy. But companies won't take that into account in making their own decisions. A tax incentive might give them the price signal to do an amount of R&D closer to that which they would have done if they were taking account of the positive spillover effects of their own decisions. Tax systems that recognize these sorts of spillovers effectively may have quite significant effects on growth and welfare. As we suggest in Chapter 12, for example, there are potentially large environmental benefits associated with a tax system better designed to capture the externalities associated with driving.

2.1.4. A Fair and Transparent Tax System

Whether the tax system is seen as 'fair' is not simply a question of redistribution. Fairness of procedure, fairness with respect to legitimate expectations, and fairness in treating similar people similarly also matter:

- A tax system is more likely to command respect, and so be widely accepted, if the process that determines tax levels and structures is seen to be fair. This is what we mean by fairness of procedure. The process and institutional context for tax policy matter, not just because they are likely to determine the outcome, but also because they affect how that outcome is perceived and even how well it is complied with. A process of policy determination is needed that ensures that even those who lose out accept the legitimacy of the outcome. Workable democratic procedures have this at their heart and are supported by a process of debate and consultation. We do not spend much time on this issue in this volume, but its importance should not be underestimated.

- Another sort of fairness, which can be related to this concept, is that of fairness with respect to legitimate expectations. Tax changes that impose unexpected losses relative to previous expectations can be perceived as 'unfair'. This is most often true of capital taxes, which, for example, might reduce the net expected capital gain from an asset, or indeed might reduce the value of assets into whose value a particular expectation of the tax rate has been capitalized. In fact, any tax change can have this kind of effect— my investment in my own human capital may become less valuable as a result of an increase in income tax, in just the same way as my house may become less valuable as the result of a tax change. While legitimate expectations matter, effects of this kind can be very hard to avoid and have to be weighed in the balance against potential longer-term benefits.

- More closely related to the idea of distributional fairness is the notion that the tax system should treat similar people in similar ways. This has been dubbed *horizontal equity* by economists. The difficulty with applying this concept in practice is defining similar individuals, and different countries define them in different ways. For example, the UK taxes individuals with similar earnings in similar ways whether or not they are part of a married couple. In contrast, the US taxes married couples with similar earnings in similar ways regardless of how individual earnings are split between the partners.

It is not even obvious that the tax system should treat people with similar levels of earnings in similar ways. If one person can earn £500 a week in 20 hours, then she is better off than someone who needs to work 40 hours to earn the same amount. Perhaps she should pay more tax. People also differ in their needs—perhaps because of health status or number of dependent children—and tax systems might reasonably differentiate accordingly. In France, for example, the number of children influences the amount of tax paid.

Ideas of fairness can also be applied to the range of economic activities that are taxed. A neutral tax system—one that taxes similar activities similarly—avoids giving people encouragement to shift from high- to low-taxed activities in a way that is economically costly. It also avoids discriminating between people who make different (but inconsequential) choices. There is unlikely to be any legitimate case for taxing silver cars at a higher rate than blue cars—that seems simply unfair. There are aspects of different VAT rates in the UK tax system which can also be seen as unfair. Those who like biscuits (subject to VAT) are in this sense unfairly treated relative to those who prefer cakes (not subject to VAT). Neutrality between goods can promote fairness as well as efficiency.

None of these senses of fairness is absolute. More or less any tax proposal will face some charge of unfairness viewed from some perspective. But this is best dealt with by trying to be open and transparent about the arguments and evidence that underpin the proposal. Tempting though it may be to disguise who gains and who loses, in the long run the cause of sensible reform is best served by being honest about the objectives and consequences of what is being proposed. This is among the reasons for seeing transparency as an important part of a good tax system. Lack of transparency can easily lead to poor process, to outcomes that lack fairness in some dimension, and eventually to a lack of legitimacy, which can fuel non-compliance.

2.2. ACHIEVING AND TRADING OFF OBJECTIVES

We want a tax system that does not unnecessarily discourage economic activity, that achieves distributional objectives, and that is fair, transparent, and administratively straightforward. How can we achieve these outcomes and how should we trade them off? In particular, how should we think about balancing efficiency loss against equity?

The question of how to trade off these objectives is the subject of optimal tax theory, to which we come in the next subsection. We then look at three 'rules of thumb'—neutrality, simplicity, and stability—which might help to guide the design of a tax system. We distinguish these from the basic criteria for a good system because, whilst generally likely to be desirable, these are not ends in themselves in the way that progressivity and efficiency are goals of the system. Rather, they are instrumental guidelines, the following of which is likely to help achieve the final goals.

Before delving into these issues, though, it is worth stressing one point which will be crucial to the messages in much of this volume—that in achieving the overall objectives of the tax system, it is important to consider all taxes (and transfer payments) together as a system. It is the redistributive impact of the system as a whole which needs to be measured and judged. Not every tax needs to be progressive.

2.2.1. Optimal Taxation and Social Welfare

Economists have expended much effort in the study of 'optimal taxation'. Much of this work is abstract and mathematical, and this volume is not the place for a detailed exposition of optimal tax theory.[6] Nevertheless, it is important for the approach taken here. It provides a methodology for designing tax systems to achieve the best outcome given the constraints

---

[6] For which see e.g. Tuomala (1990).

faced by the government. As such, it is the foundation of the idea of 'tax by design'.

Optimal tax theory is all about the choice of a system of taxation that balances efficiency losses against the government's desire for redistribution and the need to raise revenue. It provides a way of thinking rigorously about these trade-offs, and ensuring that value judgements reflecting concerns about income distribution and well-being are made explicit while the efficiency costs of achieving that redistribution are properly taken into account. The seminal theoretical work in this area[7] was carried out some years ago—in the early 1970s—but its impact on practical tax design continues to build, along with important developments in both theory and applications. The theory of optimal taxation begins by clarifying the *objectives* of policy and identifying the *constraints* under which it operates. The tax system that best achieves the objectives whilst satisfying the constraints is identified as the optimum.

What matters for these value judgements is the effect of the tax system on welfare rather than only on income. With a revenue-neutral reform, our judgement of the effects will depend upon the weights we give to the welfare of people at different points in the income distribution. The resulting changes in tax liabilities will redistribute income from some points in the distribution to others and this will be welfare enhancing only if we weight welfare gains to the recipients more strongly than we weight welfare losses from the losers. If we care more about the welfare of the poor than the rich, then, other things equal, we will prefer a world in which the rich pay more tax. How much more will depend on how much we care about inequality.

We also need to evaluate behavioural changes induced by changes in tax rates. In general, welfare is lost by taxing someone who responds to that tax by reducing their work effort or by putting effort into reorganizing their affairs to reduce tax payments. These behavioural responses constrain what can be achieved via the tax system. There are costs associated with work, but if individuals would have chosen to work in the absence of taxation, then the benefits of work must outweigh those costs, and reduction in work effort as a result of taxation is welfare reducing. This loss of welfare is referred to as the *deadweight loss* or *excess burden of taxation*. It too has distributional aspects

[7] Mirrlees, 1971.

since the magnitude of the deadweight loss will differ across the income distribution. We can assess the magnitude of the deadweight loss at any point by considering how much more tax we could have raised from individuals at that point without leaving them worse off if, hypothetically, we had had the information needed to raise those taxes without basing them on income. The size of that loss will depend both on those individuals' wages and on the responsiveness of their behaviour to tax changes. A beneficial tax reform is one that has a positive impact on social welfare taking all of these effects into consideration.

It is worth being a little more concrete about how optimal tax theory helps to inform views about the best system.

Consider the structure of tax rates on labour earnings. A good deal of the concern about progressivity in the tax system is motivated by the fact that inequality is primarily determined by disparities in employment opportunities. A progressive system will set taxes on earnings at higher levels for higher earners. Such higher tax rates impose distortions and disincentives. But these need to be balanced against the gain in achieving progressivity. Just how far tax rates can be raised depends on how responsive earnings are to tax changes. And, as we have already seen, we may want to vary tax rates where some groups are known to be more or less responsive to taxation over the life cycle. An income tax system is optimal when the gain through desired redistribution, and raising revenue, is offset in an optimal way against the cost induced by lowering labour earnings.

Optimal taxation also helps in thinking through the right structure of tax rates on goods and services. The principle is the same as for labour earnings. There are distortions induced by taxes but there are also distributional effects. But optimal tax theory does not always support taking the latter into account by differentiating rates on commodities. And this is a perfect example of why the systemic view is important. If taxes on earnings are well designed, then they can do the heavy lifting as far as achieving progressivity is concerned.

We need to approach the taxation of savings with a similar mindset. Higher earners tend also to be higher savers. But this does not automatically imply that they should face a higher tax rate on their savings. That again depends on looking at the system and assessing whether progressivity can be achieved in a more efficient way by adjusting the rate schedule. In general, taxing savings is an inefficient way to redistribute. As we shall see in Chapter 13, though, there may be circumstances—for example, where saving behaviour reveals something additional about the underlying earning potential of individuals—in which taxing the return to savings does become optimal.

In general, there is little clear rationale for trying to use the tax system to influence when people consume in their lifetime rather than focusing on progressivity based on the overall resources that they have available. This logic is particularly compelling when inequality is mostly generated by labour market opportunities and an optimal income tax can be designed. Particularly where inherited wealth makes a big difference to the welfare of some groups, on the other hand, taxes on wealth transfers may be part of an optimal system—an issue we explore further in Chapter 15.

A broad concept of optimality should include other considerations too. Administrative and compliance costs should ideally be brought into optimal tax calculations.[8] Social welfare can embody value judgements other than those associated with the distribution of welfare. Most governments put a high rate of tax on tobacco products to discourage smoking even if most smokers belong to low-income groups. Such multiple objectives imply the need to think about how a tax system performs with respect to several criteria simultaneously.

Ideally, we would begin tax design by coherently laying these objectives out and constructing the tax system that best reflects these goals.

As we have seen, the optimal tax approach emphasizes all the constraints under which the government must operate, particularly those imposed by the behavioural responses of individuals and companies to the taxes that are levied. Constraints are also imposed on the tax system by the government's *limited information*. Limited information impacts directly upon the choice of *what* to tax. For example, governments can observe people's actual earnings but cannot know about each individual's underlying ability to earn income. This is a constraint, since it would arguably be better to tax on the basis of ability to earn rather than actual earnings since the former is not subject to manipulation in the face of tax changes. On the whole, we would expect high-ability individuals to earn more. But they could choose to earn less if

---

[8] Shaw, Slemrod, and Whiting (2010) provide a very insightful analysis.

the taxes that they face are too high. Optimal taxes on earnings have to take this into account and it limits the degree of progressivity that can be achieved.

Much recent progress in tax analysis has come from a better understanding of these responses and the constraints they place on policy. In some areas, better economic understanding and better policy have gone hand in hand. But there are some constraints and behavioural responses that governments still appear to struggle to comprehend. In subsequent chapters, we shall see how the tax and benefit system has led to much lower employment rates among older men in France than in the UK (Chapter 3), how the pattern of savings is influenced by the tax treatment of different forms of savings (Chapter 13), how generous tax treatment led many self-employed people in the UK to incorporate (Chapter 19), and how the tax credit system has quite different effects on the work incentives of different groups of people (Chapter 4). There are many, many more examples of apparently unintended effects of tax design on people's behaviour.

Optimal tax theory has its limitations. It cannot readily take account of many of the concepts of fairness that we have discussed. And whilst it can be adapted to incorporate issues of administrative costs, in practice it rarely is. It is nevertheless a powerful tool and, throughout this volume, the conclusions of optimal tax theory will inform the way we discuss policy. We will see in Chapter 3 what optimal tax theory has to say about the structure of marginal income tax rates. It informs our discussion on the structure of indirect taxes generally in Chapter 6 and of VAT specifically in Chapter 9. Optimal tax theory will also be important to our discussion of the tax treatment of savings in Chapters 13 and 14 and of the taxation of company profits in Chapters 17, 18, and 19.

2.2.2. Rules of Thumb

Beyond the overall objectives of a tax system, and the details of the trade-offs that optimal tax theory forces us to think about, there are several instrumental guidelines, or rules of thumb, which can help in system design. Other things being equal, a tax system is likely to be better if it is simple, neutral, and stable. But none is necessarily the right thing to aim for at all times, which is why they are guidelines against which to assess a tax system rather than always objectives.

Neutrality

A neutral tax system is one that treats similar activities in similar ways. For example, a system that taxes all consumption the same would achieve neutrality over choices that people make about what to consume. A system that treats all income the same achieves neutrality over the form in which income is received. A system that taxes all forms of savings the same achieves neutrality over the form in which savings occur. A system that imposes the same present value of tax on consumption now and consumption in the future will be neutral with respect to the decision over whether to save or consume out of current income.

So a neutral system minimizes distortions over people's choices and behaviour. In general, it therefore minimizes welfare loss. In a non-neutral tax system, people and firms have an incentive to devote socially wasteful effort to reducing their tax payments by changing the form or substance of their activities.

But the promotion of neutrality in the tax system is not always an appropriate end for policy. There are times when a lack of neutrality is valuable. We do not want to be neutral towards environmental bads—we want to tax them more than other things. There is likely to be a case for offering tax relief for corporate research and development activity. There are strong and respectable arguments for treating some forms of consumption— particularly those, such as childcare, that are complementary to work—more leniently than others. The same is true of some forms of savings. We do not, in the end, believe that pension savings should be taxed in exactly the same way as other savings.

But the tax system in the UK, like that of most modern economies, is full of non-neutralities which are hard to justify, wasteful, and ripe for reform. It distorts choices between debt and equity finance, between capital gains and other forms of capital income, between owner-occupied housing and other assets, between different forms of remuneration for work effort, between different forms of carbon emissions, and between different forms of business organization. These distortions create complexity, encourage avoidance, and add costs for both taxpayers and governments.

They are not generally inevitable and often stem from the lack of clear underlying economic principles in the design of the tax system. The problems that stem from differential treatment of debt and equity under the corporate and personal tax systems illustrate this point, reflecting the lack of any economic principle that distinguishes these two forms of business finance. Similarly, if the tax system draws unnecessary dividing lines between items that are difficult to differentiate or are close substitutes—such as dividends and salary for owner-managers of small firms or cash and fringe benefits for National Insurance contributions—taxpayers will be gifted opportunities to select the more favourable tax option. In these circumstances, governments commonly respond with an over-elaborate, tangled web of legislation that seeks precise definitions to minimize avoidance opportunities and ends up concealing within its length and complexity whatever policy objective the legislation was originally designed to achieve.

Very often, greater neutrality leads to both greater simplicity and greater fairness. Achieving it requires a holistic view of the tax system which recognizes the interdependencies between different parts of the tax system— personal and corporate taxes, taxation of dividends and earnings, taxation of debt and equity. In particular, it requires a consistent understanding of what it is we are trying to tax—the tax base. In the UK, as in most countries, the tax base for individuals remains a mix between an income base and an expenditure base, creating distortions in people's decisions over savings. The corporate tax base both creates distortions over how firms raise funds— between debt and equity finance—and how, where, and to what extent they invest, and fails to be well aligned with the personal tax base, creating distortions over the legal form that small businesses in particular may choose.

So while there will be occasions on which we might want to diverge from neutrality, and occasionally we will argue that specific non-neutralities are justified, in general these do not align with the non-neutralities we observe in the tax system. But aiming to increase the efficiency of the tax system by moving towards greater neutrality remains a good principle in guiding reform.

Simplicity

It is often said that a good tax system should be a simple one. And surely a simple one is better than a more complex one if it achieves the same ends. A simple tax system is likely to be relatively transparent and impose low administrative costs.

But the world is complex enough that no tax system is likely to be truly simple. And just as there are occasions when we might want to deviate from neutrality, so there will be times when we have to accept more complexity. Indeed, the two concepts are linked—a neutral tax system will tend to be a simple one and vice versa. The less differentiation there is between the taxation of similar activities, the more neutral and the simpler the system will be.

Lack of simplicity and neutrality invites tax avoidance. Individuals and firms strategically arrange their affairs in response to changes in taxes, so as to reduce their liability even though the underlying economic nature of the activities does not change. But if complexity creates opportunities for avoidance, so avoidance activity invites a complex set of rules to close loopholes. And so the process of avoidance becomes a game of cat and mouse played between the revenue authority and taxpayers. Each revision to the system is followed by the introduction of new avoidance schemes. Some schemes are demonstrated to be illegal while others are rendered redundant by new revisions to the legislation. The process then begins anew. The perpetual revision of tax law and litigation against avoidance schemes add to complexity and to the cost of implementation. Compliance costs are increased by the search for avoidance schemes and the consequences of litigation. Avoidance activity results in an addition to deadweight loss. A tax system that minimizes avoidance activities—which a simpler and more neutral system will often, though not always, do—will tend to reduce the total economic cost of taxation.

Avoidance (and evasion—illegal activity that leads to lower tax payments) also cost the revenue authorities money directly. How much is inevitably hard to judge, but HMRC estimated the *tax gap* between actual revenues and the amount that the authorities think they should be receiving for 2008–09 at approximately £42 billion, which is 8.6% of the tax that should have been collected.[9] This is similar in value to the US estimate of a direct tax gap of 14% in 2001 and a Swedish estimate of 8% in 2000. Much larger tax gaps have been estimated for developing countries.[10]

As well as creating direct compliance costs and opportunities for avoidance, complexity can lead to costly behavioural change. As behavioural economists have been stressing for some time, complexity can also create additional unintended consequences. People are inclined to focus on problems that are easier to solve, on today rather than tomorrow, and on what other people are doing. This is an important issue for the political economy of tax reform and is one reason for the inordinate public and political focus on one particular aspect of the system—the basic rate of income tax. Complexity makes useful and informed debate difficult. Unfortunately, governments often increase complexity as they add provisions and special cases to the tax system.

If policymakers have multiple objectives for the tax system, then a substantial degree of complexity is unavoidable. Even so, we do need to justify with quite strong evidence any move towards greater complexity. In all that follows, we start from a presumption in favour of simplicity if it is clear that doing so generates significantly greater benefits than costs.

In any case, any tax system will involve a compromise between what policymakers would like to do and what they are able to do with the information and administrative tools available. The ability to levy a tax relies on being able to measure the relevant tax base—the quantity of income, expenditure, and so on—against which tax liability is assessed. The standards currently achieved have required major investment in administrative and compliance capacity. The costs of administering the tax system, and complying with it, matter a great deal. They impose significant limitations on tax design. At one extreme, we can't tax people directly on what we can't observe directly—for example, their ability. More pragmatically, not even all forms of income are easily assessed. The incomes of the self-employed are difficult to measure, as are some forms of capital gains.

The main bases for tax have changed over time as society has evolved. In the 19th century, most revenue was raised from excise and customs duties. Taxes on income only came to provide the majority of revenues in the

---

[9] HM Revenue and Customs, 2010d.
[10] Schneider and Enste, 2000.

second half of the 20th century. In many developing countries, levying an income tax is very challenging and, by western standards, high proportions of revenue come from taxing what is easily taxed—typically, internationally traded products as they pass through ports. Such taxes distort trade and are particularly damaging to economic efficiency.

In the longer term, what is considered feasible may change again. Might our reliance on taxing income and spending decline once other options become available? Might changes in our capacity for making genetic assessments of ability (or longevity or willingness to work) provide a new base for taxation? Perhaps not. But it is worth bearing in mind that relying on taxes levied on income seemed equally unlikely 300 years ago.

Stability

Tax systems that continually change impose greater compliance costs on those who are taxed. They lead to difficulties in making long-term plans. Lack of stability can impact negatively on investment decisions by firms and on saving and investment decisions by individuals. Changing capital taxes in particular can lead to a sense of unfairness if the current structure and rates are capitalized into asset values. For all these reasons, a stable tax system is, other things equal, preferable to an unstable one.

But this must not be an excuse for permanent inaction. There are costs associated with change. But there are also costs associated with keeping a poorly designed system in place. This is a book about tax reform and we are not writing it to conclude that the virtue of keeping everything as it is outweighs the virtue of seeking something better. As we will see later on, the scale of the welfare gains available as a result of reform is, in some cases, very large indeed.

But there is virtue in having a clear and transparent method of making changes to the tax system, and a clear long-term strategy for change. Certainty is valuable, and does not require stagnation. So the process of tax reform matters as well as the content. And the failure of successive governments in the UK and elsewhere to be clear about the long-term strategy and direction for tax policy has been very costly.

2.3. CONCLUSIONS

The concepts discussed in this chapter are at the heart of the economic approach to tax design and are used frequently in this volume. In the UK, many of the problems involving lost revenues, unintended consequences, and policy U-turns that have characterized tax policy in recent decades have resulted from ignoring or giving too little weight to these ideas. And the UK is not alone.

If there are three ideas worth holding on to from all those discussed in this chapter, they are:

- *The need to think of the tax system as just that—a system.* The way that different taxes fit together matters, as does being clear about the role of each tax within the system.

- *The central role of redistribution in the tax and benefit system.* The extent of that redistribution will be determined by society's preferences and the impact of the system on efficiency. The trade-off between redistribution and efficiency is at the centre of very many debates about tax policy.

- *The importance of neutrality as a benchmark.* While we don't always want neutrality, it is often valuable and will always be an important benchmark for assessing the system.

In some ways, it is remarkable that governments in rich countries manage to raise such substantial tax revenues from a largely compliant population. If they want to continue to do so, they will need to take account of these principles and ensure that the tax system is seen to be efficient and fair as part of the bargain between citizens and government. As we will see in the chapters that follow, there are real opportunities to improve the current system—to make it more coherent and efficient and often, as a result, more equitable. In some cases, this involves getting rid of obvious anomalies; in some cases, it means fundamentally rethinking the tax base; in some cases, it means taking proper account of the system as a whole; and in some cases, it just means making better use of our understanding of different groups' responses to incentives in designing the system.

3

———

The Taxation of Labour Earnings

The taxation of earned income accounts for more revenue than any other form of taxation across most OECD countries. Alongside the benefit and tax credit system, it also does most of the heavy lifting in redistributing resources from richer to poorer households. Not surprisingly, it occupies a special place in debates about levels and structures of taxation.

In this and the next two chapters, we look in detail at earnings taxation, and relevant aspects of the welfare benefit system which are intended to support those who are out of work or earning little. In this chapter, we provide some relevant background on earnings inequality and labour force participation. We go on to explain the inevitable trade-offs between redistribution to those with low incomes and/or high needs and the need to promote economic efficiency, especially work incentives. We consider how to think about those trade-offs in an optimal tax framework and in the context of the family, not just the individual. The key role that the limited information available to the government plays in restricting policy options is emphasized. In the subsequent chapters, we look explicitly at reform options for the UK.

In doing that, we need to bear in mind throughout that it is social welfare we are interested in. That depends on much more than measured income. There is a cost to people in working more hours. Needs vary and income may be more valuable to some than to others. Governments will tend to value income being transferred from rich to poor and society may care about how (un)equal is the well-being of different people.[1] Measures of social welfare tend to acknowledge that society generally places more weight on gains to the poor and needy.

The maximization of this measure of 'social welfare' stands a long way from the maximization of some crude measure of aggregate income. It allows for work effort, needs, and inequality. However, by acknowledging that people may respond to tax changes by adjusting the level of their work effort, it also explicitly acknowledges the importance of incentives to generate income in the economy. A balance has to be struck between the level of work effort generating earnings in the economy—the size of the pie—and the degree of redistribution to the poor and needy.

If society cares about inequality and poverty, there will always be some willingness to sacrifice a part of national income in order to achieve distributional objectives. The fundamental design issue is to minimize such losses while raising sufficient revenue to finance desired public services and satisfy concerns over inequality and poverty.

Our goal in this chapter is to lay out principles for balancing economic efficiency and redistributive objectives in a coherent tax and benefit system. To do this, we will need to address two key questions. The first is positive: how do individuals' earning decisions respond to taxes and benefits? The second is normative: given how people behave, what tax and benefit system would best meet policy goals?

In choosing a set of tax rates, a government may not be concerned only with redistribution and economic efficiency. It may also make social judgements—for example, wishing to favour the working poor over the non-working poor, or married parents over cohabiting ones. Even so, some tax arrangements dominate others by achieving the particular social objectives in a more efficient manner.

Over the longer term, the taxation of earnings can also affect choices over careers, education, and training and over whether to be self-employed or an employee. All affect the pattern of earnings and employment over the working life of an individual. Consequently, in our design of the rate

---

[1] The objective of maximizing the aggregate of all individuals' well-being is the form of utilitarianism proposed by Bentham (1789). At the other extreme, the view that so much weight should be given to equality that the quality of a society should be judged only by the well-being of its worst-off member is often attributed to Rawls.

Tax by Design

schedule, we have to balance a broad set of incentive effects with the goal of raising tax revenue and redistributing to those with greater needs. By looking at the tax system as a whole, the aim of this book is to present recommendations for a tax system that provides a coherent treatment of savings, pensions, human capital investments, and earnings.

3.1. EMPLOYMENT AND EARNINGS

In this section, we describe very briefly two important underlying trends which will inform much of the rest of what we say about earnings taxation— changes in employment rates and changes in the distribution of earnings.

Employment rates have changed a lot over the last three decades. Figure 3.1a shows this for men in the UK. There is a systematic fall in employment at nearly all ages over this period. Even though employment rates edged up in the last decade before the recent financial crisis, they did not come close to

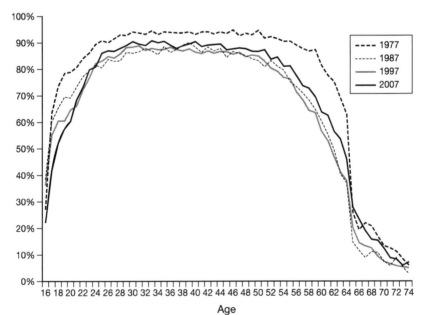

Figure 3.1a. Employment rates by age in the UK over time: men

Source: Blundell, Bozio, and Laroque, 2011.

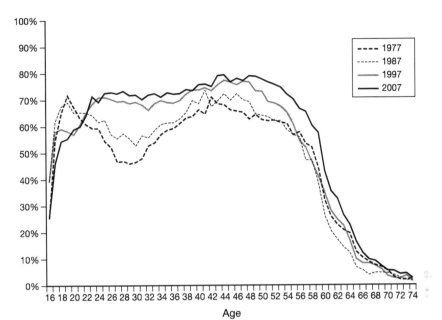

Figure 3.1b. Employment rates by age in the UK over time: women

Source: Blundell, Bozio, and Laroque, 2011.

matching the employment rates for men in the 1970s. At younger ages, the increase in education has resulted in a continual fall in employment at ages up to 21. At older ages, there has been rather more in the way of 'catch-up'. In 2007, UK men over 65 were employed at close to the same rate as they were in 1977.

For women, almost everything is reversed. Figure 3.1b shows that apart from those younger than 22, there is a higher rate of employment in 2007 than at any point since 1977. The fall in employment among women in their 20s and early 30s that was so distinct in the 1970s has largely disappeared.

The rise in female labour supply reflects a fall in fertility rates, a trend towards later marriage, and an increase in the proportion of mothers in paid work. The decline in male employment reflects less-educated and lower-skilled workers withdrawing from the labour market in the years before they reach state pension age, as well as more early retirement among higher earners (often with generous pension arrangements). Finally, the expansion of post-16 school and university/college education has increased the average

age at which working life starts and increased the skills of the working population.

Looking at labour supply differences across countries can also be very informative.[2] Figure 3.2a demonstrates that the main differences between the UK, France, and the US in male employment are concentrated at younger and older ages. Perhaps most remarkable is the stability in employment rates among men aged between about 30 and 54 across all three countries. Figure 3.2b suggests a little more variation in female employment but a strikingly similar alignment among women in their peak earning years (their 30s and 40s) across these three countries.

For many women with children in particular, a key question is not just whether to work (a decision at what we call the extensive margin), but how many hours to work (a decision at the intensive margin). Figure 3.2c shows that hours of work still dip at ages when there tend to be younger children in the family, and this dip is more pronounced in the UK than in the US or

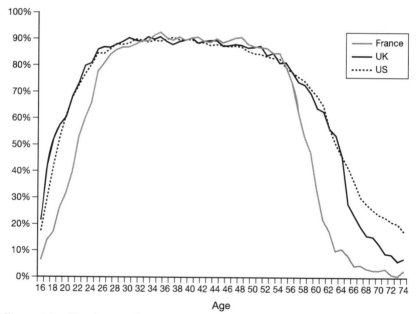

Figure 3.2a. Employment by age in the UK, the US, and France in 2007: men

Source: Blundell, Bozio, and Laroque, 2011.

---

[2] See Blundell, Bozio, and Laroque (2011) for a more detailed breakdown of hours and employment across the UK, the US, and France.

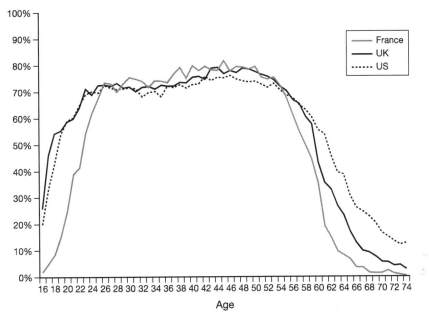

Figure 3.2b. Employment by age in the UK, the US, and France in 2007: women
Source: Blundell, Bozio, and Laroque, 2011.

France. These patterns in labour supply at the extensive and intensive margins for women with children reflect, in part, the different tax systems operating in the different countries. Differences at the extensive and intensive margins will bear heavily on our suggested directions for earnings taxation reform in the next chapter.

A dominant characteristic of these figures is the strong variation in labour supply for men and for women in their late 50s and 60s. In most developed countries, labour market activity has fallen at older ages—with some reversal recently. In the UK, individuals who are relatively poor or wealthy are more likely to leave employment early than those in the middle of the wealth distribution. Figure 3.3 shows this clearly. Broadly speaking, the poor are more likely to move onto disability benefits, while the rich are more likely to retire early and live on private pension income. Those in the middle are more likely to remain in paid work.

Figure 3.1a suggested that, in the years before the recent financial crisis, the trend toward early retirement among men in the UK had partly reversed.

Tax by Design

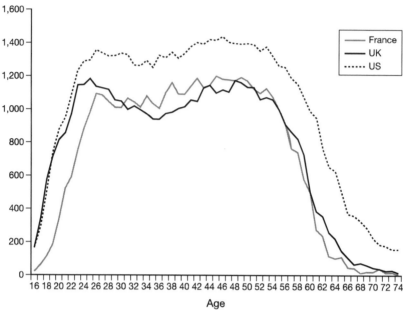

Figure 3.2c. Average total hours of market work done in 2007 by age in the UK, the US, and France: women

Source: Blundell, Bozio, and Laroque, 2011.

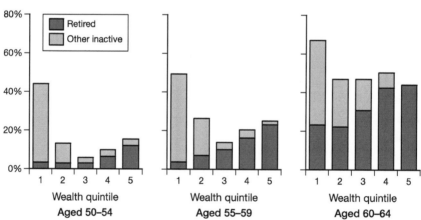

Figure 3.3. Early retirement and inactivity by age and wealth quintile in the UK: men

Note: Wealth quintiles are defined *within* each five-year age group.

Source: Banks and Casanova (2003), based on sample of men from the 2002 English Longitudinal Study of Ageing.

Tax and pension incentives have been shown to be a key determinant of employment at older ages[3] and may be expected to continue to be important in the longer run.

These changes in employment rates for different groups have been accompanied by dramatic changes in the underlying distribution of earnings. It is important to understand these changes because part of the rationale for earnings taxation is to generate revenue from high earners so that tax credits and benefits can redistribute to those with lower earning potential. Many industrial countries saw a relative decline in the wages of the low-paid at the end of the 20th century. This phenomenon was particularly acute in the UK and the US during the 1980s and 1990s.[4] 'Make work pay' policies, such as Working Tax Credit in the UK, have in part been introduced and expanded in response to these trends.[5]

Table 3.1. Male 90–10 wage ratios across countries, 1980–2000

	1980	1990	2000
Australia	2.73	2.71	3.16
Finland	2.44	2.57	2.47[f]
France	3.38	3.46	3.28[e]
Germany	2.53[b]	2.44	2.86[e]
Italy	2.09[b]	2.38	2.44[c]
Japan	2.60	2.84	2.74[f]
Netherlands	2.32[a]	2.48	2.83[f]
New Zealand	2.72	3.08	3.55[d]
Sweden	2.11	2.07	2.35[e]
UK	2.63[b]	3.24	3.40
US	3.58	4.41	4.76

Notes: Weekly earnings. OECD data for the relevant year except as denoted by: [a]1985; [b]1986; [c]1996; [d]1997; [e]1998; [f]1999.

Source: Machin and Van Reenen, 2008.

[3] Blundell, Meghir, and Smith, 2004; Gruber and Wise, 2004.
[4] Machin and Van Reenen, 2008.
[5] Blundell and Hoynes, 2004.

Table 3.1 shows the evolution of wage inequality across various developed economies. It uses the ratio between the wages at the 90th percentile and at the 10th percentile of the wage distribution. (If households were lined up from the highest to the lowest wage, these would be the level of wages one-tenth of the way down from the top of the distribution and one-tenth of the way up from the bottom.) The UK and the US stand out as economies where wages have risen much more strongly at the top than at the bottom. Changes of the scale shown here are very large indeed by historical standards. As the further details given in Table 3.2 demonstrate, changes are even more dramatic if we look further up the earnings distribution—earnings at the 95th percentile grew considerably faster than those at the 90th. (And indeed earnings at the 99th percentile grew faster still.) In the UK, we see some catch-up by those right at the bottom of the earnings distribution in the 2000s, perhaps as a result of the introduction and uprating of the minimum wage.

The important point about these trends is that they place increased pressure on redistributive parts of the tax and benefit system. They mean that workers on low wages have fallen further behind and are more likely to fall below any relative poverty line. If benefits are increased in line with (or

Table 3.2. Hourly wage inequality in the UK and the US: real wage trends by percentile (annualized percentage points)

	UK			US		
	1980s	1990s	2000s	1980s	1990s	2000s
5th percentile	1.8	1.0	3.0	−1.6	1.3	1.8
10th percentile	1.6	1.1	2.6	−0.6	1.5	1.4
25th percentile	1.8	1.2	2.3	0.0	0.9	0.4
50th percentile	2.3	1.5	2.4	0.3	0.8	1.1
75th percentile	3.0	1.9	2.8	0.6	1.0	1.6
90th percentile	3.5	2.1	3.0	1.3	1.3	1.9
95th percentile	3.8	2.2	3.5	2.0	1.3	1.9

Notes: UK derived from New Earnings Survey (NES) data; US derived from Current Population Survey data (the Outgoing Rotation Group, ORG, data from the National Bureau of Economic Research, NBER). Data are for full-time workers. The time periods used are: 1980s—1979 to 1989; 1990s—1989 to 1999; 2000s—2000 to 2004.

Source: Machin and Van Reenen, 2008.

close to) average earnings, wages in work for the low-skilled compare increasingly unfavourably with the benefit income they would receive if out of work. This weakens work incentives, creating pressure for policies to 'make work pay'. Our discussion of earnings tax reform in the next chapter highlights the importance of underlying inequality in earnings for the design of the tax and benefit system for the low-paid.

Understanding the drivers of inequality in earnings (a topic well beyond our scope) also matters for determining the overall policy response. Changing demand for skills, changing extent of collective bargaining, the level of globalization, and the supply and quality of education all play a part. The importance of each, and the pattern of inequality, change over time. For example, since the mid-1990s, the rapid growth of employment incomes among top earners has been an important explanation for the continued rise in income inequality[6] and has led to increased policy interest in the setting of tax rates on 'top' incomes. Even more recently, researchers have documented an apparent fall in demand for mid-range vocational skills in Britain and in the US.[7] Modern information technology in these countries has tended to replace jobs that require some numeracy, such as bank clerks, rather than the traditionally low-paid unskilled service jobs such as cleaning. All of these external pressures on the earnings distribution put strain on the tax and benefit system. Any discussion of reform has to be mindful of these trends in inequality.

3.2. DESIGNING THE TAX RATE SCHEDULE

In most developed economies, the schedule of tax rates on earned income is rather complex. This may not always be apparent from the income tax schedule itself, but note that what really matters is the total amount of earnings taken in tax and withdrawn benefits—the *effective* tax rate. The schedule of effective tax rates is made complicated by the many interactions between income taxes, earnings-related social security contributions by employers, welfare benefits, and tax credits.

---

[6] Atkinson and Piketty, 2007b; Brewer, Sibieta, and Wren-Lewis, 2008.
[7] Manning and Goos, 2007; Autor and Dorn, 2011.

The combination of these taxes and benefits will affect people's work effort in two ways: through the *income effect* and the *substitution effect*. Take the example of a reduction in a tax rate. For any workers earning enough to pay this rate, the cut will increase their income, allowing them to work fewer hours (or, more generally, to supply less effort) by making it easier to maintain a given standard of living. This is the income effect. At the same time, workers who now face a lower *marginal* tax rate will take home more of every extra pound they earn, encouraging them to work more. This is the substitution effect. The two effects offset each other and theory alone cannot tell us which will dominate. An exception occurs at the extensive margin. Consider someone currently out of employment; a reduction in a tax rate on earnings cannot make work less attractive. In both cases, however, credible evidence is required to tell us how powerful these effects will be.

Where we are looking at revenue-neutral reforms, the income effects will tend to balance out across the population: while some receive a giveaway and can afford to work less, others must pay correspondingly more and might therefore work harder to make up the loss.[8] But there is no reason the substitution effects will necessarily balance in this way: for example, a revenue-neutral flattening of a linear budget constraint[9] would increase the marginal tax rate for the rich *and* for the poor. The impact on the marginal wage is the same for all workers. But those with lower gross earnings will see their net income rise whereas for those on higher earnings the amount paid in tax will rise. Thus while for any single individual both income and substitution effects may be relevant, across the economy as a whole it is the substitution effects that will tend to dominate for revenue-neutral reforms.

What is really important in designing tax rate schedules is to take account of evidence on the effects of the tax schedule on different groups of people. Summarizing these comments, the main points that emerge from this evidence are the following:[10]

---

[8] It is possible that one group's labour supply will respond more to income changes than the other's, but the net outcome of differential income effects is likely to be second-order in magnitude.

[9] Meaning an increase in the lump sum paid when income is zero plus an increase in the marginal tax rate.

[10] For a more comprehensive summary of this evidence, see Blundell and MaCurdy (1999), Blundell and Shephard (2011), and Meghir and Phillips (2010).

- Substitution effects are generally larger than income effects: taxes reduce labour supply.
- Especially for low earners, responses are larger at the extensive margin—employment—than at the intensive margin—hours of work.
- Responses at both the intensive and extensive margins (and both substitution effects and income effects) are largest for women with school-age children and for those aged over 50.

In designing a tax schedule, we also need to consider other ways in which people respond to tax changes. They may change the amount of effort they put into each hour they work. They may decide on a different occupation or to take more training, or perhaps to become self-employed. They may respond by finding ways of avoiding or evading tax. Some of these effects will only become visible over long periods. Others should be observable more quickly as a change in the tax rate affects the level of taxable income declared—the taxable income elasticity is a measure of the effect. The taxable income elasticity subsumes the intensive and extensive margins and the income and substitution effects: by definition, it captures any response that affects tax payments. In general, it also provides a simple and direct measurement of the welfare cost of earnings tax reform.[11]

The more taxable income responds to a change in the tax rate, the lower is the revenue yield from any given tax change: taxing elastic behaviour yields less revenue. The larger the elasticity, the larger is the welfare loss per unit of revenue. This is true whether the action an individual takes is to work less hard or to engage in tax avoidance.

Of course, for some purposes, differences between different kinds of behavioural response matter and a single taxable income elasticity does not contain all the relevant information. An increase in tax-deductible pension contributions will reduce taxable income in the current year, but will increase future taxable income when extra pension is received, so just looking at *current* taxable income will give an incomplete picture. Similarly, some kinds of behavioural response will affect only income tax revenue whereas others will affect revenue from other taxes as well. Working less hard and reducing earnings will mean less spending (and so VAT revenues)

---

[11] Feldstein, 1999.

as well as less taxable income, whereas earnings merely reclassified to avoid income tax might still have VAT taken out of them when they are spent.[12]

Unfortunately, while the amount of evidence on the size of the taxable income elasticity is growing, it is still rather limited. Indeed, the elasticity itself is not best viewed as a fixed quantity. It can be changed by reforming the rules governing the tax base. The fewer opportunities there are in a tax system to reduce declared taxable income through exemptions, deductions, and channelling income through lower-tax jurisdictions, the easier it is to raise revenue from an increase in the tax rate and the smaller is the resulting taxable income elasticity.[13]

There is, however, a vast empirical literature on the measurement of hours and employment responses to hourly wage and other income changes, particularly for lower earners. For them, hours and employment are likely to represent the main avenues in which they can respond to tax reform, at least in the medium run. For high earners and the self-employed, on the other hand, where hours of work and employment may not be the important margins of response, we will use evidence on the size of the taxable income elasticity to examine the setting of top tax rates.

3.2.1. The Trade-Off between Work Incentives and Redistribution

So earnings taxes and welfare benefits affect work incentives. The higher the tax and benefit rates, the more they will affect incentives, and other behaviour. Nevertheless, we may well want to set them at significant levels because we are concerned about redistribution. There is a trade-off. In general, the more redistribution we carry out, the greater will be the behavioural response.

This is perhaps most readily illustrated by considering the simplest kind of 'negative income tax' system: a 'flat tax' combined with a 'social dividend'.[14]

---

[12] Similarly, some kinds of behavioural response will themselves have significant dynamic and macroeconomic effects; others merely reclassify income and will not (see Carroll and Hrung (2005)).

[13] Kopczuk, 2005.

[14] The classic proposals are Friedman (1962) and Rhys Williams (1943) respectively, though the ideas have older roots. See Meade (1978), Dilnot, Kay, and Morris (1984), Creedy and Disney (1985), and Atkinson (1995) for enlightening examinations of the ideas.

In this system, illustrated in Figure 3.4, an individual with no earnings receives a social dividend of £5,000 from the state.[15] Each additional pound the person earns is taxed at a constant effective marginal tax rate. At the break-even point, where the lines cross, the individual's tax payment is equal to £5,000 and she is neither a net contributor to nor a net recipient from the Exchequer. After this point, her earnings continue to be subject to tax at the same flat marginal rate.

In this negative income tax system, there is still a good deal of redistribution possible and the problem confronting the policymaker is to decide at what level to set the social dividend or guaranteed income and the effective marginal tax rate. The more generous the guaranteed income, the higher the tax rate needed to pay for it. We would like to redistribute to the poor, by having a high guaranteed income and a high tax rate. But a higher guaranteed income will reduce the incentive to take a job at all, while a higher marginal tax rate will reduce the incentive to earn more if the substitution effect is more powerful than the income effect.

In this simple system, it is likely that the tax rate required to provide a reasonable guaranteed income would be so high as to create a powerful

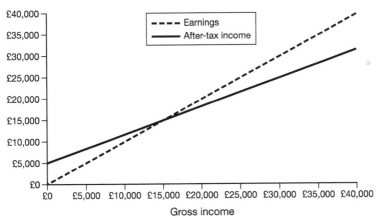

Figure 3.4. A linear negative income tax schedule

---

[15] A 'social dividend' is sometimes known as a 'citizen's income' or 'basic income'—not to be confused with a 'minimum income', which, far from being universally provided, imposes a 100% withdrawal rate as it tops up income to a given level, like Income Support does in the UK.

disincentive to work for many individuals.[16] The required tax rate is simply given by out-of-work income as a percentage of average income. So to provide non-workers with one-third of average income would require a tax rate of 33% *in addition to* that required to raise tax revenue for all other purposes. In the UK, the total flat tax rate required would be around 67% to finance existing public services and provide a social dividend of one-third of average income. That is before taking into account any behavioural responses to such a reform.

In order to provide reasonable incomes to those out of work, most real-world systems withdraw benefits at quite high rates for those on low incomes. This reduces the tax rate that needs to be imposed on middle to higher incomes to finance a given income guarantee. So the incentive to earn an extra pound is weaker for people on low incomes than for those on higher incomes. The low-paid also face reduced incentives to take work at all.

This is the inevitable trade-off. If benefits are not withdrawn quite fast from the low-paid, everyone faces a high tax rate. The alternative is that benefits are withdrawn quickly, thereby creating very significant disincentive effects for the poorest. Much policy debate centres around where best to settle on this trade-off.

3.2.2. An Optimal Tax Schedule

From society's point of view, a good tax rate schedule should seek the least distortionary way of achieving distributional objectives while raising a required amount of revenue.

The optimal tax approach requires that, for a schedule of tax rates to be 'optimal', there should be no change in tax rates that can make society better off given a fixed amount of tax revenue to be raised. By fixing the amount of revenue, the choice of schedule is deliberately posed in a revenue-neutral setting. Revenue neutrality avoids 'false' improvements in the tax schedule through unfunded government giveaways. For example, in the simple negative income tax case described above, to fund an increase in the level of guaranteed income an offsetting increase in the tax rate is required. Precisely what increase in guaranteed income could be afforded from a specific rise in

---

[16] See Creedy and Disney (1985) and references therein.

the tax rate will depend on how people choose to adjust their labour supply in response to the increase in the tax rate and the change in the guaranteed income.

The larger the substitution effect—the more people reduce their work effort in response to an increase in the marginal tax rate—the harder it is to meet a revenue requirement from a rise in the tax rate. A tax change that would have been revenue neutral in the absence of a reduction in work effort will instead produce a revenue loss. It is the size of this revenue loss that determines the 'excess burden' of taxation. A stronger preference for equality will make society willing to accept a higher excess burden and therefore a higher tax rate but, for any given preference for equality, the stronger the substitution effect the lower will be the optimal tax rate.

The way in which the optimal tax approach helps us think about the appropriate pattern of tax rates is best illustrated by considering when a small rise in the tax rate for some *small band* of income is a good idea. The tax rise increases the taxes paid by every taxpayer with incomes in or above the small band. However, it is a rise in the effective marginal tax rate only for those taxpayers in the band. Since the band of income is small, for them the substitution effect is dominant. For those workers with incomes above the tax band, there is no change in their effective marginal tax rate, so there can be no substitution effect. But they do pay a higher share of their income in taxes: their average tax rate is increased. This generates a revenue gain to society, but also a welfare loss for those individuals who pay the extra taxes.

In terms of labour supply responses, we can now separate three groups. For individuals below the band of income where the tax rate was changed, there is no effect. Those in the band face a higher marginal tax rate on any income earned. For them, the substitution effect will imply a reduction in their labour supply. Finally, those with incomes above the band will be subject to a reduction in income but no substitution effect.

It is the size of the substitution effect in labour supply and the number of people in the small band of income that determine the efficiency loss from the tax increase. However, the 'optimal' choice of tax rate for the chosen band of income will also depend on the proportion of the population with incomes above the band. The higher this proportion, the greater is the amount of revenue available for redistribution to the poorest. Finally, the optimal tax rate will depend on the welfare weights afforded to people on different incomes. The greater the existing inequality, the greater is the relative weight attached to those who gain from redistribution.[17]

That at least is a good way of thinking about changes at the *intensive* margin—how much to work. Now consider the extensive margin—whether to work or not. The evidence on labour supply responses is that, particularly for some groups such as low-earning parents, this margin matters a great deal.[18] This is an important observation for tax design. It can imply low, even negative, optimal tax rates for low earners.[19]

If a reduction in a tax rate induces individuals to move into employment, this will add to the potential gains from the reform. There is then a balance between the extensive response and the intensive response. When the extensive labour supply response is sufficiently high, it can become optimal to give an earnings subsidy. This is precisely the aim of in-work benefits such as Working Tax Credit in the UK.

There is, though, a trade-off that prohibits taking this argument too far. Reduced tax rates on low earners will have to be balanced against lower incentives to work among those on higher earnings. Knowledge of labour supply responses across the earnings distribution becomes a key input into tax design. In our analysis of the UK income tax schedule in the next chapter, we will use evidence on labour supply responses to suggest directions of reform.

3.2.3. The Tax Base and Taxable Income Responses

How people respond to taxes depends not only on the structure of marginal rates but also on the tax base. The tax base determines how much scope there is for people to reduce their taxable income in response to higher tax rates by shifting between taxed and untaxed forms of income. There is good evidence that the base-broadening reforms in the US in the 1980s made it easier to raise revenue by increasing the tax rate on higher incomes.[20] Indeed, one

[17] For further details, see the exposition in Heady (1993).
[18] See e.g. Blundell and Shephard (2011).
[19] See e.g. Saez (2002) and Laroque (2005b).
[20] Kopczuk, 2005.

argument for looking at the tax system as a whole, as we do in this book, is to bring tax base and tax rate design issues together.

In principle, the earnings tax base should include all forms of remuneration, including benefits in kind, and deduct all costs of generating earnings, such as work expenses (whether paid by the employer or by the employee). Favouring some forms of remuneration over others is potentially unfair on those only in a position to receive more heavily taxed earnings, and it encourages people to shift remuneration to less-taxed forms, with a loss to both the employee (who might have preferred cash) and the Exchequer (which sees revenue reduced). The costs of generating earnings should be deducted since they are not part of the profit from working.

Neither remuneration nor expenses are always easy to measure. Putting a value on non-cash remuneration can be difficult, and distinguishing work expenses from consumption expenditure even more so. How should laptops, suits, and company cars, which might be used for both business and personal purposes, be treated? To what extent is childcare expenditure a necessary cost of work? To what extent is spending on education an investment in generating future earnings as opposed to a consumption activity valued for itself? How far is providing a pleasant working environment—anything from less crowded desks to office plants, a subsidized canteen, car parking spaces, a recreation room, or flexible working hours—a cost of enabling people to work productively, and how far is it a form of remuneration, substituting for a higher salary?

This is not just an issue for income taxes: distinguishing consumption expenditure from business (or work-related) costs poses problems for a value added tax (VAT) as well.

Considering such problems, it is easy to see how tax systems can become complicated. To these complications—unlike many others we will encounter in this book—there is no straightforward solution. The UK income tax broadly follows the principle of taxing remuneration less costs, although the general rule that expenses are deductible only if they are incurred 'wholly, exclusively and necessarily in the performance of the duties of the employment'[21] is strict even allowing for the caution that should rightly accompany policy in this area given the difficulty of accurately identifying

---

[21] Income Tax (Earnings and Pensions) Act 2003, section 336.

work-related expenses.[22] More significant overall, though, is the appropriate taxation of savings (linked to the taxation of earnings particularly through deferred remuneration such as occupational pensions), which is the subject of Chapters 13 and 14.

In general, the more exemptions, deductions, and opportunities there are to take income in less-taxed forms, or to pass it through lower-tax jurisdictions, the more difficult it is to raise revenue from taxing labour market earnings. To quote Slemrod and Kopczuk (2002, 92):

> When personal tax rates on ordinary income rise, evasion may increase, businesses may shift to corporate form, there may be a rise in the consumption of deductible activities such as charitable giving, and individuals may rearrange their portfolios and compensation packages to receive more income as tax-preferred capital gains. These responses to higher taxes, and all others, will show up in declines in taxable income, and there is a growing body of evidence that, at least for high-income individuals, the elasticity of taxable income to the marginal tax rate is substantial.

This response of taxable income to a change in the tax rate provides a measure of deadweight loss—the excess burden of taxation. And for some types of people—the self-employed and those on higher incomes in particular—hours and employment are not the most important means they have to respond to tax reform. We devote specific attention to the self-employed and the relevant tax base and rate schedule for them in our discussion of small business taxation in Chapter 19. Here we focus on the taxation of top incomes.

Consider the choice of marginal tax rate for the top bracket of taxable income. If taxable income did not respond to changes in this rate, increasing the top rate would increase government revenue and the amount raised would depend on the number of people in the top income bracket. However, increasing the top rate may also induce top-bracket taxpayers to reduce their taxable earnings (but not taxpayers below the top bracket unless they expect to move into the higher bracket, because nothing has changed below this

---

[22] This rule—at least as interpreted in practice—is stricter than that applied to the self-employed and those applied in many other countries. See Freedman and Chamberlain (1997) for references and a discussion. Travel expenses and certain other expenses are covered by specific rules. Bizarrely, earnings are defined differently for National Insurance purposes, as discussed briefly in Chapter 5 and in more detail in Adam and Loutzenhiser (2007).

point).[23] This reduction in earnings has a cost to society, as tax revenues will be lower. The higher the taxable income elasticity, the larger is the tax rise needed to raise a given amount of revenue.

As we have seen, increasing the marginal rate at a particular point in the distribution has two social welfare effects. On the plus side, it results in a revenue gain from those higher up the distribution. On the minus side, it increases the distortion at that point. The schedule is optimal if these two effects are balanced all the way along the distribution. This leads to the famous theoretical insight that, at a point in the distribution where there is no one higher up, there is only the negative effect and the optimum tax rate has to be a deadweight-loss-minimizing rate of zero.[24]

More practically, as a guide to how high the top rate can go, we might consider the revenue-maximizing top rate. This ignores the welfare of those individuals in the top income bracket and is equivalent to placing a zero value on their (marginal) welfare. The revenue-maximizing top rate will be higher (a) the less taxable income falls when the top tax rate rises and (b) the higher the proportion of taxpayers in the top tax bracket. Of course, if society places some positive value on the welfare of those with incomes in the top tax bracket, then a lower rate—raising less revenue—will be preferred.

This sounds straightforward, but drawing policy recommendations from this analysis is fraught with difficulty. The taxable income elasticity—the proportionate change in taxable income for a given change in the tax rate—is notoriously hard to measure for high earners and will vary with the ease with which taxpayers can move their earnings out of the tax base. In the next chapter, these difficulties are highlighted as we consider the setting of tax rates on higher incomes in the UK.

---

[23] If education and career choices are significantly affected by top-bracket taxes, then this argument needs refining.

[24] This is often described as the theoretical zero top rate result. Here we are considering a band capturing a number of taxpayers, so it does not apply. Note that if the top band is small enough (so that it captures only one person), then: (i) if the highest income earner has a positive welfare weight, then the revenue-maximizing top marginal tax rate will be zero; and (ii) if the highest income earner has a zero welfare weight, then zero will be as good as any positive marginal rate.

3.3. THE TAX SCHEDULE FOR FAMILY EARNINGS

So far, we have thought of the tax and benefit system largely in terms of its impact on individuals and have not directly addressed the way in which it should treat families. This is of course a matter of great importance.

A central issue is whether the tax and benefit system should tax the income of family members jointly or independently. Do we want to treat people differently depending on whether or not they are in couples? Do we want to redistribute only towards families with low incomes overall or also towards families where there is at least one low-income person? Joint taxation and joint means-testing of benefits create very different work incentives, and have quite different distributional consequences, from independent taxation and individualized benefits. The policy judgement is as much about what seems fair in the way we treat different family types relative to each other as it is about work incentives.

To be neutral with respect to whether two individuals form a couple or not, the tax and benefit system would have to treat them as separate units. But to treat all couples with the same combined income equally, the tax and benefit system would have to treat couples as a single unit. If an individualized system is progressive, so that the average tax rate rises with income, then two couples with identical joint incomes but different individual incomes would pay different amounts of tax. If there is joint assessment and the system is progressive, then a couple would have a higher joint income if they separated.

A tax system cannot simultaneously be progressive, neutral towards marriage/cohabitation, and tax all families with the same joint income equally.[25]

The UK has a mixed system, in which entitlement to means-tested benefits and tax credits is assessed on joint income while liability to income tax and National Insurance contributions is assessed on individual income. The tax system is progressive but does not tax all families with the same joint income equally. This is because the average tax rate for the family depends on the way income is split between the partners—the more equal the split, the lower the tax bill. But the tax system is neutral over the marriage decision—two

---

[25] Rosen, 1977.

people living apart will pay the same tax as they would if they married. (Though if two adults living together enjoy a higher standard of living for a given joint income than two adults living apart, this arguably justifies taxing the couple more heavily.) The benefit and tax credit system, on the other hand, penalizes partnership.[26] If a non-earner marries, or moves in with, an earner, she will lose benefit entitlement. There is a balance to be struck here. We probably do not want to give benefits to the partners of millionaires—that would cost a lot and, at least when comparing the incomes of family units, look regressive. On the other hand, we know that families do not fully pool their resources and so not providing benefits to non-earners in couples may result in less redistribution than intended to individuals with low resources.[27]

It is not just how we think about redistribution that matters for decisions over the taxation of families. Evidence shows that women's work decisions, at least when they have dependent children, respond significantly to tax rate changes.[28] Other things being equal, this suggests that women with dependent children should be taxed at lower rates.[29] But a balance has to be struck between the implicit tax rates on workers in low-income families with children and the desire to redistribute to such families. If we do not worry too much about the fair sharing of income and resources within the family, the mixed system in the UK can provide such a balance.[30] For example, if a woman is working and has a partner with high earnings, the tax and benefit system would not distort her earning decisions unnecessarily by attempting to redistribute income to her.

In practice, the tax rate may be too high for low-earning secondary workers in the UK, certainly if they have low-earning partners.[31] If the extensive labour supply elasticity of a woman with children is sufficiently large, then it may even be optimal to introduce an earnings disregard for the

---

[26] Adam and Brewer, 2010.

[27] See Browning et al. (1994); also Lundberg, Pollack, and Wales (1997), who show that the 1977 reform of child benefits in the UK, which switched payment 'from wallet to purse', resulted in increases in spending on children's and women's clothing.

[28] See Blundell and MaCurdy (1999) and Meghir and Phillips (2010).

[29] See related arguments in Alesina, Ichino, and Karabarbounis (2007).

[30] Kleven, Kreiner, and Saez, 2009b.

[31] Brewer, Saez, and Shephard, 2010.

second earner. In the next chapter, we consider reforms to address these issues.

So the structure of family taxation matters for work incentives and for 'fairness'. Over the course of his or her life, any particular individual will very likely appear in many different family types: as a child, as a single adult, as a parent, etc. So perhaps what matters most is that we treat individuals fairly from a lifetime perspective rather than worry too much about specific family types. But the third way in which the tax and benefit system matters is that it may itself influence an individual's marriage and fertility decisions. Systems that are progressive and assess income tax and benefit awards on the basis of joint incomes inevitably create a marriage (or cohabitation) subsidy or penalty. The total income after tax and benefits of two adults might change if they decide to marry or cohabit.[32]

Although the marriage penalty/subsidy attracts substantial public attention, it only becomes particularly relevant for tax design if the decision to marry is sensitive to those fiscal incentives. Hoynes (2010) concludes that 'Overall, the research finds tax effects on marriage that are consistent with the theoretical predictions but are small in size'. It should be noted, though, that, even if marriage or partnership decisions are relatively insensitive to tax or welfare advantages, people might change how they *report* their relationship status to the tax authorities.[33]

It is also possible that the decision on whether to have children (and, if so, how many) is affected by the generosity of child-contingent taxes and welfare benefits. If so, this introduces another aspect of behaviour that can be influenced by the design of the family earnings tax system. Some recent UK evidence[34] concludes that generous tax or welfare treatment does encourage childbearing but that the effect is modest.

Over the long term, family formation and composition could very well be sensitive to economic incentives,[35] and any discussion of tax design should at least lay out what those incentives are and be cognizant of the impact of such behaviour responses.

---

[32] Adam and Brewer, 2010.

[33] Brewer and Shaw, 2006.

[34] Brewer, Ratcliffe, and Smith, 2010.

[35] As Becker (1991) so eloquently argues.

3.4. USING ADDITIONAL INFORMATION (TAGGING)

If the tax authority could observe an individual's potential earning capacity and needs directly, the tax design problem would be considerably eased. For example, taxes could be levied on those with a high capacity to earn— irrespective of their actual earnings—thereby preventing them from reducing their tax payments by working less. In the real world, immutable measures of productive ability and needs are not available. That is why measures of actual earnings, income, or expenditure are typically used to approximate ability or earning capacity, while characteristics such as family size and age are used to approximate needs. At root, this is what drives the equity–efficiency trade-off: if the tax rate on earnings is set too high, individuals may choose to earn less. The more the government can make the tax system contingent on observable factors closely related to abilities and needs, the smaller the welfare losses from taxation. In this section, we look briefly at the question of whether it is possible to use more information about people to approximate the redistribution we would ideally like to achieve with less distortion to behaviour than by using information on income alone.

If we can complement income with other indicators of ability and needs, we can redistribute more accurately and with correspondingly less need to use income and therefore disincentivize work.[36] If we know which groups are most responsive to taxation, we can adjust tax rates to generate a more efficient tax system. In sum, using additional information can relax the trade-off between work incentives and redistribution. This approach is known as *tagging*.[37]

Governments do this already. For example, they provide additional support for people with disabilities because disability is a good indicator both of having unusually low earning capacity and of having unusually high needs. Tax and benefit payments vary by many other demographic characteristics as well (and, indeed, by tastes for different goods, through differential indirect taxes), although not all differentiation is in line with the principles of tagging.

However, there are serious limitations to this approach:

---

[36] See Dilnot, Kay, and Morris (1984, 71–77) for a simple graphical illustration.
[37] Akerlof, 1978.

- *Complexity.* Nothing is costlessly observable. The more characteristics tax and benefit payments depend on, the less transparent and comprehensible the system becomes and the higher the administrative and compliance costs involved in its implementation.

- *Privacy.* In some cases, information that might be very useful for efficient redistribution might be considered an undue invasion of people's privacy, or it might be thought that the government cannot be trusted with such information. Such concerns grow as advancing technology, from store cards to DNA testing, expands the scope of characteristics that could potentially be used.[38]

- *Incentives to acquire tags.* Redistributing towards people with *any* characteristic provides people with an incentive to acquire or keep that characteristic. The context in which we usually think of this is that redistributing from high-income to low-income people encourages people to keep their income low. But tagging does not simply remove this problem: rather, it replaces the incentive to have low income with an incentive to have whatever 'tag' is used instead. How far people are likely to respond to this incentive will depend on what the tag is: it is hard to envisage people responding to an incentive to be old, but they might respond to an incentive to have more children; they are unlikely to make themselves (more) disabled, but they might be tempted to pretend they are less healthy than they really are. Other things being equal, such distortions of behaviour are undesirable; they must therefore be balanced against the disincentives to work created by income taxation.

- *Horizontal equity.* In some cases, people would consider it simply unfair to discriminate between individuals on the basis of particular characteristics. Nobody questions redistribution based on disability. On the other hand, membership of certain minority ethnic groups is an excellent indicator of poverty,[39] but there is little prospect of any government introducing a 'black person's benefit', for example. Height is a surprisingly good predictor of earnings,[40] but few would advocate introducing a height tax to reduce the need for distortionary income taxation.

---

[38] See Slemrod (2006) for a discussion.

[39] Kenway and Palmer, 2007.

[40] Case and Paxson, 2008.

It is hard to reach definitive conclusions on questions of fairness in this context.[41] Kay (2010) considers a selection of characteristics and concludes: 'I can see no obvious criterion for distinguishing those variables which seem to be found generally acceptable and those which are generally unacceptable: words such as "arbitrary" and "inappropriate" simply reiterate intuitive feelings'. Hall (2010), reflecting on Banks and Diamond's (2010) discussion of the considerable theoretical potential for height taxation to improve the efficiency of tax design, concludes similarly: 'Neither they nor I have a totally coherent framework for explaining why we oppose taxation of height'.

There is a vast literature—in economics and far beyond—addressing this and related questions from a variety of angles, and it is a central part of political debates about 'fairness'. There is scope for continuing philosophical inquiry (and, indeed, for focus groups and polls[42]) to play a major role in informing judgements about what characteristics are considered acceptable to use. But in this book, we will largely duck the philosophical complexities and value judgements that are inherent in this question by restricting our attention to characteristics that governments already use, such as family composition and children's ages, to determine tax liabilities and benefit entitlements. In the next chapter, we consider how they could be used better.

3.5. CONCLUSIONS

By creating a wedge between the cost to the employer and the reward to the worker, the taxation of earnings has a direct impact on the efficient running of the economy. At the same time, it is a core policy instrument in achieving society's distributional objectives. There are several important messages from this chapter which set up the later discussions of reform.

First, the pre-tax distribution of earnings matters a great deal for the appropriate structure of the tax system. That distribution has become much more unequal in the UK, and in many other countries, over the past three decades.

---

[41] See Banks and Diamond (2010) and the associated commentaries by Hall (2010), Kay (2010), and Pestieau (2010).

[42] As Kay (2010) suggests.

Second, the responsiveness of different population groups to incentives varies considerably and this can be seen quite clearly in the different levels of labour supply and changes over time for different groups.

Third, there is an inevitable trade-off between redistribution and incentives. Greater redistribution will generally reduce economic efficiency. Across the population, the substitution effect—which causes people to work less hard in response to a higher *marginal* tax rate—will generally outweigh the income effect—which increases effort in response to an increased *average* tax rate.

But fourth, taking account of how different population groups respond to incentives allows any particular level of redistribution to be achieved at a minimum efficiency cost.

Fifth, in thinking about earnings taxation and welfare benefits, it is important to distinguish between their effects on the decision to work at all (what we call the extensive margin) and their effects on decisions over how much to work (the intensive margin). In addition, tax changes may affect neither of these behaviours but may change recorded levels of taxable income as, in response, some people reorganize their affairs to minimize tax payments.

Sixth, overall taxable income elasticity—the extent to which taxable income as a whole responds to tax changes—depends not only on tax rates but also on the tax base. It is not immutable and can be changed by bringing more (or fewer) sources of income into tax.

Seventh, and as stressed in the previous chapter, in assessing changes we ideally want to account not only for their effects on income levels and labour supply but also for their effects on the distribution of income and on welfare.

Finally, there are inescapable trade-offs to consider in designing the taxation of family income. A tax system cannot simultaneously be progressive, neutral towards marriage (or cohabitation), and tax all families with the same joint income equally.

4

Reforming the Taxation of Earnings
in the UK

In the previous chapter, we looked at some of the theory and evidence on the taxation of earnings. In this chapter, we delve into a more practical assessment of the UK system and consider some changes to the rates and thresholds of existing taxes and benefits, illustrating the trade-offs involved and looking at promising avenues for improving work incentives where it matters most. In the next chapter, we go on to consider whether the set of taxes and benefits that currently exists is the right one at all: whether the way in which the taxation of earnings is implemented could be made not only simpler but also more conducive to achieving a sensible pattern of incentives.

The direct tax and benefit system is the main route through which the tax system as a whole achieves progressivity and redistributes from rich to poor. We have made a deliberate decision not to construct our analysis and proposals around a particular view of how much to redistribute. This is an issue over which reasonable people can and do disagree. But some ways of redistributing create more inefficiency, complexity, and work disincentives than others. The question we address is how to design the system to be as efficient as possible for a given degree of redistribution.

In this chapter, we focus on those elements of the tax and benefit system that depend directly on people's current earnings.[1] Other parts of the tax

---

[1] As with the rest of the book, this was largely written over Summer 2010, and descriptions of the tax and benefit system generally relate to the system in place in April 2010. Estimates of

system also affect work incentives and the income distribution, and ultimately it is the impact of the tax system as a whole that matters. But, clearly, those parts that depend directly on earnings are best suited to fine-tuning the pattern of work incentives and finessing the trade-off between work incentives and redistribution. In subsequent chapters, we emphasize the potential for adjusting the rate schedule at which earnings are taxed to offset the distributional and work incentive effects that arise as a by-product of efficiency-improving reforms in other areas.

4.1. INCOME-RELATED TAXES AND BENEFITS IN THE UK

At first sight, the UK would appear to have a pretty simple system for taxing earnings. Income tax becomes payable at a 20% rate once earnings exceed £6,475 (in 2010–11). That rises to 40% £37,400 later. Until April 2010, that was pretty much the end of the story as far as income tax was concerned. We now, though, have the rather odd situation in which the income tax rate rises to 60% on earnings between £100,000 and £112,950, before dropping back to 40% and then rising to 50% once earnings reach £150,000. This schedule is illustrated in Figure 4.1.

But, of course, income tax is only one part of the overall story. We have an entirely separate direct tax system, National Insurance contributions (NICs), which layers an additional 11% tax rate on employees' earnings between £110 and £844 a week and 1% thereafter, with an additional 12.8% of salaries above £110 also payable by employers. Note that NICs are payable only on

distributional effects, effective tax rates, and so on, for both the 'current' system and simulated reforms, are based on the tax and benefit system in place at the end of 2009–10. More recent changes have done little to alter the arguments for reform; we indicate where significant reforms have been announced by the coalition government that took office in May 2010, but we do not analyse those announcements in depth.

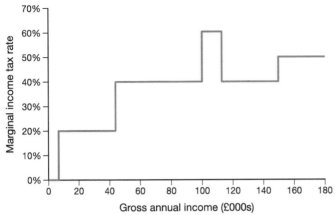

Figure 4.1. Income tax schedule for those aged under 65, 2010–11

earnings and not, unlike income tax, on other sources of income. Note also the oddity that whilst income tax thresholds and allowances are defined in annual terms, NICs thresholds are weekly.

The UK has means-tested benefits that top up the incomes of non-working families to a certain basic level, with a withdrawal rate of 100% (above a very small amount of earnings that does not reduce entitlement). Several separate benefits provide substantial additional support (regardless of work status) for housing costs (rent and council tax), children, and old age. These are withdrawn only once income reaches certain levels and at more moderate rates (though in combination with each other, and with income tax and NICs, they can yield extremely high effective tax rates overall, as we discuss later). Working Tax Credit provides extra means-tested support for low-income working families (with or without children).

Box 4.1 provides further details of each of these taxes and benefits, and the next chapter considers whether it is necessary to have so many of them, interacting in such complicated ways. But taking them all into account creates an overall rate schedule which, at least for low and moderate earners, looks quite unlike the income tax schedule illustrated in isolation in Figure 4.1. This overall schedule varies widely according to family type and a range of other characteristics, but as just one illustration, Figure 4.2 shows the relationship between gross earnings and net income—the 'budget constraint'—facing a low-wage lone parent with a particular set of circumstances.

Box 4.1. The main income-related taxes and benefits in the UK, 2010–11

Income tax: each individual has a tax-free personal allowance of £6,475. The next £37,400 of income is taxed at 20%, with income above that taxed at 40%. From 2010–11, the personal allowance is reduced by 50p for each £1 of income above £100,000 (creating an effective 60% band until the personal allowance has been completely removed at incomes of £112,950), and income above £150,000 is taxed at a new 50% rate. Those aged 65 or over have a higher personal allowance, though the extra allowance is gradually reduced by 50p for each £1 of income above £22,900 (creating an effective 30% band above this point).

National Insurance contributions (NICs) are in effect a tax on earnings (other income is exempt). Employers are charged 12.8% of the earnings above £110 per week of each person they employ; the employees themselves pay a further 11%, falling to 1% on earnings above £844 per week. Reduced rates apply if an employee 'contracts out' of the State Second Pension and instead belongs to a recognized private pension scheme. Much lower rates of NICs apply to the self-employed.

The main **means-tested benefits** and **tax credits** are as follows (in all cases, such means-testing is based on family income, unlike the individual-based taxes described above, and many have rules that reduce or eliminate entitlement for those with substantial financial assets):

Income Support and **income-based Jobseeker's Allowance (JSA)** top up the incomes of eligible working-age families to a minimum level—£64.45 per week for singles and £102.75 for couples in 2010–11, with additions for carers, those with disabilities, and those with a mortgage—provided the claimant (and any partner) is not in full-time paid work. Since additional income is offset one-for-one by reduced benefit, the means test in effect imposes a 100% tax rate on small increases in claimants' family incomes (above a very small amount of earnings that is disregarded for the means test). Lone parents with young children, carers, and people with disabilities can claim Income Support; others can claim the same amount in income-based JSA provided they satisfy various work-search conditions. Individuals who meet the work-search conditions and who have paid enough NICs in the recent past can claim a non-means-tested £64.45 per week in **contribution-based JSA** for up to six months, even if their family income would disqualify them from income-based JSA (e.g. because of savings or a partner's earnings). Individuals with a disability that prevents them from working may be entitled to **income-based Employment and**

Support Allowance (ESA), which is gradually replacing Income Support for those with a disability. Entitlement to income-based ESA is calculated in a similar way to entitlement to Income Support and income-based JSA, but with different conditions.

Pension Credit fulfils a similar safety-net role for those aged above the female state pension age (currently rising from 60 in 2010 to 66 in 2020) to that played by Income Support for working-age families. But it tops up family income to a much higher level—£132.60 per week for singles and £202.40 for couples, again with various additions—and, for those aged 65 or over, the 100% withdrawal rate is replaced by a 40% withdrawal rate on income above the level of the Basic State Pension.

Housing Benefit and **Council Tax Benefit** help to cover low-income families' rent and council tax[a] respectively. Those with incomes low enough to qualify for Income Support (or the Pension Credit safety net, for those aged 60 or over) have their full rent (up to a cap) and council tax covered; above that income level, Housing Benefit is reduced by 65p, and Council Tax Benefit by 20p, for each £1 of after-tax income.

Child Tax Credit (CTC) provides up to £545 (the 'family element') plus £2,300 per child (the 'child element') for low-income families with dependent children, regardless of employment status. **Working Tax Credit (WTC)** provides support for low-income workers, with or without children: up to £1,920 for single people without children and £3,810 for couples and lone parents, with an extra £790 for those working 30 hours or more per week. Those without children must be working at least 30 hours per week and be aged 25 or over to qualify for WTC at all; those with children need only work 16 hours and can be of any age. If all adults in the family are working 16 hours or more per week, WTC can also refund 80% of registered childcare expenditure of up to £300 per week (£175 per week for families with only one child). A means test applies to CTC and WTC together: the award is reduced by 39p for each £1 of family income above £6,420 (£16,190 for those not eligible for WTC), except that the £545 'family element' is not withdrawn until income reaches £50,000, and then only at a rate of 6.7p for each £1 of pre-tax income.

Non-means-tested benefits are available for the elderly (**state pensions** and **Winter Fuel Payment**), families with children (**Child Benefit**), and people with disabilities and their carers (**Incapacity Benefit / contributory Employment and Support Allowance, Disability Living Allowance, Attendance Allowance**, and **Carer's Allowance**).

[a] Council tax is a local property tax, discussed in Chapter 16.

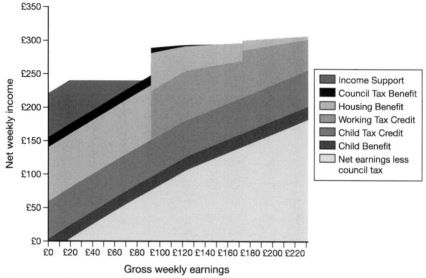

Figure 4.2. Composition of an example budget constraint in 2010–11

Notes: Example is for a lone parent, with one child aged between 1 and 4, earning the minimum wage (£5.80 per hour), with no other private income and no childcare costs, paying £80 per week in rent to live in a council tax band B property in a local authority setting council tax rates at the national average. 'Net earnings less council tax' is earnings after deducting income tax, employee NICs, and council tax. Figure does not show negative amounts for 'net earnings less council tax' on the left-hand side where council tax exceeds net earnings: with zero earnings, 'net earnings less council tax' is –£15.77, with Child Benefit making up the difference from what is shown. Employer NICs and indirect taxes are not shown, though they are included in work incentive measures in the rest of the chapter, as detailed in Box 4.2.

Source: Authors' calculations using the IFS tax and benefit microsimulation model, TAXBEN.

The main points to see in Figure 4.2 are the following:

- First, over a significant range, additions to gross weekly earnings make no difference to net weekly income. This reflects pound-for-pound withdrawal of Income Support as earnings rise.

- Second, there is then a jump in net income at 16 hours a week of work as Working Tax Credit (WTC) becomes payable. That jump in total income, though, is less than the receipt of WTC because Housing Benefit and Council Tax Benefit receipt falls in response to the WTC receipt. Nevertheless, there is a clear addition to income from working for this lone parent once she works 16 hours.

- Third, there is, however, little incentive to work more than 16 hours, as WTC and Housing Benefit are withdrawn as earnings rise further.

In addition, Figure 4.2 illustrates the complexity of the current system, with lots of different overlapping elements. That is why the coalition government has announced an intention to introduce a Universal Credit, integrating many of them into a single benefit. We discuss the idea of benefit integration in the next chapter.

Figure 4.2 shows only one example, however. Given the bewildering variety of ways in which the different taxes and benefits interact, depending on individual and family circumstances, we must be wary of extrapolating too much from this single case. We therefore turn now to summarize the impact of the tax and benefit system across the whole population, looking first at the extent to which it redistributes from rich to poor and then at its effects on work incentives.

4.1.1. The Effect of Taxes and Benefits on the Distribution of Income

The UK tax and benefit system as a whole redistributes significantly from high-income to low-income households. This is illustrated in Figure 4.3. The figure shows that benefits net of taxes (including indirect taxes) make up nearly 40% of the disposable incomes of households in the bottom tenth of the income distribution. This proportion falls over the next three deciles. The fifth decile pays slightly more in tax than it receives in benefits. Thereafter, net contributions rise rapidly such that what the richest tenth of the population pay in taxes (net of benefits) amounts to more than 60% of their disposable income.

Figure 4.4 shows how different elements of the tax and benefit system contribute to the redistribution we see in the system overall. Benefits and tax credits are overwhelmingly important for the poorest households, making up 85% of the disposable incomes of the lowest-income tenth of households and steadily declining in importance further up the distribution. Conversely, direct personal taxes become increasingly important further up the distribution. The income tax, NICs, and council tax paid by the highest-income tenth of households (or by their employers on their behalf) amount to more than half of their disposable income.

Tax by Design

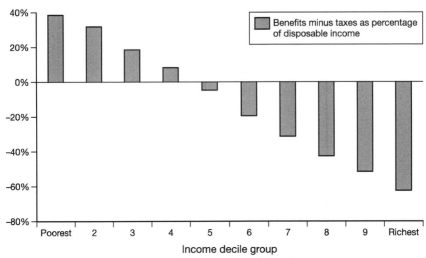

Figure 4.3. Distributional impact of the UK tax and benefit system in 2009–10

Notes: Income decile groups are derived by dividing households into ten equal-sized groups based on their disposable income adjusted for family size using the McClements equivalence scale. Assumes full take-up of means-tested benefits and tax credits. Excludes most 'business taxes' (notably corporation tax and business rates, though not employer National Insurance contributions) and capital taxes (notably inheritance tax, stamp duties, and capital gains tax).

Source: Authors' calculations using the IFS tax and benefit microsimulation model, TAXBEN, run on uprated data from the 2007 Expenditure and Food Survey with indirect taxes calibrated to aggregates from HM Treasury (2010b).

It is immediately clear that the benefit system is largely responsible for the redistribution towards those on the lowest incomes. Direct personal taxes—mostly income tax and NICs, but also, for these purposes, council tax—are responsible for redistribution away from those with high incomes. This is not surprising—the direct tax and benefit system is explicitly redistributive. It is also quite appropriate that these are the elements of the system as a whole which do the heavy lifting in terms of redistribution.

Indirect taxes—VAT and excise duties—are regressive on this measure. They take up more of the disposable income of the poorest than of the richest. This arises mainly because, at any given point in time, low-income households typically spend a lot (and therefore pay a lot in indirect taxes) relative to their incomes. But VAT in fact is a smaller share of *expenditure* for poorer households in the UK, since goods subject to zero or reduced rates of VAT are mostly necessities such as food and domestic fuel. So, if

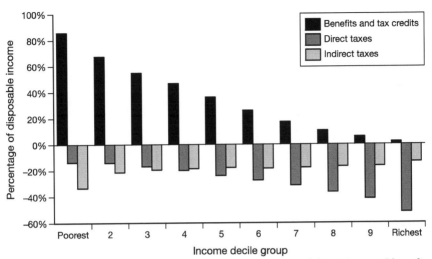

Figure 4.4. Distributional impact of different components of the UK tax and benefit system in 2009–10

Notes and source: As for Figure 4.3. 'Direct taxes' includes income tax, employer and employee NICs, and council tax. 'Indirect taxes' are VAT and excise duties.

lifetime income and lifetime expenditure are equal, as they will tend to be (the main difference being bequests given and received), VAT must actually take up a smaller share of lifetime resources for lifetime-poor households, and in that sense it is progressive.[2]

We will return to this issue in the context of VAT reform in Chapter 9. But it highlights more broadly the importance of taking a lifetime perspective on the tax system. Besides the particular pitfalls of examining indirect tax payments by income rather than expenditure, the redistribution shown in Figures 4.3 and 4.4 is a snapshot of money being transferred at one point in time. Many people will find themselves in different parts of the income distribution, and with different demographic characteristics, at different stages of their life, and much of the redistribution done by the tax and benefit system can be thought of as redistribution across the life cycle rather than between people. This idea of taking a lifetime perspective is one that will recur throughout this book.

[2] Some excise duties, however—notably tobacco duty—are regressive on any measure.

The main point to bear in mind for the purposes of this chapter is that direct taxes and benefits are what make the tax system as a whole redistributive. It is straightforward to vary the amount of redistribution they do by changing tax rates and benefit levels. But, by reducing work incentives, these taxes and benefits also impose costs, and there is often a trade-off between the degree of redistribution achieved and the impact of the system on incentives. For the rest of this chapter, we focus mainly on the incentive effects of direct taxes and benefits. We start by describing these incentive effects, before going on to assess the system and consider possible reforms.

4.1.2. The Effect of Taxes and Benefits on Work Incentives

The tax and benefit system can affect the incentive to be in paid work at all and the incentive for someone already in work to earn a little more. The first effect is measured by the participation tax rate (PTR), the second by the effective marginal tax rate (EMTR). Box 4.2 explains in more detail how we calculate these effective tax rates.

Someone for whom an extra £1 of earnings is not only subject to basic-rate income tax and standard-rate NICs, but also reduces their entitlements to tax credits, Housing Benefit, and Council Tax Benefit, faces an effective marginal tax rate of over 96%. Low earners entitled to generous out-of-work benefits, but little in-work support, can face similarly high participation tax rates. These cases are not typical: they mainly serve to illustrate that the interactions between different taxes and benefits can lead to extraordinary outcomes.

Box 4.2. Measuring work incentives[a]

We measure the incentive to be in paid work at all by the participation tax rate (PTR), the proportion of total earnings taken in tax and withdrawn benefits. This can be calculated as

$$PTR = 1 - \frac{\text{Net income in work} - \text{Net income out of work}}{\text{Gross earnings}}.$$

We measure the incentive to increase earnings slightly by the effective marginal tax rate (EMTR), the proportion of a small increase in earnings taken in tax and withdrawn benefits.

To calculate PTRs and EMTRs for individuals in couples, we look at how the couple's net income changes when the individual in question stops work or changes their earnings slightly, holding the other partner's employment and earnings fixed.

Throughout this book, measures of PTRs and EMTRs incorporate income tax, employee and employer NICs, all the main social security benefits and tax credits, and the main indirect taxes (VAT and excise duties).[b] They do not incorporate capital taxes (corporation tax, inheritance tax, stamp duties, capital gains tax, or income tax on savings income) since, although they may affect work incentives, the extent to which they do so is difficult to assess even in principle and impossible to estimate with the data available.

Since we incorporate employer NICs and indirect taxes, what we are measuring is not just the gap between gross earnings and disposable income; it is the gap between how much labour costs the employer (i.e. earnings plus employer NICs) and the value of what the wage can buy (i.e. disposable income less the tax component of purchase costs). Not all past analysis has done this; but since employers presumably care about the overall cost of employing someone, while employees presumably care about what working (or working more) can buy them, including the impact of employer NICs and indirect taxes produces a more accurate measure of the disincentive to work created by the tax and benefit system than ignoring them does.

When calculating effective tax rates, we consider only the payments made at a particular level of earnings, ignoring any future benefit entitlement that payment of NICs in particular may confer and which offsets the disincentive effect of having to pay NICs. In practice, the link between NICs paid and future benefits received is rather weak in the UK, as discussed in the next chapter, so this simplification will not lead to major inaccuracies, but in some cases (notably the State Second Pension) the omission may be significant.

[a] Adam (2005) and Adam and Browne (2010) discuss the methodology used here in more detail.

[b] To incorporate indirect taxes, we estimate consumption tax rates (CTRs)—indirect taxes paid as a percentage of household expenditure—in the Expenditure and Food Survey and use those to impute CTRs in the Family Resources Survey used in this chapter. Note that CTRs will not quite be an accurate measure of how indirect taxes affect work incentives unless the average tax rate on what additional income is spent on is the same as that on existing purchases. More details are given in an online appendix available at http://www.ifs.org.uk/mirrleesReview.

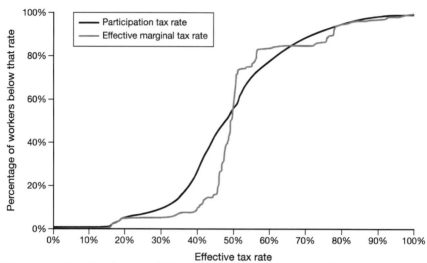

Figure 4.5. The distribution of PTRs and EMTRs among UK workers, 2009–10

Source: Authors' calculations using the IFS tax and benefit microsimulation model, TAXBEN, run on uprated data from the 2006–07 Family Resources Survey, and using estimated consumption tax rates from the 2007 Expenditure and Food Survey.

The distribution of PTRs and EMTRs among UK workers is shown in Figure 4.5.[3] Reading across, we can see that (for example) about 10% of workers have PTRs below 30%, and 10% have EMTRs below 40%. A rough rule of thumb is that people's earnings (or additional earnings) are typically worth to them about half of what they cost their employer: the mean and median PTR and EMTR are all close to 50%. But while this rule of thumb is right for many people, it is far from universal. Half of workers have PTRs between 40% and 60%, but the other half are outside this range, with slightly more below this range than above it. The distribution of EMTRs is more concentrated: three-quarters of workers face an EMTR of between 40% and 60%. But 15% of workers—about 3.5 million individuals—face an EMTR above 75%, so that earning a little more buys them less than a quarter of what it costs their employer.

---

[3] Adam, Browne, and Heady (2010) and Adam and Browne (2010) estimate PTRs for non-workers as well, showing that non-workers tend to face weaker incentives than workers.

Table 4.1. Distribution of PTRs among workers, 2009–10

	Mean	Percentile of distribution					Number (millions)
		10th	25th	50th	75th	90th	
Single							
No children	55%	39%	49%	53%	63%	75%	6.8
Children	50%	16%	38%	56%	67%	76%	1.0
Couple, partner not working							
No children	52%	31%	38%	48%	64%	79%	2.1
Children	66%	44%	53%	69%	79%	86%	1.8
Couple, partner working							
No children	41%	30%	37%	41%	45%	52%	8.3
Children	47%	27%	38%	48%	57%	66%	6.6
All	49%	31%	39%	47%	58%	72%	26.7

Source: Authors' calculations using the IFS tax and benefit microsimulation model, TAXBEN, run on uprated data from the 2006–07 Family Resources Survey.

Table 4.2. Distribution of EMTRs among workers, 2009–10

	Mean	Percentile of distribution					Number (millions)
		10th	25th	50th	75th	90th	
Single							
No children	50%	41%	47%	50%	50%	73%	6.8
Children	71%	38%	56%	76%	87%	92%	1.0
Couple, partner not working							
No children	50%	34%	42%	49%	56%	78%	2.1
Children	65%	45%	49%	72%	78%	92%	1.8
Couple, partner working							
No children	47%	41%	46%	49%	50%	56%	8.3
Children	52%	40%	46%	49%	55%	76%	6.6
All	52%	40%	46%	49%	53%	77%	26.7

Source: Authors' calculations using the IFS tax and benefit microsimulation model, TAXBEN, run on uprated data from the 2006–07 Family Resources Survey.

Tax by Design

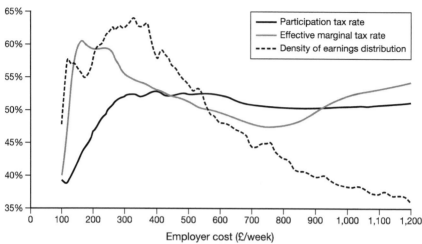

Figure 4.6. Average PTRs and EMTRs across the earnings distribution, 2009–10

Notes: Non-parametric regression (lowess) estimates for PTRs and EMTRs; kernel density estimate of the earnings distribution, for which no scale is shown. Employer cost = Gross earnings + Employer NICs.

Source: Authors' calculations using the IFS tax and benefit microsimulation model, TAXBEN, run on uprated data from the 2006–07 Family Resources Survey, and using estimated consumption tax rates from the 2007 Expenditure and Food Survey.

These EMTRs and PTRs vary both by income level and by other characteristics, notably housing tenure and family type. The variation by family type is illustrated in Tables 4.1 and 4.2. Sole earners in couples with children have the weakest incentives to stay in work (the highest PTRs), while people with working partners and no dependent children have the strongest. But single parents have the highest EMTRs, implying the weakest incentives to earn a little more; those in couples without children tend to have the lowest EMTRs. Both PTRs and EMTRs vary most widely among single parents, and least widely among single people and dual-earner couples without children.

The differences between family types shown in Tables 4.1 and 4.2 reflect different earnings distributions as well as different tax and benefit treatments: groups with high effective tax rates at any given level of earnings may still face low effective tax rates on average.

Figure 4.6 shows how average PTRs and EMTRs vary by earnings, measured in terms of the cost to an employer. The figure also overlays the frequency, or density, of workers at different earnings levels—the peak, or mode, being at an employer cost of around £330 per week. EMTRs tend to be high at low levels of earnings as means-tested support is withdrawn, then fall at moderate-to-high levels of earnings where people face only basic-rate income tax, NICs, and indirect taxes, and then finally rise again as higher rates of income tax take effect—though never to the extraordinary levels faced by some low earners.[4]

Despite high EMTRs, PTRs are relatively low on average for low-paid workers.[5] This is because tax-free income tax allowances and NICs thresholds cover a large fraction of their total earnings (even if *additional* earnings would then be taxed at full income tax and NIC rates), and because moving into work often attracts WTC awards (even if *additional* earnings would then see these awards sharply reduced). Average PTRs are higher for those earning more, as the loss of out-of-work support is compounded by substantial income tax and NICs, rather than being offset by WTC.

But it should be stressed that these patterns are only averages at each earnings point. For example, the PTR associated with a particular level of earnings can depend on how many hours are being worked to earn it, since Income Support and JSA are not available to those working 16 hours or more while WTC is only available to those with (without) children if they work at least 16 (30) hours. Work incentives at a given level of earnings also depend heavily on family type and housing costs.

We have already mentioned the importance of family type. Most obviously, low-income people with children tend to face weaker work

---

[4] Note that Figure 4.6 only shows earnings up to the equivalent of about £60,000 a year. Even at the £100,000 point at which there is a brief 60% income tax rate, and at incomes over £150,000 where the 50% rate takes effect, marginal tax rates never come close to those experienced by the lowest earners. Even at £60,000 a year, the earnings distribution is becoming considerably less dense.

[5] Figure 4.6 does not show effective tax rates on earnings of less than £100 per week, however. At these extremely low levels of earnings, people without a working partner typically face very high PTRs, since earnings would barely (if at all) exceed out-of-work benefits and WTC is not available for jobs of less than 16 hours per week (the minimum wage makes it difficult to earn much less than £100 if one works 16 hours or more). There are exceptions (such as students, who are not eligible for out-of-work benefits), but in general these high PTRs mean we would expect few people without working partners to choose to work for less than £100, and some apparent cases of people doing so look suspiciously like errors in the data rather than genuine examples. The weak incentive for lone parents to take 'mini-jobs' in the UK is documented and discussed in Bell, Brewer, and Phillips (2007).

Tax by Design

incentives than those without children, since Child Tax Credit provides substantial means-tested support which is then withdrawn as income rises. But the presence and work status of any partner are also important. Because means tests are assessed on couples' joint incomes, the pattern of work incentives for second earners in couples is often different from that for first earners.

If one partner is in low-paid work, he will often be entitled to WTC, which gives him a low PTR—the point of the WTC system. But this creates a disincentive for the spouse to enter work because doing so will reduce the couple's entitlement to WTC. She will have a high PTR. On the other hand, if the first worker in a couple earns enough to exhaust the family's entitlement to means-tested support, a low-earning second worker can face a

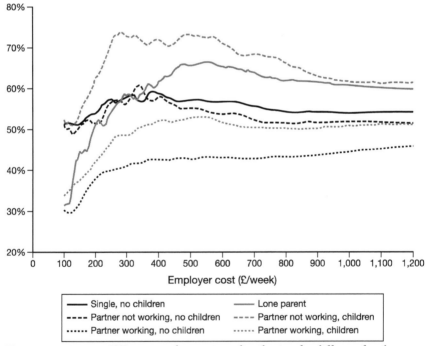

Figure 4.7. Average PTRs across the earnings distribution for different family types, 2009–10

Notes: Non-parametric regression (lowess) estimates. Employer cost = Gross earnings + Employer NICs.

Source: Authors' calculations using the IFS tax and benefit microsimulation model, TAXBEN, run on uprated data from the 2006–07 Family Resources Survey, and using estimated consumption tax rates from the 2007 Expenditure and Food Survey.

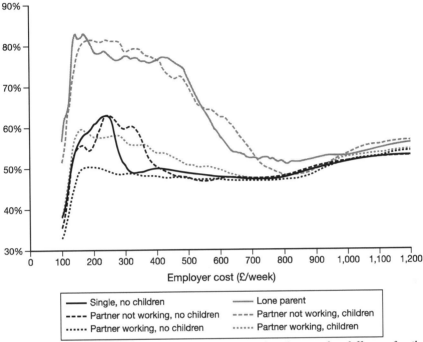

Figure 4.8. Average EMTRs across the earnings distribution for different family types, 2009–10

Notes: Non-parametric regression (lowess) estimates. Employer cost = Gross earnings + Employer NICs.

Source: Authors' calculations using the IFS tax and benefit microsimulation model, TAXBEN, run on uprated data from the 2006–07 Family Resources Survey, and using estimated consumption tax rates from the 2007 Expenditure and Food Survey.

very low EMTR (with no benefit or tax credit withdrawal), far from the high EMTRs shown in Figure 4.6. Figures 4.7 and 4.8 show how average PTRs and EMTRs vary with earnings for different family types. It is clear from Figure 4.8 how the tax credit system affects EMTRs for the first earner in a family with children, with average EMTRs for this group above 70% up to earnings of around £500 a week.

Finally, the role of support for housing costs in determining the work incentives people face deserves to be highlighted. The government expects to spend £21.5 billion on Housing Benefit for renters in 2010–11, about the same as on Child Tax Credit and more than on any other benefit except the

Basic State Pension.[6] By providing support for potentially large rental costs when income is very low, and then withdrawing this support sharply as income rises, Housing Benefit is responsible for some of the weakest work incentives in the UK tax and benefit system. Tables 4.3 and 4.4 show that, on average, workers who rent accommodation have PTRs 13 percentage points higher, and EMTRs 11 percentage points higher, than those who own their homes outright (though some of this difference may reflect differences in their incomes and other characteristics as well as their housing tenure).

The position is more complicated for those with a mortgage. Out-of-work benefits can include a Support for Mortgage Interest (SMI) component,

Table 4.3. Average PTRs among workers by family type and housing tenure, 2009–10

	Rent	Own with mortgage		Own outright
		SMI	No SMI	
Single				
No children	60%	56%	50%	48%
Children	48%	54%	39%	35%
Couple, partner not working				
No children	65%	55%	50%	46%
Children	70%	66%	56%	52%
Couple, partner working				
No children	45%	40%	40%	39%
Children	58%	46%	45%	45%
All	57%	48%	45%	44%

Notes: 'SMI' and 'No SMI' columns give average PTRs for the same people with and without Support for Mortgage Interest included in their out-of-work income. Table excludes people with housing tenure not recorded in the data.

Source: Authors' calculations using the IFS tax and benefit microsimulation model, TAXBEN, run on uprated data from the 2006–07 Family Resources Survey, and using estimated consumption tax rates from the 2007 Expenditure and Food Survey.

---

[6] Sources: Department for Work and Pensions, Benefit Expenditure Tables, http://research.dwp.gov.uk/asd/asd4/index.php?page=medium_term; HM Treasury, 2010b; HM Revenue and Customs, 2010f.

Table 4.4. Average EMTRs among workers by family type and housing tenure, 2009–10

	Rent	Own with mortgage		Own outright
		SMI	No SMI	
Single				
No children	54%	49%	49%	50%
Children	79%	65%	65%	62%
Couple, partner not working				
No children	60%	50%	50%	47%
Children	78%	61%	61%	61%
Couple, partner working				
No children	48%	47%	47%	46%
Children	61%	51%	51%	51%
All	60%	51%	51%	49%

Notes: 'SMI' and 'No SMI' columns give average EMTRs for the same people with and without Support for Mortgage Interest taken into account in the (few) relevant cases. Table excludes people with housing tenure not recorded in the data.

Source: Authors' calculations using the IFS tax and benefit microsimulation model, TAXBEN, run on uprated data from the 2006–07 Family Resources Survey, and using estimated consumption tax rates from the 2007 Expenditure and Food Survey.

covering an assumed interest rate (regardless of actual interest paid) on the outstanding balance (capped at £200,000) of mortgages taken out before the claimant moved onto benefits. But non-pensioners can receive SMI only after three months on benefit—a significant delay for those with mortgage payments to make and no private income—and those on JSA can receive it only for two years.[7] Since SMI is available only for certain time periods, it is

[7] The precise rules on SMI have been subject to rapid change since Autumn 2008; the details in the text are accurate at the time of writing (April 2011), but some of the recent changes are explicitly temporary. The cap was increased from £100,000 to £200,000; the three-month waiting period used to be either six months or nine months, depending on circumstances; the two-year limit for JSA claimants is a new feature; and the assumed interest rate used to be set at 1.58 percentage points above the Bank of England base rate, was then frozen at 6.08% when the base rate fell during the recession, and from October 2010 is based on average bank and building society mortgage interest rates.

not clear whether one should include it in potential out-of-work income when estimating PTRs for workers with a mortgage. In the preceding analysis and the rest of this chapter, we treat all those with a mortgage as if they would be eligible for SMI—so we arguably overstate their PTRs—but Tables 4.3 and 4.4 show the work incentives such people would face with and without SMI.[8]

SMI makes almost no difference to average EMTRs, since people working 16 hours or more per week are not eligible for out-of-work benefits. It is largely irrelevant to the PTRs of people with working partners, for similar reasons. But it can have a big effect on PTRs for the first earner in a family, and particularly for those with children (who are more likely to have larger mortgages than other groups).[9] The average PTR is 15 percentage points higher for a working lone parent with a mortgage if they would qualify for SMI than if they would not, and 10 percentage points higher for the sole earner in a couple with children.

SMI is often overlooked, as very few people actually receive it—only 4% of Income Support claimants and 3% of income-based JSA claimants, for example[10]—and its cost is a tiny fraction of that of Housing Benefit. But SMI matters more for work incentives than this implies, because while more non-workers rent their accommodation than have a mortgage, most workers have a mortgage. The *potential* availability (or otherwise) of SMI can thus be important for many people currently in work.

---

[8] We do not model the £200,000 cap on mortgages subject to SMI, so the true SMI-inclusive PTRs would be slightly lower than those shown.

[9] In the case of single parents, an additional factor is that they have lower average earnings than single people without children, so a given cash amount of SMI would make a bigger difference to the PTR. The opposite is true for sole earners in couples, however: those with children earn more on average than those without children.

[10] Source: DWP's Tabulation Tool (http://research.dwp.gov.uk/asd/index.php?page=tabtool), based on 5% sample data for February 2010. Corresponding figures for Pension Credit are not given, but they are likely to be rather higher: Pension Credit claimants make up the majority of SMI recipients.

4.1.3. Assessing the System

We have seen that the tax and benefit system is both significantly redistributive and creates important disincentives. Given the desire to redistribute, how does the pattern of work incentives described stack up against an 'optimal' pattern?

In broad terms, the pattern of work incentives outlined in the previous subsection corresponds surprisingly well to what would be demanded by the theory and evidence described in the previous chapter.

In the last chapter, we argued that for many groups—particularly single mothers, women with working partners, and the low-skilled—financial incentives affect the number in work more than they affect the earnings of those in work. This would tend to imply a strong case for keeping PTRs low at low levels of earnings. And indeed we find that PTRs are relatively low at low levels of earnings, on average, and especially for low-wage single parents and those with working partners, whose employment decisions are particularly responsive to financial incentives. The highest PTRs apply to sole earners in couples with children, and to a lesser extent to single people and sole earners in couples without children—the types of people who are likely to stay in work even if the incentive to do so is relatively weak.

The pattern of EMTRs shown in Figures 4.6 and 4.8—a 'U-shape', with high EMTRs at very low earnings, falling to a trough at employer costs of around £750 per week before rising again—is consistent with the lessons of optimal tax theory set out in the previous chapter for how the rate schedule should depend on the shape of the earnings distribution: that EMTRs should be highest when there are few people *at* that earnings level but many people *above* that earnings level.

Looking at Figure 4.6, we can see that EMTRs are highest, on average, at an employer cost of about £170 a week, just before the peak of the earnings distribution: there are relatively few people at that point (who might reduce their incomes in response) but many people above that point (so the high EMTR delivers a lot of revenue). Average EMTRs are lower at, say, £400, around the peak of the distribution. There are many people at that point (so strong disincentives would be damaging) and fewer people above it. The design problem is more complicated than that, of course—it must also take into account how responsive people at different earnings levels are, the extensive as well as intensive margin of labour supply, possible variation between different demographic groups, and society's redistributive preferences. But the broad pattern of EMTRs does not stand out as obviously flawed.[11]

But while these broad patterns may look sensible, there remain problems for certain groups. And even where effective tax rates are low on average, they may be too high for some.

Although not all low earners face weak work incentives, the weakest work incentives are found at low earnings levels. The effective tax rates of 90% or more faced by some low earners as a result of several benefits and tax credits being withdrawn at once are surely too high: even without reducing effective tax rates on average, it might be possible to reduce the dispersion shown in Figure 4.5 and in Tables 4.1 and 4.2. Naturally, high PTRs and EMTRs apply to people who stand to lose a lot of state support if they work—usually because they have children and/or substantial housing costs, and do not have a working partner whose earnings exhaust entitlement. This includes not only primary earners, but also some second earners: as mentioned in the previous subsection, low-wage second earners (or potential second earners)—a highly responsive group—face relatively low PTRs on average, but high PTRs if their partners are also low earners since the tax credits the family receives with one person in low-paid work are withdrawn when a second person moves into work. Very high PTRs also apply to low earners who do not qualify for Working Tax Credit—those without children who are under 25 or who are working (or contemplating work of) less than 30 hours per week, and those with children working (or contemplating work of) less than 16 hours per week.

Further up the earnings distribution, we do not find quite such high effective tax rates—though it seems unlikely that the bizarre pattern of rising

---

[11] Indeed, the pattern of a U-shape with a trough around £750 per week is remarkably similar to the simulated optimal EMTR schedules for the UK shown in figures 2.4A and 2.4B of Brewer, Saez, and Shephard (2010). These simulations should not (and were not intended to) be taken too seriously as a precise guide to policy—they ignore the extensive margin of labour supply, do not allow for any variation by demographics, and assume a uniform labour supply elasticity—but the broad pattern, driven by considerations of the shape of the earnings distribution, is certainly suggestive.

and falling marginal income tax rates shown in Figure 4.1 is optimal. Tax rates at the very top of the distribution are particularly important to get right because of the very large amount of revenue being extracted from a very small number of people. In Section 4.3, we consider the appropriate choice of top tax rates in detail.

Finally, looking beyond the broad family types we have considered so far, it is not clear that tax and benefit rates reflect demographic characteristics as well as they could, i.e. that the system makes full use of what we know about the labour market characteristics of different groups.

In what follows, we look first at possible reforms for low earners and then at the position for moderate and high earners. Finally, we turn to the question of whether demographic characteristics—specifically, age—could be used more intelligently than at present to target incentives where they are most effective.

4.2. EFFECTIVE TAX RATES FOR LOW EARNERS

Some low earners face very high PTRs and/or EMTRs as means-tested support is withdrawn. But reducing these effective tax rates clearly has costs as well as benefits: in simple terms, withdrawing this support from low earners can be avoided only by not providing as much support in the first place (which makes the poorest worse off) or by extending the support to those with higher incomes (which costs money that must ultimately come from someone). This is the central dilemma for policy, though there are nuances that make both the problem and the available policy options somewhat more complex in the real world.

To examine in more concrete terms the dilemma that policymakers face, we can consider some specific proposals put forward by Brewer, Saez, and Shephard (2010). They argue that PTRs and EMTRs are too high for many low earners, and suggest a set of reforms to the existing set of means-tested benefits and tax credits:

- increasing to £50 per week the amount that can be earned before means-tested benefits start to be withdrawn;

- doubling (from £6,420 to £12,840 per year) the amount that two-earner couples can earn before tax credits start to be withdrawn;
- reducing the rate at which tax credits are withdrawn from 39p to 34p per £1 of earnings;
- increasing WTC rates to the level of Income Support / JSA rates (except for lone parents, for whom WTC is already higher than Income Support).

Figure 4.9 shows how these reforms would affect the budget constraint facing the same low-wage single parent shown in Figure 4.2, with and without the reforms in place.[12] In this example, what stands out is the rise in in-work income—and thus the strengthening of the incentive to be in work—resulting from the first of the reforms listed above, the increase to £50 in the amount that can be earned before means-tested benefits start to be withdrawn and the budget constraint flattens out.

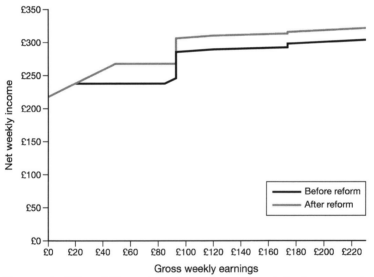

Figure 4.9. Effect of illustrative reforms on an example budget constraint in 2009–10

Notes and source: As for Figure 4.2.

[12] The 'Before reform' line of Figure 4.9 is not quite identical to the top line of Figure 4.2 because Figure 4.2 was drawn for 2010–11 while the reforms illustrated here are to the 2009–10 tax and benefit system. The difference is minimal, however.

As ever, no one example tells the full story—indeed, only two of the four changes listed above apply to lone parents at all, though they would be important for other groups. Broadly speaking, these proposals were designed to increase the incentives for people to move into work—focusing on lowering PTRs and EMTRs at very low levels of earnings. But there is a cost to this. Means-testing and high EMTRs are pushed further up the earnings distribution. The proposals highlight a number of delicate trade-offs:

(i) *Incentives to be in work versus incentives to increase earnings.* All four components of this reform act to increase the net incomes of low-paid workers and therefore reduce their PTRs. But the result of means-testing less aggressively and increasing WTC is that means tests extend further up the income distribution, reducing the incentive for many of those in work to increase their earnings. The fundamental rationale for the reform is that this increase in EMTRs is a price worth paying for the reduction in PTRs.

(ii) *Incentives for first earners versus incentives for second earners.* Entitlement to means-tested support is generally assessed on the basis of a couple's combined income. Increasing support for low-earning families increases the incentive to have a first earner in work. But if that support is withdrawn against additional earnings, it can reduce the incentive for families to have a second earner in work. In a system of joint assessment, policies that reduce PTRs for first earners will therefore increase PTRs for many second earners.[13] The second component of this set of policies, introducing a higher tax credit threshold for two-earner couples, is designed to counteract this feature of the other three components and of the existing system—essentially by departing from the principle of pure joint assessment. It is particularly important given the evidence that employment responses are especially large among second earners.

---

[13] This can be thought of as a special case of the previous point: with a jointly assessed system, the trade-off is between the incentive for *families* to have someone in work and the incentive for *families* to increase their earnings, and one way in which single-earner families can increase their earnings is to have a second earner in work.

(iii) *Very weak incentives for a few versus quite weak incentives for many.* Reducing the rate at which tax credits are withdrawn means that those facing the highest EMTRs would see them reduced. But the price for this is that the withdrawal is spread over a wider range of income and high (albeit not quite as high) EMTRs affect many more people. On the one hand, spreading high EMTRs more evenly is valuable: the distortion imposed by taxes rises more than proportionately to their rate,[14] so having two people face 50% tax rates is generally preferable to having one person taxed at 30% and another at 70%. On the other hand, as tax credit entitlement and means-testing are extended, they start to affect income ranges that are more densely populated. This means that the cost to government rises and that many more people face higher EMTRs than lower EMTRs. Brewer, Saez, and Shephard (2010) argue that current EMTRs are so extraordinarily high for some low earners that a little spreading-out is justified.

(iv) *Theoretical optimality versus practical considerations.* A major extension of means-testing has practical downsides quite apart from its effect on EMTRs, including extra administration for government, hassle and stigma for claimants, and widespread non-take-up of entitlements. These practicalities matter—perhaps more than getting the theoretical trade-offs precisely right. That is why we devote the next chapter to the administration and integration of taxes and benefits.

Of course, alternative policies could be chosen to finesse these trade-offs. One obvious way to reduce PTRs at relatively low (but not the lowest) levels of earnings, without extending means-testing, would be to increase income tax allowances (perhaps financed by increasing the basic rate of tax, thus trading off reduced PTRs against increased EMTRs). This would have the additional practical advantage of taking people out of the tax system altogether. But this alternative does less to address the problems identified in the existing system, since it would affect only those earning above the current personal allowance whereas the argument for reducing PTRs is strongest at even lower levels of earnings than this.

---

[14] See Auerbach (1985) for an exposition; the idea has been traced back to Dupuit (1844).

Another possible reform, which would more fully address concerns about support for first earners weakening incentives for second earners, would be to make WTC entirely individually assessed. There would be a separate credit for each working individual, means-tested on their individual income, irrespective of any partner's circumstances. As noted in the discussion of family income taxation in Section 3.3, the obvious downside of this is the cost of paying tax credits to large numbers of people in relatively affluent families.

To illustrate the potential for reform more concretely, we focus here on the set of changes[15] that we outlined above.

To make a fair comparison with the current system, we need to recognize that all the components of this reform have a monetary cost—collectively, some £12.3 billion, if no one changed their behaviour in response to the reform[16]—and this must be paid for.[17] For illustration, we assume that they are financed through a combination of:

- a 12% cut in all the main means-tested benefits and tax credits except Pension Credit (offsetting the more targeted increases listed above);
- a 1 percentage point increase in the basic rate of income tax.

Having chosen a set of reforms to rebalance the system between non-workers, low earners, and higher earners, we try to upset the new balance as little as possible by sharing the burden of paying for them between all three groups: non-workers lose from the reduction in benefits, higher earners from the increase in income tax, and low earners from a combination of the two. These changes would raise the required £12.3 billion, again assuming no one changed their behaviour in response.

---

[15] Those proposed by Brewer, Saez, and Shephard (2010).

[16] This is rather higher than the £8.8 billion costing given by Brewer, Saez, and Shephard (2010). They ignored free school meals, Support for Mortgage Interest, the childcare element of Working Tax Credit, the 'baby bonus' in Child Tax Credit and Housing Benefit / Council Tax Benefit, and the Sure Start Maternity Grant; we take all of these into account. The expansion of means-testing entailed by their reform would extend eligibility for all of these benefits to more families, increasing the overall cost of the reform.

[17] Brewer, Saez, and Shephard (2010) set out a long-run reform which was revenue neutral, but did not suggest how to pay for their short-run reforms.

By their nature, these reforms are not distributionally neutral. Strengthening incentives to enter low-paid work must increase support for low-paid workers (broadly the lower-middle of the income distribution) at the expense of the poorest and the rich: there is no escaping these distributional consequences.

Given this inevitable 'inverted-U-shaped' pattern of gains and losses, the relative sizes of the tax rise and the benefit cut used to finance the reform were chosen to minimize the overall distributional shift: it seems to us that the pattern of gains and losses shown in Figure 4.10 strikes a balance that is neither strongly progressive nor strongly regressive overall.[18] In financing

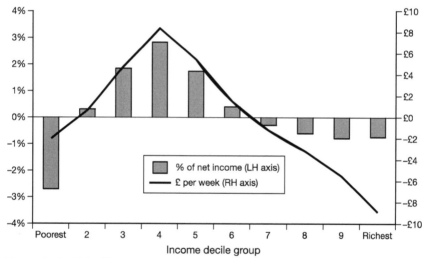

Figure 4.10. Gains/Losses across the income distribution

Notes: Reform as described in the text. Income decile groups derived by dividing families into ten equal-sized groups according to their disposable income adjusted for family size using the McClements equivalence scale.

Source: Authors' calculations using the IFS tax and benefit microsimulation model, TAXBEN, run on uprated data from the 2006–07 Family Resources Survey.

[18] Standard measures of inequality bear this out. The Gini coefficient and the coefficient of variation are slightly reduced by the reform, whereas the Theil mean log deviation is increased. These differences reflect different weights put upon extremely high and extremely low incomes by the various measures of inequality, but there is certainly no clear message of increased or reduced inequality that emerges.

gains for the lower-middle, the rich lose most in cash terms; the poorest lose most as a percentage of income.[19]

Whether the distributional pattern shown in Figure 4.10 is considered balanced—or acceptable—is a matter for political debate. Our intention is not to advocate the precise distributional outcomes associated with this particular variant of reform, but to illustrate the economic effects of moving in this broad direction.

Figures 4.11 and 4.12 show the effects of the reform on work incentives, illustrating some of the trade-offs discussed above. Figure 4.11 shows that average PTRs fall for low earners and rise for high earners.[20] But the overall average falls (by 1.5 percentage points, from 49.0% to 47.5%), and the fall is concentrated on the highest PTRs. In fact, the number of workers facing PTRs above 75% falls by 40% (800,000). By contrast, the average EMTR rises by 2.3 percentage points, from 51.6% to 53.9%; average EMTRs rise right across the earnings distribution, and especially for low-to-moderate earners (Figure 4.12). Again the highest effective tax rates are reduced: the number of people facing EMTRs above 75% falls by 900,000. But the number facing EMTRs between 50% and 75% rises by 4.9 million: overall, a 38% increase in the number of workers for whom any extra earnings are worth less than half what they cost their employer. This illustrates the trade-off between improving extremely weak incentives for a relatively small number of people and weakening already quite weak work incentives for a lot of people.

These overall patterns hide significant variations between family types. For example, the average PTR rises by nearly 3 percentage points for two-earner couples without children but falls for all other demographic groups—especially one-earner couples with children, for whom it falls by 9 percentage points. The average EMTR falls by 4 percentage points for lone parents but rises (by rather less than this) for all other groups.

---

[19] Brewer, Saez, and Shephard (2010) restricted their attention to working-age families; we include pensioners as well. In practice, this makes little difference.

[20] Average PTRs rise for high earners partly because of the income tax rise, but also because many of these high earners have low-earning partners and so would be entitled to means-tested support if they did not work. Since support for families with a single low earner is increased by the reform, more support is then lost by the higher earner's being in work.

Tax by Design

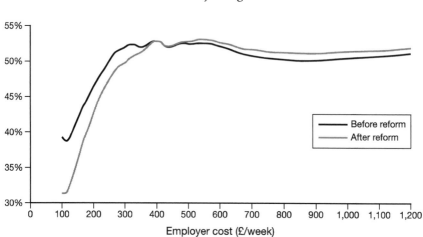

Figure 4.11. Effect of reform on average PTRs across the earnings distribution

Notes: Non-parametric regression (lowess) estimates. Reform as described in the text. Employer cost = Gross earnings + Employer NICs.

Source: Authors' calculations using the IFS tax and benefit microsimulation model, TAXBEN, run on uprated data from the 2006–07 Family Resources Survey, and using estimated consumption tax rates from the 2007 Expenditure and Food Survey.

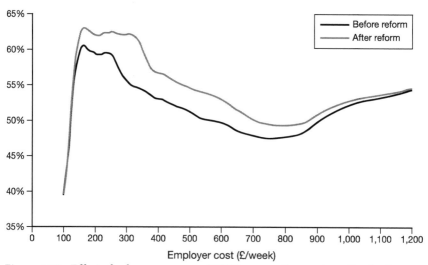

Figure 4.12. Effect of reform on average EMTRs across the earnings distribution

Notes: Non-parametric regression (lowess) estimates. Reform as described in the text. Employer cost = Gross earnings + Employer NICs.

Source: Authors' calculations using the IFS tax and benefit microsimulation model, TAXBEN, run on uprated data from the 2006–07 Family Resources Survey, and using estimated consumption tax rates from the 2007 Expenditure and Food Survey.

Using evidence (discussed in the previous chapter) about how responsive different types of people are, we can estimate the magnitude of the likely responses to these changes in work incentives, in terms of employment, hours worked, and total earnings.[21] While there is inevitably considerable uncertainty surrounding our assumptions, our central estimate is that this reform would lead to a remarkable 1.1 million (or 4.2%) net increase in employment. There is obviously a lot of uncertainty associated with this precise number: it is quite sensitive to assumptions, and the elasticities involved are not precisely measured and could themselves be changed by large reforms. The key point is just that the effect on employment could be large.

But those moving into work would predominantly be low earners, while the increase in average PTRs for high earners means that some of them would stop working. The increase in EMTRs also means that many of those who stayed in work would reduce how much they earned. So aggregate earnings (including employer NICs) across the economy would grow by much less: only 0.5%, or £3.5 billion. About £3.0 billion of this would accrue to the household sector in terms of higher consumption, while the Exchequer would gain £0.6 billion in higher tax revenues and lower benefit spending than in the absence of the reform.

To summarize: if the diagnosis is that net incomes in low-paid work are too low relative to net incomes out of work, then the treatment is to increase in-work incomes for the low-paid. But this treatment has undesirable side effects, the principal one being the extension of means-testing to many more people: around a million more families would be entitled to a means-tested benefit or tax credit as a result of this reform (from a base of around 14.6 million who we estimate are entitled now, about a third of whom are pensioners). The practical implications of such an extension of means-testing, quite apart from the associated weakening of incentives for low earners to increase their incomes, might make this reform a difficult pill for policymakers to swallow. The pros and cons are finely balanced.

---

[21] Details of our methodology and assumptions are available in an online appendix available at http://www.ifs.org.uk/mirrleesReview. The same assumptions are maintained for labour supply estimates throughout this chapter and the rest of the book.

There may be ways to sugar the pill. To minimize (or avoid altogether) the extension of means-testing, reductions in effective tax rates could be focused more precisely where they are needed: rather than means-testing less aggressively overall, we could reduce effective tax rates specifically for those who are currently subject to several taxes and means tests simultaneously, which is where the biggest problem lies. That requires reforming the way in which different taxes, tax credits, and benefits interact—reforms which could also make means-testing less objectionable in the process. We address that subject in the next chapter.

4.3. TAXATION OF MODERATE AND HIGH EARNERS

We know quite a lot about how those on low earnings respond to incentives in the tax and benefit system. We know less about higher earners in general, though we do know that across the earnings distribution, labour supply adjustments seem to occur mainly at older ages, around retirement, and, for women, during years of child-rearing. For other groups, and particularly perhaps for the highest earners, less of their response to the tax system seems to be about changes in labour supply, and more of it about changes in taxable income. This might arise through effort being put in to avoiding (or evading) tax payments, or even through decisions over whether or not to locate in this country. Labour supply seems to be relatively inelastic for the most part; but recent evidence suggests that taxable income elasticities remain positive and significant throughout the earnings distribution.[22]

For some, short-run labour supply responses might well be less important than longer-term choices over, for example, education, training, and occupation. These relationships, while likely to be important, have proven harder to estimate empirically.[23]

The level of uncertainty about the way in which people in the middle of the earnings distribution respond to tax changes makes it difficult to fine-tune delicate trade-offs of the kind discussed in the previous section.

---

[22] Chetty, 2009.
[23] Heckman, Lochner, and Taber, 1999.

The government can change how it raises a given amount of revenue by adjusting the tax-free personal allowance, the basic and higher rates of income tax, the higher-rate threshold, and the equivalent NICs rates and thresholds. In doing so, it can, albeit with limited knowledge, trade off the degree of progression against concerns over work incentives and long- and short-run taxable income elasticities. In general, raising allowances will be more progressive than cutting the basic rate of tax, and much more progressive than cutting the higher rate. On the other hand, higher marginal rates above the personal allowance could have negative effects on incentives to earn more. Note that within the tax system itself, little can be done for the very poorest. Around a quarter of adults live in households where nobody has a high enough income to pay tax.[24]

Two specific features of the income tax schedule merit further comment: the complexity of the rate schedule and the taxation of the very highest earners.

4.3.1. A Straightforward Income Tax Schedule

A basic requirement for any system of taxing earnings is that the rate schedule should be transparent. The UK tax system is far from meeting that requirement, and reforming income tax itself would be a good place to start.

The biggest offender is the tapering-away of personal allowances as income rises. At present, the extra personal allowances available to those aged 65 or over (and 75 or over) are reduced by 50p for each £1 of income above £22,900, so that the personal allowance for people of 65 or over is the same as that for under-65s once income is above £28,930 (£29,230 for those aged 75 or over). Many people are unaware of this; far more do not realize that it is equivalent to applying a 30% marginal income tax rate in this income range.[25] Similarly, from 2010–11, the main personal allowance is reduced by

---

[24] Adam, Browne, and Heady, 2010.

[25] In fact, for married couples and civil partners aged 75 or over, there is an added complication: they can claim a married couple's allowance, which reduces their tax liability by £696.50; this is reduced by 5p for every £1 of income above £29,230 until it reaches a minimum

Tax by Design

Table 4.5. Income tax schedule for those aged 65–75, 2010–11

Income range	Marginal income tax rate (%)
£0–£9,490	0
£9,491–£22,900	20
£22,901–£28,930	30
£28,931–£43,875	20
£43,876–£100,000	40
£100,001–£112,950	60
£112,951–£150,000	40
£150,001+	50

50p for each £1 of income above £100,000 until it is eliminated entirely once income reaches £112,950. That is equivalent to a 60% income tax rate in this range.

If setting these effective tax rates is the objective, then it should be explicit in the marginal rate schedule, not described opaquely as a phased withdrawal of the personal allowance: this peculiar mechanism serves no purpose except to obscure what the tax system is actually doing. Table 4.5 shows the effective income tax schedule for someone aged between 65 and 75, for whom both allowances can be tapered.[26] We doubt that many ministers and officials

of £267.00 at incomes of £37,820. This in effect applies a 25% marginal income tax rate between £29,230 and £37,820—though only for the lower-income spouse, since couples can choose which of them claims the allowance (or can claim half each) and so can always save by allocating it to the lower-income spouse if only one has income above £29,230. The absurdity and obscurity of this situation speak for themselves.

[26] Even Table 4.5 is a simplification of the true position. The 10% starting rate of income tax was not completely abolished in 2008–09: it remains in place, but only for savings income and only where that savings income, treated as the top slice of income except for dividends, falls into the first £2,440 of income above the personal allowance. Again, describing this situation in detail is perhaps the best way of illustrating how ridiculous and indefensible it is.

within government are consciously aware they are inflicting this absurd tax schedule, let alone that many taxpayers understand it.

There is little chance that Table 4.5 describes an optimal schedule—though it is not necessarily the case that an optimal income tax schedule is a very simple one, at least if we put to one side issues of practicality. When defining the tax *base*, applying similar tax rates across the board tends to achieve not only simplicity but also efficiency, as it minimizes distortions to the form of economic activity.[27] When setting the *rate* schedule, there is no such presumption. As we described in the last chapter, optimal tax theory prescribes how the tax rate at each level of earnings should depend on factors such as the number of people at that level of earnings and their responsiveness to tax rates, as well as the degree of concern for redistribution. If those factors vary by earnings in a complicated way, the optimal income tax rate schedule could be complicated, and there is certainly no reason to expect a single marginal rate of tax at all levels of earnings to be optimal.

Yet even if the theoretically optimal rate schedule were to be a complicated function of earnings, it is generally possible to approximate such a schedule closely with just two or three rates and an allowance: a great variety of outcomes can be achieved with relatively few tools. A 'flat tax', with just one marginal rate above a personal allowance, is unnecessarily inflexible, so having separate basic and higher income tax rates does serve a useful purpose. A case could conceivably be made for a third tax band above the personal allowance (such as the 50% tax rate on the highest incomes that was introduced in 2010–11). But beyond that, adding more bands and rates achieves nothing that could not be approximated almost exactly by adjusting the rates and thresholds of a relatively simple system. For example, the starting rate of tax that was in place between 1992–93 and 2007–08 achieved a pattern of payments that could have been replicated almost perfectly by extending the personal allowance to cover the bottom part of that band and applying the basic rate of tax to the top part. Certainly a system as

---

[27] Economic theory can suggest ways in which departing from uniformity could enhance economic efficiency, and we discuss such arguments (and whether any increase in economic efficiency justifies the associated complexity) in later chapters. Nevertheless, a presumption in favour of uniform taxation is generally a good rule of thumb.

convoluted as that shown in Table 4.5, with tax rates rising and falling seemingly at random, is patently absurd.

The income tax schedule is clearly more complicated than it needs to be. But the rate schedule for earnings taxation as a whole is far more complicated than that for income tax alone, because it consists of many different components which do not fit together harmoniously. To take the simplest example, the thresholds for income tax and NICs are not aligned with each other, so the two taxes in combination have several more bands than income tax alone. Once tax credits and benefits are brought into the equation as well, the complexity becomes quite bewildering, and seemingly arbitrary patterns of effective tax rates proliferate. That is just one reason to address the interaction between the different elements of earnings taxation—something to which we devote the next chapter.

4.3.2. The Top Tax Rate

From 2010–11, a new 50% rate of income tax applies to incomes above £150,000. The government estimates that this directly affects only 275,000 individuals, out of an adult population of about 49 million. Yet the income tax rate applying to the very highest earners has an importance out of proportion to their numbers, simply because they are such an important source of revenue: even before this reform took effect, a quarter of income tax was paid by the top 1% of income tax payers, just over 300,000 individuals.[28] That is a fact worth repeating. One pound in every four collected by the income tax system comes from just 1% of income tax payers. Of course, this largely reflects just how much more pre-tax income the top 1% of taxpayers earn than the bulk of the population do.

---

[28] Sources: For the number facing the 50% income tax rate—HMRC statistics, table 2.1, http://www.hmrc.gov.uk/stats/income_tax/table2-1.pdf; for the top 1%'s share of income tax revenue—HMRC statistics, table 2.4, http://www.hmrc.gov.uk/stats/income_tax/table2-4.pdf; for total population—ONS 2008-based national population projections, http://www.statistics.gov.uk/downloads/theme_population/NPP2008/NatPopProj2008.pdf; for the number of dependent children in the population—HMRC, *Child Benefit Statistics: Geographical Analysis, August 2010*, http://www.hmrc.gov.uk/stats/child_benefit/chb-geog-aug10.pdf.

As noted in the previous chapter, the responsiveness of taxable income, and hence tax receipts, to tax rates may be quite high at the top of the earnings distribution—not because high earners' employment decisions or hours of work are particularly responsive, but because they may find other ways to minimize the amount of tax they pay: by reducing their effort per hour worked or by, for example, changing the form of their remuneration, contributing more to a pension or to charity, converting income into capital gains, setting themselves up as a company, investing in tax avoidance, illegally hiding their income, or even leaving the country altogether (or not coming here when they otherwise would have).

In fact, it is not clear whether the 50% rate will raise any revenue at all. There are numerous ways in which people might reduce their taxable incomes in response to higher tax rates; at some point, increasing tax rates starts to cost money instead of raising it. The question is, where is that point? Brewer, Saez, and Shephard (2010) addressed precisely this question for the highest-income 1%. Their central estimate is that the taxable income elasticity for this group is 0.46, which implies a revenue-maximizing tax rate on earned income of 56%.[29] This in turn (accounting for NICs and indirect taxes) corresponds to an income tax rate of 40%. So, according to these estimates, the introduction of the 50% rate would actually reduce revenue.[30]

However, there is no escaping the uncertainty around the estimate of a 40% revenue-maximizing income tax rate. It was based primarily on what happened to incomes when tax rates changed in the late 1980s; but people's ability to respond to tax changes may well have changed since then. Increases in international mobility and in the availability of complicated financial products may have increased people's scope to respond, while a succession of anti-avoidance measures may have reduced it. Changes to capital gains tax have at different times made it easier and harder to escape tax by converting income into capital gains.[31] And the government increased the likely yield of the 50% income tax rate by also announcing a limit on the tax relief that high

---

[29] Brewer and Browne, 2009.

[30] Increases in rates of NICs and VAT announced since this analysis was done will further reduce the income tax rate that corresponds to a given overall tax rate on earnings.

[31] We return to this issue in Chapter 19.

earners can obtain by saving their income in a pension.[32] So the elasticity might have risen or fallen. And even if nothing had changed since the late 1980s, statistically there was only a two-thirds chance that the revenue-maximizing rate was somewhere between 33% and 57%.[33]

So we do not know with confidence what the revenue-maximizing top tax rate is. But governments do not have the luxury of stopping there: policy must be decided, so, in the absence of compelling evidence, they must take a best guess. The Treasury's best guess is that the 50% rate will raise some revenue. That is certainly not impossible, but it is certainly uncertain.

Whatever the precise revenue-maximizing tax rate, it seems unlikely that much additional revenue can be raised simply by increasing the income tax rate for the very highest earners. But it is important to realize that this is not the only tool available for extracting money from this group. Widening the income tax base—removing reliefs and clamping down on avoidance—not only raises money directly but also reduces the scope for shifting income into tax-free forms and thereby makes tax rate increases more effective revenue-raisers. And there are, of course, other taxes aimed at the wealthy (notably inheritance tax), which might have the potential to raise revenue.

In addition, we should not forget that the revenue-maximizing rate is itself not necessarily the rate that we should impose on this group. If we value their welfare at all, or have concerns over long-term behavioural effects, then we might want a rate below the revenue-maximizing rate in any case.

---

[32] An issue to which we return in Chapter 14.

[33] Brewer and Browne, 2009. The estimate of the revenue-maximizing top tax rate also relies on two other debatable assumptions. The first is that, were it not for tax changes, the incomes of the top 1% would have evolved in the same way as those of the next-richest 4%, which we cannot know. The second is that any reduction in taxable income would be matched one-for-one by a reduction in spending (and therefore indirect tax revenues)—likely to be broadly accurate if the reduced taxable income reflected a real reduction in economic activity in the UK (less work effort or less net immigration, for example), but not if it reflected more tax avoidance or evasion, say.

4.4. TARGETING INCENTIVES AT DIFFERENT POINTS IN THE LIFE CYCLE

In Section 3.4, we argued that redistribution could be achieved more efficiently by varying tax rates by characteristics that are known to indicate people's ability, needs, or responsiveness to taxation—the approach known as tagging. We also noted that tagging can potentially have disadvantages in terms of complexity, infringement of privacy, and incentives to acquire whatever characteristics are used, and that the use of some characteristics would be widely ruled out as constituting improper discrimination.

In this section, we look at two examples of policies designed to focus on particular groups that exhibit the advantages while suffering few of the disadvantages. They are based on using information about the ages of family members: specifically, applying lower effective tax rates to families whose youngest child is of school age, and to those around retirement age, than to others. We have strong evidence that labour supply is particularly responsive at these points in the life cycle, which makes reducing effective tax rates at those points a powerful tool.

Governments in the UK and elsewhere already vary tax and benefit payments according to these characteristics. The reforms would raise few new problems of privacy or improper discrimination, and our illustrative reforms add little if any complexity to the existing system. In addition, age cannot, of course, be changed in response to incentives (though the timing of childbearing can be). But while tax and benefit payments currently vary with the ages of family members, they do so in a way that does not make best use of what we know about people's responsiveness, so significant improvements are available, increasing labour supply without being any less progressive overall. Targeting particular points in the life cycle also means that what distributional effects there are can in large part be thought of as shifting resources over a family's life cycle rather than between different families.

4.4.1. Age of Youngest Child

Mothers' decisions over whether and how much to work are more responsive to incentives when all their children are of school age than when they have a child under 5 years old.[34] The tax and benefit system should provide stronger work incentives for people who are more responsive to them: we can afford to redistribute more from rich to poor among less responsive groups, because the damage that redistribution does to work incentives is less important for them than for more responsive groups. So a simple way of tilting the system to reflect the differential responsiveness of parents with children of different ages is to make Child Tax Credit more generous (and so means-testing more extensive) for families with any children under the age of 5, and less generous (with less means-testing) for families whose youngest child is aged 5 or older.

In 2009–10, one revenue-neutral reform (assuming no behavioural change) would have been to increase the child element of CTC from £2,235 to £3,100 where the youngest child in a family was under 5 while reducing it to half that, £1,550, where the youngest child was 5 or older.[35]

Figures 4.13 and 4.14 show how average work incentives were already somewhat stronger for families with older children, and how this reform would make the differential greater. For parents with older children, this reform reduces average PTRs by about 1 percentage point and average EMTRs by a similar amount. There would be a corresponding weakening of work incentives for parents with pre-school children: their average PTR would rise by 1.0 percentage point and their average EMTR by 1.5 percentage points. But we would expect this group to respond less to these weakened incentives than the parents of older children would respond to their strengthened incentives. We estimate that some 72,000 parents of older children would enter work, while only 21,000 parents of younger children would stop work: an overall increase of 52,000, or roughly 0.2% more workers. Those working more have lower average wages than those working

---

[34] Blundell and Shephard (2011) find that the elasticity of employment for single mothers in the UK is 0.85 when their youngest child is aged 5 or older, compared with around 0.5 for those with younger children.

[35] Our modelling also includes a symmetric reform to child additions to Housing Benefit and Council Tax Benefit. Otherwise, the effect of the reform would be severely dampened for families facing withdrawal of these benefits as any increase (reduction) in CTC would be offset by a reduction (increase) in these benefits. This is typical of the kind of complication that could be removed by benefit integration, as discussed in the next chapter.

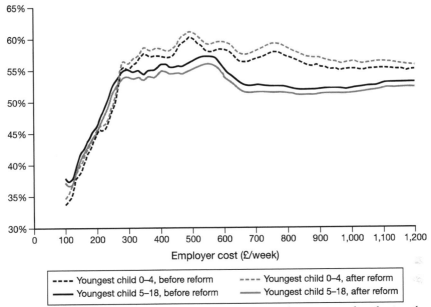

Figure 4.13. Effect of reform on average PTRs across the earnings distribution, by age of youngest child

Notes: Non-parametric regression (lowess) estimates. Reform as described in the text. Employer cost = Gross earnings + Employer NICs.

Source: Authors' calculations using the IFS tax and benefit microsimulation model, TAXBEN, run on uprated data from the 2006–07 Family Resources Survey, and using estimated consumption tax rates from the 2007 Expenditure and Food Survey.

less, so aggregate earnings (including employer NICs) would increase by somewhat less—about 0.1% or £0.8 billion, of which about £0.5 billion would accrue to households and £0.3 billion to the Exchequer.

Policymakers will have regard to more than just the effects of reforms on work incentives. In particular, they are likely to be concerned with distributional effects. In any given year, this reform clearly redistributes from parents with older children to parents with younger children, taking about £1.5 billion per year from the latter group and giving it to the former. But this is largely redistribution over the life cycle: since everyone's children start off aged 0 and get older, what families gain when the children are young will

Tax by Design

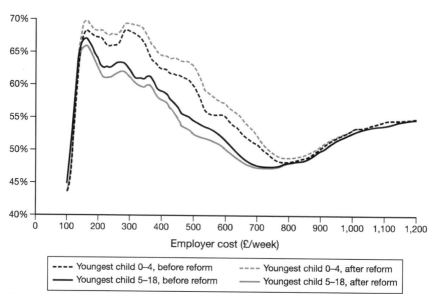

Figure 4.14. Effect of reform on average EMTRs across the earnings distribution, by age of youngest child

Notes: Non-parametric regression (lowess) estimates. Reform as described in the text. Employer cost = Gross earnings + Employer NICs.

Source: Authors' calculations using the IFS tax and benefit microsimulation model, TAXBEN, run on uprated data from the 2006–07 Family Resources Survey, and using estimated consumption tax rates from the 2007 Expenditure and Food Survey.

generally offset what they lose when the children are older. A government introducing a reform like this could consider increasing the rate for young children a few years before reducing that for older children, so that families suffered from the cut only if they previously benefited from the increase.

Of course, the distributional picture is slightly more complicated than merely bringing forward a given amount of support. Families might have too much income to qualify for tax credits when their children are older but not when their children are younger (or, less likely, vice versa). Effects will also vary if marital status changes and according to how spread out the ages of children in the family are. Nevertheless, for many families the main effect would be that support was received earlier on, an effect that might be rather helpful given evidence that spending on children is more valuable when the children are young.[36]

4.4.2. Retirement Age

Continuing in the same vein, there is powerful evidence that people's decisions about whether and how much to work become much more responsive to financial incentives when they are around retirement age—roughly 55–70.[37] It may therefore be more important to keep work incentives strong for people in this age range than for those in their 30s, 40s, and early 50s.

Older workers already tend to have somewhat stronger work incentives, partly because they are less likely to have dependent children and so to face losing Child Tax Credit if they work (or increase their earnings). If we were to target means-tested support on families with younger children, as advocated in the previous subsection, this would also strengthen work incentives for parents in the 55-plus age range, whose children are typically older.

But it is possible to focus incentives on older workers more directly. The tax and benefit system already contains several important features that change around retirement age and thereby transform the effective tax rates that individuals face:[38]

- Employee and self-employed NICs stop being payable at state pension age (currently 65 for men, and in the process of rising from 60 to 65 for women by 2018 and then to 66 for both men and women by 2020).

---

[36] See e.g. Heckman (2006) and Fiszbein and Schady (2009). Note, however, that these studies are concerned not with simple financial support, but with education policy or with *conditional cash transfers*—financial support provided on condition of 'good behaviour' by the parents.

[37] Gruber and Wise, 1999 and 2004.

[38] Another age-related feature is due to take effect in April 2011: the 2009 Pre-Budget Report announced that those aged 65 or over will be required to work for only 16 hours per week, rather than 30, to be eligible for Working Tax Credit. This will encourage people to work part-time rather than retiring, but also to work part-time rather than full-time.

- The income tax personal allowance rises substantially (from £6,475 to £9,490) at age 65[39]—with this extra allowance reduced by 50p for each £1 of income above £22,900.

- Income Support and JSA are replaced by the much more generous Pension Credit at the female state pension age, becoming even more generous at age 65.

For illustrative purposes, we consider simply changing the age at which each of these changes takes place so as to strengthen work incentives for 55- to 70-year-olds, in each case raising the money required (or spending the money generated) by a roughly mirror-image reform for under-55s. Thus the reform we model is to:

- end employee and self-employed NICs at age 55, rather than at state pension age; this would cost £5.2 billion, paid for by increasing the main rates of employee and self-employed NICs by 1.2 percentage points for those (aged under 55) who would still be paying them;

- apply the higher personal allowance from age 55 rather than 65, meeting the £1.7 billion cost by reducing the personal allowance from £6,475 to £6,145 for under-55s;

- raise the age requirement for receiving Pension Credit to age 70, using the £3.1 billion raised to increase rates of Income Support and JSA by 19%.[40,41]

Obviously, there are other possible reforms, including reforms that would be revenue neutral within the 55–70 age group. In the reform we have illustrated, the combination of changes would mean gains for 55- to 70-year-olds on average, at the expense of under-55s, in any one year. But the pattern depends strongly on income. The rate schedule for 55- to 70-year-olds would

---

[39] Rising further to £9,640 at age 75.

[40] As in the previous subsection, our modelling also includes symmetric reforms to Housing Benefit and Council Tax Benefit to prevent these benefits offsetting the changes for many families.

[41] In fact, much of this increase in the age requirement for Pension Credit is already due to happen as the female state pension age rises from 60 to 66 between 2010 and 2020. The 2007 Pensions Act also provides for the state pension age and Pension Credit age to rise further to 68 by 2046, although the coalition government has said that it will bring forward proposals 'to manage future changes in the State Pension Age more automatically' (HM Treasury, 2011).

become less progressive, with those on low incomes losing and those on higher incomes gaining, while the rate schedule for under-55s would become more progressive, with non-workers on low incomes gaining and those on higher incomes losing.

Since the reduction in the progressivity of the tax and benefit schedule for 55- to 70-year-olds is mirrored by an increase in progressivity for under-55s, there would be little change in the progressivity of the system as a whole. Nevertheless, this reform undoubtedly involves big changes to the tax and benefit payments of each family at each point in time: more than half of families would gain or lose more than £5 per week. But, as with the reform in the previous subsection, these distributional effects look less stark when considered in a life-cycle perspective. For many people, what they lost (or gained) when aged under 55 they would later gain (or lose) when aged 55–70: much of the redistribution is over the life cycle rather than between groups. This would not be true for everyone: those experiencing lengthy

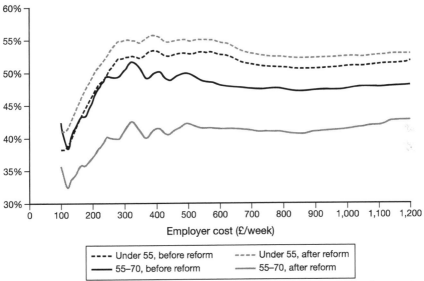

Figure 4.15. Effect of reform on average PTRs across the earnings distribution, by age

Notes: Non-parametric regression (lowess) estimates. Reform as described in the text. Employer cost = Gross earnings + Employer NICs.

Source: Authors' calculations using the IFS tax and benefit microsimulation model, TAXBEN, run on uprated data from the 2006–07 Family Resources Survey, and using estimated consumption tax rates from the 2007 Expenditure and Food Survey.

Tax by Design

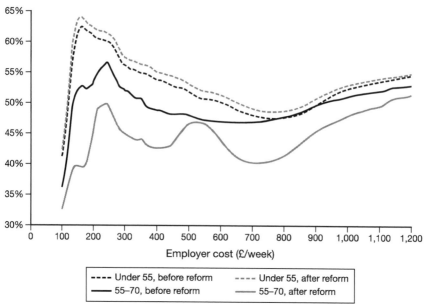

Figure 4.16. Effect of reform on average EMTRs across the earnings distribution, by age

Notes: Non-parametric regression (lowess) estimates. Reform as described in the text. Employer cost = Gross earnings + Employer NICs.

Source: Authors' calculations using the IFS tax and benefit microsimulation model, TAXBEN, run on uprated data from the 2006–07 Family Resources Survey, and using estimated consumption tax rates from the 2007 Expenditure and Food Survey.

spells out of work and on low incomes but then earning a good living later in life would gain significantly, while those earning decent salaries but then falling into low income later in life would lose. But certainly the large number of people gaining or losing large amounts at any given point in time dramatically overstates the long-run distributional impact of the reform.

Figures 4.15 and 4.16 show what effect this set of reforms would have on average PTRs and EMTRs of under-55s and of 55- to 70-year-olds earning different amounts. For 55- to 70-year-olds, both incentives to stay in work at all and incentives to earn more are strengthened right across the earnings distribution, and this strengthening is marked: the mean PTR falls by 7.0 percentage points and the mean EMTR by 5.3 percentage points. There is a smaller weakening of incentives for under-55s, but the effect hits far more people (the mean PTR and EMTR rise by 2.2 and 1.2 percentage points respectively).

We estimate that these reforms could lead to a net increase in employment of around 157,000, or 0.6% of the workforce—the balance of 535,000 more 55- to 70-year-olds and 378,000 fewer under-55s in work, although in practice such a large shift would not happen overnight. Aggregate earnings (including employer NICs) would increase by £1.9 billion, or 0.3%. In fact, households' purchasing power would increase by £2.5 billion and the Exchequer would lose £0.7 billion: this is because, as shown in Figures 4.15 and 4.16, effective tax rates are lower for those aged 55–70 than for under-55s, so the government would collect less revenue from the extra work the older people do than it would lose from the reduction in work among under-55s.

This illustrative reform is limited to changing rates and thresholds within the existing tax and benefit system. No new complexities are introduced. If this particular reform looks difficult, alternatives could readily be devised, such as a more generous Working Tax Credit for those aged 55 or over.[42] Given how many of those who stop working before state pension age move onto disability benefits rather than retiring (see Section 3.1), the design of these benefits is another area worthy of attention. But the design of disability benefits is beyond the scope of this book. Our intention here is merely to illustrate the potential advantages of ensuring work incentives are strong at this critical point in the life cycle.

As a broad direction for reform, we do think that the changes in tax and benefit rates that take effect as people enter their later years could take better account of what we know about people's responsiveness around retirement age. It seems particularly perverse that Pension Credit provides a large increase in the level of out-of-work support available at exactly the time that people's decisions as to whether to continue working are most sensitive. If the distributional implications are considered acceptable, the process currently in train to increase the age at which Pension Credit becomes

---

[42] There is already a 50+ bonus in WTC, but it is payable only to those who move off benefits into work and only for a year, and the June 2010 Budget announced its abolition from April 2012. Note that increasing WTC does not unambiguously strengthen work incentives because it reduces second earners' incentives to be in work and it increases the number of people facing high EMTRs through tax credit withdrawal.

available from 60 to 66 (and then beyond) is very much a move in the right direction.

4.5. CONCLUSIONS

The shape of the rate schedule is the most political part of the tax system—the forum in which different views about the trade-off between achieving higher average living standards and achieving a more equal distribution of living standards play out. Indeed, we see direct taxes and benefits as the key part of the system for achieving the redistribution society desires. But we are deliberately not making recommendations over just how progressive the system should be. It is straightforward to see how more or less progressivity could be introduced. We have focused instead on how to maximize the efficiency with which redistribution is achieved, by minimizing disincentives where they matter most.

Designing a rate schedule is hard, and, for all the criticisms in this chapter, the overall rate schedule faced by most people in the UK is a lot less bad than it could be: almost nobody faces an effective marginal tax rate above 100% (it wasn't always thus), and, to a significant extent, it is already true that effective tax rates are lower for more responsive groups. Nevertheless, there is considerable scope for improvement.

The income tax schedule could be made simpler by abolishing the practice of tapering away allowances: the bizarre pattern of rising and falling marginal rates it creates is patently absurd, and the obscure language of tapered allowances only serves to hide that absurdity from the public.

The choice of income tax rate for top earners depends partly on political preferences: how much one values, or objects to, the satisfaction the rich derive from getting even richer. Even if the only thing that mattered were the amount of revenue raised, we know rather little about what the right level of the top rate should be. But without base-broadening, a 50% top income tax rate is at the upper end of what estimates suggest might maximize tax receipts.

At the other end of the income scale, there is a case for saying that PTRs are too high for many low earners—their gain from entering work is too low.

This could be addressed by means-testing less aggressively: we examined one option, which involved having much larger earnings disregards in benefits and tax credits, separate disregards for first and second earners, and a lower tax credit withdrawal rate, along with more generous Working Tax Credit. There are major disadvantages to this approach. It would involve a significant extension of means-testing, which has practical disadvantages over and above the disincentive it implies for working families to increase their earnings. And it would cost money, which could only come from some combination of tax rises (weakening work incentives for those affected) or benefit cuts (which make the poorest worse off). But if these disadvantages can be borne, it does look possible to achieve a sizeable increase in employment rates. The trade-offs are finely balanced.

We can more confidently recommend changes to the way in which the tax and benefit system affects families with children of different ages and people around retirement age. Reforms are available that could improve economic efficiency by minimizing work disincentives for those most responsive to them. Specifically, we recommend that work incentives should be strengthened for parents whose children are of school age and for older workers, perhaps balanced by weakening them for other groups, and we have illustrated ways in which this could be achieved.

There remain many things that we do not know about the precise effects of taxing earnings, and especially the longer-term effects, such as on education and career choices. These might be important and should not be ignored— for example, the fact that observed hours of work seem to be unresponsive to taxation for large sections of the population does not necessarily mean that their tax rates can be increased indefinitely with no loss to the economy. The important point is that system design needs to remain sensitive to what we do know about how people respond to incentives, even if in some cases that is frustratingly little.

5

Integrating Personal Taxes and Benefits

The last chapter discussed how we might alter rates and thresholds of the existing set of taxes and benefits in order to improve work incentives where it matters most. In this chapter, we focus on reforms to the architecture of the system: the instruments used to implement taxation of earnings. Specifically, we look at whether and how the different direct taxes and benefits in the UK system might be integrated.

How the taxation of earnings, and the payment of benefits, are delivered matters. Taxes and benefits are costly for the government to administer and costly for taxpayers and benefit recipients to deal with; we would like to keep those costs as low as possible.

Effective delivery is also essential to ensure that people pay the tax, and receive the support, that policymakers intend. Tax evasion and avoidance, benefit fraud, innocent errors by government or individuals, and non-take-up of entitlements all prevent the tax and benefit system that is written down on paper from translating into outcomes in the real world.

To some extent, these kinds of frictions can be measured. For example, according to the UK government's most recent estimates:

- The government spends about 4p on administration for each £1 it pays out in working-age benefits and tax credits. Collecting income tax and National Insurance contributions (NICs) costs the government 1.24p and 0.35p respectively per £1 collected.[1]

------

[1] Sources: Department for Work and Pensions, 2010b; HM Revenue and Customs, 2009. The figure for benefits and tax credits is only approximate, since the amounts spent on

- The cost to employers of operating PAYE (see Box 5.1) is around 0.6p per £1 paid.[2] Compliance costs for individuals who fall under self-assessment are unknown but likely to be far higher.[3]

- For every £1 of revenue from income tax, NICs, and capital gains tax, 5.4p is lost to evasion, avoidance, and error, while for every £1 of entitlements to benefits and tax credits, 3p is overpaid and 1p is underpaid due to error and fraud.[4]

- Out of each £1 of entitlements to means-tested benefits and tax credits, 20p goes unclaimed by eligible families.[5]

But keeping the delivery mechanism simple also matters for reasons that are harder to quantify. Transparency is a virtue in itself. We would generally prefer people to understand the consequences of their decisions. Transparency can also help to make work incentives effective. Carefully designed patterns of work incentives are of rather less value if people do not understand the financial implications of changing the work they do. And having a simple set of instruments makes it easier to achieve coherent policy design. Policymakers are only human; with a complicated set of interacting taxes and benefits, it is more likely that well-intentioned reforms will have unintended consequences, creating anomalies and an irrational rate schedule. Well-designed tools are easier to use.

administration are heavily rounded, HMRC's administration costs are a lower bound, and the administration costs seem to include the whole of Housing Benefit and Council Tax Benefit while the benefit spending might include only payments to working-age recipients.

[2] Sources: Cost of operating PAYE—HM Revenue and Customs (2010c); total PAYE receipts—HM Treasury (2010b).

[3] The cost to individuals of claiming benefits and tax credits has never been quantified, but see Bennett, Brewer, and Shaw (2009) for a discussion.

[4] Sources: HM Revenue and Customs, 2010a and 2010d; Department for Work and Pensions, 2010c. Note that tax credit overpayments and underpayments due to error and fraud are not the same as the much larger amounts that are overpaid and underpaid in the normal course of operation of tax credits but reconciled at year-end, as discussed in Section 5.3.1.

[5] Source: Authors' calculations from Department for Work and Pensions (2010a) and HM Revenue and Customs (2010b). Midpoints of ranges used where point estimates not provided.

Box 5.1. PAYE

The Pay-As-You-Earn (PAYE) system of withholding income tax from earnings (and from private and occupational pensions) is unusual internationally in that it involves exact cumulative deduction: that is, when calculating tax due each week or month, the employer considers income not simply for the period in question but for the whole of the tax year to date. Tax due on total cumulative income is calculated and tax paid thus far is deducted, giving a figure for tax due this week or month. The cumulative system means that, at the end of the tax year, the correct amount of tax should have been deducted—at least for those with relatively simple affairs—whereas under a non-cumulative system (in which only income in the current week or month is considered), an end-of-year adjustment might be necessary.

About 85% of income tax revenue is collected through PAYE.[a] Tax on some other sources of income such as bank interest is collected through a simpler withholding system that operates under the assumption that this income is not subject to higher-rate tax. Those with more complicated affairs—such as the self-employed, those with very high incomes, company directors, and landlords—must fill in a self-assessment tax return after the end of the tax year, setting down their incomes from different sources and any tax-privileged spending such as pension contributions or gifts to charity; HM Revenue and Customs will calculate the tax owed, given this information.

PAYE works well for most people most of the time, sparing two-thirds of taxpayers the need to fill in a tax return. However, in a significant minority of cases the wrong amount is withheld—typically when people have more than one source of PAYE income during the year (more than one job/pension over the course of the year, for example), especially if their circumstances change frequently or change towards the end of the year. Such cases can be troublesome to reconcile later on, which is one reason the government has embarked on a substantial, and potentially very important, PAYE modernization programme.[b]

National Insurance contributions for earnings from employment are not an annual system; thus liability is calculated separately for each pay period, with neither cumulation during the year nor an end-of-year reconciliation.

[a] Source: HM Treasury, 2010b, table C11.

[b] On the PAYE modernization programme, see HM Revenue and Customs (2010c and 2010e). For an assessment of PAYE, see Shaw, Slemrod, and Whiting (2010) and the associated commentaries by Highfield (2010) and Mace (2010).

There are some basic principles against which we might want to assess mechanisms for delivering earnings taxation. We should probably aim to do the following:

- *Maximize transparency*: as few programmes as possible, as simple as possible. People should know what they are paying/receiving and ideally why (i.e. how it has been calculated).
- *Minimize the number of different returns or applications that must be submitted, and their length.*
- *Minimize the number of different things that need to be measured or calculated*: for example, avoid multiple definitions of income, assessment periods, and so on where possible.
- *Minimize duplication of information provision and processing*: do not collect the same income information, for example, for several benefits, tax credits, and taxes.
- *Deal with as few agents as possible*: for example, it is easier for the authorities to deal with one employer than many employees.
- *Ensure people are dealing with the same organization, and even the same named official, as much as possible.*
- *Obtain information from verifiable market transactions where possible*: for example, use payslips rather than self-declaration of income.[6]
- *Minimize 'gaps' between programmes*: for example, reduce delays between stopping payment of out-of-work benefits and starting payment of in-work benefits.
- *Ideally, avoid separating out a few people as needing to apply for special help*, which can be stigmatizing and demeaning.

These guidelines could inform many aspects of policy design at a level of detail we do not pursue here. However, one more general conclusion seems to follow almost directly from them: integrate separate but similar programmes into a single programme. The UK has a plethora of different taxes, tax credits, and benefits, apparently aiming to achieve very similar objectives. This makes the system complicated for people to understand and comply with, hard for the government to administer, and not conducive to

---

[6] The crucial role of third-party monitoring as a deterrent to evasion is discussed in Kleven, Kreiner, and Saez (2009a).

coherent design and desirable outcomes. Simply reducing the number of
separate schemes has the potential to bring improvements on almost every
one of the criteria listed above. This chapter discusses the options for
integrating parts of the tax system, parts of the benefit and tax credits system,
and the tax system with the benefit system.

5.1. INCOME TAX AND NATIONAL INSURANCE[7]

The UK has two taxes on income—income tax and National Insurance
contributions. Though different in origin, they are now very similar.
Maintaining separate systems yields little benefit, but makes their combined
effect less transparent and imposes extra burdens on employers, who must
calculate earnings on two definitions, duplicate record-keeping, and so on.
There is therefore an obvious case for merging them. Remaining differences
between the two taxes could be retained if that were considered desirable (for
example, a combined tax could be charged at a lower rate on items that are
currently subject to one tax but not the other); but integration would
underline the illogicality of most of the current differences between the two
taxes and provide an opportunity to remove them. It is patently absurd, for
example, to have one tax assessed on earnings in each individual pay period
and another assessed on income over the whole year.

Successive governments have rejected integration of income tax and
National Insurance (NI).[8] The main reason given is the so-called
'contributory principle'—the idea that NI is supposed to embody a form of
social insurance in which contributions create rights to benefits. Certainly,
NICs originated as a payment made in return for specific benefit

[7] The discussion here draws heavily on work by Adam and Loutzenhiser (2007), who discuss
these issues in more detail and provide full references.

[8] As this text was being finalized, the government announced that it would consult on
'options, stages and timing of reforms to integrate the operation of income tax and NICs' (HM
Treasury, 2011). At the time of writing, it is not clear what this might involve, but it seems that
the crucial phrase is 'the operation of': initial indications are that reforms will be restricted to
operational matters rather than more fundamental integration.

entitlements. But, in practice, the link between contributions and entitlements is now vanishingly weak. Contributions rise with earnings, benefits do not. By far the biggest NI benefit is the state pension. But it is now rather hard to live in the UK and not earn entitlement to a full basic pension. The unemployed, the sick, and those caring for children are credited with contributions, and recent changes mean that only 30 years of contributions or credits are required to earn a full pension. As a result, the government estimates that 90% of those reaching state pension age in 2025 will be entitled to the full pension.[9] And those who are not entitled to full contributory benefits will often be fully, or almost fully, compensated through entitlements to means-tested benefits. The incremental value of additional NI benefits is often very small. There may be a case for a social insurance system. It is just that we don't have one.

This matters. If NI were real social insurance in which additional contributions earned additional benefits, there would be a case for keeping it separate from income tax. And there would be a case for analysing its effects on incentives and labour supply differently since it might act more like an insurance or savings vehicle than a tax. But that is not the world in which we find ourselves.

By simplifying the system, integration would bring two main benefits: reduced administration and compliance costs—likely to be significant, albeit difficult to quantify[10]—and greater transparency.

The tax schedule that people actually face on their earnings reflects the combination of income tax and NICs. Transparency requires that it is the combined schedule that should be described and debated. When politicians debate whether the current 20% basic rate, 40% higher rate, and 50% additional rate of income tax are appropriate, people should not have to

---

[9] HM Treasury, 2007.

[10] A report for the government (KPMG, 2006) put the incremental cost to employers of operating NICs on top of income tax at £179 million per year. But this study focused on only a narrow range of costs, excluding e.g. costs for employers associated with determining what their obligations were, dealing with changes, and tax planning, as well as all costs borne by employees, the self-employed, and the government itself. See Adam and Loutzenhiser (2007) and Shaw, Slemrod, and Whiting (2010) for more detail.

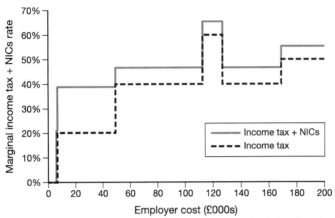

Figure 5.1. Combined income tax and NICs schedules for those aged under 65, 2010–11

Notes: Includes employer and employee NICs. Assumes individual not contracted out of State Second Pension.

remind themselves (or be reminded) that the true rate schedule includes NICs on top of that, nor should they have to do the calculations. It is rare in popular discourse to hear discussion of the 31%, 41%, and 51% rates that (in 2010–11) apply once employee NICs are taken into account, let alone consideration of the effect of employer NICs (or the different rate schedule that applies to the self-employed). Because attention is often restricted to headline income tax rates (which rise from 20% to 40% and then 50% at higher incomes), ignoring NIC rates (which fall from 11% to 1% for employees), the degree of progression towards the top of the distribution is easily overstated. Figure 5.1 shows that the gap between the rates of income tax alone and the combined effective rates of income tax, employee NICs, and employer NICs is much larger at modest levels of earnings than for high earners. The two lines convey quite different impressions.

Regrettably, governments may see the lack of transparency in the current system as a positive rather than a negative. Just one example of the way in which the separation of the systems can lead to confusion (to put it generously) was the Labour Party's 2001 general election manifesto. This included a pledge not to increase rates of income tax, but contained no such pledge on NICs. Labour was re-elected and, in its first Budget after the election, promptly announced an across-the-board increase in NIC rates. It is hard to believe that the government had decided after careful deliberation that tax rates on earnings (subject to NICs as well as income tax) should increase but that the tax rate on other income (subject only to income tax) should not, and that the manifesto pledge had been intended to guarantee the latter while leaving open the former. Such an intention was certainly not made clear to the public during the election campaign. Whether the shortcoming was duplicity, incoherence, or merely poor communication, we should strive to make such episodes unrepeatable.

The separation of income tax and NICs is also an obstacle to making the combined rate schedule sensible and straightforward. For example, a simple combined rate schedule would have the thresholds for income tax and NICs aligned, so as to minimize the number of bands of earnings to which different rates applied. After many years of gradual convergence, the alignment of income tax and NI thresholds was finally announced in the 2007 Budget.[11] But only a few weeks after this had been implemented in April 2008, it became politically expedient to break it again. The government preferred to compensate losers from the abolition of the 10% tax rate by increasing income tax allowances alone, leaving NI thresholds unchanged. Further changes have been announced since then, so that from April 2011 income tax, employee NICs, and employer NICs will all become payable at different levels of earnings. The ease with which alignment was abandoned demonstrates that it is a poor substitute for genuine integration.

In so far as income tax and NICs are fundamentally the same, transparency and administrative simplicity would clearly be well served by merging them. But the differences that do remain between the two tax bases arguably make the case for integration even stronger.

Some categories of income are subject to income tax but not to NICs (or only to employer NICs): savings income, certain state benefits, most non-tradable forms of remuneration, gratuities, and the earnings and pension income of individuals over state pension age (or under 16).[12] These

---

[11] Subject to the significant limitations that the alignment was still between weekly thresholds for NICs and their nearest equivalents for an annually assessed income tax and that the two taxes continued to be levied on different bases.

[12] Similarly, some items are deductible for income tax but not for NICs: most importantly, employee pension contributions, but also e.g. employment-related expenses not reimbursed by

categories of income are in effect taxed at an intermediate rate, above zero but below the full (combined) rate charged on ordinary earnings. It may be that an intermediate tax rate is appropriate (for example, in the last chapter we suggested that there might be a case for applying a lower tax rate to older workers), though in practice it is hard to see a justification in most cases.[13] But, at present, the level of the intermediate rate is an accidental by-product of decisions made for other reasons, driven largely by misperceptions that make NICs politically easier to increase than income tax.

The level of the intermediate rate applied to forms of income subject to one tax but not the other is not only an unintended feature of the system; it is also a particularly opaque one. If some forms of income are to be taxed at an intermediate rate, this treatment should be made explicit. A single integrated tax would achieve this, and thereby prompt open debate about whether each form of income should be taxed in full, not at all, or at an intermediate rate. The level and coverage of the intermediate rate are little discussed at present because they are largely invisible.

One central difference between income tax and NICs is that NICs are levied 'on employers' as well as 'on employees'. The previous chapters have made clear that this distinction in law and terminology has little economic significance. Both are taxes on earnings, driving a wedge between the cost to the employer of hiring someone and the take-home pay the employee receives. With a given overall tax wedge, employer cost and take-home pay will, in the long run, be determined by the supply of and demand for labour, not by whether the wedge in between is labelled an 'employer' or an 'employee' tax.

Aside from increasing administrative and compliance costs, having separate employer and employee taxes disguises the size of the overall tax wedge and hinders sensible discussion of the appropriate shape for the overall rate schedule. It invites people to treat the employer tax as somehow

---

the employer, the business-use component of assets used for both business and private purposes, and entertainers' agents' fees.

[13] The appropriate tax regime to apply to savings and pensions is discussed in Chapter 14.

fundamentally different, or else to ignore it entirely. There is therefore a strong case for phasing out the employer contribution altogether, merging it with income tax and employee NICs to form a single tax levied on the individual.[14] If we did not already have separate employer and employee taxes, we would certainly not want to introduce them.

That said, given where we start, such a transition would be painful. The immediate effect of an overnight shift from employer to employee taxes is that take-home pay would fall and employers' profits increase. Earnings would eventually rise to return take-home pay and employer cost to their previous levels, but this could take a long time. The transition could be made easier by announcing and publicizing the change well in advance of its implementation, allowing earnings to adjust in tandem with the shift; indeed, the government could explicitly advise employers and employees what adjustment to earnings would be needed to offset the reform. But it would still be likely to cause friction, particularly if there were a perception that employers were taking advantage of the reform to short-change their employees.

In addition, while the new regime would be simpler than the current one, the changes required to get there would not be simple. Offsetting the abolition of 12.8% employer NICs would not simply require a 12.8 percentage point increase in employee NICs. Because of the way employer NICs fit into the current system (specifically, being assessed sequentially rather than simultaneously, a distinction discussed in Section 5.3.2), it would require changes of different sizes to several rates and thresholds.[15] Further adjustments, such as to the minimum wage and to certain state benefits, would also have to be considered.

---

[14] The logic of the irrelevance of formal incidence suggests that they could equally well be merged into a single tax levied on the employer. This would not work, however, if we wished to levy a progressive tax on the individual's entire income, since, where someone has more than one income source (e.g. income from a second job or from savings), there is no good way to determine which slice of income falls within the tax base of any given employer.

[15] Adam and Loutzenhiser (2007, 25) identified no fewer than nine adjustments that would be needed, and there would now be more. But that was for a shift from employer to employee NICs, holding everything else unchanged; if there were not separate income tax and NICs thresholds, and if tax credits were assessed on after-tax rather than before-tax income (both changes proposed in this chapter), then far fewer adjustments would be needed.

If such transitional difficulties were thought prohibitive, income tax and employee NICs could be merged while leaving a separate employer tax in place. But retaining an employer tax has a price beyond simply forgoing part of the benefits of integration. Since it is necessarily confined to employment income, it has consequences for the tax system as a whole. For example, suppose we wanted to apply the same overall tax schedule to all forms of income, not just employment income—something we will argue for in later chapters. Employment income is currently taxed more heavily than self-employment and capital income (and capital gains), largely because NICs apply only to earnings. For all forms of income to be subject to the same overall rate schedule, NICs or something equivalent to them would have to be extended to other forms of income. It is easy to see how this could be achieved for employee NICs, the scope of which could simply be extended. The same would apply to employer NICs if they too were brought within a merged tax. But if employer NICs were kept as a separate tax, it could apply only to employment income; so to achieve equal treatment, additional tax equivalent to employer NICs would have to be levied on capital income, self-employment income, and so on. This would add further complexity to the system, and it hardly seems politically appealing either. Whether it is a more attractive prospect than phasing out employer NICs and raising income tax instead is a moot point.

For the fiscal purist, a system with no separate employer payroll tax has strong attractions: it is simpler in itself, and makes it simpler to achieve coherence of the system as a whole. Political pragmatists may find the choice more finely balanced. Whether or not employer NICs remain separate, however, the case for some form of integration of income tax and NICs seems overwhelming.

5.2. INTEGRATING THE BENEFIT SYSTEM

The benefit and tax credit system is much more of a mess of complicated overlapping programmes than income tax and NICs. The list of programmes intended to provide support for low-income families currently includes Income Support, income-based Jobseeker's Allowance, income-based

Employment and Support Allowance, Housing Benefit, Council Tax Benefit, Pension Credit, Working Tax Credit, and Child Tax Credit—and these come on top of benefits intended to provide non-means-tested support for certain contingencies, such as Child Benefit, state pension, Winter Fuel Payment, contribution-based Jobseeker's Allowance, Disability Living Allowance, Carer's Allowance, and contribution-based Employment and Support Allowance. Many families claim several of these simultaneously.

One implication of there being so many programmes is that it is harder to achieve a sensible structure for the system as a whole. For example, the interaction of several means tests can create extraordinarily high effective tax rates on earnings for some people. The detailed rules are also different for different schemes (for example, what qualifies as 'work' and how income is measured), and there are swathes of complicated rules and design features that exist purely to deal with people claiming support under more than one scheme or moving from one scheme to another.

Another consequence of the plethora of programmes is that people often do not know what they are entitled to, let alone what they would be entitled to if their circumstances were different. Many out-of-work families are unaware that they could continue to claim Housing Benefit and/or Council Tax Benefit if they moved into low-paid work.[16] People might therefore be discouraged from working by a perception of lost entitlements that exceeds the reality. And since many of those in work never find out that they can claim Housing Benefit and Council Tax Benefit, the support reaches only a limited proportion of the intended recipients: only around half of working families that are entitled to Housing Benefit claim it, compared with over 90% of non-working families.[17] Similar problems arise because people do not realize that Working Tax Credit can be claimed by those without children and that Child Tax Credit can be claimed (for now) by those with relatively high incomes.[18]

Finally, the separation of the different programmes can lead to hassle for claimants and administrative problems for government. People have to make

---

[16] Turley and Thomas, 2006.

[17] Department for Work and Pensions, 2010a.

[18] Up to £58,000 at the time of writing. See McAlpine and Thomas (2008) for details on people's understanding.

multiple applications, providing much the same information to different branches of government. Most benefits are the responsibility of the Department for Work and Pensions (DWP), but tax credits and Child Benefit are run by HM Revenue and Customs (HMRC), while Housing Benefit and Council Tax Benefit are administered by local authorities.[19] And when families' circumstances change (starting work or recovering from illness, for example), not only do they often have to apply for support under a different scheme, but there is often a delay between the moment at which payment of one benefit ceases and the moment at which payment of another starts. This can lead to hardship for families at a time of transition and upheaval.

Of course, government agencies can take steps to ease the burden on claimants or to spread information. But such processes are costly, and most add to the complexity of the system rather than reducing it.

A more radical approach would be to integrate as many of these different structures as possible into a single benefit, with a coherent structure and a single set of rules. This is in fact an approach that was adopted in 2003 with the introduction of Child Tax Credit, which replaced all or part of no fewer than nine different benefits. Before 2003, families with children might have been entitled to Children's Tax Credit and/or Working Families' Tax Credit; furthermore, almost all other benefits, from Income Support to Incapacity Benefit to the Basic State Pension, included extra payments for children. The government's idea was to replace almost all of these child-related payments (though not universal Child Benefit) with a single means-tested programme. Thus the same programme would provide support for the vast majority of families with children from the time the first child was born to the time the youngest child became too old for eligibility, with entitlement continuing (albeit not at the same level) almost regardless of changing circumstances in the meantime. Since so many would be entitled, people would be more likely to know they were entitled and there would be less stigma attached to claiming; and since a single programme covered a wide variety of circumstances, people could be secure in the knowledge that their entitlement would continue even if their circumstances changed, with no

---

[19] There are other variants too, such as war pensions operated by the Ministry of Defence and the Education Maintenance Allowance run by the Department for Education.

need to fill in different forms and no administrative problems moving from one programme to another.

The advantages of this approach are clear, and we see no reason why they should apply only to child-related support.[20] There is a strong case for integrating all means-tested support—and possibly non-means-tested benefits as well—into a single benefit. The basic purpose of all of the different benefits and tax credits is to provide support for families with high needs and/or low resources. The logical approach is therefore to make a single integrated assessment of a family's needs and a single integrated assessment of its resources, and compare the two.

An integrated benefit could share many features of the current system, if that were thought desirable. Maximum entitlement could consist of a basic allowance (replacing Income Support, income-based Jobseeker's Allowance, income-based Employment and Support Allowance, and Working Tax Credit), plus additional elements for children (replacing Child Tax Credit), old age (replacing Pension Credit), local housing costs (replacing Housing Benefit and Council Tax Benefit), and disability (replacing disability components of existing programmes). Existing non-means-tested benefits could either be merged in as well or be kept separate.

The level of benefit could be conditional on actively seeking work or other work-related activities (like Jobseeker's Allowance and some Employment and Support Allowance), on working a minimum or maximum number of hours (like Working Tax Credit and Income Support / Jobseeker's Allowance respectively), or on past behaviour such as years living in the UK, paying taxes/NICs, or caring for dependants (like contributory benefits). And the means test could involve any range of different withdrawal rates at different income levels for different groups.

An integrated benefit need not imply a higher or lower cost to the government, or any particular pattern of winners and losers. But integration would be an opportunity to make the design of the whole system simpler and

---

[20] The problems associated with the implementation of Child Tax Credit (and Working Tax Credit) in 2003 were caused not by this integration, but primarily by the government's decision to use a complicated assessment system that involved making retrospective adjustments to people's entitlements (as discussed in Section 5.3.1) and by severe problems with IT in the first few months; see Brewer (2006).

more coherent and to think about whether the system is well designed to achieve its objectives. The transparency brought about by integration would focus a spotlight on anomalies and help rationalize the system.

Perhaps the greatest opportunity afforded by benefit integration would be to rationalize the pattern of effective tax rates for those on low incomes. In the previous chapter, we showed that the highest effective tax rates are created by the simultaneous withdrawal of several benefits or tax credits, often in conjunction with income tax and NICs as well. Even if individual withdrawal rates are not especially high, in combination they can be enormous. Benefit integration opens up options for moderating the very highest effective tax rates without necessarily expanding means-testing overall. Very high and low effective marginal tax rates (EMTRs) would no longer arise arbitrarily as a result of the way that withdrawal of different benefits starts and finishes at different points.

Instead, the income level at which support started to be withdrawn could be set the same for everyone, and the rate of withdrawal could be the same for everyone and at all income levels until support was completely withdrawn; or they could vary systematically according to the total amount (or the specific elements) to be withdrawn or according to the characteristics of the family. In short, the means test could be rationally designed. Integration would not remove the need to make trade-offs of the kind explored in Chapters 3 and 4, but it would make achieving a sensible rate schedule much easier.

Of course, integration cannot remove all complexity. A single integrated benefit would surely have a long and complicated application form. But, as with income tax returns, most sections would be irrelevant for most people and could be skipped. Designing the process appropriately, making it as easy as possible, and using appropriate online technology would be crucial.

The case for benefit integration has become increasingly influential among policymakers and commentators, and numerous proposals have been put forward.[21] In November 2010, the government announced plans to integrate all or most means-tested working-age benefits and tax credits into a new

[21] For example, Freud (2007), Sainsbury and Stanley (2007), Select Committee on Work and Pensions (2007), Martin (2009), Centre for Social Justice (2009), Brewer, Saez, and Shephard (2010), and Taylor et al. (2010).

Universal Credit.[22] This will be a highly complex operation but the prize is substantial enough to make these hazardous waters worth navigating.

5.3. THE JUNCTION OF TAXES AND BENEFITS

So far, we have discussed integration of income tax with National Insurance and integration of different benefits into a single one. The holy grail of integrated design, however, has always been the integration of taxes with benefits.

This finds its purest expression in proposals for a 'negative income tax' or for a 'social dividend' (as described in Section 3.2.1). The defining feature of such proposals is that there is no distinction between income taxation and benefit withdrawal; instead, there is just a single schedule for how payments vary with income. This could mean that support for low incomes is achieved through tax refunds (as in the negative income tax) or that benefits are paid to everyone regardless of income, with tax rates correspondingly higher in order to finance them (as in the social dividend). Although typically described with a single flat tax rate and a single level of support for those with no private income, these systems can easily be modified to allow more than one tax rate and/or payments that vary with household characteristics.

The attractions of integrating taxes with benefits are similar to those of integrating taxes or benefits more narrowly: it makes the rate schedule more transparent, and hopefully more coherent as a result; and it removes the need to separate out means-tested benefits as a special mechanism whereby poor people must suffer the hassle and perceived indignity of asking the state for a handout.

The main barrier to integration in the UK is that the bases of assessment for taxes and benefits differ in two ways that make them hard to reconcile:

---

[22] Department for Work and Pensions, 2010d. See Brewer, Browne, and Jin (2011) for a preliminary analysis. The proposals are contained in the 2011 Welfare Reform Bill, which is before Parliament at the time of writing.

- First, income tax is largely based on individual income, while benefits and tax credits are assessed on the basis of a couple's joint income. A combined system could not be both at once.[23]

- Second, income tax depends on actual annual income, in the sense that liability for a given year depends on income in that year. Benefits— particularly those providing a safety net for those with no other income— are usually assessed on a much shorter time horizon, typically on a week-by-week basis. The UK's attempt (discussed in Section 5.3.1) to provide tax credits for low-income families using a within-year income assessment, while remaining responsive to changing characteristics, shows how thorny this problem can be.

Of course, these differences in unit and period of assessment are not immutable. But there are good reasons for each. Tax payments should reflect individuals' overall ability to pay, best gauged by their income over a relatively long period. Benefits, on the other hand, are intended to meet immediate need: they should provide support to people in temporary hardship even if their income in other periods is higher.

The case for assessing benefit entitlement on a joint basis is also strong—it would be very expensive indeed for the state to provide support through the benefit system to individuals with high-income partners.

The case for using the individual, rather than the couple, as the basis for income taxation is less clear-cut. There are trade-offs. As we discussed in Chapter 3, a tax system cannot simultaneously be progressive, neutral towards marriage (or cohabitation), and tax all families with the same joint income equally. Individual taxation ensures that the tax system (unlike the benefit system) is neutral over marriage and partnership decisions—tax bills are not affected by marital status or cohabitation. But it does not tax families with the same joint income equally. Couples where incomes are unequally shared face higher tax bills than those where the two partners have similar incomes. There are incentives to ensure that income is received by the

---

[23] The distinction between individual and joint assessment collapses only in the special case of a single flat tax rate and a social dividend / break-even point that is twice as high for couples as for single people; governments might reasonably not want to accept such severe restrictions on the pattern of distribution and incentives they can achieve. See Adam and Brewer (2010).

spouse facing the lower marginal rate—particularly important for investment incomes and for those running small businesses. An individual basis for taxation also means that a couple will pay the same amount in tax as two single people with the same incomes, despite probably benefiting from some economies of scale in the household budget.

Ultimately, the choice between individual and joint taxation depends on political value judgements about how far people should be viewed as independent individuals and how far as couples. Rather than making a judgement of our own, in this book we simply take the current individual, annual assessment for taxes and joint, short-term assessment for benefits as given. In these circumstances, there is certainly no scope for full integration, but is there scope for making them fit together better? Routes to this target could involve either greater administrative integration or integration of the rate schedules.

5.3.1. Administrative Integration

The main feature of proposals for administrative integration tends to be the withdrawal of means-tested support through the tax system. Benefit withdrawal would not become indistinguishable from taxation—as now, benefits would be withdrawn until they were exhausted and thereafter only tax would be payable—but the two processes would be administratively combined.[24] Some proposals involve giving all claimants the maximum entitlement for their circumstances (that is, the amount they would be entitled to if they had no private income) and then using the tax system to administer the means test, clawing back 'excess' benefits from those with incomes high enough to reduce their entitlement. Other proposals involve using the tax system not just to withdraw 'excess' benefits but actually to pay out benefit entitlements, 'netting off' income tax and benefits so that employers pay wages with a single addition/deduction reflecting a net contribution from/to state coffers.

---

[24] This was a feature of the proposals of Dilnot, Kay, and Morris (1984), and more recently those of the Select Committee on Work and Pensions (2007), Centre for Social Justice (2009), and Brewer, Saez, and Shephard (2010).

But benefits and tax credits, unlike income tax, depend on a couple's joint income and on a range of other characteristics such as number of children, childcare costs, housing costs, and disability. Providing such support through the tax system—or ensuring that withdrawal of support stops at the right point—would require the tax system to respond to all these characteristics. The challenge is much greater now that it is the norm for couples to have two earners. If the right amount of support could not be delivered at the right time, underpayments and overpayments would presumably have to be rectified following an end-of-year reconciliation.

Tax credits in the UK have provided two instructive experiences in this context, illustrating both the difficulty of achieving administrative improvements and the problems that can arise if entitlements are not delivered accurately at the point they arise:

- When first introducing tax credits in 1999–2000, the then government considered integrating their administration with income tax by delivering tax credits through PAYE codes, but concluded that 'PAYE codes could not deliver the necessary accuracy and reliability'.[25] However, the government remained committed to paying tax credits via employers where possible, in order to make them look and feel like part of the tax system, so instead the government calculated entitlement and simply told employers how much to adjust salary payments. This 'effectively added an additional link in the payment chain without simplifying administration', and, faced with high administrative and compliance costs, payment via employers was abandoned in 2006.[26]

- A new system for calculating and paying tax credits, adopted in 2003, based entitlements on circumstances in the current year, like income tax. It was intended to be responsive, with claimants encouraged (and, in some cases, obliged) to notify HMRC when their circumstances changed. But since claimants did not usually inform HMRC of changes in circumstances as they happened, provisional payments were based on past information, generating underpayments and overpayments to low-income families on a large scale. When actual circumstances had been confirmed,

---

[25] Inland Revenue (1999, 5), cited in Shaw, Slemrod, and Whiting (2010, 1140).

[26] Shaw, Slemrod, and Whiting, 2010, 1140.

typically at the end of the year, these underpayments and overpayments were corrected. The recovery of overpayments in particular gave rise to widespread discontent and in many ways undermined the whole tax credit system, providing a salutary warning of the dangers of relying on an 'approximate now, reconcile later' approach to support for low-income families. Reforms introduced in 2006 somewhat reduced the problem of overpayments, but at the cost of increasing the extent of underpayments, further increasing the complexity of the system, and retreating from the responsiveness that was supposed to be the hallmark of the 2003 reform.[27]

The current UK income tax system is not well suited to making and withdrawing payments that need to adjust rapidly to changes in the recipient's circumstances and that depend on the income of the recipient's partner, the number of children, and potentially many other characteristics. That said, technology is advancing apace. As it becomes easier to transfer large amounts of information in real time, this should open up new ways to join up the administration of benefits with that of taxes. Recently suggested reforms to the PAYE system[28] would move in this direction. If employers (and others) who withheld tax notified HMRC monthly of their payments to each individual, it might become possible to link that information to any partner's income information and use it to check and adjust benefit awards. The longer-term suggestion that the government, rather than employers, would calculate and deduct income tax and NICs raises the distant prospect that the administration of tax and benefits could be more profoundly integrated. Full administrative integration does not seem practical at present, but administrative improvements should certainly be sought.

5.3.2. Integrating Rate Schedules

A common complaint is that many people both pay taxes and receive benefits. The complaint is understandable: it is natural to think that a situation in which the government gives someone £100 while simultaneously

---

[27] See Brewer (2006) for details and analysis.

[28] HM Revenue and Customs, 2010c.

taking £50 from them (or vice versa) could be improved upon. There are attractions to approaching this in a more fundamental way than simply looking for administrative reform. Could income tax liability start only after benefits have been completely withdrawn?

Unfortunately, such a move would be hampered by just the same differences between the bases for taxes and benefits that we have already discussed.

The different assessment periods mean that some people with moderate incomes over the course of a year—enough to bring them into the income tax net—might still have periods in which their income is low enough to qualify for means-tested support (which is precisely the intention of policymakers).

More important is the fact that benefits and tax credits, unlike income tax, depend on family income and a range of other characteristics. To have no one paying tax and receiving benefits at the same time, the income level at which tax became payable would have to be at least as high as the income level at which benefit entitlement ran out. But the benefit run-out point varies widely according to family circumstances. In the UK in 2010–11, for a single under-25-year-old with no children and no housing costs, entitlement would run out at an income of less than £3,000 per year; in contrast, a working family spending £300 a week on formal childcare for their four children could have an annual income of over £70,000 and still be entitled to tax credits. Unless tax allowances are to vary with personal circumstances in similarly complicated ways, removing all overlap would require a tax allowance at least equal to the highest possible run-out point. Increasing the tax allowance to achieve this would, of course, be prohibitively expensive, and cutting benefits and tax credits dramatically enough to achieve it is equally implausible.

As long as taxes are assessed on a different basis from benefits, it is inevitable that they remain separate entities and that some people will face both tax and benefit withdrawal. The number of people in that position could be reduced—either by reducing the number paying tax or by reducing the number eligible for benefits—but the options for doing so all have downsides. For example, raising the income tax allowance and NICs thresholds to £10,000 (from their starting points of £6,475 and £5,720 respectively) in 2009–10, holding fixed the point at which higher-rate tax becomes payable, would cost in the order of £40 billion (ignoring any changes to behaviour in response to the reform). Doing so would reduce the numbers entitled to means-tested benefits or tax credits while also paying tax by around 1.8 million, just a fifth of the total number in that position. Whatever its other merits, increasing the personal allowance is an enormously costly way to reduce the overlap between taxes and benefits.

Given this, one useful guideline which can help avoid the highest EMTRs is to make the income assessments sequential rather than simultaneous:[29] in other words, to calculate one of them on income measured after the other, rather than using the same income measure for both. If there is one tax and one means-tested benefit, this means either means-testing on after-tax income or making the benefit taxable. This makes the combined EMTR less than the sum of its parts.

Table 5.1 illustrates how this would work for someone earning an extra £100 if we had a tax rate of 31% (the current basic rate of income tax plus employee NICs) and a withdrawal rate of 39% (the current tax credit withdrawal rate). If the tax and the benefit were assessed simultaneously—both based on gross earnings—then someone facing both tax and benefit withdrawal would have an EMTR of 70%,[30] leaving them with only £30 from an extra £100 earned. But if, instead, they were assessed sequentially, the individual would be left with £42, an EMTR of only 58%.[31]

Table 5.1. Sequential versus simultaneous income assessments

	Simultaneous assessment	Tax assessed first (means test on after-tax income)	Benefit assessed first (benefit taxable)
Extra earnings	£100	£100	£100
Extra tax due	31% of 100 = £31	31% of 100 = £31	31% of (100−39) = £19
Benefit withdrawn	39% of 100 = £39	39% of (100−31) = £27	39% of 100 = £39
Extra net income	100 − 31 − 39 = £30	100 − 31 − 27 = £42	100 − 19 − 39 = £42

---

[29] Or multiplicative rather than additive.

[30] $0.31 + 0.39 = 0.7$.

[31] $1 - (1-0.31) \times (1-0.39) = 0.58$.

Sequential assessment can sometimes be more complicated to understand and administer than simultaneous assessment, but its advantages in terms of moderating the highest EMTRs are clear from this example. And in situations with more than one tax and/or more than one means test, making sequential rather than simultaneous income assessments becomes even more important. If we added a 65% Housing Benefit withdrawal rate into the example above, the combined EMTR would rise from 70% to 135% under simultaneous assessment, but 'only' from 58% to 85% under sequential assessment.

Sequential assessment makes it impossible for individual withdrawal rates below 100% to combine into overall EMTRs above 100%. EMTRs above 100% were a problem in the UK before 1988, when income tax, employee NICs, and various means tests all operated simultaneously. Happily, much of the UK tax and benefit system does now operate sequentially. Employer NICs are first in sequence: all other taxes and benefits are assessed on earnings excluding (i.e. after deducting) employer NICs. The main means-tested benefits are assessed on income after deducting income tax and NICs and after adding tax credits. (And VAT is automatically last in sequence, since the money people spend is their disposable income after all taxes and benefits.)

The most significant case of simultaneous assessment now to be found in the UK is that tax credits are assessed on pre-tax income—a change introduced in 2003 which seems a step in the wrong direction.[32] Reversing this would be a well-targeted way to reduce the highest EMTRs—much better targeted than simply reducing individual tax or withdrawal rates—since it addresses precisely the interaction between different taxes, tax

[32] In fact, the then government reduced the tax credit withdrawal rate from 55% to 37% at the same time as introducing simultaneous assessment, to keep the combined EMTR at 70% for someone on the tax credit taper who was also paying basic-rate income tax and employee NICs. But for those not paying income tax (or paying it at the 10% starting rate which applied then), this was a genuine reduction in their EMTR, and thus a giveaway: in other words, rather perversely, the reform spent money on reducing EMTRs for everyone *except* those facing the highest EMTRs. This money could have been spent more efficiently by reducing the withdrawal rate from 55% while continuing to assess on net income, thus cutting EMTRs for all those facing tax credit withdrawal, including those paying tax as well and therefore facing the highest EMTRs of all.

credits, and benefits, which is what gives rise to the highest EMTRs. The effect is that shown in Table 5.1: it would reduce the EMTR from 70% to 58% for someone facing tax credit withdrawal at the same time as paying income tax and NICs, while not spending money to reduce EMTRs for those facing one but not the other.[33] Moving to sequential assessment delivers improvements where they are most needed.

The choice between simultaneous and sequential assessment affects more than just the EMTRs of those facing more than one assessment. For example, making benefits taxable is a reduction in generosity, and assessing them on after-tax income is an increase in generosity, to those who both pay tax and receive benefits. Offsetting this by simply adjusting tax or benefit rates would affect all taxpayers or all benefit recipients, not just those who fall into both categories. Some wider distributional and incentive effects are therefore inevitable, although with judicious adjustments to rates and thresholds of different taxes and benefits they can be kept small.

The UK already uses sequential assessment in most cases, and while, 'pound for pound', changing the measure of income on which tax credits are assessed would be a well-targeted measure, it is not a major reform and would not generate large improvements. The priority in terms of rationalizing the rate schedule and avoiding the highest EMTRs should be to integrate the different benefits and tax credits as discussed in Section 5.2— tackling the problem of people facing withdrawal of multiple strands of support at its source rather than just mitigating the worst of its consequences.

---

[33] This reform would also reduce EMTRs for those facing benefit withdrawal as well and therefore subject to even higher EMTRs at the moment: it would reduce the EMTR from 90% to 85% for those also facing Housing Benefit withdrawal; from 76% to 66% for those also facing Council Tax Benefit withdrawal; and from 96% to 94% for those facing both Housing Benefit *and* Council Tax Benefit withdrawal as well as income tax, NICs, and tax credit withdrawal. For consistency with the simple illustration in Table 5.1, these figures ignore employer NICs and indirect taxes.

5.4. CONCLUSIONS

The way in which any chosen rate schedule is delivered really matters. It matters particularly for those on low incomes who face the day-to-day complexity of the benefit system and may have the least ability to deal with it. The chaos—and that is not too strong a word—that accompanied the administration of tax credits in the UK after 2003 is just one of the most salient examples of the cost of getting policy and delivery wrong.

The UK has two separate taxes on earnings, their separation serving little purpose save to obscure the true effective marginal tax rate and increase employers' administrative burdens. We have multiple benefits designed to achieve the same objective—to provide an income to people currently unable to support themselves in the labour market. The benefit system, tax system, and tax credit system are designed and operated largely in isolation from each other. Indeed, different parts of the benefit system are administered separately and do not join together properly. This piecemeal approach is costly for the people dependent on benefits, it is costly for employers, and it dampens the effectiveness of reforms to the rate schedule designed to improve work incentives.

In this chapter, we have set out several changes to the UK tax and benefit system that would help:

- Income tax and employee NICs—and perhaps employer NICs as well—should be integrated into a single tax.

- As many benefits as possible, and certainly the main means-tested benefits and tax credits, should be integrated. But these integrated benefits should remain separate from the income tax.

- Having argued that the tax and benefit systems should remain separate, and accepting that achieving only one tax and one benefit may not happen in the short run, we should also ensure that we avoid the extremely high EMTRs that arise when multiple benefits overlap, or overlap with the tax system. We therefore recommend that, where possible, individual taxes and benefits should be assessed sequentially, not simultaneously. The most immediate reform that implies is that tax credits should be assessed on after-tax income (with appropriate adjustments to the rates and thresholds of tax credits, or indeed income tax, if they were thought necessary).

Finally, it is worth saying something here about the role of policymakers in delivering a transparent system. Structural integration might avoid, for example, the unfortunate experience of 'keeping' promises not to increase income tax rates and then promptly increasing the largely equivalent NICs rate. But incoherent rate schedules—such as those emanating from the tapering-away of allowances described in the last chapter—would still be possible however much integration there is. And no amount of administrative simplification and integration can stop a government using fiscal drag or other hidden measures to raise taxes in opaque ways. The number of higher-rate income tax payers in the UK has increased almost unnoticed from 763,000 in 1978–79 to 3.3 million in 2010–11,[34] in large part because governments have quietly failed to index thresholds in line with growing earnings, and the number is on course to rise more quickly in future as higher-rate tax affects increasingly dense parts of the income distribution.[35]

In the end, if government chooses obscurity and incoherence over transparency and coherence, we are all losers. Too often, governments have chosen the wrong path.

[34] Sources: HMRC statistics, table 2.1, http://www.hmrc.gov.uk/stats/income_tax/table2-1.pdf; *Inland Revenue Statistics 1994*.

[35] Projections by Browne and Phillips (2010) suggested that there would be 5.4 million higher-rate taxpayers by 2015–16. This rise reflects pre-announced real cuts to the higher-rate threshold as well as 'normal' fiscal drag. Since this projection was made, the June 2010 emergency Budget announced cuts to the higher-rate threshold, which will increase the number even further.

6

Taxing Goods and Services

Taxes on goods and services—excise duties, stamp duties, and, most importantly, VAT—raise nearly 30% of tax revenue in the UK and are important parts of all modern tax systems. VAT especially has become an increasingly important part of the tax system in the UK and elsewhere. Over 150 countries worldwide, including every OECD country apart from the US, employ VAT systems.

Of course, a tax on consumption levied at a uniform rate on goods and services is economically equivalent to a flat-rate expenditure tax, as described in Chapter 2 and which we look at in detail in Chapters 13 and 14.

We organize our discussion of indirect taxes into four chapters. In the next chapter, we look at the design of VAT, explaining why VAT is, in general, a well-designed consumption tax. In Chapter 8, we give particular consideration to the taxation of financial services. Then, in Chapter 9, we look at a particular reform to VAT in the UK. In this chapter, we consider the choice of *base* and *structure* for indirect taxes.

The first question to consider concerns what should be taxed. We will argue in favour of taxing goods and services when they are purchased to consume, but not when they are purchased to use as inputs in the production of other goods and services. We will also argue against the use of transactions taxes, such as stamp duties, on the sale or purchase of assets.

The main issue we address in considering the structure of indirect taxes is whether the same tax rate should be levied on all goods and services. The current VAT system in the UK uses several different rates. We look at whether the efficiency arguments favour a uniform or a differentiated VAT system, and then consider issues of equity. There are some quite subtle and complex arguments here, but, in practice, the case for differentiated rates looks weak and that for a broader, more uniform, structure looks strong. Imposing a uniform rate avoids distorting the choices people make between different goods. And the case for imposing lower VAT rates on goods and services consumed disproportionately by poorer people is weakened in a modern tax system where we have income taxes and benefit payments available to achieve distributional goals more effectively.

Tax rates are also differentiated by imposing excise duties in addition to VAT on a small number of goods, such as tobacco products, alcohol, and motor fuel. A strong case for this can be made when the consumption of particular goods and services generates externalities, i.e. when consumption has positive or negative spillovers to other people's welfare. But we should recognize that a large part of the argument for high alcohol tax and, especially, high tobacco tax is behavioural, based on the negative effects of their consumption on the consumer herself—the 'internality' effect.

6.1. WHAT TO TAX

The starting point for our analysis is that it is the consumption of goods and services which is the appropriate tax base. This fits closely with our arguments in Chapter 2. In general, consumption and expenditure by consumers can be considered the same thing—though in the case of very long-lived goods such as housing, consumption occurs over such long periods that we might prefer to levy a tax as consumption occurs rather than when the house is first built and sold.

VAT is structured such that it is paid in the end by consumers. Businesses in general do not pay VAT when they buy inputs into their production processes. VAT is also designed to be a tax on consumption, not a tax on transactions. We will see in the next chapter how VAT is designed such that these statements are true. We show here why, in general, it is appropriate to have a tax neither on inputs into the production process nor on transactions.

6.1.1. The Production Efficiency Argument against Taxing Inputs

Production efficiency occurs when the economy cannot increase the output of one good without having to produce less of another. In an idealized market economy without any taxes, the prices of inputs act as signals that guide individual firms to make choices that ensure production efficiency is achieved.

Taxes can be levied on produced inputs[1] as well as on final consumption goods. However, taxes on produced inputs would distort the input choices of firms and result in a loss of production efficiency. In a famous paper, Diamond and Mirrlees[2] show that the tax system should be designed to ensure production efficiency is attained. This implies that produced inputs should not be taxed, so that all taxes should fall on final consumption goods.

The reasoning is straightforward. What matters for the welfare level of the economy is the amount of consumption enjoyed by each consumer. Consumption choices are determined by the prices of final goods relative to the wage rate. Any set of prices for final goods that can be obtained using a combination of input taxes and final goods taxes can be achieved by final goods taxes alone. Taxes on input prices are therefore superfluous in respect of their effects on consumption choices. They can, however, affect production decisions in a way that creates production inefficiency. If the tax system results in production inefficiency, then welfare can be easily increased: more of a good that someone enjoys can be produced and consumed without using any additional labour. A tax system that places the economy in a position where there are such unexploited gains cannot be efficient.

In fact, when there are externalities or other market failures, the strict conditions needed for this result may often not be met. The case for taxing environmentally damaging inputs into production remains. But this apart, the requirement for production efficiency is powerful and a key reason for the use of VAT in preference to taxes that burden intermediate transactions.

---

[1] A produced input is an input into the production process that is itself the output of an earlier production process. Such inputs can equally be called *intermediate inputs*.

[2] The argument is demonstrated in Diamond and Mirrlees (1971) for an economy with no market failures.

The UK tax system (in common with many others) does indeed tend to eschew taxation of inputs.[3] But there is a set of taxes levied not on final consumption but on transactions. These are stamp duties. We come to these briefly now.

6.1.2. Should We Tax Transactions?

Taxes on share dealing, house purchase, and land sales are an important part of the fiscal landscape in the UK. These 'stamp duties' have a long history and their continued use reflects the ease with which such taxes can be levied, given the need for people to register their ownership of these items. However, they are unattractive from an economic point of view.

This lack of attractiveness stems from the fact that any tax on transactions will reduce expected welfare by discouraging mutually beneficial trades. Welfare is maximized when assets are owned by the people who place the highest value on them. Taxing transactions will affect who owns an asset, and so can disrupt the efficient pattern of ownership.

The value of a good or service is determined by the flow of benefits that are derived from owning it. So a consumption tax can be levied either on the purchase price of the good or service when it is first sold or on the flow of benefits over time. A transactions tax does not do this and it always seems preferable to tax the benefits directly. For example, if the benefit of owning the asset comes in the form of income, as in the case of share dividends, then it can be taxed as income. Alternatively, if the benefit comes in the form of a flow of consumption services, it can be taxed along the lines that we discuss for housing in Chapter 16. In no case do we find the arguments for a transactions tax compelling.

Of course, if a good is sold only once before final consumption, then a transactions tax (on the value of the transaction) and a VAT have the same economic effect: they raise the price of the good by the rate of tax. The difference between the two taxes arises when the good is sold more than once before consumption. A durable good, such as a house, can be sold

---

[3] With one major exception—the taxation of business property through the business rate (see Chapter 16).

many times over its lifetime. A financial asset can have an unlimited potential lifetime and be traded many, many times—hence potentially being liable for a transactions tax many, many times. A transactions tax will reduce the price of assets that are traded relatively frequently, it will reduce the number of mutually beneficial trades, and it will fall arbitrarily heavily on those who, for whatever reason, engage in more transactions.

Stamp duty on house transactions, for example, taxes according to the number of times a house changes hands over its lifetime. Houses vary considerably in the number of times they are traded, but there is no good economic argument for taxing more-frequently-traded housing more. Worse still, a tax on transactions reduces the incentive to trade in housing and leads to less efficient usage of the housing stock. A tax on the consumption value of housing would make sense (as we see in Chapter 16) but a stamp duty on transactions does not.

An argument for a transactions tax has been put forward, however, in cases where transactions may not always be efficiency enhancing. In particular, this case has been made for a tax in some financial markets, where it is argued that trade is excessive and in some situations destabilizing: the transaction itself induces a negative externality. Then a transactions tax can be seen as a way to reduce excessive speculative activity, and consequent price volatility. This was the justification for the original 'Tobin tax' on financial transactions,[4] which involved the taxation of transactions on foreign exchange markets at a very low rate, but which can be applied to any financial transaction.

While superficially appealing, there are reasons to doubt the premise on which this argument is based. It has been argued that speculation could only be profitable if it reduced volatility, while empirical research has not found any clear link between speculation and volatility.[5] There is some evidence, though, that greater use of financial transactions taxes would affect incentives to trade. The prices of more-frequently-traded shares appear to be responsive to announcements of changes in stamp duty in the UK.[6] So, for

---

[4] Tobin, 1978.
[5] A recent contribution to this literature is Radalj and McAleer (2005).
[6] Bond, Hawkins, and Klemm, 2004.

better or worse, transactions taxes are likely to have an impact, even when levied on purely financial assets.

The Tobin tax has gained renewed support in the wake of the recent financial crisis,[7] though not, it seems, because of any convincing evidence that its existence would have reined in the growth of banks' balance sheets or dealt with the kind of asset market inflation that spawned the crisis. It is now seen more as a means to obtain additional tax revenue from the financial sector. But it is important to be clear on where the incidence will lie. There is no particular reason to believe that the owners of financial sector companies would bear the burden of a tax on foreign exchange transactions. It might well be passed on to consumers in the form of higher import prices. More general financial sector transactions taxes would likely be passed on to savers in the form of lower returns.

This is not to deny that we might want to rethink the taxation of the financial services sector, in particular because it is currently undertaxed as a result of not being subject to VAT. Moreover, the degree of undertaxation grows as the standard rate is raised. We consider this in Chapter 8. But, in general, there is a weak economic case for taxing transactions rather than the income from, or consumption of, the asset or good that is changing hands. While current anger at the financial sector may be justifiable, it is difficult to make a compelling case for using a transactions tax to deal with what are essentially regulatory issues. It is preferable to start by removing the favourable treatment of financial services in VAT.

Ultimately, the existing transactions taxes on housing and share dealing have little compelling economic logic behind them.

6.2. EFFICIENCY, EQUITY, AND UNIFORMITY

So, taxes should only be levied on goods and services used for consumption. But should the same tax rate be applied to all, or are there good reasons for applying different rates to different goods and services?

---

[7] In fact, even before the current episode, Stiglitz (1998) was making this argument.

There are some goods—alcohol, tobacco, petrol—where a case for a high rate of tax can readily be based on the harmful effects of their consumption on others. Indeed, in the case of tobacco especially, the long-term harmful effects on the consumer herself can also be the basis for a high tax rate. We discuss these issues briefly in Section 6.3. But first we consider the arguments for and against uniformity in situations where there are no such spillover effects.

In general, of course, there is an initial presumption in favour of uniformity to avoid distortion of consumption decisions. It is costly in welfare terms if the tax system results in me buying a different set of goods from the ones that I would have bought had all goods been treated the same. Uniformity also avoids the complexities and political lobbying that are inevitable concomitants of a differentiated regime. It can reduce both the administrative and compliance burdens of the tax system. It has practical advantages for businesses, which currently need to work out the VAT categories into which their products and purchases fall. They face much more complicated calculations and paperwork if more than one category applies. Uniformity avoids the sometimes farcical process of deciding exactly which goods should be taxed at which rates. It would allow us to dispense with the need for court cases to establish whether Jaffa Cakes are cakes or biscuits.[8]

Uniform taxation also simplifies the politics of decision-making and makes tax policy less vulnerable to lobbying pressure and short-term political considerations. A system with differentiated rates invites interest groups to lobby for lower rates for their own products, or at least rates as low as those on other preferentially treated commodities.[9] Arguably, this has been important in past decisions to create concessions in the VAT base, such as the reduced rate on domestic energy.

---

[8] Chocolate-covered biscuits are subject to VAT, while chocolate-covered cakes are not. McVitie's produced a giant Jaffa Cake for the court to illustrate that their product was really a miniature cake, not a biscuit, arguing that cakes generally go hard when stale while biscuits go soft. The VAT Tribunal ultimately upheld the makers' claim. United Biscuits (UK) Ltd (VTD 6344).

[9] This argument is made very strongly by Buchanan in Buchanan and Musgrave (1999).

These arguments in favour of a simple uniform system seem persuasive. But there are important arguments against.

First consider just the efficiency issues. Suppose the government has to raise a certain amount of revenue and cares only about the total deadweight loss caused by the tax system but not its distribution across people. As we saw in Chapter 2, a lump-sum tax, with everyone paying a fixed amount, would be efficient. But it is generally impractical. Now suppose that purchases of commodities can be taxed. In a world in which indirect taxes are passed straight on to consumers in the form of higher prices, the efficiency loss resulting from a commodity tax will depend on the extent to which the rise in price reduces people's demand for the good or service in question.

The deadweight loss or 'welfare cost' of a tax is greatest where it has the largest impact on people's purchasing behaviour. It follows that the deadweight loss is smallest when higher rates of indirect tax are imposed on goods for which demand is relatively inelastic (in other words, where the higher price will do relatively little to deter people from buying them) than on those for which there is relatively elastic demand. This *inverse elasticity rule*[10] suggests that since goods generally differ in their price elasticity,[11] optimal tax rates would be differentiated across commodities.[12] In practice, accurately implementing the recommendations of the inverse elasticity rule would require knowledge about the responsiveness of demand to price for individual goods. It would also require decisions on the level of disaggregation at which to distinguish between different goods and services, and on how often to vary the tax rates as market conditions change and alter the optimal rates. The more closely the authorities want to adhere to the

---

[10] For a formal demonstration of this result, see Atkinson and Stiglitz (1980) or Myles (1995). The inverse elasticity rule is valid when there are no substitutability or complementarity relationships between commodities. When such relationships are admitted, the efficient tax system is described by the *Ramsey rule*. This rule is more general but has the same overall consequences as the inverse elasticity rule.

[11] Blundell, Pashardes, and Weber, 1993.

[12] Because there is a budget constraint relating labour income to total expenditure, we can generally relate conditions on demand elasticities to work and leisure choices. Uniformity will be efficient when all goods are 'equally substitutable' for leisure. Otherwise, goods that are more complementary with leisure time will bear higher taxes.

most efficient set of tax rates over time, the greater the costs both of administering the system and of complying with it. But, in general, this rule would suggest a case for higher tax rates on goods such as basic foodstuffs, which are 'necessities' and for which price elasticities tend to be relatively low, than on other goods.

This is the main efficiency argument for having differential tax rates.[13] In fact, much of the deviation from uniformity we see in the UK VAT system and elsewhere is driven by considerations of equity—goods such as food and domestic fuel, which form larger parts of the budgets of poorer people, are taxed at zero or reduced rates as a means of promoting 'fairness'. Such concerns for fairness lie behind most opposition to the notion of a uniform VAT.

It is worth distinguishing three egalitarian arguments for differentiated VAT. The main one relies on the fact that poorer people spend a larger portion of their income on certain goods. A slightly different argument suggests that there are some goods that should face lower tax rates because they are in some sense 'essentials for life'. A third and separate argument is that, separate from income, spending patterns might themselves reveal something particular about a person's needs. The second and third of these arguments we consider separately in the next subsection. Here we focus on the first.

When indirect taxation is considered in isolation, and when there are concerns for equity, there looks to be a strong case for differentiating tax rates to help low-income households by imposing lower taxes on goods that they consume disproportionately. But indirect taxes should *not* be considered in isolation from the rest of the tax and welfare system. Where the government is able to levy a progressive income tax and pay welfare benefits that vary according to people's needs and characteristics, this will generally prove a much more effective means of meeting its equity objectives.

However, there are some circumstances in which governments cannot levy progressive income taxes at all effectively. The income tax (and benefit)

---

[13] There are others, including the suggestion that lower taxes can offset the effects of market power where firms are able to charge above the efficient price (Boadway and Pestieau, 2003), but we do not pursue those here.

system may be constrained, for administrative reasons, to be relatively simple. This might typify a developing country that has relatively few direct tax and benefit instruments available. In this case, a government might care about distribution but can only use indirect taxation to achieve its redistributive goals. It will then want to tax at a lower rate (and possibly even subsidize) the necessities, which make up a larger share of the expenditure of the poor. Since necessities, such as basic food items, also tend to be price inelastic, the government faces a trade-off between efficiency and concerns for redistribution. This can result in keeping tax rates on price-inelastic goods such as food relatively low even though, for pure efficiency reasons, one would want to tax these goods at higher rates.

But the UK and other developed economies do have access to sophisticated direct tax and benefit systems. As we demonstrate in Chapter 9, it is possible to introduce a uniform VAT in the UK whilst changing the direct tax and benefit system to produce an outcome with similar distributional (and work incentive) features to those that are achieved with extensive zero-rating.

However, there does remain a more subtle argument for indirect tax differentiation which relies on the fact that even a sophisticated direct tax and benefit system cannot achieve a 'first-best' outcome. Underlying abilities and needs are not observed with perfect accuracy. A high-ability person may put in little work effort and earn the same amount as a low-ability individual who works very hard. If both have the same earnings, both will pay the same tax even though the high-ability person works less. This information constraint limits the redistribution that can be achieved via an income tax.

In this case, there may be an argument for distorting choices across commodities if the preferences for some commodities are related to work and leisure choices or to earning capacity.[14] To develop this argument, note that the government would like to redistribute from the more able to the less able, but the extent to which this can be done is limited since a high-wage individual can always work less and benefit from the redistribution. These are the incentive compatibility constraints that enter any modern discussion of tax design. The higher the tax rate on higher earned incomes, the more the high-wage individual will choose to work less. Out of this comes the simple

---

[14] Technically referred to as 'non-separabilities with work'; see Atkinson and Stiglitz (1976).

rule—tax goods that are 'complementary' to leisure as this will discourage the high-wage individual from taking too much leisure. Of course, since there is a deadweight loss to such tax distortion, there is a limit to the extent to which we want to tax such complementary goods. But some degree of higher taxation of goods that are 'complementary' to leisure activities and, conversely, lower taxation of goods that are 'complementary' to work will be warranted.

The argument here is quite straightforward. Goods that take more time to consume, such as restaurant meals or theatre performances, require more leisure time. Hence, taxing them more highly is a form of leisure tax and will encourage those who consume them to work longer hours and take less leisure. In general, by taxing goods and services that are associated with leisure more heavily—and goods and services associated with work more lightly—we can partially offset the disincentives to work that a redistributive tax system inevitably creates. A similar effect is possible by imposing lower tax rates on goods that are associated with longer hours of work (ready meals, for example).

Assessing the practical significance of this argument is not easy, although there are some instances where it might be compelling. For example, taxing childcare services (during working hours) less heavily than other goods and services would help offset the disincentive to work created by other parts of the tax system. The same might apply to some kinds of public transport (particularly peak-time travel). Subsidy of goods that increase the time available for work, or its effectiveness, such as (some) medicines, can be justified. Perhaps less compelling, goods and services that are most useful during leisure time (such as fishing rods, suncream, and cooking ingredients) are candidates for higher tax rates, while reduced tax rates on takeaway and ready meals, dishwashers, and repair services might encourage people to do more paid work instead of doing these activities themselves.

6.2.1. Egalitarianism and Horizontal Equity

A conceptually different argument for differentiation rests on what James Tobin has described as *specific egalitarianism*[15]—the idea that there are specific domains in which we seek to limit inequality as an end in itself. For example, differentiation of tax rates could be justified to avoid taxing 'life's essentials'. Poorer households spend more of their money on cigarettes than rich households, but one rarely hears calls for these items to be given preferential treatment: concerns about 'fuel poverty' have greater resonance than concerns about 'cigarette poverty'. What distinguishes commodities such as food and domestic fuel (along with the likes of water and sewerage services and burial and cremation) is not that they take up a larger share of poorer households' budgets but that they are essentials of life. Unlike cigarettes, people must unavoidably buy a certain amount of these goods.

Many goods where such egalitarian sentiments prevail, such as education and health care, are provided by the state. However, many are allocated through the operation of the market. To distinguish specific egalitarianism from the argument for generalized redistribution, we must believe that people will still choose to buy 'too little' of these goods even if they have the money to do so. The goal is to encourage people to buy these goods in particular rather than giving them enough money in general. In one sense, this is a more coherent argument for differentiation than is the general equity argument, since we could not achieve this outcome more efficiently using other tools that we currently have. On the other hand, it is an argument that sits uncomfortably with a belief that people are generally able to make the right decisions for themselves.

The third egalitarian argument for a differentiated VAT is that some spending patterns might convey extra information about consumers' abilities or needs and hence might be useful 'tags' for the tax system to achieve specific distributional ends. A good example in the current UK tax system is that vehicles for people with disabilities are exempt from VAT on the cost of adaptation and exempt from payment of the annual vehicle excise duty. As with broader distributional objectives, the case for differentiating indirect tax rates for this reason depends on there not being more efficient alternatives.

---

[15] The concept of specific egalitarianism is discussed in Tobin (1970).

This might be so if other distributional tools have undesirable disincentive effects or if it is difficult to target certain groups using them.

There may be one or two exceptions of this sort, but, in general, when other more direct instruments exist, using differentiation in the indirect tax system to achieve distributional objectives is likely to be costly and inefficient.

We should round off this discussion by reminding ourselves that there is, in fact, another type of equity for which uniformity is important. This is what we described in Chapter 2 as *horizontal equity*, or the desire to tax similar people in similar ways. Individuals with the same income or wealth may differ in the way that they like to spend their money. When the rate of tax is differentiated across goods, some individuals are rewarded and others penalized in a way that can appear rather arbitrary. At present in the UK, we subsidize those who spend large amounts of money on designer clothes for their children but tax those who spend similar amounts on, perhaps rather educational, toys. Those with a taste for music are taxed; those with a taste for magazines are not. We clearly want to avoid differentiating rates between people who differ only in *inconsequential* characteristics (such as a taste for Jaffa Cakes rather than chocolate-covered biscuits).[16]

At the extremes, non-uniform taxation can even appear discriminatory when differences in tastes and needs mirror characteristics such as age and gender, where society has explicit anti-discrimination policies.

6.2.2. Balancing the Arguments

For efficiency reasons, it is always a good thing for consumer prices to line up with marginal costs. If markets are competitive, then non-uniformity

---

[16] This consequence of this approach is demonstrated in Atkinson and Stiglitz (1976). Assume there are two consumers. One consumer has a strong taste for vanilla ice cream relative to chocolate ice cream but does not care greatly about the choice between red and white wine. The other consumer has a strong taste for red wine but does not mind about ice cream. It is then efficient (applying the inverse elasticity rule) to tax vanilla ice cream and red wine at a higher rate than chocolate ice cream and white wine. The taxes are differentiated, but the two consumers have the same level of welfare.

drives prices and costs apart in a way that is always undesirable in itself and can be justified only by some countervailing consideration.

Where the government is looking to raise revenue, and price elasticities of demand for different goods differ, then there is an efficiency case for imposing high taxes on those goods with lower price elasticities. This will generally mean higher taxes on necessities. On the other hand, if the government is concerned about equity, and does not have an effective direct tax and benefit system to achieve redistribution, then there is a case for imposing lower taxes on those goods that take a greater part of the budget of the poor. However, where there are effective progressive direct taxes and benefits available, these will do a better job at redistributing. In this case, differential commodity taxation will enable more redistribution only where commodity purchases reveal something about effort. Lower taxation on goods that are complementary to work may allow more effective redistribution.

In general, though, it is hard to implement most of these distinctions. With the likely exception of childcare, the case for the greater complexity associated with differentiated tax rates is not proven. The equity and revenue-raising goals of any differentiated indirect tax plus an income tax can be achieved more efficiently by replacing these taxes with a uniform indirect tax and a more progressive income tax. The progressivity of the income tax achieves redistribution; the lack of differentiation in indirect taxes avoids distortions in choice of commodities; both help raise revenue.[17] This is not surprising. Income taxes and benefits can be closely designed to achieve distributional outcomes. Indirect taxes are generally very blunt instruments. While we do not doubt the case for redistributing to low-income households, differential commodity taxes are an inefficient way to achieve that end, for the reasons that we have outlined.

Differentiation of the tax rates on commodities redistributes on the basis of how much people spend *on particular items*. But if we wish to redistribute from those most able to pay to those least able to pay, we can do so more accurately based on the level of people's *total* expenditure—or their earnings,

---

[17] This statement is justified in Laroque (2005a) and Kaplow (2008).

income, or wealth.[18] Unless someone's spending on particular items can tell us something about his ability or his needs that his overall spending and income cannot, differential indirect tax rates cannot help us achieve the redistribution we want. So, the general case for differentiating commodity tax rates as a way of achieving redistribution is, in the presence of other tools such as an income tax, a weak one.

In Chapter 9, we will explore the implications of extending the VAT base while looking for ways of compensating some of the households that lose. While we cannot compensate each and every household, we will find that, for the most part, the argument that there are better ways of dealing with distributional concerns is largely borne out in practice. This result is somewhat complicated, but not undermined, by the potential for a progressive income tax to create work disincentives.

In sum, the efficiency arguments for differential tax rates are important but, in our view, can be very hard to operationalize in practical terms. The one exception to this is that there is probably a strong case for exempting childcare costs from VAT because, in many cases, spending on childcare is so closely related to the choice over how many hours to work. The equity arguments might also be powerful in the absence of other parts of the tax and benefit system that can redistribute more effectively. But those other parts do exist, and they can redistribute more effectively without creating the distortions that differential VAT rates bring with them. In addition, considerations of horizontal equity—treating similar people similarly—argue in favour of uniformity.

6.3. SPILLOVERS AND BEHAVIOURAL CHANGE

So far, we have avoided discussion of the most significant divergences from uniformity. In the UK, and in most other countries, alcohol, tobacco, and automotive fuels (petrol and diesel) are subject to taxes in addition to the standard VAT. These are usually levied as excise duties—a tax per unit

---

[18] Chapter 13 discusses which—or what combination—of these is the most appropriate tax base.

bought, rather than a tax proportional to value (though there is also an additional *ad valorem* element to the taxation of tobacco products in the UK). These duties continue to account for a substantial element of UK exchequer revenues. In 2010–11, fuel duties were expected to raise over £27 billion, tobacco duties over £9 billion, and various alcohol duties £9.5 billion.[19] There are also a series of smaller environmentally related taxes, insurance premium tax, and additional taxes on betting and gaming.

There are convincing arguments for these sorts of differentiated tax rates where the consumption of a particular good or service creates spillover costs or benefits for individuals other than the consumer. An obvious example is the imposition of higher tax rates on products, such as petrol, the consumption of which harms the environment. We devote separate chapters to considering environmental taxes in some detail (Chapters 10–12).

The basic principles for taxing spillovers are straightforward. In general, the additional or reduced taxation on any good should reflect the damage or benefit that the consumption of a little more of it creates. This ensures that the private decision about how much of the good to consume takes into account the impact on others. In practice, there are limits to this. Estimating the damage or benefit—and the appropriate tax differential—is often difficult. Indeed, the external effects of consumption may vary dramatically according to where, when, and by whom the consumption is taking place. Most moderate drinkers, for example, impose no costs on the rest of society. But the costs imposed by a minority, through associated accidents and crime, may be very high.

Importantly, even though taxation can be an effective tool with which to influence the amount of socially costly or beneficial consumption in the economy, it may not always be the *best* tool. If the harm is large enough, an outright ban would likely be the best policy: for example, alcohol is taxed, while drugs perceived as more damaging are prohibited. Similarly, compulsion may sometimes be the best way to achieve beneficial spillovers: for example, it seems preferable to require vehicle owners to take out motor insurance rather than merely to impose a lower tax rate on it.

---

[19] HM Treasury, 2010b, table C11.

But it would be a mistake to think that taxes on tobacco and alcohol in particular are entirely, or even largely, about reducing negative effects on others. They are actually in some part justified by the rather more contentious argument that the consumption of alcohol and, especially, tobacco harms the consumers themselves. Rather than creating an externality—an impact on other people—the consumption of these goods may create what some authors have called an *internality*[20] and others refer to as 'an externality to one's future self'[21]—an impact on the consumer. The idea is that taxes can encourage people to avoid acting against their own self-interest. They might act against their own self-interest, and might require action to prevent them doing so, either because they do not understand the costs of their consumption decision, or because the goods are addictive (and, in particular, addictive in ways that are not fully anticipated), or because the decision is in some sense not rational.

In all these cases, the government can act paternalistically and use taxes to change prices and encourage people to change their behaviour. The general principle is similar to the case of spillovers: tax rates should include a component to reflect self-harm, with a larger tax where self-harm is deemed to be larger. Such arguments are certainly influential in the taxation of alcohol and tobacco, although (as with spillovers) it is hard to know what level of taxation would be proportionate to the costs to the individuals concerned. The costs of consuming a particular product may also differ across different groups. Children and young adults, for example, might be thought particularly susceptible to the consequences of drinking and smoking. As it happens, there is also evidence that such groups may be the most responsive to taxes.[22]

Underlying many of these arguments is the observation that individuals make inconsistent choices at different times during their life. This may be especially true at the point at which smoking begins. The majority of smokers start smoking when they are young. They are unlikely to make the decision to do so with a clear view about the future. This is well illustrated by a survey that followed a group of school seniors in the US who smoked a

---

[20] Gruber, 2003a.

[21] Viscusi, 1995.

[22] See e.g. Chaloupka and Wechsler (1997).

pack or more a day. Of those who expected still to be smoking in five years' time, 72% were still smoking. Of those expecting *not* to be smokers five years hence, 74% were still smoking.[23]

If consumers cannot control their short-term desire to smoke, even though they would expect it to be of long-term benefit to control it, then in more reflective moments a smoker might actually prefer higher taxation as a counterweight to his or her short-term lack of control. This is a plausible view of human psychology (and indeed supported by experimental evidence[24]), but the implications for policy are not straightforward. The tax rate required to offset people's lack of self-control would vary widely. Taxation could also be seen as penalizing fully-rational individuals who choose to smoke and drink when they are entirely cognizant of the (current and future) benefits and costs.

Similar sorts of arguments have also been made for taxing fatty foods. This is much more complex than taxing alcohol and tobacco, in part because, of course, moderate consumption of most foods is beneficial, but perhaps even more importantly because of the extreme difficulty in defining a category of fattening or harmful foods different from all others. We already have a situation in the UK in which certain unhealthy foods are standard rated for VAT while others are zero rated. Ice creams, biscuits, and potato crisps fall into the first category; cakes, tortilla chips, and chocolate cookies bought from a bakery fall into the second. This illustrates both the use of taxation to deter consumption of unhealthy foods and the difficulty of making a clear assignment into healthy and unhealthy categories.

6.4. CONCLUSIONS

The main conclusion from the analysis in this chapter is that there is a strong case for a move to a broader-based and more uniform system of indirect taxation. There are a few clear-cut situations where there should be deviations from uniformity—taxes on environmental harms, and taxes on

---

[23] Gruber, 2003b.

[24] Gruber and Koszegi, 2001.

goods such as alcohol and tobacco that can have damaging effects on the consumer and on other people, are the obvious examples. But the case for the widespread differentiation in indirect tax rates that we see in the UK at present is not strong. In particular, if we are concerned about equity, then it is much better to use the direct tax and benefit system to achieve the distributional outcomes that we favour than it is to use differential indirect tax rates. We will look in detail at how this might be done in Chapter 9.

There are reasons other than equity for favouring differential tax rates, including a desire to tax more lightly the consumption of those goods associated with work. This is likely to provide a strong case for a low (perhaps zero) VAT rate on childcare. One could make a case for some other goods and services in this category, but, in the absence of strong evidence to the contrary, our view is that the advantages in terms of simplicity of a single rate are likely to outweigh any possible advantage from differentiating tax rates for this or other reasons of efficiency.

Prior to these conclusions is the conclusion that economic efficiency is best served by taxing consumption goods and not by taxing either produced inputs or transactions per se. We tackle some of the issues associated with this principle in Chapter 16, where we consider stamp duty (a transactions tax) and business rates (a tax on a produced input). In this context, the question of what we might do with financial services is dealt with briefly in Chapter 8.

Finally, indirect taxes need to be seen in an international context. Significant changes to the economic environment in recent years have brought international tax issues to the fore. For EU member states, for example, the most important of these was the completion of the single European market in January 1993, which directly affected the operation of the VAT system. In an international context, there is a fundamental question over *where* taxation should take place. In practice, indirect taxes are almost exclusively levied on a destination basis at present—that is, in the country where purchases take place rather than in the country where production occurs (as would happen if taxes were levied on an origin basis). While this is likely to continue to be the case, it does create a number of inefficiencies associated with cross-border shopping and problems of administration, to which we return in the next chapter.

7

———

Implementation of VAT

In the previous chapter, we discussed the principles of indirect taxation. In this chapter, we focus on some of the practical issues in its implementation, and in particular in the design and operation of VAT. These issues of implementation are important to policy design, and in particular to considering possible reforms to VAT. Once we have been through the important design issues in this chapter, we will look at two sets of reforms in the next two chapters—first the specific issue of VAT and financial services, and then extending VAT coverage to other goods and services in general.

In terms of revenue raised, VAT is by a long distance the most important indirect tax in the UK, and in most other OECD countries. Since its introduction in France in 1954, it has proved an exceptionally successful form of taxation and has been adopted by many countries worldwide, including all OECD countries other than the US. Bird (2010, 363) calls it 'unquestionably the most successful fiscal innovation of the last half-century … perhaps the most economically efficient way in which countries can raise significant tax revenues'.

In this chapter, we first explain how VAT works and why it has such appeal. We then go on to discuss its more problematic aspects: rate differentiation and exemptions, the scope for non-compliance, and difficulties applying VAT in the context of international trade.

7.1. HOW VAT WORKS

VAT taxes all sales, whether wholesale or retail, but allows registered traders to deduct the tax charged on their inputs. It is therefore a tax on the *value added* at each stage of the production process. Since the value of the final product is the total of the value added at each stage of production, the tax base—total value added—equals the value of final sales. Consequently, the tax is in effect imposed on the value of the final product but is collected in small chunks from each link in the supply chain. VAT charged on sales to registered traders who sell on an item or use it in production can be reclaimed by the purchaser; only VAT on retail sales cannot be reclaimed. VAT therefore taxes only final consumption and leaves production decisions undistorted.

It is worth illustrating how the system works with a very simple example. Suppose firm A makes a sale to firm B for £100 plus 20% VAT—£120 in total—remitting the VAT to the tax authorities.[1] Firm B uses what it has bought to make products worth £300; £60 VAT is due when these products are sold to firm C, but B can also reclaim the £20 VAT charged on its inputs. And, similarly, C can in turn reclaim the £60 VAT on its input purchases. Firm C, a retailer, sells its products to final consumers—households—for £500 plus £100 VAT.

Table 7.1 illustrates the VAT payments in this simple supply chain from two perspectives which bring out the two key features of VAT. The top panel shows the VAT payments associated with each transaction. When firm A makes a £100 sale to firm B, A charges £20 VAT on the sale, but B can reclaim the same £20, so there is no net revenue raised from the transaction. Similarly, the £60 VAT due on B's sale to C is reclaimed by C. Only sales to final consumers generate a net VAT liability, and the total revenue raised is 20% of the value of this final consumption. No net tax is levied on intermediate inputs; the pattern of activity in the supply chain generating the final product is irrelevant to the tax burden, and so is not distorted.

---

[1] VAT is usually expressed in *tax-exclusive* terms: a 20% VAT rate means that liability is 20% of the price excluding VAT (20% of £100 = £20). This is unlike income tax, for example, which is expressed in *tax-inclusive* terms: as a percentage of income including (i.e. without deducting) the tax itself. A 20% tax-exclusive rate is equivalent to a 16.7% tax-inclusive rate (16.7% of £120 = £20).

Table 7.1. A simple supply chain with 20% VAT

	VAT charged on sales	VAT reclaimed on input purchases	Net VAT liability
Analysis of transactions			
Sale from firm A to firm B for £100[a]	£20	£20	£0
Sale from firm B to firm C for £300[a]	£60	£60	£0
Sale from firm C to consumer for £500[a]	£100	£0	£100
Analysis of firms			
Firm A	£20	£0	£20
Firm B	£60	£20	£40
Firm C	£100	£60	£40

[a] Price excluding VAT, which is shown separately in the next column.

The bottom panel of Table 7.1 shows the VAT remitted by each firm. Firm A makes sales of £100 plus VAT with no purchased inputs in our example, so it simply remits the £20 VAT on the sale. Firms B and C each add £200 to the value of the goods, and so each has a net liability of 20% of that (£40). B transforms £100-worth of inputs into £300-worth of outputs, so deducts £20 input VAT (20% of £100) from its £60 output VAT (20% of £300), remitting a total of £40. C is liable for £100 output VAT on its £500 sales, less £60 input VAT on its £300 purchases, also remitting £40 in total. Each firm pays 20% tax on the value it adds; in other words, responsibility for remitting the £100 tax on the total value of the final product is divided across the supply chain in proportion to the value added at each stage.

An alternative, which achieves the objective of taxing only final consumption but without dividing liability across the supply chain in this way, is to make a legal distinction between wholesale and retail sales and tax only the latter. This is the approach of the retail sales tax (RST) which currently operates in most states of the US. This would appear more straightforward, and means that only firms selling to retail customers (firm C in our example) need face the cost of complying with the tax. But the RST approach suffers from significant disadvantages.

First, drawing the distinction between wholesale and retail sales is difficult in practice. An RST requires sellers to establish whether their customers will use their products for business or consumption. But there is little incentive for sellers to draw the distinction correctly, making misclassification and significant loss of revenue possible. In contrast, VAT requires buyers to establish whether they have used their *purchases* for business rather than consumption. Since only registered traders deduct VAT on their purchases, misclassification of purchases as inputs rather than consumption would normally require people to register for VAT and commit outright fraud. Despite taking a less direct approach than the RST to taxing only final consumption, VAT is more likely to be successful in achieving this goal.[2]

More importantly, dividing VAT liability across all links of the supply chain means that any one trader evading VAT escapes with only the tax due on the value added in that part of the supply chain, not the VAT due on the whole value of the product. This lessens the incentive for traders to attempt evasion. Traders' claims for deduction of input VAT also require an output VAT invoice from their supplier, so traders buying inputs have an incentive to ensure that their supplier invoices the VAT in full (if not necessarily remitting it to the authorities). If the supplier does not do so, the input buyer ends up paying both parties' VAT liabilities—which is undesirable for the input buyer, but at least means that the government gets the revenue it is due. The symmetric invoices—each claim for input VAT can be checked against the supplier's recorded output VAT—also provide a useful audit trail for the government.

For these reasons, a VAT is a very attractive way for governments to raise revenue. Sadly, it does not always operate smoothly in practice. In the rest of this chapter, we look at some of the more important design problems with the UK VAT. We focus on two issues in particular: first, the widespread use of zero-rating and exemptions, the latter of which in particular causes significant deviations from the 'ideal' described above; and second, the scope

---

[2] Distinguishing between business expenditure and consumption expenditure is not always straightforward under a VAT, as e.g. when a firm buys gym memberships for its employees or when a self-employed person buys a computer for personal as well as business use. These blurred borderlines—unlike the more mundane monitoring problem discussed in the text—create difficulties for VAT and RST equally, and indeed for other taxes too: there are close parallels between these boundary issues and the difficulties in identifying work-related expenses for income tax purposes, as discussed in Section 3.2.3.

for non-compliance and the closely related question of how to implement VAT in an international context.

7.2. ZERO RATES, REDUCED RATES, AND EXEMPTIONS

In practice, many goods and services are not subject to VAT at the standard rate (20% from January 2011) in the UK. Some are zero rated, some are subject to a reduced rate of 5%, and some are exempt. The distinction between zero-rating and exemption is that zero-rating allows registered traders to reclaim the VAT on any inputs used in the production process. As a consequence, there is no component of taxation in the final price of a product that is zero rated. Goods and services that are exempt are not subject to VAT when sold, but the producer of an exempt product cannot reclaim the VAT paid on purchases of inputs. The VAT on inputs means that the sale price does include a component of taxation, so is higher than it would be with zero-rating. If a good or service is zero rated, then it is subject to VAT, but the VAT rate is 0%. If it is exempt, then its production is in effect ignored completely for VAT, with no VAT charged on sales or credited on inputs.

Table 7.2 provides a brief summary of the main goods and services that are zero rated for VAT, those facing a reduced (5%) rate, and those that are exempt, alongside government estimates of the revenue forgone by not charging VAT at the full rate on these goods and services (though note that the full rate was 17.5% and 20% during different parts of the year in question). While this table may look relatively straightforward, the reality is that there is a huge amount of detail and complexity in the rules determining exactly what qualifies as, for example, an exempt financial service, zero-rated food, and so on.[3]

---

[3] Note that Table 7.2 excludes public sector bodies (and others) that are outside the scope of VAT—a status equivalent in effect to exemption. We discuss the treatment of public sector bodies below, but the net revenue implications are small since it mainly affects how much VAT is paid by one part of government to another.

Table 7.2. Estimated revenue cost of zero-rating, reduced-rating, and exempting goods and services, 2010–11

	Estimated cost (£m)
Zero rated:	
Food	14,250
Construction of new dwellings[a]	5,400
Domestic passenger transport	3,250
International passenger transport[a]	150
Books, newspapers, and magazines	1,600
Children's clothing	1,300
Water and sewerage services	1,700
Drugs and supplies on prescription	1,850
Supplies to charities[a]	200
Certain ships and aircraft	550
Vehicles and other supplies to people with disabilities	450
Reduced rated:	
Domestic fuel and power	4,250
Women's sanitary products	50
Energy-saving materials	50
Residential conversions and renovations	200
Exempt:	
Rent on domestic dwellings[a]	4,850
Supplies of commercial property[a]	350
Education[a]	1,150
Health services[a]	1,500
Postal services	200
Burial and cremation	150
Finance and insurance[a]	9,050
Betting, gaming, and lottery duties[a]	1,150
Businesses below registration threshold[a]	1,650

[a] Figures for these categories are subject to a wide margin of error.

Notes: These figures refer to 2010–11. VAT was levied at 17.5% during most of that year, rising to 20% for the last three months. With a standard rate of 20% throughout the year, the costs are likely to be around 10–15% higher. Some zero-rated goods (e.g. cycle helmets), reduced-rated goods (e.g. contraceptives, smoking cessation products, and children's car seats), and exempt goods (e.g. cultural admissions charges), where costs are very low or unknown, are not included here.

Source: HMRC statistics, table 1.5 (http://www.hmrc.gov.uk/stats/tax_expenditures/table1-5.pdf).

The overall extent of deviations from uniformity, along with the degree of non-compliance (discussed in Section 7.3 below), can be measured by the ratio of actual VAT revenues to the VAT that would have been levied if all private consumption were successfully taxed at the standard VAT rate. The OECD estimates this ratio at 46% for the UK in 2008, well below the (unweighted) OECD average of 58%.[4]

The list of zero- and reduced-rated goods is extensive. It exists as a result of a combination of distributional concerns and a desire to encourage consumption of particular goods.[5] The reduced rate on domestic fuel illustrates where these two goals may conflict. It is there for distributional reasons despite the fact that for environmental reasons we might want to discourage, rather than encourage, the consumption of domestic fuel.[6] In the last chapter, we noted the practical disadvantages of departing extensively from a uniform VAT rate, and the weakness of distributional arguments for zero- and reduced-rating when there are flexible income-related taxes and benefits which can achieve redistribution more precisely and more efficiently. A detailed practical illustration of that is the subject of Chapter 9. The fact that children's clothes are taxed at 0%, children's car seats at 5%, and educational toys (and clothes for children who happen to be big enough to need adult sizes) at 20% is just one of many possible examples of the difficulty in rationalizing the list as it currently appears.

To illustrate specifically how zero-rating works, let us return to our previous example. If firm C's output is zero rated, it need no longer add £100 VAT to the £500 price of its sales, but it can still reclaim the £60 VAT charged on its purchase from firm B. Thus C in effect reclaims the VAT remitted further up the supply chain (£20 by A and £40 by B) and charges no VAT on its own sales. Production in this case is entirely VAT free and the consumer pays a price unaffected by VAT. However, as we shall see in the international context in Section 7.4, the fact that there are firms such as C, which can claim significant net refunds from HMRC as a result of zero-rating, can create opportunities for fraud.

---

[4] OECD, 2011.

[5] The large category of construction of new dwellings does not readily fit either of these explanations. We consider it in more detail in Chapter 16.

[6] We explore this in more detail in Chapter 11.

Exemption is different. It means that sales are not subject to VAT but, in contrast to zero-rating, the firm cannot reclaim the VAT paid on its inputs. If firm C is selling VAT-exempt goods, it would charge no VAT on its sales but would not be able to reclaim the £60 VAT paid on the inputs it purchased from firm B. Although C's outputs no longer bear VAT, its production costs are now £60 higher, perhaps passed on in a higher price to the consumer. With a final product worth £500, this £60 irrecoverable input VAT represents an effective tax rate of 12%. It should be clear, then, that the effective rate of VAT on the final product depends on the proportion of total value that is added before the exempt link of the supply chain.[7] The effective VAT rate will always be below the standard rate, but by differing amounts depending on the structure of the supply chain.

Although exempt goods and services bear less than the full rate of VAT, exemption is very different from a reduced rate of VAT. For one thing, exemption is not always more generous than taxation. Where exempt goods and services are sold directly to final consumers, this lower effective rate of VAT is payable *instead of* the standard VAT rate on those sales. But where exempt products are sold to other VAT-registered businesses, the irrecoverable input VAT comes *on top of* the VAT that will be charged on sales to final consumers by businesses further down the supply chain.

If, in our example, it were firm B's output that was exempt from VAT, the £20 VAT on A's sale to B would now be irrecoverable. Crucially, the fact that £60 VAT would no longer be levied on B's sale to C is irrelevant since C could have recovered it anyway; and C's sale to final consumers would be subject to VAT. So the overall VAT payable on this chain of production would be increased by the £20 irrecoverable input VAT; coming on top of the £100 already due on C's sale to final consumers, this means that the final product bears *more than* the full VAT rate.[8]

---

[7] Specifically, the effective rate of VAT as a fraction of the full rate is equal to the share of value added before the exempt link. In our example, the goods are worth £300 by the time C acquires them, and the final product is worth £500, so the effective VAT rate is 60% (300 ÷ 500) of the full 20% rate, or 12%.

[8] In this case, the share of value that is added before the exempt link in the supply chain is 20% (the £100 value of B's inputs is 20% of the £500 value of the final product), so the effective tax rate generated by the irrecoverable input VAT is 20% of the standard 20% rate, 4%. Coming on top of the standard 20% VAT charged on the sale to final consumers, this makes a total

Whether exemption is more or less generous than applying the standard rate thus depends on whether the exempt products are sold to final consumers—in which case the lack of output VAT outweighs the irrecoverable input VAT—or to other businesses—in which case any output VAT would have been recoverable anyway, so the irrecoverable input VAT is a pure extra cost.

Exemption is anathema to the logic of the VAT. It breaks the chain of tax and offsetting credit, leading to distortions of production patterns since taxes on produced inputs cannot be reclaimed. In Section 6.1.1, we stressed the importance of production efficiency and that intermediate inputs to production should not be taxed. The Australian description of exempt activities as 'input-taxed' is a good one and immediately draws attention to the inefficiencies that can be created.

We noted above that the effective tax rate entailed by exemption is related to the share of total value that is added before the exempt link in the supply chain. But this share is not fixed, so there is an incentive to minimize it. Exemption creates an incentive to 'self-supply'—that is, it encourages firms producing VAT-exempt outputs to undertake as many links of the supply chain as they can themselves to ensure that value added at intermediate stages is not taxed. So, for example, firms whose outputs are VAT exempt have a strong incentive to supply their own security services, technical support, cleaning services, and so on, rather than contract them out and face irrecoverable VAT bills. Exemption can create distortions in competition when exempt firms compete with non-exempt firms—favouring exempt over non-exempt firms when selling to final consumers, and favouring non-exempt over exempt firms when selling to other traders—or when competing exempt firms in different EU countries face different costs as a consequence of being charged different VAT rates on their inputs.

Finally, exemption can create additional administration and compliance burdens (and opportunities for tax avoidance) through the need to allocate

---

effective VAT rate of 24% on the £500 pre-tax price of the final product: £100 output VAT and £20 irrecoverable input VAT making £120 in total.

input VAT between taxable and exempt outputs (credit being available for the former but not the latter) for producers selling both.

While the total cost of these complexities and distortions is hard to ascertain, it is likely to be substantial. Indeed, Maurice Lauré, nicknamed 'father of the VAT' for developing the first fully fledged VAT system (introduced in France in 1954), went so far as to describe exemption as 'the cancer of the VAT system'.[9] Given this, the natural question to ask is: why is it used? One simple, if unhelpful, answer is that most of the UK's exemptions, including those for financial services and for health and education services, are mandated by EU rules. The UK government says that 'A number of goods and services are exempt from VAT because it is considered inappropriate to tax them (including public services such as health, education and welfare) or they are too technically difficult to tax (including financial services)'.[10]

We come back to the issue of financial services—important because of its sheer size as well as the unusual problems it poses for VAT—in the next chapter. For other exemptions, the 'inappropriateness' referred to in this quote appears to imply some combination of concern about distribution and a view that it is somehow obviously wrong to charge VAT on public services. If the exemptions reflect distributional concerns, then, given the additional distortions created by exemption, our arguments for using other parts of the tax and benefit system to address these apply with even more force than they do to zero-rating. And even if there is some other compelling reason why public services should be treated preferentially, it is far from clear why this preferential treatment should take the form of exemption, which, as we have argued, is far more damaging than, say, applying a zero or reduced rate.

The exemption for services in the public interest, such as health, education, postal, and cultural services, is closely related to the effective exemption applied to many public sector bodies. But the two are not the same, and the relationship between them is becoming more important and more complicated as various forms of privatization, liberalization, outsourcing, and public–private partnerships increase private sector involvement in the provision of public services and blur the boundaries between the two sectors. To some extent, what we have is a VAT system which has just not adapted

---

[9] Cited in European Commission (2010c, 28).
[10] HM Treasury and HM Revenue and Customs, 2010, para. 4.2.

with the economy. Blurred boundaries between public and private sectors lead to arbitrary differences in the tax treatment of similar organizations doing similar things. If public and private sector bodies are competing, they might not do so on a level playing field: public sector bodies may have an advantage in providing services to final consumers or to other exempt bodies because of the lack of output tax, whereas private firms' ability to recover input VAT may give them an advantage in providing services to taxable firms.

When public sector bodies are selling something—whether or not in competition with private firms—it might be thought that charging VAT is equivalent to simply adjusting the price: after all, passing the VAT on to HMRC is merely a transfer from one government agency to another, which could (at least in principle) be offset by adjusting the funding of the agency concerned. However, this is not always true: if a public sector body is selling something (for example, parking spaces) that is used both for consumption and as a business input, then charging VAT is not equivalent to a price adjustment as businesses could reclaim the VAT whereas households (and, indeed, exempt bodies paying for the parking space) could not. Since only final consumption should be taxed, prices ought to be higher for households than for businesses. The VAT mechanism achieves this, whereas a simple price adjustment cannot.

Finally, regardless of whether their outputs are sold or provided free to users, exempt public sector bodies have an incentive to self-supply rather than purchase taxed goods and services from private sector suppliers.

In all these cases, distortions could be avoided if VAT were applied to the public sector.[11] Studies have shown how this could be done and the benefits it would have,[12] and Australia and New Zealand provide practical examples.

There is one important exemption, though, that is more readily defensible—that for firms (including self-employed individuals) with sales

---

[11] Rules are in place at both EU and UK levels to mitigate some of the distortions, in effect by moving away from exemption. For example, some activities of public sector bodies are classed as 'business activities' and taxed; exemption does not apply where it is deemed that it would lead to a significant distortion of competition; and a special scheme refunds input VAT to some public sector bodies (notably local authorities). However, the scope of these provisions is far from complete and, in practice, many distortions remain.

[12] Aujean, Jenkins, and Poddar, 1999; Gendron, 2005; Copenhagen Economics and KPMG, 2011.

below the VAT registration threshold (£70,000 per year in 2010–11). Registration for VAT is optional for traders with sales below this level. Firms choosing not to register do not remit VAT on their sales, nor can they reclaim VAT on their input purchases, so they are in effect VAT exempt. This is in fact the position of most UK businesses—the government estimates that 2.9 million small businesses are not registered, compared with a total of 1.95 million businesses registered for VAT[13]—although since they are, by definition, small, these unregistered businesses account for only a small minority of sales and revenue. However, many firms with turnover below the threshold choose to register, because if they don't they cannot reclaim VAT paid on inputs. For firms selling mostly to registered traders, any output VAT charged is unimportant because their customers can reclaim it anyway, whereas irrecoverable input VAT could be a significant extra cost. So voluntary registration can often make sense for such firms— although they must also take account of the compliance costs entailed by being registered for VAT.

It is these compliance costs, and the corresponding administrative costs to government, that provide the rationale for a threshold of this kind. The costs of ascertaining VAT liabilities, record-keeping, and so on are substantial, and particularly important for small businesses since many of these costs are fixed rather than proportional to turnover, while the revenue at stake is small. A trade-off needs to be made between the administration and compliance costs of imposing VAT on small businesses, on the one hand, and the loss of VAT revenue and distortion of production activities created by exempting firms below a threshold, on the other. Exempting small firms has all the downsides of exemption generally, discussed above, and the threshold itself brings additional distortions, including creating an incentive for traders to remain below the threshold and giving retailers below the threshold an unfair competitive advantage over taxed retailers. These costs and benefits are difficult to quantify. Crawford, Keen, and Smith (2010) provide some indicative calculations that weigh administrative and compliance costs against lost revenue (but ignore distortions). The results prove highly sensitive to difficult-to-measure parameters, but on balance we

---

[13] HM Treasury and HM Revenue and Customs, 2010, para. 4.9.

agree with them that 'there is good reason to suppose that the relatively high threshold should be counted as a strength of the UK VAT'.

Another route, used in many countries, to minimizing administration and compliance costs is to apply a simplified scheme to small businesses. Such a scheme has existed in the UK since 2002 for small firms (those with non-exempt sales below £150,000, excluding VAT, in 2010–11), which have had the option of using a simplified flat-rate VAT scheme. Under the flat-rate scheme, firms pay VAT at a single rate on their total sales and give up the right to reclaim VAT on inputs. The flat rate, which varies between 4% and 14.5% depending on the industry,[14] is intended to reflect the average VAT rate in that industry after taking into account recovery of VAT on inputs, zero- or reduced-rating of some outputs, and so on. This scheme has problems. By disallowing the recovery of VAT on inputs, it distorts production decisions in the same way as exemption. The differentiation of rates between 55 categories of industry creates distortions and policing problems at the boundaries between them. And the scheme may not even succeed on its own terms, in reducing compliance costs for relatively small businesses. It is not clear how much easier it is to comply with the flat-rate scheme than with the standard scheme; more importantly, optional schemes of this kind naturally encourage firms to estimate (at least roughly) their liability under both regimes to see which is lower—indeed, tax advisers often insist on doing both sets of calculations for fear of being found negligent if clients choose the wrong option. This increases compliance costs—ironic when the scheme exists precisely to reduce them—as well as ensuring the maximum revenue loss for the government.

While the merits of an optional flat-rate scheme are questionable, the case for a substantial registration threshold is strong. In other areas, though, there is a powerful case for reform. In general, we agree with the view expressed by Crawford, Keen, and Smith (2010, 301) that 'the extensive rate differentiation still found in the VATs of EU members is coming to look increasingly quaint'. It reflects an outdated view of what it is possible to do within a VAT system and does not reflect lessons learned by those countries, including Australia and New Zealand, that introduced VATs more recently and with many fewer exemptions and less rate differentiation than are seen

---

[14] This is the range of rates from January 2011, when the main VAT rate rises to 20%.

either in the UK or in many other European countries. The UK's long list of exemptions and extensive zero-rating are increasingly hard to justify. Some of the changes needed are substantial and complex and we don't deal with them all in this chapter. Rather, we devote Chapter 9 to illustrating how the use of zero and reduced rates of VAT can be drastically reduced without adverse consequences for either redistribution or work incentives. We discuss in detail in Chapter 8 how the major issue of the exemption of financial services might be dealt with. And the treatment of housing is dealt with in Chapter 16. For the rest of this chapter, we focus first on some of the general compliance issues that are thrown up by the design of VAT and then on the international context and particular compliance issues surrounding the treatment of exports.

7.3. NON-COMPLIANCE

Evasion and fraud are important issues in the administration of VAT. Keeping up with what remains a vast paper trail of invoices is a formidable task. HMRC estimates that the 'VAT gap' was £11.5 billion in 2009–10.[15] That is the difference between tax actually collected and the tax that would have been paid if all individuals and companies complied with both the letter of the law and HMRC's interpretation of the intention of Parliament in setting law. At 14% of the potential revenue yield—higher than for most other taxes—it is clearly a cause for concern.

Not all of the VAT gap represents outright fraud: a significant part of it reflects innocent error or legal tax avoidance, for example. But illegal evasion is significant. In general terms, evasion falls into two main categories:

- traders understating taxable sales and/or overstating creditable inputs;
- traders disappearing without paying a VAT bill they owe.

The first category involves a range of different practices. These include working cash-in-hand and not recording sales that ought to be taxable, or failing to register for VAT despite being liable. Invoices for input purchases can be faked, or it is possible to claim that sales are zero rated (for example, by faking export invoices) when they should not be. Evaders can also exploit the different rates of VAT on different forms of transaction, taking advantage of the difficulty in policing borderlines between different activities (for example, consumption versus business expenditure; inputs to exempt versus non-exempt activities; inputs from registered versus unregistered suppliers; taxable versus zero-rated inputs). Some of these problems are inherent to a VAT system, though many are concrete and expensive examples of the consequences of the complexity created by deviations from uniformity. The way VAT works does limit the scope for evasion because it is harder to understate sales when the buyer wants an invoice with which to reclaim input VAT and, correspondingly, it is harder to overstate inputs when one needs an invoice from the seller. Broadening the VAT base would further help, since reducing the number of boundaries would leave less scope for misclassification—reducing error and avoidance as well as evasion. It would also be harder to claim zero-rated sales if fewer products were zero rated. Other aspects of VAT policy—such as the choice of registration threshold, the speed with which payment is demanded and refunds are given, and the sheer level of resources devoted to HMRC's enforcement activities—could also have an impact on evasion, though of course there are also other considerations involved in each of these choices.

The second form of evasion mainly arises when individual traders have large net VAT liabilities. The fractional nature of VAT is designed precisely to deal with this problem: the VAT liability on a final consumption sale is divided across the supply chain so that no individual trader gains that much by disappearing. Of course, where a single trader genuinely creates significant value added, there is still a substantial incentive to disappear, but much less so than under a retail sales tax. And the very fact that the value added is genuine must reduce the incentive to sacrifice the long-term benefits of remaining active for short-term fraudulent gains.

Those traders with the biggest incentive to evade VAT in this way are those with large liabilities relative to their turnover. These will generally be firms that produce taxed outputs using untaxed inputs. There is not much scope for this in a purely domestic context because most zero-rated items are final consumption goods. But, as we shall see, the zero-rating of exports does create significant possibilities for fraud in an international context.

7.4. THE INTERNATIONAL CONTEXT

So far, we have considered the implementation of VAT in a purely national context. But the international dimension, and particularly the EU dimension, is central to the operation of VAT. For one thing, the EU is a major player in VAT policy—indeed, the UK adopted a VAT in 1973 largely because it was a precondition for entry to what was then the European Economic Community. As well as setting out standardized definitions and rules, the EU mandates a minimum standard rate of 15%, restricts the use of reduced rates, forbids the extension of zero-rating to new items, and insists on various exemptions. But significant changes to the economic environment in recent years have brought international tax issues ever more to the fore. For EU member states, the most important of these was the completion of the single European market in January 1993, which directly affected the operation of the VAT system. The completion of the single market also contributed to the wider impact of globalization in increasing trade. Particularly marked have been the very large increase in cross-border trade in services and the birth and rapid expansion of e-commerce, both more difficult to tax than traditional trade in physical goods. These changes have highlighted weaknesses in the current tax system and constrain the design of an alternative system.

In an international context, there is a fundamental question over *where* taxation should take place—in the country in which consumption takes place (the *destination principle*) or in the country of production (the *origin principle*).

It is worth clarifying what taxation 'in the country of' consumption or production means. First of all, while consumption generally takes place at a single location, production of a good or service is often split between several countries. Under origin taxation, the final price paid by the consumer would include some VAT at the rates charged in each country, in proportion to where the value was added. But, as we shall see, difficulties in identifying where the value was really added can cause problems.

Second, the country whose tax rate determines the final burden of tax on a product may not be the country that initially collects the revenue or the country that ultimately receives the revenue. In line with the economic literature (but unlike much EU policy discussion in recent years), we use origin and destination taxation to refer to the first of these three. But while current international practice is for VAT to be destination-based in all these senses, some reform proposals involve separating these different aspects, and terminology often becomes confused.

A uniform tax levied on a destination basis is a tax on the value of aggregate consumption, while a uniform tax levied on an origin basis is a tax on the value of aggregate production. In principle, there need not be any stark contrast between the two. When trade is balanced—as ultimately it must be—these are the same thing. Moving from a uniform destination-based VAT to a uniform origin-based VAT would leave trade patterns and economic welfare unchanged as exchange rates and/or prices in the different countries would adjust to offset any impact on the price of each country's products to purchasers in other countries.

Reality is not so neat.[16] In practice, VAT systems are far from uniform, so an across-the-board adjustment to a country's exchange rate or aggregate price level could not be a perfect offset for all goods.[17] And, to be neutral, a shift to the origin basis would have to be applied—unilaterally if necessary —to trade with all countries, which is unlikely to be politically popular because it would give the appearance (in fact illusory) of making exports uncompetitive on international markets, and would probably be inconsistent with World Trade Organization agreements. Thus origin and destination bases for taxation are not fully equivalent in practice; but what these arguments bring home is that the considerations involved in choosing between them are subtler than it might first appear.

The standard international practice of using a destination basis has the advantage that businesses and consumers are indifferent between imports and domestically produced goods, and between imports from different countries that levy different tax rates. In both cases, the only tax payable is that imposed in the country of consumption. This means that it should not distort decisions over where to produce.

The most problematic aspect of the destination basis is how it can be implemented in the context of an EU without internal border controls. The

---

[16] The conditions for equivalence are set out in Lockwood, de Meza, and Myles (1994).
[17] The precise condition for equivalence is in fact slightly weaker than full uniformity, but it is still far from being met.

problem arises for both sales to other businesses and cross-border shopping by individuals.

At present, the VAT system ensures that goods are taxed only in the country of consumption by zero-rating exports (thus freeing them of all VAT levied on the supply chain up to that point) and subjecting all imports to tax. In the EU prior to 1993, this involved the use of border controls to monitor exports and imports. Since then, border controls within the EU have been abolished to facilitate free trade and create a level playing field between firms operating across member states. But this means that it is no longer possible to apply at borders the tax adjustments that are fundamental to the operation of the destination principle. We discuss the problems this creates, and possible ways to deal with them, below.

As far as individual cross-border shopping is concerned, if two countries set different tax rates on a product, then, when there are no borders (and so no way to enforce limits on what individuals can bring home from abroad having paid tax only at the foreign-country rate), consumers can purchase the product in the country with the lower rate of tax and ship it home. This form of cross-border shopping is clearly an inefficient outcome. The origin principle does not suffer from this disadvantage: since tax liability depends on where the goods are produced rather than where they are consumed, consumer prices will tend to be equalized across countries, which would not distort where goods are consumed. There is simply no need to go abroad to buy goods more cheaply if the tax rate is the same wherever they are purchased. However, an origin-based tax would affect the pattern of production. Whether it is more important to avoid distortions to production patterns or to consumption patterns is still an issue for debate.[18] But an important downside of the origin approach is that it encourages producers to use mechanisms such as transfer prices (the prices at which part of a firm in one country 'sells' its output to another part of the firm in another country) to lower their tax bills artificially. Since, as mentioned above, pure origin taxation involves taxing the value added in each country at that country's tax rate, firms can use transfer prices to shift measured value added into

---

[18] Key contributions to the debate include Lockwood (1993), Keen and Lahiri (1998), Haufler and Pflüger (2004), Keen and Wildasin (2004), Haufler, Schjelderup, and Stahler (2005), and Hashimzade, Khodavaisi, and Myles (2005). Crawford, Keen, and Smith (2010) provide a summary of the arguments.

jurisdictions with low tax rates, just as they have an incentive to use transfer pricing so that profits appear to be earned in jurisdictions with low corporation tax rates. The problems associated with transfer pricing in corporation tax suggest that this is a potentially major drawback.

Since corporation tax is levied essentially on an origin basis (the usual terminology is 'source basis' in that context, but there is little difference), the pros and cons of origin and destination principles are relevant not just for the design of the VAT system itself, but also for governments deciding how much to rely on direct (corporate and personal) versus indirect taxes. At present, there is little prospect of the EU (let alone the UK unilaterally) moving to a pure origin basis for VAT, or for that matter a destination basis for corporation tax.[19] From the point of view of the UK (and the rest of Europe) in 2011, the most important international issue in VAT implementation is that of how best to manage a destination-based system in the absence of border controls. This has confronted the operation of VAT in the EU with some significant challenges, including frauds that have exploited the zero-rating of exports. We look now at this issue in more detail.

7.4.1. Export Zero-Rating and Compliance

We have already seen that zero-rating leads to opportunities for evasion. Zero-rating of goods at export involves tax authorities paying out large-scale refunds to exporting companies, since there is no tax on their sales and they can reclaim input VAT on their purchases. If this reclaim is accompanied by fraud or failure to pay VAT further down the chain, then not only can the revenue authorities collect less tax than intended, they can even end up paying more in refunds than they collect in tax.

In the early and middle years of the 2000s, missing trader intra-community (MTIC) fraud, including so-called carousel fraud, which exploited this possibility, became a widespread problem across the EU. In 2004, the European Commission reported that losses from fraud, of which carousel fraud is the best-known (but not the only) manifestation, amounted

---

[19] Auerbach, Devereux, and Simpson (2010), however, argue that shifting corporation tax to a destination basis deserves serious consideration. The international dimension of corporation tax is the subject of Chapter 18.

to 10% of net VAT receipts in some member states. One result for the UK was that, in the middle years of the 2000s, the Treasury was consistently forecasting VAT receipts several billions of pounds greater than actual out-turns because of losses to fraud. HMRC estimates that MTIC fraud in 2005–06 is likely to cost the Exchequer between £2.5 and £3.5 billion.[20] This was enough to distort trade statistics. The Office for National Statistics estimates that there were a staggering £20.7 billion of trade flows associated with MTIC fraud in the first half of 2006 alone[21]—though that appears to have been the peak. For an otherwise rather abstruse part of the tax system, these issues have certainly received a remarkable amount of press coverage,[22] in part because of the large totals involved and in part because some spectacular cases appear to have made some individuals very rich very quickly.

Whilst the scale of this fraud appears to have dropped dramatically in recent years, to between £0.5 and £1.5 billion in 2009–10,[23] it is worth explaining how it works since it provides a very clear illustration of some of the weaknesses in the VAT system, and in particular why the issue of the appropriate treatment of exports for VAT purposes has been the subject of considerable attention.

A carousel fraud is operated by importers purchasing products that are zero rated and selling them on with VAT added to another trader. The purchasing trader reclaims the input VAT, but the seller does not pay the VAT due and disappears. The way this works is illustrated in Figure 7.1. The importing company (company B) pays no VAT on its purchase because the import is zero rated. It then sells the goods to another company (company C), legitimately charging VAT on the sale. It should then remit this VAT to the tax authorities. Company C may well be an entirely innocent 'buffer' in the fraud. In the simplest version, it then sells goods on to company D, again charging VAT. Company D then exports the goods back to the original company, A, charging no VAT on the sale since exports are zero rated, but claiming a refund of input VAT on its purchase of the exported goods.

---

[20] HM Revenue and Customs, 2010d, table 2.4.

[21] Page 8 of http://www.statistics.gov.uk/pdfdir/trd1007.pdf.

[22] For example, 'Revealed: the £5bn-a-year tax fraud', *The Guardian,* 9 May 2006. The BBC *Panorama* programme on 16 July 2006, 'Do you want to be a millionaire?', also investigated carousel fraud; details at http://news.bbc.co.uk/1/hi/programmes/panorama/5366914.stm.

[23] HM Revenue and Customs, 2010d, table 2.4.

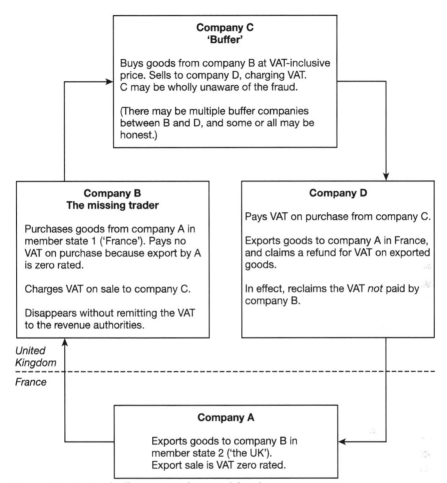

Figure 7.1. A simple illustration of carousel fraud

Source: Crawford, Keen, and Smith, 2010.

This is all fine unless the original importing company, B, 'disappears' before remitting VAT to the authorities. If this happens, then, in effect, company D is claiming a refund for VAT which was never actually paid. If there were no zero-rating of exports, then the importing company would have been charged VAT by the original exporter, which it could not then reclaim as input VAT if it disappeared without remitting its output VAT. And the final exporter would not be entitled to any refund of VAT if its sales were not zero rated. The opportunity for this type of fraud would not exist.

7.4.2. Responses to the Break in the VAT Chain at Export

Fundamentally, it is the break in the VAT chain created by the zero-rating of exports which allows this type of fraud to occur. It is particularly problematic for tax authorities because it involves not just reduced revenue but also an actual payment out from the system—revenue is negative. It has been a particular issue within the EU since completion of the single European market in January 1993. Before 1993, the border controls between member states permitted a destination system to operate, with commodities taken out of tax in the exporting country and brought into tax in the importing country. This was achieved by the zero-rating of exports, combined with subjecting all imports to VAT at the border. Since 1993, border controls within the EU have been abolished. So the ability to raise tax at the border has been lost, and the system depends upon a paper trail of invoices—account auditing plays the role previously performed by frontier controls. This has undermined the operation of the destination system and opened up the potential for abuse. Imports from outside the EU are, of course, still captured at borders.

The government's preferred solution to MTIC fraud has been *reverse charging*. In business-to-business transactions, this places the VAT liability on the buyer rather than the seller. This would deal effectively with the carousel fraud illustrated, because the VAT due on the sale by company B (the missing trader) would become the responsibility of the buyer, C. In turn, the tax due on the sale from C to D would be the responsibility of D. The zero-rating of the subsequent export sale would then offset D's tax liability on its purchases from C, reducing the tax payment by D but not requiring outright refunds. The opportunity to make fraudulent gains by claiming refunds of tax that has not in fact been paid would thereby be eliminated.

So reverse charging reduces the possibility of fraud by preventing the purchaser claiming back input VAT which has not actually been paid. But it also fundamentally undermines the fractional nature of the VAT, which we have argued is a crucial part of its attraction. If reverse charging applies all the way down the line, then nothing is collected until the final transaction and we effectively have a retail sales tax. Nevertheless, the UK has implemented reverse charging for mobile phones, computer chips, and some other easily transported and high-value goods which have been particularly prone to carousel fraud. Other member states (Austria and Germany, for example) have made applications for more comprehensive systems of reverse charging, but these applications have been rejected by the European Commission.

Reverse charging does appear to have met with some success, at least in the short term, in reducing MTIC fraud. But by undermining the fractional nature of VAT collection and creating further distinctions between those goods and services that are subject to it and those that are not, it potentially opens up the route to more mundane forms of evasion. It also leaves open the possibility that the carousel fraud itself could move to other goods which are not subject to reverse charging. It looks more like an interim solution plugging a hole than a fundamentally stable solution.

To understand what the more fundamental reform options are, recall that zero-rating of exports has the following features. All VAT in the exporting country is 'washed out' of the good at the point of export—the exporter receives a VAT refund. The good is then brought into the VAT system of the importing country. All VAT on the final product is paid at the rate of the country where consumption occurs and all revenues are collected by, and enjoyed by, the country where consumption occurs. This is a pure destination system.

The most radical option would be to move to a pure *origin* system, the advantages and disadvantages of which we discussed earlier. In practical terms, this would involve exporters remitting VAT on their sales at the exporting country's VAT rate (rather than zero), while importers would claim credit from the importing country's tax authorities at the destination country's VAT rate, irrespective of the VAT charged in the country of export. Note that this would mean not only that the burden of VAT on the final product reflected the rate in the country of production, but also that the revenue accrued to that country, so it would involve a redistribution of revenues between countries, as exporting countries would gain revenue and importing countries would lose revenue.

A variant on this is *exporter rating*. Under this system, exports would again carry the VAT of their country of origin, but now it would be this origin-country rate of VAT that could be reclaimed as input VAT in the destination country. Because the VAT could be reclaimed at the original rate charged, the VAT charged to the final consumer would still be that of the destination country. Exporter rating therefore has the underlying economic characteristics of destination-based taxation—for example, in avoiding the transfer pricing problems that could be introduced by a full origin system.[24] And unlike zero-rating of exports, it would avoid breaking the VAT chain at export. But it would create its own problems, most important of which would be the incentives that would be created for countries to impose high VAT rates on goods that are primarily exported. The country of production would collect the VAT. The importing company wouldn't worry about the high VAT rate because it could claim that VAT back in full. But the government in the importing country would clearly lose revenue. This could be avoided by having a 'clearing house' which would reallocate revenues to match revenue collection under the current system. But this would undermine the enforcement incentives for individual countries: tax authorities have little incentive to devote resources to ensuring that exporters remit their full tax liabilities if this revenue is then to be handed over to the importing country's government. Enforcement incentives could be reinstated by fixing flows from the clearing house at some agreed level (perhaps based on statistics for aggregate consumption or trade) rather than transferring the actual VAT collected on exports, but then countries would again be incentivized to increase VAT rates to increase revenues from the taxation of exports. So while a form of exporter rating has long been envisaged as a goal of the European Union,[25] no such scheme has been adopted, because of these incentive and administrative difficulties.

An alternative way to avoid the break in the VAT chain is to set a single EU-wide VAT rate (the 'intermediate' rate)—no higher than any current VAT rates—either on all business-to-business transactions or on all cross-border supplies within the EU, with countries free to set their own tax rate

---

[24] Confusingly, however, discussions of exporter rating in the EU context often refer to it as 'taxation at origin', since that is where the revenue would be collected.

[25] In 1987, the European Commission proposed that exporter rating be adopted after the abolition of border controls. A subsequent proposal (European Commission, 1996) involved exporter rating based on the place of establishment of the seller rather than the physical movement of goods. Both attempts were unsuccessful, though a formal commitment remains (in the VAT Directive—Council Directive 2006/112/EC of 28 November 2006 on the Common System of Value Added Tax) to replace the current system—still described as 'transitional'—with a 'definitive' regime.

above the EU-wide rate for domestic sales to final consumers if they wish. This system of *uniform rating* has been proposed in a number of variants, each with its own disadvantages.[26] It could apply either just to exports (the 'CVAT' proposal[27]), which means sellers would still face different procedures for domestic and cross-border sales, or to all transactions between registered traders (the 'VIVAT' proposal[28]), which would require making a distinction between business-to-business and business-to-consumer sales. It could be operated as a separate EU-level mechanism (as proposed for CVAT), which would require a new EU-level bureaucracy, or be incorporated into the VAT administrations of member states (as proposed for VIVAT and for a variant of CVAT examined by the European Commission in 2008). The latter would require reallocation of revenues to importing countries through a 'clearing house' mechanism similar to that envisaged for exporter rating, except that the commonality of the intermediate rate allows formula-based revenue allocations to be used with no scope for countries to respond to tax-setting incentives. But all of these variants would retain the economic properties of destination-based taxation, fix the break in the VAT chain between member states (to an extent that would depend on the level of the EU-wide intermediate rate), and leave incentives for enforcement and rate-setting unaffected, without diminishing the current ability of member states to choose the rate applied to domestic sales to final consumers and hence how much revenue they raise.

7.4.3. Future Directions

Whilst VAT is in many ways a successful tax, the audit trail that is required to collect it accurately and effectively is complex. As we have seen, scope for fraud and evasion is significant, particularly in the context of intra-EU trade, where a combination of zero-rating of exports, the lack of internal frontiers, and a reliance on paper invoices has allowed significant frauds. There are

---

[26] As well as the variants mentioned here, there are others, such as the 'DVAT'. DVAT is discussed in Crawford, Keen, and Smith (2010), on which this section draws heavily.

[27] The 'compensating VAT', proposed by Varsano (2000) for Brazil and McLure (1999 and 2000) more generally.

[28] The 'viable integrated VAT', proposed by Keen and Smith (1996 and 2000).

no easy solutions. Reverse charging has been effective in the short run. Increased auditing has also helped. More fundamental changes have their own problems, creating different sets of problematic incentives and/or requiring additional bureaucracy to keep national VAT revenues in line with current levels. Of the reform options, some form of uniform rating looks the most promising. But it would not be in any sense straightforward to implement.

It is possible that a longer-term solution does exist, though, based on a much more effective enforcement system using new technology. The current system remains heavily reliant on paper invoices. It is very hard to follow the VAT payment trail through the supply chain. There are also significant delays between the point at which firms charge VAT to their customers and the point at which they remit the VAT to the authorities. (Recall that the basic problem in the carousel fraud illustrated in Figure 7.1 was that the importing firm 'disappeared' before it had remitted the VAT it owed.)

One increasingly plausible possibility is that developments in electronic payment systems might overcome many of these problems. They could allow—and the authorities could insist upon—direct payments of VAT at the point of any transaction. They could also allow automatic reconciliation between the VAT liabilities of firms at different points in the production chain. The temptation to put one's faith in new technology often leads to disappointment, but there do seem to be good reasons for thinking that many of the current difficulties in the system, and the bureaucracy around exports, could be overcome in this way. If that were possible, then the balance of advantage between the different possible VAT structures we have been looking at would change. Effectively, the current system of zero-rating of exports could work much more readily—electronic checking and payments would stand in the place of the dismantled border controls.

It may be that the best approach for the next few years will be to use the necessary sticking plasters—such as reverse charging for some goods—to keep the current system operating, while planning a technological overhaul of the administration to put the current system on a stable long-term footing. But we are not best placed to judge the viability of alternative technologies. Unless the view is taken that a technological solution is genuinely feasible and planning begins accordingly, policymakers should instead look to move away from zero-rating exports, probably towards some form of uniform rating. The status quo cannot hold indefinitely.

7.5. CONCLUSIONS

VAT is an appealing way to raise revenue. In its purest form, it taxes only final consumption. Because it is collected at stages through the supply chain, scope for wholesale evasion, such as can exist with a retail sales tax where all the revenue is collected at the point of sale to the final consumer, is limited. But many difficulties remain which limit its effectiveness in practice. VAT is complex to administer, and depends for its operation on careful auditing and enforcement. Evasion remains a problem. Rate differentiation and the use of exemptions create welfare-reducing distortions as well as adding to complexity.

Some of its difficulties are perhaps largely unavoidable. Trade-offs need to be made over the scale of business that should be brought within the ambit of VAT—we believe a relatively high threshold, such as in the UK, has much to commend it, minimizing as it does compliance costs for small businesses. The appropriate treatment of exports within the EU in the context of no border controls requires one to trade off advantages and disadvantages of different systems—though it is no surprise that the current system of zero-rating of exports has always been considered interim. Interim, however, is looking increasingly permanent.

But there are clear directions for reform that would make the VAT system much better. The first, and most important, is a wholesale removal of most of the exemptions and zero- and reduced-rating of goods and services which add so much complexity and distortion to the current system. The next two chapters look at the specific issue of applying VAT to financial services and the more general issue of how the scope of zero- and reduced-rating can be much reduced whilst maintaining equity and work incentives. It should be possible, and is certainly desirable, to move in this direction even in the case of activities, such as public services, that have traditionally been seen as outside the scope of VAT.

The choice for the treatment of intra-EU trade seems to come down to either continuing the current sticking-plaster solution of selective reverse charging whilst waiting for, or rather actively planning for, a revamp of administration and enforcement through electronic payment systems, or else a fundamental overhaul of the EU system, moving towards a system of uniform rating of the kind we have outlined.

8

VAT and Financial Services

When I open a current account at the bank, I do so in part because the bank will store my money more safely than leaving it under the mattress. It will also give me a cheque book and a debit card which enable me to withdraw and spend my money at will without needing to carry the cash around with me; and it will save me the trouble of finding someone who can put my money to productive use until I need it. Often, the bank will give me car breakdown cover or discounts on rail tickets as well. My consumption of all these services should be taxed.[1]

If the bank charged me explicitly for these services, this would be straightforward: it would be selling me a money-storage facility, a debit card, a borrower-finding service, and car breakdown cover, and VAT could be charged on the sale. But it does not. Instead, the bank gives me a paltry interest rate on my account. If I open a savings account that does not provide instant access to my funds and all the other perks, the bank will pay me a somewhat higher rate of interest.

Meanwhile, if I wish to borrow money, the bank will charge me interest at a much higher rate, reflecting the fact that, rather than doing me the service of storing and using funds I have but don't immediately need, the bank is now doing me the service of finding and providing funds I need but don't immediately have. It is through such interest rate 'spreads'—the interest rate

---

[1] Some have argued that financial intermediation services should not be taxed (e.g. Grubert and Mackie, 1999; Lockwood, 2010), but we are not convinced that there is any fundamental difference between financial services and other services.

charged to borrowers in excess of that given to savers—that the bank covers the cost of providing its services and makes profits.

Standard VATs cannot cope with this. Borrowers and savers are not explicitly buying financial services from the bank, so there is no sale on which VAT must be charged. To date, most governments around the world, including the whole of the European Union (EU), have resigned themselves to this, and have exempted financial services from VAT.[2] Exemption is seen as taxing what can be taxed: anything the bank purchases from registered traders to enable it to provide its services bears VAT that the bank cannot reclaim, so the government gets some revenue, paid for by customers if the bank passes on this VAT in its interest rates.

But exemption taxes only the value of the inputs the bank purchases; it does not tax the additional value added by the bank through the labour and ingenuity of bankers in transforming those inputs into the services I enjoy. And we discussed in Chapter 7 the other problems caused by banks' inability to reclaim VAT on their inputs:

- overpricing of financial services provided to other businesses, which ought not to bear any tax;

- a bias towards sourcing financial services (and anything produced using them) from countries that have lower VAT rates or that have a narrower (i.e. more generous) interpretation of what are non-creditable inputs;[3]

- difficulty identifying which inputs are attributable to exempt activities, where firms undertake a combination of taxable and exempt activities (as financial institutions typically do);

- a bias towards minimizing the use of taxed inputs—specifically, towards the use of zero-rated inputs and towards vertical integration as banks do

---

[2] Not all countries exempt financial services: Zee (2006) and Bird and Gendron (2007) describe other approaches used around the world, though none is equivalent to standard VAT treatment in the way described in the rest of this chapter. South Africa levies VAT on those services banks do charge explicitly for, which of course results in incentives to move towards even greater use of implicit charges.

[3] There is also a bias towards sourcing financial services from countries that in effect zero-rate exports of financial services. Services provided across borders within the EU are not zero rated in this way, however.

as much as possible in-house (provide their own cleaning and security services, for example) to avoid paying VAT on purchased inputs.

These are serious problems. It could even be argued that zero-rating would be an improvement on exemption: that it might be worth forgoing the revenue currently collected on inputs to financial services—and making financial services to consumers even more underpriced—in order to avoid these problems.

But in fact there is a logically straightforward way to bring financial services within the scope of VAT.

8.1. CASH-FLOW TAXATION

The government could treat my entire deposit as buying a bundle of financial services ('an account') from the bank, and charge VAT on the bank's 'sale' to me; when I withdraw the money, I am selling the account back to the bank, so it could reclaim VAT on this 'input purchase'.[4] If the money I get back is worth less in present-value terms than the money I deposited—because, in exchange for providing financial services, the bank withholds the interest I could normally expect to receive for delaying consumption and supplying funds—then the VAT on my deposit will be worth more than the VAT refund on my withdrawal. Whatever the bank charges me for its services will be reflected in the VAT payments.[5]

Borrowers could be treated symmetrically: giving them a loan is treated as the bank purchasing an input from them, while their repayment of the loan and interest is treated as buying something from the bank. If borrowers pay a high interest rate and savers receive a low interest rate, reflecting the services

---

[4] Note that, unlike with normal input purchases, the bank should be able to reclaim input VAT even though the depositor is not a registered trader. An alternative analogy that captures this is to imagine that I am returning my account to the bank much like I might return unwanted clothes to a shop, where my refund would include the relevant VAT on the item.

[5] This mechanism is presented in Hoffman, Poddar, and Whalley (1987), Merrill and Edwards (1996), and Poddar and English (1997), though the idea can be traced back at least as far as Meade (1978).

being provided to them, then the VAT paid on the saver's deposit and the borrower's repayments will exceed the VAT refunded on the saver's withdrawal and the loan to the borrower. VAT is in effect charged on the interest rate spread—the implicit charge for financial services provided.

A standard VAT taxes the cash traders receive for selling goods and services, less the cash they pay for purchasing inputs. The idea presented here is that all cash inflows to the bank—including deposits, interest on loans, and repayment of principal on loans—would be taken to represent taxable sales, while all cash outflows from the bank—including loans made, interest on deposits, and withdrawals of principal—would be treated as reflecting input purchases carrying creditable VAT.

To illustrate the basic concept, suppose that in year 1, one household deposits £1,000 and another borrows the same amount. In year 2, the latter repays the loan with interest at 15% and the former withdraws the principal with interest at 5%. The VAT rate is 20%. The cash received (and paid out) by the bank is shown in Table 8.1, along with the VAT due.

There is no net VAT due in year 1: £200 would be due in respect of the deposit (20% of £1,000), this being treated as a taxable sale, but a credit of £200 would be due in respect of the funds the bank loans out, treated as a deductible purchase. In year 2, repayment of the loan creates a VAT liability of £230 (20% of principal plus interest of £1,150)[6] while withdrawal of the interest-augmented deposit gives a credit of £210 (20% of £1,050). The only net VAT collected, all in year 2, is thus £20. This is equal to the VAT rate applied to the value of the bank's spread (£100), and works irrespective of

Table 8.1. Cash-flow VAT with a 20% tax rate

| | Deposit (5% interest rate) | | Loan (15% interest rate) | | Overall | |
| | (1) | (2) | (4) | (5) | (7) | (8) |
	Cash inflow	VAT	Cash inflow	VAT	Cash inflow	VAT
Year 1	£1,000	£200	(£1,000)	(£200)	£0	£0
Year 2	(£1,050)	(£210)	£1,150	£230	£100	£20

Note: Negative numbers in parentheses.

[6] If a loan were not repaid in full, the value of any assets claimed in lieu by the lender should be treated as a cash inflow.

whether this £100 represents pure profit or is used to pay the wages of bank employees.

The illustration in Table 8.1 is for saving and borrowing by final consumers. Financial services provided by one business to another will automatically be taken out of tax: the idea is just an extension of VAT, and it avoids taxing intermediate production in exactly the same way as VAT generally. For cash flows between registered traders, anything that is a taxable sale for one trader is a creditable input for the other; only cash flows to and from final consumers give rise to net tax liabilities. If the borrower in the example above were a registered trader, he would be charged the same £200 VAT on his borrowing that the bank was credited with in year 1, and would reclaim the same £230 that was charged on his repayment in year 2. The VAT credits and liabilities in respect of the loan cancel out in both years; the net revenue flows that are left are those in respect of the retail depositor: a £200 liability in year 1 and a £210 credit in year 2.

This cash-flow treatment could in principle apply not only to simple bank deposits and loans, but also to insurance and to more sophisticated financial products. The definition of what currently counts as exempt financial services is extraordinarily lengthy and complex—a very good example of the difficulties created by not having a standard VAT treatment of all goods and services. Such definitions would not matter if financial services were treated like other products.

Not quite all cash flows should fall within the tax. Wages, of course, are not a deductible input for a VAT. And equity transactions—dividend payments and sales and purchases of shares—must also be excluded from the tax, since money paid out to shareholders represents the profits generated by providing financial services, not the financial services themselves; if we were to bring shareholder transactions within the scope of the tax, anything paid by the bank's customers would be deducted when it was passed on to shareholders. Equity transactions are not normally part of VAT; all we are saying here is that, when bringing financial services within the scope of VAT, equity transactions should not be among them.

The principle of applying a cash-flow VAT to financial services is coherent and straightforward. In practice, this approach might have drawbacks. But we can exploit equivalences between different tax bases to devise mechanisms that achieve the same result in other ways. The key thing is to keep focused on the logic and principles of what is achieved by this approach; *how* it is achieved can then be tailored for practicality. A clear understanding of what we are trying to achieve, and of how different taxes relate to each other, opens up possibilities for achieving the same outcome in ways that might be more administratively appealing.

One potential practical concern with the mechanism described so far is that the complexity and sheer number of financial transactions in modern economies—and especially the UK—may put strain on administrative mechanisms. Another is that the system outlined above would be a major change in the VAT system—introducing new, unfamiliar concepts and mechanisms into a tax with which businesses and revenue authorities are familiar and comfortable at the moment, and in a way that affects all traders, not just a few financial firms. A final concern is how the transition to a new system would deal with existing financial positions—deposits and loans already made, insurance contracts already written, and so on. These are all serious concerns, but we are not convinced that any of them is necessarily fatal to the underlying idea.[7] A number of suggestions have been made to

---

[7] An additional concern sometimes raised (e.g. Poddar and English, 1997, 98; Kerrigan, 2010) is that the tax would create cash-flow difficulties: if a business wanted to borrow £100, it would be charged £20 VAT on that cash inflow precisely when it was in need of cash, and only receive credit for loan repayments much later. But it is not clear how much of a problem this really is: the lender would receive a corresponding credit of £20 on the loan, and so should be just as willing to transfer £120 to the borrower as he was to transfer £100 to the borrower without the tax. In the absence of the tax, the lender would simply give £100 to the borrower. In the presence of the tax, the lender would instead give £120 to the borrower; the borrower would hand over £20 of this to HM Revenue and Customs (HMRC), while the lender could immediately reclaim £20 as input VAT. The only change to anyone's net payments arises from any short delay between the lender–borrower transaction and the settlement of tax and credit with HMRC—which, note, is a cash-flow *benefit* to the struggling borrower in this case. The much longer time lag between loan and repayment is irrelevant as long as the size of all cash flows is scaled up to reflect tax. Of course, the circular transfer of £20 from lender to borrower, on to HMRC, and back to the lender might seem like rather unnecessary bureaucracy; that would be eliminated by zero-rating business-to-business (B2B) transactions or adopting a tax calculation account (TCA) approach, two of the options discussed below. But, in any case, this circular flow is no different from that which arises at the moment, when one trader remits output VAT on a sale while another trader reclaims the same amount as input VAT; it is not clear that applying a cash-flow VAT to financial services would create significant cash-flow

alter the pure cash-flow VAT mechanism described above in order to achieve the same economic outcomes while dealing with these practical concerns, and we now discuss some of the key ideas.

8.2. SEPARATING OUT THE TAX ON FINANCIAL SERVICES

The cash-flow approach described above essentially extends the existing VAT to apply to financial services as well as to sales of 'real' goods and services. But rather than extending VAT to cover financial services, the tax on financial services could be introduced as a separate tax. Thus the familiar, tried-and-tested VAT would continue largely unchanged; but a separate tax would be levied on financial flows that did not represent 'real' sales or input purchases of the kind already subject to VAT.[8]

Separating the tax on financial services from the main VAT opens up possibilities for calculating and administering it in a different way. At the administrative level, for example, rather than requiring invoices for every transaction—taxing each cash inflow and crediting each cash outflow—it would be possible simply to add up net cash flow over the course of a year (say) and levy a tax on that. In the example in Table 8.1, a standard VAT would involve calculating the tax (or credit) due on the deposit and the tax (or credit) due on the loan each year (columns 2 and 5) before netting them off to give the overall VAT due (column 8). Instead, the bank could just look at its net cash flows (column 7) and do a single calculation based on that.[9]

---

problems, any more than applying a VAT to B2B transactions (rather than adopting a retail sales tax) does at the moment.

[8] In the terminology of the Meade Report (Meade, 1978): rather than replacing the current R-based VAT with an R+F-based VAT, VAT could continue to be R-based and a separate F-based tax introduced.

[9] These mechanisms are known as the 'invoice-credit' method and the 'subtraction' method respectively; see Ebrill et al. (2001) for a fuller description.

The attractions of a single consolidated calculation for a bank with millions of customers are obvious. On the other hand, doing the calculations separately for each account may have advantages in terms of the audit trail it provides: in the last chapter, we noted the advantages of requiring each claim for input VAT to have an invoice that can be traced to another trader's matching output VAT (though note that such stringent procedures are not required for companies to deduct purchase costs from profits for corporation tax purposes, for example).

Perhaps the biggest difficulties with taxing financial services through a separate tax rather than by extending the existing VAT arise in ensuring that VAT and the separate tax interact appropriately. These obstacles do not seem insurmountable, however. For example, there might be boundary issues in deciding which cash inflows and outflows reflect 'real' activities and which 'financial' activities; but as long as the two taxes are charged at the same rates, there is no need for precision in defining this distinction and allocating cash flows to one category or the other. Indeed, some difficult distinctions that are currently required for VAT would cease to be sensitive as they would no longer affect overall tax liabilities—for example, identifying which particular services are exempt, and identifying which inputs are used in the production of financial services and are therefore non-creditable. The crucial thing is to ensure that any cash flow is subject to one, and only one, of the taxes; the tax base for the financial tax could be defined as any cash flows not subject to the VAT.[10]

---

[10] We should recognize that extending VAT to financial services, while removing many problems associated with the current regime, would create at least one awkward new boundary problem, arising from the fact that financial outflows (unlike input purchases at present) would generate a deduction even if the recipient were not a registered trader. Cash outflows to households in respect of financial products would be deductible, but purchases of inputs from unregistered traders would not be. This creates a potential avoidance opportunity: if an unregistered trader provided widgets to a bank, and the bank paid 1p for the widgets but instead gave the trader an interest-free loan or paid massive interest on the trader's bank account, the widget supply would effectively be taken out of tax by the negative VAT on the financial transaction. But this hardly seems like an enormous problem. Note that no such difficulty arises if the widgets are acquired from a registered trader, since either payments to registered traders would not be deductible for the VAT or the trader's symmetric VAT payments would offset any credit.

In the following sections, we introduce alternatives to the pure cash-flow VAT described so far which change not merely the administration of the tax (as with consolidated versus transaction-by-transaction approaches) but the amount of tax that is remitted by each firm in each year. Yet these alternatives are designed to be economically equivalent to a cash-flow VAT, and they have the same properties in terms of alleviating rather than exacerbating difficult distinctions that tax authorities must draw.

Separation would also allow the two taxes to be more fundamentally different: for example, it might be possible for the financial tax to be levied on an origin basis while the rest of VAT continues on a destination basis. We do not pursue these possibilities here, except to note that any difference such as this in the underlying properties of the tax (as opposed to the timing, administration, and so on of payments) would reopen troublesome questions around the definition of financial services.

8.3. ZERO-RATING BUSINESS-TO-BUSINESS TRANSACTIONS

With pure cash-flow taxation, business-to-business (B2B) transactions are automatically taken out of tax because what is a taxable cash inflow ('sale') for one firm is a deductible outflow ('input purchase') to another. Only transactions with households have no such offset and therefore give rise to a net VAT liability.

An alternative way to take B2B transactions out of tax is for financial services to registered traders to be zero rated.[11] With respect to financial services, only cash inflows from non-business customers would be taken to represent taxable sales, and only outflows to those customers would be treated as purchasing inputs. In effect, this converts the financial services tax from a VAT to a retail sales tax.

The advantage of this approach is that the new tax regime could be restricted to retail financial firms. Non-financial firms—those whose dealings with households all relate to real goods and services and whose

---

[11] Huizinga, 2002; Poddar, 2003. As usual with VAT, traders below the registration threshold should be treated much like households.

experience of financial services relates entirely to their bank (or to other businesses)—would not have to do anything new. And the vast swathes of financial transactions between firms—not only bank loans to businesses, but also wholesale funding, interbank lending, and the overwhelming majority of the derivatives trades taking place daily in the City of London, for example— would be irrelevant for the tax.

In the numerical example in Section 8.1, the loan was treated as reflecting a taxable sale by the firm to the bank, with a £200 VAT liability for the trader and a £200 input credit for the bank in year 1; the repayment of the loan with interest led to a £230 credit for the trader and a £230 liability for the bank in year 2. In each year, the liability and the credit cancelled each other out. But if instead these business-to-business transactions were zero rated, there would simply be no liabilities or credits at all for the bank or the firm. Only the cash flows associated with the household's deposit would be measured and taxed.

As we discussed in the previous chapter, a retail sales tax also has disadvantages relative to a VAT, in requiring sellers (in this case, financial institutions) to distinguish between supplies to businesses and supplies to households, and in concentrating all revenue collection at the final (retail) link in the supply chain so that more revenue is lost if a transaction escapes tax. However, the balance between advantages and disadvantages may be different in the case of financial services from in the wider economy.

8.4. TAX CALCULATION ACCOUNTS

Rather than collecting tax on inflows of principal (respectively, crediting outflows) up front, it is clearly possible to achieve an outcome that is the same in present-value terms by carrying that tax forward with an appropriate interest markup and collecting (refunding) it later. One particularly interesting possibility is to let the carried-forward principal deposited (loaned) cancel out the principal later withdrawn (repaid), and offset the interest associated with the carry-forward against the actual interest paid on the deposit (received on the loan). This is the essence of the 'tax calculation account' (TCA) method of implementing VAT proposed by Poddar and English (1997).

Crucially, for this approach to work—for the changed pattern of tax payments to be equivalent to a cash-flow VAT—the interest rate with which the principal is carried forward must reflect the 'true' value of money today versus money tomorrow: the pure time value of money, not necessarily the actual interest rate at which the bank borrows or lends to customers, which may include an implicit charge for its services.

To implement such a system, the government must therefore take a view on what a 'normal' or 'pure' rate of interest would be in the absence of any charge for financial services. The interest rate on government bonds—the interest rate at which the government can borrow—might be a suitable guide in normal circumstances.

With payment and withdrawal / repayment of principal cancelling each other out, the government is taxing the difference between actual interest payments and this 'normal' rate of interest: taxing the interest on loans to the extent that it exceeds a 'normal' interest rate, and taxing the shortfall in interest on deposits below a 'normal' rate.

In a sense, this system offers a more direct answer to the problem posed at the start of this chapter: how to identify the charge for financial services when it is hidden in an interest rate spread. In effect, the government directly estimates what component of interest rates represents a charge for financial services, and taxes it. The government decides that a 'normal' rate of return is, say, 8%. Then any interest above 8% charged on loans, and any shortfall of interest below 8% paid on deposits, are taken to represent a charge for services and are taxed accordingly.

Note that if the values of loans made and of deposits taken are the same, then the overall tax base will just be the difference between interest received and interest paid by the bank, irrespective of what 'normal' rate of return is used: it is a tax on the interest rate spread which reflects the implicit charge for financial services. If loans exceed deposits or vice versa, then an adjustment is needed to reflect the imputed value of the balance.

As with a cash-flow VAT, B2B transactions should be taken out of tax to avoid taxing intermediate production; and again this can be done either by applying the TCA to all firms—allowing business customers to reclaim input tax on any 'excess' interest paid on loans and 'shortfall' received on

Tax by Design

deposits—or by 'zero-rating' B2B transactions so that only transactions with households are measured and taxed, and only firms that undertake financial transactions with households need be subject to the tax.

Table 8.2 compares a cash-flow VAT with a TCA, building on the simpler example in Table 8.1.

Consider first the saver, who deposits £1,000 in year 1. The account has a 5% interest rate, so in year 2 £50 is paid out to her; in year 3 she receives a further £50 interest and closes the account, thus taking out £1,050 in total in that year. These transactions between the bank and the customer are shown in column 1.

Under a cash-flow VAT (column 2), the £1,000 deposit is treated as a taxable sale by the bank, generating a £200 liability. The £50 and £1,050 paid out to the saver are treated as deductible input purchases, generating VAT refunds at the 20% tax rate. The tax calculations are straightforward: they are just 20% of cash flows.

Column 3 shows liability under a TCA approach under which a 'normal' return is assumed to be 8%. The deposit and withdrawal of principal have no tax consequences. But any shortfall in interest paid below the 8% normal return is taxed. An 8% return on £1,000 would be £80; since only £50 is actually paid, the remaining £30 (the 3 percentage point gap between the actual interest rate paid and the 'normal' rate of return) is attributed to financial service and taxed at 20%, giving a tax liability of £6 in each year for which it is paid.

Table 8.2. Cash-flow and TCA approaches with a 20% tax rate and an 8% 'pure' interest rate

	Deposit (5% interest rate)			Loan (15% interest rate)			Overall		
	(1)	(2)	(3)	(4)	(5)	(6)	(7)	(8)	(9)
	Cash inflow	VAT	TCA	Cash inflow	VAT	TCA	Cash inflow	VAT	TCA
Year 1	£1,000	£200	–	(£500)	(£100)	–	£500	£100	–
Year 2	(£50)	(£10)	£6	£75	£15	£7	£25	£5	£13
Year 3	(£1,050)	(£210)	£6	£575	£115	£7	(£475)	(£95)	£13
Present value	£53.50	£10.70	£10.70	£62.41	£12.48	£12.48	£115.91	£23.18	£23.18

Notes: Negative numbers in parentheses. Present value = Year 1 value + (Year 2 value / 1.08) + (Year 3 value / 1.08^2).

At first sight, the VAT and the TCA look like completely different taxes: the patterns of payments in columns 2 and 3 seem completely unrelated. But now look at the bottom row, 'present value'. This shows the value in year 1 of the stream of payments in each column, assuming that money received a year earlier is worth 8% more.

With that 8% discount rate, the interest and principal returned to the saver are worth only £946.50 in year 1 terms: the bank is implicitly charging £53.50 for its services. The cash-flow VAT, since it taxes all cash flows as they occur, naturally generates payments with a present value of 20% of this, or £10.70; but, crucially, £10.70 is the present value of the payments under a TCA too. The seemingly unrelated patterns of payments in columns 2 and 3 turn out to have the same present value.

The relationship between columns 2 and 3 can be thought of as follows: rather than handing over £200 in year 1, the bank carries it forward to offset against £200 of credit due in year 3 when the saver withdraws her money. But to reflect the time value of this delay, the bank pays 8% (£16) interest each year. Deducting from this £16 the £10 credit due on its actual interest payments to the saver leaves it facing a net liability of £6 in each year.

The second panel of Table 8.2 shows the corresponding calculations for a £500 loan on which 15% interest is charged.[12] In this case, the cash-flow VAT involves a refund in year 1 (the loan is an input purchase by the bank) followed by payments in years 2 and 3 (the interest and repayment on the loan are treated like income from sales). With an interest rate as high as 15%, the VAT on interest and repayment is worth more than the VAT refund on the £500 loaned out. Under a TCA, tax is due on the excess of 15% interest (£75) over an 8% 'normal' interest rate (£40). Again the present value of these tax payments is the same as that of the cash-flow VAT payments.

Taking the deposit and the loan together, overall figures for VAT and TCA payments (columns 8 and 9) can be derived either by summing the payments

---

[12] The £500 loan is less than the £1,000 deposit taken: one could imagine that the remaining £500 is held as reserves, or lent out to a VAT-registered business customer (if B2B transactions are zero rated). Alternatively, loans could exceed deposits if they are financed from the bank's equity capital, or from wholesale funding (if B2B transactions are zero rated). The example was chosen to demonstrate that (and how) the cash-flow VAT and TCA work when loans and deposits are not equal.

for the deposit and loan or by applying the VAT/TCA calculations to the bank's net cash flows to and from customers shown in column 7. In other words, as with a cash-flow VAT, the TCA can be calculated separately for each deposit/loan for each customer, or with a single consolidated calculation: the value of the bank's net financial assets (outstanding loans less outstanding deposits) could be recorded at the start of the year, and the bank's net interest income (interest received from borrowers less interest paid to savers) for the year could be taxed in so far as it exceeded 8% of net assets. (In this case, deposits exceed loans, so 8% of the balance is added to net interest income to form the tax base.)

The TCA is somewhat harder to calculate than simply taxing cash flows: it is easier to arrive at the figures in column 5 than in column 6 of Table 8.2. Its neutrality also relies on the choice of the 'normal' rate of return being accurate: using a 'normal' interest rate that is too high would overtax saving and undertax borrowing, and vice versa, with obvious implications for distorting the pattern of financial activity in the economy.

On the other hand, the TCA has significant advantages. Comparing the VAT and TCA columns in Table 8.2, it is striking that the TCA involves much smaller gross tax payments, and much less use of refunds, to arrive at the same present-value tax payments. This has two important implications.

First, taxing all cash inflows and deducting all outflows might be thought to pose a revenue risk—for example, if a saver/lender claims a VAT refund on the principal they deposit/lend, but then disappears (or perhaps emigrates, depending on how international flows are treated) without paying VAT when the principal is withdrawn/repaid. The TCA gives much less exposure to such risks.

Second, by avoiding such large payments and refunds, the TCA can deal more smoothly with changes in tax rates—the most important of which is the change from zero to 20% when the reform is introduced. Introducing a cash-flow VAT raises a transitional problem of how to deal with existing financial positions—deposits and loans already made, and so on. We might not want to give input-VAT credits for withdrawals by savers if we had not taxed the deposit when it was made, or tax mortgage interest paid to the bank if we had not given credit when the loan was made. Giving windfall gains to households with existing savings and imposing windfall losses on households with existing debts is not an appealing proposition.

A TCA could be introduced by simply noting the current outstanding balance of a loan or deposit on the day the new system was introduced (call it A-day) and operating the system from there. Any interest on loans received by the bank after A-day would be taxed in so far as it exceeded a normal return to the A-day balance; any interest paid on deposits would be taxed in so far as it fell short of a normal return to the A-day balance.

In principle, this transitional arrangement has a cash-flow counterpart. The equivalent under a pure cash-flow regime would be to levy a windfall tax on A-day on the balance of deposits, with a windfall refund on the balance of loans. In effect, this amounts to a retrospective tax/refund on the past cash flows to balance out the cash-flow tax applied in future: it is as if all the loans and deposits were made on A-day. These windfall taxes and refunds are equivalent in present-value terms to taxing/crediting a stream of imputed 'normal' returns to the existing position under a TCA. In principle, it is hard to see any obstacle to imposing such a windfall levy on banks' loans less deposits. But, in practice, governments may be understandably squeamish about doing so.

We will revisit these advantages and disadvantages when we come to examine the merits of ACE (allowance for corporate equity) versus cash-flow corporation taxes in Chapter 17 and RRA (rate-of-return allowance) versus cash-flow expenditure tax treatments of savings in Chapter 13. There are close parallels between these systems, and many of the same issues recur.

8.5. THE FINANCIAL ACTIVITIES TAX

We have noted that either the pure cash-flow approach or the TCA approach could in principle be implemented either separately for transactions with each customer or by looking at firms' consolidated accounts. In fact, with a consolidated rather than transaction-by-transaction approach, the tax base could be calculated in a more radically different way: as the sum of profits and wages. At first glance, profits and wages might seem to have little to do with a VAT. But value added is actually the sum of profits (on one definition) and wages. If a firm sells its outputs for more than it buys its inputs, the surplus—the value it adds—is either paid to employees in wages or is profit for the firm. Profits are the income that is left over after buying inputs and paying wages.[13]

We have seen clues to this already: in describing the cash-flow VAT in Section 8.1, we mentioned two exceptions to the rule that all cash flows are taxed: those in respect of equity and labour. These flows represent the profit and wages we are seeking to tax. Rather than taxing all cash inflows and deducting all cash outflows except those to shareholders and employees, we could just tax net outflows to shareholders and employees.

The relationship between a VAT and a tax on profits plus wages becomes clearer when one considers that the starting points for calculating profits and value added have much in common. In both cases, the basic calculation consists of recording income from sales and deducting expenditure on inputs. The biggest difference is that wages are treated as a deductible expense for corporation tax, but not as a creditable input for VAT: thus, to be equivalent to a VAT, a tax on profits must be supplemented by a tax on wages.

Closer examination of what exactly constitutes taxable income and what costs can be deducted—in particular, how the purchase cost, depreciation, and resale price of capital assets are treated—shows that a VAT is identical to a tax on profits plus wages only with a particular definition of profits: not surprisingly, a cash-flow definition. In Chapter 17, we will discuss the cash-flow corporation tax in more detail. We will also introduce—and advocate— a form of corporation tax based on another definition of profits, with an allowance for corporate equity (ACE), which is equivalent in present-value terms to a cash-flow definition of profits. A tax on the sum of wage costs plus profits on one of these two definitions is equivalent to a tax on value added.

In fact, the ACE system of corporation tax is closely related to the TCA system of VAT, apart from the deduction of labour costs. The ACE bears the same relation to a cash-flow corporation tax as the TCA bears to a cash-flow VAT.

A recent IMF report on the taxation of the financial sector called for precisely such a tax on profits plus wages, which it called a 'financial

---

[13] Indeed, calculating value added by summing wages and profits is one of the three ways of implementing a VAT listed by Ebrill et al. (2001)—the 'addition' method, to go alongside the 'subtraction' method and the 'invoice–credit' method mentioned in footnote 9.

activities tax' (FAT), noting explicitly its potential to substitute for VAT on financial services.[14]

In principle, taxes on profits and wages could replace the entire current VAT structure. But there is no reason for such an upheaval: for the most part, VAT works passably well as it is. If introducing a new tax on financial services, however, it is sensible to ask which way of calculating it is most practical, and taxing profits plus wages has some appeal in that both revenue authorities and taxpayers are accustomed to operating corporate taxes and wage taxes in the financial sector; the cash-flow VAT and TCA approaches described above might be less familiar and involve bigger changes.

However, to be equivalent to a VAT on financial services, and therefore avoid unnecessary distortions, a FAT should have two features that are unusual when calculating profits:[15]

- First, if a tax were introduced on the *total* profits and wages of financial firms, it would involve the double taxation of any of their activities that are currently subject to VAT, from the provision of investment advice to the provision of safety-deposit boxes. To be neutral, only the profits and remuneration associated with their VAT-exempt financial activities should be taxed.[16] (Note that this would alleviate, rather than create, pressure on the definition of financial services, since a particular activity would now always be subject to either VAT or FAT, never both or neither, so the categorization would not matter as long as the tax rates were the same.)

- Second, some mechanism would be needed for taking B2B transactions out of tax—either excluding financial transactions with business customers from the calculation of profits for the FAT, or else allowing

---

[14] International Monetary Fund, 2010. The variant discussed here is what is called 'FAT1' in appendix 6 of the report. The FAT is discussed in more depth in Keen, Krelove, and Norregaard (2010).

[15] These issues are mentioned in the IMF reports (International Monetary Fund, 2010; Keen, Krelove, and Norregaard, 2010), but the IMF's baseline exemplar of FAT1 (on which its numerical estimates are based, for example) seems to assume conventional calculation of profits.

[16] This also implies that inputs on which VAT has been reclaimed should not be allowed as deductible expenses in the definition of profits for FAT purposes.

business customers to claim a FAT refund (or a VAT deduction) for the losses they make in their financial dealings with banks.

The partitioning of profit implied by these features—separating out financial activities, and perhaps financial transactions with business customers, from other profits—clearly moves it a step away from the familiar calculation of profits that these firms will be doing anyway. But the partitioning and the calculations are not difficult or sensitive—tending, as with all of these equivalent treatments, to alleviate rather than exacerbate awkward boundaries in the current system.

8.6. CONCLUSIONS

A number of taxes are already successfully applied to the financial services sector. For all the volume and complexity of financial trades conducted in the City of London and other financial centres, the calculation of profits for corporation tax purposes and wages for income tax and NICs purposes proceeds fairly smoothly, and has succeeded in raising large amounts of revenue.

Imposing VAT on financial services is admittedly more difficult. There are real barriers to treating financial services just like any other product for VAT. But there are potential routes to achieving an equivalent outcome. Whether by extending VAT or introducing a separate tax; whether B2B transactions are taken out of tax by zero-rating them or by allowing non-financial firms to reclaim tax; whether the calculations are transaction-by-transaction or based on firms' consolidated accounts; whether by subtracting inflows from outflows or summing profits and wages; whether operated on a cash-flow or TCA/ACE basis: we do not claim to have studied the practical implications of each of these (let alone all combinations) in detail, and we do not have a single preferred mechanism. The unfamiliarity of the systems and the complexity of the financial services industry are such that serious investigation would be warranted before leaping into any particular option. We have laid out the concepts here, rather than exploring the details: our discussion has barely touched on the international dimension, for example, which would be important in practice. But we are optimistic that a practical solution can be found.

The FAT is the option that has attracted most attention since the IMF proposed it. The UK's coalition government's first Budget after it was formed in Summer 2010 said that it would 'explore' such a tax,[17] and the European Commission has also said it 'believes that the FAT option is worth exploring in the EU context'.[18] Yet it is notable that the IMF staff analysing the FAT themselves concluded: 'it should be stressed that it is better to fix the VAT treatment of financial services than to use a FAT1 as fix'.[19]

Both the cash-flow VAT and the TCA were tested in experimental pilots with volunteer banks in Europe during the 1990s and were found to be conceptually robust and administratively practical.[20] The hostility that there is, and the fact that these proposals are not currently on the European Commission's agenda, are more to do with resistance to unfamiliar concepts and concerns over compliance costs. But the concepts are clear and conducive to explanation, and familiarity would come with time; and it is by no means obvious that compliance costs need be prohibitively high if the appropriate combination of mechanisms described above were chosen. It would be worth putting up with some administrative and compliance burden to reap the benefit of economic efficiency and the revenue gain; and the benefits of removing the administrative and compliance burdens imposed by the current system of exemption should not be forgotten.

Tentative government estimates imply that exempting financial services costs about £10 billion (with a 20% VAT rate),[21] although around a third of

---

[17] HM Treasury, 2010b, para. 1.99.

[18] European Commission, 2010a, 7. See also European Commission (2010b).

[19] Keen, Krelove, and Norregaard, 2010, 138.

[20] See Poddar (2007).

[21] Source: Authors' calculations using HMRC statistics, table 1.5 (http://www.hmrc.gov.uk/stats/tax_expenditures/table1-5.pdf), adjusting the 2010–11 estimate to reflect the fact that the VAT rate was 17.5% for part of that fiscal year and 20% for the rest. The IMF report (International Monetary Fund, 2010) estimates that the tax base for a FAT in the UK would be about 6.1% of GDP, which implies that a 20% FAT would raise around 1.2% of GDP, or about £18 billion in 2010–11. Note, however, that this estimate is for a version of the FAT which, as discussed above, appears to tax non-exempt activities of financial firms and financial services to VAT-registered businesses, both of which we argue should be removed from the tax base. Precise magnitudes aside, both the HMRC and IMF estimates are consistent with earlier

this is recouped through insurance premium tax, a tax currently levied on insurance premiums as a proxy for VAT which could be abolished (a further simplification) if insurance were subject to a cash-flow VAT (or equivalent) along with other financial services. Note that this £10 billion figure is not a good guide to the scale of the problem caused by the current exemption: it is the net revenue effect of undertaxing financial services to households and overtaxing financial services to businesses. The revenue effects of these offset each other, but both are distortions in their own right. Two common complaints are that it has been too cheap and easy for households to borrow, but too expensive and difficult for businesses to obtain finance. Moving from exemption to a cash-flow VAT (or equivalent) treatment would alleviate both of these problems. And that is even before considering the other problems that exemption creates: the bias towards vertical integration, the distortion to international trade, the difficulty identifying each firm's untaxed outputs and non-creditable inputs, and so on.

The exemption of financial services, like other VAT exemptions, is mandated by EU law. It may therefore be that reform must be pursued at an EU level, though it may be that an equivalent tax (such as a FAT) could be introduced unilaterally. In any case, international coordination would be desirable to minimize the risk of financial services being actually or notionally relocated in response to the tax.

In the wake of the recent financial crisis, many commentators and some governments have argued for the imposition of other taxes on financial services in general, and banks in particular.

Some proposals are aimed at changing the behaviour of financial institutions and correcting specific market failures. The UK is one of several countries (including the US, Germany, France, and Sweden) that have recently adopted, or propose to adopt, a tax on banks' liabilities, generally excluding core equity capital and some other low-risk sources of funds. Along with the FAT discussed above, this is the second tax advocated by the

---

studies (Genser and Winker, 1997; Huizinga, 2002) in finding that a move from exemption towards more standard VAT treatment of financial services could raise significant sums.

IMF, who called it a 'financial stability contribution';[22] the UK's coalition government has stated that its proposed tax is 'intended to encourage banks to move to less risky funding profiles'.[23] The UK and France also imposed temporary taxes on certain bank bonuses; the stated aim of the UK's tax was to tackle 'the remuneration practices that contributed to excessive risk taking by the banking industry' and to 'encourage banks to consider their capital position and to make appropriate risk adjustments when settling the level of bonus payments'.[24] We do not explore these issues here. The complex issue of market failure in the financial services sector is beyond the scope of this book, and consideration of any fiscal measures must be intimately linked with consideration of the regulatory regime, which is the main means of providing appropriate safeguards in the financial system.

Other proposals are motivated by a more general desire to extract more revenue from the financial sector—to punish banks for recent events, to recoup the costs of the bail-out, to build up funds to deal with any future crisis, or to shrink a sector that is argued to have become too big. Of course, *any* additional tax could play a role if the objectives are stated in such general terms. These arguments can be developed more fully—some more coherently than others. But even if such arguments are accepted, serious attention must be paid to the design of any additional tax in order to avoid creating new problems. For example, in Chapter 6, we explained why we would not be comfortable with the idea of a financial transactions tax, which is one of the more popular suggestions. Introducing VAT (or an equivalent) on financial services would go some way towards addressing these objectives, but by removing existing distortions rather than adding to them. If there is a concern that the financial services sector is undertaxed, we should ensure that banks are at least subject to the same taxes as other businesses before we think of applying special additional taxes.

---

[22] International Monetary Fund, 2010.

[23] HM Treasury, 2010b, para. 1.63.

[24] HM Treasury, 2009, box 3.2.

9

Broadening the VAT Base

Value added tax (VAT) is an important and, on the whole, well-designed tax. But in the UK, zero rates are applied to an unusually wide range of goods and services. There may be convincing arguments to justify a few of these departures from uniformity, but not most. For the reasons we have set out in Chapters 7 and 8, we favour a broadening of the VAT base in the UK, applying the standard rate to a wider range of goods.

This is not simply a preference for textbook tidiness. Moving towards a more uniform rate would increase consumers' welfare by distorting their spending decisions less. People would make choices based on relative prices that reflect the underlying costs of producing the goods rather than differences in tax rates. Our calculations suggest that if almost all zero and reduced rates of VAT in the UK were removed, the government could (in principle) compensate every household to leave them as well off as they were before and still have about £3 billion of revenue left over.[1]

Removing zero and reduced rates in isolation would raise considerable revenue and would inflict proportionately larger losses on low-income families than high-income ones. The challenge is to design a reform package that would spend the proceeds on direct tax cuts and benefit increases in a

---

[1] Authors' calculations, assuming a 17.5% standard rate of VAT. The welfare gain would rise with the new standard rate of 20%. The estimation assumes that uniformity would be optimal, in the sense that it ignores the point made in Chapter 6 that it may be efficient to tax time-saving goods more lightly and goods that require lots of leisure time more heavily in order to reduce overall disincentives to work; taking this into account could either increase or reduce the estimated welfare gain from base-broadening.

way that is both broadly distributionally neutral and, importantly, would avoid worsening work incentives. In this chapter, we show how this challenge can be met. Note that even in the absence of a net financial giveaway, households should feel significantly better off as a result because the basket of goods and services they could buy after the reform would be worth more to them than the one they could buy before the reform.

We also look at a second potential reform which would use the proceeds of base-broadening to raise net revenue for the Exchequer and to redistribute more resources from better-off households to less-well-off households. But this has much less to recommend it since it would deal a double blow to work incentives, unwinding some or all of the welfare gains generated by the more uniform VAT rate. This is a point that has been missed in much previous literature. Designing a reform that avoids these work incentive effects and that does in fact increase welfare is not straightforward.

Note that we are not suggesting—nor are we modelling here—a completely uniform system of indirect taxation. As we have seen in Chapter 6, there are good reasons for taxing the consumption of alcohol, tobacco, and petrol more heavily than the consumption of other goods, and here we assume no changes to the structure of the excise duties applied to them. We also maintain the current tax-advantaged treatment of childcare, because to do so helps offset the disincentives to work created by other taxes. For the purposes of this chapter, we are also assuming no change to the treatment of the various VAT-exempt goods and services, most notably financial services, which were discussed in the previous chapter.[2] Housing is addressed separately in Chapter 16.

9.1. SPENDING THE PROCEEDS ON DIRECT TAX CUTS AND BENEFIT INCREASES

The central component of both reform packages we look at is a broadening of the VAT base such that goods and services now subject to zero and

---

[2] In part reflecting the complexity of both modelling and introducing such changes, and in part reflecting the fact that many exempt goods have 'administered' prices.

reduced rates of VAT—principally food, passenger transport, books and other reading matter, prescription drugs, children's clothing, and domestic fuel and power—would be taxed at the standard rate after the reform. Our calculations in this volume assume the standard rate of 17.5% which applied for nearly 20 years until January 2011. (The arguments for more uniformity are only reinforced by the introduction of the 20% rate.) If people continued to buy the same goods and services, they would pay an additional £24 billion in VAT[3] and the aggregate price level would increase by a one-off 3.4%.[4]

In our first reform, we look at the consequences of spending that £24 billion on a range of direct tax cuts and benefit increases, so as to create a package that has minimal effects on work incentives and is broadly distributionally neutral in the sense that the gains and losses for households with different levels of incomes and spending would, on average, be relatively modest. Specifically, we model the following changes to the tax and benefit system in place at the end of 2009–10:

- an increase of 3.4% in all tax allowances and thresholds and in rates of all benefits and tax credits (this would happen automatically following the changes to VAT, as allowances, thresholds, and rates are indexed to inflation);

- further increases of 3.4% in the main means-tested benefits (but not tax credits), 2% in the Basic State Pension, and 10% in Child Benefit (making total increases of 6.9% (because of rounding), 5.4%, and 13.4% respectively);

- a £1,000 increase in income tax allowances, which would take 1½ million people out of income tax;

- a £4,530 cut in the basic-rate limit for income tax and the upper earnings limit for National Insurance contributions (leaving them £2,000 below their current nominal level, given the other changes above);

- a 2p cut in the basic rate, and a 1½p cut in the higher rate, of income tax.

---

[3] Source: HM Revenue and Customs statistics.

[4] Source: Authors' calculations using the IFS tax and benefit microsimulation model, TAXBEN, run on uprated data from the 2007 Expenditure and Food Survey.

Spending the proceeds in this way offsets the regressive impact of broadening the VAT base, while avoiding harm to work incentives. On its own, broadening the VAT base weakens work incentives, as it reduces the amount that can be bought with the proceeds of working, in much the same way as would an increase in income tax rates.[5] Redistributing the revenue in a way that left the package more progressive in its overall impact—by increasing means-tested benefits, for example—would tend to exacerbate this weakening of work incentives (see Section 9.2). The reform package described above seeks to alleviate this in particular through the increases in tax allowances and reductions in tax rates.

Assessing the distributional implications of a move from direct to indirect taxation of this sort is not straightforward. On average, in any given year, this reform package leaves people with low spending better off and those with high spending worse off—which looks progressive. But at the same time, on average, it leaves people with low incomes worse off and those with high incomes better off in any given year—which looks regressive.

It is in the nature of indirect taxes that they bear heavily on those with high expenditures. And while there is a correlation between expenditure and income levels, it is not by any means perfect. In any shift from direct to indirect taxation, people who spend a lot relative to their income in any given year will lose and people who spend little relative to their income will gain. The important point is that, for many people, the amount they spend in a particular year is probably a better indicator of their lifetime living standard than the level of their income in that year. While some people are persistently poor, many have volatile earnings, are temporarily unemployed, are studying, are taking a break from the labour market to raise children, or are retired but with access to significant savings. In these circumstances, their spending may be high relative to their current income because they are borrowing in the expectation of income being higher in the future (such as students) or they are drawing down savings accumulated from past earnings (such as pensioners).

---

[5] There is also an income effect from a simple increase in VAT, but of course our compensation package offsets that effect fully.

Of course, over a lifetime, a person's income and spending must be equal (bequests, dying in debt, and inheritances aside).[6] One cannot have spending greater than income forever. Those who are losers in the current year, because they are spending a lot relative to their income, will often experience corresponding gains in future years when their income is high relative to their spending. They may well be able to adjust their saving patterns to smooth this out themselves.

It is particularly notable that right at the bottom of the income distribution, income looks like a rather poor measure of welfare. Many households in the bottom tenth of the income distribution have spending patterns (and other characteristics) that are more similar to those of households near the middle of the distribution than to those of other low-income households.[7] Of course, there are still people with low incomes and relatively high spending who are genuinely poor: those who are in danger of getting into unmanageable debt and those who have no future prospect of increased incomes, for example.

Given this disparity between income and expenditure in any given year, our first reform is designed to ensure that, particularly for low-income groups, their percentage rise in income from the compensation measures would at least match their percentage rise in expenditure as a result of the VAT increase. This is a natural way of thinking about the problem and is a similar principle to that embodied in the standard indexation of benefits: benefits are increased in line with economy-wide inflation to maintain their purchasing power. If the cost of living increases by 5%, then benefit income is increased by 5%. Benefit recipients enjoy the same percentage increase in their benefits as in their cost of living, even though the cash increase in income would not cover the cash increase in their costs if their spending were higher than their income. In fact, what we do matches household circumstances much better than standard RPI indexation of benefits. In the

[6] In our discussion of the taxation of wealth in Chapter 15, we argue for maintaining a tax on wealth transfers, albeit on a fairer basis than under the current inheritance tax.
[7] Studies that have examined the use of expenditure rather than income for looking at distributional outcomes include Goodman, Johnson, and Webb (1997), Blundell and Preston (1998), Meyer and Sullivan (2003 and 2004), Goodman and Oldfield (2004), Brewer, Goodman, and Leicester (2006), and Brewer et al. (2009).

first place, it directly relates average percentage increases in incomes for each part of the income distribution to that group's actual price increase, as opposed to the population average; and second, we seek to increase the whole of income in line with the relevant price increase, not just benefit income.

Where the compensation package does not cover the increase in spending, adjustments to saving and borrowing could help to smooth out the change. There are two important groups for whom this may not be true, however. First, those who are credit constrained may not be able to borrow more to pay for their higher immediate costs, unless the expectation that their future income will be taxed less makes it easier for them to obtain credit. Second, as a transitional issue, those who have already gone through their period of high income and low spending, and are now in a period of low income and high spending, may see a rise in their costs but have no expectation of an increased income in future.

Shifting from income taxes to consumption taxes in effect imposes a windfall tax on 'old capital': the purchasing power of people's existing assets is reduced. This is highly efficient—since the assets already exist, the revenue they provide does not involve discouraging any new activity—but it might reasonably be seen as unfair on those who lose out. Such windfall losses (or gains) for old capital are an issue we have to confront many times in tax reform. In this case, those over pension age are the obvious group who might be in this position, although in fact our modelled reform is designed so as to not leave pensioners worse off on average.

This discussion of how to think about the difference between spending and income as measures of welfare is rather important in understanding the impact of our proposed reforms. Our presentation in Figures 9.1 and 9.2 reflects the discussion.

Figure 9.1 sorts the population by income decile from the lowest-income tenth to the highest-income tenth. The bars, measured against the left-hand axis, show the percentage rise in spending as a result of the VAT rise (left side, light shaded bar) and the percentage rise in income as a result of the compensation package (right side, dark shaded bar). The line, measured against the right-hand axis, shows the pounds-per-week cash gain or loss as a result of the reform.

Tax by Design

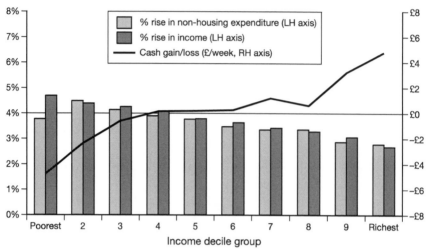

Figure 9.1. Effect of reform by income decile

Note: Income decile groups derived by dividing households into ten equal-sized groups according to their disposable income adjusted for household size using the McClements equivalence scale.

Source: Authors' calculations using the IFS tax and benefit microsimulation model, TAXBEN, run on uprated data from the 2007 Expenditure and Food Survey.

Looking at this line first, we see the familiar effect of an indirect tax rise. Even with compensation, the two lowest income deciles make significant cash losses, whilst the highest income deciles make cash gains. The reform looks decidedly regressive. But the bars tell a somewhat different story. For each decile group, the percentage rises in income and spending are much the same, except in the bottom decile where income rises rather more than spending. So, on our test as to whether income rises as much as spending in percentage terms, the reform looks very slightly progressive.

Note in passing that the lowest income decile sees a smaller percentage rise in spending than the second, third, or fourth deciles. This must be because people in this group devote a smaller proportion of their budget to zero- and reduced-rated goods than those in the deciles immediately above them. Arguably, this is further evidence that they do not, on average, have the lowest living standards, since one would usually expect those with the lowest living standards to spend the largest proportion of their budgets on 'necessities', which tend to be subject to zero or reduced rates.

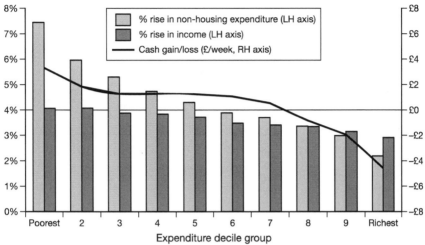

Figure 9.2. Effect of reform by expenditure decile

Note: Expenditure decile groups derived by dividing households into ten equal-sized groups according to their non-housing expenditure adjusted for household size using the McClements equivalence scale.

Source: Authors' calculations using the IFS tax and benefit microsimulation model, TAXBEN, run on uprated data from the 2007 Expenditure and Food Survey.

Now consider Figure 9.2, in which the population is ranked not by income but by spending level. Here, the group on the far left is the group with the lowest spending and that on the far right is the group with the highest spending. The pattern is completely different from that in Figure 9.1. This time, it is the lowest decile that enjoys the greatest cash gain and the highest decile that sees cash losses. On the other hand, spending in the lowest decile rises by a much bigger percentage than does income. (This reflects the fact that people in this expenditure group have low spending relative to their income and do not benefit as much from the benefit increases aimed at those on low incomes.) So, while this group becomes better off in cash terms, it appears to become worse off in the sense that its cost of living is rising faster than its income.

Though complicated, it seems to us that this pattern could be described as broadly distributionally neutral on average if we consider income and spending together as a guide to lifetime resources. It is also broadly neutral between different types of household. There is no significant redistribution between the main demographic groups—so, for example, neither lone parents nor pensioners gain or lose significantly on average—and the distributional patterns *within* each demographic group roughly match those shown in Figures 9.1 and 9.2.

Whatever its average impact may be on different income bands, spending bands, and family types, when we disaggregate them this reform has large effects on individual households in any given year. Indeed, barely one in ten households are broadly unaffected (with a cash gain or loss of less than £1 a week), while around half of households gain or lose more than £5 per week. There are more winners than losers in every demographic category, but there are nevertheless almost 10 million households losing more than £1 per week, of which nearly 6 million are losing more than £5 a week. The political difficulties of such a reform are obvious.

Some of these gains and losses arise, no doubt, because our compensation package is imperfectly designed. However, the two principal reasons for such large, widespread gains and losses are more fundamental:

- First, households that are currently spending a lot relative to their incomes are likely to lose out, and vice versa. But, as we have noted, this state of affairs cannot be permanent: such households must spend less relative to their incomes at other times, so to a large extent the distributional effects over a lifetime will balance out. This element of the gains and losses is in part an artefact of taking a snapshot view of the population.

- Second, at any given level of overall income and expenditure, some households will buy more zero- and reduced-rated goods than others. Those with a strong taste for such goods will lose out (over a lifetime, not just in a single year), while those who prefer standard-rated goods will gain. In one sense, imposing these gains and losses is the purpose of the reform. Why should the tax system favour people who like reading magazines more than listening to music, or who buy their children more expensive clothes and less expensive toys than others? Unless the government wishes to defend such preferential treatment *given overall levels of income and expenditure*, the gains and losses implied by removing these inequities should be positively welcomed.

While a degree of distributional neutrality was one aim of the compensation package, avoiding damage to work incentives was another.

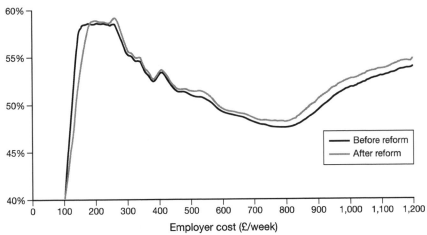

Figure 9.3. Effective marginal tax rate before and after reform

Notes: Kernel regression (lowess) estimates. Employer cost = Gross earnings + Employer NICs.

Source: Authors' calculations using the IFS tax and benefit microsimulation model, TAXBEN, run on uprated data from the 2007 Expenditure and Food Survey.

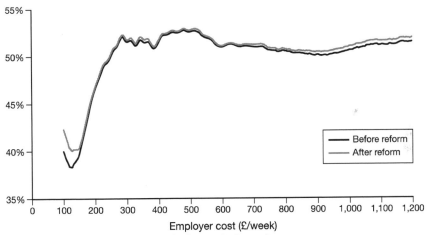

Figure 9.4. Participation tax rate before and after reform

Notes: Kernel regression (lowess) estimates. Employer cost = Gross earnings + Employer NICs.

Source: Authors' calculations using the IFS tax and benefit microsimulation model, TAXBEN, run on uprated data from the 2007 Expenditure and Food Survey.

Figures 9.3 and 9.4 show how the reform has minimal effects on work incentives.[8] Figure 9.3 shows that effective marginal tax rates (EMTRs) for workers change little, on average, at any level of employer cost (that is, gross earnings plus employer National Insurance contributions), with only slight rises for the highest earners and slight falls for the lowest. Figure 9.4 shows that pre- and post-reform participation tax rates (PTRs, which measure the incentive to enter paid work) would be even more closely aligned. On average, the PTR rises by only half a percentage point and the EMTR by less than a quarter of a percentage point.

In fact, this reform package closely replicates the existing pattern of work incentives by earnings not only overall but for each type of worker (single people and one-earner and two-earner couples, with and without children).

Having spent the entire proceeds of broadening the VAT base on measures to compensate poorer households for the increase in living costs they would suffer and to avoid weakening work incentives, it is important to remind ourselves what the point of the exercise was in the first place. Even though the government would not be offering a net financial giveaway, people should feel an improvement in their material well-being because the basket of goods and services they could buy after the reform would be worth more to them than the basket they could buy before the reform. This is because the government is no longer spending its money encouraging them to buy more of some goods and services than they actually want.

9.2. RAISING REVENUE AND REDISTRIBUTING MORE

If a government wished to raise additional revenue, and did not believe that the sort of reform described in Section 9.1 would give it the 'political permission' to do so by generating an offsetting welfare gain, then it could design the reform package explicitly to raise net revenue. It could also design the package explicitly to be more redistributive.

---

[8] The measures of work incentives used here are defined and discussed in Chapters 3 and 4.

One way to do so would simply be to accompany the VAT-base-broadening with a 15% increase in all the main means-tested benefits and tax credits.[9] This costs only about £13 billion, whereas the base-broadening raises £24 billion, so the reform package in total raises net revenue of £10 billion (after rounding), or just under £400 per household per year.

Not surprisingly, a revenue-raising reform creates more losers. Whereas in our previous reform there were more winners than losers, now only a third of households gain, 2% are unaffected within £1 per week, and almost two-thirds lose. Almost three-fifths of households lose more than £5 per week (15 million compared with 6 million in Section 9.1).

The pattern of gains and losses across the income and expenditure deciles would also be dramatically different, as illustrated in Figures 9.5 and 9.6, which are comparable to Figures 9.1 and 9.2. This second reform is much more redistributive—offering cash gains on average to the bottom three income deciles and substantial cash losses to the top deciles.

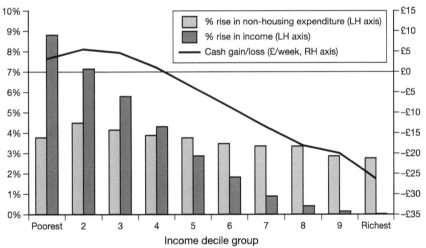

Figure 9.5. Effect of alternative reform package by income decile

Note: Income decile groups derived by dividing households into ten equal-sized groups according to their disposable income adjusted for household size using the McClements equivalence scale.

Source: Authors' calculations using the IFS tax and benefit microsimulation model, TAXBEN, run on uprated data from the 2007 Expenditure and Food Survey.

---

[9] This is the package illustrated in Crawford, Keen, and Smith (2010).

Tax by Design

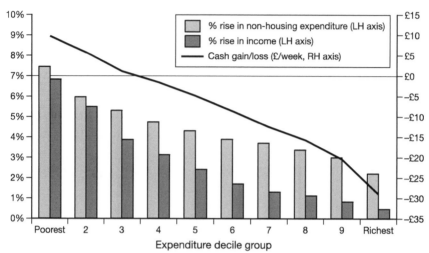

Figure 9.6. Effect of alternative reform package by expenditure decile

Note: Expenditure decile groups derived by dividing households into ten equal-sized groups according to their non-housing expenditure adjusted for household size using the McClements equivalence scale.

Source: Authors' calculations using the IFS tax and benefit microsimulation model, TAXBEN, run on uprated data from the 2007 Expenditure and Food Survey.

So we have a reform that, like our first package, involves a broadening of the VAT base. Unlike our first reform, it raises money from the better-off while redistributing to the least-well-off and adds £10 billion to the government's coffers. But the price of doing so is a double hit to work incentives, because the weakening of incentives implied by the VAT extension itself is exacerbated by the weakening of incentives created by a major increase in the generosity of means-tested benefits. Therefore we cannot claim an overall efficiency gain.

On average, effective marginal tax rates rise by 2.8 percentage points and participation tax rates rise by 3.3 percentage points as a result of this reform, with the biggest increases being for low earners. To put this in context, our simulations suggest that such a weakening of work incentives could result in total employment levels falling by several hundred thousand.

This illustrates nicely the difficulties in designing effective tax reforms. Broadening the VAT base increases economic efficiency and increases consumers' welfare. And it is easy to target direct tax and benefit reforms that, on average, compensate those on low incomes and that leave behind money for the government. But if not very carefully designed, these reforms can create a new inefficiency and source of welfare loss—in this case, weakened work incentives. Our first reform showed that it is possible to achieve the degree of redistribution and the strength of work incentives that we currently have and to get rid of the undesirable distortion of consumption choices that our current VAT system imposes. But VAT-base-broadening does not in itself provide an escape from the fundamental trade-offs between work incentives, redistribution, and revenue-raising. Broadening the VAT base can generate an efficiency gain, which, like the other efficiency-enhancing tax reforms described in this volume, allows the government to raise more revenue without reducing overall welfare. However, beyond this efficiency gain, it cannot be used to raise net revenue without either hurting the poor or weakening work incentives (or both).

9.3. CONCLUSIONS

There is a strong case for broadening the VAT base and moving towards a uniform rate. This would increase consumers' welfare by distorting their spending choices less. We have illustrated one possible reform package, designed to broaden the base of VAT by moving goods from zero and reduced rates to the standard rate. This would inevitably raise the cost of living, but we can design a set of compensating changes to the direct tax and benefit system so that the overall reform package would avoid worsening work incentives and would be broadly distributionally neutral. This distributional neutrality is achieved by ensuring that gains and losses for households with different levels of incomes and spending would, on average, be relatively modest.

But achieving distributional neutrality in this sense would not avoid creating large numbers of winners and losers at the level of individual households. Some will be affected because they happen to have a preference for the zero- or reduced-rated goods that the government is currently trying to encourage them to buy: our proposal gets rid of an anomaly that currently favours those who prefer these goods and punishes those who prefer goods that attract VAT at the standard rate.

Beyond the fact that a shift to a more uniform system of VAT is both feasible and desirable, two really important conclusions flow from the analysis in this chapter.

First, any reform needs to be very carefully thought out and structured if we are not to lose any efficiency gain from a more uniform VAT to worsened work incentives. We have been very careful to design a package to avoid this happening and have illustrated the dangers of ignoring these considerations.

Second, it is really important to think carefully and clearly about what we mean by progressivity and redistribution. The reform package shifts the structure of the tax system away from direct taxation and towards indirect taxation. This inevitably means that households that have high spending relative to their income in any given year will also lose, and vice versa. That is why the reform leads to different patterns of cash gains and losses when viewed by income decile and by expenditure decile. It is a regressive reform when household welfare is measured by income, but progressive when welfare is measured by expenditure. Of course, over the lifetime of a household, income must equal expenditure (bequests, dying in debt, and inheritances aside). So high spending relative to income cannot be sustained indefinitely. Those households that lose in the current year because they are spending a lot relative to income will often experience corresponding gains in future years when their income is high relative to their spending. They may well be able to adjust their saving patterns to smooth out this fluctuation.

The bottom line is that a carefully designed reform of the current UK VAT system could offer a golden opportunity to unlock a significant improvement in consumer welfare. Unfortunately, any government contemplating such a reform may fear that the electorate will fail to give credit where credit is due, given the intangible nature of the welfare gain, a problem exacerbated by the fact that a significant minority of households would suffer financial losses.

10

———

Environmental Taxation

Much of this book discusses how to design the tax system to avoid unintended or undesirable effects on people's decisions about how much and in what way to work, spend, save, and invest. In this and the next two chapters—focusing on climate change and motoring—we consider taxes in a rather different light: as instruments specifically designed to alter behaviour in ways deemed desirable by the policymaker. Taxes are among the most important economic instruments available to deal efficiently with pollution and thereby help protect the environment. Some[1] also believe that environmental taxation has the potential to transform the tax system by raising large sums of money that could be used to finance significant cuts in other taxes.

The basic rationale for environmental taxation is clear. Pollution imposes costs on society that are not borne by the polluter. Imposing a tax[2] ensures that the polluter takes account of (or 'internalizes') these wider costs when deciding how much to pollute. On this basis, a reasonable goal is to reduce pollution to a level that takes full account of both the costs of the pollution and the benefits of the polluting activity. Taxes are often more effective than regulation as a way to achieve this.

In this chapter, we address some of the main economic issues in the design of environmental taxes. We do see a greater role for environmental taxation, but not to the extent that it will transform the composition of the tax system.

---

[1] e.g. the Green Fiscal Commission (http://www.greenfiscalcommission.org.uk/).

[2] Often known as a Pigouvian tax, following Pigou (1920).

We are also clear that taxes alone will often not be enough. There is a role for other policies to achieve the desired outcome.

10.1. PRINCIPLES AND PRACTICE OF ENVIRONMENTAL TAXATION

The use of regulations to improve the environment has a very long history. Londoners were complaining about the noxious effects of burning sea coal as early as the 12th century.[3] The first environmental legislation in the UK was the Smoke Nuisance Abatement (Metropolis) Act of 1853, with landmark Clean Air Acts following in 1956 and 1968. This was highly effective in reducing harmful health effects. The Air Pollution Control Act was passed in the US in 1955. Similar regulatory tools have been used throughout the world to deal with pollution.

More recently, taxes and other instruments that work by changing prices have become much more prominent in dealing with environmental externalities. In 2006, there were about 375 environmentally related taxes in OECD countries plus another 250 or so environmentally related fees and charges.[4] The UK is reasonably typical. There have been three new national environmental taxes in the UK in recent years, on landfill (the landfill tax introduced in 1996), on industrial energy use (the climate change levy introduced in 2001), and on the extraction of aggregates (the aggregates levy introduced in 2002). In addition, a new tax on travelling by plane (air passenger duty) was introduced in 1993 and has been increased and restructured more recently. Company car taxes and the annual vehicle excise duty have both been restructured, with differential rates reflecting the different environmental attributes of vehicles. In London, a congestion charge for vehicle use in the central area was introduced in 2003.

Table 10.1 shows the revenues from the main environmentally related taxes in the UK in 2009–10. The vast majority of revenues come from taxes

---

[3] Newbery, 2003.
[4] OECD, 2006.

Table 10.1. Environmental tax revenues, 2009–10

Tax	Estimated revenue (£ billion)
Fuel duties	26.2
Vehicle excise duty	5.6
Climate change levy	0.7
Landfill tax	0.8
Aggregates levy	0.3
Air passenger duty	1.9
Total	35.5

Source: HM Treasury, 2010b, table C11; with additional information from http://budgetresponsibility. independent.gov.uk/wordpress/docs/hmrc_receipts_300610.pdf.

on motoring (which were not originally conceived as 'environmental' taxes). This is typical of OECD countries, though tax rates are higher than average in the UK. The small amount of revenue raised by the other taxes comes mostly from energy production and consumption.

When polluters take account only of the private costs of their activities, ignoring the social costs, they will pollute more than is socially efficient. Taxes change the prices faced by polluters and they change their behaviour in response. A tax on pollution emitted by firms during production allows firms with different business models and adjustment costs to react differently. Crucially, a tax encourages adjustments where they are most easily or cheaply enacted. Firms with lower adjustment costs will do more to reduce pollution than firms where costs are greater. This is efficient, whereas insisting that all firms do the same thing can be very costly.

In principle, we want to increase the tax on pollution until the marginal cost for the firm of emitting pollution is equal to the marginal environmental benefit of the additional abatement the tax induces. (This would not normally reduce pollution to zero, as the costs of abatement would typically outweigh the benefits since some polluting activities may be valuable.) In reality, we lack the information to achieve this optimal solution precisely. Taxes can easily be set too low or too high. Badly designed or excessive taxes can be damaging. As Fullerton, Leicester, and Smith (2010, 439–40) say,

The key to achieving the potential gains from environmental taxes does not lie in the indiscriminate introduction of taxes with a vaguely defined environmental justification. Rather, it lies in the effective targeting of incentives to the pollution or other environmental problems that policy seeks to influence. Poorly targeted environmental taxes may increase the economic costs of taxation, while offering little in the way of environmental gains.

This is illustrated by the different forms of environmental tax that are possible. Taxes on measured emissions can, in principle, be very closely targeted on environmental objectives. Swedish taxes on nitrogen oxide emissions and Dutch charges for water pollution are good examples. But the information requirements for such taxes can be quite severe, limiting their general applicability. Emissions are not generally measured or traded, so costly special mechanisms may need to be set up to allow them to be taxed. An alternative is to tax observable market transactions that are related to pollution—taxes on batteries or fertilizers might fall into this category. Administratively, such taxes may be much cheaper, but they are less directly targeted and they may prompt unintended or inefficient responses from polluters.[5]

Such concerns may lead one to prefer a *multi-part instrument*—a combination of taxes and/or subsidies which between them are easier to implement than a direct tax on emissions but avoid some of the adverse consequences of a simple tax on a market transaction. For example, an excise tax on the sale of a commodity and a subsidy for clean technology may be better together than either on its own. Similarly, taxing motor vehicle emissions directly may not be feasible, but the combination of a tax on petrol, a subsidy to new car purchases (or a tax on older cars), and a tax on cars with low fuel efficiency or high emission rates may together be broadly as effective.[6]

These practicalities in designing environmental taxes are crucial and all too frequently overlooked. The right tax structure will depend on circumstances. Taxing coal burned in power stations on the basis of its sulphur content would be a mistake because flue gas desulphurization is a viable and effective way to remove sulphur from emissions. There is no incentive to remove the sulphur if the input rather than the emission is taxed. But taxing fuels on the basis of their carbon content looks a much better bet—at least so long as

---

[5] Sandmo, 1976.
[6] Fullerton and West, 2002.

there are no viable technologies to remove carbon dioxide (CO_2) after combustion. This position may change as technology advances, so the tax structure must be dynamic and responsive to changes in technology and circumstances.

Note also the distinction between 'stock' and 'flow' pollutants. Flow pollutants cause damage as they are produced and the damage ends when their production ends. Emissions of nitrogen oxides and sulphur dioxide are like this—they cause health damage when emitted and the damage falls rapidly when the emissions stop. Carbon dioxide, on the other hand, is a classic stock pollutant—it is the stock of CO_2 (and other greenhouse gases) which causes global warming. Flow pollutants are easier to price, as all we need to know is the damage they do immediately. The damage done by stock pollutants builds up and can last over long periods. As we discuss in Chapter 11, in the case of greenhouse gases a large number of assumptions—for example, about future emissions, the consequences of those emissions, and how to value the welfare of future generations—may need to be made to set an appropriate price.

10.2. TAXES AND TRADING

In a world in which all benefits and costs are known for sure, any reduction in pollution can be achieved either by restricting the quantity of pollution or by increasing its price. The former can involve direct limits on polluters or allocating a limited number of pollution licences. The latter can involve a price on each unit of pollution or a tax on polluting activity. Whatever the method, the goal is to achieve the efficient level of pollution, where the cost to society of polluting slightly more or less is equal to the benefit of doing so.

How can this be achieved by quantity restriction? The government can use its knowledge of the costs and benefits directly to order firms to make the efficient level of adjustment or it can issue licences to the required overall quantity and allow them to be traded. Trading ensures that licences are ultimately used by the firms that most value the right to pollute, which is the most efficient outcome.

In a 'cap-and-trade' system, tradable emissions permits are allocated to polluting firms. Each permit allows the firm a certain quantity of emissions (pollution). What makes this different from direct regulation is allowing the firms to trade these permits. Firms with lower abatement costs will sell permits to firms with higher abatement costs. The need to buy a permit will raise the cost of polluting in much the same way as a tax, and an efficient trading system will achieve much the same outcome as a tax. Emissions will be reduced where it is cheapest and most efficient to do so. And, to labour the point, this is the beauty of the price mechanism.

Politicians and environmentalists sometimes argue that every sector of the economy should 'bear its fair share' of cutting (for example) carbon emissions—that more planes or cars or lorries are incompatible with concern about the environment. But the role of government should be to decide what costs it thinks emissions impose and, hence, what overall level it wants to achieve. Taxes or trading mechanisms can then achieve the most efficient allocation of reductions. If it then turns out that the most efficient way to reduce emissions across the economy is to cut emissions from cars to zero whilst emissions from planes continue to grow, or vice versa, then so be it.

Placing a tax upon a polluting activity, or allowing pollution only if a licence is held, produces an incentive to innovate over time, both by introducing new technology and by using available technologies more effectively. If a textile factory faces an increased cost of pouring chemicals into the river, it will look to find new ways of disposing of them or new ways of producing textiles without producing so many chemicals. A stronger effect can be achieved by announcing that quantity restrictions will become increasingly onerous over time. Such a strategy was particularly effective in encouraging innovation in the motor industry. For example, the adoption of regulations on vehicle emissions in California beginning in 1966 was at least partly responsible for the introduction of the catalytic converter in 1975.

Unlike regulation, environmental taxes also raise revenue. In the case of 'cap-and-trade', the same level of revenue can be raised by selling—generally auctioning—the initial allowances. While most policies to reduce pollution increase people's welfare by doing so, they also impose costs on consumers by increasing the price of the goods on whose production regulations or taxes have been imposed. If the government restricts pollution without raising revenue (which it can then recycle), it risks losing much of the welfare gain associated with improved environmental performance through other costs imposed on consumers.

'Grandfathering' pollution permits—giving them free to polluting firms which can then trade them—will have the same impact on the total level of pollution and the distribution of polluting activities as auctioning them. Introducing pollution permits encourages firms to produce less, because the firms have to pay for them or because they can sell those they have already been allocated rather than undertake the production the permits would allow. In fact, grandfathering is equivalent to the case where permits are auctioned, but with the revenues given back to firms as lump-sum transfers. Firms are required to restrict output and pure 'windfall' profits arise. If permits are auctioned, then the government can capture these economic rents and use them to compensate consumers for higher costs or to reduce other distortionary taxes. With grandfathered permits, the economic rents are captured by producers. This was what happened—apparently to the surprise of some governments—when the EU's Emissions Trading Scheme was introduced.

We have so far emphasized situations in which taxes and cap-and-trade are equivalent. But when there is uncertainty over abatement costs, this equivalence is lost. The most salient difference is that cap-and-trade systems provide certainty over the amount of pollutant that will be emitted, whereas tax systems provide certainty for emitters over the costs they will face.

In principle, taxes are preferable where the benefits of reductions change less with the level of pollution than do the costs of delivering the reductions. Conversely, quantity mechanisms are preferable where the benefits of further reductions increase more with the level of pollution than do the costs of delivering reductions.[7] If there is significant uncertainty over the costs of delivering a particular level of emissions reductions, then cap-and-trade may impose higher costs than intended. But if we are concerned by risks to welfare arising from higher-than-intended emissions, then a quantity cap may be preferable to a tax since it can guarantee emissions falling to the desired level. In practice, the relative costs may be hard to determine and, in most circumstances, the choice between price and quantity intervention is

---

[7] Weitzman, 1974.

likely to be determined as much by practical and political considerations as by a clear understanding of the relative risks involved.

In fact, a combination of price and quantity regulation may perform better under uncertainty than reliance on just one or the other.[8] This might involve an emissions trading system with upper and lower 'safety valves'. At a high price the authorities might issue additional permits, while at a low price they would buy back permits. Alternatively, an emissions tax could be used to set a floor to the marginal incentive for abatement.

Such considerations do matter—cap-and-trade systems are now a popular policy tool. As well as being at the centre of the Kyoto climate change programme, they are in common use in fisheries management and have increasingly been used to control other forms of atmospheric pollution, most notably sulphur emissions in the US.

Taxes and cap-and-trade systems have many virtues, but there are still circumstances in which 'old-fashioned' regulation of behaviour will be more appropriate. Taxes may be difficult to implement or ineffective where pollution damage varies with the source of the emissions. If emission of some gases is much more damaging when close to large population centres, or discharging effluent is much more damaging in some stretches of water than in others, then, while very complex tax or trading structures could be designed, direct regulation is likely to be more efficient and effective. We might also worry that taxing or charging industries that are competing internationally might encourage some to move abroad. In that case, international agreements are likely to be necessary. This risk can be real but should not be overplayed. In addressing climate change, for example, large increases in energy prices are likely to impact significantly on location choices for only a small proportion of industries—cement manufacture and oil refining, for example.

Finally, and crucially, price signals do not work in all circumstances. Where individuals or firms are 'locked in' to particular technologies, imposing a tax may simply make them worse off. There may be other market failures that mean that incentives do not feed through to behaviour change. For example, there may be market failures in the rental market, where it may

---

[8] Roberts and Spence, 1976.

not be in the interest of a landlord to invest in better insulation if it is the tenant who pays the heating bills. For owner-occupiers, payback periods for substantial investments—for example, solid wall insulation—may be longer than their expected occupancy of the property and they may not believe that their investment will be reflected in the price they can get for the property when they come to sell it. It may also be difficult to persuade firms that the price imposed by a tax or trading system will be maintained. Investments by energy producers, for example, are very long lived and a lack of certainty over future policy may significantly reduce the effectiveness of price signals.

Whilst policymakers should be very careful in the choice of policy instrument, it *is* clear that there are areas where regulation, subsidy, or other intervention will be optimal alongside or instead of taxes or trading. In most areas where environmental taxes are beneficial, other forms of intervention can also be effective.

10.3. REVENUES AND THE DOUBLE DIVIDEND

Advocates of environmental taxes often argue that there is a 'double dividend' to be had by raising revenue from taxing pollution. The idea is straightforward and initially seductive: environmental taxes increase welfare *both* by reducing socially damaging activities *and* by reducing the need to raise tax revenues in other welfare-reducing ways. For example, environmental tax revenues can be used to pay for cuts in taxes on labour income which harm work incentives.

There are in fact many reasons to reject this view of a double dividend. But before we discuss them, bear in mind that the double dividend is not necessary for taxes on pollution to be welfare improving. The single dividend—the reduction in levels of pollution towards socially optimal levels—should be enough for that.

The intuition for the existence of a double dividend looks appealing, so what is wrong with it? The problem is similar to the incorrect argument that taxes on income reduce work incentives while taxes on spending do not. Because taxes on spending reduce the real buying power of wages, they have a similar incentive effect to labour income taxes. Similarly, environmental taxes tend to increase the price of goods consumed somewhere in the economy and so will have distortionary effects of their own. These effects may be bigger or smaller than the welfare effects of any taxes that are cut in response to the increased revenues from the environmental taxes. For a double dividend to exist in this sense, there would need to be 'no regrets' even if the expected environmental benefits did not arise.

Now, it might be the case that the current tax system is suboptimal in other ways—that goods with negative spillovers are not taxed highly enough (even ignoring the pollution consequences) and that other taxes are too high. In that case, raising taxes on the polluting activity *would* provide a double dividend, but only because of the original poor design of the tax system. The opposite case is also possible. Raising environmental taxes on goods or activities that are currently overtaxed will tend to reduce welfare, i.e. even part of the single dividend will be lost.

From the UK perspective, for example, there is one major potential environmental tax proposal which could unlock more than a single dividend because the current structure is suboptimal even ignoring environmental questions. Currently, the UK does not charge the full rate of VAT on domestic energy use, which an optimal system would do[9] *even ignoring effects on carbon emissions*. So raising tax on domestic energy might well involve a double dividend. We would move the tax system towards an optimal structure and (ignoring for the moment the complicating issue of the impact of the EU's Emissions Trading Scheme) also cut carbon emissions towards optimal levels. Even here, though, we would most likely accompany the increased tax with some form of compensation package which, if not designed carefully in the way we illustrated in Chapter 9, could itself worsen work incentives and dampen the overall welfare gain.

This argument underlines how important it is to look at the tax system as a whole when thinking about the effects and appropriate design of new taxes. The revenue raised from environmental taxes (or auctioned allowances) does allow other taxes to be cut, which provides an additional welfare gain alongside the environmental gains. But the double dividend argument overstates what is an already strong argument by ignoring the potential

---

[9] See Chapters 6, 7, and 9.

welfare *costs* of environmental taxes, which tax cuts elsewhere may or may not offset.

10.4. SOME PRACTICAL POLICY

We consider the implications of the principles we have discussed for policy towards climate change and motoring in the next two chapters. Actual and potential taxes on motoring, and potential taxes on energy use, are more substantial by far than any other existing or currently feasible environmental tax. The other relevant taxes in the UK are air passenger duty, the landfill tax, and the aggregates levy. Each of these smaller taxes is interesting in its own right.

Air passenger duty (APD) was first introduced in the November 1993 Budget. Since then, the rates at which it is levied have been increased, cut, increased again, and restructured. Expected to raise £2.3 billion in 2010–11,[10] it is charged on a per-person-per-flight basis, varying according to the class of ticket and according to whether the destination is more or less than 2,000 miles from London. Several features are noteworthy:

- First, despite its relatively recent origin, it was not introduced as an explicitly environmental tax, but rather because air travel was seen as undertaxed relative to other sectors thanks to its zero-rating for VAT. Indeed, Treasury ministers continue, at times, to argue that it is not essentially an environmental tax.[11]

- Second, most of the externalities associated with flying—noise and greenhouse gas emissions—are more closely related to the number of flights and the characteristics of the planes than to the number of people

---

[10] Source: HM Treasury, 2010b, table C11.

[11] John Healey, then Financial Secretary to the Treasury, argued that '[APD] has never been an environmental tax.... it does, however, contribute to the recognition that ... the aviation industry has to pay the costs, the externalities if you like, that it imposes on society and on the environment' (House of Commons Environmental Audit Committee, 2006, Q185 on Ev 73).

on board the planes. So APD is levied on only a very rough proxy for the relevant externality.

- Third, continued zero-rating of domestic aviation for VAT looks very odd in the face of concerns about environmental impacts.

The even smaller landfill tax is also interesting in terms of looking at how policy can actually develop. Research on the external costs of disposing of waste in landfill[12] was used to justify a tax rate on 'standard' waste of £7 a tonne and a reduced rate for 'inactive' waste of £2 a tonne from October 1996. But since then the standard tax rate has been increased time and again, reaching £40 a tonne in 2009 and due to increase to £80 a tonne by 2014. This is several times greater than any reasonable estimate of the external costs associated with landfill. Brought in originally as a tax with a rate set at something close to the best estimates of the external cost it was intended to internalize, the landfill tax has been forced up to levels that may be economically hard to justify, in an attempt to meet externally imposed targets set under the 1999 European Landfill Directive. To help meet those targets, the Landfill Allowance Trading Scheme (LATS) has also been introduced. This allocates a landfill tonnage (for biodegradable municipal waste) to each local authority in England up to 2020.

A number of issues arise from this example. Precise and effective targeting is difficult, and damaging avoidance behaviour is a possibility. The government acknowledges that 'there is some evidence that rising costs of legitimate disposal, including landfill sites, can lead to increases in flytipping'.[13] In addition, price signals may be rather ineffective in changing behaviour here. The biggest payers are local authorities disposing of household waste, but they are not able to charge households. So while councils have an incentive to find other methods of disposal, there is no price signal for households that might lead to any change in their behaviour. Using two instruments in this way also means that one is effectively redundant. Given that the LATS places a binding cap on landfill (or biodegradable municipal waste), the tax plays no role in reducing landfill. In addition, the high tax levels and the quantity cap have been imposed to meet

---

[12] CSERGE, 1993.
[13] http://archive.defra.gov.uk/environment/quality/local/flytipping/flycapture-qa.htm.

given targets, rather than because the tax rates have been economically justified by the environmental damage associated with landfill.

For completeness, we should also mention the aggregates levy, which was introduced in 2002 explicitly to address the environmental externalities associated with the commercial exploitation of aggregates. Companies subject to the levy were granted a reduction in National Insurance contributions to make the policy revenue neutral. To some extent, the levy has been successful. The use of recycled aggregates has risen from an estimated level of 10 million tonnes per year in 1990 to 36 million tonnes in 2003.[14] On the downside, there has been an increase in illicit quarrying.

A more general lesson from environmental taxes internationally is that it is extraordinarily hard, *ex ante*, to know what effects taxes at different levels will have. Leaving scope for evaluation and experimentation is important.

What of possible new environmental taxes or permit regimes? Leading contenders in the UK include reform of licences for abstraction of water and discharging of waste water. Currently, such licences are provided in a way that covers administration costs but that does not reflect either scarcity value or environmental costs and that does not facilitate trading. There is scope to use price signals and trading so that decisions do incorporate economic and environmental costs.[15]

The introduction of a plastic bags tax, as in Ireland, is another contender. The Irish experience suggests that such a tax, introduced there at €0.15 a bag, can be effective at influencing behaviour. The tax is estimated to have reduced plastic bag use by more than 90%—and as a result, of course, it has raised minimal revenue. It has involved some unintended consequences—including an increase in theft of baskets and trolleys—and its overall environmental impact has probably been small.[16] But it certainly indicates the scope for pricing to change behaviour in quite dramatic ways.

It is beyond the scope of this review to consider these or numerous other possible taxes in more detail. Experience internationally has been mixed. Certainly—outside of energy and transport—there seems little scope for raising large sums of money. Some schemes have had positive effects, but

[14] British Aggregates Association, 2005.
[15] See the Cave Review (Cave, 2009).
[16] Convery, McDonnell, and Ferreira, 2007.

most are quite costly to run and some have been driven more by political than by economic considerations.

10.5. CONCLUSIONS

The case for using taxes or cap-and-trade mechanisms to counter environmental externalities is strong. Using the price mechanism in this way can lead to firms and consumers internalizing the costs they are imposing on others and can result in a more efficient outcome than regulation. The government can use the revenues that arise to reduce the distortionary effects of other taxes. While this need not give rise to a 'double dividend', the welfare gain associated with efficient reduction of the externality justifies the tax.

The choice between taxes and cap-and-trade is not straightforward. In principle, they can achieve the same outcome, so long as permits are auctioned in the cap-and-trade case so that the government captures the rents created. When there is uncertainty about abatement costs, the case for a tax may be stronger if there is a risk that the costs of achieving a particular level of abatement may be very high. The case for cap-and-trade is stronger if the costs of not meeting a particular level of abatement are high. A hybrid system that places a floor and/or ceiling on prices in a cap-and-trade system may have particular attractions in these circumstances.

The precise design of the tax or trading scheme, and how it sits alongside other environmental policy, is important. Getting the price or quantity 'right' is likely to be difficult and to require a degree of experimentation. There will be cases where the existence of other market failures requires the use of instruments other than taxes.

While a role for more environmental taxation undoubtedly exists, it is not a magic bullet that will either transform the tax system or sort out all environmental problems by itself. The principles that have guided other elements of our conclusions are certainly relevant here. Complicating the tax system is easy in this area. There are undoubtedly gains to be had from this complication, but there are costs too—both immediate compliance and administrative costs and longer-term costs in lobbying and special pleading.

Whilst the UK government has been good at setting out aspirations and principles, it remains a pity that no serious, comprehensive, and public review and analysis of the potential options in this area have been undertaken.

We move on to consider the two biggest areas of environmental taxation in practice in the next two chapters, on climate change and on motoring.

11

———

Tax and Climate Change

The main reason for the recent reawakening of interest in the economics of environmental taxation has been concern about climate change. Man-made emissions of carbon dioxide and other greenhouse gases have harmful environmental spillovers. The analysis in the previous chapter suggests policymakers should aim to achieve a consistent price for carbon (equal to the cost to society of emitting a little more of it) through a tax or a system of traded permits.

In fact, things are much more complex than that. This chapter begins by setting out briefly the most important facets of climate change which should drive policy choices. We go on to consider the role of pricing, the choice between taxes and tradable permits, and how the price should be set. The role of other instruments is then briefly considered and a way forward for policy in the UK is suggested.

11.1. CLIMATE CHANGE—THE ISSUES

This is no place to go into the science or indeed all the economics of climate change in any detail.[1] However, it is important to understand the nature of the challenge that requires policy action.

---

[1] An overview of the science is provided by the report of the Committee on Climate Change (2008) and by the Intergovernmental Panel on Climate Change (2007). An exposition of the economics can be found in the Stern Review (Stern, 2006).

First, climate change is distinguished from other environmental issues by the potential scale of the problem and the current degree of uncertainty about the process. There is broad scientific consensus that climate change is occurring as a result of the accumulation of carbon dioxide (CO_2) and other greenhouse gases (GHGs) in the atmosphere. What is uncertain is the effect that this accumulation will have on global temperatures, the level at which the accumulation will stabilize if no corrective action is taken, and the economic and social damage that will result. The choice of appropriate policy has to be framed in the context of this uncertainty.

The quantity of GHGs in the atmosphere is generally measured in terms of parts per million (ppm) of carbon dioxide equivalent (CO_2e).[2] Since the mid 19th century, atmospheric concentrations have grown from 285ppm to about 430ppm CO_2e. Over the past decade, concentrations have been growing at about 2.5ppm a year. Without action, economic growth (particularly in developing countries) is forecast to increase this rate to 3–4ppm a year over the first half of this century. This would take atmospheric concentrations to 580–630ppm by mid century and 800–900ppm by the end of the century.[3] Table 11.1 provides estimates of the probability of global temperature increases at different concentration levels of CO_2e.[4]

Second, this is a global issue in two senses. Climate change would affect the whole world, though some parts would suffer more than others—notably the poorer countries of Africa and the developing countries of Asia. The problem is also global in the sense that it is the total worldwide emission of GHGs that matters, not where they are emitted.

No single country (other than perhaps the US and China) can make a significant impact on this global problem just by cutting its own emissions.

---

[2] Other GHGs have different effects on global warming by comparison with CO_2. For example, one molecule of methane has an effect on global warming (over a 100-year horizon) 25 times that of one molecule of CO_2, while nitrous oxide has an effect 298 times that of CO_2 and the rarer HFCs, PFCs, and SF_6 have effects many thousands of times as great (Intergovernmental Panel on Climate Change, 2007, table 2.14). Total concentrations of all these GHGs are generally shown as CO_2 equivalents.

[3] These figures are taken from Stern (2009, 25–6).

[4] These estimates change as the science advances. The recent past has seen an increase in the estimated probability of higher temperature rises.

Tax by Design

Table 11.1. Probabilities (%) of exceeding temperature increases, relative to 1850, at various stabilization levels of CO_2e

Stabilization level	Temperature increase					
(ppm CO_2e)	2°C	3°C	4°C	5°C	6°C	7°C
450	78	18	3	1	0	0
500	96	44	11	3	1	0
550	99	69	24	7	2	1
650	100	94	58	24	9	4
750	100	99	82	47	22	9

Source: Stern, 2009, 26.

Certainly, the UK, responsible for about 2% of global emissions, cannot.[5] So a global solution is required. The construction of such a solution is well beyond the scope of this book. We focus on the appropriate domestic UK response and the role of tax and pricing within that. The international context is relevant, though, when assessing the relative merits of taxes and trading.

Third, to return to one of the distinctions mentioned in the previous chapter, the problem of greenhouse gases is a *stock* problem rather than a *flow* problem. Most GHGs, in particular CO_2, remain in the atmosphere for a long time. And the scientific evidence shows that it is the quantity in the atmosphere that matters for the impact—rather than, for example, the amount that is emitted in any one year. This, in addition to the timescales and uncertainty involved, makes selecting an appropriate price for emissions particularly tricky.

One final issue that needs to be borne in mind is that there are two different ways to think about a country's emissions. One is to consider only emissions that occur domestically—resulting from coal burnt or petrol consumed in the UK, for example. The other is to consider the embedded carbon content of what is consumed in the UK—i.e. to take account of, say, coal burnt in the manufacture of goods produced in China but consumed in the UK. Nearly all policy debate is framed in the former way and UK targets

[5] Source: US Energy Information Administration, http://tonto.eia.doe.gov/cfapps/ipdbproject/IEDIndex3.cfm?tid=90&pid=44&aid=8.

refer to emissions that actually occur in the UK. But ideally we might want to focus on the latter.[6] Reducing emissions in the UK by shifting high-carbon manufacturing abroad does not address the global problem.

This is not an issue we focus on here. The complex web of global trade agreements makes imposing additional taxes on imports with high levels of 'embedded carbon' formidably difficult. This difficulty is greatly enhanced by the huge complexity in measuring the embedded carbon. There are great advantages, in this situation, in imposing taxes 'upstream', i.e. using an origin system to tax emissions at the point at which they are produced. This points again to the need for global agreements to make that happen.

11.2. PRICING MECHANISMS

The central policy challenge in controlling the accumulation of GHGs is to impose a consistent price on emissions. This should result in efficient decisions over how, when, and where emissions reductions take place, removing the need for politicians to make decisions about where cuts should occur.

In an ideal world of full information and perfectly competitive markets, that would be all that was required. But in the real world, other policies will also be needed. But the more we deviate from the price mechanism, the greater the danger of high policy costs, pork-barrel politics, and inefficient distributions of reductions in emissions. As Helm (2008, 233) has argued, 'Economic efficiency and political expediency are likely to conflict in climate-change policy … the case for market-based instruments is especially great'.

11.2.1. Taxes or 'Cap-and-Trade'

As we have seen, pricing can occur through either tax or cap-and-trade mechanisms. In an international context, two practical considerations favour

---

[6] This is a version of the 'origin' versus 'destination' debate that we also discuss in relation to VAT and corporate taxation.

trading. The first is that it already exists. The Kyoto Protocol is, in effect, an attempt to apply emissions trading between sovereign states, while the EU's Emissions Trading Scheme (EU ETS) has created a well-established and active carbon trading market within Europe. The second reason to favour trading is that applying taxes on any kind of international, let alone global, basis is not likely to be popular with sovereign states.

Trading mechanisms can also create substantial flows of private money around the globe, which may be desirable if we see value in helping poorer countries to reduce emissions. Under current arrangements, a scheme under the Kyoto Protocol called the Clean Development Mechanism (CDM) allows rich countries effectively to pay for emissions reductions in poorer countries through, for example, the use of cleaner technology in power generation and to set those reductions against their own targets.[7]

In addition, our previous analysis of the different properties of tax versus cap-and-trade systems also points to preferring a cap-and-trade-type solution at a global level because the consequences of emitting 'too much' could be exceptionally serious. That said, experience of the EU ETS would also suggest that there might be a case for a price floor in the system, perhaps provided through the tax system. A hybrid between price- and quantity-based mechanisms may have attractions both theoretically and in practice.

Finally, credible global caps on emissions may be necessary to overcome one of the particular problems created by the fact that emissions result from the burning of exhaustible resources—oil and coal. An expectation of rising taxes clearly increases the incentive to extract and sell fossil fuels now rather than wait for a time at which taxes may be high enough to significantly reduce the pre-tax price that can be achieved by producers.

The global nature of the climate change problem, then, probably pushes us towards international cap-and-trade systems as the main way to achieve a sensible carbon price. But there may well be a case for a hybrid system with some price underpin. And in the end, the relative roles of tax and trading are likely to be determined on a pragmatic basis. Taxes may be easier to implement in particular circumstances, countries, or regions. The main point is that pricing carbon is vital.

---

[7] The current CDM is most imperfect and has, with some justification, been subject to criticism. It is not our purpose here to review that, simply to state that some form of effective mechanism is important.

11.2.2. The UK Context

Policy in the UK has a long way to go to achieve a consistent price for carbon. Indeed, the range of policies and emissions sources is so complex that it is hard to say what the effective carbon prices are. To start with, consider where emissions in the UK are physically created (for example, at a power station) and the purpose for which they were created (for example, for domestic or business use). Table 11.2 shows figures for emissions in 2006 broken down in both ways. Since 1990, on the source measure, emissions from energy supply, business, and agriculture have been falling fairly rapidly as a result of changing fuel mix in energy supply and changing mix of businesses and agricultural practices. Emissions from transport and domestic heating have risen.

But emissions from these different sectors are priced very differently. Those from electricity supply are priced through the EU ETS. Those created by business directly may be: caught by the ETS if large enough; priced at a low level through the climate change levy (CCL); covered by Climate Change Agreements (see later); or entirely unpriced. Electricity used by business may be priced through both the ETS and the CCL. Businesses and public sector organizations that are large energy users, but not large enough to be covered by the CCL, are covered by a trading scheme known as the Carbon

Table 11.2. Greenhouse gas emissions by source and by end user, 2006

Source	Emissions (MtCO$_2$e)	End user	Emissions (MtCO$_2$e)
Power stations	185	Business	211
Transport	153	Transport	158
Industry	122	Residential	156
Residential	85	Agriculture	52
Agriculture	45	Public	22
Services	28	Waste management	22
Waste management	22	Industrial process	18
Refineries	16	Exports	16
Land use change	−2	Land use change	−2

Note: MtCO$_2$e = million tonnes of carbon dioxide equivalent.
Source: Committee on Climate Change, 2008, xxiii.

Reduction Commitment (CRC). Their electricity use will be priced through both the EU ETS and the CRC. Emissions from agriculture—mostly non-CO_2 gases, particularly methane and nitrous oxide—are not subject to any pricing at present.

Emissions from road transport are priced at a very high level through excise duties on fuel, though to what extent these duties are intended to reflect GHG emissions, as opposed to their impact on congestion spillovers, local air quality, and accidents, is unclear (we come to this in the next chapter). Air transport is about to be brought into the ETS and is also subject to a separate air passenger duty. Emissions from electricity consumed by households are priced through the ETS, whilst those from gas used principally in domestic heating are not priced at all. In effect, emissions from domestic gas and electricity use are subsidized because VAT is not charged at a full rate.

Other policies affect electricity prices too. The Renewables Obligation requires electricity suppliers to source a certain proportion of their electricity from renewable generation. This is more expensive than conventional generation. In 2009, the then government estimated, on central assumptions, that its total Renewable Energy Strategy would increase domestic electricity bills by 15% and domestic gas bills by 23% by 2020.[8]

One way of quantifying differences in implicit taxes is illustrated in Table 11.3. This shows, for 2009–10, how the implicit tax per tonne of CO_2 varies not only between gas, electricity, and transport fuel, but also between electricity from different sources and between business and domestic users. VAT is not included in these calculations—either as an additional tax or, because it is charged at a reduced rate, as a subsidy.

The first column in the table is an estimate of CO_2 emissions per kilowatt-hour (kWh) of energy produced.[9] For gas and electricity, the second column is an estimate of the impact of the Renewables Obligation (RO) on electricity prices per kWh.[10] The third column is simply the 2009–10 rate of the climate

---

[8] Department of Energy and Climate Change, 2009a.

[9] Source: Annex A of *Digest of United Kingdom Energy Statistics, 2010*.

[10] The buyout price in 2009–10 was £37.19 per megawatt-hour (MWh), the obligation was for 9.7% of electricity to be from renewables, and all suppliers purchased buyouts. So the effective 'tax' on the marginal MWh is 9.7% of £37.19 per MWh, which is 0.36p per kWh.

change levy. For the EU ETS, we take the government's central estimate[11] of £22 per tonne of CO_2 to estimate the cost of the ETS per kWh of electricity.[12]

Table 11.3. Implicit carbon taxes, 2009–10[a]

Fuel type	CO_2 emissions: g/kWh	RO: p/kWh	CCL: p/kWh	ETS: p/kWh	Implicit tax: p/kWh	Implicit tax: £/tonne CO_2
Electricity (business)						
Coal	910	0.36	0.47	2.00	2.83	31.13
Gas	393	0.36	0.47	0.86	1.70	43.14
Nuclear	0	0.36	0.47	0.00	0.83	∞
Renewables	0	0.00	0.00	0.00	0.00	–
Gas (for heating, business)	184	0.00	0.16	0.00	0.16	8.91
Electricity (domestic)						
Coal	910	0.36	0.00	2.00	2.36	25.96
Gas	393	0.36	0.00	0.86	1.22	31.18
Nuclear	0	0.36	0.00	0.00	0.36	∞
Renewables	0	0.00	0.00	0.00	0.00	–
Gas (for heating, domestic)	184	0.00	0.00	0.00	0.00	0.00

Transport fuel	CO_2 emissions: g/kWh	CO_2 emissions: g/litre	Fuel duty: p/litre	RTFO: p/litre	Implicit tax: £/tonne CO_2
Petrol	240	2,303	56.19	0.54	246.33
Diesel	250	2,639	56.19	0.54	214.96
Aviation gasoline	238	2,226	34.57	0.00	155.30
Aviation turbine fuel	245	2,528	0.00	0.00	0.00

[a] The table should be interpreted with care. Electricity consumers, for example, do not buy their power from a particular power station that generates electricity using a single fuel, but rather from a supplier that has a particular mix of fuels. In terms of electricity, the interpretation of the table should be: 'In a world where all electricity were produced from the same fuel source (coal, gas, nuclear, etc.), what impact would various policies have on the price and what implicit carbon tax does this give for that source given the CO_2 emissions it generates?'.

Source: Johnson, Leicester, and Levell, 2010.

[11] See Department of Energy and Climate Change (2009b).
[12] e.g. coal-fired power generates 910g CO_2/kWh. This is 0.00091 tonnes of CO_2, which, at a price of £22 per tonne, would cost 2.00p/kWh.

The motor fuel taxes are simply duty rates applying at the end of fiscal year 2009–10 plus a small addition for the Renewable Transport Fuels Obligation (RTFO), a scheme similar to the RO in electricity supply which requires fuel suppliers to include a proportion of biofuel (3.6% in 2009–10) in their fuel.[13]

The results are rather telling, with very big differences in implicit carbon tax by source. Gas directly used by domestic consumers attracts no carbon tax, while electricity used by business and produced from gas attracts a tax of £43 per tonne of CO_2. Electricity from different sources differs in implicit tax because of the way in which neither the RO nor the CCL distinguishes between different fossil fuels but the ETS does.

While it is difficult to put the implicit subsidy from the reduced VAT rate in the same format, one way of looking at its relative importance is to observe that the electricity bill for a consumer with average consumption was £461 in 2009.[14] The cost with a full rate of VAT would have been £515.88. The difference, £54.88, is an estimate of the subsidy households receive from the reduced VAT. Ofgem estimates that the cost of the RO and ETS for the same consumer would have been £36.[15] So the VAT subsidy is bigger than the total implicit carbon tax. This is for electricity consumption—there is no implicit carbon tax on gas for the VAT subsidy to outweigh.

Finally, note that the very large numbers calculated for petrol and diesel should be taken with a little pinch of salt since the main externality associated with driving is actually the congestion caused, and hence a large part of this tax should be seen as a tax on congestion rather than on carbon.

In sum, policy towards the pricing of greenhouse gas emissions remains highly inconsistent, creates different prices for different sources of emissions, and even effectively subsidizes some. There is scope for considerable improvement. We now discuss some of the main pricing instruments in turn.

---

[13] The figure in the table is based on this 3.6% obligation and a buyout price of 15p a litre. In fact, no buyouts were purchased in 2008–09 and only two in 2009–10, so this represents an upper-bound estimate.

[14] Department of Energy and Climate Change, 2010.

[15] Ofgem, 2009.

The EU Emissions Trading Scheme

The EU ETS covers about half of total emissions in the UK and three-quarters of industrial emissions—largely those from electricity generators and other energy-intensive firms. Figure 11.1 illustrates.

The scheme was established in 2005, with a first phase covering the period 2005–07, a second phase from 2008 to 2012, and a planned third phase to cover 2013–20. The price of the tradable emission allowances (EU allowances or EUAs) fell to zero in 2007 as it became clear that permitted emissions exceeded annual emissions. Some tightening in the second phase needs to be followed by still tighter caps in the third if significant cuts in emissions are to be achieved.

Because it puts a cap on emissions across the EU (other than through the ability to purchase project credits, which allow reductions to be bought from other countries), the ETS limits the value of other policy instruments applied to the same emissions. Consider, for example, the role that a domestic tax on electricity consumption might play in reducing carbon emissions. It will push up the price of electricity in the UK, thereby reducing demand. However, electricity generators in the UK are members of the ETS. So any cut in demand for the electricity they produce, and therefore in their

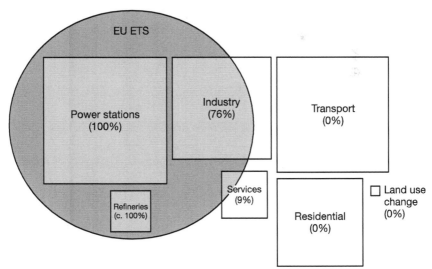

Figure 11.1. Coverage of the EU Emissions Trading Scheme by UK sector

Source: Committee on Climate Change, 2008, 150.

demand for EUAs, will *increase* the availability of EUAs in other member
countries and have no effect on overall emissions across the EU. So any
additional policy that increases the price of electricity in the UK can only
have positive environmental consequences if it has a *dynamic* effect in the
sense of making it easier to reduce future emissions caps.

It is not clear that a number of policies implemented by the UK
government have been thought through in this context. The Carbon
Reduction Commitment is one. It targets energy use by large non-intensive
users of electricity—large retail businesses and service industries, for
example—creating a cap-and-trade mechanism amongst them. This may
reduce electricity use in this sector but it *cannot* reduce emissions across the
EU unless either the ETS cap is not biting (in which case the central plank of
policy has failed) or there are genuine dynamic effects on future caps (for
which there is little firm evidence, and which seem a shaky basis on which to
introduce an expensive new policy).

More generally, for as long as the ETS remains a central plank of policy, a
national carbon tax is not likely to be effective in reducing overall emissions.
It would reduce emissions in one country by subsidizing emissions
elsewhere. That is not to say that such a tax may not be efficient or necessary
to help meet *domestic* targets. This serves to illustrate a problem to which we
will return—that of how to assess the role of national targets in the context of
an international trading scheme.

Whilst this is not a book about the design of cap-and-trade systems, the
ETS is so central to the pricing of carbon emissions that it requires some
attention. The way in which it interacts with other pricing policies is
particularly important, as is the fact that its coverage is less than complete.
The setting of emissions caps and the allocation of permits also matter.

In the first two phases of the ETS, individual countries proposed national
emissions caps to the EU, based on their calculations of the level of emissions
implied by 'business as usual'. There are obvious incentives to 'game' the
system here. In the first phase, there was a shortage of allowances in only a
small number of countries (including the UK). For the second phase, the
European Commission rejected the proposed caps initially put forward by
most member states because they would not between them have created
enough scarcity. A more centralized allocation mechanism is proposed for

the third phase.[16] Even so, the difficulties in setting caps and the extent to which the system is open to political lobbying can hardly be exaggerated.[17]

Once caps are set, permits have to be allocated to firms. This has been done by 'grandfathering'. Polluters are given permits reflecting their past levels of emissions. This may have been important in the early years of the scheme to ensure acceptance by industry, but it is clearly undesirable going forward. During the second phase, it is estimated that free allowances will create windfall profits of £1.6 billion annually for the UK power sector.[18]

Auctioning is preferable. It raises revenue for the government and it does not confer competitive advantages on incumbents. The current plan is to auction half of allowances in 2013, with all allowances in the power sector being auctioned by 2020.

A system that covers a greater proportion of total emissions is also preferable. We currently have a dual pricing system: half of emissions are in the ETS and half out, with aviation due to join in 2012. The result is a range of effective carbon prices. As we discuss in Section 11.2.3, the dual system can create particular problems in the context of 'binding' emissions targets, which are now key pillars of climate policy.

Finding some way to increase price stability and certainty going forward is also likely to be important. Uncertain and variable prices may render the price signal too weak to drive major investment decisions by energy and other companies. Figure 11.2 illustrates this by showing how prices changed over the period 2005–08, including the collapse in price to zero during the first phase of the ETS.

Two strategies might increase the degree of stability. One is to expand carbon markets across activities, time, and regions so as to deepen them and increase information flows and liquidity. Deeper and more liquid markets tend to be more stable. In line with our more theoretical discussion in the previous chapter, a price floor (and perhaps a ceiling) is also likely to be valuable, at least in the shorter term.[19]

---

[16] See http://europa.eu/rapid/pressReleasesAction.do?reference=MEMO/08/796.

[17] There are many complexities to this issue, including the role of project credits allowing reductions to be bought from other countries, which we ignore here.

[18] Committee on Climate Change, 2008, 149.

[19] Also proposed by the Committee on Climate Change (2008, 156).

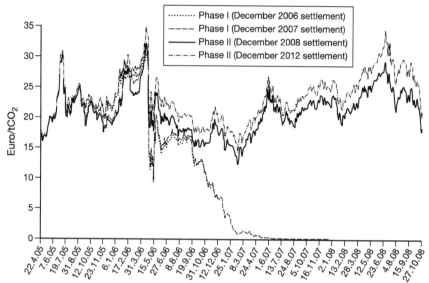

Figure 11.2. Allowance price evolution in the EU ETS, 2005–08

Source: Committee on Climate Change, 2008, 150.

Taxes on Domestic Energy Consumption

As we have argued, the existence of the ETS makes the case for the imposition of an additional tax relatively weak unless it is the only way of achieving a reasonable degree of price stability.

But important sectors of the economy are not currently covered by the ETS, including the use of gas in domestic heating. There may be specific areas where tax incentives can motivate further behavioural change—for example, to buy more energy-efficient goods. And then, of course, we need to confront the fact that the imposition of VAT at a reduced rate of only 5% on domestic energy (gas and electricity) effectively *subsidizes* energy use relative to other forms of consumption.

In this respect, the UK differs from most other EU countries. Largely because we impose VAT on domestic fuel at such a low rate, taxes account for less than 5% of the cost of domestic electricity in the UK, which is very low by EU standards.[20] The result is that while the pre-tax electricity price in

---

[20] Source: Eurostat, *Data in Focus 23/2008: Environment and Energy* (http://epp.eurostat.ec. europa.eu/cache/ITY_OFFPUB/KS-QA-08-023/EN/KS-QA-08-023-EN.PDF).

the UK is slightly above the average of the EU-27, the post-tax price is below the average.

The main reason for eschewing taxes on domestic energy consumption has always been distributional. On average, poorer households devote a higher proportion of their spending to energy than do richer households. This is illustrated in Figure 11.3. Domestic fuel has become a much less important part of total spending over time, and particularly so for poorer households, but it still takes three times as big a share of the spending of the poorest households as of the richest. So concerned was the last government about the fuel costs for poorer households that it had a specific target to reduce numbers in 'fuel poverty'.[21] But bear in mind that since 1970, average internal home temperatures have increased by a remarkable 6°C, from 12°C to 18°C.[22]

From an economic point of view, we might want to distinguish between those who simply have a preference for using more energy (for example, to keep the house warmer or to run more electric goods), those who need to use more energy because their house is poorly insulated, and those who need

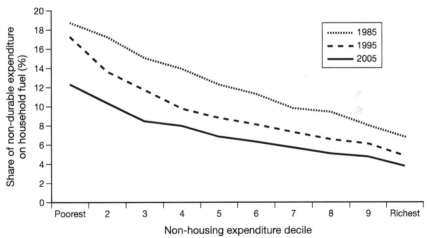

Figure 11.3. Share of non-durable expenditure devoted to domestic fuel, by expenditure decile

Source: Fullerton, Leicester, and Smith, 2010.

[21] Fuel poverty is defined as a situation in which a household needs to spend more than 10% of household income on all domestic fuel to heat its home to an adequate level of warmth.
[22] Committee on Climate Change, 2008, 217.

more energy because they are old or sick. There is no obviously good reason to subsidize the first group. The second group might need help to make their homes more energy efficient. If their homes cannot be made more fuel efficient, they may simply need financial support, as is likely to be the case for the last group.

Some of the money raised by taxing domestic energy use could be used to compensate poorer households by raising benefits and cutting other taxes. The problem is that, whilst this would compensate people *on average*, it would still leave many poorer households (i.e. those that use significantly more energy than the average) somewhat worse off. As we discussed in Chapter 9, one would also need to be very careful about potential effects on work incentives from such a reform.

The problem is illustrated in Figure 11.4, which shows the pounds-per-week losses that would be experienced by households at different points in the income distribution if VAT on fuel were to be increased from 5% to 17.5%. For each income decile, the bars show average losses and the lines

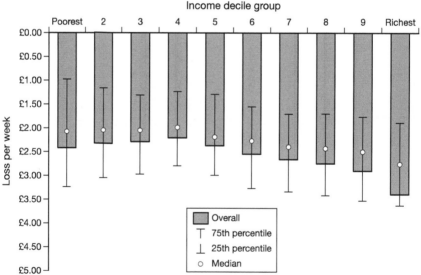

Figure 11.4. Losses from imposing VAT at 17.5% on domestic energy consumption, by income decile

Note: Income decile groups derived by dividing households into ten equal-sized groups according to their disposable income adjusted for household size using the McClements equivalence scale.

Source: Authors' calculations using the IFS tax and benefit microsimulation model, TAXBEN, run on uprated data from the 2007 Expenditure and Food Survey.

show losses at the 25th, 50th, and 75th percentiles. For the poorest group, median losses are just over £2 per week, but a quarter of households in this group would lose well over £3 per week.[23]

As Simon Dresner and Paul Ekins—long-time proponents of a carbon tax—have shown,[24] it is not possible to provide effective compensation through the benefit system to *all* low-income households by using money raised from such a tax. They conclude that a long-term programme of improving energy efficiency in such households would be a prerequisite for a significant tax rise. Such an approach might help avoid some of the opposition that stymied the attempt to impose the full rate of VAT on domestic fuel in the early 1990s.

That said, it is worth remembering that many other countries have bitten the bullet and imposed VAT on energy consumption. Raising VAT to the full rate of 20% would increase effective energy prices by just over 14%. Market fluctuations and the apparent long-term increase in energy prices since 2006 have been much more dramatic than that. As of 2008, three existing policies—the EU ETS, the Renewables Obligation, and the Carbon Emissions Reduction Target[25]—already increased electricity bills by an estimated 8%,[26] but in a way that is much less visible to the general public and which therefore excites less opposition (even though there has been no explicit compensation). And, as we have seen, proposals to increase the use of renewable energy sources will lead to this cost increasing over time.

Overall, there is a strong case for extending VAT at the full rate to domestic fuel consumption—just as there is a strong case for a more uniform VAT generally. While there is a functioning ETS, there is not a strong case for any additional tax on electricity consumption. But while gas remains outside the ETS, there is a case for an additional tax on gas consumption. To equate roughly to the effect of the ETS in 2009, such a tax would need to be in the region of 10% of gas price. This would require some of the money raised to be used on compensation and measures to improve insulation and energy efficiency.

---

[23] Though see Chapter 9 for a discussion of how to interpret these sorts of figures.

[24] Dresner and Ekins, 2006.

[25] A description of the last can be found at http://www.decc.gov.uk/en/content/cms/what_we_do/consumers/saving_energy/cert/cert.aspx.

[26] Ofgem, 2009.

Climate Change Levy

There is one particular tax in the UK that it is worth dwelling on briefly here, if only because of its name. The climate change levy, introduced in April 2001, is a tax on the supply of energy to business, paid by users. Electricity is taxed at the same rate whether generated by gas, coal, or nuclear power, despite their very different carbon emissions. Lower rates are charged on direct use of gas, solid fuel, or liquefied petroleum gas (LPG), and some exemption is available for electricity generated from renewable sources. The CCL was forecast to raise around £700 million in 2010–11.[27]

The CCL has a number of interesting features. First, it is closer to being a tax on energy consumption than a tax on greenhouse gas emissions. Second, its introduction was accompanied by a 0.3% cut in employer National Insurance contributions (NICs) so as not to increase the overall tax burden on business; in fact, the cut in NICs has been worth rather more than the money raised by the CCL. Third, it was accompanied by Climate Change Agreements (CCAs) that allowed energy-intensive businesses to reduce their CCL liabilities by 80% in exchange for agreeing to meet energy efficiency targets. Fourth, some of the money raised by the CCL (already more than exhausted by the National Insurance cut) was hypothecated to funding the Carbon Trust,[28] an organization set up by government to provide advice and support to business on saving energy. Fifth, the CCL applies only to business. Finally, in the first five years of its operation, it was not indexed in line with inflation, thereby reducing its real value (and presumably impact) year on year.

In these respects, the CCL has interesting parallels with other actual and proposed 'green taxes'. The political economy of their introduction seems to be such that cutting other taxes, hypothecating revenues, and focusing on business tend to be important elements of their design. And taxes that require annual uprating are less likely to maintain their real value than proportional taxes—such as VAT—which automatically rise with prices. The use of Climate Change Agreements alongside the main CCL reflects both

---

[27] http://budgetresponsibility.independent.gov.uk/wordpress/docs/hmrc_receipts_300610.pdf.
[28] The logical conundrum created by the hypothecation of revenues that were more than negated by the reduction in another tax is just another of the absurdities that tend to go with efforts to hypothecate tax revenues.

concerns over international competitiveness of energy-intensive industries and a view that there is a role for improved information and advice in reducing firms' energy use. Like many other aspects of tax policy in the environmental field—including the free allocation of emissions trading allowances—the scope and structure of CCAs and the scale of the reduction in the main tax rate that goes with them inevitably attract intense lobbying.

The CCL is a flawed tax. In the compromises that are central to it— exempting households entirely and energy-intensive industries by 80%, cutting other taxes, hypothecating non-existent revenues, creating opportunities for lobbying—it mirrors the compromises that governments have deemed necessary to many environmental taxes. But it forms a small and complex part of a rather incoherent overall system.

11.2.3. The Carbon Price

We have so far avoided discussing the appropriate level of the carbon price. The unwary reader might think that this is a relatively straightforward issue.

Much effort has been expended in the calculation of a so-called social cost of carbon (SCC), defined as the present value of the future costs associated with the emission of an additional tonne of carbon. Unfortunately, the SCC is likely to have only limited use in informing policy decisions, not least because of the range of estimates produced. Watkiss and Downing (2008, 101) conclude that estimates of the SCC 'span at least three orders of magnitude, from zero (or even below) to over £1000/tC, reflecting uncertainties in climate impacts, coverage of sectors and extremes, and choices of decision variables (notably over discount rate, equity weighting and climate sensitivity)'. It is indeed possible to take a range of different views about all these things, which is why there is considerable disagreement among economists about the appropriate response to climate change, and in particular over how much effort it is worth investing in abating emissions now, as opposed to in the future, and hence what price we should effectively be putting on carbon.

To complicate matters further, estimates of the SCC also depend on the assumed path of future emissions. The damage caused by additional carbon emissions depends on the level at which GHGs stabilize in the atmosphere.

For example, if we end up with concentrations of GHGs stabilizing at 450ppm CO_2e, then the damage done by each additional tonne emitted will be less than the damage done by each additional tonne emitted if we end up stabilizing at 650ppm. Damage rises more than in proportion to the increase in atmospheric concentration.

The problem relates to risk and uncertainty and how they are taken into account. An explicit way of doing that, adopted by the Stern Review, is to choose a target for atmospheric GHG concentrations, on the basis of what we know about the costs of possible climate change scenarios at various levels of concentration and what we know about the costs of meeting that target. If we go along with Stern's recommendation, that a target in the broad range between 450 and 550ppm CO_2e would be appropriate, then an appropriate price for carbon would be the marginal abatement cost of the most expensive technology required to achieve that outcome.

A target stabilization level in effect underlies many countries' approaches to climate policy, not least in the UK where the government has taken on a 'binding' commitment to reduce emissions by 34% below 1990 levels by 2020. These targets frame the debate about policy and the role of prices and other instruments in reaching the targets. In this context, the UK government has moved away from thinking about setting appropriate carbon prices by reference to measures of the SCC, towards defining prices by reference to the price needed to achieve the targets. There is an internal consistency to this position, but of course it depends on a belief that the targets are themselves in some sense 'right'. And most of the uncertainties and judgements that make calculating the SCC so difficult and controversial also make determining the correct emissions target difficult and controversial. But if we do have reduction targets, then it makes sense to price carbon so as to achieve those reductions.

The EU has also set itself targets, for 20% emissions reductions by 2020 (or 30% if a global agreement is reached), and caps within the ETS itself will need to be set so as to ensure the ETS sectors play their appropriate roles in meeting these targets. One important issue for countries such as the UK, which have set themselves stringent domestic targets, is that the effective price put on emissions reductions outside the ETS will need to be higher than that on those inside. Indeed, the most recent government guidance on this subject[29] suggests that while the traded price of carbon in the EU ETS might be £25 per tonne of CO_2, the appropriate price to use in the non-traded sector in order to achieve UK targets would be £60 per tonne of CO_2. Going forward, the appropriate carbon price will likely increase as the cost of technologies required to meet increasingly stringent targets rises.

This divergence results from the fact that half of UK carbon emissions are traded across the EU and half are susceptible only to UK policy, whilst UK targets are set independently. This creates obvious inefficiencies. Too much will be done in the non-traded sector and not enough in the traded sector. Furthermore, there are no plans to impose a consistent carbon price through a tax or any other mechanism on the non-traded sector. The importance of bringing more emissions within the ETS, of pricing those left outside, and of setting UK targets as consistently as possible with EU policy should be obvious.

11.2.4. Other Policies

This is a book on tax, and we have focused on the role of taxes and other pricing mechanisms in climate change policy. In a perfect world, pricing might be sufficient. But it is worth noting, briefly, that this is not a perfect world and these are not the only policies that will be needed either nationally or internationally 'given the risks, urgency, inertia in decision making, difficulty of providing clear and credible future price signals in an international framework, market imperfections, unrepresented consumers, and serious concerns about equity'.[30]

Internationally, policy will need to focus on supporting and accelerating technological change and it will need to take account of market failures and problems in information, transaction costs, and so on. In any case, the abundance and cheapness of coal in countries such as China suggest that technological solutions, including especially developing means of capturing the CO_2 that is emitted in producing electricity, will also be needed. Indeed, support for such technology is absolutely crucial to climate change policy.

---

[29] Department of Energy and Climate Change, 2009a.
[30] Stern, 2008, 23.

In non-energy-intensive sectors, pricing through the tax system is unlikely to be enough to drive action. There are multiple barriers to households and non-energy-intensive businesses responding to increased energy prices, including lack of information and 'hassle costs' associated with improving energy efficiency—for example, through installing insulation. The costs of any kind of trading schemes for such large numbers of small emitters will be excessive.[31] Pricing will also be difficult to implement in some sectors, such as agriculture, where there are multiple sources of emissions and where very particular behaviour patterns matter a lot—for example, in determining the quantity of nitrous oxide emissions, it matters not only how much fertilizer is applied but also when it is applied. Regulation is probably the right *economic* instrument in many of these instances.

Governments use numerous non-price policies. In the UK, these include support for technology (particularly demonstration carbon capture projects), obligations on energy suppliers to improve the energy efficiency of many of the households to which they deliver, obligations on use of biofuels in petrol, increasingly stringent building regulations, and direct support for renewable sources of electricity generation. There are also various minor tax policies in these domains, with a range of tax breaks and subsidies for energy efficiency investments and, for example, stamp duty exemptions on zero-carbon homes.

It is not for us, here, to judge the right combination of non-tax policies, but two points are important. First, the range of policies needs to be coherent and related to the specific market failures in each case. The case for using policies other than a consistent price signal always needs to be made. Second, and more important, it is crucial that other policies do not get in the way of pricing. At EU level, there are real dangers of this happening. Not only do we have the ETS, but we also have a 20% emissions reduction target, a 20% renewables target for energy supply, and a 20% energy efficiency target, all for 2020. This gives the wonderful '20-20-20 by 2020' slogan. (There is also a 10% target for biofuels by 2020.) Unfortunately, while this might make a lovely slogan, it does not make for great policy. If policy is really designed to meet these targets, there is every chance that the ETS itself will be undermined by the renewables target and that GHGs will be abated at much

---

[31] See e.g. Department for Environment, Food and Rural Affairs (2008).

higher cost than would have been achieved with the ETS as the main instrument.

11.3. CONCLUSIONS

We are a very long way from having a coherent approach to the pricing of greenhouse gases in the UK, as in most countries. Many emissions are not priced at all—those from domestic gas use being the most obvious, but also those from agriculture. Indeed, the reduced rate of VAT on gas and electricity consumption implies a significant subsidy. There is a wide range of effective prices on other emissions. And we ignore completely emissions 'embedded' in imports. On the other hand, there is a trading system up and running at the European level, which is moving to embrace more sectors and to include more auctioning of allowances. It is likely that an ETS extended to other sectors, with allowances auctioned and with caps set more effectively, will be crucial to achieving an effective and consistent treatment of emissions in an international context. Wider international agreements on pricing and emissions trading are also needed.

As we have stressed throughout, consistent pricing is necessary but not sufficient for dealing with climate change. The list of other policies in place in the UK is a long and complex one. An inchoate mass of regulation and subsidy has been built up bit by bit, budget by budget, ministerial announcement by ministerial announcement. This is partly a political failure, but it also reflects failures in the markets for research and technology development and in the provision of information to consumers, as well as concerns about the effects of pricing on incomes of the poor and on competitiveness.

But only by getting pricing right can we have any confidence that we will make the right choices over which sectors can and should bear particular shares of the carbon reductions that policymakers deem necessary to deal with climate change. That matters because other routes lead to much higher-cost carbon reductions and potential loss of political support. There can be few other places where getting the economics right matters as much.

Specifically with regard to taxes and pricing carbon, we would start by introducing VAT at the full rate on domestic energy consumption alongside, or preceded by, significant investment in energy efficiency and an appropriate compensation package. The EU ETS needs to be improved, bringing domestic gas supply within it if possible. If that does not prove feasible, then an additional tax equal to the expected ETS price should be levied on gas consumption. Full auctioning of ETS allowances needs to be introduced as soon as possible. An important part of the strategy must be to bring much more stability to the ETS price, if necessary by imposing a price floor. A much simpler single pricing system for emissions not covered by the ETS is also required.

Between them, these policies should both bring some more rationality to the pricing of carbon and raise substantial sums of money. The Committee on Climate Change has estimated that auctioning of allowances in the EU ETS could raise up to £8 billion a year in the UK by 2020.[32] The amount raised depends on the carbon price (assumed to be £40 a tonne of CO_2 for the purposes of this calculation) and the proportion of allowances auctioned. Less than 100% auctioning and a lower carbon price could reduce these revenues substantially—to £3 billion with a price of £21 a tonne of CO_2 and some exempt sectors. In the short run, before 2013, sums of well below £1 billion annually will be available. Policy should clearly aim at the top end of this range. Our calculations suggest that charging tax on direct consumption of gas at £40 a tonne of CO_2 could raise around another £3 billion.

In addition, imposing VAT at its full rate on domestic fuel should raise around £5 billion (with a 20% VAT rate)[33] before the cost of any compensation package for poorer households.

---

[32] Committee on Climate Change, 2008, box 11.3.

[33] Source: Authors' calculations using HMRC statistics, table 1.5 (http://www.hmrc.gov.uk/ stats/tax_expenditures/table1-5.pdf), adjusting the 2010–11 estimate to reflect the fact that the VAT rate was 17.5% for part of that fiscal year and 20% for the rest.

12

Taxes on Motoring

By far the most significant 'environmental' taxes in the UK (and virtually all other countries) in terms of revenue raised are on motoring—in particular, taxes on petrol and diesel, but also taxes on car ownership. UK fuel duties were expected to raise £27 billion and vehicle excise duty to raise a further £6 billion in 2010–11—about 6% of all tax revenues.[1]

Road transport is responsible for many environmental and other spillovers, the most costly of which is congestion. Others include accidents (the annual death toll on the roads is about 2,600 in the UK[2] and well over 30,000 in the US[3]), local air pollution (carbon monoxide, nitrogen oxide, and particulates), noise pollution, harm to the landscape and biodiversity, and greenhouse gas emissions (cars are responsible for 13% of the UK's carbon dioxide (CO_2) emissions, with other forms of road transport responsible for a further 9%[4]).

That said, none of the existing taxes on motoring was introduced for environmental purposes. The first taxes on road fuel in the UK were raised in 1909 and the Road Fund Licence (the precursor of the current vehicle excise duty) was first introduced in 1921 as a charge hypothecated to the maintenance and construction of roads. But taxes on motoring should now

---

[1] HM Treasury, 2010b, table C11.

[2] 2008 figure from http://www.roadsafetycouncil.com/stats.htm and http://webarchive. nationalarchives.gov.uk/+/http://www.dft.gov.uk/pgr/statistics/datatablespublications/accident s/casualtiesmr/rcgbmainresults2008/.

[3] National Highway Traffic Safety Administration, http://www-nrd.nhtsa.dot.gov/Pubs/ 811291.PDF.

[4] Quoted by King (2007).

be considered in light of their effectiveness in addressing the various spillovers created by driving. From this perspective, we look at the issues around the design of motoring taxes, and in particular at congestion charging and 'second-best' options in the absence of such charging.

12.1. DESIGNING TAXES ON MOTORING

Two problems make the optimal design of taxes on motoring especially difficult. First, driving causes multiple spillovers, and different instruments are likely to be appropriate for the different problems. Second, for a number of the externalities that driving causes, there is no simple link between either the amount of fuel consumed or the distance driven and the cost imposed on society. Greenhouse gas emissions are approximately proportional to the quantity of fuel consumed and so a tax on petrol and diesel should capture this effect directly. Congestion costs, on the other hand, depend on when and where driving takes place. The cost of adding to local air pollution varies both by location and by the particular features of the vehicle. The relationship between accidents and amount of driving is unclear.

Table 12.1 reports some (now rather dated) estimates of the spillover costs of driving an extra kilometre. It illustrates three points. First, there are several different costs. Second, there is considerable uncertainty over the

Table 12.1. Estimated marginal external costs of driving (pence per vehicle-kilometre, 1998)

Externality	Low estimate	High estimate
Operating costs	0.42	0.54
Accidents	0.82	1.40
Air pollution	0.34	1.70
Noise	0.02	0.05
Climate change	0.15	0.62
Congestion	9.71	11.16

Source: Sansom et al., 2001.

costs, as illustrated by the differences between the high and low estimates. Third, congestion costs are, by some distance, the most important. (Note that the climate change costs were calculated before recent upward revisions to estimates of climate sensitivity, but more up-to-date figures would still show that congestion is a far more costly spillover.)

As always, it is important to consider tax instruments in the wider context of available policy instruments. In the EU, Japan, and the US, vehicle emissions levels are also targeted by a range of regulations and voluntary agreements with manufacturers. These may be relatively effective ways of meeting environmental objectives, especially where consumers are less than fully informed over (or do not take full account of) the long-term costs of their buying decisions. Indeed, the evidence that is available does suggest that such regulation has an important place alongside the tax system and that costs of the regulation are often much more modest than expected.[5]

One interesting example of regulation was the requirement to fit catalytic converters to new cars.[6] This led to a reduction in particulate emissions, forced all new cars to move to unleaded fuel, and encouraged the adoption of fuel injection and electronic engine management—both technological advances that further reduced emissions. Simultaneously, a tax incentive encouraged owners of existing cars to move from leaded to unleaded petrol. Regulating to make all cars run on unleaded petrol would have resulted in a significant amount of uneconomically early scrapping of cars that could not readily be altered to run on unleaded petrol. Introducing a tax differential in favour of unleaded petrol, by contrast, provided incentives to alter engines or buy new cars capable of running on unleaded petrol, without forcing swift and costly scrapping of all old cars. In that sense, it was a good example of a well-designed environmental tax change introduced alongside regulation.

The UK now has only two significant taxes on motoring (plus the company car tax regime discussed in Section 12.3.2). Fuel duty raises the cost of driving an extra mile or of buying a less fuel-efficient car. Vehicle excise duty (VED) is levied annually and varies according to the CO_2 emissions— and hence fuel efficiency—of the vehicle. This variation can be seen as an incentive to encourage the purchase of more efficient cars and the early scrapping of less efficient ones. Fuel duty and VED between them may be

---

[5] Harrington, Morgenstern, and Nelson, 1999; King, 2008.
[6] From 1993 in the EU.

effective in influencing emissions, but they are not at all well targeted on congestion, local air pollution, noise, or accidents. Cars that use very little petrol or diesel create just as much congestion as gas guzzlers. Congestion would be equally problematic even if entirely new forms of car that produced no pollution on the road—electric, for example—replaced the existing stock. Electric cars incur no fuel duty and are not subject to VED, so the current tax system provides no discouragement to driving them even though they still add to congestion, which is the biggest spillover cost of driving.

Considering the different spillovers suggests that we, in principle at least, might want:

- a tax on fuel varying with the output of all harmful emissions;
- a congestion charge varying with the time and place of driving;
- a noise charge varying according to time and place of driving;

plus perhaps:

- an *ad valorem* tax on the accident-related element of insurance premiums.

We do not focus on all these issues, but rather on the biggest—the case for a congestion charge.

12.2. CONGESTION CHARGING

Taxing just fuel consumption and car ownership, no matter how the taxes are differentiated by emissions and engine size, cannot result in anything approaching an optimal tax because neither is a good proxy for the impact of car use on congestion. Many journeys occur on relatively empty roads. These journeys are overtaxed because the congestion costs imposed on other road users are minimal. In that sense, rural road users are overtaxed relative to those who regularly drive in towns during busy periods. The result is too much driving in towns relative to the amount of driving in less congested areas.

The economic costs of congestion are very large. Estimates generated for the UK government suggested that annual welfare benefits of up to £28 billion (or about 1% of national income) may be available by 2025 if a road pricing scheme could be implemented that could vary charges by place and time of day to accurately reflect actual congestion levels and costs.[7] These numbers assume a very sophisticated system, and are themselves subject to considerable uncertainty, but they do indicate that the scale of possible gains is very substantial.

Another reason to favour congestion charging (and one that might persuade a government to risk the attendant unpopularity) is that, over time, fuel duty will do a less and less good job of capturing the externalities associated with driving. At current rates, it will also raise less revenue as time goes by. The Committee on Climate Change (2008) has estimated that additional action to improve vehicle fuel efficiency could reduce revenues from fuel duty by £2.5 billion annually by 2020, on top of reductions to be expected anyway as cars become more efficient. The Committee envisages a future after that in which technology drives petrol and diesel cars off the roads almost entirely. In that world, no tax will be levied on driving, yet the main externality—congestion—will remain, and indeed is likely to grow. In addition, governments are unlikely to view the loss of £27 billion of fuel duty revenues with equanimity. Developing other forms of charging, preferably congestion charging, is a matter not just of economic efficiency. It is also likely to be viewed as a matter of fiscal necessity.

Of course, this makes the economic efficiency case for congestion charging even stronger. If we cannot tax car use effectively through a tax on fuel—and do not replace that tax—then, in the absence of a congestion charge, we would offset, through pricing, few if any of the negative spillovers created by driving.

Introducing national road pricing would be a huge and complex undertaking. It would involve significant political risks. But the scale of gains available is enough to persuade us that further steps towards road pricing must be a priority.[8] With the congestion costs of driving an extra mile varying dramatically according to when and where people travel, the current

---

[7] Estimated benefits are in 2002 prices. The scheme modelled allowed 75 different levels of charges, capped at 80p/km, varying by time of day, area, and road type. Of the £28 billion in welfare benefit, about £15 billion was estimated to show up in higher national income. Source: Department for Transport, 2006.

[8] As it has persuaded many others, including Sir Rod Eddington in his review for government of priorities for transport (Eddington, 2006).

range of taxes is nowhere close to being able to reflect the costs that different motorists impose on others. Moving to a system of charges would also open up the possibility of changing quite radically how the highway network is owned and financed. Proposals to switch to a system of user charges for a road system owned, regulated, and charged for in much the way we currently charge for other utilities deserve to be taken seriously.[9]

Experience of road pricing of one kind or another is quite widespread internationally, from long-established tolls on motorways in much of Europe, to time- and place-varying charges in Singapore and radical proposals for the Netherlands. Up to now in the UK, we have only one significant experience of road pricing in an urban area—the London Congestion Charge. This is a very crude scheme involving a single payment triggered when a vehicle enters the central zone between 07:00 and 18:00 hours, Monday to Friday. Beyond this, it does not vary according to where, when, and how far people drive. Even this has been described as 'a triumph of economics. It represents a high-profile public and political recognition of congestion as a distorting externality and of road pricing as an appropriate policy response'.[10] The same author suggests that traffic delays within the zone decreased and journey time reliability improved.

This and international experience suggest that, short of a full national scheme, significant benefits could come from making the London scheme more responsive to traffic conditions, introducing schemes in other congested cities, and introducing charges on some main trunk routes.[11]

Politicians are likely to be wary of such reforms. In December 2008, the people of Manchester rejected congestion charging by a remarkable four-to-one majority despite the promise of a big increase in public transport investment alongside the scheme. Inevitably, potential losers from such a scheme will resist its introduction, and there seem to be widespread concerns, and misperceptions, about the levels of taxes on motoring, the distributional consequences of change, and the impact on privacy.

The facts that fuel duty is not targeted at congestion and that it is excessive relative to the emissions of vehicles imply that it should be reduced if a

---

[9] See e.g. Newbery and Santos (1999) and Newbery (2005).

[10] Leape, 2006, 158.

[11] The example of the M6 Toll—building a toll road parallel to an existing road— is unlikely to be widely copied due to lack of space.

coherent congestion charge policy is introduced. Linking reductions in fuel duty to the introduction of congestion charging would also increase the chances of gaining political acceptance. One problem with a piecemeal, city-by-city approach is that the appropriate policy would be to accompany the introduction of charging with local offsetting reductions in fuel duty. But fuel duty almost certainly has to remain uniform across the country—reducing it only where congestion charging was introduced would encourage drivers to drive to that area specifically to fill up.

However it is done, we do not underestimate the political difficulties of introducing road pricing nationally. But in addition to the long-standing case for such a move, we need urgently to wake up to the fact that, if the UK and other countries are to meet their targets for reductions in greenhouse gas emissions, petrol and diesel use by motor vehicles is likely to have to fall and eventually end as alternative technologies are introduced. This will leave the UK with no tax at all on the very high congestion externalities created by motorists. So, if we all end up driving electric cars, it seems that we shall have no choice but to charge for road use. It will be much easier to introduce such charges while there is a quid pro quo to offer in terms of reduced fuel taxes.

12.3. SECOND-BEST OPTIONS

Congestion charging will not be with us on a substantial scale for some years, even if government and voters have the courage to commit to it now. In the meantime, we face more immediate choices over the level and structure of taxes on motoring. Are current tax levels too high, too low, or about right? How should taxes vary across different fuels? And can other taxes play a role?

12.3.1. The Level of Taxes

Determining the correct level of taxes is not straightforward, in part because the taxes are such poor proxies for the damages being caused. The

Table 12.2. Marginal external costs and taxes paid by road users (pence per kilometre)

	Marginal external cost of congestion	Environment and safety costs	Fuel duty and VAT on duty	Uncovered externality
2000	7.3	2.2	5.2	4.3
2010	12.3	1.6	3.9	10.1

Source: Department for Transport, 2004, figure B1.

appropriate tax on the fuel consumed by someone driving mostly in central London would be many times that for someone driving mostly in rural Yorkshire. However, if we take either the figures quoted in Table 12.1 from the study by Sansom et al. or the figures shown in Table 12.2 that underlie the government's feasibility study of road pricing, current levels of fuel duty are somewhat below their optimal level on average.[12] The last column in Table 12.2, the uncovered externality, shows government estimates of the gap between the optimal tax per kilometre and the actual tax charged. Note in particular how much this rises over time both as traffic increases, and therefore the congestion level rises, and as cars become more fuel efficient so that fuel duty falls *per kilometre driven*. This gap grows the further into the future we look. For example, analysis for the Eddington Review, again from within UK government, suggested that total vehicle-kilometres travelled might rise by 31% and congestion by 30% between 2003 and 2025, while fuel costs could fall by 26% as a result of improved vehicle efficiency.[13]

One response to this analysis is to conclude that, *in the absence of a major shift to congestion charging*, there is a case for increasing fuel duties in the UK (despite the fact that fuel taxes in the UK are high by international standards). The case becomes stronger year by year as increasing fuel efficiency reduces the effective tax on driving and more driving creates higher congestion costs. (The fact that emissions of harmful particulates

[12] In contrast, Parry and Small (2005) find that UK fuel taxes are excessive. One factor explaining this difference in result is that Parry and Small use a central estimate of 2.9p/km for the marginal external cost of congestion. This is much smaller than the figures reported in Table 12.2.

[13] Department for Transport, 2006, table 2.1 and page 24. Congestion is measured as seconds lost per vehicle-kilometre relative to the free-flow speed.

(PM_{10}) and nitrogen oxides are expected to continue falling[14] is not enough to outweigh these effects.) The case against, of course, is that the congestion component of the tax on fuel would also fall on users of non-congested roads. This would penalize them needlessly and unfairly. Fuel duty is a very blunt instrument—which returns us to the long-term case for congestion charging.

These observations are made against the background of taxes (and some other costs of motoring) having fallen in recent years after very sharp increases over the 1990s. This is illustrated in Figure 12.1. The pattern is illustrative of some of the difficulties associated with continuing to increase duties ahead of inflation. The turnaround in real duty levels from 2000 followed nationwide protests at fuel prices and duty levels. The impact of these protests on policymaking is clearly visible for several years afterwards.

Estimates suggest that a 10% rise in the petrol price cuts the amount of petrol consumed by 2.5% in the short term and by 6% in the long term, once

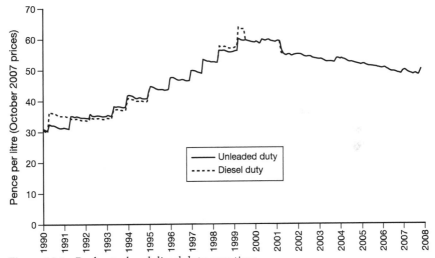

Figure 12.1. Real petrol and diesel duty over time

Notes and source: Calculated from Department for Business, Innovation, and Skills (BIS; formerly the Department for Business, Enterprise, and Regulatory Reform, BERR) data; duty rates are deflated to October 2007 prices using the all-items retail price index. This graph updates figure 5.5 of Leicester (2006).

[14] By 53% and 60% respectively between 2003 and 2025, according to Department for Transport (2006, table 2.1).

people have the chance to switch to smaller or more fuel-efficient cars.[15] This suggests that if fuel duties had remained at their 1999 peak in real terms, petrol consumption might now be around 10% lower than current levels. Encouraging the purchase of smaller or more efficient cars also means that the impact on petrol consumption in the long term is bigger than the impact on miles driven, underlining the fact that fuel duties are more effective at reducing CO_2 emissions than reducing driving or congestion.

The fact that fuel duties are very imperfectly targeted at the externalities created by driving is one objection to the conclusion that fuel duties should be raised. But what of the fact that pre-tax fuel prices have risen substantially over the last decade? Estimates suggest that a 10% rise in prices leads to about a 1% reduction in vehicle-miles travelled in the short term.[16] If higher fuel prices reduce traffic levels, then the optimal fuel duty level will fall as price rises (though not by much). This suggests that there is some economic case for varying fuel duty with the fuel price. The same logic suggests that fuel duties should increase over time since the amount of driving, and therefore the amount of congestion, rises with income.

Another consideration, as with other environmental taxes, is that increasing fuel duty may result in undesirable distributional consequences. On average, these might not be too severe. In the UK at least, car ownership is strongly related to the level of household expenditure. Over 90% of the highest tenth of households ranked by expenditure are car owners; indeed, half of them own more than one car. By comparison, fewer than 30% of the lowest tenth of households by expenditure own a car, and very few (less than 5%) in this group own more than one car.[17] However, we need to be careful before drawing conclusions from these figures. The poorest households also tend to own the oldest cars. These cars are less efficient and more polluting than comparable new cars. This makes the tax charge per mile driven higher and these cars attract the highest rates of VED. Furthermore, the recent introduction of increased differentiation of VED has reduced the market value of many of the old cars owned by poorer households. For some, this has represented a significant reduction in wealth—an unintended consequence of well-intentioned legislation.

[15] Hanly, Dargay, and Goodwin, 2002.
[16] Hanly, Dargay, and Goodwin, 2002.
[17] Fullerton, Leicester, and Smith, 2010.

We have so far ignored the fact that there are different fuels that motor vehicles use—primarily unleaded petrol and diesel, but also biofuels. Many countries charge a lower rate of tax on diesel than on unleaded petrol. The UK is unusual in not following this practice.[18] There are also significantly lower tax rates on biofuels, although so far these have had very limited market penetration.

Carbon emissions from a litre of diesel are less than those from a litre of petrol, which might suggest a lower tax on diesel. On the other hand, the local health impacts of diesel are larger because of higher particulate emissions. Newbery (2005) estimates that, taking account of these two offsetting effects, there is a case for a tax on diesel about 4p a litre higher than that on petrol. More recent higher estimates of the social cost of carbon might narrow that differential, but there seems at first sight no environmental case for having a lower tax on diesel.

In practice, it may be the fact that diesel is the main fuel used by commercial vehicles which leads many countries to charge lower taxes on it. Commercial vehicles are frequently driven across national borders, which gives a choice of where to buy fuel. In the UK, Northern Ireland provides a relevant case study. HM Revenue and Customs (2010d) estimates that between 25% and 32% of diesel used had non-UK duty paid, i.e. it was bought across the border in the Irish Republic, with revenue losses of between £140 million and £180 million in 2008–09. This cross-border shopping for fuel constrains the extent to which UK policy can deviate from that of our neighbours. The greater opportunities that exist in countries with longer land borders may explain the relatively lower taxes on diesel in those countries.

The environmental case for a lower tax on biofuels is unresolved. There has been recent controversy over whether biofuels do indeed provide environmental benefits, or whether they can be positively harmful. Until this question is resolved, there is a potential danger involved in creating an

---

[18] Even without fiscal incentives, diesel's share in the UK fuel market rose from 38% of fuel sales in 1997 to 53% in 2008 as improved engine technology made diesel cars more appealing (figures derived from figures 3.3 and 3.4 at http://www.ukpia.com/files/pdf/ukpia-statistical-review-2010.pdf).

incentive through a lower tax without a full understanding of the likely effect.[19]

12.3.2. Taxes on Car Ownership

It is the use of vehicles which creates externalities. But most countries impose taxes not just on petrol but on the ownership of motor vehicles. In the UK, vehicle excise duty is such a tax, levied annually and varied according to CO_2 emissions, with higher rates of duty on the more polluting cars.

The case for an annual tax such as this is perhaps unclear. A tax on car *purchase*, differentiated by car size or level of CO_2 emissions, might have an effect additional to annual vehicle excise duty by virtue of its visibility and timing. There is evidence[20] that consumers give much more weight to the purchase cost of a vehicle than to future fuel and other costs. If this is the case, it justifies the introduction from 2010 of high first-year VED rates for more polluting cars in the UK. It certainly explains the introduction of legislation in France which, from January 2008, sees those purchasing cars with the lowest emissions receiving *rebates* of up to €1,000, while those buying the highest-emitting vehicles pay a purchase tax of up to €2,000.

From an environmental perspective, VED is poorly targeted and does not raise the marginal cost of driving (and hence causing negative spillovers). It is an observable fact that the proportions of new cars in the different VED bands have changed. In 1997, 45% were in the top two, most polluting bands. This had fallen to 10% by 2009. The proportion in the top three bands fell from 77% to 21%. Average new car emissions fell over the period from 190 grams of CO_2 per kilometre to 149.5g/km.[21] But there is no evidence of the role played by differential VED rates in this, as opposed to the role played by higher petrol taxes and prices and exogenous increases in car engine efficiency.

One last part of the tax system which may also have played a role in changing fuel efficiency is that which applies to the taxation of company

---

[19] See Gallagher (2008) for a comprehensive review.
[20] Quoted by King (2007 and 2008).
[21] Society of Motor Manufacturers and Traders, 2010.

cars.[22] In 2006 in the UK, purchases of new cars for private use accounted for only 44% of sales. Sales for fleets and business use accounted for the remaining 56%.[23] The tax rules applied to company cars matter in determining the composition of the car fleet, and those rules have changed over time to impose higher taxes on cars with higher CO_2 emissions—though with higher taxes on diesel cars than on petrol ones, reflecting their effects on the local environment. Again, we know of no robust evaluation of the impact of these rules.

12.4. CONCLUSIONS

Driving imposes a range of spillover costs on other road users, local residents, and the local and global environment. Getting the structure and level of taxes correct requires understanding and estimating each component of these costs, and designing taxes and charges that are equal to the costs. By some distance, the biggest spillover cost created by driving, especially in a crowded country such as the UK, is on other road users through congestion—and hence wasted time.

Taxes on fuel use and car ownership are not well designed to target congestion costs, which vary by the time and location of journeys. Nevertheless, most countries rely almost exclusively on such taxes. If we continue to rely on them, they will need to rise, and at an annual rate well above inflation. The amount and costs of congestion are rising and the fuel efficiency of cars is also rising. In addition, we in all likelihood start with fuel taxes below the optimum.

Much better would be to make real progress towards congestion charging. This is complex and potentially expensive, but has huge potential welfare benefits. In any case, the current system of motoring taxes will simply become unsustainable in the medium term. Fuel consumption per mile

---

[22] HM Revenue and Customs describes a company car as follows: 'There is a tax charge where, because of their employment, a car is made available to and is available for private use by a director or an employee earning £8,500 a year or more, or to a member of their family or household'.

[23] Source: Society of Motor Manufacturers and Traders data service.

driven is falling and will continue to do so, possibly at an accelerating rate, eventually falling close to zero as new technologies replace petrol and diesel engines. A tax system based on fuel consumption will lose the ability to capture any of the remaining spillover costs created by driving. Of all the challenges raised in this volume, this seems to us one that is simply inescapable. It may be another ten years before change becomes urgent, but urgent it will become and the sooner serious advances are made to move the basis of charging to one based on congestion the better.

13

The Taxation of Household Savings

The taxation of savings plays a central role in how economists evaluate a tax system. There are five reasons for this.

First, the way in which savings are taxed is a key characteristic of the *tax base*. If the tax base is defined as including income from savings as well as labour earnings, and all components of the tax base are taxed equally, this yields the so-called 'comprehensive income tax'. Alternatively, if earnings that are saved, and the returns to savings, are not taxed until such time as they are used for consumption, then the resulting tax system will be an 'expenditure tax' or a 'consumption tax'. The difference in the tax treatment of savings is the critical difference between these two tax bases.

Second, the tax treatment of savings is an important determinant of the extent to which the tax system recognizes interpersonal differences in *lifetime income*, as opposed to annual income. Careful design of the tax treatment of savings is one way of trying to equalize the tax burden on taxpayers with similar lifetime incomes but different income patterns over their life courses.

Third, taxation of savings stands right on the boundary between taxation of personal income and taxation of company profits. How we tax savings can influence the behaviour of small firms and the self-employed, as well as the allocation of capital to large firms.

Fourth, savings taxation can affect both the total amount of savings in the economy and, probably more importantly, how those savings are allocated across different assets. This can directly affect the amount of capital invested and how efficiently it is invested.

Finally, for individuals, the taxation of savings affects their decisions on how much to save, when to save, and how much risk to take when allocating their savings between assets. It therefore directly affects their welfare and particularly their welfare in periods of retirement or unemployment, when they may need to rely on accumulated savings.

This chapter examines the economic arguments for different possible systems of savings taxation. In the next chapter, we focus on some specific directions for reform in the UK context.

We start our discussion with some evidence on people's actual saving behaviour. This is important in understanding what we might want to achieve through taxation. We go on to look at the case for exempting tax on the normal return to savings. The case for exempting the normal return to savings from taxation is likely to depend on, among other factors, the reasons that people save in the first place. Many do so in order to consume at one period of their lifetime rather than another. By sacrificing consumption today, saving is a way of generating future income and, like other forms of investment, there is a case for exempting the normal return. The taxation of the normal return to savings distorts the timing of lifetime consumption and labour supply. A timing-neutral tax system would not create such distortions, and there are a number of tax systems that achieve such neutrality.

A consumption tax does not create distortions in the timing of consumption, while a comprehensive income tax does. This is because the latter reduces the after-tax rate of return relative to the pre-tax return, and because the rate of return the consumer receives determines the effective price of future versus current consumption. Since one of our objectives is to avoid distorting intertemporal choices, at least for a large fraction of the population, we explore three possible routes to savings taxation that maintain neutrality over when consumption occurs. We explain these and contrast them with some of the difficulties inherent in a comprehensive income tax and with the additional distortions—for example, over whether returns to savings are taken as income or capital gains—that are almost inevitably introduced by such a tax.

In spite of a vast body of research on the appropriate taxation of savings, we recognize at the outset that economic theory does not provide an unequivocal recommendation on the issue of optimal tax design. We therefore rely in part on broadly-attractive concepts, such as tax neutrality, in framing our analysis. We view neutrality as a constructive benchmark in understanding the issues surrounding the design of savings taxation. There is potentially a rich array of ways in which individuals differ with regard to saving behaviour based on underlying preferences and opportunities. In the absence of such detailed knowledge, it seems sensible to begin from this benchmark and look for justifications for deviating from it.

The different routes to neutral taxation involve collecting taxes at different times. In simple terms, one route involves collecting tax up front and not taxing the later return to savings. Another route involves not levying tax on any income that is saved, but then taxing withdrawals (rather as pensions are taxed in the UK today). A third route is to exempt a 'normal' return to savings but to tax 'excess' ('supernormal') returns. These obviously have different cash-flow consequences for governments.

An important further difference between these systems from the point of view of individuals arises when income taxes are progressive or, in general, when individuals expect to face different marginal tax rates at different times of their life. Then the different systems will have different effects on people's incentives to save according to the pattern of their income and consumption over time. One possibility we examine is to allow people to choose between the different systems and thereby to smooth their taxable income between periods. In some circumstances, that can move us towards the ideal of taxing lifetime income.

When considering the taxation of savings, it is also important to consider the taxation of borrowing (negative savings) and the taxation of 'human capital'. If financial investments and investments in the future through education are treated differently, then choices may be distorted across this margin.

Having discussed tax structures that achieve tax neutrality, we conclude this chapter by examining the economic case for tax neutrality. We note that there are a number of potential justifications for deviating from the timing-neutral tax benchmark, and observe that the optimal taxation of capital income is a very active area of ongoing research.[1] A number of recent studies suggest that the economic case for taxing the normal return may be more

---

[1] See Banks and Diamond (2010) for a review.

ambiguous than many analysts have suggested, and, as a result, our
conclusions on this issue cannot be completely clear-cut. We do retain
neutrality as a useful benchmark and suggest that there are many practical
reasons for assigning a presumption to a neutral system.

In the next chapter, we go on to apply some of these insights to the current
UK policy context, with some recommendations for changes to the tax
regime as it applies to particular asset classes. In both these chapters, we
focus only on life-cycle savings—that is, savings that are accumulated in one
part of an individual's life in order to increase consumption at a later date.
The analysis does not necessarily follow through to situations in which
savings derive from, or are used to provide, gifts and inheritances. Motives
for bequests and the extent to which individuals save in pursuit of dynastic
wealth are poorly understood. We look at the taxation of wealth transfers
separately in Chapter 15.

13.1. SAVING BEHAVIOUR

It is worth starting by looking at some general evidence on people's actual
saving behaviour. If we were to find that people neither make any attempt to
smooth their consumption over their lifetime, nor change their behaviour in
the face of different taxation of different assets, we might conclude that how
savings are taxed matters little. What we show here is that, in fact, people
generally do both these things—suggesting that taxation does matter. There
is also a very extensive formal literature that confirms the impressionistic
evidence presented here.[2]

13.1.1. Saving over the Life Cycle

In broad terms, people tend to save less when their incomes are low and their
needs are high—for example, when they have children and take paternity or
maternity leave—and save more when incomes are high and needs are low—
the period between children leaving home and retirement, for example. On

---

[2] See Poterba (2002), Attanasio and Wakefield (2010), and Attanasio and Weber (2010).

the whole, many people do a fair job of maintaining stable consumption levels during their working life and in retirement. Of course, this is not true for all. Government policy in general, and tax policy in particular, cannot rely on individuals always making optimal saving decisions. One consequence is that a balance has to be struck between avoiding distortions to saving behaviour and providing a safety net for those who do not prepare well for the future.

Individuals save (or repay debts) or dissave (either borrowing or running down their existing wealth) when the amount they choose to consume differs from the amount of income they receive in a particular time period. As Figure 13.1 shows, people's incomes tend to rise and then fall on average over the course of their lives. Although this pattern also holds for consumption (here measured by expenditure on non-durables and services), there is much less variation. Consumption of non-durables and services is flatter than income over the life cycle.

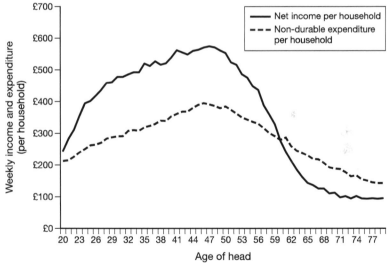

Figure 13.1. Net income and net expenditure per household

Notes: Average weekly net income is after-tax-and-National-Insurance take-home pay plus benefits and other unearned income. Average weekly expenditure on non-durables and services.

Source: Authors' calculations using the IFS tax and benefit microsimulation model, TAXBEN, run on uprated data from the UK Family Expenditure Survey / Expenditure and Food Survey, 1974–2008.

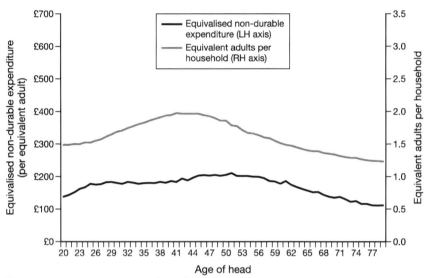

Figure 13.2. Consumption and needs

Notes: Average weekly expenditure on non-durables and services. Number of equivalent adults is computed using the modified OECD scale.

Source: Authors' calculations using the IFS tax and benefit microsimulation model, TAXBEN, run on uprated data from the UK Family Expenditure Survey / Expenditure and Food Survey, 1974–2008.

Of course, a family will not aim to smooth consumption exactly; it will wish to vary consumption with family size. Figure 13.2 shows how the number of 'equivalent adults' in a typical household varies over the life cycle. This is a measure of household size that takes into account the fact that a child is less costly to support than an adult.[3] The figure also shows how expenditure per equivalent adult varies much less than family size and is reasonably constant across families with heads of different ages. This is direct evidence of the way that consumption is smoothed to adapt to needs over time.

The net effect is that there is usually a desire to borrow, then to save, and then to draw down savings as the stages of the life cycle progress. Figures 13.1 and 13.2 suggest that people on average do a reasonably good job of

[3] An equivalence scale assigns weights to households of different compositions, intended to reflect the different resources they require to reach the same standard of living. We use the modified OECD scale in which the first adult in a household has a weight of 1 and the second and subsequent adults each have a weight of 0.5. Children aged 14 and over also have a weight of 0.5, and children 13 and younger have a weight of 0.3.

'consumption-smoothing', once we adjust for changes in needs as family size changes. But, of course, people's behaviour is not quite as straightforward as this account suggests.

The standard economic model assumes that consumers make sophisticated decisions based on well-founded expectations and beliefs about future economic events. In reality, even if people think hard about the long-term decisions they face, they are likely to take decisions on the basis of only limited information.

Some individuals and families will find consumption-smoothing hard to achieve, especially if they have limited access to credit (which is more often the case for younger and poorer households than for older and richer ones). Others may be myopic, so they save too little for the future and have to either consume less in retirement or delay retirement. More specifically, people's decision-making may be driven less by long-term thinking and more by the desire for immediate gratification than the traditional model assumes.[4]

It is, perhaps, not surprising that apparently myopic behaviour occurs most often among individuals and families with relatively poor educational qualifications and low wealth. Recent experimental studies suggest that individuals with higher ability (and earning potential) tend to be more patient and better able to make complex decisions.[5] Intellectual ability and numeracy are both associated with higher likelihoods of holding stocks and of having a private pension, and not just because able and numerate people tend to have more financial wealth in total.[6]

There is particular policy concern over the extent to which people save enough to support themselves, and maintain their standard of living, in retirement. There is, in fact, a well-documented fall in consumption at the time of retirement.[7] While two-thirds of this drop can be explained within the context of a life-cycle consumption plan (for example, a fall in work-related expenditures, or less spending on expensive prepared foods as people have more time to cook), the remaining third does appear to indicate that some people do not save enough for retirement. Concerns about

---

[4] See Ainslie (1975) and Thaler and Shefrin (1981).

[5] See e.g. Parker and Fischhoff (2005), Kirby, Winston, and Santiesteban (2005), and Bettinger and Slonim (2006).

[6] Banks and Oldfield, 2006.

[7] Banks, Blundell, and Tanner, 1998.

undersaving for retirement have led the UK government to propose to 'nudge' people into saving by ensuring that everyone is automatically enrolled into an employer-sponsored pension. They will have to make an active decision not to save, rather than an active decision to save.

In designing the taxation of savings, we need to recognize that patience, self-control, and the ability to take long-term decisions in a sensible way vary from person to person. We cannot rely on all individuals to make considered provision for their long-term needs through their own private decisions.

It is this apparent lack of rationality by some people that can drive government policy on savings, pensions, and social insurance. At one extreme, government can simply tax everyone in work and provide incomes in retirement that are unrelated to tax payments. But linking benefits to contributions can improve the efficiency of a tax system.[8] At the other extreme, where future provision is provided solely through private savings and private insurance contributions, there would no longer be any distortions to the timing of consumption produced by such contributions. However, there are limits to the ability of individuals and families to make life-cycle provisions through voluntary insurance contributions and private savings. The income tax and benefit system will continue to be called upon to provide a floor for living standards.

13.1.2. Allocation of Savings between Assets

We need to distinguish between the issue of how much people choose to save and the variety of assets or financial instruments through which they save. The most recent estimates from the Office for National Statistics (ONS)[9] are that households in the UK held around £9 trillion of wealth in 2006–08, of which 39% was held in private pensions and a similar amount in property, largely owner-occupied housing. Pensions and housing are, of course, two relatively tax-favoured ways of holding wealth.

Evidence from the English Longitudinal Study of Ageing (ELSA) provides more detail on the distribution and composition of savings, specifically for

---

[8] See Bovenberg and Sørensen (2004) and Bovenberg, Hansen, and Sørensen (2008).
[9] Office for National Statistics, 2009.

Table 13.1. Fraction of financial wealth held in different assets in England, 52- to 64-year-olds, 2004

Decile of gross financial wealth	Range of gross financial wealth (£'000s)	Percentage of wealth held in:		
		Private pensions	ISAs, PEPs, and TESSAs	Other assets
Poorest	<1.7	12.6	9.1	78.3
2	1.7–16.6	54.8	13.8	31.5
3	16.6–39.1	65.2	11.0	23.8
4	39.1–75.9	68.2	10.8	21.0
5	75.9–122.3	69.7	7.9	22.3
6	122.3–177.2	74.7	6.8	18.5
7	177.2–245.4	78.1	6.2	15.7
8	245.4–350.3	81.8	4.6	13.6
9	350.3–511.2	79.0	5.7	15.3
Richest	>511.2	68.4	4.4	27.3
All		73.6	5.5	20.9

Notes: Benefit units with at least one member aged 52–64 in the 2004 English Longitudinal Study of Ageing. Private pension wealth comprises current fund value of defined contribution (DC) pensions and the value of accrued entitlements to date of private defined benefit (DB) pensions (based on assumption of no further real earnings growth). Percentages are ratios of means for each decile group, not group means of individual ratios. Numbers do not always sum exactly, due to rounding.

Source: Wakefield, 2009.

individuals aged over 50.[10] Table 13.1 considers the non-housing wealth of individuals in a key part of their lifetime as far as savings are concerned— those aged 52–64. Those with low levels of gross financial wealth hold the largest proportion in 'other assets', mainly interest-bearing accounts, which are subject to taxation as interest is credited and have no tax advantage when savings are deposited. These are the most heavily taxed savings assets, particularly in an inflationary environment.

When the tax system changes, people respond. When tax-privileged accounts such as Individual Savings Accounts (ISAs; and their predecessors TESSAs and PEPs) were introduced, billions of pounds rapidly flowed into them.[11] In the late 1980s, the government introduced a reform that provided

---

[10] Banks, Emmerson, and Tetlow, 2007.

[11] Attanasio and Wakefield (2010) and references therein.

young people with very large incentives to 'contract out' of the State Earnings-Related Pension Scheme (SERPS) into personal pensions. Young people did exactly that, with 40% of those in their 20s moving into personal pensions, along with remarkable numbers of 16- to 19-year-olds. As the incentives were withdrawn, so coverage fell. In the early 2000s, there were also marked responses to changes in tax limits that accompanied the introduction of stakeholder pensions.[12]

The key point is not that everybody at all times responds rationally to tax incentives, but rather that there is compelling evidence that such incentives are major drivers of individual decision-making and of the allocation of resources across the economy. Large and salient changes in the savings tax system change behaviour.

13.2. THE NEUTRALITY PRINCIPLE

As the discussion of actual saving behaviour has illustrated, two distinct concepts of neutrality matter with respect to the taxation of savings. The first is neutrality over the level and timing of saving—if the tax system is neutral in this sense, it does not distort people's choice over when to consume their income. The second is neutrality between different types of savings vehicles or assets—a neutral tax system in this sense does not distort people's choices over the assets in which they save.

A tax system that levies a tax on the 'normal return to savings'—the return that just compensates for delay in consumption (without any additional return related to risk-taking, for example, which we discuss below)—cannot satisfy the first neutrality criterion. It taxes people who choose to consume later in life more heavily than people who choose to consume earlier in life.

Taxing the normal return to savings means taxing consumption tomorrow more heavily than consumption today. In some contexts, having different tax rates on consumption according to when it occurs is conceptually rather like having different tax rates on different forms of consumption. The arguments over the merits of such different tax rates would then be directly

---

[12] Chung et al., 2008.

parallel to the arguments discussed in Chapter 6 over whether to tax some consumption goods more heavily than others.[13]

Recall that, in an ideal world, we would like to tax people according to their lifetime earning capacity—broadly equivalent to their potential consumption. The problem for policymakers is that ability cannot be observed directly, so we use actual earnings or expenditure as an imperfect proxy, which has the unfortunate consequence of discouraging people from earning (or spending) as much as they would otherwise like: we distort their behaviour towards choosing more leisure time instead. Taxing the normal return to savings can only improve on this if it allows us to target high-ability people more accurately or with less distortion to labour supply.

It might appear that taxing savings is an effective way to redistribute—after all, aren't people with large savings wealthy almost by definition? But someone with savings is not necessarily better off over their lifetime than another person without savings. The two might earn and spend similar amounts over their lifetimes, but at different times: one earns his money when young and saves it to spend when he is old, while for the other the timings of earning and spending are close together. We can tax people on their total resources by taxing their money at its source (taxing earnings) or when it is finally used for consumption (taxing expenditure).[14] We can tax better-off people more heavily by making the rate schedule applied to earnings or expenditure more progressive. If—given what we already know from their actual income and expenditure—people's saving decisions tell us nothing more about their underlying earning capacity, just about their taste for consuming tomorrow rather than today, then taxing savings cannot help us to target high-ability people more accurately than taxing earnings or expenditure. By taxing the normal return to savings, we are not taxing the better-off; we are taxing those who spend their money tomorrow rather than today. That seems both unfair and inefficient, unless there is a relationship between when individuals choose to spend their money and other attributes that might be a basis for taxation, such as their underlying earning capacity.

---

[13] See Atkinson and Stiglitz (1976).

[14] If people inherit money rather than earn it, or bequeath it rather than spend it, then (although ultimately the money must have been earned by someone and must be spent by someone) different considerations apply. These are the subject of Chapter 15.

Broadening the tax base to include savings might seem like it allows us to reduce tax rates on earnings and reduce disincentives to work. But work decisions involve trading off consumption against leisure. If someone is working in order to finance *future* consumption, then taxing savings—reducing the future consumption that can be bought with earnings—discourages work just like taxing earnings directly. Why discourage work more among those who prefer to consume the proceeds later?

Arguments about consumption today versus tomorrow only apply to taxation of the normal return to savings—the return that just compensates for delaying consumption. In Section 13.2.2, we will see that there are strong arguments for taxing returns in excess of this. In Section 13.3, we will discuss cases where the logic even for exempting the normal return breaks down—for example, where people's saving decisions do tell us about their earning capacity, or where taxing future consumption does not reduce labour supply in the same way as taxing current consumption—and consider whether such cases justify departing from neutrality in practice. But neutrality over the timing of consumption is, at the very least, a reasonable starting point for tax design.

The second type of neutrality—neutrality between different assets—is lost if different assets (housing, pensions, other financial assets) are taxed differently. One would generally need rather strong reasons for deviating from this form of neutrality—tax policy shouldn't really be influencing whether I decide to save in gilts, shares, or a savings account. One potentially substantial exception is that there may be a case for treating pensions more generously than other forms of savings so as to encourage people who may not plan well for the long term to save for retirement in a form that will provide them with a regular income.

While there are limitations to the standard arguments in support of both neutrality concepts, and particularly the first, understanding what types of tax system will achieve neutrality is a natural benchmark for any reform discussion.

We look now at why a comprehensive income tax cannot achieve either of these types of neutrality, then outline three different approaches to achieving neutrality, before going on to look at complications to this story created by income tax systems with more than one tax rate.

13.2.1. Why Standard Income Taxation Cannot Achieve Neutrality

A standard income tax treatment of savings achieves neutrality neither over time nor across assets. An income tax deters saving by making future consumption more expensive than current consumption. Because it taxes earnings as they are received and then taxes any return to savings, the present value of the income is greater if it is used for consumption now than if it is used for consumption in the future. Furthermore, unless there is full indexation for inflation, the degree to which this occurs will vary over time in an arbitrary way with fluctuations in the rate of inflation because the nominal return will be taxed, not just the real return. If inflation is high, interest rates will tend to be high in nominal terms to compensate for the fact that the real value of the principal will be falling. Taxing that nominal return implies that the effective tax rate on the real return to interest-bearing assets tends to increase with the rate of inflation.[15]

The phenomenon of compound interest means that a tax that reduces the effective rate of return on savings looks increasingly penal—reduces the final wealth generated more—the longer the time horizon involved. For a young person saving for much later in life, this can make a startling difference to the value of wealth generated by a given amount saved. Even ignoring inflation, a tax that reduces the net interest rate on a bank account from 5% to 4% will reduce the value of the account by around 1% after one year (from £105 to £104), but by around 9% after ten years and by 38% after 50 years. For quite plausible saving over an individual's life, the combination of inflation and compound interest means that standard income taxes reduce the future consumption that can be bought by forgoing consumption today to a far greater degree than one might suspect from looking at statutory tax rates.

It is difficult to design an income tax that is neutral across assets, particularly when capital gains are taxed at realization and without any adjustment that makes a realization-based tax equivalent to a tax on accruing gains. Capital gains are a return to savings in just the same way as interest

---

[15] It is possible to design a tax system based on realization accounting that achieves a uniform capital tax. Indeed, Auerbach and Bradford (2004) develop a generalized cash-flow tax that avoids having to measure capital income while at the same time effectively imposing an income tax at a constant rate on all capital income.

income or dividends. Under a comprehensive income tax, capital income (including capital gains) should be taxed as it accrues, or in a way that is equivalent to accrual taxation. So capital gains need to be taxed at the same rate as other components of income, which is clearly possible (though not what happens in the UK). In the standard formulation of a comprehensive income tax, capital gains are taxed at the same time as other forms of income from savings. That implies taxation on accrual (when the rise in value occurs) rather than on realization (on disposal of the asset). For an asset that increases in value and is then held for several more years before being sold, the effect of taxation on realization is to defer the tax payment on the accrued capital gain for several years. While it is possible to design realization-based capital gains taxes that provide investors with the same incentives as a tax on accruals, such taxes would require modifying the asset's tax basis by an amount that depends on rates of return since the asset was purchased.

Deferring or delaying tax payments is valuable to taxpayers—this can be thought of as the equivalent of an interest-free loan from the government to the taxpayer, from the time the asset increases in value to the time it is sold. This delay reduces the effective tax rate on capital gains, particularly for assets that are held for long periods. This unequal treatment favours assets that generate returns in the form of capital gains over assets that generate returns in the form of cash income. This also creates incentives for cash income to be converted into capital gains, which may be particularly important in the context of business assets, and therefore favours some individuals over others. Taxing capital gains on realization without any 'accrual-equivalent' adjustment also creates a 'lock-in' effect—once an asset has risen in value, there is an incentive to hold on to it, to shield the accrued gain from tax for a longer period. Taxing capital gains on accrual would, though, be extremely difficult for two reasons: first, all assets would need to be 'marked-to-market' or valued in periods when they are not traded; and second, individuals may be required to pay tax on accrued gains in periods when they lack the liquid financial resources to make these payments.

In practice, then, taxing the return to savings under a standard income tax implies accepting arbitrary distortions to the pattern of saving both over time and across assets. As we shall see, an expenditure tax avoids distorting the choice between assets that yield cash income or capital gains, and the holding-period distortion, even though gains are taxed only when they are realized and consumed.

13.2.2. Alternative Routes to Savings-Neutral Taxation

A comprehensive income tax cannot take us to a savings-neutral system of taxation. But there is in fact more than one route to a savings-neutral system. We consider three here. In doing so, and in order to facilitate the discussion, we find it very useful to make use of some simple notation. We describe each stage in the life of the asset in which savings are invested as taxed (T) or exempt from tax (E).

There are three stages to consider: first, when income is received (i.e. before or at the point at which it is paid into a savings account or used to purchase an asset); second, as the returns (interest, capital gains, or distributable profit) accrue; and third, when the funds are withdrawn from an account or an asset is sold.

In this notation, a (cash-flow) expenditure tax is defined as EET. Tax is simply paid on income used for consumption at the time the expenditure is made. This is equivalent to saving in a tax-deferred account and most pension saving operates in this way. In contrast, the comprehensive income tax is TTE. That is, savings are made out of taxed income; all returns are taxed, including the normal return; but no further tax is due when the savings are withdrawn.

With these concepts in mind, there are three potential alternative savings-neutral forms of taxation. They are:

- a 'cash-flow expenditure tax', which taxes only income used for consumption when it is spent—EET;

- a 'labour earnings tax', which excludes all savings income from taxation, but with no exemption for savings when first made—TEE;

- an 'income tax with a rate-of-return allowance' (RRA), which taxes labour earnings and supernormal returns to savings—TtE. The lower-case 't' in TtE denotes the exemption for the normal return.

The three savings-neutral approaches are broadly equivalent in the absence of supernormal returns. All three leave the normal risk-free return untaxed and consequently leave the choice between consumption today and consumption tomorrow undistorted.[16]

The different forms do, however, have different implications for the tax treatment of returns in excess of the normal return, as well as for the time path of government revenue. The normal return is a central concept here. It can be thought of as the return obtained by holding savings in the form of a safe, interest-bearing asset. For this reason, it is often called the normal risk-free return.[17] It is this return that we want to avoid taxing in order to avoid distorting decisions over the timing of consumption. It is because it taxes the normal return that the income tax distorts these decisions.

Returns above the normal return may reflect differential risk across different investments or some form of rent earned by investors. The source of excess returns may have an important effect on the economic consequences of different approaches to achieving neutrality. The earnings tax (TEE) leaves excess returns untouched by the tax system. It doesn't matter how well my investments do, I pay no further tax. The expenditure tax (EET) and rate-of-return allowance (TtE) bring excess returns into the tax base (and both raise revenue by taxing rents). This is a crucial difference. Widespread application of the TEE system would allow successful investors to earn unlimited rewards without being taxed. It is quite inappropriate as a general regime for business assets and other risky investments. The TEE regime, of course, also requires a very sharp differentiation between earned income and investment income, since the former is taxed and the latter not.

Earnings tax (TEE) and expenditure tax (EET) treatments of savings are widely used for certain assets. Private pension plans in the UK approximate an EET treatment. This is also the case for human capital investments where the investment of time in education is not taxed but the returns are. Roth 401(k) plans in the US and ISAs in the UK are examples of assets that are given a TEE tax treatment. Owner-occupied housing in the UK and most durable consumption goods attract a TEE treatment too, since they are bought out of after-tax income but there is no tax paid on returns, even 'excess' returns.

---

[16] At least for consumers who can borrow at the normal return and face a constant tax rate over time (we address these caveats in Section 13.2.3).

[17] In most developed countries and most time periods, this can be well approximated by the interest rate on medium-maturity government bonds (Sørensen, 2007).

A standard income tax (TTE) taxes all the returns from capital investments, including the normal return.

An EET base can be thought of as giving tax relief for saving up front. The rate-of-return allowance can be viewed as an expenditure tax with deferred rather than immediate tax relief for saving. Their common feature is that, unlike the comprehensive income tax (TTE), they do not tax the normal return to savings. Indeed, the RRA and the EET can be viewed as two special cases of a more general savings-neutral tax base.[18,19] The RRA has gained increasing attention in the economic literature and has been introduced in Norway.[20] We believe it should be taken seriously in the savings tax reform debate. It achieves the neutrality we are looking for. It has the potential to be less disruptive to implement than a traditional consumption tax. It maintains government revenues up front. And it allows the same tax rates to apply to (above-normal) returns to savings as apply to labour income.[21]

These different tax regimes for savings can all be applied to borrowing as well, as described in Box 13.1.

To help understand the different systems, we develop a simple example that compares a standard income tax (TTE) with the three alternative savings-neutral tax regimes. In our example, we look at an individual who is considering saving in an asset that provides a 5% annual return. For every £100,000 of this year's income saved, the following year there is interest income of £5,000 plus principal of £100,000, a total of £105,000.

A standard income tax at 20% gives tax on interest income of £1,000, after-tax interest income of £4,000, and a return of only 4%. This is a disincentive to save. The TTE case is displayed in the first column of numbers in Table 13.2. In the remaining columns, we draw out the comparisons for the savings-neutral tax systems.

---

[18] In much the same way that cash-flow corporation taxes and ACE-type taxes are two special cases of a more general investment-neutral corporate tax base (see Chapter 17).

[19] An intermediate case would give immediate tax relief for part of the individual's net saving, with deferred tax relief (with the same present value) for the remainder.

[20] Sørensen, 2009.

[21] It should be added that the full 'general equilibrium' effects of moving between these different savings-neutral tax systems still need to be fully worked out.

Box 13.1. Tax regimes for borrowing

Borrowing can be thought of as negative saving, and the same four tax treatments we consider for savings could all, in principle, be applied.

- **TEE—a labour earnings tax** simply ignores borrowing, like it ignores saving. Neither taking out a loan, nor making payments of interest or principal, has any effect on tax liability.
- **EET—a cash-flow expenditure tax** involves taxing all cash inflows and deducting all outflows, hence adding the loan to taxable income for the year when it is taken out and then deducting all payments of interest and principal.
- **TTE—a comprehensive income tax** treatment of borrowing allows full deductibility of interest payments from taxable income (but does not add the amount borrowed to taxable income or deduct repayments of principal), just as it fully taxes interest income on savings. A comprehensive income tax thus taxes saving and subsidizes borrowing.
- **TtE—a rate-of-return allowance** regime allows deductibility of interest payments, like TTE, but only in so far as they exceed a 'normal' rate of interest on the outstanding principal. (Unlike with TTE, there is no difference in present-value terms between making interest payments and making repayments of principal. If a payment is labelled interest, it is deductible; if it is labelled principal, it is not deductible but, by reducing the value of the outstanding debt, it reduces the stream of 'normal' interest allowances to offset against future interest deductions.)

Table 13.2. Comparison of savings tax regimes with normal returns (assumed 5%)

	TTE	TEE	EET	TtE
Purchase price	100,000	100,000	100,000	100,000
Tax relief in year 1	0	0	20,000	0
After-tax contribution	100,000	100,000	80,000	100,000
Value of asset in year 2	104,000	105,000	105,000	105,000
After-tax withdrawal	104,000	105,000	84,000	105,000
Tax paid in year 2	1,000	0	21,000	0
Present value of year 1 tax relief	0	0	21,000	0
Present value of tax paid	1,000	0	0	0

Under an earnings tax (TEE), the purchase again costs £100,000 in terms of consumption forgone, but no tax is then levied on the return, so £105,000 can be withdrawn. An expenditure tax (EET) can be thought of as providing a tax relief of 20% on the purchase price. Hence the cost of the asset in terms of consumption forgone is £80,000. That is, the expenditure tax gives tax relief of £20,000 on saving of £100,000 in the first year. It then taxes the withdrawal of £105,000 in the second year, resulting in a tax payment of £21,000. After tax, the saver gives up £80,000 this year and gets £84,000 next year, a return of 5%. Put another way, the present values of tax relief in period 1 and tax payment in period 2 are equal. There is no distortion to the intertemporal allocation of consumption.

Now suppose that instead of giving tax relief of £20,000 this year, we carry this forward, marked up at the interest rate of 5%, and give tax relief of £21,000 next year. The saver then gives up £100,000 this year and gets £105,000 next year, just as in the TEE case, a return of 5%. This is displayed in the final column of Table 13.2. The EET and TtE approaches are equivalent provided the individual is indifferent between tax relief of £20,000 in year 1 and tax relief of £21,000 in year 2. We can achieve this here, and more generally, by providing a rate-of-return allowance, calculated as the risk-free (nominal) interest rate multiplied by the stock of savings (at historic cost) at the end of the previous year—5% of £100,000 = £5,000 in the example.

The situation changes when there is a return above the normal rate. To illustrate, suppose that the normal return is 5% but that the asset purchased provides a return of 10%. We assume in this case that the excess return is a rent earned by the investor. This situation is illustrated in Table 13.3 for each system that we are considering. We see that TtE and EET are equivalent, while TEE is different. This is because under TtE there is only an allowance of £5,000 in year 2 to set against the return of £10,000. In this case of supernormal returns, the return above £5,000 is taxed at 20%.

This stylized example is useful for understanding basic principles, though of course there are other important differences between the systems. For example, in the case of a risky asset, both the timing and riskiness of government revenue receipts are different between the systems. With the TEE treatment, all revenues are certain and are received in the first period.

Table 13.3. Comparison of savings tax regimes with excess returns (assumed 10% with normal at 5%)

	TTE	TEE	EET	TtE
Purchase price	100,000	100,000	100,000	100,000
Tax relief in year 1	0	0	20,000	0
After-tax contribution	100,000	100,000	80,000	100,000
Value of asset in year 2	108,000	110,000	110,000	110,000
After-tax withdrawal	108,000	110,000	88,000	109,000
Tax paid in year 2	2,000	0	22,000	1,000
Present value of year 1 tax relief	0	0	21,000	0
Present value of tax paid	2,000	0	1,000	1,000

In contrast, revenues with the expenditure tax come only in the second period and will depend upon actual returns. The RRA ensures government receives some revenue up front and receives a share of any excess returns.

The RRA effectively provides a tax-free allowance equal in value to the normal risk-free rate multiplied by the amount invested. Operationalizing it would create some complexities, including over the choice of the normal risk-free return, increased record-keeping requirements, and the treatment of 'losses'.

As mentioned above, the normal return can generally be well approximated by the interest rate on medium-maturity government bonds. This interest rate fluctuates, and to maintain neutrality across assets and across time, one would ideally like to ensure that the risk-free rate allowed by the tax code varied closely with it. But this clearly complicates administration, and there will always be a trade-off between varying the rate too frequently and maintaining strict neutrality.

The record-keeping required with an RRA system would be somewhat more onerous than under some other systems, but no more than under a standard capital gains tax. And there is also the question of dealing with returns below the normal rate. Giving an allowance for a normal rate of return would give rise to a tax loss when the return realized in a given year is below the normal return. The RRA allowance would then be higher than the return it is supposed to be deducted from, giving rise to 'unutilized' RRA allowances.[22]

Unutilized RRA allowances are analogous to losses that can arise under a standard income tax, but 'losses' relative to a normal rate of return will be more prevalent than the losses in absolute terms that arise in standard income and capital gains taxes: nominal returns are below a positive rate-of-return allowance more often than they are below zero. Loss offsets are a vital aspect of the way an RRA deals with risky returns, preventing asymmetric treatment of gains and losses creating an important disincentive for risky investments.[23]

Finally, it is worth noting that the labour earnings tax, expenditure tax, and RRA approaches all achieve equal treatment of capital gains and cash income, and do not require indexation for inflation. Hence they avoid distortions to the form and timing of saving. This is immediately obvious for the EET regime. I pay tax on the value of my savings at withdrawal. It makes no difference whether they have grown as a result of accumulated interest or capital gains. The same is true for an RRA. An allowance of, say, 5% of the initial investment is carried forward. If either interest or capital gains are realized in the next period, any tax liability is set against the allowance. If capital gains are not realized until a future period, then the unused allowance is carried forward, uprated at the normal rate of return. The result is that normal returns are not taxed, whether they arise from interest or capital gains. Above-normal returns are taxed and the net present value of tax paid is unaffected by the form or timing of the returns.

13.2.3. Tax-Smoothing and Different Marginal Rates

In laying out the details of the various savings-neutral tax systems, we have so far simplified our discussion significantly by assuming that underlying tax rates are constant—a flat tax system—whereas in actual fact all modern tax systems have tax schedules with a marginal rate that is not constant.

---

[22] We adopt the standard terminology of 'unutilized RRA allowances' here, but it should be recognized that the 'unutilized RRA allowance' would, in fact, be more than the full RRA allowance if there were nominal losses.

[23] See e.g. Cullen and Gordon (2007).

Table 13.4. The impact of progressive taxation (40% when saving, 20% on withdrawal)

	With normal 5% return		With 10% return	
	EET	TtE	EET	TtE
Purchase price	100,000	100,000	100,000	100,000
Tax relief in year 1	40,000	0	40,000	0
After-tax contribution	60,000	100,000	60,000	100,000
Value of asset in year 2	105,000	105,000	110,000	110,000
After-tax withdrawal	84,000	105,000	88,000	109,000
Tax paid in year 2	21,000	0	22,000	1,000
Present value of year 1 tax relief	42,000	0	42,000	0
Present value of tax paid	−21,000	0	−20,000	1,000

Consider first a system in which tax rates are higher when incomes are higher—one like the UK's, with a basic rate and one or more higher rates. Suppose, in the example in Tables 13.2 and 13.3 above, that the saver is a higher-rate taxpayer in year 1 and a basic-rate taxpayer in year 2. Then the calculations for the EET and TtE systems look quite different, as Table 13.4 shows.

The EET system subsidizes saving in a way that encourages people to save at times when their tax rate is high and to access the returns when their tax rate is low. Conversely, saving would be discouraged at times when the individual temporarily faces a low tax rate. This creates a non-neutrality when the tax system is progressive. The tax system affects the level and timing of saving.

In principle, we should not seek to impose more tax on someone whose annual income fluctuates between £20,000 and £60,000, averaging £40,000, than on someone who earns £40,000 every year. But in fact at present in the UK we do. Put another way, suppose there is a threshold for higher-rate tax of £40,000. In period 1, someone earns £80,000, saving £40,000. In period 2, he earns nothing and consumes only that £40,000. Annual consumption is never above the higher-rate threshold, any more than it would have been had earnings and consumption equalled £40,000 in each period. It is not clear why the higher rate of tax should ever be payable in this example.

The example individual in Table 13.4 pays a lower rate of tax on income in the second period because his income has dropped below the threshold for higher-rate tax payments. An individual whose lifetime income is high enough to be a higher-rate taxpayer in both periods would pay more tax than the individual in our example.

Under the TtE regime, by contrast, tax at the higher rate is paid in the first period, and the fact that the tax rate is lower in the second period is immaterial (at least if only the normal return is earned). The fact that income drops does not impact on total tax paid on the savings.

This illustration shows that with non-linear tax systems, the savings neutrality underpinning the three alternative tax treatments we have considered thus far is not guaranteed. Neutrality only strictly holds if the marginal rate of tax on expenditure is constant.

In our example, saving is subsidized by a consumption tax. Equally, if the marginal rate rises as expenditure rises, then this can result in an implicit tax on saving during those parts of the life cycle in which consumption is low. Consider someone deciding whether to save some income now and spend later. Perhaps she is thinking that she might be supporting young children in the future and hence expects higher consumption needs. With constant income, this would imply that her consumption will be higher tomorrow than it is today. If there is a progressive pure (EET) expenditure tax, then she may face a higher marginal rate on her (higher) consumption tomorrow than she does on her (lower) consumption today. Consumption tomorrow is more costly—exactly the impact of a tax on savings and clearly a removal of the neutrality condition that left the timing of consumption undistorted.

Again the reverse is true with a TtE (or TEE) regime. In this case, saving in the period of lower consumption and withdrawing savings at periods of higher consumption reduces the overall tax payment.

If there is a straight choice between implementing a pure EET system and a pure TtE (or TEE) system, then it seems that, in the face of a tax system with more than one marginal rate, one group of savers must be advantaged and another group disadvantaged. If we choose EET, then those, for example, saving from high incomes now who will be facing a lower tax rate in retirement will be provided with a major incentive to save. But those wishing to save from lower income now to finance a period of higher consumption when marginal rates are higher will be disadvantaged. On the other hand, a TtE (TEE) regime would disadvantage someone facing a higher rate now and saving for retirement when the marginal rate is lower—their average rate would be 'too high' from a lifetime perspective.

One strategy for resolving this tension would be to offer taxpayers the choice between EET and TtE regimes. This would in principle allow full 'tax-smoothing', an idea with a distinguished history in economics.[24] In the example above, if the individual with increasing expenditure could also invest in a TEE-taxed asset, this would allow her to 'smooth out' the tax rate across today's and tomorrow's consumption. Tax-smoothing permits changes in the marginal tax rate to be evened out over the lifetime.

If people have variable earnings and variable spending needs over their lives, as they surely do, then a 'pure' earnings tax (TEE) penalizes people with variable earnings. On the other hand, a 'pure' expenditure tax (EET) penalizes people with variable spending. If people had perfect foresight, faced no uncertainty in their earnings, and had complete flexibility to save (and borrow) as much as they liked within each regime, they could smooth their tax base across years, meaning that people with the same lifetime earnings would pay the same lifetime taxes (in present-value terms). This would give, in effect, a lifetime tax base—which, as we noted at the beginning of this chapter, has significant attractions.

But there are disadvantages to allowing complete flexibility. Not everyone has the foresight, the certainty, the financial sophistication, or the access to credit to smooth their tax payments perfectly. Is it fair and efficient to favour those who do? In addition, we might not want to be neutral over the timing of labour supply and consumption. For example, we might want to provide stronger work incentives around the time people are considering retirement. We will revisit this question in Section 13.3.

There is no overwhelming argument in favour of allowing any particular degree of smoothing. Even more analytically difficult is the question of how to allow for the effect of means-tested benefits (and tax credits) on saving incentives and possible gains from tax-smoothing. The analytical problem is that means-tested benefits mean that those with low incomes face higher marginal tax rates than those with higher incomes. In practice, means-tested benefits are likely to have much greater effects on saving incentives than the

---

[24] Dating back to Meade (1978) and Bradford (1982).

variation in income tax rates.[25] This adds great complexity, and certainly leaves no simple analytic solutions. We discuss the policy issues that arise in some detail in the next chapter.

13.3. THE ECONOMIC CASE FOR A SAVINGS-NEUTRAL TAX SYSTEM

We noted at the start of this chapter that neutrality provides a useful baseline from which to judge savings tax reform, but that the economic case for the optimality of a neutral tax system remains an active topic of research. A savings-neutral tax code has the potential to provide a tax base that raises revenue without distorting the timing of consumption. But should the timing of consumption be sacrosanct, or could some deviation from the savings-neutral benchmark be part of the optimal tax system?

As we have already seen, a progressive rate structure can undo the neutrality of a consumption tax in any case. We have also argued that our reasoning applies to life-cycle savings and not to inheritances and bequests. Moreover, we have made the case for taxing excess returns and will suggest pensions are subject to a separate tax treatment. There are several other quite sophisticated arguments for considering departures from the principle of savings neutrality across time. In considering directions for tax reform, we need to ask whether the benefits of such departures outweigh their costs, particularly given our limited knowledge of exactly what departures would be optimal.

Here we look at four arguments for deviating from neutrality.

First, it may be that people who save are more patient or have higher cognitive ability than those, with the same earnings, who don't. If patience or cognitive ability is associated with earning capacity, then taxing savings may be an indirect way of taxing those with high earning capacity.

Second, if individuals are choosing between investing in human capital and investing in financial capital, and if there are market failures that make it difficult for individuals to access credit in order to invest in their own human

---

[25] See Blundell, Emmerson, and Wakefield (2006).

capital, then a zero rate of tax on savings may distort decisions in favour of financial investments over human capital investments.

Third, if there is uncertainty about future earning ability, then individuals may save to hedge against a bad outcome. If the world turns out well, they will have 'oversaved', and in that situation they may reduce their labour supply. Some form of tax on savings can increase efficiency in such settings.

Finally, if future consumption (saving today) is complementary to leisure today, there may be a case for taxing savings, in just the same way as there may be a case for higher rates of indirect tax on goods and services the consumption of which is complementary to leisure (see Chapter 6).

The next subsections explore these arguments in more detail. Each is, in principle, a coherent argument against savings-neutral taxation. How far these arguments can be translated into practical policymaking will likely depend on empirical evidence that is still in the early stages of development.

13.3.1. Patience, Cognitive Ability, and Self-Control

Different people have different attitudes towards the future and towards risk. They also have different abilities to process information. As a result, saving behaviour varies. Some people save more for the future than others because they are more patient. Some save more because they have a greater understanding of the options available and the consequences of saving, or not saving. Some will be willing to bear more risk in their savings portfolios.

If it is the case that those with more patience or cognitive ability do save more, and they also have higher earning capacity, then a case for taxing the normal return to savings might emerge.

The standard argument against taxing the normal return to savings rests on the assumption that taxing savings creates inefficiencies and cannot help with redistribution. But if the observed level of saving is a good proxy for earning capacity, then taxing savings might be a useful way of redistributing. At the margin, by taxing savings the government could raise revenue and redistribute from those with higher earning capacity while reducing tax rates on labour supply and effort.

In fact, there is good evidence from experimental psychology of a significant relationship between cognitive ability and patience.[26] Those with higher ability value the future more, and will therefore save more, independently of actual earnings levels.

Higher-ability (and, particularly, more numerate) individuals are also able to process information and make complex decisions more easily. Experimental evidence suggests that they are less susceptible to framing effects (such as failing to realize that '25% fat' and '75% fat-free' mean the same thing) and generally draw stronger or more precise meaning from numbers and numerical comparisons.[27] This makes it easier for them to make rational decisions over saving and may in part explain why cognitive ability has been shown to be associated with a higher likelihood of holding stocks, and of having a private pension, even when controlling for the overall level of financial wealth and earnings.[28] This evidence also suggests that people with higher cognitive ability show more self-control.

From this sort of evidence, it is also possible to discern an additional argument for making sure that we tax any above-normal returns to savings. Higher-skilled individuals appear to be less risk averse than the lower-skilled. They may therefore invest in assets with more risk but a higher expected return. Ensuring supernormal returns are taxed can then aid efficient redistribution.

Behavioural arguments[29] such as these also suggest a case for taxing savings because saving is an indicator of having high earning capacity. The converse is that those with low earning capacity may not save enough and we might then want to subsidize, compel, or otherwise encourage them to save. In the UK, in fact, much debate has centred on apparent undersaving, and new measures have been enacted[30] that will lead to automatic default into employer-sponsored private pension saving. That is, all employees will automatically save in a pension unless they actively choose not to. The framing of the decision has been changed and the expectation (based on

---

[26] See the detailed evidence and arguments in Banks and Diamond (2010).

[27] See the review in Bernheim and Rangel (2005).

[28] The evidence is reviewed in Banks and Diamond (2010).

[29] Bernheim, 2002; Bernheim and Rangel, 2005.

[30] HM Treasury and Department for Education and Skills, 2007.

evidence of the effectiveness of auto-enrolment[31]) is that many more people will engage in pension saving as a result.

13.3.2. Neutrality between Financial and Human Capital Investments

People do not only have the option of investing in financial assets. They can also invest in their own 'human capital'—that is, education and skills. Such investment should earn a return in the long run, just as savings earn a return. There is no obvious reason why we should wish to distort people's choices between these two forms of investment.

In some cases, a savings-neutral treatment of human capital investment occurs in a fairly natural way. Suppose I reduce my hours of work, or delay entry into work, in order to invest in learning. No tax is levied at the time the investment occurs. The return is taxed only when income from the investment is earned—exactly the EET or consumption tax treatment we have described. (Though, just as with the consumption tax, a rising marginal rate over time may create a disincentive. If I am facing a 20% tax rate now, but that rises to 40% later as a result of my investment in human capital, neutrality is lost.)

A problem occurs if I lack access to credit. In that case, I might invest less than I would like because I can't borrow to finance consumption while undertaking the education or training. Savings-neutral taxation of financial investments may then make things even worse, since alternatives to human capital investments that reap early rewards become even more attractive. This may lead me to choose an occupation with large earnings up front rather than invest in a longer-term career that involves human capital investments.

It should be obvious why this is potentially a serious distortion. Of course, it is not just related to the savings tax system—we would like to address the lack of access to credit, but the reluctance of creditors to lend to individuals without satisfactory collateral is hard to overcome. This helps explain why so much of the costs of education and human capital investments are covered

---

[31] See the influential study by Choi et al. (2004).

through public provision. In the UK, as elsewhere, much formal education is free at the point of use at least until the age of 18. While this does not directly address the cost of earnings forgone, it can go some way to removing underinvestment due to borrowing constraints.

Even so, the difficulty of borrowing against prospective earning capacity means that, in practice, it is difficult to ensure full neutrality between human and financial capital. The costs of education and human capital investments should also be fully deductible for tax purposes. But many of the costs of human capital investments are difficult to measure. If it is impossible to provide a tax treatment of savings that does not distort the choice between human capital investment and financial capital investment, some taxation of the normal risk-free return from financial capital investment may be desirable.[32]

13.3.3. Earnings Risk

None of us can be certain about how much we will be able to earn in the future. We may save not just to smooth our consumption over predictable life events—having children or retiring—but also to protect ourselves in case something goes wrong—being made redundant or getting sick, for example. This will be especially true when adequate products are not available on the insurance market.

Those of us lucky enough to maintain a high earning capacity (to avoid getting sick, becoming disabled, or being made redundant) may find ourselves with more wealth than we had planned. A natural response would be to choose to work less (or less hard) and run down this unexpected wealth. The more redistributive is direct taxation, the more attractive is this option. At the margin, taxing savings or introducing an assets test—reducing access to benefits when assets exceed a certain level—will weaken the desire to take this course of action and will therefore reduce the distortionary effects of redistributive taxation.

Beyond the treatment of savings, this argument has direct application to the way we might think about making incapacity and other benefits available at later ages. It depends, of course, on the inability of governments to fully

---

[32] Jacobs and Bovenberg, 2008.

measure an individual's true productive ability. Imposing an assets test[33] effectively imposes a tax on savings. It reduces the incentive to build up assets and then falsely claim disability benefits.

Although the earnings risk argument is quite compelling, the practical importance of this effect will depend on how risky earning capacity is and the observability of ability (or disability).[34]

13.3.4. Interactions between Work and Savings

Finally, it is worth noting a further argument for taxing savings, which harks back to the relatively simple idea that if specific expenditures are directly related to labour supply, then they should be taxed differently from other types of consumption goods. We considered this in the discussion of the pros and cons of a uniform VAT in Chapter 6. In principle, consumption of goods or services that are complements to leisure should be taxed more heavily so as to increase work incentives.

But a similar argument will hold when we consider consumption today and consumption tomorrow. It may be efficient to discriminate against (or, indeed, in favour of) saving if, given the level of earnings, the way in which people want to divide their expenditure between consumption today and consumption tomorrow depends upon how many hours they work. By acting as a tax on future consumption, taxing savings may increase the incentive to work if consumption tomorrow is complementary to leisure today.

I may, for example, want to defer more consumption into my retirement if, during my working life, I have spent time investing in mastering and gaining pleasure from leisure activities, activities that I will be able to spend time and money on in the future. If this is the case, taxing savings may increase labour supply. On the other hand, if long hours of work today are associated with more consumption in the future, perhaps because I don't have time to consume much today, then the case is reversed and there is an argument for subsidizing saving. Whether this argument applies in practice with much force depends on empirical magnitudes that have yet to be well determined.

---

[33] See Golosov and Tsyvinski (2006).
[34] See Farhi and Werning (2007).

13.3.5. Taking These Arguments to Policy Design

All of these arguments are well founded in economic theory. They justify levying some tax on the normal return to capital, though not necessarily at full labour income tax rates, as in a comprehensive income tax.[35] However, there are several reasons to be cautious in applying these arguments immediately to policy.

First, in all cases, achieving the most efficient outcome requires calibrating tax rates to particular, difficult-to-measure, behavioural parameters: how much greater earning capacity savers have than non-savers with the same level of actual earnings; how much more or less complementary to work consumption tomorrow is than consumption today; and so on. In some cases (such as complementarity to leisure), it is not even obvious in which direction the departure should go—should we tax or subsidize saving?—and it is possible that some of the arguments might offset each other. Being unable to estimate the parameters of interest precisely is not on its own a good argument for persisting with neutrality: taking a best guess would presumably be better than not even trying. And as empirical economic and psychological research progresses, more accurate approximations to the optimal treatment are becoming achievable. But a degree of humility is in order: we are still some way from a robust and accurate quantitative understanding of all the relevant aspects of behaviour, and we should be mindful that a rough approximation would only yield part of the efficiency improvements that the theoretical arguments suggest might be attainable.

Similarly, even where we can be confident taxation of the normal return ought in principle to be positive, the optimal policy to achieve that may not be obvious, even theoretically. For example, a tax that reduces the net rate of return to savings (like standard income taxes) has effects that compound over time, as we discussed in Section 13.2.1. The alternative of applying an additional tax (or reduced relief) on contributions or withdrawals would also imply a net tax on the normal return (as with the case of varying marginal tax rates discussed in Section 13.2.3), but without this compounding property. Which time profile is right can be difficult to judge. Savers may be more able than non-savers, but are those who save for long periods more able than those who save for short periods? It may be that the optimal tax

---

[35] Banks and Diamond (2010) make this case.

profile is more complicated than either of these alternatives, or it may involve different instruments entirely, such as assets tests for disability benefits or intervention in the provision of education. The general point is again that unless the tax response can be designed to target precisely the objective identified, departing from neutrality may result in little efficiency improvement. Note again that we are considering neutral taxation for lifetime savings and not for generational transfers. We are also arguing for a system that captures excess returns.

Not only must we be cautious about how much of the potential benefits of departing from neutrality can be realized in practice; we must also be mindful of the costs of doing so. Taxing the normal return to capital as it arises inevitably reintroduces the difficulties of dealing with inflation and capital gains that plague standard income taxes. And all of the arguments are reasons for deviating from our first kind of neutrality: neutrality over the timing of consumption. They provide little, if any, rationale for departing from neutrality across assets. Yet we have already seen that a major difficulty with taxing the normal return to capital is precisely that it is difficult to be consistent across all assets. Unless the tax on the normal return can be applied consistently to defined benefit pensions, housing and other durable goods, human capital, derivatives, and so on, it will come at the cost of neutrality between assets.

A case could be made that the benefits of some (even very approximate) movement towards the theoretically superior positions described in the previous four subsections justify accepting some of the problems it would reintroduce. But taking all of the counter-arguments together, we think it would be better to make neutrality the central goal of savings tax policy.

13.4. DIRECTIONS FOR REFORM

Whilst not everyone is by any means fully 'rational' in their decisions of how much to save and in what form, it is evident that tax incentives can have a large impact on behaviour. Getting the taxation of savings right matters a lot on both equity and efficiency grounds.

The argument for taxing income from savings on the grounds that 'all income should be taxed the same' does not stand up. Saving simply defers consumption, so taxing savings means taxing earnings spent tomorrow more heavily than earnings spent today. And standard income taxes not only fail to achieve neutrality in the choice over when consumption should occur, but also make it extremely difficult to achieve neutrality between different forms of savings.

Trying to make the tax system savings neutral is a constructive benchmark. Neutrality can be achieved through a cash-flow expenditure tax (EET in our notation), a labour earnings tax (TEE), or a rate-of-return allowance (TtE). These systems differ in several important respects:

- The consumption tax and rate-of-return allowance impose a tax on above-normal returns. The earnings tax does not.

- The timing of tax payments and revenues differs, with the consumption tax involving no tax payment (revenue receipt) until consumption occurs.

- With more than one income tax rate, a consumption tax penalizes those with variable consumption, while the earnings tax and the RRA penalize those with variable earnings.

We have argued that a pure earnings tax (TEE) is inappropriate for assets with returns that may exceed the normal level. Widespread use of an earnings tax for such assets could see much effort devoted to avoidance and would allow the effort of those who are skilled at, for example, stock-picking to go untaxed.

For assets where there are likely to be significant excess returns, there is a strong case for using either a rate-of-return allowance or a cash-flow expenditure tax. Either would bring excess returns into the tax base and treat capital income and capital gains in a consistent and uniform way.

There are in fact arguments for having some element of each of the three within the tax system. As we shall see in the next chapter, in purely practical terms we are already close to an EET treatment of pensions and it would be difficult to move away from that. On the other hand, an RRA treatment of other assets may be easier to introduce in the short to medium term than a full consumption tax, not least because of transition difficulties and the timing of revenue flows to the Exchequer. But there is a principled argument for allowing a choice between these treatments in any case. Giving people the choice allows them to 'tax smooth' so as to allow the tax system to approximate a tax on lifetime income.

But we have also seen that there are arguments against allowing full smoothing and, indeed, against a fully neutral tax treatment of savings. As far as full smoothing is concerned, the main issue is one of equity. It seems likely that only the unusually well-informed, and relatively well-off, would take full advantage. In addition, allowing full smoothing would prevent us from having tax rates that vary with age, a flexibility which we argue in Chapter 4 is potentially very valuable.

The arguments against full neutrality are rather more subtle. It may be that the decision to delay consumption tells us about someone's earning capacity. Those who are more cognitively able may be more likely to save. Savings-neutral taxation may distort decisions in favour of financial saving over human capital investment if there are credit constraints or if it is hard to measure and offset the full costs of human capital investment. It may be that taxing savings will increase the labour supply of those who have saved against the possibility of losing earning capacity but who find, *ex post*, that they didn't need to save for that reason. Or it may be that future consumption is a complement to current leisure.

These are important arguments, but we maintain neutrality as a useful benchmark as it is hard to know how to fully operationalize them from a policy point of view. Particularly given that we start with a tax system that is a long way from a tax system that is savings neutral, it seems to us to make sense to move towards neutrality. But these arguments may be enough to suggest some limits on the extent to which people can access tax-neutral savings. We therefore develop in this book a set of proposals that would provide a tax system with a neutral treatment of life-cycle savings for the vast majority of taxpayers. It would also retain—indeed, increase—taxes on capital income and gains in excess of the normal rate of return for substantial asset holdings.

Importantly, the focus of all this analysis has been on lifetime savings. The arguments for not distorting the timing of consumption for the most part concern life-cycle savings and not transfers across generations. Different arguments come into play with transfers of wealth and we dedicate the whole of Chapter 15 to the issue of how to tax inheritances and other transfers.

In the next chapter, we look in much more detail at how tax treatment currently differs between assets, and some of the practical issues in savings tax reform. We will also look at some important issues that we have barely mentioned here—including the role of means-tested benefits—and others, notably the role of National Insurance contributions, that we have avoided altogether so far.

14

Reforming the Taxation of Savings

The current system of savings taxation in the UK is beset by complexity and unequal treatment. Saving in many forms is discouraged. Simple interest-bearing accounts are treated particularly harshly. Other forms of savings receive rather generous tax treatment. This complexity and unequal treatment have spawned a thriving industry advising people on how to allocate their savings, not on the basis of the best underlying investments but on the basis of tax treatment.

In setting out some practical directions for reform, we start by providing a brief overview of savings taxation in the UK, with a particular focus on explaining how the different tax treatments of different assets lead to different effective tax rates. The difficulty of taxing capital gains within the current system, and the problems this creates, are substantial. There are also complexities created by the progressive structure of the income tax and, in particular, by the effects of means-tested benefits and tax credits.

We go on to look at directions for reform. One obvious step is to move to an earnings tax treatment (TEE) of interest-bearing accounts. In addition, we propose that the rate-of-return allowance (RRA, which we denoted TtE) described in the last chapter should be made available to those with substantial holdings of risky assets such as shares. We make some arguments in favour of an RRA treatment over an EET expenditure tax treatment for these assets, but the main thrust of our reform package could be achieved with an EET or RRA form of tax-neutral treatment of these assets.

We also look in some detail at the taxation of pensions, which is currently close to a consumption tax (EET) regime, and make some suggestions regarding how the current tax treatment could be modified. Importantly, in the case of both pensions and the RRA, we need to consider not just income tax but also National Insurance contributions (NICs). For supernormal returns to be taxed at the same rate as earnings, that rate should be the rate inclusive of NICs. Equally, we cannot neglect the effect of NICs in the taxation of pensions, where the current system provides a large subsidy to employer contributions to pensions.

We end by looking at the issue of the extent to which we can or should seek to maximize opportunities for 'tax-smoothing' by allowing free access to different forms of tax treatment of savings (and borrowing).

In this chapter, we try to keep things simple at least to the extent of focusing on just three classes of assets—simple risk-free assets such as interest-bearing accounts, riskier assets such as equities, bonds, and unit trusts, and pensions. Other assets such as life assurance could be brought within our framework fairly straightforwardly. The taxation of financial savings is, of course, intimately bound up with the taxation of housing, small businesses, and inheritance, all issues we look at in detail in other chapters.

14.1. OVERVIEW OF THE CURRENT SITUATION IN THE UK

A description of how different forms of savings are taxed requires us to take account of not only income tax but also NICs and capital gains tax (CGT). Table 14.1 summarizes the treatment of a limited range of assets for each of these taxes. For ease of exposition, we avoid discussion of more esoteric assets and of a range of specific assets and schemes which have, over the years, attracted a complex and changing array of tax advantages.

For owner-occupied housing and for cash and shares held in ISAs, saving is out of taxed income and there is no tax on returns and no tax on withdrawals (the proceeds of sale in the case of housing): a TEE treatment. This treatment is very limited in the case of Individual Savings Accounts (ISAs), into which just over £10,000 can be placed each year. Of this, a maximum of half can be in a cash ISA, though one can choose to place the whole amount in an equity ISA. Rather oddly, then, TEE treatment is more widely available for equity investments than for cash savings.

Tax exemption is provided in a different way for pensions: saving is out of untaxed income, fund income is untaxed, but withdrawals are taxed: EET. This regime for pensions would produce the same effective tax rate of zero

Table 14.1. Tax treatment of different assets (in 2010–11)

Asset	Income tax and NICs on contributions	Returns		Income tax and NICs on withdrawals
		Income tax on interest/dividends	Capital gains tax[a]	
Pension—employee contribution	Exempt from income tax, not exempt from employer and employee NICs	Exempt	Exempt	Taxed except for a 25% lump sum, no NICs
Pension—employer contribution	Exempt from income tax and employer and employee NICs	Exempt	Exempt	Taxed except for a 25% lump sum, no NICs
ISA	Taxed	Exempt	Exempt	Exempt
Interest-bearing account	Taxed	Taxed at 10%, 20%, 40%, or 50%	n/a	Exempt
Direct equity holdings	Taxed	Taxed at 10%, 32.5%, or 42.5%, but offsetting dividend tax credit means effective rates are 0%, 25%, and 36%	Taxed	Exempt
Housing—main or only house	Taxed	Exempt[b]	Exempt	Exempt
Housing—second or subsequent house	Taxed	Rental income taxed	Taxed	Exempt

[a] CGT was charged at 18% for basic-rate taxpayers and 28% for higher-rate taxpayers on gains above an allowance of £10,100. Note that a flat rate of 18% was in place before 23 June 2010 (http://www.hmrc.gov.uk/cgt/intro/basics.htm#6).

[b] Dividends are effectively the imputed value of income from owner-occupation—this was taxed on the basis of the notional rental value of the property until 1963. Note that income tax is payable on income received from letting out part of a main residence while the owner resides there, although the first £4,250 per year is tax free.

on the normal return to savings;[1] but the 25% lump sum that can be withdrawn from pension funds tax free means that pension saving is in effect subsidized. In addition, employers' pension contributions are particularly tax favoured since they are not subject to employer or employee NICs either at the point of contribution or at the point of withdrawal.

National Insurance contributions are not charged on the returns to any form of savings; nor is relief from NICs available for contributions to any form of savings other than employer contributions to pensions. This means that the NICs treatment of all other savings is effectively TEE. Savings are made from income on which NICs have already been charged, but returns are not subject to NICs.

Perhaps unsurprisingly, most of the wealth held by the UK population is in pensions, housing, and ISAs. Saving in other forms is discouraged by the tax system. Cash in ordinary interest-bearing accounts is saved out of taxed income, and income tax is then applied to the full nominal return: TTE. The same is true of equities held outside ISAs, with CGT also applicable to capital gains.

Given this set of tax treatments, under certain assumptions, we can calculate the effective tax rate (ETR) on savings in each of the different asset types: the percentage reduction in the annual real rate of return caused by tax.[2] Table 14.2 illustrates ETRs for basic- and higher-rate taxpayers if all assets earn a 3% real rate of return before tax and inflation is 2%. The ISA regime (TEE in our earlier notation) can be taken as the base case with an effective tax rate of zero because there is no tax on the real return.

Note that the ETR on an interest-bearing account is 33% for a basic-rate taxpayer, not the statutory income tax rate of 20%. This is because tax is charged on the nominal return, not the real return. With a 3% real return and 2% inflation, £100 of savings yields nominal interest of about £5; 20% tax on this, £1, represents 33% of the £3 increase in the real purchasing power of the deposit. Inflation does not, however, affect ETRs on pensions, ISAs, and owner-occupied housing, where the return is tax exempt.

---

[1] Assuming that the individual faces the same marginal tax rate in retirement as when making the contribution—the implications of relaxing this assumption are discussed below.

[2] The calculation of ETRs here broadly follows that of IFS Capital Taxes Group (1989). For more detail of methodology and results, see Wakefield (2009).

Table 14.2. Effective tax rates on savings in different assets

Asset		Effective tax rate (%) for:	
		Basic-rate taxpayer	Higher-rate taxpayer
ISA		0	0
Interest-bearing account		33	67
Pension—employee contribution	– invested 10 years	−21	−53
	– invested 25 years	−8	−21
Pension—employer contribution	– invested 10 years	−115	−102
	– invested 25 years	−45	−40
Housing—main or only house		0	0
Rental housing	– invested 10 years	30	50
	– invested 25 years	28	48
Direct equity holdings	– invested 10 years	10	35
	– invested 25 years	7	33

Notes: Assumes 3% annual real rate of return and 2% inflation. Calculations for rental housing and direct equity holdings assume that real returns accrue as rental income or interest or dividends while capital gains match price inflation and are realized at the end of the period in question. Rental housing is assumed to be owned outright, with no outstanding mortgage. Calculations for employer pension contribution assume that the employee is contracted into the state second pension. Saver is assumed to be a basic- or higher-rate taxpayer throughout the period in question, to have exhausted the CGT exempt amount where appropriate, and to have no entitlement to means-tested benefits or tax credits.

Source: Wakefield, 2009.

Pension savings are treated more favourably than by a pure cash-flow expenditure tax and are therefore shown as having a negative ETR. This arises because of the tax-free lump sum and from the fact that employer contributions are exempt from NICs whilst no NICs are charged on withdrawal. The measured ETR depends on the period for which the pension is held because the ETR is a measure of the tax as a percentage of the real return. Over longer periods, the real return is greater, so the value of a tax subsidy to the contribution (the NICs treatment) or the final withdrawal (the lump sum) is lower as a proportion of the total return.

The ETRs on direct equity holdings and on rental housing represent a combination of income tax and capital gains tax.[3] The ETRs are lower for longer holding periods because CGT is levied when an asset is sold rather than when the rise in value occurs. This interest-free deferral of the tax liability is worth more the longer the asset is held, reducing the ETR over time and creating an incentive (the 'lock-in effect' introduced in the last chapter) for people to hold on to assets for longer than they would in the absence of the tax.

Table 14.3. Contribution to a range of assets required to match TEE return

Asset		Required contribution for:	
		Basic-rate taxpayer	Higher-rate taxpayer
ISA		100	100
Interest-bearing account	– invested 1 year	101	102
	– invested 10 years	110	121
	– invested 25 years	127	163
Pension—employee contribution		94	86
Pension—employer contribution		72	75
Owner-occupied housing		100	100
Rental housing[a]	– invested 10 years	109	116
	– invested 25 years	122	142
Stocks and shares[b]	– invested 10 years	103	111
	– invested 25 years	105	127

[a] We have assumed capital gains that match price inflation, and real returns that accrue as rent. We assume rental housing is owned outright, with no outstanding mortgage. We assume that a CGT liability is incurred. If no CGT were incurred, then the figures for the basic-rate (higher-rate) taxpayer would be 106 and 116 (112 and 134) for the respective horizons. With a CGT liability, if we were to incorporate mortgage interest that could be offset against half the rental income, then the figures for a basic-rate (higher-rate) taxpayer would be 106 and 113 (109 and 122), instead of 109 and 122 (116 and 142).

[b] We have assumed capital gains that match price inflation, and real returns that accrue as interest or dividends. We assume that a CGT liability is incurred. If no CGT were incurred, then the figures for the basic-rate (higher-rate) taxpayer would be 100 and 100 (108 and 120) for the respective horizons.

Source: Wakefield, 2009.

---

[3] For simplicity, we assume that asset price inflation matches general inflation and that real returns are received as interest or dividends or rental income.

The ETRs in Table 14.2 illustrate the effect of tax on annual rates of return. Perhaps a more intuitive way of thinking about this is to ask the question 'What contribution would be required to match the net return to an ISA?'. In other words, what amount of money do I need to put in an ordinary interest-bearing account, or into a pension, so that I would end up with the same net value of asset as I would have done had I contributed £100 to an ISA, assuming some underlying pre-tax return? Answers are provided in Table 14.3 for basic- and higher-rate taxpayers. In this case, the answer depends on the holding period for interest-bearing accounts. Taxes on the return to savings compound over time. So the longer an interest-bearing account is held, the more has to be invested to match the return to an ISA. Taxes on initial contributions or final withdrawals do not have this property, so the net tax subsidies for pensions are invariant to the length of holding.

Despite these differences between the treatments of different assets, there has in fact been a narrowing in the dispersion of effective tax rates over the past three decades, as illustrated in Figure 14.1. This partly results from lower and less dispersed income tax rates and lower levels of inflation. But there has also been a series of more specific reforms. Importantly, the introduction of personal pensions and ISAs (previously PEPs and TESSAs) has extended the range of tax-free savings vehicles available. But as we saw in

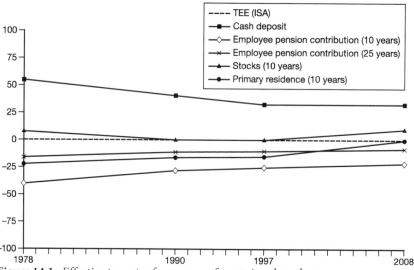

Figure 14.1. Effective tax rates for a range of assets in selected years

the last chapter, whilst most savings are indeed held in these tax-free forms, a significant minority are still held in tax-disadvantaged forms, and this is particularly true for lower-wealth households.

It is worth briefly mentioning the taxation of capital gains. As we saw in the last chapter, the standard approach to taxing capital gains at realization within an income tax system creates a lock-in effect favouring holding assets for longer than in a world without tax. This arises because tax is levied only on the realization of the gain and there is no adjustment of tax liability to make it equivalent to an accrual-based tax system. In practice, there are other problems created by the way in which we tax capital gains. As with the rest of the savings tax system, there is no allowance for inflation, so nominal gains are taxed.

In the UK in 2010–11, CGT was charged at 28% for higher-rate taxpayers and 18% for basic-rate taxpayers,[4] on realized capital gains in the year of more than £10,100. The effective value of these rates varies between assets since there is no allowance made for corporation tax paid as there is when income tax is due on dividends.

The high additional tax-free allowance for CGT unambiguously makes taking returns as capital gains relatively attractive. The allowance means that for many people with significant asset holdings, who can divest themselves of their holdings over a period of time, there is effectively no tax at all on capital gains. Whilst capital gains realized in any year remain below £10,100, no tax is payable.

Particularly attractive are gains in the value of personal business assets, the first £5 million of which, through 'entrepreneur's relief', are entirely exempt from CGT. The existence of this relief is, of course, in complete contravention of the principles for an effective tax system which we discussed in the last chapter. It ensures that, for a small group, a significant part of the return to effort is not captured in the tax system and a very big incentive is created to take returns in the form of capital gains. These issues are compounded by the fact that there is a complete exemption from CGT at death.

The result has been a great deal of tax planning focused around capital gains. The ability of some of the very wealthy, including many private equity

---

[4] See note a to Table 14.1.

fund managers, to take returns in the form of capital gains has generated controversy and concern around the equity of the whole tax system.[5] All of this makes CGT a highly unsatisfactory tax. Possibly more than any other tax, it has been subject to frequent, dramatic, and often controversial changes, despite accounting for less than 1% of all revenues.[6] Within the current tax system, this reflects the fundamental tension between the desire for a tax regime that does not penalize saving and one that treats similar levels of income similarly. It is this tension that we argue can be overcome in an expenditure tax or rate-of-return allowance regime.

14.1.1. Progressive Taxes and Means Tests

There is one other complication which makes the potential differences in effective tax rates much greater than those illustrated. Thus far, we have assumed that the income tax rate faced at the point of saving is the same as that faced at the point of withdrawal. As we saw in the last chapter, the fact that we have a progressive income tax schedule means that, in practice, this is often not the case.

Consider saving in a pension. Putting earnings into a pension fund in effect defers the tax on those earnings until they are withdrawn from the fund. If the tax rate at withdrawal is different from the rate when the income was earned, the deferral of tax can make a dramatic difference to the amount of tax actually paid. Many of those facing a 40% marginal rate while in work will face the basic rate of 20% in retirement. Their incentives to save in a pension are substantial. Indeed, there are substantial incentives to adjust the timing of pension saving to take advantage of differential tax incentives— much better to save when you are facing the higher tax rate than when you are a basic-rate taxpayer.

In Table 14.2 above, we showed the effective tax rates on employee pension contributions into a pension fund held for 25 years. The tax rates were –8% and –21% for basic- and higher-rate taxpayers respectively, on the assumption that they paid the same rate of tax in work as in retirement. If instead they make contributions when paying 40% tax and withdraw when

---

[5] See House of Commons Treasury Committee (2007).
[6] Source: HM Treasury, 2010b, table C11.

facing a 20% tax rate, the effective tax rate on their pension savings is −48%. The lower tax rate in retirement is a reflection of the fact that lifetime income is not so high as to justify taxation at the higher rate in all periods. To that extent, we may not worry too much about the apparent generosity of this incentive for higher-rate taxpayers to save in a pension. As we saw in the last chapter, in principle, with a standard progressive tax system, a free choice between EET and TEE savings vehicles could allow full consumption-smoothing for any individual, irrespective of their pattern of income receipt.

This picture, though, is much complicated by the existence of means-tested benefits and tax credits. To the extent that accumulated savings reduce entitlement to benefits, the incentive to save is reduced. On the other hand, if contributions to savings products are deducted from income in assessing entitlement to benefits, then incentives to save are enhanced. The way in which the benefit system in the UK takes account of savings is complex and inconsistent. The most important points to note are that entitlements to means-tested benefits are reduced at quite high marginal rates in the face of income from private pensions. Entitlement to Pension Credit, for example, is reduced by 40p for every pound of pension income and Housing Benefit entitlement is reduced by 65p in every pound. This matters since just under half of pensioners are entitled to some form of means-tested benefit.[7] In addition, having stocks of savings above quite low limits results in reductions in means-tested benefit entitlement. On the other hand, owner-occupied housing is ignored in all means tests.

For pension savings, it also matters how contributions are treated for calculating benefit or tax credit entitlement. Pension contributions are in fact not counted as part of the income on which tax credit entitlement is calculated, just as they are excluded from income when calculating tax due. This potentially provides a significant saving incentive for tax credit recipients since it effectively costs a tax credit recipient only 39p in lost income to save £1 in a pension.[8]

More details are provided in Box 14.1.

The potential impact of tax credits and Pension Credit, along with different income tax rates, on the incentive to save in a pension is illustrated in Table 14.4. The table shows how much you would need to contribute to a

---

[7] Department for Work and Pensions, 2006, ch. 3.

[8] This and other statistics here refer to the 2010–11 tax and benefit system.

pension to match the return to saving £1 under a TEE regime. The differences are dramatic. There is clearly a very strong incentive for anyone on the tax credit taper to contribute to a pension. Equally, there is a strong disincentive to pension saving for basic-rate taxpayers expecting to end up on the Pension Credit taper. In terms of scale, however, note that the

---

Box 14.1. Means-tested benefits and tax credits

Different financial assets are treated differently by different parts of the means-tested benefit and tax credit system. Tax credits are assessed on the same measure of income as is income tax, so most forms of savings income are counted for the means test but any savings held in an ISA, for example, do not affect entitlement. For other means-tested benefits—principally, Housing Benefit, Income Support, Pension Credit, and Council Tax Benefit—any actual income generated by financial assets is ignored in calculating entitlement. But an income is *deemed* on any asset-holding above £6,000, with every £250 in assets above this level (£500 for those aged over 60) assumed to provide an income of £1 a week for the purposes of the means test. Those with assets of more than £16,000 are not eligible for means-tested benefits at all. These rules, combined with the high withdrawal rates of means-tested benefits, create a very strong disincentive for those who are on means-tested benefits, or consider themselves likely to be eligible for them in the future, to build up financial assets worth more than £6,000.

In terms of contributions, the treatment of different benefits is also inconsistent. Whilst all pension contributions are excluded from income when calculating tax credit entitlement, only half of employee contributions are deducted when calculating entitlement to means-tested benefits.

One way of summarizing these different treatments is to use our standard notation and apply it to means-tested benefits. In broad terms, we can say the following:

- housing is subject to a TEE regime for all means-tested benefits and tax credits;

- pensions are subject to an EET regime for tax credits and a ½TET regime for means-tested benefits;

- other savings (including ISAs) are subject to a TEE regime for means-tested benefits but with an assets test on top that rapidly reduces entitlement once savings exceed £6,000;

- ISAs are subject to a TEE regime for tax credits;

- other savings are subject to a TTE regime for tax credits.

Table 14.4. Employee contribution to pension (ten-year investment) required to match £1 contribution to TEE vehicle for different combinations of working-life and retirement tax rates

Tax rate in work	Tax rate in retirement	Required contribution (p)
Basic rate (20%)	Basic rate (20%)	94
Higher rate (40%)	Higher rate (40%)	86
Higher rate (40%)	Basic rate (20%)	71
Basic rate (20%)	Pension Credit taper (40%)	114
Tax credit taper (59%)	Basic rate (20%)	48
Tax credit taper (59%)	Pension Credit taper (40%)	59

Note: Assumes 3% annual real rate of return and 2% inflation.

Source: Wakefield, 2009.

disincentive for pension saving in the face of the Pension Credit taper is not much greater than the disincentive that basic-rate taxpayers face from saving in an ordinary interest-bearing account for ten years. (Compare the required contribution of 114p in Table 14.4 to the 110p in Table 14.3.)

As illustrated in Box 14.1, the current regime treats different assets in different ways, and it gives rise to some peculiar saving incentives. That said, no easy reform presents itself. It would be nice if we could adopt one or more of the approaches we have discussed for income taxation (TEE, TtE, or EET). But this turns out to be much more problematic for means-testing than for taxation. There are two reasons for that. First, there is little correlation between being in receipt of any particular benefit when saving and when withdrawing the savings. Second, unlike a standard progressive tax schedule, means-testing implies levying higher effective tax rates on those with lower incomes.

A TEE-type regime makes little sense in the context of means-testing. If Pension Credit, for example, were not reduced in the face of higher private pension income, it would no longer be a means-tested benefit. One could conceive of a system in which a saver sacrifices Pension Credit now in order to enjoy the benefits of that saving, and of Pension Credit, in the future. But that is not consistent with the usual pattern of behaviour: almost nobody saves in a pension while in receipt of Pension Credit.

An EET regime suffers from the mirror-image problem. Many of those on means-tested tapers when they withdraw the savings (receive a pension) will have been facing just the basic tax rate when saving (in work). They will face the 'T' without ever having benefited from the 'E'. And because means-testing involves higher effective tax rates when incomes are lower, saving to smooth consumption will result in an overall higher level of tax paid than would have occurred in the absence of saving. This is the opposite effect of an EET regime in the face of a tax system with rising marginal rates. In this case, as we have already seen, saving when income (and the tax rate) is higher and consuming when income is lower allows the overall tax paid to be smoothed, at least to some extent, to reflect income over a longer period.

There is no easy way around the issue of means-testing and savings. Obviously, less reliance on means-testing would help. But that can only be achieved either by reducing the generosity of benefits or by increasing universal benefits. The first makes poor people worse off; the second requires increases in taxes to pay for the benefits. Another path is to make some level of saving compulsory. If this leads to very small increases in eventual incomes because of the action of means-testing, then it has much the same effect as an increase in direct taxes on those affected.

14.2. REFORMS

There is a strong case for substantial reforms to the taxation of savings. In keeping with our goal of promoting neutrality toward savings for the majority of taxpayers, we favour an approach that exempts the normal return to savings from taxation. As we have seen, for many assets, this can be achieved in two ways. We could implement a consumption tax (EET) in which contributions to savings are made gross of tax and tax is paid on withdrawal. Or we could implement a rate-of-return allowance (TtE) in which savings are made net of tax, but with tax then charged only on any returns above the normal rate. For assets such as interest-bearing accounts, where no supernormal returns can be earned, an earnings tax (TEE) is also equivalent.

In the next subsections, we outline some of the issues in applying these regimes to different assets, arguing that the TEE regime is the only one appropriate to ordinary interest-bearing accounts, and looking at the RRA particularly in the context of shareholdings and the consumption tax in the context of pensions.

14.2.1. TEE and Cash Savings

Ordinary interest-bearing accounts are currently subject to a standard income tax treatment, with no allowance for the effect of inflation on nominal interest rates. Savings are made out of taxed income and tax is levied on any returns. This violates the neutrality principle discussed in Chapter 13. Such a system is particularly punitive at times of high inflation, since a large part of the tax burden then falls on the component of the return that is simply compensating holders for inflation.

Cash ISAs already allow returns to be accumulated free of tax (TEE) on contributions up to an annual limit of £5,100 (in 2010–11). The argument for moving towards a more general TEE treatment of cash accounts is persuasive. They will not achieve 'supernormal' returns and there is little scope to disguise labour income as bank interest, so TEE treatment is entirely appropriate. This form of savings also tends to be the focus of less well-off and perhaps less sophisticated savers, though of course in absolute terms the biggest winners would be those who currently have substantial savings—simple interest-bearing accounts may form a higher *share* of total financial assets for those with lower levels of income and wealth, but wealthier individuals tend to have more in absolute terms.

It might appear that an alternative would be to allow consumption tax (EET) or RRA (TtE) treatment of such accounts. Given that we are going to go on to suggest such treatment for other assets, it is reasonable to ask why we would want an earnings tax treatment of savings accounts. There is, in fact, one rather important reason for this, related to our discussion of the taxation of financial services in Chapter 8. Suppose we were to offer RRA treatment on bank accounts. It would then be straightforward for such accounts to offer a range of services in exchange for a low or zero return. Under an RRA, this 'loss' could be offset against gains elsewhere. Equally, under EET, no tax would be paid on the implicit value of the financial services received. To avoid these distortions and the associated opportunities for tax avoidance, we therefore support the use of a TEE regime for these savings.[9]

14.2.2. The RRA and the Treatment of Risky Assets

Broader application of the TEE regime would fail to tax supernormal returns, and it would result in very different marginal tax rates being applied to labour income and capital income. TEE treatment of business income would be especially problematic. Exempting trading profits or dividends from taxation while seeking to tax self-declared labour income creates a range of obvious avoidance opportunities.[10] In order to avoid creating such tax avoidance opportunities, we focus on alternatives to general TEE treatment.

Introducing either an expenditure tax (EET) or a rate-of-return allowance (TtE) ensures that whilst the normal return remains untaxed, any excess returns are taxed. As we saw in the last chapter, these tax treatments can also ensure neutral treatment between income and capital gains. From our point of view, a crucial part of their attraction is that they can achieve neutrality while setting the tax rates on income, and capital gains, from investments equal to the tax rates on labour income. So there is no incentive to take income in one form rather than another. This is an important neutrality property and central to our proposals on small business taxation (Chapter 19).

This neutrality is only achieved if the rates of tax applied to above-normal returns are set not at current income tax rates but at rates equal to the income tax plus full (employee and employer) National Insurance contribution rates. Otherwise, a substantial incentive remains to transform earned income into capital income. Of course, for the RRA, this rate

---

[9] For all the same reasons, TEE is also suitable for cash borrowing such as bank loans—simply ignoring them for tax purposes, neither taxing the principal borrowed nor deducting repayments of interest or principal—as is already standard practice. Box 16.1 discusses the tax treatment of mortgages specifically.

[10] These issues are discussed further in Chapter 19.

schedule would apply only to returns above the normal return. So whilst the proposal might seem to involve a punitive increase in rates relative to the current system, the reality is that the RRA allows these rates to be aligned whilst ending the taxation of the normal return. By complete contrast to the current situation, both an expenditure tax and an RRA would allow capital gains to be treated wholly consistently with income.

In principle, a rate-of-return allowance (TtE) and an expenditure tax (EET) confer similar advantages. We have shown how they are economically equivalent. As we explain in the next subsection, there remains a strong case for keeping (and improving) the current EET treatment of pension savings. But it may make sense to offer the rate-of-return allowance for savings in other risky assets. In part, the transition to, and implementation of, such a regime are likely to be easier than the transition to EET for all. In part, as we discuss in Section 14.3, there may be benefits in having both regimes in existence for different assets and allowing people some degree of choice.

That said, there are several potential implementation complications to deal with under an RRA regime. These include the record-keeping requirements, the relative complexity or unfamiliarity of the calculations required, and the treatment of 'losses'—or, more properly, returns below the normal rate. On the other hand, one of the attractions of the RRA is that the transition to it is likely to be easier, both technically and politically, than the transition that would be required to move us to a cash-flow consumption tax.

One particular practical issue worth mentioning briefly is that if we plan to tax people making high (above-normal) returns on their assets, we should equally provide relief to those making 'losses' (below-normal returns). If we fail to do this, then we introduce a different distortion because the expected tax on returns to risky assets would be positive, undermining neutrality both over the timing of consumption and between more and less risky assets. More generally, the effect of this approach to taxing the returns to risky investments on the incentives to invest in risky assets is likely to depend on the structure of capital market opportunities available to investors as well as on the tax rules applying to loss offsets, for example. This is a topic of ongoing study.

To achieve neutrality on the timing and risky-versus-riskless asset dimensions would require that losses (i.e. net returns below the RRA allowance) be offset in some way. In principle, this could take the form of outright tax refunds, setting losses on one asset against gains on another (or perhaps against labour earnings), or carrying losses forward or back to set against taxable income or gains in other years. We do not discuss further the detailed economic and practical considerations surrounding these different ways in which loss offsets could be implemented.[11] But it is worth emphasizing that, unlike current practice, losses offset in other periods should be carried forward or back with interest, thereby maintaining the value of tax relief.

An RRA regime could simplify the capital tax system as a whole by reducing opportunities for avoidance, and hence reducing the plethora of concomitant laws and regulations designed to minimize avoidance. But, not just because of the issue of losses, it would be more complex for some people than the current regime. It would require more record-keeping for some— though no more than is needed for CGT to operate—and the calculations involved would be unfamiliar. We make two proposals to ensure that this does not become a barrier to implementation.

First, we would propose maintaining a limited TEE vehicle, such as an equity ISA, with limits like those currently in place or somewhat reduced. That would avoid unlimited availability of tax-free returns for those skilful or lucky enough to do well by investing in risky assets. And, like ISAs at present, the TEE vehicle would only be available for arm's-length assets: it would not be possible for people to put shares in their owner-managed business into a tax-free wrapper as a way to convert their labour income into untaxed capital income. But it would ensure that a simple vehicle remains for the vast majority of people wanting to invest in equities. This is in keeping with our goal of savings neutrality for most taxpayers.

And second, for holdings above the limit on the TEE vehicle, investors could opt to use a rate-of-return allowance. But if they do not take that option, their investments would, by default, be taxed under a comprehensive income tax regime similar to the one currently in place. There would clearly be an incentive to use the RRA regime, but no obligation for those with relatively small holdings or a strong aversion to extra record-keeping and calculations.

---

[11] For such discussion, see Devereux (1989) or Altshuler and Auerbach (1990).

14.2.3. Pensions and the Consumption Tax

The UK currently has something close to an EET taxation treatment of pensions. We see no reason to move away from that system, which delivers savings-neutral tax treatment for those who save through pensions. Indeed, there are many practical reasons for believing this is much the best way of approaching the tax treatment of pensions. Both because pensions account for by far the majority of non-housing wealth and because they play a central role in government policy aimed at ensuring adequate incomes in retirement, getting their tax treatment right is extremely important.

It is worth starting with some context. Unlike all the other assets we consider in this book—equities, housing, interest-bearing accounts, and so on—a pension is not defined by the underlying assets in which money is invested. In fact, money saved in a 'pension' can be invested in virtually any underlying asset. The main defining characteristic of a pension is that access to the savings contained therein is allowed only from a certain age (55 in the UK from 2010). Additional rules regarding requirements to purchase annuities also often exist—though in some countries (Australia, for example), there are no such constraints. If people are to save voluntarily in a form subject to these limitations, they will need to be encouraged to do so, either with more generous tax treatment than is available for alternatives or through some other incentive.

Public policy towards pension saving spans many issues beyond tax treatment. The level and design of the basic state pension, the role of state earnings-related pensions, and the design of means-tested benefits in retirement all have a major impact on the amount and form of private pension saving. There are also quite different types of pension saving. From our point of view, it is the difference between 'defined benefit' and 'defined contribution' pensions that matters. The latter are more straightforward, effectively acting like savings accounts which are directly attributable to individuals. They are savings accounts with severe restrictions, though, in terms of the age at which they can be accessed and the form in which income can be withdrawn. Defined benefit pension arrangements are more complex. They are employer-sponsored schemes in which the eventual pension in payment is not linked directly to an individual's contributions and the performance of her particular fund. Rather, the pension is usually defined according to some measure of final salary and years of service. For example, some schemes will offer an annual pension of one-sixtieth of final salary for every year worked, with the result that someone with 40 years in the scheme will receive two-thirds of their final salary as a pension. The tax treatment of defined benefit schemes needs to be considered in light of the fact that the value of the employer contribution in respect of each individual is not straightforward.

This is the context in which, in the UK, we have a tax regime for pensions which is close to a consumption tax. Contributions are made free of income tax, investment returns accumulate free of tax, and the pension in payment is taxed. The reality, however, diverges from a strict consumption tax in three important ways. First, there are limits on how much can be contributed to a pension in any year, and on how much can be accumulated in total before tax penalties apply. Second, while it is right to describe the income tax treatment of pension saving as close to EET, the NICs treatment of pension saving is quite different. Indeed, it differs according to whether the pension contribution comes formally from the employer or from the employee. Third, a quarter of the accumulated pension balance in a defined contribution scheme can be withdrawn as a lump sum free of tax. (A roughly equivalent rule works for defined benefit schemes too.) The result is that a quarter of contributions are effectively subject to a very generous EEE treatment for income tax purposes. We now look at each of these in turn.

Limits

In brief, the limits to the availability of tax relief for pension saving apply both to the amount that can be contributed in any one year and to the total that can be accumulated in the pension account before penalties are applied. These limits have been subject to some change and review. In late 2010, the most recent decisions were that tax relief should be available on contributions of up to £50,000 a year with a limit on the value of the accumulated pension balance of £1.5 million before penalties are paid.[12] This annual contribution limit in particular is much less generous than the £255,000 annual limit previously in place. The reason for the change is quite explicitly to raise revenue and, in particular, the reform represents an

---

[12] http://www.hm-treasury.gov.uk/consult_pensionsrelief.htm.

attempt to limit the responsiveness of taxable income to the income tax rate. Its timing, following the introduction of a new highest income tax rate of 50%, is no accident.[13]

Are limits of this kind desirable? There are three possible principled arguments in favour of limits in general. One is that a limit on the amount that can be saved in a tax-neutral environment may be desirable if we would like to tax bequests and other wealth transfers but cannot do so adequately. Then limits on tax-neutral accumulation up to some level that could be considered adequate for life-cycle savings may be one, albeit very much second-best, response. This argument, of course, bears much less weight in respect of pensions than for other forms of saving. A second argument refers back to concerns about ever being able to collect the tax. The tax authorities might have legitimate concerns if it were possible to place unlimited amounts of money into an EET vehicle, and then avoid domestic tax by taking up residence elsewhere. Of course, this is a general issue for consumption taxes, including VAT. Third, in the last chapter, we considered a range of relatively subtle arguments against a general presumption in favour of tax-neutral treatment. One reasonable response to these arguments could be to impose some limits on the availability of tax-neutral savings instruments. Note, though, that all these arguments would seem to apply more naturally to limits on the total amount that can be saved rather than limits on annual contributions.

Of course, if we were to reform savings taxation more fundamentally, it would be important that any limits on saving in tax-neutral pension vehicles be lined up sensibly with limits on other savings vehicles. If we were to allow unlimited access to vehicles with RRA (or, for cash accounts, TEE) treatment, limits applied only to pension saving would just lead to more savings in those other forms by those who are affected by the limits.

Within these limits, though, the tax regime for pensions is more generous than a pure consumption tax in respect of the NICs treatment and in respect of the tax-free lump sum. We now turn to these.

---

[13] These changes stand in place of alternative proposals laid out by the previous government which, broadly, would have restricted the rate of tax relief available to those paying the new 50% income tax rate. Restricting rates of tax relief is complex and sits very badly with attempts to achieve rational tax treatment.

NICs Treatment

As we have stressed, getting the taxation of savings right involves not only getting the income tax treatment right, but also getting the NICs treatment right. At present, NICs are charged on *employee* contributions into private pensions. They are not charged on pension withdrawals. This is a TEE regime. The situation is different for employer contributions. These are subject neither to employer NICs nor to employee NICs. Again, pensions in payment are not subject to NICs at all. This is an EEE regime.

This difference in treatment between employer and employee contributions creates a very substantial incentive for contributions, formally, to come from employers. For those facing the main rates of NICs—12.8% for employers and 11% for employees in 2010–11—a net contribution to a pension of £100 costs an employer £100 if he makes the contribution, but costs him nearly £127 if the contribution comes from the employee.[14] Looking back at Tables 14.2 and 14.3, this helps explain why employer contributions to pensions are much the most tax-favoured form of saving. It also helps explain why HMRC records (income tax relief on) employer contributions as two-and-a-half times as great as employee contributions.[15] Some might argue that encouraging saving through workplace pensions is a particularly effective way of raising personal saving, but it is not clear whether this warrants net saving incentives of the magnitude currently in the tax code.

Could we move to a full EET treatment of pensions for NICs as well as income tax? To do so would mean exempting employee as well as employer contributions from employer and employee NICs. There would then need to be an additional tax (NICs) payment on pensions in payment. If this were to reflect the main 2010–11 NICs rates in full, it would need to be set at about 21.1% on pensions in payment below the upper earnings limit for NICs.[16]

If we wanted to move in this direction, though, it would not be appropriate simply to start charging this full rate of NICs on pensions currently in payment. That would imply double taxation—NICs will have been levied on

---

[14] $100 \times 1.128 / (1 - 0.11)$.

[15] HMRC statistics, table 7.9, http://www.hmrc.gov.uk/stats/pensions/table7-9.pdf.

[16] Note that employee and employer NICs rates are multiplicative, not additive (assessed sequentially, not simultaneously): employee NICs are charged on gross earnings excluding employer NICs. This distinction is discussed in Section 5.3.2.

any employee contributions already made—and undermine the legitimate expectations of those who have saved up to now.

What one would need to do would be to start providing relief for employee contributions now and gradually phase in additional payments in retirement over an extended period. One attractive way to do this would be by date of birth. In other words, those reaching 65 before, say, 2015 would be unaffected. Then NICs could be imposed on private pension income in retirement at, say, 0.5% for those reaching 65 in 2016, 1% for those reaching 65 in 2017, 1.5% for those reaching 65 in 2018, and so on until a final target rate is reached (15% would be reached by 2045, 20% by 2055). Quicker phase-in would be possible, though anything short of 40 years to reach 21.1% risks some (albeit small) element of double taxation. In principle, one might consider it reasonable to phase this reform in more quickly to take account of the historic exemption from NICs of employer contributions, though inevitably those who had had to rely on their own contributions would lose out—and no doubt concerns would be expressed over 'retrospective' taxation.

Two points are worth making with regard to this proposal. First, because employee contributions would be moving from a TEE to an EET regime, it would cost the government money up front—though it would raise money in the long run by getting rid of the EEE treatment of employer contributions. Second, there can be no denying that reforms of this kind raise uncertainty about future taxes and place the tax treatment of savings at some political risk. If a government were to set out on the path of gradually increasing tax rates on pension income over a long period, there would clearly be a temptation for successor governments to deviate and to increase rates more quickly or tinker in other ways. There is no obvious way to tie the hands of future governments and reassure people they would not succumb to the temptation.

Moving to a full EET treatment of pensions for NICs as well as income tax still seems to us the most appropriate way forward, particularly in the context of our proposals in Chapter 5 to move towards integration of income tax and National Insurance contributions. It provides a sustainable and transparent rate schedule, does not require valuation of employer contributions to defined benefit schemes, and ensures that excess returns are taxed. But if the transition is seen as too painful, there is a partial alternative which might be more palatable, especially to governments concerned about short-term costs. This would be to maintain the current TEE NICs regime for employee pension contributions and to move to a TEE regime for employer contributions as well. Employer NICs are already virtually flat rate (other than the earnings threshold) and could readily be charged at a flat rate on any contributions made by the employer. From the employer's point of view, pension contributions would then be treated like any other form of remuneration paid to the employee. This solution would, however, be harder to implement with respect to charging *employee* NICs on *employer* pension contributions. The non-flat-rate structure of employee NICs would require employer contributions to be allocated to individuals. That is possible for defined contribution schemes, but difficult for defined benefit schemes.

The Tax-Free Lump Sum

Under current rules, part of a pension can be taken as a tax-free lump sum—a quarter of the accumulated balance in a defined contribution scheme (and a roughly equivalent rule applies for defined benefit schemes). The part taken as a lump sum in effect receives EEE income tax treatment, i.e. is fully tax exempt at every point.

The existence of such a 'bonus' is usually defended as being compensation for the fact that pensions are constructed to be a highly inflexible form of savings, available only after a certain age. If, for reasons of public policy, we do want people to lock money away for long periods, we are likely to have to provide them with a good reason for doing so. The case for a bonus of some sort would be strengthened if the other reforms we have suggested, opening up more opportunities for saving in a tax-neutral environment, were to be implemented. But encouraging withdrawal of a tax-free lump sum seems a perverse way of encouraging people to build up a pension if one of its main purposes is to provide a regular annual income (and keep people off reliance on means-tested benefits). The current system also provides a significantly bigger bonus for higher-rate taxpayers than for basic-rate taxpayers. And allowing a quarter of the accumulated sum to be taken tax free makes this very valuable for those with the biggest pension pots.

There are many alternative ways of incentivizing pension saving that do not have this perverse effect. One would simply be to reduce the rate of tax on pensions in payment by a quarter. This would have to go alongside a reduction in benefit withdrawal rates to be of value to all. This may be less salient, and therefore less effective in influencing behaviour, than the lump sum. A more salient alternative, which would be similar in effect, would be for government to top up pension funds at the point of annuitization. For a basic-rate taxpayer, a 5% top-up (20% of 25%) would be broadly equivalent in value to the tax-free lump sum.

14.3. THE OVERALL SYSTEM AND THE OPPORTUNITY TO SMOOTH

We have recommended ending taxation of interest income in cash accounts and introducing a rate-of-return allowance for direct holdings of equities and similar assets.[17] We have also recommended keeping and improving the EET treatment of pensions. Between them, these proposals, which would represent steps toward a savings-neutral tax system, would substantially improve the savings tax system in the UK.

One feature of these recommendations is that the combination of TEE/RRA treatment of cash and equities with an EET pension vehicle would also allow some people access to opportunities for the kind of tax-smoothing we described in Chapter 13. That is, they could choose which to use depending on their expected future consumption and earnings paths. Those expecting to face lower tax rates in retirement than during working life would use a pension. Anybody expecting the reverse would find it beneficial to save through the TEE and RRA regimes.

But the opportunity for smoothing would not extend to those with variable incomes during working life. Ideally, someone earning £50,000 this year and £20,000 next year should pay the same tax as someone earning £35,000 in each year. Under TEE or TtE regimes, they would pay more tax. If the person with variable earnings had access to an EET savings account such that they could place £15,000 into the account in the first year and withdraw

---

[17] In Chapter 16, we also run through how an RRA regime could apply to housing. In Chapter 19, we show how important it is in lining up the taxation of individuals and companies.

it in the second, then they would pay the same tax as the person with the stable earnings.

If we wanted to allow this—and we set out the pros and cons of allowing full smoothing in the previous chapter—there are two routes we could follow. One would be the introduction of a separate EET savings vehicle. This might allow taxpayers to place a certain amount of money into an account this year, with tax relief, and allow them to withdraw it, and pay tax on the withdrawal, at any point in the future. The second option would be to allow more flexible access to current pension vehicles. For example, a taxpayer might be allowed to access current pension savings at any age. In principle, this access might only be allowed subject to having a minimum (age-varying) total level of pension savings. This condition could help balance the value of the additional flexibility against the policy imperative of ensuring that as many people as possible have 'adequate' incomes in retirement, or at least incomes that take them off means-tested benefits.

Either route should be perfectly practicable and looks attractive from the point of view of getting the tax system closer to taxing a measure of lifetime income. The attractiveness of doing this depends on three considerations: first, the extent to which there is a case for maintaining a clearly differentiated treatment specifically for pension saving; second, the extent to which we are concerned about equity implications in the sense that perhaps only a minority of the better-off and better-educated might be able to take advantage of these opportunities; and third, the extent to which the additional flexibility around EET savings would lead to permanent loss of tax revenue, perhaps through movements abroad.

Finally, we should note that in order to allow the full smoothing that the combination of these savings tax treatments is aimed at providing, we should also consider the tax treatment of debt. At present, debt is given an earnings tax (TEE) treatment. Neither taking a loan nor paying it back makes any difference to tax paid. This clearly has the benefit of simplicity. The EET equivalent would involve taxing all cash inflows and deducting all outflows, hence adding the loan to taxable income for the year when it is taken out and then deducting all payments of interest and principal when repaid. The EET treatment would allow tax-smoothing in the sense that if I borrow when my earnings are low, I will be taxed at a low rate, or perhaps not at all. If I repay when my earnings are high, then the deduction against my income tax may be more valuable. Returning to the last example: instead of saving to cushion a fall in earnings from £50,000 to £20,000, suppose a taxpayer borrows to smooth consumption as earnings rise from £20,000 to £50,000. Under the TEE system, there is no smoothing and the borrower pays more tax than the person on £35,000 each year. Under EET, the loan of £15,000 is added to taxable income in year 1, but the repayment is deducted in year 2. In this case, the borrower is treated exactly as the person earning £35,000 in each year.

If the goal is to smooth, then logic pushes us towards allowing this kind of EET treatment for borrowing as well as allowing wider availability of EET treatment for saving. The relative complexity, or at least unfamiliarity, of this change to the taxation of borrowing, some of the arguments against free choice of savings vehicle, and the fact that means-testing implies that full smoothing for all is never likely to be practicable suggest to us that a focus on achieving this kind of total smoothing may not be a priority. But it could remain a long-term goal for tax reform.

14.4. CONCLUSIONS

The taxation of savings in the UK is distorting, inequitable, and complex.

Reforms in recent years have not been governed by any broad strategy or direction. There remain substantial differences between the ways in which different assets are taxed. Ordinary interest-bearing accounts are harshly taxed. There is, bizarrely, more limited availability of TEE tax treatment for cash than for equities. The taxation of capital gains continues to be contested and continues to provide substantial incentives to take returns as capital gains rather than as income. The taxation of pensions has been beset by uncertainty as governments worry more about tax revenue than maintaining the integrity of the system. And the treatment of employer contributions to pensions provides a substantial tax subsidy for saving in that form.

In these circumstances, a coherent package of reform is needed. In our view, the priority should be to move towards a system that is much more neutral in its treatment of savings as a whole—neutral between consumption now and consumption in the future—and one that limits the distortions between different types of assets. Getting there is not straightforward and does not mean treating every asset the same.

To reduce opportunities for tax avoidance, it is important to align the tax rates on earned income and on investment income in excess of the normal rate of return. This would remove numerous complexities and opportunities for avoidance. It requires National Insurance contributions to be charged on returns to savings in the same way as they are charged on earnings. We have shown specifically how this might be achieved for pensions.

Aligning the tax treatments of returns to savings in the form of income and of returns in the form of capital gains is also important. This is difficult to achieve under an income tax (TTE) treatment because there is a natural benefit to be had from the 'lock-in' effect of capital gains tax. In addition, the current system fails to index gains for inflation, offers a substantial additional tax-free allowance for capital gains, charges capital gains tax at below standard income tax rates, offers very generous 'entrepreneur's relief' to those owning their own business, and forgives CGT entirely at death.

The way we suggest achieving the desired neutral treatment is through a combination of a straightforward TEE system of taxation for ordinary bank and building society accounts, a reformed EET treatment of pensions, and the introduction of a rate-of-return allowance for holdings of shares and similar assets.

This combination of reforms would achieve a great deal more rationality in the savings tax system. The RRA system for shares would ensure that returns above the normal return, and only those returns, are taxed. These returns could be taxed at the full (income tax and National Insurance) rates applied to labour income. To ease the possible compliance burden of such a regime, we propose that equity ISAs remain in place for the vast majority of people, who have relatively small holdings of shares. In addition, those who do not choose to use the RRA would, by default, be subject to tax on the full returns.

Ordinary bank and building society accounts should just face a straightforward TEE system—saved out of taxed earnings and then no more tax applied. This is appropriate for assets on which 'supernormal' returns cannot be earned. Indeed, it would be inappropriate to apply an EET or RRA treatment to such assets because of the failure to tax financial services that this would imply.

The current consumption tax (EET) treatment of pensions should be maintained. This should be accompanied by the removal of the excessively generous, and distorting, treatment of employer contributions to pensions for NICs purposes. The tax-free lump sum is an odd method of providing an additional incentive for saving in a pension. There is a strong case for replacing it either with a reduction in the tax rate paid on pensions or with a government top-up to the fund that is annuitized.

The combination of reforms that we consider would result in a savings-neutral tax system for most taxpayers. It would increase taxes on some—those who benefit from generous CGT treatment, those who benefit from employer pension contributions, and, perhaps, those who are very lucky or skilled in their stock-picking. It would reduce taxes for others—those reliant on cash savings and those with substantial stocks of shares or similar assets held outside ISAs.

Finally, we have looked at the difficult issue of the degree of 'tax-smoothing' that the system should allow and at the impact of means-tested benefits on saving incentives. With a tax system in which tax rates increase with incomes, EET and RRA regimes have different implications for tax payments depending on the pattern of income receipts. EET regimes, such as the pension tax system, favour those saving when incomes (tax rates) are high to consume when incomes (tax rates) are lower. RRA (or TEE) regimes do the reverse. The free existence of both, alongside a consumption tax treatment of borrowing, would allow full tax-smoothing. That is, people with variable earnings would be able to arrange their affairs so as to pay the tax that they would have done had their earnings been the same in total and spread evenly across years. Full tax-smoothing would allow us to tax a measure of lifetime income.

Our proposals—allowing a combination of RRA and TEE treatment for some assets and an EET treatment of pensions—would get us some of the way towards a lifetime base. But they would help neither those who would benefit from an EET treatment of pre-retirement saving, nor those who need an EET treatment of borrowing in order to achieve smoothing. While reform to achieve a lifetime base may not be an immediate priority, there is a strong case for considering it a benchmark for future reform.

The interaction with the means-tested benefit system, though, creates formidable problems. If benefit entitlements are reduced in the face of accumulated savings, the incentive to save is reduced. Most people who are saving are not entitled to benefits while they contribute, and so ignoring savings contributions for benefit purposes does not create the desired neutrality. The effect can be that a saver with a relatively low lifetime income can face a high effective tax rate. While there are ways of bringing greater coherence to the current interactions between savings and means-tested benefits, none of them, as far as we can see, is likely to take us very far down the road to a savings-neutral system in respect of means-testing.

15

Taxes on Wealth Transfers

Taxation of wealth is a topic that excites strong passions. Some view it as the most direct means of effecting redistribution and key to achieving equality of opportunity. Others see it as the unjustified confiscation of private property by the state. Given these opposing viewpoints, it is not surprising that this is an area of taxation where international practice differs dramatically. Most OECD countries have taxes on income, spending, corporate profits, and so on, with recognizably similar goals. Practice with taxes on wealth varies widely. Some countries levy taxes directly upon wealth holdings, while others only tax transfers of wealth. There are some countries that do not tax wealth at all.

In this chapter, we focus specifically on the taxation of wealth transfers. Levying a tax on the stock of wealth is not appealing. To limit avoidance and distortions to the way that wealth is held, as well as for reasons of fairness, the base for such a tax would have to be as comprehensive a measure of wealth as possible. But many forms of wealth are difficult or impractical to value, from personal effects and durable goods to future pension rights—not to mention 'human capital'. These are very serious practical difficulties. And where attempts have been made to levy a tax on a measure of current wealth—in France, Greece, Norway, and Switzerland, for example—practical experience has not been encouraging.

There is also a persuasive economic argument against taxing the stock of wealth. A wealth tax in this form would tax not only inherited wealth but also wealth representing the individual's accumulated savings from taxed income. Taxing the stock of accumulated savings is closely related to taxing the returns to savings, and raises many of the same issues. We have already argued in favour of exempting a 'normal' return to savings but taxing 'excess' returns. A tax on the stock of accumulated savings does the opposite of this: it is equivalent to taxing the normal return to savings but exempting excess returns. To see this, suppose that I save £100 and the normal rate of return is 5%. A tax of 20% on the normal return is equivalent to a tax of 1% on the stock of wealth: both raise £1 from me (20% of £5 or 1% of £100) irrespective of the actual return I earn on my £100. It therefore discourages me from saving, but it taxes me no more if I manage to earn extremely high returns on my savings.[1] This seems exactly the wrong policy.

Wealth transfers are different. We explicitly excluded them from consideration when going through the theory and practice of the taxation of lifetime savings. Some of the arguments for and against their taxation are similar to those applying to taxes on lifetime savings, but some are quite different. An appropriate treatment of wealth transfers is an important complement to an appropriate tax treatment of lifetime savings.

Wealth transfers can come in the form of gifts between the living (*inter vivos* transfers) and bequests on death. Taxes on the latter are more common. There is an easily identified event where the vesting of ownership of the deceased's property in the hands of the heirs can be made conditional upon payment of the tax. In practice, taxing *inter vivos* transfers is difficult partly because it requires those concerned to report the taxable event. There are also many ways in which money can effectively be spent for the benefit of others without involving any direct transfer of money.

Views about the appropriateness of inheritance taxation remain sharply polarized. Those who are instinctively hostile to this form of taxation typically look at it from the perspective of the donor. They consider that individuals should have the right to leave their assets to whomever they choose without suffering a tax. If asset accumulation occurs from income that has already been subject to tax, inheritance taxation is seen to constitute 'double taxation'. Why should I be encouraged to spend my money before I die rather than providing for my children? Reflecting such views, estate taxes

---

[1] Except in so far as I will be taxed if I choose to save that money—adding to my stock of wealth, and the normal return thereon, to be taxed in the next period—rather than spending it. Note that this tax liability arises from more money being saved, not from excess returns being earned: no tax is levied on the excess returns if I spend them immediately.

in the US have brought forth the marvellous call to arms 'no taxation without respiration'.[2]

On the other hand, those who favour significant inheritance taxation often tend to look from the perspective of the recipient, arguing that it is anomalous to tax people on money they have earned while exempting from taxation money that comes to them through no effort of their own (except perhaps the effort expended in being kind to elderly loved ones). This is a very different perspective on social justice: one which tends to emphasize equality of opportunity. In addition, high levels of inheritance are frowned on as they can reduce effort among recipients—something which is often referred to as the *Carnegie effect* after the philanthropist Andrew Carnegie who observed that 'the parent who leaves his son enormous wealth generally deadens the talents and energies of the son, and tempts him to lead a less useful and less worthy life than he otherwise would'.

In this chapter, we lay out some of the economic principles behind the taxation of wealth transfers and clarify some of the issues around using taxation of wealth transfers to pursue equity objectives. We then consider some of the practical barriers to an effective system, before looking at some possible policy directions. But we start by providing a few statistics and some evidence of the potential importance of this subject.

15.1. THE DISTRIBUTION OF WEALTH

In the UK, the controversy over the legitimacy of wealth taxation has led to a somewhat half-hearted tax, with many loopholes and opportunities for avoidance through careful organization of affairs. This leads to charges of unfairness and makes a principled defence of the current inheritance tax difficult. But this is an issue of importance. Wealth is very unequally distributed in most countries, much more so than income. Figure 15.1 illustrates the extent of wealth inequality between households in the UK. The richest 10% of households own a staggering £4 million on average—more than ten times the average for all households—while the poorest 10% are net

---

[2] Steve Forbes, quoted in Gale and Slemrod (2001b).

debtors on average. The top 10% own almost five times as much wealth as the bottom half put together. Figure 15.1 also shows that wealth holdings are dominated by pensions and housing, which together account for more than three-quarters of households' wealth.

Much of the difference in wealth between households is simply a result of their being at different stages of their life. In Chapter 13, we showed how people typically save during their working life and run down their assets in retirement. This would create the appearance of substantial cross-sectional inequality of wealth even if there were no inheritances and everyone followed the same earnings trajectory over their lives. Figure 15.2 shows that households do indeed reach their peak wealth in the run-up to retirement.[3] But it also shows substantial wealth inequality even within age groups: among households in the 55–64 age bracket, for example, a quarter have more than £800,000 of net assets while a quarter have less than £175,000.

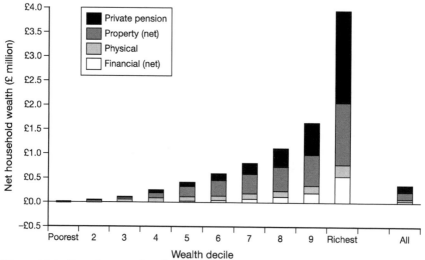

Figure 15.1. Distribution of net household wealth, 2006–08

Note: Excludes state pension rights.

Source: Office for National Statistics (2009), using data from the Wealth and Assets Survey 2006–08.

---

[3] Although these patterns may also reflect differences between cohorts in the amounts earned or inherited at a given age. Separating these out would require tracking the wealth of the same people over the course of their life cycle.

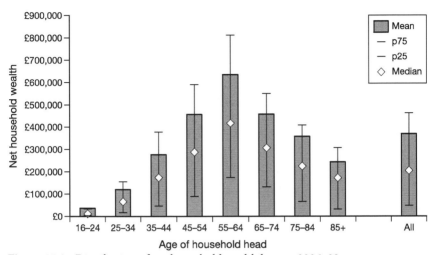

Figure 15.2. Distribution of net household wealth by age, 2006–08

Note: Includes private pension wealth but excludes state pension rights.

Source: Office for National Statistics (2009), using data from the Wealth and Assets Survey 2006–08.

The concentration of wealth has increased in recent years, following a longer period of gradual equalization.[4]

Receipts of gifts and inheritances are also, like wealth itself, unequally distributed. Those with more wealth to begin with are also those who are more likely to inherit. For example, the wealthiest fifth of people in their 50s consider themselves more than four times as likely to receive an inheritance of £100,000 or more than do the least wealthy fifth.[5] And it is clear that the existence of wealth transfer taxes has the potential to affect both how much wealth is built up and the form it takes, so that the level and structure of the tax do matter.

15.2. ECONOMIC PRINCIPLES AND OBJECTIVES

Of course, the fact that wealth is unequally distributed is not in itself enough to tell us how, or indeed whether, wealth transfers should be taxed. Taxing

---

[4] Atkinson and Piketty, 2007a.

[5] Banks, Karlsen, and Oldfield, 2003, figure 3.11. See also Rowlingson and Mackay (2005).

wealth transfers is fraught with practical difficulties. As UK experience shows, it can lead to considerable resources being diverted to tax planning, distortions being created by different treatments of activities and assets, and ultimately failure to tax the target group effectively. We address some of these practical issues later in the chapter. But before we do so, it is important to give careful consideration to what we are trying to achieve. Without a coherent objective, the prospects for implementing a successful tax are slim.

We start by looking at how the effects of wealth transfer taxes, and the case for employing such taxes at all, depend in some measure on the motive for the transfer, and on how the government views donor and recipient and the relationship between them. We then look at the objectives for wealth transfer taxes.

Four different motives have been identified and each has a different consequence for what we might think is the appropriate tax treatment.[6]

Some bequests are accidental or unintended. Some people die before they have consumed their accumulated stock of wealth, perhaps because they saved for contingencies that did not occur or because they were constrained in annuitizing their wealth. There clearly are uncertainties around timing of death, and there does seem to be at least some unintended bequeathing of assets in this sense.

At the other extreme, wealth transfers may be calculated and strategic in nature. That is, they may be made as a reward for services provided during life. They are 'strategic' in the sense that I might hold out the prospect of a bequest in order to encourage a relative to behave in a particular way.

Some gifts and bequests are made for more noble reasons, of course. The donor might be motivated by pure altruism—that is, the donor directly values the welfare of the recipient. If I am purely altruistic, I may value the happiness of my heirs in just the same way as I value my own future happiness. I could be said to be considering my heirs as extensions of myself. So households become 'dynasties' that behave (in terms of decisions made) like a single individual with a very long life. In this case, there is a close relationship between wealth transfers and life-cycle savings. Each dynasty can be thought of as acting like a single individual, with inheritances playing

---

[6] Following Cremer and Pestieau (2006).

the same role as savings for the standard household: I transfer money to my heirs much like saving transfers money to my future self.

Pure altruism is subtly different from our fourth motive, that of 'joy of giving': I get pleasure from giving, but my satisfaction is not determined by the recipient's enjoyment of the transfer—rather, I might get a 'warm glow' from a sense of acting virtuously, or perhaps I care paternalistically about the recipient's financial security (rather than about how much *they* value the money).

Unfortunately, available empirical evidence does not give terribly clear guidance as to which motive is most important,[7] and it seems likely that all are relevant to some degree. We care about our children and our children's children, but we don't tend to see our descendants as simply continuations of ourselves. Some bequests will be unintended and some will have a strategic element, but it is hard to observe whose and how much.

Given that not all bequests are accidental, there undoubtedly will be an extent to which taxes on inherited wealth do affect saving and consumption decisions, and thereby create distortions in the same way that taxing the return to savings can create costly distortions. The idea that inheritance tax involves 'double taxation' of assets that have already been bought out of taxed income, and thereby reduces incentives to work and save, certainly seems to be behind some of the public unpopularity of inheritance taxes, according to work done with focus groups.[8] Of course, there is also an income effect on the recipients of transfers, who have an unambiguously reduced incentive to save and work. If you expect to receive a large inheritance, why save yourself?

In practice, there is limited empirical evidence on the effects of this. Some studies from the US suggest some small negative effects of estate taxes on the wealth accumulation of potential donors and some negative effects of anticipated receipt of inheritances by potential recipients.[9] One study suggested that receipt of an inheritance of $350,000 might reduce labour force participation rates by 12% and reduce the probability that both

---

[7] The literature surveyed in Gale and Slemrod (2001b) and Kopczuk (2010) neither confirms nor refutes any of the motives.

[8] Lewis and White, 2006; Prabhakar, 2008.

[9] Weil, 1994; Kopczuk and Slemrod, 2001.

members of a couple work by 14%.[10] By extension, taxes that reduce receipts should increase work incentives.

The motive for transferring wealth makes a big difference in analysing how wealth transfers should be taxed—but the implications of different motives for policy are not always clear-cut, and in some cases depend on how we frame the government's objectives.

Since purely accidental bequests are, by definition, not made by choice, taxing them would not change donors' behaviour. There would be no economic efficiency cost in taxing such unintended transfers, so that a tax rate of 100% could, in principle, be levied without distorting choice. Obviously, this could not apply to *inter vivos* transfers—this is the only motive that would directly justify taxing bequests on death differently from *inter vivos* gifts.

In the case of strategic bequests, one can draw an analogy between the bequest and a market transaction—a sale of services from one person to another—and argue that such transfers (the income from the sale) should be taxed. Indeed, one could argue that, in principle, VAT should be payable on the transfer.

Transfers motivated by altruism or by 'joy of giving' are the most difficult to analyse.[11] Theoretical policy prescriptions turn out to depend critically on the precise nature of the donor's motivations. For example, if I get a warm glow from giving, is my pleasure determined by the (before-tax) amount given or the (after-tax) amount received? The recipient's feelings also matter: do they care about the lost consumption that the donor suffered in order to transfer the wealth—or indeed the pleasure the donor may have got from doing so? And exactly how should the motivations of donor and recipient (and perhaps others) figure in governments' decision-making?

If donor and recipient behave as continuations of the same individual and transfers to the next generation are made much like saving for one's own future, we might apply the conclusions that we drew on savings taxation: that the normal return to capital should not be taxed; taxes should arise

---

[10] Holtz-Eakin, Joulfaian, and Rosen, 1993.

[11] For extensive discussion—and often heated debate—of the relationship between individuals' motivations, government objectives, and theoretically optimal policy, see e.g. Hammond (1988), Kaplow (1995 and 1998), Cremer and Pestieau (2006), Farhi and Werning (2010), and Boadway, Chamberlain, and Emmerson (2010).

either when labour income and excess returns are earned or when consumption occurs.[12] If there is an expenditure tax, then my children or later generations will pay tax on what they inherit when they come to spend it.[13] But there is no role for taxing transfers: consumption by different people (just like consumption at different times or consumption of different goods) should not be taxed differently.[14] However, this policy implication is not inevitable: even if donor and recipient behave as if they are continuations of the same individual, it is not clear that policymakers must think of them, or treat them, that way. As we shall see, governments might have other reasons for treating transfers to the next generation differently from savings.

While exploring the implications of different bequest motives is interesting and throws light on the issues involved in deciding upon the appropriate taxation of gifts and bequests, it is clear that on its own it does not take us very far in forming a practical policy recommendation. In our view, such considerations are certainly not enough to rule out taxing transfers. But with this conceptual background in place, we believe more progress can be made by looking at what the government's objectives for wealth transfer taxation might be.

The ethical case for taxation of inherited wealth is important. It was put thus by John Stuart Mill:

I see nothing objectionable in fixing a limit to what anyone may acquire by mere favour of others, without any exercise of his faculties, and in requiring that if he desires any further accession of fortune, he shall work for it.[15]

The Meade Committee took a very similar view:

Inherited wealth is widely considered—and we share the view—to be a proper subject for heavier taxation on grounds both of fairness and of economic incentives. The citizen who by his own effort and enterprise has built up a fortune is considered to deserve better tax treatment than the citizen who, merely as a result of the fortune

---

[12] This result is demonstrated in Cremer and Pestieau (2006) and Farhi and Werning (2010). The latter paper also demonstrates how it is sensitive to the definition of social welfare.

[13] Hashimzade and Myles (2007) have shown that an expenditure tax achieves more redistribution than an income tax precisely because it ultimately taxes initial wealth holdings (or 'old capital') when they are spent.

[14] This argument would, of course, still be subject to the same caveats as those about taxation of different goods (see Chapter 6) or at different times (see Chapter 13), e.g. if consumption by some people was more complementary to labour supply than consumption by others.

[15] Quoted in Reeves (2007, 210).

of birth, owns an equal property; and to tax the former more lightly than the latter will put a smaller obstacle in the way of effort and enterprise.[16]

Many people see pursuing equality of opportunity as an important goal for policy. Inequality in inheritance runs directly counter to that agenda. Whilst inequality resulting from differential ability and effort may be acceptable, inequality resulting from differences in opportunity may be less so. This provides a powerful argument for taxing transfers of wealth between generations, to reduce the advantage that some people get from being born into a well-off family. The fact that the ownership of inherited wealth is extremely concentrated may also add a further attraction to this argument for a wealth transfer tax. Further, there may be concerns about the access to power and status that access to wealth brings. (These concerns, of course, are not limited to inherited wealth.)

If it is equality of opportunity in this sense which matters, then three considerations for the design of a tax system follow. First, from the point of view of equity, it is the amount of money received by an individual which matters, rather than the amount given by the donor. It makes sense to think of the tax base as receipts by beneficiaries rather than gifts and bequests from donors. We should not tax a bequest of £1 million that is divided equally among ten recipients at a higher rate than a bequest of £100,000 given to one recipient. In each case, the impact on the recipient is the same—they receive £100,000. And if the argument for a wealth transfer tax is one of equality of opportunity, then it is the increased wealth of the recipient which should be the base for the tax. Second, again because it seems to make sense to look at this from the perspective of the recipient, one would ideally want to consider the total amount received in inheritance from all sources. If I receive £1 million from each of five rich uncles, I should be treated no differently from my sister who receives a single sum of £5 million from one rich aunt. Third, it is possible that if equality of *opportunity* is our concern, then we might want to distinguish between inheritance received when young and that received when old or, to take this a step further, we might want to vary taxation according to the age gap between the donor and the recipient. There is a stronger case for taxing wealth passed down to the next generation than for taxing gifts to people of the same age—let alone contributions to the

[16] Meade, 1978, 318.

care of an elderly relative. And it is not obvious that we should want to tax transfers directly from grandparents to grandchildren less heavily than transfers that happen in two stages (from grandparents to parents, then from parents to children), as would be implied by a system that taxed each transfer of wealth separately.

But we also need to keep in clear view what is and is not possible to achieve through the taxation of gifts and bequests. There are many drivers of inequality of opportunity that are not to do with direct transfers of wealth. Time spent with children, housing and material goods, education expenditure (in particular, private education), and much else vary between families and have a material effect on children's life chances. We need to be clear whether, and why, inheritance or other transfers of wealth are different and should be subject to taxation. The answer may well be that, practically, this is all that can be taxed, in which case we have to recognize that one consequence of only taxing direct transfers is that decisions may be distorted towards, for example, greater investment in education or other less tangible or earlier transfers—it being particularly hard to imagine that gifts received during childhood could be taxed effectively.

Of course, there is a great deal of public expenditure on welfare benefits, social services, early education, and schooling, which in large part is driven by various equity concerns. One might want to view taxation of wealth transfers as a complement to these activities of the state. Together with state education and so on, taxation of wealth received provides those in the next generation with a measure of insurance against particularly fortunate or unfortunate circumstances of birth.

Our view is that there is a case for wealth transfer taxation as one part of an overall policy aimed at reducing inequalities of opportunity. We have also emphasized in this volume the importance of taking a life-cycle perspective on taxation. Whilst recognizing the limitations, the logic of this position drives us to suggest a tax based on the recipient rather than on the donor, and a tax based on total receipts over a lifetime. The question then arises as to the practicability of such an approach.

15.3. WEALTH TRANSFER TAXES IN THE UK

The main effort to tax wealth transfers in the UK is inheritance tax, which is, so far as we know, the only tax in the UK that around half the population seriously believes should be abolished altogether,[17] with most of the rest wanting significant cuts. Yet the political difficulty and controversy created by the tax are out of all proportion to its importance as a source of revenue. In the UK, even after a decade of rapid growth in housing wealth, inheritance tax was paid on only 3% of estates on death in 2009–10 and raised less than 0.5% of all tax revenue.[18] The position is similar in the US, where only about 2% of estates were subject to the federal estate duty in 2009.[19] Given this apparently limited scope and impact, the degree of political salience is at first sight surprising.

And it is not because the idea and practice of taxing transfers at death are new. In the UK, and internationally, this area of taxation has a longer history than many. Inheritance taxes were established in a number of European countries by the 17th century and probate duty was introduced in the UK in 1694, a century before newfangled ideas such as taxing income received much of a hearing. One attraction, which was true then and remains so today to some extent, is the practical legal necessity of transferring the deceased's property to his or her heirs. That provides an opportunity both to value the wealth of the deceased, and to collect the tax by ensuring that the inheritors can only claim title to the estate once the tax is paid.

The UK inheritance tax (IHT) is levied at a rate of 40% of assets in excess of a tax-free allowance of £325,000 in 2010–11. Assets bequeathed to spouses or civil partners are entirely exempt from tax[20] and, since October 2007, unused tax-free allowances have been transferable between spouses, so that married couples and civil partners can collectively bequeath double the

---

[17] Hedges and Bromley, 2001.

[18] Out of a total of 555,000 deaths (Office for National Statistics, *Monthly Digest of Statistics*, table 2.4, http://www.statistics.gov.uk/statbase/TSDSeries1.asp), some 15,000 estates were taxed (HMRC statistics, table 1.4, http://www.hmrc.gov.uk/stats/tax_receipts/table1-4.pdf). A further 4,000 lifetime transfers were taxed. Revenue figures from HM Treasury (2011, table C.3).

[19] Gale and Slemrod, 2001.

[20] The exemption is limited if the spouse or civil partner is not domiciled in the UK, reflecting the fact that foreign assets are outside the scope of the tax if owned by a non-domiciled person.

allowance (i.e. £650,000 in 2010–11) tax free even if the first to die leaves their entire estate to the surviving partner. Gifts made within seven years of death are also subject to some tax, charged at a rate that is lower the further from death the gift is made, but otherwise *inter vivos* gifts between individuals are not subject to tax.[21] The other main exemptions from tax relate to gifts to charity and bequests of businesses, unquoted shares, and agricultural property. These reliefs between them are estimated to have reduced IHT liabilities by £770 million in 2010–11—a substantial amount in the context of a tax raising just £2.7 billion in total.[22]

Table 15.1 gives an indication of how assets were distributed in 2007–08 (the latest year for which data are available). The table only covers estates notified for probate, thus excluding around half of estates either (broadly speaking) because they were worth less than £5,000 or because they were jointly owned and passed automatically to a surviving spouse or civil partner—in both cases meaning there would be no IHT liability. Even excluding these, the large majority of estates were small—below £200,000 in value—and therefore not within the IHT net. Owner-occupied housing made up a large part of total assets and especially for those estates with

Table 15.1. Composition of estates by size (estates passing on death in 2007–08)

Size of estate (£ million)	Number of estates	Residential buildings	Cash	Securities	Other[a]
Below 0.2	162,954	61%	32%	5%	2%
0.2–0.3	54,795	63%	26%	5%	6%
0.3–0.5	32,786	56%	25%	11%	8%
0.5–1.0	14,615	44%	23%	20%	13%
1.0–2.0	4,045	35%	17%	30%	19%
Above 2.0	1,443	25%	12%	35%	29%
All	270,639	52%	24%	14%	10%

[a] Including other buildings and land, and insurance policies.

Note: This table includes information on estates notified for probate before 1 July 2010 of people who died in the year to 5 April 2008, before reductions for reliefs and exemptions.

Source: Authors' calculations based on HMRC statistics, table 12.4 (http://www.hmrc.gov.uk/stats/inheritance_tax/table12-4.pdf).

[21] There may be a lifetime tax charge at a lower 20% rate for a gift into a trust.
[22] http://www.hmrc.gov.uk/stats/tax_expenditures/table1-5.pdf; HM Treasury, 2011, table C.3.

between £200,000 and £500,000 in total assets, which are those estates close
to or just over the tax threshold (£300,000 in 2007–08).

This concentration of wealth in housing among those with modest estates,
alongside rapid house price increases, was largely responsible for the increase
in the number of estates taxed on death from 18,000 to 34,000 (from 3% to
6% of estates) between 1998–99 and 2006–07.[23] It is also likely to be
responsible for some of the apparent discontent over IHT. The biggest
estates had the largest amounts in shares and other assets. In trying to
understand both the impact and the perception of IHT, it is important to
recognize that it is harder to organize one's affairs so as to avoid paying tax
when the main asset one owns is the house in which one lives. The fall in the
number of estates liable for inheritance tax after 2006–07, down to 15,000 in
2009–10, was caused primarily by the introduction of transferable allowances
between spouses, along with a cooling of the housing market from its
Autumn 2007 peak and above-inflation increases in the inheritance tax
threshold.

The current UK system does not stack up terribly well against any
reasonable set of principles for the design of a tax on inherited wealth. We
have already suggested that the logic behind a system of wealth transfer
taxation implies that tax should be levied on the recipient and should be
levied irrespective of whether the transfer was made at or before death. Of
course, inheritance tax is not designed to meet these criteria, but even on its
own logic it is not well designed. It ought to be as comprehensive as possible,
both as a matter of fairness and in order to minimize opportunities for
(economically costly) tax planning and avoidance. And it should presumably
be designed in a way that garners public acceptance. There are specific and
important ways in which the current system fails to conform to these criteria.

The first is the existence of reliefs, in particular for agricultural land and
unquoted business assets. The UK is unusual in offering unlimited 100%
relief on business assets—this is not available in France, Germany, or the US.
These reliefs create just the sort of non-neutrality the tax system ought to try
to avoid, pushing up the price of agricultural land and of certain offerings on
the AIM market, and providing a large incentive to keep businesses going

---

[23] HMRC statistics, table 1.4, http://www.hmrc.gov.uk/stats/tax_receipts/table1-4.pdf and
Office for National Statistics, *Monthly Digest of Statistics*, table 2.4, http://
www.statistics.gov.uk/statbase/TSDSeries1.asp.

and in the family even if there are good financial reasons for disposing of them sooner. This is damaging economically. At the very least, the rules should be significantly tightened up to limit reliefs to a certain level and to, for example, active farmers and genuine sole or majority owners of businesses. Even here, however, we see no real merit in granting special treatment to preserve the wealth of a particular occupational group.[24]

Second, the current IHT regime introduces another non-neutrality—and, arguably, horizontal inequity—into the tax system through its treatment of marriage (and civil partnership). If I am married and leave my estate to my spouse, no tax is payable, and indeed I bequeath to her my tax-free allowance. If I leave my estate to my unmarried partner, tax is payable. This is unquestionably the biggest tax advantage for marriage in the current tax system.

Third, the UK system has a significant threshold, but then imposes tax at 40% on all bequests above that tax-free allowance. This is a rate twice the current basic rate of income tax. There is merit in a system with a high allowance and then a substantial marginal rate, but it seems likely that an initial lower rate would command greater public acceptance.

There is also a practical issue around how to deal with *trusts*. A trust is a relationship created by the donor that requires a *trustee* to hold property for the benefit of others. While trusts are often set up for entirely different reasons, they can potentially be used to avoid the payment of inheritance tax since they confer the benefits of wealth without transferring the ownership— they frequently operate to separate the entitlement to the income that trust property generates from the entitlement to the trust property itself. It is then necessary to decide how each interest should be taxed. In addition, and more importantly, an individual's interest under the trust may be uncertain. It may depend upon the occurrence of some future contingency—such as whether the individual survives to a particular age. Or it may depend upon the exercise in favour of an individual of some discretion vested in the trustees or another person. Trusts can continue over many years, during which it may not be known who will ultimately benefit from the trust property, and possibly skipping a generation entirely. Hence, special measures are needed

---

[24] There may be a case, which we do not consider here, for special measures to enable tax to be paid over time, rather than immediately, when the gifted or inherited assets are to be retained by the recipient and are otherwise illiquid.

to ensure that any tax on the transfer of inherited wealth from one individual to another cannot be avoided altogether through judicious use of trusts.

Trusts may be established for entirely legitimate personal or family reasons—for example, to provide for a disabled individual, to prevent family assets falling into spendthrift hands, or simply to ensure that an individual is only given the freedom to deal with assets as their own once they reach whatever age the donor regards as suitable. While the way in which particular trusts are taxed necessarily affects these personal and family decisions, we see no reason to devise a taxation regime that sets out to discourage the use of trusts or to express some moral view on the legitimacy or otherwise of particular trust objectives. Ideally, the regime for taxing transfers into and out of trusts and of property while it is held in trust should be compatible with whatever regime applies to the straightforward transfer of inherited wealth between individuals.

Unfortunately, this is extremely difficult to achieve. Experience clearly illustrates the obvious point that if certain trust arrangements are taxed more favourably than straightforward transfers of assets between individuals, the system will provide a significant incentive to adopt trust arrangements rather than making more straightforward choices. That is why the government now imposes a 20% tax on lifetime transfers of wealth into most kinds of trust.

All this aside, the fundamental practical issue raised by the current inheritance tax is that it is easily avoided by those—generally the very wealthy—who are able to transfer significant proportions of their wealth during their lifetime. The principal targets of the tax are frequently able to plan their affairs to minimize the impact of the tax before the occasion of its charge, provided they do not suffer the misfortune of an untimely and unexpected death. This planning is not open to the vast majority of us whose wealth is mainly tied up in the house in which we live, our pension, and modest assets over which it is important for us to retain control, especially as life expectancy and care costs increase. Maintaining an inheritance tax while not taxing lifetime gifts makes any justification of the tax much harder. It creates horizontal inequity according to when transfers are made. It results in vertical inequity because the wealthy are most likely to be able to exploit the differences. It encourages transfers to occur at a time dictated by the tax system.

So the biggest barrier to the effective operation of inheritance tax is the failure to tax *inter vivos* transfers. If one were to move to a tax on gifts and bequests received, the case for treating all receipts the same would be strong. There is no particular reason for distinguishing between wealth received from a living donor and that received from a dead one. Receipts can, in principle, be accounted for on a lifetime basis, with the tax being levied progressively. Moreover, the recipient would be taxed on all kinds of wealth they receive and not just bequests. Taxing the recipient accords well with the intuition that we discussed in the last section that the beneficiary of the inherited wealth should pay. So the same-sized stock of wealth should be taxed less when it is distributed more widely.

The downside, and it is a serious one, is that it is difficult to monitor the process of wealth acquisition. For a tax on receipts to work, it would be necessary for individuals to inform the tax authorities of all receipts over some minimum. Policing such a system would be hard—though some countries, such as Ireland, have some experience of such a system.[25] We would also have to accept some horizontal inequity and distortions around whatever boundary is chosen between taxable transfers of wealth and the kind of parental provision for children that could not possibly be taxed.

There are also significant practical difficulties in moving away from a tax that can be withheld from estates at the time of death. For a brief period, from 1975 until 1986, the UK had a gifts and bequests tax known as capital transfer tax, which sought to charge both lifetime gifts and bequests on a cumulative lifetime basis. It remained, however, a donor-based tax—the tax was charged by reference to the cumulative amount of the donor's gifts and bequests rather than by reference to the cumulative receipts of the beneficiary. The short life of the capital transfer tax illustrates one of its difficulties: namely, that with no political consensus on how to tax gifts and bequests, individuals may decide to await the next change of government in anticipation of a more favourable regime.

Logic dictates that if we are to have a tax on wealth transfers, it is best levied on the recipient. Ideally, such a tax would be levied on lifetime receipts, or at least receipts over a significant period, so as to minimize

---

[25] The capital acquisitions tax is currently charged at 25% to the extent that the aggregate of gifts or inheritances exceeds the relevant threshold, which depends upon the relationship between the donor and the recipient.

opportunities to avoid the tax by transferring assets over time. How difficult this may be to achieve remains unclear. It is a very long time since a thorough review of the system of wealth transfer taxation was carried out, and we are certainly not aware of any studies that have looked seriously at how, and whether, a change from taxing the donor to taxing the recipient could be made. It is surely time to devote some serious resources to determining the feasibility of such a move.

Finally, we should note that while the current inheritance tax represents a flawed attempt to tax wealth transfers on death, the UK simultaneously maintains an equally flawed subsidy to certain wealth transfers on death: 'forgiveness' of capital gains tax (CGT). The deceased's estate is not liable for CGT on any increase in the value of assets prior to death, and those inheriting the assets are deemed to acquire them at their market value at the date of death, so any rise in value that occurs before death escapes tax completely. This cost the Exchequer £690 million in 2010–11[26]—equivalent to a quarter of the total yield from IHT.

Forgiveness of CGT at death reflects the presence of IHT: politicians understandably baulk at the idea of imposing (say) 28% CGT on top of 40% IHT. But that is a weak argument. CGT exemption does not, and should not, offset the impact of IHT.

In purely practical terms, the current system does not eliminate double taxation or zero taxation. Assets transferred in the seven years before death can still attract both IHT and CGT. Conversely, CGT is forgiven even when estates are below the IHT threshold and so no IHT would be paid anyway. And the two taxes exempt different asset classes: people's main homes are exempt from CGT, while agricultural property and unquoted businesses are not (though entrepreneur's relief does provide a reduced rate for owner-managed businesses).

More fundamentally, the two taxes serve different purposes. CGT is a tax on returns to savings, not on wealth transfers. As Boadway, Chamberlain, and Emmerson (2010, 801) put it,

the aim of capital gains tax is to ensure that capital gains are treated on a par with other forms of income such as dividends and interest which will already have been taxed as they accrue (and are also then subject to a wealth transfer tax). Wealth transfer taxation has different ends.

---

[26] HMRC statistics, table 1.5, http://www.hmrc.gov.uk/stats/tax_expenditures/table1-5.pdf.

'Double taxation' of wealth that was already taxed as income (or will be taxed as expenditure) is inherent to wealth transfer taxation. The principles discussed in the previous section essentially concerned whether there is a case for such double taxation. Coexistence of CGT with wealth transfer taxation would merely make this double taxation more explicit.[27] If policymakers do not accept the argument for taxing transfers, then they should not tax them: simply abolish inheritance tax. But if there is an argument for taxing transfers, that must be on top of the regime for taxing returns to capital.

The regime for taxing returns to savings should be designed appropriately on its own merits, while wealth transfer taxation should tax the value of wealth transferred; it should not depend on the historical returns earned on those particular assets. Forgiveness of CGT at death looks like another half-hearted reluctance to adopt a principled position. But it is highly distortionary. It encourages people to hold on to assets that have risen in value, even if it would be more profitable to sell them and use the proceeds in some other way before death (at which point other assets, including the proceeds from selling the original assets, could be passed on instead) and even if it would be preferable to pass on the assets (or the proceeds from selling them) immediately. If people expect to be able to bequeath assets on death, it also encourages them to buy assets that yield returns in the form of capital gains and to convert income into capital gains where possible.

Wealth transfer taxation may affect how much people save, but it should not unnecessarily distort asset allocations in this way. Whatever kind of wealth transfer tax one does (or does not) want, there is no case for forgiveness of CGT on death.

---

[27] Note also that ending forgiveness of CGT at death need not necessarily mean that CGT would be payable at the same time as IHT. If an asset were retained by the recipient, the system could be designed so that CGT liability was triggered only on sale of the asset, with the base price deemed to be the original purchase price rather than the market value when the asset changed hands. That is how *inter vivos* transfers between spouses and civil partners are already treated for CGT purposes.

15.4. CONCLUSIONS

The arguments against taxing the normal return to life-cycle savings do not apply with equal force to the taxation of bequests and other transfers of wealth. There may be a particular case for taxing inherited wealth on equity grounds. Yet the current system of inheritance taxation in the UK is something of a mess. Its notable failings are largely to do with the fact that it is half-hearted and hence fails to tax the wealthiest.

By taxing transfers only on or near death, it allows the richest to organize their affairs to avoid taxation. Only those with very large amounts of wealth can afford to give most of it away several years before they die. And by exempting business assets and agricultural land, IHT creates distortions that have no economic justification and promote avoidance among those who can engage in tax planning. As Kay and King noted in 1990, inheritance tax favours 'the healthy, wealthy and well advised',[28] and nothing much has changed in the 20 years since then to affect that judgement. Few can aspire to be rich enough to avoid inheritance taxation, but many aspire to wealth levels at which they would end up paying it. As currently structured, it therefore resembles a tax on aspiration.

It is not so surprising, therefore, that IHT is unpopular. Some countries have responded to similar concerns by abolishing their inheritance and transfer taxes altogether. Such responses inevitably make the retention of such taxes in other countries more problematic (in particular in the form adopted by the UK), given the increasing mobility of those who might otherwise find themselves subject to such taxes.

We do not believe the UK should move towards abolition. It is not required by the dictates of efficiency; nor is it justified in the face of great, and growing, inequality in wealth. But while there is a case to maintain some form of tax on inherited wealth, the argument for leaving things as they are is weak.

Whatever else is done, forgiveness of capital gains tax at death should be ended. As a way to offset the impact of inheritance tax, it is poorly targeted. But, in any case, no choice of a tax regime for wealth transfers justifies

[28] Kay and King, 1990, 107.

creating the bizarre distortions to asset allocation decisions that this policy does.

A minimal reform to inheritance tax itself would be to maintain it in more or less its current form but to widen its base to include business assets and agricultural property. There may in addition be a case for levying it at a lower rate than 40%, at least on an initial tranche of assets.

But the biggest barrier to the effective working of inheritance tax as it currently stands is that it is levied only at or close to death, allowing the wealthy to avoid it altogether by the simple expedient of passing on wealth well before they die. Put this fact together with the logic of such a tax, which suggests that a tax on the recipient makes more sense than a tax on the donor, and the case for a tax on lifetime receipts looks strong. That case does need to be balanced against the practical difficulties of implementation. Such a tax would have to depend on self-assessment. There may be particular issues arising from international mobility. But a movement towards a tax on lifetime receipts would be more defensible than the current system, both on grounds of fairness and on grounds of economic efficiency. The present halfway house simply provides ammunition to the abolitionists.

16

———

The Taxation of Land and Property

Most taxes nowadays are levied on flows of income and of expenditure. But land and property have been taxed for centuries—certainly for longer than income—and they continue to form an important part of the tax base in most advanced economies.

There are good economic reasons for this. The supply of property, and especially land, is not very responsive to its price, which means that it can be taxed without significantly distorting people's behaviour. The ownership of land is also generally visible and easily established, which makes it relatively straightforward to identify who should be paying the tax. The fact that land and property have identifiable and unchangeable geographic locations also makes them natural tax bases for the financing of local government.

But deciding exactly *how* to tax land and property is particularly complex, because they combine a number of characteristics that each suggest different tax treatments. Take a house. It sits on land, the value of which we might want to tax because the land is completely fixed and the return to it is an economic rent. But the house also provides services that are consumed by the occupier—just as a fridge or a car does. So it is natural to think that the value of this consumption should be subject to VAT. The house is also a valuable asset, whose value rises and fluctuates like those of stocks and shares. So we might see homeownership as a form of saving that should be taxed consistently with other savings. Also important is the distinction between owner-occupied and rented property. Ideally, we would want to treat these consistently. But, at present, their tax treatments are quite different in the UK, providing a clear bias towards owner-occupation.

Business property also combines characteristics that suggest different tax treatments. We would ideally like to tax the commercial use of land consistently with other uses, while treating the property built on it consistently with other inputs into the production process.

To understand how to tax land and property, it is important to keep these issues and themes distinct. To be clear:

- **Land**, whether used for business or residential property, can be taxed at an arbitrarily high rate on economic efficiency grounds.

- **Business property** is an input into the production process and, on efficiency grounds, should not be taxed.

- **Owner-occupied housing** combines the features of an investment and a consumption good, and we should consider its taxation from both these points of view.

- **Rental housing** is an investment good from the point of view of the owner and a consumption good from the view of the renter. Overall, there is a presumption in favour of taxing it at a similar level to owner-occupied housing.

In this chapter, we start with a discussion of the case for land value taxation and the practical difficulties that may pose. We contrast the strong case for taxing land values with the strong case against taxing business property. We go on to look at the taxation of the consumption value of housing and conclude that, in the UK context, council tax should be reformed so that it more closely resembles a genuine tax on the consumption value of housing. The asset-like properties of housing mean that it should also be brought into the savings tax regime outlined in Chapter 13. Finally, we consider stamp duty land tax, finding little to say in its defence.

It is worth noting two further issues that are important in the taxation of land and property, though we do not pursue them further.

First, taxes on land and property have strong historical ties to local taxation. This is, in part, due to the widespread view that such taxes are partly 'benefit taxes', a charge for the goods and services provided locally. It also reflects the immobility of property—it is clearly associated with the location. In the UK, council tax—an annual tax imperfectly related to the value of domestic property—is the main tax base for local government, though the majority of local government income comes directly from central government. A very complex system of 'equalization' exists, giving larger grants to those local authorities with a more limited tax base—where properties are less valuable—to try to ensure that, if all local authorities spent at the level judged appropriate by central government, they would all levy the same tax rate on properties of a given value. We do not explore these issues further. For the most part, the question of how to tax land and property can be separated from where the power to tax is located. For example, reforms to council tax could be accompanied by adjustments to grants that maintain the existing distribution of spending power across local governments.

Second, land and property are hugely important socially and economically. Having enough housing available to accommodate the population comfortably matters. Decisions over whether to develop land for business or housing use contribute to the structure of the economy. The impact of the housing market on the macroeconomy is great enough both to have influenced the decision not to take the UK into the euro and to influence regular decisions over interest rate policy. Changes to the tax system aimed at increasing the availability of housing and of business land have been proposed, as have changes that, it is claimed, will reduce volatility in the housing market. We note these issues below in relevant sections, but they are not the focus of our considerations. Other policy choices, in particular over the planning regime—the desirable reform of which is well outside the scope of this review—are likely to be more important in this context.

16.1. THE TAXATION OF LAND VALUES

16.1.1. The Economic Argument

Land and property should be thought of as distinct bases for taxation, although in most countries taxes are levied on the combined value of property and the land on which it is located. William Vickrey, a Nobel Prizewinning economist, argued that 'The property tax is, economically speaking, a combination of one of the worst taxes—the part that is assessed on real estate improvements ...—and one of the best taxes—the tax on land or site value'.[1] Later in this chapter, we argue that there are in fact good reasons for taxing housing as well as the land on which it stands; but as far as business property is concerned, Vickrey had it exactly right.

The economic case for taxing land itself is very strong and there is a long history of arguments in favour of it. Taxing land ownership is equivalent to taxing an economic rent—to do so does not discourage any desirable activity. Land is not a produced input; its supply is fixed and cannot be affected by the introduction of a tax. With the same amount of land available, people would not be willing to pay any more for it than before, so (the present value of) a land value tax (LVT) would be reflected one-for-one in a lower price of land: the classic example of *tax capitalization*. Owners of land on the day such a tax is announced would suffer a windfall loss as the value of their asset was reduced. But this windfall loss is the only effect of the tax: the incentive to buy, develop, or use land would not change. Economic activity that was previously worthwhile remains worthwhile. Moreover, a tax on land value would also capture the benefits accruing to landowners from external developments rather than their own efforts. Henry George, the political economist, writing in the mid 19th century, argued that land taxes are equitable because the value of land is determined by community effort, not by individual effort.[2] Winston Churchill, speaking in the House of Commons in 1909, put this argument eloquently:

Roads are made, streets are made, services are improved, electric light turns night into day, water is brought from reservoirs a hundred miles off in the mountains—and all the while the landlord sits still. Every one of those improvements is effected by the labour and cost of other people and the taxpayers. To not one of those improvements does the land monopolist, as a land monopolist, contribute, and yet by every one of them the value of his land is enhanced. He renders no service to the community, he contributes nothing to the general welfare, he contributes nothing to the process from which his own enrichment is derived.

One wrinkle in the argument that an LVT would not distort behaviour is that there is, in effect, some elasticity in the supply of land because of planning regulations. Governments in the UK and most other countries specify the uses to which particular pieces of land can be put—for example, residential, business, or agricultural. So land that is designated for

---

[1] Vickrey, 1999, 17.
[2] George, 1879.

agricultural use, for example, cannot be used for house-building. In general, land with planning permission for residential use is much more valuable than adjacent land with an agricultural designation. In January 2009, the average value of a hectare of arable farming land in south-east England was £20,000, compared with £1.3 million for a hectare of industrial land and £2.5 million for a similar area of residential building land.[3] A tax on land value might, at the margin, reduce the incentive to apply for permission to change the designation. But the scale of gains available suggests this is unlikely to be a major issue. And, in any case, planning permission is a policy variable, not a market good: a government concerned that an LVT might discourage valuable development could compensate by relaxing planning regulations so that applications were more likely to succeed. This could be done directly or achieved by giving local authorities, which generally make planning decisions, some incentive to accept applications by, for example, allowing them access to some portion of the additional receipts created by an extension of their tax base.[4]

It is worth noting in passing that a number of unsuccessful attempts have been made to capture the rents arising from *change* in designation through the introduction of 'development taxes' or 'betterment taxes', in 1947, 1967, 1973, and 1976. Each attempt has ended in failure, in large part as a result of lack of credibility over the long-term sustainability of the tax.[5] There has been a clear incentive to wait for a reversal of the policy before applying for planning permission. More recent proposals to introduce a Planning-Gain Supplement[6] were worked up and consulted on in some detail but were eventually dropped in 2007 in favour of an extension to the less formal

---

[3] Valuation Office Agency, 2009.

[4] Bentick (1979) and Oates and Schwab (1997), in contrast, argue that an LVT can create a bias towards excessively rapid development: more specifically, towards land uses that deliver returns early, since returns of equal present value that accrue more slowly are still capitalized into land prices immediately and therefore taxed every year even before they are realized. This bias could be avoided by taxing the 'best use' value of the land rather than its market value (though 'best use' value would be even harder to assess); but, in any case, it does not seem to us to be a sufficient reason to reject LVT.

[5] The history is well set out in the Barker Review (Barker, 2004, box 4.2).

[6] http://customs.hmrc.gov.uk/channelsPortalWebApp/channelsPortalWebApp.portal?_nfpb= true&_pageLabel=pageLibrary_ConsultationDocuments&propertyType=document&columns =1&id=HMCE_PROD1_024845.

system of planning charges. These do capture some of the value uplift from granting of planning permission but, historically, have been less transparent, predictable, and consistently applied than either a national planning-gain supplement or an LVT would be.

Since LVT would be levied annually rather than just at the point planning permission was granted, it would not create the same incentive to delay development in the hope that the policy would be reversed. Even if the LVT were abolished again, delaying a planning application for a year to wait for its abolition would save at most only a proportion (the tax rate) of the value of having planning permission for the one extra year. Unlike with a planning gains tax, the main gain from the abolition of LVT—the removal of all future years' liabilities—would be felt whether planning permission were granted before or after its abolition, so there is no advantage to be had by waiting.

16.1.2. Practical Issues

The economic case for a land value tax is simple, and almost undeniable. Why, then, do we not have one already? Why, indeed, is the possibility of such a tax barely part of the mainstream political debate, with proponents considered marginal and unconventional?

One issue, no doubt, is the simple lack of political attractiveness. If a land tax is seen as a new and additional tax, then it is likely to be about as popular as any other new tax. So it should be seen as an alternative to other existing property taxes, not as a way to raise additional revenue. Moving from a property-based tax to a land-based tax would also create numerous gainers and losers. This is politically difficult. But then a major revaluation exercise just to bring current domestic property taxes up to date would also create winners and losers, which is perhaps why politicians have avoided doing it and why relative domestic property tax liabilities in England and Scotland bear increasingly little relation to relative property values.

As well as any political difficulty, introducing an LVT would also pose practical challenges. Valuing all land at an adequate level of disaggregation sounds like a formidable task. But before concluding that it is not possible, it is worth looking at how non-domestic property is valued for the purposes of business rates. There already exists a considerable apparatus designed

specifically to record land and property values. The basis for valuation is a
'rating list' for each local authority, identifying every relevant non-domestic
property in the area and estimating its annual rental value based on its
location, physical properties, and other relevant economic conditions.[7] There
are approximately 1.7 million non-domestic properties in England and
100,000 in Wales. The rating lists are compiled and maintained by the
Valuation Office Agency (VOA), which employed the equivalent of just over
4,000 full-time staff in 2009–10.[8] The rating lists are updated during their
lifetime to reflect changes in properties, and new lists are compiled every five
years.

We thus have a considerable machinery designed to value business
properties and update those values regularly. We have, or can obtain without
excessive cost, a measure of the land area occupied by each property. The
Land Registry holds information on the boundaries of each property and this
could be converted into area measurements. No doubt there would be some
initial disputes over the size of assigned areas, but this should be a one-off
transitional problem. Once the measurement of each property was agreed, it
would become part of the description of that property. If we are then able to
supply a land value per acre (or hectare, or square metre), it is possible to
combine this with the area of the property to compute the implied land
value.

The biggest practical obstacle to the implementation of a land value tax,
though, is that it would require the valuation of land separate from any
structure erected on it. If there were a competitive market for land, with a
high number of transactions, then the value of land would be directly
observable. But in most areas and sectors, the number of transactions in land
(separate from any buildings thereon) is low. In the absence of a sizeable
market, it is difficult to determine what the market price would be.

It is worth noting that since we are looking at taxing a rent, the figure for
land value does not have to be exact—or even approximate—for the LVT to
be efficient. The value of each plot of land falls by the present value of the tax
imposed on it; in principle, each plot could be taxed at an arbitrarily
different rate without compromising the efficiency of the tax. However, to

---

[7] Properties for which the concept of a market rent is tenuous, such as public utilities, are
valued using a statutory formula.

[8] Valuation Office Agency, 2010.

the extent that valuations are not accurate, inequities will be created between taxpayers—just as they can be created by inaccurate valuations under the current property tax regime, but the inequities will be worse if the valuation is less accurate.

So is it possible to determine the value per acre of land given the thinness of the market? We cannot answer that for certain, but there are reasons to believe that it may not be impossible. There are some transactions to work with—enough, indeed, for the VOA even now to publish estimates of land values for residential and industrial land at some level of disaggregation (by town, for example). There are recognized methods for determining land value where the market is thin: where similar buildings are valued differently according to their location, for example, it is not hard to imagine that the difference in overall value reflects the difference in land values. We are also encouraged by the considerable international experience of land valuation—in Denmark and in various US and Australian states, for example.[9]

As Kate Barker concluded in her comprehensive review,[10]

A national land value tax would also require additional administrative resources in order for a national land ownership and value register to be created. Given the volatility of land prices over recent years, regular valuations would be needed in order to tax accurately the underlying value of land assets. Such a system would not be impossible to envisage, however—… Denmark operates a system of nationwide land taxation. Indeed, given the information shortages concerning land ownership and land value in the UK, there are arguments for a more comprehensive land registry in any case.

A recent review of US evidence[11] suggests that successfully implementing and administering a land value tax is feasible. We are not in a position to make such a judgement for the UK, but we propose that government should study the feasibility of such a tax. As we will see below, there is a much stronger case for having a separate land value tax in the case of land used for non-domestic purposes, so the feasibility needs first to be studied for commercial and agricultural land rather than for land on which housing sits.

---

[9] Japan, South Korea, and Taiwan also have experience of LVT. Andelson (2001) contains details on international experience.

[10] Barker, 2004, paragraph 4.14.

[11] Dye and England, 2009.

16.1.3. Replacing Business Rates

In the UK, business property is taxed through the national non-domestic rate (NNDR or business rates), which is levied as a percentage of the estimated rental value of the property, with reduced rates for low-value properties. It raised about £24 billion in 2009–10, more than 4% of total revenue.[12] Although locally administered, it is a national tax, with the rate set centrally and all receipts flowing into national coffers.

The business rate is not a good tax. It discriminates between different sorts of businesses—agriculture is exempt, for example. More fundamentally, from an economic perspective, business property is an input to the productive process of a company. Further, it is a produced, or *intermediate*, input with the same economic properties as other forms of physical capital. As we discussed in Chapter 6, it is an important principle of the economics of taxation that an efficient tax system should not distort choices firms make about inputs into the production process, and hence that intermediate goods—those used in the production process—should not be taxed. The principal effect of business rates is that economic activity in the UK is artificially skewed away from property-intensive production.

Another effect of business rates in practice arises from the treatment of unused or undeveloped land, on which business rates are levied at reduced or zero rates. This provides a clear and perverse incentive to use land inefficiently. Indeed, this has led to a rash of garish press headlines about property-owners demolishing property in order to avoid business rates. This puts the issue in rather stark perspective. If property is subject to tax and land is not, then, if the property is not being used, a tax incentive for demolition is created. If empty or unused property is taxed at a lower rate than property being used, then a tax disincentive to use it is created. An LVT avoids these problems.

Taxing non-domestic property is inefficient, and should not be part of the tax system. But abolishing business rates now that they already exist would, on its own, provide a windfall gain to the owners of business land and property. Handing out windfall gains is an inefficient use of taxpayers' money, and the distribution of these gains would be unfair: in general, those receiving windfalls will not even be the same people who were previously

---

[12] HM Treasury, 2010b, table C11.

made worse off by business rates, since the beneficiaries will probably have acquired the property at a lower price reflecting the expected tax bill (i.e. business rates will have been capitalized into the purchase price of properties).

If business rates were replaced by an LVT, however, the windfall gains from abolishing business rates would be offset by windfall losses from introducing LVT. The offset would not be exact for individual properties: owners of highly developed properties would gain while owners of undeveloped land would lose. But in so far as the value of property is largely determined by the value of the land on which it stands, the offset will be close. And if the reform is revenue neutral, there would at least be no windfall gains or losses on average.

To mitigate transition costs, the reform should be implemented gradually, with transitional protection for those most affected, similar to what already happens with business rate revaluations. While not essential to such a reform, in our view agricultural land should be brought within the net— although much of it may be of low enough value that it would in reality be subject to little or no tax.

Given available data, it is hard to be precise about what rate of LVT on commercial land would be required to replace business rates on a revenue-neutral basis. Some basic calculations[13] suggest that a rate somewhere in the region of 4% of land value levied once a year might achieve this. One could clearly introduce this gradually whilst reducing business rates, perhaps starting at ½% of land value and rising. Ideally, such a tax would also replace stamp duty land tax on business properties, the inefficiency of which is discussed in Section 16.3.

We do not go further in our prescriptions here. We cannot say conclusively that the administrative hurdles to such a reform could be overcome at reasonable cost, but we cannot see any fundamental problems. This is such a powerful idea, and one that has been so comprehensively ignored by governments, that the case for a thorough official effort to design a workable system seems to us to be overwhelming. In particular, significant

---

[13] Following Muellbauer (2005). He recommends imposing an LVT at 2% of land value on business land whilst keeping business rates at half their current level, and estimates that this would be roughly revenue neutral. He suggests an exemption for land worth less than £20,000 a hectare, which would exclude most agricultural land.

adjustment costs would be merited if the inefficient and iniquitous system of business rates could be swept away and replaced by an LVT.

But what should be done if a move to a system of land value taxation were to be deemed politically or practically infeasible? Currently, business rates are becoming gradually less important, as they are constrained by legislation to grow by no more than price inflation, rather than with the economy and other tax bases. Hastening their demise looks attractive because of their distorting effects, but two considerations make us wary of recommending this in the absence of an acceptable alternative such as an LVT.

First, as we have already mentioned, there is the undesirable windfall gain to the owners of business land and property that abolishing business rates in isolation would imply. Second, even though business rates have many undesirable features, they are at least to some extent incident on land values. To paraphrase Vickrey, business rates are a combination of a desirable tax on the land and an undesirable tax on the buildings. If we cannot treat these two components differently, some tax on the combination may be preferable to leaving land values wholly untaxed.

16.2. HOUSING

We devote the rest of this chapter to the complex and contentious issue of the appropriate tax treatment of housing. Whilst there are not good reasons for taxing business property, there are good reasons for taxing housing. Housing has two main attributes that are relevant for tax design:

- First, by living in a house, you consume a flow of services. If we have a consumption tax such as a VAT, a reasonable presumption is that housing should in some way be covered by it.

- Second, homeowners also own a valuable asset; indeed, it is usually their *most* valuable asset. The value of the house may go up and down. In that sense, owner-occupied housing is like any other asset, and much of our discussion in Chapter 13 on the taxation of savings should apply.

The distinction between these two attributes is explicit in the case of private rented property: the landlord invests in the asset, while the renter consumes (and pays for) the flow of services. But the two attributes are just as surely present in owner-occupied housing: in effect, the owner-occupier is both landlord and tenant simultaneously. At present, the tax system treats rented and owner-occupied properties differently, creating a distortion in favour of owner-occupation. If, instead, we could treat all housing consistently both as a form of consumption and as a type of asset, such distortions could be removed. As we will see, achieving such ideal treatment in practice would be difficult. But it is important to be clear what we would like to aim for.

We take the first of these attributes—the consumption properties of housing—first. We then move on to consider how housing should be taxed as an asset.

As with business property, the taxation of land and the taxation of buildings can, in principle, be separated. In particular, regardless of the efficient taxation of housing as a consumption good or an asset, the land on which it stands could efficiently be taxed at an arbitrarily high rate. A 'two-tier' housing tax could tax residential buildings at one rate and residential land at a different (presumably higher) rate. Some US cities have such a tax. But we are wary of proposing this largely because, unlike with business property, there is a strong case for taxing buildings as well as land. So there is obvious merit in avoiding the considerable additional complexity associated with valuing and taxing residential land and buildings separately.

In what follows, therefore, we discuss taxation of the land and buildings taken together, though if an LVT could first be successfully implemented in the non-domestic sector, there may in future be a case for reconsidering its application to domestic property as well.

16.2.1. Taxing the Consumption Value of Housing

Housing can be thought of as a large consumer durable, like a very big fridge or car. When considering the taxation of most consumer durables, we start from the presumption that it would be appropriate to impose VAT on their price when new. This is because the price of the durable itself reflects the present value of the stream of services it is expected to yield. VAT paid on the newly bought good is, in effect, a prepayment on the stream of services yielded. A natural starting point is that the same approach should be applied to housing. Yet, at present, the UK, alone among OECD countries, applies a zero rate of VAT to the construction and sale of residential property.[14]

Houses differ from other consumer durables not only in size. For one thing, they last a very long time—hundreds of years in many cases. This raises two possible difficulties for imposing VAT.

First, because houses are so long lived, their consumption value may change a great deal over time. Hence, their up-front price may prove to be a bad approximation to the value of consumption services they eventually provide. Ideally, if a house delivered more (less) valuable services than was originally envisaged and built into the purchase price, we would like to tax (subsidize) this difference. This is true in principle for all durables, but on a much larger scale for housing.

Second, even if we wanted to impose VAT on newly built housing, we would still fail to impose any tax on the majority of UK housing for many decades to come. Taxing newly built housing while failing to tax the stream of consumption services that existing housing continued to provide would be problematic. It would artificially encourage overuse of existing properties and discourage new construction, while forgoing revenue from the existing housing stock means giving windfall gains to current homeowners at the expense of non-owners. An alternative[15] would be to levy VAT both on newbuild and on existing properties the next time they are sold—taxing the stream of consumption services they are expected to yield thereafter without retrospectively taxing the consumption services enjoyed to date. But this would act to discourage mutually beneficial transactions as people sought to defer the tax[16] and has the potential, like a planning gains tax, to be avoided altogether by the simple expedient of waiting for a future government to repeal the tax, before entering into any transaction.

If we want to tax the consumption value of housing, therefore, it is probably best to do so at the point at which the services are consumed rather

---

[14] Since VAT is generally charged on refurbishing existing properties but not on building new ones, the current system also incentivizes developers to build new properties rather than redevelop derelict sites.

[15] Proposed by Crawford, Keen, and Smith (2010).

[16] Another way of thinking about this effect is that, since only housing services consumed after the next transaction would be taxed, the tax would be minimized by delaying a transaction as long as possible.

than at the point of first purchase. That suggests an annual tax related to the (consumption) value of the property.

One immediate point to note is that such a tax should not be levied on any increase in property value resulting from improvements on which VAT has been levied. To do so would involve double taxation. This could, in principle, be avoided either by zero-rating such expenditure—spending on constructing extensions, for example—or by taxing only the consumption value of the 'unimproved' property. This latter solution seems wholly impractical over the long run. It would be odd indeed to be charging tax on a property in 2050 on the basis of its condition in 2010, for example. The former solution—not charging VAT on improvements—is preferable: the guiding principle should be that only those kinds of improvements that will affect the property valuation should be zero rated (or, in other words, valuations should only take account of improvements that were zero rated). Nevertheless, it may be difficult to define and police qualifying improvements in practice. This may be an area in which we have to accept some imperfection in the system.

Council Tax

A tax related to the consumption value of a property bears some resemblance to a tax we already have in Britain: council tax. Given that we want to levy a tax on the consumption value, it makes sense to build upon what is already in place.

Council tax is charged to all occupiers of domestic property.[17] In England and Scotland, council tax operates by placing every house into one of eight bands (A to H): the higher the band, the higher the council tax paid (see Table 16.1). The valuation bands are based on the estimated market value of each house on 1 April 1991—there has been no revaluation of properties at all in England or Scotland since the tax was introduced.[18] The ratios between the council tax bills charged for each band are set centrally, but the overall level of council tax is set locally (although central government can choose to cap it) and the revenue from the tax is locally retained.

---

[17] Strictly, not all occupiers—most students and some other groups are exempt.
[18] Though a revaluation was carried out in Wales, and a ninth band (band I) introduced there, with effect from April 2005 (based on April 2003 property values).

Table 16.1. Council tax bands and rates in England

Band	Value as at 1 April 1991	No. of properties in band in England at September 2010 (millions)[a]	Tax rate as a proportion of that in band D	Charge in local authority setting English average band D rate in 2009–10
A	Up to £40,000	5.7	$6/9$	£959
B	£40,001 to £52,000	4.5	$7/9$	£1,119
C	£52,001 to £68,000	5.0	$8/9$	£1,279
D	£68,001 to £88,000	3.5	$9/9$	£1,439
E	£88,001 to £120,000	2.2	$11/9$	£1,759
F	£120,001 to £160,000	1.1	$13/9$	£2,079
G	£160,001 to £320,000	0.8	$15/9$	£2,398
H	More than £320,000	0.1	$18/9$	£2,878

[a] Source: http://www.communities.gov.uk/localgovernment/localgovernmentfinance/counciltax/ and http://www.voa.gov.uk/publications/statistical_releases/council-tax-valuation-list-1993-england.html.

A 25% discount is applied where there is a sole occupant; second and empty homes are also subject to discounts, determined locally. A specific social security benefit—Council Tax Benefit—is available to ease the burden of the tax on those with low current incomes. In 2009–10, council tax, net of Council Tax Benefit, raised £25 billion and the average annual levy on a property in England was £1,175.[19]

Three things are immediately evident from Table 16.1. First, properties are heavily concentrated in the lower bands: two-thirds of all properties are in the bottom three bands, while less than a tenth are in the top three bands. Second, charges rise more slowly than values—the charge in band H is twice the charge in band D, whereas the house at the bottom of band H is worth more than four times the house at the bottom of band D. So the tax is designed to be regressive relative to its base—the more the house is worth, the less as a proportion of the value is paid in council tax. Third, the highest band covers all properties worth more than £320,000 in 1991, including those worth many times more, while the lowest band covers all properties

[19] Revenue figure from HM Treasury (2010b, table C11); average levy from Communities and Local Government, http://www.communities.gov.uk/documents/statistics/xls/1349754.xls.

worth less than £40,000 in 1991. The width of the top band, and the number of properties lumped into the bottom band, highlight the failure of council tax to differentiate between properties in the same band. In addition, of course, being based on values from so long ago, current tax bills take no account of subsequent changes in price relativities and hence do not capture even the original intention of the tax.

Council tax is an unpopular tax. There are a number of possible reasons for this. It is highly visible: 88% of tax is remitted by firms,[20] so for the vast majority of people council tax is one of the only taxes they are asked to pay personally.[21] This means people overestimate its importance. It also lacks buoyancy, which means that 'increases' have to be announced each year just to keep up with inflation, let alone growth in GDP. Council tax can seem particularly onerous for the 'asset-rich, cash-poor' since, unusually, it is not linked to a pre-existing cash flow. But there is also evidence that people just find the idea of a tax linked to the value of their property unfair.[22] This seems to reflect the fact that perceptions of fairness in tax are more closely linked to the relationship of the tax to flows of income than to stocks of wealth. But, both because consumption of housing services is as legitimate a tax base as any other consumption, and because it is a good complement to current income as an indicator of lifetime income or ability to pay, this does not seem to us to be a good objection—at least not economically.

The unpopularity of council tax has been one major factor behind the unwillingness of government to undertake revaluations. The other is the fact that any revaluation inevitably creates losers and winners—and losers tend to be very vocal. This is one of the most egregious demonstrations of the 'tyranny of the status quo' as a block to desirable change. In this case, the problem only gets worse over time as relative property prices diverge more and more from the 1991 position. Part of the problem now is that a revaluation has been avoided for so long that changes in relative tax liabilities would be very substantial. But as council tax valuations have passed the milestone of being 20 years out of date, the absurdity of the status quo becomes ever more apparent. Any property tax requires regular revaluations, and this process should begin as soon as possible.

[20] 2006–07 figure. Source: Shaw, Slemrod, and Whiting, 2010.

[21] The other being vehicle excise duty.

[22] Lyons, 2007, 226.

Housing Services Tax

Council tax clearly has important shortcomings, and housing is not currently subject to VAT as it probably should be. So we now propose a reform that addresses both these problems and would create what we call a 'housing services tax'.

We have already noted in Chapter 6 that the purpose of a VAT is to tax final consumption. This is generally accomplished by levying the tax when goods are initially purchased, but in the case of housing it is better achieved by taxing the flow of housing services on an annual basis. In an efficient market with no uncertainty, the market value of a house is the capitalized value of these housing services, so a tax on the flow is equivalent to a VAT on the market price when the house is new. A tax on the flow of services has the advantages that it can capture housing services that (for whatever reason) were not reflected in the initial price, and that it can be applied to the existing stock of housing with none of the transition problems associated with a VAT. Furthermore, an annual tax on housing services would be similar in operation to council tax, which would further reduce problems of transition.

In fact, a tax on housing services would bear an even closer resemblance to one of council tax's predecessors, domestic rates, which were charged as a percentage of the estimated rental value of properties. Interestingly, a reformed system of domestic rates is still in place in Northern Ireland, levied as a proportion of properties' 2005 capital values—though with various reliefs, and a cap that means that any property worth more than £400,000 in 2005 is treated as though it were worth just £400,000.

A housing services tax (HST) should be levied as a simple, flat percentage of the rental value of each property, whether it is rented or owner-occupied. According to Communities and Local Government, the average house price in England in 2009 was about £200,000 and the average council tax bill in England in 2009–10 was £1,175. This suggests that a tax of around 0.6% of property value would leave the average bill unchanged and therefore be revenue neutral.[23] If annual rental values are about 5% of capital values, that

---

[23] There is considerable uncertainty around this figure, however: different calculations based on various published statistics suggest different revenue-neutral rates, some higher and some lower than that used here. In any case, as discussed below, the revenue-neutral rate would have

would correspond to an HST rate of about 12% of the value of housing services. However, the rate could also be increased to pay for the abolition of stamp duty on residential property transactions, discussed in Section 16.3. The volatility of stamp duty revenues makes it difficult to say reliably how much this would add to the HST rate, but it would probably still leave it somewhat below the current 17.5% VAT rate. In the long run, further increasing the HST rate towards 17.5% might make sense, but given the windfall losses that that would entail and the political sensitivity of reforms to housing taxation, we think revenue neutrality with the current regime is a more pragmatic medium-term goal.

Figure 16.1 illustrates how tax bills would change under an HST designed to replace the revenue from council tax only, while Figure 16.2 shows the effect that this change would have on house values if it were to be fully capitalized into market prices. The vast majority of properties are on the left-hand side of these graphs. For houses with a market value less than about £250,000—a large majority—tax bills would fall and house prices rise modestly. Conversely, for houses with a market value above that, tax bills would rise and house values fall. The change in value would not be significant for many properties, although a house with a current value of £1 million would lose around 6% of its value. Note, however, that single-person households would see their tax bills rise at rather lower property values than £250,000, since they currently receive a 25% discount on their council tax that is not shown in Figure 16.1.

To be clear, there are four major differences between council tax and an HST:

(a) Council tax provides discounts for single occupants and for second and empty properties. These encourage inefficient use of the housing stock (among other distortions). An HST would not have this feature.

to be quite different in different years to yield the same revenue as council tax, since property prices rise and fall. For comparison, the rates levied in Northern Ireland in 2009–10 ranged from 0.55% to 0.74% of value, depending on district.

Tax by Design

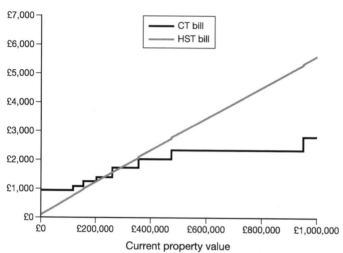

Figure 16.1. Comparing a 0.6% tax on property values with council tax (CT) in a local authority setting average band D rate in England, 2009–10

Note: Figures for council tax assume household not eligible for single-person discount and uniform growth of 185% in property prices since April 1991.

Source: Authors' calculations.

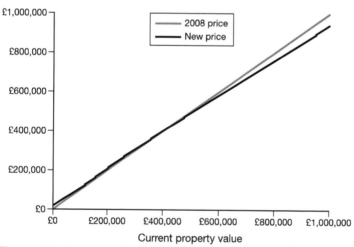

Figure 16.2. Impact on house prices of replacing council tax with a 0.6% tax on property values in 2009–10

Note: Assumes council tax rates at average level across England, no effect of single-person discounts on property prices, and uniform growth of 185% in property prices since April 1991.

Source: Authors' calculations.

(b) Council tax band rates are not proportional to band values. This unfairly and inefficiently favours more valuable properties, and particularly the most valuable properties of all.

(c) Council tax bills do not vary within bands. This again favours more valuable properties in each band. A pure HST would have taxes based on a continuous measure of value.[24]

(d) Council tax bills are based on relative property values in 1991 rather than today. This unfairly and inefficiently favours properties that have seen above-average price rises since then.

Figures 16.1 and 16.2 do not take account of (d), since we lack comprehensive data on relative house price changes. To look more closely at the kind of households that would gain and lose from the reform, we must also ignore (c), since the data on household characteristics do not contain information on the distribution of property values within council tax bands. We therefore model an approximation, shown in Figure 16.3, in which the

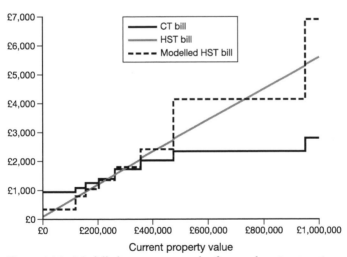

Figure 16.3. Modelled revenue-neutral reform to housing taxation

Notes: Assumes uniform growth of 185% in property prices since April 1991. Figures for council tax assume household not eligible for single-person discount.

Source: Authors' calculations using the IFS tax and benefit microsimulation model, TAXBEN, run on uprated data from the 2006–07 Family Resources Survey.

---

[24] There may be a case for some banding on administrative grounds, though we note that this was not deemed necessary in Northern Ireland or under the old domestic rates system.

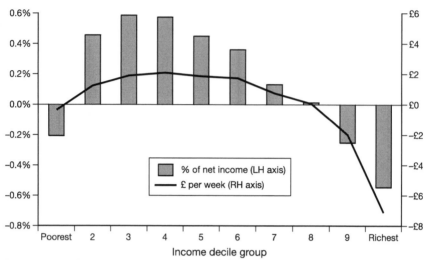

Figure 16.4. Gains/Losses across the English income distribution from modelled reform to housing taxation

Note: Income decile groups are derived by dividing all households in England into ten equal-sized groups according to net income adjusted for household size using the McClements equivalence scale.

Source: Authors' calculations using the IFS tax and benefit microsimulation model, TAXBEN, run on uprated data from the 2006–07 Family Resources Survey.

tax rate for each existing council tax band is adjusted to be proportional to the value of properties at the midpoint of each band (and in which the single-person discount is abolished). The rates that achieve this in a revenue-neutral way are consistent with a tax rate of about 0.6% of value at the midpoint of each band.[25]

Overall, a reform of this type would be progressive. In general, better-off people live in more expensive houses. Figure 16.4 shows that there are gains, on average, for households in the second to eighth income decile groups, with losses in the ninth and, especially, highest income decile groups. The average loss for the lowest income decile group requires a word of explanation, however. Most of those on the lowest incomes would be unaffected by the reform, as they are entitled to Council Tax Benefit (and, we assume, would be entitled to a corresponding HST rebate) to cover their tax

---

[25] The top band, band H, has no midpoint; we assume a value of £400,000 in 1991—£80,000 above the bottom of the band, which is the same distance above the bottom as the band G midpoint is above the bottom of band G.

bill.[26] Those on low incomes who are *not* entitled to Council Tax Benefit are excluded from entitlement because they have too much financial wealth: those with non-pension financial assets of more than £16,000 are not eligible for Council Tax Benefit.[27] The average loss for the bottom decile group reflects the fact that people with little current income but substantial financial wealth also tend to have big houses. They are low-income losers, but they may not be people we would ordinarily consider poor.

Table 16.2. Average gains/losses and numbers gaining/losing from modelled reform to housing taxation

	Average weekly gain/loss	% gaining > £5 per week	% losing > £5 per week
All-pensioner households	−£1.41	9%	13%
Of which:			
Lowest income quintile	−£0.35	4%	5%
2nd income quintile	+£0.63	9%	3%
3rd income quintile	+£0.31	11%	6%
4th income quintile	−£0.52	11%	12%
Highest income quintile	−£7.10	9%	38%
Working-age households	+£0.49	25%	12%
Of which:			
Lowest income quintile	+£0.88	14%	4%
2nd income quintile	+£2.72	34%	4%
3rd income quintile	+£2.45	36%	8%
4th income quintile	+£0.88	28%	13%
Highest income quintile	−£4.47	14%	28%

Note: Income quintile groups are derived by dividing all all-pensioner households in England, or all working-age households in England, into five equal-sized groups according to net income adjusted for household size using the McClements equivalence scale.

Source: Authors' calculations using the IFS tax and benefit microsimulation model, TAXBEN, run on uprated data from the 2006–07 Family Resources Survey.

[26] We assume full take-up of these benefits, which means that we understate the progressivity of the reform since most of those who do not take up their benefit would see falls in their bills.

[27] Entitlement is also reduced for those with less wealth than this: each £250 (£500 for those aged 60 or over) of assets above £6,000 is assumed to yield £1 per week of income for the purposes of the means test.

Table 16.3. Characteristics of households in England by council tax band, 2009–10

	Bands A–D	Band E	Band F	Band G	Band H
Number of all-pensioner households	4,195,000	499,000	315,000	215,000	33,000
Of which:					
In bottom half of overall income distribution	2,967,000	284,000	152,000	68,000	[a]
In bottom fifth of overall income distribution	1,163,000	134,000	80,000	40,000	[a]
Number of working-age households	13,200,000	1,514,000	811,000	558,000	82,000
Of which:					
In bottom half of overall income distribution	6,459,000	400,000	228,000	95,000	[a]
In bottom fifth of overall income distribution	2,553,000	148,000	97,000	46,000	[a]

[a] Sample size too small to yield reliable estimate.

Note: Official figures for the total number of households in each band (shown in Table 16.1) differ slightly from those shown here, but they do not allow disaggregation by income or demographic group.

Source: Authors' calculations using the IFS tax and benefit microsimulation model, TAXBEN, run on uprated data from the 2006–07 Family Resources Survey.

While the reform is progressive on average, however, there would be many losers and gainers at all parts of the income distribution, as illustrated in Table 16.2.

To illustrate some of these issues in a different way, Table 16.3 provides some details of the characteristics of those currently in different council tax bands. A majority of those in bands A to D are in the lower half of the income distribution. This is true of a much smaller proportion of those in higher bands. But even so, 30% of pensioners in band G are in the bottom half of the income distribution and approaching 20% are in the poorest fifth by income.

There would clearly be a large number of losers from a reform of this kind. The losers would include those, often older people, on low incomes who live in expensive houses. This would undoubtedly make such a reform politically difficult. On the other hand, its desirability comes from the fact that those living in expensive houses are consuming something valuable that, in other circumstances, we would not hesitate to tax. Such people are unlikely to be lifetime poor, and taxing people in proportion to the full value of the property they occupy would lead to a more rational use of the existing housing stock. However, neither the politics nor the ethics are straightforward.

There are, though, a number of ways of mitigating losses from the reform. We have assumed, in the first place, that a benefit like the current Council Tax Benefit would be maintained. This would ensure that those with very low incomes and little in the way of other savings would be protected.[28] Second, one would likely want to implement the reform over some transition period such that bills rose only gradually. The lengthy phasing-out of mortgage interest tax relief shows that reforms with potentially significant effects on prices can be achieved given an appropriate timescale. Finally, it would be possible to allow people, in specified circumstances, to roll up liabilities (with interest) either until the property is sold or until death, in order to alleviate cash-flow problems. A system along these lines operates in Denmark.

Political difficulties would also no doubt arise from the fact that a well-functioning HST would require a full revaluation of domestic properties and a credible commitment to further revaluations every three to five years (at least). But this, of course, would be desirable even if we were to keep council tax.

Any property tax—be it council tax, HST, business rates, or LVT—with regular revaluations will see the size of the tax base rise and fall as property prices generally rise and fall. If tax payments correspondingly rose and fell, some would consider that a good thing, acting as an 'automatic stabilizer' in the property market. Others would see the instability in bills as undesirable for households and the instability in revenue as undesirable for the government.

But it is not necessarily the case that tax payments would change in line with the tax base. At present, council tax rates are set locally, and we see no good reason for HST to be different. Under the current system of local government finance, bills would not rise and fall with prices. The revenue

---

[28] With no other changes, such a benefit would be smaller than Council Tax Benefit, reflecting the fact that an HST would be more progressive than council tax. There is separately a case for reforming this benefit, perhaps decoupling it from actual bills, but a discussion of its possible reform is well beyond the scope of this book.

that local authorities must raise—and therefore the amount that households must pay—is simply the difference between what they wish to spend and the grant they receive from central government. If property prices rose, councils would simply reduce the tax payable at any given property value so that household bills, and the revenue generated, were unchanged. Grant from central government might be redistributed between areas if relative property prices changed, but what was gained by one would be lost by another; if total grants remained the same and total local authority spending remained the same, then total revenue to be raised from the local property tax (and so average bills) would also remain the same.

For a centralized property tax, revenues could potentially rise and fall with the property market—much as revenues from stamp duty already do.[29] But if this were thought undesirable, the government could prevent it by automatically adjusting tax rates to keep revenues on a stable path: a formula that tied the annual overall increase in payments to something like the historical long-run trend rate of house price growth might be one such revenue-stabilizing mechanism. This is similar to the current business rates formula, which allows changes in relative payments in response to changes in relative property values, but which constrains total payments to rise in line with retail price inflation even if property prices on average fall or rise significantly.

To summarize, our basic proposal is straightforward: council tax as it currently exists should be replaced by a housing services tax which would, eventually, be charged in full proportion to the value of the property—and hence would leave the majority, who own less valuable property, somewhat better off and those owning more valuable property worse off. We do not propose a separate tax on residential land value. Ideally, the tax rate might be set at 17.5%, since it is intended to substitute for VAT on the consumption of housing; but a more pragmatic medium-term goal might be to replace the revenue currently provided by council tax and stamp duty on residential properties, which would probably imply a slightly lower rate than this.

---

[29] Though note that if local property taxes were simply replaced by, say, a local income tax as the main locally controlled tax, local income tax rates would rise and fall to keep revenue at the desired level exactly as described above for local property tax rates. Thus the greater cyclicality of property tax revenues would be offset by reduced cyclicality of overall income tax revenues.

16.2.2. Taxing Housing as an Asset

Gross housing wealth in the UK stood at £3.5 trillion[30] (£3,500,000,000,000) in 2007, with about £1.1 trillion of loans secured against it.[31] Gross financial assets stood at around £3.7 trillion in 2008.[32] In other words, housing is as important as an asset as all financial assets combined. And it dwarfs the less than £300 billion held in tax-free Individual Savings Accounts (ISAs).[33] Seventy-two per cent of households own the property they live in.[34]

The sheer scale of the value of housing makes its tax treatment as an asset very important. To begin our discussion, it is worth summarizing two other key features of housing wealth:

- First, people's net housing wealth varies across the life cycle. Looking at the population today, people under the age of 30 tend to have small amounts of housing wealth. Even among 40- to 45-year-olds, barely 10% own a property outright (without a mortgage), compared with over 70% of 65- to 69-year-olds. Those with the greatest housing wealth on average are in their 50s—they have had a chance both to 'trade up' and to pay off their mortgages. The elderly own somewhat less housing—in part because they come from a generation where ownership was less common, relative to living in social housing, and in part because they may have 'traded down' to smaller properties.[35]

- Second, ownership of housing wealth is closely correlated with lifetime income and wealth, but not necessarily with current income. Those in their 60s own more housing wealth than those in their 30s but have lower incomes. But among retirees, those with substantial housing wealth have, on average, both higher total wealth and higher incomes than those of the same age with little in the way of housing wealth: among owner-occupiers

---

[30] Not including social housing.

[31] http://www.cml.org.uk/cml/publications/newsandviews/8/10.

[32] Office for National Statistics, *United Kingdom National Accounts: The Blue Book 2009*, http://www.statistics.gov.uk/downloads/theme_economy/BB09.pdf. The household sector is 'households and non-profit institutions serving households' (hh&npish).

[33] HMRC statistics, table 9.6, http://www.hmrc.gov.uk/stats/isa/table9-6-onwards.pdf.

[34] Office for National Statistics, *Social Trends No. 39, 2009 Edition*, http://www.statistics.gov.uk/downloads/theme_social/Social_Trends39/Social_Trends_39.pdf.

[35] Numbers and statements based on our analysis of British Household Panel Survey (BHPS) data.

over the age of 60, the highest-income tenth own properties worth on average almost £400,000, while those in the lowest-income fifth have properties worth around a third of that.[36]

Our concern in this section, though, is more with changes in housing wealth. The extent of gains over the past 35 years is shown in Figure 16.5, which plots real house prices since 1975. The trend line shows a real capital gain on housing of 2.9% per year. It is also clear from the figure that domestic property is an asset with a risky financial return. There are several periods of capital losses, most notably from 1989 through to 1995. House prices have also fallen since autumn 2007. Nevertheless, over the long run, there do appear to be significant, and arguably predictable, gains. Note that these gains are just part of the overall return to housing, which includes the return that comes in the form of housing services—a crucial point to which we return below.

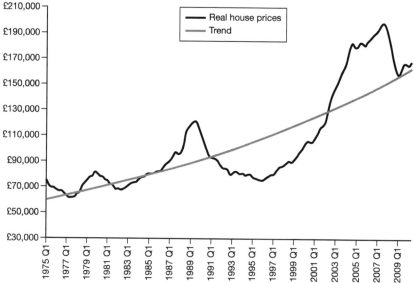

Figure 16.5. Real house prices and trend from 1975 Q1 to 2010 Q2

Notes: Prices in 2010 Q2 terms, uprated using the retail price index. Trend real growth rate is 2.9% per year.

Source: Nationwide Building Society, http://www.nationwide.co.uk/hpi/historical.htm.

---

[36] Our analysis of BHPS data.

Many factors influence house price changes. In local areas, there are unforeseen changes in local services and amenities that affect prices. Similarly, there are changes in the number of households, in the number of houses, and in lending conditions in financial markets. Given the relatively fixed stock of housing, increases in the number of households and the granting of bigger mortgages can increase both the demand for houses and their price.

House price growth has varied widely both between and within regions of the UK. Those who have been lucky—or perhaps particularly adept—in the property market have seen their wealth grow, tax free, by far more than others.

The question that we tackle here is whether and how the taxation of housing can be brought more into line with the system of taxation we are proposing for other assets.

A Rate-of-Return Allowance for Housing?

In Chapter 13, we characterized savings tax regimes according to the tax treatment of income saved, returns generated, and income withdrawn. Applied to the case of housing, the elements of this taxonomy are as follows:

- Income saved means the income used to buy the property (which is equal to the cost of buying).

- Returns generated take two forms: income from the consumption services provided by the property (either rental income received by landlords or the in-kind reward enjoyed by owner-occupiers) and any capital gain (or loss).

- Withdrawals include both the consumption services (which are, by their nature, 'withdrawn' and consumed at the same time as the property generates them) and receipts from selling the property.

Owner-occupied housing is currently subject to what we earlier described as an earnings tax or TEE tax treatment. It is bought out of taxed income, but no tax is payable on any returns or at the point of sale.[37] In contrast, housing

---

[37] Here and below, we use 'owner-occupied housing' to mean principal private residences; capital gains on second homes are taxable, though there is some flexibility in designating which is one's main home.

that is bought to rent out is subject to something closer to a comprehensive income tax (TTE) treatment. Returns in the form of rental income and capital gains are subject to tax.

This difference in treatment creates a major bias in favour of owner-occupation, albeit less so since the tax-deductibility of mortgage interest payments was gradually removed for owner-occupiers but retained for landlords (see Box 16.1). The treatment of owner-occupied and rental property should be levelled out.

Box 16.1. The tax treatment of mortgages

The tax treatment of mortgages can be characterized in terms of the same three stages as other borrowing and saving, with the same main options for charging tax at a combination of these stages:

- **TEE—an earnings tax** simply ignores all borrowing and saving. Neither taking out a mortgage, nor making payments of interest or principal, has any effect on tax liability.

- **TTE—a comprehensive income tax** treatment of mortgages would allow full deductibility of mortgage interest from taxable income (but not add the amount borrowed to taxable income or deduct repayments of principal), just as it would fully tax interest income on savings. A comprehensive income tax thus taxes saving and subsidizes borrowing.

- **EET—a cash-flow expenditure tax** involves taxing all cash inflows and deducting all outflows, hence adding the loan to taxable income for the year when it is taken out and then deducting all payments of interest and principal.

- **TtE—a rate-of-return allowance** regime would allow deductibility of mortgage interest payments, like TTE, but only in so far as they exceeded a 'normal' rate of interest on the outstanding mortgage. (Unlike with TTE, there would be no difference in present-value terms between making interest payments and making repayments of principal. If a payment were labelled interest, it would be deductible; if it were labelled principal, it would not be deductible but, by reducing the value of the outstanding mortgage, it would reduce the stream of 'normal' interest allowances to offset against future interest deductions.)

In the UK, mortgages taken out on rental properties are given a TTE treatment: mortgage interest payments are treated as a business expense to be deducted against rental income, just like companies can deduct interest payments from their profits for corporation tax purposes. This is an appropriate counterpart to the current TTE treatment of rental housing itself.

Mortgages for owner-occupied housing were formerly also given TTE treatment. This may have been appropriate when (prior to 1963) the imputed rental income from owner-occupation was taxed under 'Schedule A' income tax; but once owner-occupied housing was itself given TEE treatment, continuing to allow mortgage interest deductibility led to a huge net subsidy for owner-occupied housing. To their great credit, successive governments responded to this by gradually restricting mortgage interest tax relief, and between 1974 and 2000 this relief was phased out entirely. The resulting TEE treatment of mortgages for owner-occupiers now matches the TEE treatment given to owner-occupied housing itself.

The current tax treatment of mortgages is therefore appropriately aligned with the current tax treatment of housing as a whole for both the owner-occupied and rental sectors. In this chapter, however, we argue for reform of the existing system, moving towards TtE taxation of rental (and, ideally, owner-occupied) housing. How should the taxation of mortgages be adjusted in line with this? Two approaches are consistent with our proposed direction of reform:

- TEE treatment—ignoring mortgages entirely in the income tax system—is certainly appropriate for owner-occupiers if owner-occupied housing continued to have TEE treatment; but it would also be a simple and viable option for mortgages on (rental or owner-occupied) properties that were given TtE treatment. Relative to the current tax treatment of mortgages, this would simply mean abolishing mortgage interest deductibility for landlords.

- For housing investment that was given TtE treatment, an alternative would be to give TtE treatment to loans secured against that property. TtE on the property would involve taxing (actual or imputed) rental income and capital gains above an allowance for a normal return on the purchase price, while TtE on the mortgage would involve deducting mortgage interest above an allowance for 'normal' interest on the outstanding mortgage. Taking the property and the mortgage together, this means taxing rental income and deducting mortgage interest payments, as happens for landlords now, while giving a rate-of-return allowance (RRA) against the purchase price net of outstanding mortgage.

TtE treatment of mortgages might be the more obvious counterpart to TtE treatment of the housing itself. But TEE has the advantage that it taxes the financial service provided by mortgage lenders. As a form of implicit charge for their services, lenders may demand more than a normal rate of interest on the mortgages they provide. Under TEE, this charge for financial services is a private matter between borrower and lender, like the provision of any other service. But under TtE, with mortgage interest above a normal rate tax deductible, the Exchequer provides the

(cont.)

Box 16.1. (*cont.*)

---

borrower with an income tax deduction for the financial services supplied to him/her. If we do not wish the consumption of financial services to be tax deductible—and there is no obvious reason to privilege financial services in this way—this gives a reason for preferring TEE treatment of mortgages. Other than this, we see no strong grounds for choosing between the TEE and TtE treatments of mortgages on TtE housing. The choice could be mandated by the government or left for borrowers and lenders to decide.

Neither the TEE treatment currently applied to owner-occupiers nor the TTE treatment applied to landlords seems appropriate for housing. TTE straightforwardly penalizes saving, as discussed in Chapter 13: investing in buy-to-let housing is currently discouraged by the tax system for no good reason. TEE does not discourage saving in this way. But since TEE exempts not just the normal return to capital saved but the entire return, it fails to capture any excess return that may arise as a result of sheer luck, rents earned, or effort and skill put into choosing undervalued properties and improving them. The deficiencies of this are most clearly seen by noting that a TEE treatment of all housing would entail leaving professional property investors, who make their living seeking these excess returns, entirely untaxed. If I buy a house that I then sell at profit, reinvesting, selling, and so on, under a TEE regime I would never be subject to tax despite the fact that I am clearly earning an income in this way.

We have observed that either an EET consumption tax or a TtE rate-of-return allowance (RRA) can tax excess returns while leaving the normal return to capital untaxed and therefore not discouraging saving.

An EET consumption tax treatment of housing—allowing houses to be bought out of pre-tax income and then taxing any value extracted from them (actual or imputed rental income and proceeds of sale)—is not appealing. It would mean that someone buying a house outright would have the entire purchase price deducted from their taxable income for the year. Since houses normally cost far more than a year's income, this would mean the person made a large loss for tax purposes that year, resulting either in a negative tax bill (a refund from the government) or in losses to be carried forward and set against income for several future years, depending on the tax treatment of losses.[38] Creating losses on such a monumental scale is something no tax authority would entertain as a practical proposition.

In our view, a TtE rate-of-return allowance provides the most promising avenue for reforming the taxation of housing as an asset. Recall that an RRA regime involves assets being acquired out of taxed income and only returns above a 'normal' or 'safe' rate being taxed.

Introducing an RRA for rental property would be fairly straightforward. It could be based on the existing system, taxing both rental income and capital gains; but landlords would now be able to claim an allowance for the normal return on their investment. This allowance could take one of two forms:

(i) In the purest form of RRA, an allowance of 5% (say) of the purchase price would be deductible against rental income each year. When the property was sold, capital gains tax (CGT) would be charged at the taxpayer's marginal rate on the full nominal gain.

(ii) Alternatively, rental income could continue to be taxed in full, as at present. But when the property was sold, the base price for calculating CGT would be stepped up by 5% per year (appropriately compounded).

These methods differ only in the timing of the allowance given; the government could choose between them or else allow each individual to choose for themselves. Method (ii) is equivalent to the landlord simply not claiming the annual allowance available in (i) but instead carrying it forward with interest and claiming it at the point of sale. Note that if a property yielded exactly the normal return, method (ii) would generate a CGT *refund* when the property was sold, with the same present value as the stream of taxes paid on rental income. In practice, housing has tended to yield more than a normal return in the UK, but method (ii) would still imply substantial refunds in many cases. This generation of widespread losses (albeit on a far smaller scale than with EET treatment) may be off-putting for revenue

---

[38] The outcome would not be this stark in all cases. Once an EET system had bedded down, those selling one house and buying another would see the sale and purchase offset each other, so they would only pay tax (or receive a refund if downsizing) on the difference in price between the two properties. If EET treatment were also applied to mortgages (see Box 16.1), those taking out a mortgage to finance a house purchase would receive a deduction only for the non-mortgage-financed part of the purchase.

authorities; on the other hand, method (ii) has the advantage of being closer to current UK practice and therefore raising fewer transitional difficulties.

To illustrate how an RRA might work, suppose it costs me £200,000 to buy a house and that the rental income from it is initially £10,000 a year. With a normal return of 5%, my allowance on method (i)—5% of the purchase cost, or £10,000—cancels out this return for tax purposes and I pay no tax. If the rent then rises to £11,000, my allowance is still £10,000, so I pay tax on £1,000's worth of housing services; if I sell the house for £220,000, I pay tax on £20,000 of capital gain. The equivalent alternative, method (ii), would be to tax the whole income of £10,000 or £11,000 each year, but only tax any capital gain above a carried-forward allowance. After ten years, tax would be paid on any capital gain over about £126,000[39] in this case, with anything less than this treated as a loss.

An RRA could be implemented for owner-occupied housing in the same two ways as for rental housing. The calculation above would work in exactly the same way, except that instead of an actual rental income there would be an imputed rental income. So, to be clear:

(i)   Imputed rental income could be taxed only where it exceeds 5% (say) of the purchase price, with CGT charged at the taxpayer's marginal rate on the full nominal gain.

(ii) Imputed rental income could be taxed in full—in effect adding the homeowner's marginal income tax rate to the HST rate—with CGT charged only on gains relative to a base price that was stepped up with interest.

Of course, it would be harder to introduce an RRA for owner-occupied property than for rental housing. The most obvious problem is that a large part of the return—the consumption services provided by the property—is received in kind rather than in cash, and is therefore difficult to value—though it is exactly what we propose to value and tax for our HST proposal above. The same valuation could be used for both purposes, although this would put an extra premium on ensuring valuations were accurate.

---

[39] The purchase price stepped up with interest would be £200,000 × 1.05^{10} = £325,779, so tax would be payable on gains above £125,779.

It is important to note the relationship between this proposal and the HST proposal. An HST, like a VAT, is designed to tax the consumption of housing itself. An RRA is designed to tax the consumption that a property purchase *finances*—whether that be consumption of the housing services themselves or whatever the cash from renting or selling the property can buy—but only in so far as it exceeds the consumption that the money used to buy the property would 'normally' be expected to finance. Tax is only paid in so far as a house delivers and finances more consumption than the money used to purchase it: if housing yields only a normal return, no tax is payable.

Starting from the UK's current position, method (i) looks much less attractive for owner-occupied property than for rental property. CGT already exists for rental property. But introducing it in full for principal residences might discourage people from selling their property if they believed there was a significant chance that the new tax would be abolished by a future government. As discussed in Section 16.1.1, this was a key factor undermining attempts to introduce development taxes in the past. The fact that a reform could be presented as bringing housing within a consistent tax regime applying to all assets might help persuade people of its durability, but there is little doubt that such a change could only be feasible with the sort of political consensus in its favour that currently looks very distant. Method (ii) may not suffer from this problem, since the expected CGT bill would be much smaller—indeed, negative in many cases. Rather, the downside of method (ii) is the political unpalatability of proposing to tax the annual consumption value of housing not just at the HST rate (offsetting the abolition of council tax and stamp duty land tax on average) but additionally at the homeowner's marginal income tax rate. Building a consensus around one of these options is important if we are to move towards a fair and efficient tax system. But we do not underestimate the challenges involved.

Once again, the taxation of improvements poses something of a problem. Spending on improvements is essentially additional investment in the property, generating returns in the form of higher (actual or imputed) rental income and capital gains. Strictly speaking, it should therefore be added to the purchase price in calculating the basis for a rate-of-return allowance.[40] This is similar to the current treatment of improvements to rental property:

---

[40] An alternative would be to treat spending on improvements as an immediately deductible expense, in effect giving EET treatment of improvements.

spending on improvements above a certain level is recorded and reported and netted off the capital gain when CGT liabilities are calculated (though note that the spending ought to be carried forward with interest, in line with method (ii) of implementing an RRA described above). However, extending this (not very heavily policed) regime from a relatively small number of such properties to the vast bulk of the population would involve very substantial additional administrative complexity.[41]

Introducing an RRA regime for rental properties would be feasible, sensible, and relatively inexpensive.[42] Introducing an RRA regime for owner-occupied housing as well would be ideal: it was surely inappropriate that the enormous returns enjoyed by homeowners during the long property boom up to 2007 went untaxed. But we recognize that this would be much more difficult and may be politically impossible in practice. Even if owner-occupied housing continued to be subject to the present TEE regime, however, bringing in a rate-of-return allowance for rental property—and, as for other assets, aligning CGT rates with income tax rates—would be a major improvement. It would bring the tax regimes for rented and owner-occupied housing much closer together, completely eliminating the bias towards owner-occupation for property that generated a normal return. It would also

---

[41] In particular, recall that the implicit rental income from owner-occupied housing is imputed (rather than observed), based on a valuation that may not take account of all improvements. If the return to such improvements in the form of higher implicit rental income is not taxed, the cost of those improvements should not generate a deduction against the tax on imputed income—just as we argued that improvements that do not affect valuations for the HST should not be zero rated for VAT. But all improvements will presumably affect the actual sale price of the property, so the returns to improvements will be subject to CGT at that stage and some deduction for the cost of improvements is warranted. The correct—rather complicated—treatment is for improvements that do affect valuations to be registered immediately (either deductible immediately, or added to the basis for the RRA, or carried forward with interest and netted off the capital gain) and for improvements that do not affect valuations to be ignored initially but netted off the capital gain (*without* interest being added) when the property is sold.

[42] The precise cost is difficult to estimate. If 2009–10 tax rates were applied to 2006–07 taxable property income and gains on disposal of property, total revenue would be about £3.5 billion; an RRA would only involve giving up that part of the £3.5 billion that reflects normal returns. However, as part of our overall package, we would also be increasing tax rates on property income and capital gains to align them with full labour income tax rates (including what are currently National Insurance contributions); this implies collecting more revenue from taxing 'excess' returns but forgoing more revenue by not taxing 'normal' returns.

bring the taxation of rented housing into line with (our proposals for) taxation of other assets.

16.3. STAMP DUTY LAND TAX

Before drawing this chapter to a close, we need to say something about a tax that is currently charged on residential and commercial property transactions—stamp duty land tax. In 2010–11, it is levied at rates of 0% on transactions up to £125,000, 1% between £125,000 and £250,000, 3% from there to £500,000, 4% between £500,000 and £1 million, and 5% above that.[43] Unlike, say, income tax, the relevant rate applies to the full sale price, not just the part above the relevant threshold—so a house selling for £500,000 would attract tax of £15,000 (3% of £500,000), whilst a house selling for £500,001 would attract tax of £20,000 (4% of £500,001): a £1 increase in price triggering a £5,000 increase in tax liability. This is, of course, an absurd structure for any tax.

Stamp duty has a long history in the British tax system, having first been introduced in 1694. It stems from a time when few other potential taxes were straightforward to implement, whereas the transactions on which stamp duty was levied were easy to identify and to measure. But, in the modern era of broadly based taxation, the case for maintaining stamp duty is very weak indeed. As discussed in Chapter 6, transactions taxes are particularly inefficient: by discouraging mutually beneficial transactions, stamp duty ensures that properties are not held by the people who value them most. It creates a disincentive for people to move house, thereby leading to potential inflexibilities in the labour market and encouraging people to live (and businesses to operate) in properties of a size and in a location that they may well not otherwise have chosen. The 'slab' rate structure described above is especially perverse, meaning that transactions of very similar value are

---

[43] The stamp duty land tax threshold is £150,000, rather than £125,000, for non-residential properties and for residential properties in certain designated disadvantaged areas. The March 2010 Budget announced that the threshold would be £250,000 for first-time buyers of residential properties in the two years up to 24 March 2012 inclusive.

discouraged to completely different degrees and creating enormous incentives to keep prices just below the relevant thresholds.

There is no sound case for maintaining stamp duty and we believe that it should be abolished. Simply removing it would create windfall gains for existing owners, as it will largely have been capitalized into property values; so a reasonable quid pro quo for its abolition is that a similar level of revenue should be raised from other, more sensible, property taxes. If stamp duty were phased out while our proposed new land value tax and housing services tax were being brought in, then those losing most through the latter change would be among those gaining most as a result of the former. Revenue neutrality would at least ensure no windfall gains or losses on average.

16.4. CONCLUSIONS

The taxation of property in the UK is currently something of a mess. As we have seen when considering the practicalities involved in implementing an ideal system, up to a point this is understandable. But it remains both desirable and feasible to clear up much of the mess. Our conclusions can be summarized thus:

- There is a strong case for introducing a land value tax. In the foreseeable future, this is likely to mean focusing on finding ways to replace the economically damaging business rates system with a land value tax.

- Council tax should be reformed to relate it more closely to actual property values—levied as a proportion of up-to-date values with no cap and no discount for unoccupied or single-occupancy properties. We have called this a housing services tax to reflect its underlying economic rationale as a tax on housing consumption to substitute for VAT.

- Taxation of rented housing should be reformed by offering landlords an allowance against the normal return to their investment (and by aligning capital gains tax rates with income tax rates, as discussed in Chapter 14). In principle, it would also make sense to move towards a rate-of-return allowance basis for the taxation of owner-occupied housing, but this may prove extremely difficult in practice.

- Finally, stamp duty land tax should be abolished and the revenue replaced by part of the housing services tax (for domestic property) and land value tax (for business property).

This is a radical set of proposals, and the changes would need to be phased in carefully. But this is also an area where the current practice is a long way from an economically rational and efficient system. Stamp duty and business rates defy the most basic of economic principles by taxing transactions and produced inputs respectively. Income tax and capital gains tax create a significant bias against the rental market in favour of owner-occupation. Meanwhile, council tax is indefensibly regressive and, thanks to spineless government refusal to undertake a revaluation, we find ourselves in the absurd position that tax bills are still based on relative property prices in 1991. Over time, this arrangement will come to be seen as more and more untenable. At some point, some government will have to grasp the challenge of making the case for intelligent reform.

17

Taxing Corporate Income

This chapter and the following two are concerned with the taxation of income derived from business profits. Business activity comes in many forms, ranging from the operations of huge international corporations to those of a self-employed trader. This diversity presents a major challenge for the design of business tax systems. In most developed countries, the profits of incorporated businesses (companies) are taxed under a separate corporate income tax—for example, corporation tax in the UK. Dividends paid by companies to their owners, and capital gains made by shareholders on the sale of company shares, may also be taxed at the personal level. The profits of unincorporated businesses and the income of the self-employed are also taxed under the personal income tax. One of the challenges is to design a system that does not result in unwarranted distortions to the choice of legal form for small business activities. At the other end of the spectrum, multinational companies may have interrelated operations in many different countries, and another important challenge is to determine how their taxable profits are allocated between different national jurisdictions. Perhaps the most important developments affecting business taxation since the Meade Report in 1978 have been the growth of multinational businesses and cross-border ownership of companies.

These developments have placed increasing strain on international elements of company tax systems. Multinational firms can relocate both real activities and taxable profits to countries that offer more favourable corporate tax regimes. This increase in the international mobility of the corporate tax base has resulted in a proliferation of complex anti-avoidance legislation, particularly in high-tax countries, and put downward pressure on corporate tax rates. The UK corporation tax rate has fallen from 52% in 1982–83 to 28% in 2010–11, with further reductions to 23% by 2014–15 announced in the Budget of March 2011. Figure 17.1 illustrates that corporate income tax rates have fallen in other major economies over the same period, with Ireland having a particularly low rate of 12.5%. There has not been the same downward trend in revenues from corporate income taxes, as illustrated in Figure 17.2. One reason is that cuts in the corporate tax rate have often been accompanied by reductions in tax allowances or other extensions to the corporate tax base, in a pattern of rate-cutting, base-broadening reforms that was initiated by the UK in 1984 and the US in 1986.

This chapter considers the rationale for having a separate tax on company profits, and the properties of alternative corporate tax bases. Chapter 18 considers how the tax base should be divided between different countries, and the influence of 'tax competition' between governments on the corporate tax rate. Chapter 19 focuses on how we should tax income derived from unincorporated businesses in relation to the taxation of company profits. This requires consideration of dividend taxation and capital gains taxes on company shares, as well as corporate income tax paid by companies and personal income tax paid by self-employed individuals and proprietors or partners of unincorporated business organizations.

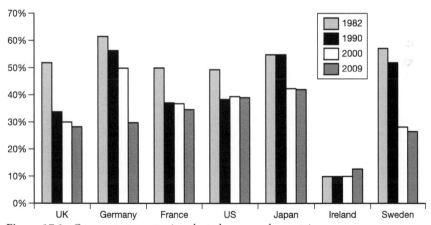

Figure 17.1. Corporate tax rates in selected years and countries

Notes: Tax rates include representative state or local corporate income taxes, where appropriate. The 10% rate in Ireland before 2003 did not apply to all sectors.

Source: Loretz, 2008. We thank Simon Loretz for providing figures for 2009.

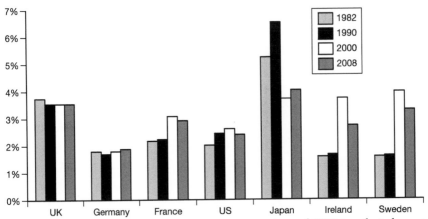

Figure 17.2. Taxes on corporate income as a percentage of GDP in selected years and countries

Source: OECD Revenue Statistics.

17.1. WHY TAX COMPANIES?

Corporations provide a convenient contractual arrangement that allows groups of individuals to own assets through a separate legal entity offering the benefit of limited liability. However, neither separate legal identity nor limited liability provides a rationale for a tax on company profits, since the terms and conditions under which creditors are willing to lend to companies will adjust to reflect this legal protection.

Perhaps the most important point to keep in mind when considering company taxation is that it is not meaningful to think about the effects of taxes on companies separately from the effects of those taxes on the individuals associated with companies. This may include not only the individuals who own companies, but also the individuals who supply goods and services to companies, including their employees, and the individuals who purchase goods and services from companies. While a successful corporate sector may be vital for the welfare of many people, we are not directly concerned about the welfare of companies. Rather, we care about the impact of company taxes on people whose living standards may be affected, as either shareholders, workers, suppliers, or customers.

We are thus interested in whether company taxes reduce the incomes of shareholders, through lower post-tax profits and dividends; or the incomes of workers, through lower real wages; or the real incomes of consumers, as a result of higher prices. Economists ask whether the 'effective incidence' of a tax on company profits is 'shifted' onto employees or customers. This will depend on the form of the corporate tax, the nature of the economy in which it is levied, and the choices open to the firms on which it is imposed. Different views about the appropriate form and level of company taxation tend to be shaped by different views about the extent to which it is borne by shareholders, workers, or consumers, particularly in open economies where much activity is conducted by multinational firms. This will also influence how corporate taxes impact on the behaviour of these stakeholders.

Why then do we impose a separate tax on company profits? Two important considerations are administrative convenience and the 'backstop' role that corporate taxation plays in the implementation of the personal income tax.

However we choose to measure company profits for tax purposes, it would in theory be possible to allocate a fraction of those taxable profits to each shareholder in proportion to his or her share in the ownership of the company, and to tax this share of the company profits under the personal income tax. Even with modern information technology, this would be administratively cumbersome, particularly in the context of large companies with thousands of small shareholders. Some shareholders may also find it difficult to pay tax on their imputed share of the underlying company profits, particularly when the company retains those profits to finance its operations and the shares are not easily traded on a liquid market. With significant ownership of UK companies by foreign shareholders, and significant ownership of foreign companies by UK residents, this would also have important implications for where company profits are taxed. Implementation would require substantially more cooperation and exchange of information between national tax administrations than the current practice of taxing the profits made by companies operating in a jurisdiction primarily in that jurisdiction, at the corporate level. Finally, the ownership of company shares by financial intermediaries such as insurance companies and pension funds, representing contingent contractual arrangements such as life insurance and future pension rights, may defy any current attribution of corporate profits to beneficial individuals.

An appropriate form of corporate taxation may also play an integral role in the effective administration of the personal direct tax system. There are two important aspects of this, relating to the personal taxation of income from savings and to the personal taxation of labour income.

In one sense, a company is a repository for the unconsumed savings of individuals. The simple mantra that we must have a corporate income tax because we have a personal income tax is weakened by the fact that in many countries, including the UK, we choose not to tax, or not to fully tax, the return on substantial components of personal savings, such as owner-occupied housing, pension plans, or assets held in tax-free accounts such as UK Individual Savings Accounts (ISAs). We do choose to tax personal income from substantial direct holdings of company shares, in the form of dividends and capital gains, and this would be undermined if we did not also tax corporate profits—in that case, owners of small companies could, for example, defer tax payments for long periods simply by retaining profits in the company. But this begs the question of why we choose to tax different forms of personal savings in radically different ways. More generally, the form and structure of the corporate income tax should be consistent with the form and structure of the personal income tax, and with policy choices for the taxation of savings in particular. The system as a whole should not present individuals with glaring opportunities to avoid taxation of their income from savings simply by holding their wealth in corporate form, nor should it penalize individuals who choose to save and invest through direct holdings of company shares.

For owner-managers of small companies, we also have to consider the possibility that labour income can be disguised as capital income and appear in the form of company profits, dividends, and capital gains. A significant difference between the individual's tax rate on labour income and the overall tax rate that applies to dividend income paid out of company profits, for example, then presents an opportunity for tax avoidance. We discuss this further in Chapter 19, but note that this is a potentially serious drawback to 'dual' income tax systems, which combine a progressive rate structure on labour income with a flat tax rate on capital income. More generally, omitting corporate income from taxation could create strong incentives for individuals to avoid tax by conducting activities in corporate form.

In an international context, taxing companies may allow tax to be imposed on foreign owners of those companies. Personal income taxes tend to operate on a 'residence-country' basis, with resident individuals liable to tax on their worldwide income, often with credit provided for taxes paid to foreign governments on income earned abroad. In contrast, corporate income taxes generally operate on a 'source-country' basis, taxing the profits of all firms operating in the domestic economy, regardless of their ownership.[1] This opportunity to tax non-resident owners may look attractive to governments and residents alike, although it also runs the risk of deterring some inward investment.

Another factor may be the perception that corporate taxes fall on anonymous companies, or at least on wealthy owners of those companies. In an open economy setting, there are good reasons for thinking that much of the burden of a (source-based) tax on corporate income will be shifted onto domestic workers in the form of lower wages and that workers would be better off if their wages or consumption were taxed directly. (We discuss these arguments further in Chapter 18.) However, this may be hard to sell to domestic voters, and, to this extent, governments may be attracted to a separate tax on corporate profits for similar reasons that they are attracted to separate social security contributions for employers—because many voters perceive these to be taxes that fall on someone else.

All OECD countries and most developing countries operate a form of corporate income tax. While corporate tax rates have fallen over the last quarter-century, most countries appear reluctant to forgo their share of this source-based taxation. Moreover, each country has an interest in the maintenance of source-based corporate taxes by other countries, as this reduces the tax advantage for its residents of investing abroad rather than at home.

In contrast, there are substantial differences across countries in the relationship between corporate and personal income taxes—that is, the

---

[1] Corporate income taxes do not necessarily operate on a pure source-country basis. For example, the taxation of foreign-source dividends under credit systems, and the application of Controlled Foreign Company rules, may introduce elements of taxation on the basis of corporate residence. These issues are discussed further in Chapter 18.

extent to which tax on company profits paid by the firm reduces tax charged on company dividends received by shareholders. Some countries, including Ireland and the Netherlands, have a 'classical system' in which dividend income is taxed at the shareholder's full marginal personal tax rate. Other countries, including Australia, have an 'imputation system', in which there is an explicit tax credit against personal tax on dividend income in recognition of tax paid on the underlying profits at the corporate level. Imputation systems commonly treat dividends received from foreign corporations and domestic corporations differently and/or treat dividends paid to foreign shareholders and domestic shareholders differently. Within the EU, the European Court of Justice has ruled such systems in breach of treaty obligations, leading to their withdrawal. Many EU countries, including the UK and Germany, now tax dividend income at lower personal tax rates than other sources of income. In this respect, the taxation of company dividends has come to resemble the taxation of capital gains on company shares, where most countries have made no explicit recognition of corporate tax on the underlying company profits but many countries tax capital gains at preferential rates.

17.2. THE STANDARD CORPORATE INCOME TAX BASE

The corporate tax base in almost all OECD countries corresponds to a measure of company profits net of allowances for interest payments and presumed depreciation costs. Two important questions are how this standard corporate income tax base affects the level of corporate investment, and how this investment is financed.

At zero inflation, and for an asset whose true decline in value over its lifetime matches the tax depreciation schedule, this standard corporate income tax base does not affect the required rate of return, or 'cost of capital', for corporate investments that are financed by borrowing. In essence, if the company can borrow at a real interest rate of 3% to finance a safe investment, the investment need only generate a net return of 3% to be viable. In contrast, the standard corporate income tax base raises the required rate of return for a similar investment that is financed by retained profits ('internal equity') or by issuing new shares ('external equity'). Shareholders require a positive rate of return on the use of their funds by the company, to compensate for the income they could have earned by investing instead in an interest-bearing asset. But unlike the interest cost of debt finance, which appears as an explicit charge in company accounts, this 'opportunity cost' of equity finance is not deductible from taxable profits. Consequently, for an equivalent equity-financed investment to be viable, the project must generate a higher pre-tax return to provide the company and its shareholders a net return of, say, 3%, after payment of corporate income tax. This implies that the standard corporate tax base favours debt rather than equity finance, and tends to discourage corporate investment to the extent that companies rely on equity finance.

These results are illustrated in Table 17.1. We consider a simple investment project undertaken by a firm that involves an outlay of £1,000 in year 1 to acquire an asset that generates a guaranteed income of £30 in year 2.[2] There is no inflation, and the asset purchased can also be sold for £1,000 in year 2, so there is no depreciation. Initially, we suppose there is no corporate income tax, and the risk-free interest rate is 3% per annum.[3]

If the firm borrows £1,000 at 3% to finance this project, the return of 3% just covers the interest payment of £30 in year 2, and the proceeds from selling the asset just cover repayment of the sum borrowed. Shareholders give up nothing in year 1 to finance this investment, and get nothing in year 2 in return. They should be indifferent as to whether the firm undertakes the investment or not. In this context, a project that just earns the required rate of return of 3% is referred to as a 'marginal' investment. If the firm could generate income in year 2 higher than the interest payment of £30, its owners would be better off if it undertakes the investment. Profits in excess of the required rate of return are referred to as 'supernormal' profits or 'economic

---

[2] This income can be thought of as sales of additional goods and services produced using the asset, minus additional current costs (wages, costs of energy, and costs of raw materials) that are incurred.

[3] 3% is close to the long-run average real interest rate on ten-year index-linked UK government bonds since they were introduced in 1984, although this measure of the *ex ante* real interest rate has been rather lower in recent years. See e.g. Joyce, Sorensen, and Weeken (2008).

Tax by Design

Table 17.1. Effects of the corporate income tax on a simple investment

	Debt finance		Equity finance	
	No tax	With tax	No tax	With tax
Investment in year 1	−1,000	−1,000	−1,000	−1,000
Borrowing in year 1	1,000	1,000	0	0
Income in year 2	30	30	30	30
Interest payment in year 2	−30	−30	0	0
Asset sale in year 2	1,000	1,000	1,000	1,000
Debt repayment in year 2	−1,000	−1,000	0	0
Proceeds in year 2 before tax	0	0	1,030	1,030
Rate of return before tax	n/a	n/a	3%	3%
Corporate tax payment @ 25% in year 2	0	0	0	7.5
Proceeds in year 2 after tax	0	0	1,030	1,022.5
Rate of return after tax	n/a	n/a	3%	2.25%

rents'. Typically, making such profits would require the firm to possess some scarce resource, knowledge, or ability that is not easily replicated by other firms.

Nothing changes in this example if the firm is subject to a standard corporate income tax, provided the tax code correctly recognizes that this kind of asset does not depreciate in value, and so provides no deduction for the cost of depreciation. The income of £30 is taxable in year 2, but the interest payment of £30 is deductible, leaving a tax base of zero and no corporate tax to be paid. No tax is levied on marginal investments, and consequently the required rate of return is unchanged. Tax would be paid on any supernormal profits. For example, if the firm could earn income in year 2 of £40, the tax base would be £10. However, for any tax rate less than 100%, shareholders would still be better off if the firm undertakes the investment. For debt-financed investments, the standard corporate income tax with depreciation allowances equal to true depreciation thus raises revenue by taxing economic rents.

The situation is quite different for equity-financed investments. If the firm did not undertake this expenditure in year 1, it could return an additional

£1,000 to its shareholders. This could be used to earn a certain return of £30 next year, giving shareholders a total of £1,030 in year 2. In the absence of the corporate income tax, if the firm uses its shareholders' funds to purchase the asset, it can also return £1,030 to its shareholders in year 2. Again shareholders should be indifferent as to whether the firm undertakes the investment project or not. But in the presence of the corporate income tax, this is no longer the case. With no interest payments to deduct, the firm now has taxable profits of £30 in year 2. If, for example, the corporate income tax rate is 25%, the firm will have to pay £7.50 in tax, leaving shareholders with a post-tax rate of return of only 2.25%. If shareholders can earn 3% by investing in a safe, untaxed asset outside the corporate sector, they will now be worse off if a taxed company invests in a project with a pre-tax return of 3%.[4]

In this example, shareholders should only be indifferent between the firm investing or not investing if the firm can generate a guaranteed income of £40 before tax, giving post-tax income of £30 and a post-tax rate of return of 3%. The corporate income tax at 25% here raises the cost of capital for equity-financed corporate investment from 3% to 4%. Some corporate investment that would otherwise be viable is likely to be deterred by a standard corporate income tax.

Two implications follow from these properties of the standard corporate income tax. All else equal, firms will be induced to use more debt finance and less equity finance. In reality, the future returns on any investment project tend to be uncertain, and the risk that lenders will not be repaid in full tends to increase as firms take on more debt relative to the value of their assets. Borrowing costs are likely to rise as firms become more indebted, and

---

[4] Note the assumption here that shareholders are not taxed at the personal level if they hold their wealth in the safe, interest-bearing asset. We are also abstracting here from personal taxation of dividend income and capital gains. Formally, we can think of this example applying where the shareholder is a pension fund (or, more accurately, an individual who saves through a tax-exempt pension fund), or an individual who saves in a tax-exempt account such as a UK Individual Savings Account (ISA). More generally, with different shareholders subject to different marginal tax rates, it is much harder to pin down the effects of personal income taxes on the required rate of return from corporate investments. Alternatively, we could think of 3% as being the safe rate of return available to shareholders in our example after personal tax on their savings income. In either case, the example illustrates the effect of the corporate income tax in isolation, holding constant the personal tax treatment of shareholders' savings income.

in practice we observe firms using a mix of debt and equity finance. Still, it is unclear why we should want the design of the corporate income tax to encourage companies to have more fragile balance sheets than they would otherwise choose.[5] As a result, more firms are likely to default in an economic downturn than would otherwise be the case. This imposes real costs, notably when firm-specific assets cannot be redeployed easily to other uses.

The second implication is that the corporate income tax raises the cost of capital and results in lower corporate investment, given that companies continue to use equity finance.[6] The key reason is that the normal return on equity-financed corporate investments is taxed under the standard corporate income tax base. We discuss the merits of this in Section 17.4 and, in the open economy context, in Chapter 18.

There are other problems with the standard corporate income tax base. Firms invest in many different assets with different useful lives and depreciation rates. It is not administratively feasible to specify a precise depreciation schedule for every asset, even if these were known with any certainty. Accordingly, corporate income tax rules typically specify depreciation schedules that can be charged for broad classes of assets, or specify maximum rates of depreciation that can be charged for broad classes of assets.[7] As a result, investment in some assets will be favoured (generating tax deductions for depreciation that are more generous than those implied by the fall in the value of the asset) and investment in other assets will be disadvantaged (being written off too slowly for tax purposes). Such disparities between the depreciation allowed by the tax code and true

---

[5] Historically, one might have argued that the tax bias in favour of debt in the corporate income tax could be offset by a tax bias against debt in the personal income tax. At least for large corporations in open economies, this kind of argument now has little merit, as the growth in share-ownership by tax-exempt institutions and foreign shareholders has weakened the link between domestic personal income taxes and corporate financial behaviour.

[6] Empirical evidence suggests that the cost of capital is an important influence on corporate investment, although estimates of the magnitude of this effect vary considerably. See Hassett and Hubbard (2002) for a review of this literature and Bond and Xing (2010) for recent cross-country evidence.

[7] The latter case generally applies when the tax code allows commercial depreciation charges to be deducted for tax purposes. Since firms then benefit in present-value terms from charging depreciation at a faster rate in their commercial accounts, maximum rates are needed to limit the extent to which this can be exploited.

economic depreciation will distort the asset composition of investment. While there may be reasons for designing a tax system that increases the required rate of return for all assets, there is little evidence of commensurate differences in social returns that would justify discouraging investment in some types of assets more than others in this way.[8]

Furthermore, tax depreciation schedules generally operate with reference to the historic cost for which assets were purchased, implying that the real value of tax depreciation allowances will be eroded by inflation. Even quite modest annual inflation rates can have a significant effect in reducing the real value of these tax allowances below the actual depreciation costs borne by firms, particularly for assets with long lifetimes.

For equity-financed investment, this can imply a substantial effect of inflation in raising the cost of capital. For debt-financed investment, this effect is mitigated by another feature of unindexed corporate income tax bases, which is that nominal rather than real interest payments on outstanding debt can be deducted against taxable profits. Per se, this reduces the real after-tax cost of borrowing. Higher inflation may have other effects—for example, raising the cost of holding inventories that appreciate in nominal value, and increasing the taxation of real capital gains on asset sales at both the firm level and the shareholder level. Even if we thought there might be good reasons why the corporate income tax should encourage firms to use debt and discourage firms from investing, it is unclear why we would want these effects to vary with the rate of inflation.

These effects of inflation could, in principle, be avoided by indexing the corporate tax base. Depreciation allowances could be specified in relation to inflation-adjusted values of assets, rather than their historic purchase prices, and interest deductions could be restricted to real rather than nominal interest payments.[9] However, no OECD country has yet adopted a fully

---

[8] Some types of investment are granted more favourable tax treatments as a result of considered policy choices that may be justified by externalities or market failures. Examples include expenditures on research and development, and on energy-saving technologies, which may e.g. be expensed immediately or benefit from further tax credits.

[9] Similarly, taxable capital gains when assets are sold could be calculated with reference to an indexed base, and adjustments could be made for the effect of inflation on the nominal value of inventories.

inflation-adjusted corporate income tax base, perhaps reflecting the additional complexity involved.

These are by no means the only problems involved in computing taxable profits under a standard corporate income tax. Because there is no uniform definition of the corporate tax base—reflecting the absence of any common definition of 'profits' for tax purposes—many detailed aspects of the corporate tax base differ across countries, even though they aim to tax broadly the same thing. Multinational firms may in some cases be able to benefit from these differences, obtaining the most generous tax allowances on offer, or even deducting the same costs against tax in more than one jurisdiction—although, conversely, in other cases they may find that the same income is taxed more than once in different countries. We discuss these international issues further in Chapter 18.

To summarize, the standard corporate income tax is likely to distort company behaviour in several ways that may be undesirable. Borrowing is favoured over retained profits or new equity as a source of finance for corporate investment, leaving firms more exposed to the risk of bankruptcy. This tax bias in favour of debt increases with the rate of inflation. The tax treatment of depreciation favours investment in particular assets where tax allowances are relatively generous compared with true depreciation costs. Overall, the corporate income tax increases the cost of capital and reduces investment. This principally reflects the inclusion of the normal return on equity-financed investment in the standard corporate income tax base.

17.3. ALTERNATIVE CORPORATE TAX BASES

Several proposals have been made to reform or replace the standard corporate income tax base, in ways that reduce or remove some or all of the distortions to corporate behaviour that we highlighted in the previous section.

17.3.1. Cash-Flow Taxes

A radical proposal, which was developed in the Meade Report, would replace a tax based on a measure of company profits or income by a tax based on a measure of net cash flow. One version of this, known as the R-base, would abolish deductions for both depreciation and interest payments, and replace them with a deduction for investment expenditure when it is incurred.[10] Investment is then treated like any other current cost and, conversely, sales of capital assets would be treated like any other cash inflow.

In the simple example we considered in Table 17.1, at a tax rate of 25%, the purchase of an asset for £1,000 in year 1 would then require the firm to finance an outlay of only £750.[11] In year 2, both the income of £30 and the revenue of £1,000 from selling the asset are taxed at 25%, leaving the firm with 75% of the net cash flow, or £772.50. In effect, this cash-flow tax contributes 25% of the investment outlay in exchange for 25% of the proceeds. Regardless of whether it is financed by equity or debt, the original project is simply scaled down from the perspective of the investor. In the case of equity finance, shareholders make a return of £22.50 on their investment of £750, matching the 3% return we have assumed they could earn elsewhere. For debt finance, this just covers the interest cost. Moreover, if the pre-tax rate of return on the project exceeds 3%, this will also be the case for the post-tax rate of return.

The R-base cash-flow tax eliminates the current tax bias in favour of debt by treating debt- and equity-financed investments identically. Marginal investments, which just earn the minimum required rate of return in the absence of tax, remain marginal investments in the presence of the tax. Consequently, the tax has no effect on the cost of capital, or minimum required pre-tax rate of return. In effect, this approach taxes only economic rents and not the normal return on corporate investments. This applies to all

---

[10] This up-front allowance for investment expenditure is sometimes called a 100% first-year allowance, or 'free depreciation'. The Annual Investment Allowance in the UK provides this expensing treatment for a limited amount of investment in plant and machinery.

[11] This assumes either that the firm has other net cash flows of at least £1,000, so that the investment allowance generates a reduced tax payment of £250 in year 1, or that the 'tax loss' of −£1,000 generates a rebate of £250 (i.e. there is a symmetric treatment of taxable profits and losses). Similar outcomes can be achieved if the 'tax loss' is carried forward to set against positive net cash flows in later years, with an appropriate interest mark-up.

types of assets, regardless of their useful lifetimes or depreciation profiles. Inflation has no effect on these properties, as the tax base in each period depends only on nominal cash flows.

The R-base version of the cash-flow tax makes a distinction between cash flows that are associated with the firm's 'real' business operations (such as revenues from the sale of goods and services, and payments for labour and other inputs used to produce these goods and services, including purchases and sales of capital) and cash flows that are associated with financing those operations (including borrowing and repayments of interest and principal to lenders, and injections of equity and payments of dividends to shareholders). Within these cash flows associated with financing, no distinction is made between debt finance and equity finance—neither payments of interest to lenders nor payments of dividends to shareholders would be tax deductible. The R-base version of the cash-flow tax is closely related to current versions of VATs that exempt financial transactions from the tax base.[12] This presents a problem for the taxation of banks and other financial intermediaries, which make a high proportion of their profits from interest spreads—charging higher interest rates to borrowers than they pay to depositors—which would not be taxed under the R-base tax. The distinction between debt and equity also plays an important role in the current operation of corporate income taxes around the world. While maintaining this distinction is administratively costly, requiring legislation to determine whether payments made by firms to financiers on 'hybrid securities' can be deducted against the corporate income tax or not, the abolition of interest deductibility could also present difficulties for a single country that introduced the R-base cash-flow tax in isolation.[13]

A variant of the cash-flow tax that addresses these issues is the R+F-base. Under the R+F-base, new borrowing would be treated as a taxable cash

---

[12] Value added taxes are discussed in Chapters 6–9. The connection follows from noting that value added can be expressed as net cash flow plus labour costs.

[13] For example, there may be uncertainty about whether payments of a reformed corporation tax along these lines by subsidiaries of international companies would continue to be creditable against domestic corporate income taxes in countries that use the credit method of international double tax relief (see Section 18.2 in the following chapter). Experience with implementing taxes very like the R-base cash-flow tax has been mainly limited to specific taxes on natural resources such as oil and gas, where high economic rents are expected and where operations in specific locations such as the North Sea can be 'ring-fenced'.

inflow, while repayments of both interest and principal would be treated as deductible cash outflows. This requires a distinction to be made between cash flows associated with debt finance and equity finance. Deductibility of nominal interest payments against the corporate tax base is then preserved, in common with corporate income taxes in other countries. Nominal interest receipts from lending would continue to be taxable, so that profits made by banks from interest spreads would still be taxed, in so far as banks earn more than the minimum required rate of return on their capital. In principle, it would appear possible, if somewhat cumbersome, to tax new borrowing and allow repayments of principal to be deductible. However, we have no experience of attempting to do this in practice. Implementation of the R+F-base cash-flow tax would raise similar issues to some of the proposals for applying VAT to financial services, which we discussed in Chapter 8.

17.3.2. An Allowance for Corporate Equity (ACE)

A different approach to equalizing the tax treatment of debt and equity finance was proposed by the IFS Capital Taxes Group (1991). The basic idea is to provide explicit tax relief for the imputed opportunity cost of using shareholders' funds to finance the operations of the company. This 'allowance for corporate equity (ACE)' can be thought of in two ways: either as a counterpart to allowing the interest cost of debt finance to be tax deductible, or as a series of deferred tax allowances which compensate for the absence of the up-front 100% allowance for equity-financed investment expenditure provided by the cash-flow taxes. These two interpretations are broadly equivalent in examples with perfect certainty about future returns, while the second interpretation turns out to be more appropriate in the presence of risk and uncertainty. The effect is again to remove the normal return on equity-financed investment from the corporate tax base.[14]

At first sight, it may seem that simply allowing a deduction for the opportunity cost of equity finance would leave the issues of tax depreciation schedules and inflation unresolved. In fact, by relating the measure of the

[14] Versions of this tax base were used in Croatia between 1994 and 2001, and introduced in Belgium in 2008.

equity base used to compute this tax allowance explicitly to the depreciation schedule used for tax purposes, this sensitivity can be avoided.

Broadly speaking, the stock of shareholders' funds used to compute the ACE allowance evolves according to:

Closing stock = Opening stock + Equity issued – Equity (re-)purchased
+ Retained profits as computed for tax purposes.

The ACE allowance for the current period is then obtained as an imputed return on the closing stock of shareholders' funds at the end of the previous period (i.e. multiplying this stock by a specified rate of interest). Here, equity (re-)purchased includes the acquisition of equity or additional equity in subsidiaries that the company acquires or whose expansion the company finances, as well as any share buy-backs. Retained profits as computed for tax purposes correspond to taxable profits (net of the ACE allowance) minus tax paid to the government and minus dividends paid to shareholders.

Now compare the sequence of depreciation allowances and ACE allowances in the case of an asset for which the tax depreciation schedule is 'right' with those for an asset where the depreciation rate allowed for tax purposes is 'too low'. For such an asset, where the tax schedule initially underestimates the true cost of depreciation, the depreciation allowances will be 'too low' in the early years of the asset's life, resulting in taxable profits and tax payments that are initially 'too high'. However, retained profits as computed for tax purposes will then also be higher than they would otherwise be, resulting in a higher stock of shareholders' funds used to compute the ACE allowance in future years. As a result, future ACE allowances will be higher, and future tax payments will be lower.[15] These two effects can be shown to offset each other precisely in present-value terms, so that the present value of the stream of tax payments under the ACE tax base does not depend on the details of the depreciation schedule used.[16]

The ACE tax base could be indexed to deal with inflation, but this is not required. The intuition here is that the same deduction for the cost of equity finance can be computed either by indexing the equity base in line with

[15] The converse applies for assets where the tax depreciation schedule over-depreciates the asset relative to true economic depreciation.
[16] This useful property of the ACE tax base was demonstrated in IFS Capital Taxes Group (1991), building on earlier work by Boadway and Bruce (1984).

inflation over the previous year and then computing the opportunity cost using a real interest rate; or more simply by not inflation-adjusting the equity base, but computing the opportunity cost using a nominal interest rate. Provided the ACE allowance is calculated by applying a nominal interest rate to the unindexed equity base, allowing nominal interest payments to also be deductible then provides the appropriate tax relief for the cost of debt finance in the presence of inflation.[17]

These properties of the ACE tax base depend on using the appropriate interest rate to compute the ACE allowance. Given that future returns on investment projects may be highly uncertain and shareholders are likely to be risk averse, this may appear to be a formidable problem. Generally, shareholders will not be willing to invest in risky projects whose expected rate of return is no higher than the interest rate they can earn on safe assets. The gap between the expected rate of return they require and the risk-free interest rate is known as the risk premium component of the required (expected) rate of return. This is likely to vary widely across different investment projects, and no single rate would be appropriate for firms that invest in many different assets. Fortunately, under quite general assumptions about the way in which risky assets are valued by investors, this information is not needed to implement the ACE corporation tax, and the appropriate rate to compute the ACE allowance turns out to be the risk-free (nominal) interest rate.[18]

The intuition for this result comes from thinking about the stream of ACE allowances for a particular investment project not explicitly as tax relief for the minimum (expected) rate of return required by equity investors in each period, but rather as an alternative to the expensing treatment of equity-financed investment under the R+F-base cash-flow tax. Suppose the firm invests £1,000 in an asset that lasts forever and that does not depreciate in value. The cash-flow tax gives an allowance of £1,000 in the first period. If we assume for simplicity that there is no inflation and the risk-free (real) interest rate is constant at 3%, the ACE tax instead gives a perpetual stream of ACE allowances of £30 per year, with a present value (discounted at 3%)

---

[17] The deduction of nominal interest payments from taxable profits will again be reflected in the computation of retained profits for tax purposes used to determine future ACE allowances.
[18] This convenient result was shown by Bond and Devereux (2003), building on earlier work by Fane (1987).

also of £1,000. Provided investors are indifferent between receiving £1,000 now or £30 per year forever, the ACE tax has the same neutrality properties as the cash-flow tax outlined in the previous subsection.[19] If instead the ACE allowance were to be calculated using a higher interest rate than the risk-free rate, the value of the tax relief provided by the ACE tax would then exceed that provided by the cash-flow tax. The effect would then be to reduce the minimum required (expected) pre-tax rate of return below that which would be required in the absence of the tax, and corporate investment decisions would be distorted.

This view of the ACE allowance as an alternative to the up-front tax relief for equity-financed corporate investment provided under the R+F-base cash-flow tax mirrors our discussion in Chapter 13 of alternative approaches to the implementation of a personal tax on consumption. The ACE approach at the corporate level has much in common with the 'rate-of-return allowance (RRA)' at the personal level, while the cash-flow tax proposals are closely related to the 'EET' treatment of savings at the personal level. In both cases, aligning the timing of tax relief for the normal return on savings and investments more closely with the timing of tax payments on actual returns reduces the need for rebates or carry-forward provisions to deal effectively with tax losses, and may reduce associated opportunities for tax avoidance. At the corporate level, the ACE proposal has the further advantage of retaining much of the structure of existing corporate income taxes.

The ACE corporation tax would allow nominal interest payments to be deducted from the corporate tax base and would tax nominal interest receipts, so that profits from interest margins are taxed in the case of banks and other financial intermediaries. The treatments of debt-financed and equity-financed investments are equivalent in present-value terms and also similar in relation to the timing of tax payments, provided tax depreciation

---

[19] Strictly, this requires investors to be certain that they will benefit from all future ACE allowances over the lifetime of the project. Bond and Devereux (2003) set out the tax rules that are needed in the event of firm closure or bankruptcy for this result to hold. A symmetric treatment of tax losses, at least in present-value terms, is also required. If these conditions do not hold, the risk premium component of the interest rate used to compute the ACE allowance should reflect *only* the risk that future ACE allowances will not be paid out in full, *not* the uncertainty about the underlying future returns on the project to equity investors.

schedules approximate true depreciation. In principle, the ACE tax should not distort financing choices.

Marginal investments pay no tax in present-value terms, regardless of how they are financed. Revenue is raised from projects that earn supernormal profits or economic rents, i.e. where profits exceed the minimum (expected) rate of return required to justify the investment. The taxation of economic rents at both the corporate and personal levels still raises important issues. If rents are exclusively the result of history or accident, then taxing them will generate revenue with no economic distortions. If, however, what appear to be economic rents today are in part the result of past investments of effort or financial capital, then high taxes may still discourage the activities that generated the apparent rents. In the international context, some economic rents may also be mobile across national borders. We discuss this further in Chapter 18.

Implementation of the ACE tax would preserve most of the structure of existing corporate income taxes, including depreciation schedules and interest deductibility. All that would be required would be to specify how the equity base used to compute the ACE allowance evolves over time, and which particular 'risk-free' nominal interest rate is used to compute the allowance. In most contexts, this could be approximated by the interest rate on medium-term government bonds.

17.3.3. A Comprehensive Business Income Tax (CBIT)

Equal treatments of debt and equity could also be achieved by including the normal return on debt-financed investments in the corporate tax base. This would imply the abolition of interest deductibility, and the taxation of a measure of corporate profits after depreciation but before interest.[20]

While the deductibility of interest payments produces different treatments of debt and equity finance under the standard corporate income tax base, simply abolishing interest deductibility would not address the other concerns about the standard corporate income tax. The resulting tax base would raise the required rate of return on both debt-financed and equity-

---

[20] A proposal for a 'comprehensive business income tax (CBIT)' along these lines was put forward in US Department of the Treasury (1992) but has not so far been implemented.

financed investments, and would do so to varying degrees depending on the rate of inflation and details of the tax allowances for depreciation. The CBIT approach does not achieve a uniform treatment of different kinds of assets that firms invest in, nor does it avoid sensitivity to inflation.

Simply abolishing interest deductibility would also present a practical problem in taxing banks and other financial institutions. Taxing interest income while giving no tax relief for interest payments would imply a huge tax increase for banks and other intermediaries that make profits from borrowing and lending. Conversely, a symmetric treatment of interest income and interest payments would imply no taxation of interest income. This would exempt from taxation the component of bank profits that results from interest spreads. Neither of these outcomes seems to be attractive. One alternative would be to make interest payments deductible only against interest income. This would make net interest income taxable if interest income exceeds interest payments, but not deductible if interest payments exceed interest income. This asymmetric approach would, though, introduce a tax incentive for banks, with taxable net interest income, to acquire companies that are net borrowers, which could still erode a significant part of the corporate tax base.

While no major country has abolished interest deductibility, there is an increasing tendency for countries to limit interest deductibility on cross-border investments. This is principally to combat tax avoidance by multinational companies, which can reduce their worldwide tax payments under the standard corporate income tax base by allowing subsidiaries in countries with relatively high corporate tax rates to borrow from, and pay deductible interest to, subsidiaries in countries with lower corporate tax rates.[21] More fundamentally, as countries have found it increasingly difficult to tax effectively the profits that companies earn abroad, and have moved explicitly to exempting foreign profits from their corporate tax bases, they have also had to consider restricting tax relief for costs of financing foreign (exempt) investment, which would otherwise only serve to reduce the domestic tax base of multinational companies.[22]

---

[21] This assumes that the firm has taxable profits in both locations.

[22] The UK introduced exemption for foreign-source dividends in July 2009 and a 'worldwide debt cap' in January 2010. The debt cap limits interest deductibility available for UK subsidiaries of multinational groups, in relation to interest expenses for the group as a whole.

17.4. THE CHOICE OF THE CORPORATE TAX BASE

Good reasons for taxing corporate profits remain. But it is important to tax them in a way that distorts as little as possible company decisions over how much to invest, what to invest in, and how to finance that investment, as well as personal decisions over how much to save and which assets to hold. The corporate tax base should be consistent with policy choices for taxing personal savings.

The standard corporate income tax base does have some consistency with the policy choice of taxing the normal return on savings. In the UK, the normal return is taxed in many instances, though not when savings are held in the form of pension plans, ISAs, or owner-occupied housing. The difference in the treatments of corporate investment financed by debt and by equity is something of an anomaly. Historically, and in a closed economy setting, this may have been consistent with the view that returns to debt can be taxed only at the personal level, while returns to equity require taxation at source, in the corporate sector. The CBIT resolves this anomaly on the basis of taxing returns to both debt and equity at the corporate level.

With different policy choices for the taxation of personal savings, it becomes more attractive to consider alternative corporate tax bases. In principle, both the cash-flow taxes and the ACE corporation tax are consistent with a personal tax that does not tax the normal return on savings, and only taxes excess returns or economic rents. The cash-flow taxes are closely related to the expenditure tax treatment of personal savings, while the ACE is closely related to the rate-of-return allowance approach. The ACE provides an explicit deduction for the cost of using equity finance, similar to the existing deduction for the cost of interest payments on debt finance. This levels the playing field between different sources of finance. Like the RRA, the ACE can be designed to eliminate the effect of the corporate tax on the required rate of return for all forms of corporate investment. Different assets that firms invest in are treated equally, with no sensitivity of tax liabilities to the rate of inflation. With this form of corporate tax base, investment projects that just earn the minimum required or 'normal' rate of return are effectively exempt from corporate taxation, and revenue is collected from those investments that earn above-normal rates of return, or economic rents.

In a closed economy setting, with no international trade or capital flows, the choice between the CBIT and the ACE approach would depend on the kind of considerations that we discussed in Chapter 13, in the context of capital income taxation more broadly. Two kinds of argument could be used to support the ACE (or indeed the cash-flow approach).

One argument, drawing on the literature on optimal taxation, would appeal to conditions under which it would be efficient not to tax the normal return on capital, minimizing distortions to the timing of consumption. A more pragmatic case would emphasize the desirability of achieving a uniform tax treatment of different forms of saving and investment, noting that this uniformity can be achieved in practice only by tax bases that exempt the normal return on all assets. Conversely, arguments in favour of the standard corporate income tax or CBIT approaches would rest on the desirability of taxing the normal return to capital outweighing any resulting distortions to the composition and timing of investment. The choice between these two corporate tax bases would then depend on how interest and other forms of income from capital are taxed at the personal level, unless discrimination between debt and equity finance is actually considered to be desirable.

While these considerations remain important, in an open economy setting there are further reasons for questioning the desirability of taxing the normal return to capital, at least on a source-country basis. We discuss these arguments in the following chapter, as well as the practical challenges of implementing a conventional corporate tax in the setting of a modern open economy with a high degree of international capital mobility and in which multinational companies account for a substantial share of business activity. We also consider the factors that influence the choice of the corporate tax rate in this context.

18

Corporate Taxation in an International Context

Tax systems are designed and administered by national governments. They developed at a time when cross-border flows of goods, services, and capital were much less important than they are today. Arrangements to deal with international trade and capital flows have been added to national tax systems on a needs-must basis. Inevitably, these arrangements tend to be complex and problematic, requiring a degree of cooperation between governments and having to reconcile different approaches to taxation in different countries, as well as differences in tax rates. Cooperation takes the form both of bilateral tax treaties agreed between countries and of more ambitious attempts at coordination of some tax rules within blocs such as the OECD and the European Union.

Few would claim that the current system is satisfactory. Some international companies complain of 'double taxation' of the same income in multiple jurisdictions, resulting in cross-border investments facing higher taxation than domestic investments, as well as the additional compliance costs of having to deal with multiple tax authorities. At the same time, some governments complain of tax avoidance by multinational firms, with taxable income being shifted out of countries with high tax rates into countries with lower tax rates, and being routed through affiliates in tax havens in ways that may make it difficult to tax at all. A high proportion of the significant legal disputes between companies and tax authorities involve the treatment of cross-border transactions.

The growth of multinational corporations, in particular, has placed increasing strains on the international aspects of national tax systems. Even if there were universal agreement on *how* the worldwide profits of a company should be taxed, for firms with operations in more than one country we face the further question of *where* those profits should be taxed—or, more precisely, of how to divide global profits between the different countries in which business is conducted. These considerations—international mobility of income and international tax competition between jurisdictions—play an increasingly central role in the design of corporate income tax systems.

Consider a simple example in which a company is legally resident in country R and is wholly owned by residents of that country. The company has a wholly owned subsidiary in country S, producing products that are wholly exported and purchased by consumers in a third country, D. Country R is referred to as the residence country, in which the ultimate owners of the company are resident. Country S is referred to as the source country, in which the company's assets are located and its production takes place. Country D is referred to as the destination country, in which the product is consumed.[1] We agree that this operation produces profits—perhaps profits in excess of the normal rate of return on the capital invested—that should be taxed. But should these profits be taxed in the residence country, the source country, or the destination country? How should the tax base be allocated between these three jurisdictions?

There is no compelling answer to this question. To appreciate this, suppose that the product can only be produced in country S and is only valued by consumers in country D, and the operation can only be financed by investors in country R. Worldwide profits would then be zero without an essential contribution from individuals located in each of the three countries. There is no sense in which we could state, for example, that 20% of the profits stem from the contribution of individuals in the residence country, 50% from the contribution of individuals in the source country, and 30% from the contribution of individuals in the destination country. In this case,

---

[1] The structure of real multinational enterprises will generally be much more complex, with shareholders resident in many countries and including institutional investors, making ultimate ownership difficult to discern. Similarly, groups may have subsidiaries and customers in multiple jurisdictions.

there would seem to be no logical basis for dividing up these global profits between the three countries. And yet the international tax system clearly requires some allocation to be adopted, if the profits of multinational companies are to be taxed at all.

It can also be noted that different components of national tax systems typically result in different allocations of worldwide profits in cases such as this. Consider first value added taxes (VATs), which generally operate on a destination basis. If it were the case that the governments of all three countries in our example relied exclusively on VATs to raise their tax revenue, then the only tax paid on the operations of our company would be paid in the destination country, D. Since value added can be expressed as the sum of labour costs and economic rent, in this case the worldwide profits of the company, in excess of the normal return on capital invested, would be taxed at the VAT rate of country D.

The outcome would be very different if, instead, all three countries relied exclusively on personal income taxes, which generally operate on a residence basis. Investors resident in country R would then be liable to tax on the dividend income and/or capital gains that they derive from their ownership of the company. In this case, the only tax paid on the operations of the company would be paid in the residence country, R, at the shareholders' personal income tax rates.[2]

The allocation would be different again if all three countries relied exclusively on corporate income taxes, which generally operate on a source-country basis. In this case, the subsidiary company in country S would be taxed on its reported profits. The parent company in country R may or may not be taxed on any dividends received from its subsidiary in country S, depending on the treatment of foreign-source income in country R. If it is not, the only tax paid on the operations of the company would then be paid at the corporate income tax rate in the source country, S.[3]

---

[2] Under a standard personal income tax, both economic rents and the normal return on capital invested would be taxed in this case; although tax payments could be deferred by retention of profits within either the subsidiary or the parent company and by individual investors delaying realization of the associated capital gains.

[3] As we discuss further in Section 18.2, this would be the outcome either if country R exempts foreign-source dividends from its corporate tax base, or if it taxes foreign-source dividends under the credit method *and* the corporate tax rate is higher in country S than in country R.

These examples indicate that the balance between taxation in the source country, the residence country, and the destination country will depend on the relative levels of corporate income tax rates, personal income tax rates, and VAT rates. The balance between these different taxes also influences the degree to which different measures of profits are taxed. Thus the trend over the last three decades towards lower corporate income tax rates and higher VAT rates in many developed countries has tended to result in a shift away from taxation of total profits (including the normal return on equity invested) in source countries, and towards the taxation of economic rents (on a cash-flow basis) in destination countries.

Our focus in the remainder of this chapter will be on corporate taxation in the context of international companies. Without a much greater degree of coordination between national governments than we can envisage in the foreseeable future, there are no simple solutions to the challenges that this presents for tax design. There are powerful intellectual arguments against source-based corporate income taxes, and enormous practical problems in their implementation. And yet in spite of these concerns, source-based corporate income taxes—many of which were introduced over a century ago—have survived and continue to raise significant amounts of government revenue in many countries.

In considering the design of the tax system in a small open economy setting, we recognize that many countries are likely to continue to operate source-based corporate income taxes for many years to come. In our view, this does not preclude significant reform of the corporate tax base. However, the pressures that have led to falling corporate tax rates in recent years suggest that this will have important revenue implications. In short, it would not be attractive to offset the revenue cost of introducing an allowance for corporate equity by raising the corporate tax rate, because such a rate increase would likely induce a substantial reallocation of income across countries by multinational firms. Rather, our analysis suggests that it would be appropriate to raise less revenue from source-based corporate taxation, and to consider this reform only as part of a revenue-neutral programme of changes to the tax system as a whole.

18.1. SOURCE-BASED CORPORATE TAXES

The current international convention in taxing corporate profits allocates the primary taxing right to a 'source country', where some element of the production of goods or services takes place. Most countries tax 'resident' companies on their locally generated profits, even if they exempt foreign profits from tax. Company 'residence' may depend upon no more than the formality of incorporation under local law. It may also depend upon whether the company's head office or principal place of business or its effective centre of management is found in the country concerned. Even if the company is not resident in a particular country, however, it is still liable to be taxed there if it conducts any aspect of its business in the country through a 'permanent establishment'. In that case, any bilateral tax treaty is likely to preserve the source country's taxing rights and give it primacy over any claim that the company's country of residence may make to tax the company's foreign profits.

Most multinational companies operate in different countries through locally incorporated subsidiaries. For large corporations with subsidiaries operating in many countries, there are major difficulties in deciding how much of the group's worldwide profits are contributed by each of its subsidiaries—particularly when these affiliated companies are supplying each other with intermediate inputs and finance. Nevertheless, this is what international tax rules seek to achieve, and elaborate rules and procedures have been developed to resolve some disputes between companies and tax authorities over where particular components of profits should be taxed. An important practical consideration favouring source-based corporate taxation may be the relative ease with which local tax authorities can scrutinize the reported profits of local subsidiaries of multinational groups; with tax revenue paid to the source-country government, local tax authorities also have an incentive to collect this revenue appropriately. In any case, this is the basis on which company profits are currently taxed, and it would be difficult for any single country to seek to tax company profits at the corporate level on anything other than a source-country basis. In particular, credit for source-country tax against any residence-country tax on the same profits will usually depend upon the source country's tax conforming to international norms.

18.1.1. Implementation Issues

The current source-based tax arrangements result in very high compliance costs for international companies, and very high administration costs for tax authorities in implementing source-based corporate income taxes. Consider a multinational group with wholly owned subsidiaries in two countries, L and H. Suppose the subsidiary in country L produces an intermediate input, which is purchased by the subsidiary in country H and used to produce a final product which is then sold to unrelated customers. By charging a higher price for this intermediate input in the transaction between its two subsidiaries, the multinational group can make its subsidiary in country L appear to be more profitable, and its subsidiary in country H correspondingly less profitable, with no effect on its worldwide (pre-tax) profits. If the corporate tax rate in country L is lower than that in country H, then the group has a clear incentive to charge as high a price for the intermediate product as it can get away with. By doing so, it shifts taxable income out of country H and into country L, lowering its total corporate income tax payments and increasing its total post-tax profits. Conversely, if the subsidiary that produces the intermediate input happens to be located in the high-tax country, H, while the subsidiary that purchases this input is located in country L, the group would then have an incentive to charge a lower price for the intermediate input, again shifting more of its taxable income into the low-tax country, L.

The prices used to value trade in goods and services between affiliated companies in different countries for the purpose of measuring each company's taxable profits on a source-country basis are known as transfer prices. Governments of countries with relatively high corporate tax rates have a particular incentive to limit the discretion given to companies to determine the transfer prices used in these related-party trades. The general principle used is that of 'arm's-length pricing', which attempts to value goods and services traded between related parties at the prices observed when the same goods and services are traded between unrelated parties. This principle may be difficult to apply, particularly when the intermediate inputs concerned are highly specialized products that may not be traded between any other parties.

In some cases, the arm's-length principle may break down completely. Suppose, for example, that the intermediate input is a mineral mined only at one location in country L, whose only use is in the production process that is used exclusively by the multinational firm in country H. There is no comparison price at which the mineral is traded between unrelated parties. Moreover, we again have a situation here in which worldwide profits would be zero without an essential contribution from the group's operations in the two countries, and there is no compelling division of these profits between the two locations. This example may appear to be extreme in the context of a physical input such as a mineral. However, this situation can arise quite naturally in the case of intangible assets, such as intellectual property— suppose, for example, that the subsidiary in country L is a dedicated commercial research laboratory, established by the multinational firm for the sole purpose of improving its production processes and products. This may become more challenging still if the group has research operations in more than one country which all make essential contributions to the development of a new product or process.

The arm's-length principle may be considered to be flawed more generally. An important reason why multinational corporations exist is likely to be that they enjoy some advantage that cannot easily be replicated by arm's-length trade between unrelated firms. In any case, given the difficulty of finding appropriate arm's-length prices, it is unsurprising that there are many transfer pricing disputes between companies and tax authorities, and that some of these result in costly litigation.

Manipulation of transfer prices is one of many ways in which multinational companies can take advantage of differences in corporate tax rates across countries. Given that interest payments are deductible against taxable profits in most countries, it is tax efficient for a multinational group to locate more of its debt in high-tax countries and less of its debt in low-tax countries. Thus, in our previous example, all else equal, we would expect more of the group's borrowing to be undertaken by the subsidiary in the high-tax country, H, and less of the group's borrowing to be undertaken by the subsidiary in the low-tax country, L. In this way, the group can shelter more income that would otherwise be taxed at the high rate, again shifting more of its taxable income into the low-tax country, L, and reducing its total tax payments. Moreover, if the subsidiary in country L lends to the subsidiary in country H, this creates a deductible interest payment in country H and a taxable interest receipt in country L. The tax saving in country H exceeds the tax payment in country L, given the difference in tax rates, again reducing the group's worldwide tax payments.

Governments, particularly those in countries with relatively high corporate tax rates, again seek to limit the extent to which multinational firms can use debt to shift taxable profits out of their jurisdictions. This may take the form of 'thin capitalization rules', which effectively cap the amount of interest that can be deducted against taxable profits, perhaps particularly in relation to interest paid to affiliated companies; or 'interest allocation rules', which seek to restrict interest deductibility to borrowing that is used to finance operations within the jurisdiction. However, such anti-avoidance rules tend to be both complex to design and somewhat arbitrary in their effects, resulting in high administration and compliance costs, and numerous legal disputes.

18.1.2. Incidence and Rationale

It is clear that retaining source-based corporate income taxes perpetuates these important administrative problems. So it is reasonable to ask whether there are powerful arguments in favour of retaining them.

One rationale emphasizes the possibility of taxing foreign owners of the corporations operating in the domestic economy. At first sight, this may seem obvious. Domestic firms are owned by foreign shareholders to some extent. Domestic subsidiaries of foreign corporations are largely owned by non-residents. Surely domestic residents will be better off if some of the government expenditure they benefit from can be financed from taxes paid by these foreign shareholders? While there are circumstances in which this could be correct, much will depend on the degree to which the effective incidence of source-based corporate income taxes is borne by the owners of corporations.

We first consider a source-based corporate income tax in the setting of a small open economy with internationally mobile capital and immobile labour. As we have seen in Chapter 17, the standard corporate income tax base includes the component of corporate profits that corresponds to the normal or required rate of return on investments financed by equity. Suppose there is an array of potential investment projects available to firms in each country, offering different rates of return to potential investors. We first assume that there are no source-based corporate income taxes in any country, and that all investment projects that offer investors a real rate of return of at least 3% attract funding, regardless of where they are located. That is, we have a world of 'perfect capital mobility', in which the location of investment is separated from the location of savings.

Now suppose that one country has a source-based corporate income tax. We focus, for simplicity, on the case where all investment is equity financed. This will then raise the pre-tax rate of return that is needed from investment projects located in that country in order to provide investors with the same post-tax rate of return of 3%. We assume that the required post-tax rate of return that is needed to attract funding in the world capital market is unchanged at 3%, i.e. the country that has this tax is small enough for the resulting change in the global distribution of available post-tax returns to have a negligible impact on the minimum required rate of return. This embodies a 'small open economy' assumption, which separates the required post-tax rate of return from the tax system of the country we are considering.

Suppose that this source-based corporate income tax raises the required pre-tax rate of return from 3% to 4% for investment projects located in that country and subject to the tax. Projects with pre-tax rates of return between 3% and 4%, which would have been attractive to investors in the absence of the tax, will not attract funding. Only those projects with a pre-tax rate of return of at least 4%, and which therefore can offer investors a post-tax rate of return of at least 3%, will attract funding. The main effect of this source-based corporate income tax is that there will be less investment in this country.

We can then ask who is worse off as a result of this source-based corporate income tax. The main implication of this analysis is that, in a small open economy with perfect capital mobility, shareholders are not affected at all by the presence of the source-based corporate income tax. Shareholders continue to earn the same after-tax rate of return on their investments—at least 3% in our example—with or without this tax. They simply invest less capital in the country with the source-based tax and invest more capital elsewhere. With perfect capital mobility, the effective incidence of the tax is fully shifted away from owners of capital, and on to owners of other inputs that are less mobile. With immobile labour, the effective incidence of the source-based corporate income tax is likely to be borne largely by domestic workers. Lower investment implies less capital per worker and therefore less output per worker, which will result in a lower real wage.[4]

Under these conditions, the source-based corporate income tax then acts as a roundabout way of taxing domestic workers. There is no advantage to domestic residents from taxing foreign shareholders, since shareholders—including foreign shareholders—are unaffected by the presence of the tax. While these assumptions may still be considered extreme, they have certainly become more realistic over time, as the world economy in general, and capital markets in particular, have become more integrated. Recent empirical studies have also supported the main prediction of this simple analysis—that higher source-based corporate income taxes are likely to depress domestic real wages.[5]

In the setting of a small open economy with perfect capital mobility, it can also be shown that source-based taxation of the normal return component of capital income is inefficient.[6] Taxing labour income directly, rather than in this roundabout way, would allow the government to collect the same revenue with more capital per worker, higher productivity, and higher output. Domestic workers could then be better off if any source-based taxes on capital income that tax the normal return to capital were replaced by higher taxes on labour income.

18.1.3. Rents, and Location-Specific Rents

The preceding discussion suggests that there may be a strong argument for not taxing the normal return on corporate investments in modern, open economies. It does not follow, however, that we should not tax corporate income at all. It is important to distinguish between the required or normal

---

[4] To some extent, the effective incidence may also be borne by owners of domestic land, through less capital per square metre, less output per square metre, and lower rental values. In this case, since rental income will be capitalized in the price of land, the affected owners would be those owning land at the time the tax is introduced or increased.

[5] See e.g. Hassett and Mathur (2006) and Arulampalam, Devereux, and Maffini (2007).

[6] See Gordon (1986).

component of returns on investments, and any surplus component over and above this minimum required return. This surplus or excess component of profits is referred to as 'economic rent'.

In a closed economy setting, it is sometimes suggested that it would be efficient to tax economic rent at a high rate. If all returns in excess of the cost of capital reflected pure rents associated with scarcity—as, for example, in the case of non-renewable natural resources—they could in principle be taxed at rates close to 100%, without distorting investment decisions.[7] Part of these apparent rents may, however, reflect returns to effort by entrepreneurs or innovators, which are not fully reflected in the compensation paid to those individuals. Taxing these 'quasi rents' at very high rates may then discourage desirable activities, although taxing them at rates close to labour income tax rates may still be appropriate.

In an open economy with mobile capital, the case for taxing rents on a source-country basis becomes weaker but does not vanish. Some sources of rents may also be highly mobile. For example, a multinational firm may have a unique product that can be produced at a similar cost in different locations and exported at low cost to many different markets. The firm has market power and so can charge a price well above its production costs, earning economic rents. In deciding where to locate production, the firm is likely to want to maximize the post-tax value of these economic rents. In choosing between two otherwise similar countries with source-based taxes on economic rents, the firm will tend to favour the country with the lower tax rate. This illustrates that taxing economic rents on a source-country basis at a high rate may deter inward investment by multinational firms, even though such taxes have no effect on the cost of capital.[8] Moreover, particularly for highly profitable activities where the normal component of returns is relatively low and the rent component of returns is relatively high, firms may prefer locations that have a standard corporate income tax at a sufficiently low rate, rather than locations that tax only economic rent but at a higher rate. As the discussion of transfer pricing concerns in Section 18.1.1 illustrates, when multinational firms can separate their research and

---

[7] The effective incidence of such a tax on pure rents would also be borne by the owners of capital, who would just earn lower post-tax rates of return.

[8] Devereux and Griffith (1998) provide further analysis and empirical evidence on the effects of corporate taxes on location choices.

production activities into distinct subsidiaries, the measured rate of return to the production division may be well above the required rate of return, even though the combined rate of return to innovation and production may not be. Such a firm would seek to locate the division with the high reported rate of return in a jurisdiction with a low source-based corporate tax rate.

At the same time, other sources of rents may be highly specific to particular locations. A leading example would be mineral deposits, such as oil and gas fields in the North Sea. In principle, governments could extract economic rents from producers by auctioning the right to develop and extract these scarce natural resources, but this is rarely done in practice. Instead, these activities are often subject to specific taxes, which in some cases aim specifically to tax the economic rents.[9] Other location-specific sources of economic rents may include the presence of workers with particular skills, to the extent that these are not fully reflected in labour costs, and proximity to large markets, to the extent that this is not fully reflected in the cost of land.

The coexistence of some sources of rents that are location specific and other sources of rents that are highly mobile presents a challenge for tax design in open economies. In principle, it would be efficient to tax rents from relatively immobile activities at a higher rate than rents from more mobile activities, since the former are less likely to relocate elsewhere. We do see some examples of such differential taxation in practice, notably in relation to natural resources such as North Sea oil, but these examples are comparatively rare. More generally, there would be considerable practical difficulties in attempting to tax income from different activities at different rates, particularly where these activities may be undertaken by the same firm. The application of special low tax rates to highly mobile business activities has also been discouraged by international agreements, such as the EU Code of Conduct on business taxation, and OECD initiatives on 'harmful tax competition'.

One rationale for these agreements lies in the view that activities that appear to be highly mobile from the perspective of an individual country may be less mobile for a larger grouping of countries, such as the European

---

[9] An example is the ring-fenced application of UK corporation tax to new North Sea fields, which has 100% investment allowances and no interest deductibility, along the lines of the R-base cash-flow tax discussed in Chapter 17.

Union or the OECD. For example, a car producer selling in the European market may be largely indifferent between locating a new plant in the UK or in Spain, but may be much less likely to choose a location outside the EU. If it is correct that a significantly higher proportion of economic rents are relatively immobile for a bloc of countries, then there could be a considerable advantage to coordination on corporate tax rates within blocs. By acting collectively, countries should be able to extract more revenue from these location-specific rents. Nevertheless, beyond these agreements to limit special tax regimes for particular activities, there seems to be little appetite for greater harmonization of corporate tax rates, even within the countries of the EU.

If we accept the constraint that a single tax rate should apply to all companies, this suggests that the appropriate rate for an individual country will reflect a trade-off between the desirability of taxing location-specific rents and the danger of taxing mobile rents, on a source-country basis, at too high a rate. Taxing immobile rents is desirable partly because such taxation will be borne to some extent by foreign shareholders, but more generally because this provides an efficient source of revenue. Taxing mobile rents risks deterring some internationally mobile investment, with implications for capital per worker and domestic wages similar to those outlined in Section 18.1.2 for source-based taxes on the normal return component of corporate income.

The increased mobility of capital and the rise of multinational companies suggest that the appropriate corporate tax rate is likely to be considerably lower today than in the past. This is broadly consistent with the downward trend in corporate tax rates over the past three decades. Importantly, in the absence of coordination between countries on corporate tax rates, the appropriate or 'competitive' rate for an open economy will depend on corporate tax rates in other countries, which are rival locations for some forms of internationally mobile investment. This is broadly consistent with concerns about a 'race to the bottom' in corporate tax rates, resulting from 'tax competition' between governments to attract investment. However, the presence of some imperfectly mobile sources of economic rent suggests that the appropriate tax rate is unlikely to fall to zero, even in the absence of greater coordination between countries. In so far as larger countries tend to have greater locational advantages for business investment, this would also suggest that higher corporate tax rates may be more appropriate in larger countries. This is broadly consistent with the pattern of corporate tax rates among developed countries, with relatively high tax rates in larger countries such as Japan and the US, and relatively low tax rates in smaller countries such as Ireland and Estonia.

18.2. DOUBLE TAX RELIEF

The vast majority of corporate income tax revenue is collected in source countries. However, when dividends are paid from a subsidiary company in one country to a parent company in another country, there may be an additional layer of corporate taxation in the residence country of the parent firm.

Within a country, it is common for dividends paid by a domestic subsidiary not to be treated as taxable income when received by the parent company. The rationale for this exemption is clear. The underlying profits, out of which such dividends are paid, are assumed to have been taxed as corporate income of the subsidiary company. These profits will thus have been taxed at that country's corporate income tax rate. If any additional tax were to be charged when such dividends are received by the parent company, this would imply that profits earned by the subsidiary and paid to the parent would be subject to more taxation than profits earned directly by the parent company. Such 'double taxation' would penalize corporate groups that structure their domestic business operations into subsidiary companies. The exemption of dividend income received from domestic subsidiaries simply ensures that profits earned by the parent company and profits earned by the subsidiary are taxed at the same rate, avoiding this distortion to the choice of organizational form.[10]

The situation may be different when dividends are received from a subsidiary company located in another country. It is still the case that the

---

[10] Conversely, in cases where company profits may not have been taxed at the subsidiary level as a result of tax incentives for research and development or particular forms of investment, this exemption of dividends received from domestic subsidiaries ensures that the intended benefit of these incentives is not withdrawn on distribution.

underlying profits, out of which these dividends are paid, can be assumed to have been subject to corporate income tax in the source country. In the cross-border context, this implies that the underlying profits have been taxed at the corporate tax rate, and according to the rules for calculating taxable profits, in the source country where the subsidiary is located. Both the corporate tax rate and the corporate tax base could be rather different in the source country from in the residence country of the parent firm.

Taxing dividend income received from foreign subsidiaries as ordinary corporate income in the hands of the parent company would still imply double taxation of the underlying profits. In most circumstances, this would imply considerably higher taxation of income generated by cross-border investments than of income generated by domestic investments. Broadly speaking, and in normal circumstances, countries adopt one of two approaches to relieving this international double taxation: the exemption method or the credit method.[11]

The exemption method, as its name suggests, simply exempts dividends received from foreign subsidiaries from corporate taxation in the residence country of the parent. This treats dividends received from foreign subsidiaries in the same way as dividends received from domestic subsidiaries, and results in taxation on a pure source-country basis, with corporate income tax paid only in the source country. This broad approach is used in France, Germany, and many other EU countries.

The credit method is considerably more complicated. Suppose, for example, that a UK parent receives a dividend of £87.50 from a subsidiary in Ireland (which has a corporate income tax rate of 12.5%). Under the credit method, the underlying profits would be deemed to be £100. UK corporation tax would then be charged at 28% on these underlying profits, but with a credit for the corporate income tax of £12.50 deemed to have been paid on these underlying profits by the subsidiary in Ireland. In principle, the UK parent would then have to pay £15.50 (i.e. £28 minus £12.50) in UK corporation tax. This UK corporation tax charge would be lower for dividends received from subsidiaries in countries with a higher corporate

---

[11] Many countries, including the UK, retain the right to tax the profits of foreign subsidiaries (whether repatriated or not) in limited circumstances under Controlled Foreign Company rules. These generally apply when the subsidiary is located in a tax-haven country, with an unusually low corporate tax rate.

income tax rate than Ireland, and would fall to zero in the case of source countries with a higher corporate income tax rate than the UK. Consequently, the credit method and the exemption method produce the same outcome in relation to dividends received from foreign subsidiaries in source countries with corporate tax rates equal to or higher than that in the residence country of the parent firm.[12] They differ in their treatment of dividends received from foreign subsidiaries in countries with lower corporate tax rates.

In principle, the credit method seeks to tax profits earned by foreign subsidiaries at a rate no lower than the domestic corporate tax rate. This would be the effect, if it were the case that profits earned by foreign subsidiaries are always repatriated immediately to the parent company, in the form of dividends paid directly from the subsidiary to the parent. However, these conditions certainly do not apply. Multinational firms can defer any taxation of foreign-source dividends in the residence country by the simple expedient of retaining profits in their foreign subsidiaries. Groups with operations in many countries can plan to avoid such taxation to a considerable extent, by ensuring that dividends paid to parent companies tend to come from subsidiaries in countries with higher corporate tax rates.

Historically, the credit method tended to be used by major capital-exporting countries, including the US and the UK. In the past, it may have been less straightforward for international firms with simpler structures to avoid paying tax on foreign-source dividends in these residence countries, and the country of legal residence of the parent company may have served as a good proxy for the residence country of the firm's ultimate owners. The rise of complex multinational businesses with global operations and the increase in cross-border share ownership have changed these conditions. Arguably, the legal residence of a parent company now provides a dubious basis for asserting any right to tax (at the corporate level) profits earned by its subsidiaries operating in other jurisdictions.[13] For EU countries, it is also unclear whether it is possible in practical terms to treat dividends received from domestic and foreign subsidiaries differently. The European Court of

---

[12] Assuming comparable methods of calculating taxable profits.

[13] Although in so far as these profits are the basis for returns on the savings of domestic residents held in the form of equities, they may be taxed on a residence-country basis under the personal income tax.

Justice has indicated that member states can continue to tax foreign dividends with credit even though they exempt domestic dividends, but only if that does not disadvantage cross-border investment relative to domestic investment.[14] In this respect, the compatibility of the UK's previous credit system with Community law remains subject to legal challenge.[15]

The UK government introduced exemption for dividends received from foreign subsidiaries in most circumstances from July 2009. The revenue cost of this reform is expected to be modest. If this proves to be correct, it suggests that in practice there is little difference between the credit method and the exemption method in the context of a modern, open economy. Recognizing this in the tax system then provides a welcome simplification.

Formalizing the exemption of dividends received from foreign subsidiaries may, however, make more transparent the opportunity for multinational companies to shift taxable income out of countries with relatively high corporate tax rates by borrowing in those jurisdictions and using the funds borrowed to equity-finance operations of subsidiaries in locations with lower corporate tax rates. This in turn may increase the pressure for restricting interest deductibility to borrowing that is used to finance domestic investment. While such restrictions may appear to be attractive in principle, the difficulty of associating any particular loan with any particular expenditure may make their design and implementation formidably complicated in practice. Formulating rules whose application is compatible with EU Treaty obligations and which do not raise the cost of debt finance for domestic firms is also likely to be extremely difficult. Conveniently, the need for such restrictions on interest deductibility may be less pressing in a corporate tax system with an allowance for corporate equity, as we explain in the next section.

---

[14] See Case C-446/04 Test Claimants in the Franked Investment Income Group Litigation v Commissioners of Inland Revenue.

[15] The issue may be the subject of a further reference to the Court of Justice following further UK litigation in the *Franked Investment Income Group Litigation* case.

18.3. ACE IN AN INTERNATIONAL CONTEXT

We now consider some issues that would arise if an open economy such as the UK were to reform its corporate income tax by introducing an allowance for corporate equity (ACE), thereby exempting the normal return on equity-financed investments from its corporate tax base.

The simple introduction of the ACE allowance would not address many of the problems that arise in the implementation of source-based corporate income taxes in the context of international firms. Multinational groups would still have an incentive to manipulate transfer prices to shift taxable profits from their UK subsidiaries to affiliates operating in countries with lower corporate tax rates. Administration and compliance costs would continue to be high as a result, though no higher than they are with a standard corporate income tax base.

If we assume that most other countries continue with a standard corporate income tax base, allowing interest payments to be deducted but with no allowance for the opportunity cost of using equity finance, we might then expect multinational groups to favour equity finance for their UK operations. Using less debt in the UK and more debt elsewhere would still allow interest payments to be deducted, while using more equity in the UK and less equity elsewhere would provide the group with a tax relief not available in most other countries. From the UK perspective, this would simply replace a tax deduction that would otherwise have been claimed in respect of an interest payment by a tax deduction for the opportunity cost of equity finance. Provided the equity is used to finance investment in the UK, this would be an appropriate use of the ACE allowance. Increased borrowing by multinational groups outside the UK may put some additional pressure on thin capitalization rules in other countries, but this is unlikely to be a major concern.

One possible concern is whether dividends paid by UK subsidiaries of foreign firms would then continue to be creditable against foreign corporate income taxes, in countries that continue to use the credit system. Experience with the operation of ACE-style reliefs for the opportunity cost of equity finance, in countries such as Belgium and Croatia, does not suggest that this would be a problem.

Another possible concern is whether multinational groups would be able to exploit an ACE allowance within the UK corporate tax to obtain tax relief in the UK for equity used to finance investments abroad. We do not think this would be a problem. If we consider first a parent company with a domestic subsidiary, we would want the ACE allowance to be claimed by the subsidiary, just as it would be if the same operation were financed by outside shareholders. Any equity issued by the subsidiary and purchased by the parent would add to the stock of equity used to calculate subsequent ACE allowances for the subsidiary, but would also be subtracted from the stock of equity used to calculate subsequent ACE allowances for the parent.

For example, suppose the parent issues equity valued at £1,000 which it uses to subscribe (i.e. purchase) shares in a domestic subsidiary, which then uses the £1,000 to acquire productive assets. The stock of equity used to calculate subsequent ACE allowances for the subsidiary increases by £1,000, while that used to calculate subsequent ACE allowances for the parent is unchanged—the parent's subscription of shares in the subsidiary just offsets its issue of shares to outside shareholders. In each case, the stock of equity used to calculate subsequent ACE allowances increases with the net issue of equity (i.e. sales minus purchases), not with the gross issue of equity.[16] Profits subsequently earned by the subsidiary, net of its ACE allowance, are then taxed at the level of the subsidiary. Dividends subsequently paid by the subsidiary to the parent are not taxed at the level of the parent, as under the current system.

The same rules would apply if a UK parent subscribes shares in a foreign subsidiary. The stock of equity used to calculate the parent's subsequent ACE allowances increases only with its net issue of equity; subscribing shares in any subsidiary, foreign or domestic, would reduce this stock. Consequently, a UK firm that issues equity (or retains profits) to invest in a foreign subsidiary would not benefit from ACE tax relief against UK corporate tax. This approach is fully consistent with the exemption of foreign-source dividends from corporate taxation when received by UK parent companies.

---

[16] The same would apply if the parent company issues shares to finance the acquisition of (the equity in) a new subsidiary. Similarly, the parent firm's ACE allowances would be reduced if the parent borrows to acquire (additional) equity in a new (or expanding) subsidiary. Importantly, this loss of UK ACE allowances would reduce the incentive for an international company to borrow in the UK to equity-finance investments by their foreign subsidiaries.

Since the treatment of domestic and foreign subsidiaries would be identical, this arrangement should also comply with EU Treaty obligations.

If the foreign subsidiary is located in a country with a standard corporate income tax, then the required rate of return on this cross-border equity-financed investment would be higher than the required rate of return on an equivalent domestic investment. But this is just a consequence of the absence of an ACE allowance in the foreign corporate income tax. Conversely, the presence of an ACE allowance in the UK corporate tax would make the UK a more attractive location for equity-financed investments. This effect of the ACE system should nevertheless not be in breach of the UK's EU Treaty obligations because it arises from the interaction of the two corporate tax systems—the standard corporate income tax in the other member state and the ACE system in the UK—rather than representing discriminatory treatment of cross-border investment by the UK.

18.4. CONCLUSIONS

Our discussion in this chapter has emphasized problems in the implementation of source-based corporate income taxes in an open economy setting. The case for source-based taxation of the normal return component of corporate profits appears to be particularly weak in this context. There are stronger arguments for retaining a source-based corporate tax that exempts the normal return component of profits and taxes only economic rents. The appropriate tax rate will depend on the extent to which the sources of these rents are location specific or internationally mobile.

While it may be tempting in light of these arguments to abandon source-based corporate taxation altogether, at least in the UK context this would be a very expensive reform. Over the period 1997–2008, revenue from corporation tax provided around 8.5% of total government revenue.[17] Without radical reform of personal taxation, it is not clear that much of this revenue would be recouped through the taxation of capital gains and dividend income.

---

[17] OECD Revenue Statistics; corporation tax as a percentage of total taxation.

A less radical approach would be to reform the corporate tax base so that the normal return component of profits would not be taxed. The introduction of an allowance for corporate equity would achieve this, together with the continued deductibility of interest payments on debt. This reform appears to be quite feasible for an open economy such as the UK, and capable of implementation in a manner that is compatible with EU law. Indeed, Belgium has recently introduced this kind of tax relief for the opportunity cost of equity finance.

This reform would narrow the corporate tax base, almost certainly resulting in lower corporate tax revenue. The revenue cost would depend on several factors that are difficult to estimate, notably the relative importance of the risk-free interest rate, the risk premium component of the required return on capital, and economic rent, in the composition of the average (pre-tax) rate of return on taxed corporate capital. If, for example, the risk-free real interest rate is around 3% and the average real return around 12%,[18] then the revenue cost could be of the order of one-quarter of corporate tax receipts, or around £9 billion in the UK in 2009–10.[19] In the longer term, any additional UK investment that results from the lower cost of capital implied by the presence of the ACE allowance would generate additional taxable profits and thereby offset part of this revenue cost.[20]

If an ACE allowance were to be introduced, should this revenue cost be recouped by increasing the corporate tax rate? Our discussion of the trade-offs in determining the appropriate rate for a source-based corporate tax on economic rents in an open economy setting cautions against this approach. The international trend in corporate tax rates has been downward, and a country that bucks this trend also risks sending a dangerous signal to

---

[18] The *ex ante* real interest rate implied by ten-year UK index-linked gilts has fluctuated in the range 1–3% over the period 1998–2008 (Joyce, Sorensen, and Weeken, 2008, chart 4). The UK Office for National Statistics estimate of the net rate of return for UK private non-financial corporations varied between 11.8% (2001) and 14.5% (2006) in the period 1997–2009.

[19] This crude estimate is only intended to give an indication of the order of magnitude and obviously neglects many factors that could be important. The effect of inflation on the current corporate tax base suggests the cost may be higher. Conversely, the fact that interest payments on debt are already deductible suggests that the cost may be lower.

[20] Simulations of the introduction of an ACE allowance reported in de Mooij and Devereux (2009) suggest that around half of the initial revenue cost may eventually be recovered in this way.

investors. If a source-based tax on the normal return component of corporate profits is undesirable, and the current UK corporate tax rate is considered more or less appropriate, the implication is that less revenue should be raised from the corporate tax.[21]

We recognize that the cost of introducing the ACE allowance could alternatively be used to simply reduce the corporate income tax rate. At a lower tax rate, all the distortions associated with a standard corporate income tax that we highlighted in the previous chapter would be correspondingly reduced. But fundamentally we would be left with an unsatisfactory tax base. By reforming the corporate tax base, these distortions would be eliminated, at a similar revenue cost.

Further downward pressure on tax rates or revenues that can be collected from source-based corporate taxes may require more fundamental reforms in the longer term. In this context, the proposal to implement a cash-flow corporation tax on a destination basis, as suggested by Auerbach, Devereux, and Simpson (2010), may have considerable appeal. Taxing company profits in the jurisdiction of final sales to consumers would eliminate corporate tax distortions to location decisions of international companies and remove most opportunities to shift taxable profits between jurisdictions. Although we note that similar results could also be achieved by increasing broad-based VATs with offsetting reductions to payroll taxes.

This chapter has focused on the taxation of large, international companies. The ACE allowance considered here has a natural counterpart in the rate-of-return allowance considered in Chapters 13 and 14, in the context of the personal taxation of income derived from savings. The next chapter considers how a tax system with a rate-of-return allowance at the personal level and an allowance for corporate equity at the corporate level would fare in the thorny area of small business taxation.

---

[21] As we discuss further in Chapter 20, the simulation analysis in de Mooij and Devereux (2009) also suggests that there may be substantial gains in productivity and economic welfare if the introduction of an allowance for corporate equity in the UK is financed by increasing a broad-based consumption tax, though not necessarily if the cost of the ACE allowance is financed by increasing the corporate tax rate.

19

Small Business Taxation

The diverse nature of small business organizations requires careful consideration in the design of the tax system. Small businesses include both self-employed sole traders, who are taxed as individuals, and small incorporated firms, which are taxed as companies. Many economic activities could be carried out either by an employee working for a company or by a self-employed individual. Similarly, many activities could be undertaken either by a self-employed person or by an individual who is the owner, manager, and sole employee of his own small company. If the tax treatment of the income derived from these activities differs substantially depending on the legal form in which they are conducted, the tax system is likely to have a significant impact on the ways in which small businesses are structured. Without good reasons for favouring one legal form over another, such distortions should be avoided. This requires both a similar treatment of income from employment and self-employment within the personal tax system and a similar treatment of income derived from small companies and from small unincorporated businesses within the tax system as a whole. The latter, in turn, requires some alignment of corporate and personal tax rates; while trading profits of unincorporated businesses are taxed at the proprietor's personal income tax rate, profits generated by small companies are taxed at the relevant corporate income tax rate, and are also subject to personal taxation when paid out to owners in the form of dividends and when any capital gains are realized through the sale of all or part of the firm.

As well as this variety of legal forms, a second fundamental reason why small businesses present important challenges for tax design is that income derived from small business activities generally reflects a mix of rewards for labour supplied by those who work for the business and returns to capital supplied by those who invest in the business. In the case of a small, owner-managed company, for example, the owner-manager has considerable discretion over the way in which he derives taxable income from the firm. Simply by choosing to pay himself a lower salary, he can increase the profits of the firm; and by choosing to distribute these profits, he can increase the share of his income that comes in the form of dividends. If the tax treatments of income in the form of wages and income in the form of distributed profits are substantially different, the tax system is likely to have a significant impact on the ways in which small business proprietors choose to take their remuneration. If, at the margin, the taxation of distributed profits is lower than the tax rate that applies to labour income, this ability straightforwardly to reclassify income for tax purposes can result in owner-managers of small firms paying less tax than self-employed individuals or ordinary employees who perform similar tasks for the same gross remuneration. This may also favour more economic activity being undertaken by small firms and less activity being undertaken by employees of larger firms, who cannot reduce their tax liabilities so easily. Avoiding these kinds of inequities and distortions will again require appropriate alignment of personal and corporate tax rates.

A separate question is whether the tax system should deliberately seek to increase the share of small businesses in overall economic activity. This could be appropriate if there are positive externalities or spillover benefits associated with activities undertaken by small businesses—for example, some small businesses may be particularly innovative, generating improvements in products or processes that can subsequently be adopted by other firms. A serious difficulty with this kind of argument, however, is the enormous heterogeneity found within the small business sector. Many small businesses may not be innovative at all and it is not clear that small size per se provides a good 'tag' for the kinds of activities (for example, innovation) that government policies may sensibly want to promote.

A different argument is that the market outcome may generate too few small businesses, or allocate too little activity to the small business sector, relative to the efficient level, as a result of barriers to entry or obstacles to growth within small businesses. For example, limited information about growth prospects of small firms, combined with high risk of failure, may make it prohibitively expensive for some small firms to raise debt or equity finance for expansion. While such financing constraints may be particularly important for small enterprises, it should be noted that there may be better policy responses than simply providing tax breaks for all small businesses. For example, loan guarantees or direct funding for particular activities may allow government support to be targeted more efficiently than through tax measures. The wide variety of firms within the small business sector again suggests that blanket support for all small businesses is unlikely to be an efficient policy response. If, for example, we were convinced that there is too little investment by small businesses as a result of financing difficulties, this would tend to favour fiscal support for investment by small businesses (for example, through enhanced investment allowances), rather than preferential tax rates for all small businesses, regardless of whether they want to invest or not.

A further argument is that complying with the tax system itself tends to impose disproportionately high costs on smaller businesses. All else being equal, some potential entrepreneurs may choose employment over self-employment if the additional burden of filing business tax returns is sufficiently high. Smaller firms may also be placed at a competitive disadvantage compared with larger firms by higher costs of tax compliance, relative to their size, and the scale of this disadvantage will tend to increase with the complexity of the tax system. There is certainly evidence that complying with the tax system involves fixed costs that are more significant for smaller businesses.[1] The extent to which this justifies preferential tax treatment for smaller businesses and, if so, what form this should take are more controversial. In particular, it is not clear that differences in compliance costs rationalize a lower tax rate on profits below some threshold level. Among the firms with profits below the threshold, this approach provides the least advantage to those with the lowest profits—yet it is far from clear that compliance costs will be lower in years when profits are temporarily low. It has also been noted that smaller businesses may have greater opportunities for tax avoidance or non-compliance—for example, by converting labour income into more lightly taxed forms of capital income, as discussed above, or by treating some forms of personal consumption as tax-

---

[1] See e.g. Sandford, Godwin, and Hardwick (1989) and Evans (2003).

deductible business expenses.[2] While the issues of differential compliance costs and differential avoidance and evasion opportunities are logically distinct, they both bear on how the size distribution of businesses may be influenced by the presence of the tax system. Ideally, both distortions should be reduced by simplifying the structure of the tax system and aligning the tax treatment of different sources of income.

Another feature of the tax system that may affect smaller and larger firms differently is the asymmetric treatment of profits and losses. When taxable profits are positive, they are taxed, but when taxable profits are negative, they generally do not attract a full tax rebate. Losses may be 'carried back' to offset against positive profits made in a limited number of previous years, which may produce an immediate tax repayment if the firm had sufficiently high positive taxable profits during the relevant period. When this carry-back provision is exhausted, however, losses can usually only be 'carried forward' to set against future taxable profits. When losses are carried forward, there is generally no compensation for the time delay before they can be used to reduce future tax payments. This implies that the value of future tax reductions associated with an additional £1 of tax losses today may be considerably lower than the tax paid on an additional £1 of positive taxable profits—particularly if there is a significant risk that the firm will cease trading before these tax losses can be used.

This asymmetric treatment of losses can discourage risk-taking by firms, since the government shares in the firm's pay-off if the investment is a success but does not fully share in the downside risk.[3] This effect may well be more important for smaller firms than for larger firms, partly because younger firms are less likely to have a past history of positive taxable profits than established firms and partly because more diversified firms are more likely to be able to offset losses on a new investment against positive taxable profits from their other operations.[4] While correct, this consideration again does not justify a preferential tax treatment for all small businesses. A more appropriate response in this case would be to allow a more symmetric

---

[2] See e.g. Slemrod (2004).

[3] Cullen and Gordon (2007) provide empirical evidence that this asymmetry has important effects on the behaviour of entrepreneurs in the US.

[4] For owner-managed firms, an offsetting consideration may be the owner's ability to convert losses into a lower salary, which permits lower tax payments immediately.

treatment of tax losses for all firms. This could be achieved either by permitting immediate rebates to be claimed in a wider range of circumstances, or by allowing tax losses to be carried forward with an interest markup to compensate for the delay before they can be utilized.

There may be some justification for targeted forms of tax support that would tend to favour some kinds of smaller businesses—for example, those undertaking significant expenditures on investment or research and development—more than a typical large company. However, it seems difficult to rationalize the nature and scale of generalized tax advantages for all small businesses that we see in the UK and in many other developed countries. The next section outlines the most significant of these tax breaks for small businesses in the current UK system. We then consider how a reformed tax system could provide a more neutral treatment of different forms of business activities, both by size and by legal form.

19.1. SMALL IS BEAUTIFUL, OR AT LEAST TAX PRIVILEGED

Over the last decade, the UK tax system has departed from the principle of applying similar tax treatments to substantively similar sources of income to a quite extraordinary degree. The most remarkable example was the zero rate of corporation tax, which applied to the first £10,000 of taxable company profits in the tax years 2002–03 and 2003–04. Combined with other features of the UK tax system—notably, the personal allowance below which personal income tax is not paid, the effective absence of personal income tax on dividend income for basic- (and lower-) rate taxpayers, and the absence of social security contributions on company dividends—this allowed the owner of a small company to earn up to £14,615 per year, in salary and distributed profits, free of any direct taxation. The entirely predictable response to this tax advantage was a sharp increase in the number of small businesses choosing to incorporate and operate as small companies.[5] Initially hailed by the government as a policy to promote enterprise, this response by small

---

[5] This behavioural response to the zero rate of corporation tax was widely predicted before the policy was implemented; see e.g. Blow et al. (2002). Crawford and Freedman (2010) provide evidence on the unusual extent of incorporations in the UK during this period.

business proprietors subsequently led to the same policy being characterized by the same government as encouraging unwarranted tax avoidance. The zero rate of corporation tax was first restricted to undistributed profits, and finally withdrawn.

Significant tax advantages for small businesses remain within the UK tax system. Table 19.1 compares the total amount paid in income tax and National Insurance contributions (NICs) by an individual who produces output valued at £400 per week, operating either as an employee, as a self-employed person, or as the owner-manager of a small company. Self-employed individuals pay significantly lower NICs than employed individuals, particularly when both employer and employee NICs are taken into consideration. This advantage is partially offset by lower entitlements to some state benefits for self-employed individuals. Nevertheless, actuarial estimates suggest that the value of additional social security benefits for a typical employee is substantially lower than the additional cost imposed by these higher NICs.[6] The absence of employer NICs results in slightly higher taxable income and hence personal income tax for the self-employed individual, but the net effect remains a significant inducement for individuals to choose self-employment over employment, in situations where they would otherwise be indifferent.

Table 19.1 also illustrates how the absence of National Insurance contributions on both company profits and company dividends provides opportunities for even greater savings for owner-managers of small companies. By paying themselves a wage below the earnings threshold for National Insurance (and also below the personal allowance for income tax), they can avoid any income tax or NICs on this component of their remuneration. By taking the rest of their remuneration in the form of dividend income paid out of company profits, the only tax paid is corporation tax on these profits. In the example, corporation tax is paid at

---

[6] For example, HMRC estimates the net cost to the government of reduced National Insurance contributions for the self-employed to be £1.5 billion in 2009–10. (Source: HM Revenue and Customs, 'Tax Expenditures and Ready Reckoners', http://www.hmrc.gov.uk/stats/tax_expenditures/menu.htm, table 1.5, updated June 2011.)

Table 19.1. Total tax and National Insurance contributions, by legal form, 2010–11 (£ per week)

	Employment	Self-employment	Small company
Value of output	400.00	400.00	400.00
Employer NICs	32.91	0	0
Gross wage/income	367.09	400.00	110.00
Employee NICs	28.28	0	0
Self-employed NICs	0	25.60	0
Taxable profits	0	0	290.00
Corporation tax	0	0	60.90
Taxable income	242.57	275.48	339.10
Income tax	48.51	55.10	0
Total NICs	61.19	25.60	0
Total tax	48.51	55.10	60.90
Total tax and NICs	109.70	80.70	60.90
Net income	290.30	319.30	339.10

Notes: The example uses: contracted-in Class 1 NIC rates of 12.8% for employers and 11% for employees; an earnings threshold of £110 per week; for the self-employed, the Class 4 contribution rate of 8% plus Class 2 contributions at the flat rate of £2.40 per week; a personal allowance of £6,475 per annum; the basic rate of income tax of 20%; and the small companies' rate of corporation tax of 21%. The individual is assumed to have no other sources of income.

Employment
Employer NICs are calculated as 12.8% of £(400–32.91–110), giving 12.8% of £257.09, or £32.91.
Employee NICs are calculated as 11% of £(367.09–110).
Taxable income is calculated as £367.09 minus £124.52, allocating a fraction ($^1/_{52}$) of the annual personal allowance to each week.
Income tax is calculated as 20% of taxable income.

Self-employment
Self-employed NICs are calculated as 8% of £(400–110), plus £2.40.
Taxable income is calculated as £400 minus £124.52, allocating a fraction ($^1/_{52}$) of the annual personal allowance to each week.
Income tax is calculated as 20% of taxable income.

Small company
The wage of £110 per week incurs neither employer nor employee NICs.
Taxable profits are calculated as £400 minus £110.
Corporation tax is calculated as 21% of taxable profits.
Taxable income comprises wage income of £110 per week and dividend income of £229.10 per week (with profits after corporation tax paid to the owner as a dividend).
Wage income of £110 per week is below the personal allowance, leaving no income tax to pay. Income tax is formally charged at 10% on dividend income for basic-rate taxpayers, but this is sheltered by the dividend tax credit, leaving no income tax to pay.

the small companies' rate of 21% on taxable profits of £290 per week.[7] For a
basic-rate taxpayer, dividend income is formally taxed at 10%, but this tax
liability is wholly offset by the dividend tax credit, leaving no personal
income tax to be paid.[8] Moreover, no NICs are charged on dividend income.
By taking a substantial share of his remuneration in the form of dividends
paid out of company profits, rather than in the form of wages or salary, the
owner-manager of a small company can thus enjoy a substantial saving in
combined direct tax and National Insurance contributions, relative to both a
self-employed individual with an unincorporated business and, still more,
relative to an employee.

   This example oversimplifies in some respects. For example, company
dividends will generally be paid out less frequently than wages and salaries,
which may limit the extent to which some small company proprietors can
take advantage of this tax saving. Joint ownership of small companies may
also restrict the ability of individuals to arrange their remuneration in the
most tax-efficient way—although, conversely, in the case of joint ownership
by couples, there are further opportunities to shift taxable income from
individuals who pay income tax at a higher rate to individuals who pay
income tax at the basic rate. Owner-managers of small companies may also
prefer to pay minimum levels of National Insurance contributions, in order
to maintain full entitlement to state social security benefits. Nevertheless,
there remains a substantial tax advantage associated with reducing the share
of income taken in the form of wages or salary and increasing the share of
income taken in the form of distributed profits.

   The advantage of being self-employed or the proprietor of a small
company over being an employee also applies to individuals who are higher-
rate taxpayers. Table 19.2 reports overall marginal tax rates, accounting for
both direct taxes and National Insurance contributions, associated with a
small increase in income (before both income tax and National Insurance).
These are shown for each of the legal forms considered in Table 19.1 and for

---

[7] From April 2010, the preferential small companies' rate of corporation tax has been
relabelled the small profits rate of corporation tax, which is more accurate if less elegant.

[8] This receipt of dividend income does not affect the (non-)taxation of the individual's wage
income in our example, as the personal allowance is used against labour income before it is
used against other sources of income.

Table 19.2. Marginal tax rates, by legal form, 2010–11

	Employment	Self-employment	Small company
Basic rate	39%	28%	21%
Higher rate	48%	41%	41%

Notes: The table shows the additional tax and National Insurance contributions payable on an additional £1 of income (before tax and NICs), expressed as a percentage of this additional £1.

Basic rate
For basic-rate taxpayers, the rates used are the same as in Table 19.1.

Higher rate
For higher-rate taxpayers, the rates used are: employer NICs at the contracted-in rate of 12.8%; employee NICs at the contracted-in rate of 1% for earnings above the upper earnings limit; the higher rate of income tax of 40%; self-employed NICs at the Class 4 rate of 1% for profits above the upper profits limit; and the small companies' rate of corporation tax of 21%. Dividend income is taxed at the formal rate of 32.5% and the effective rate of 25% (after accounting for the dividend tax credit).

both basic-rate and higher-rate taxpayers.[9] Higher-rate taxpayers pay some personal income tax on dividend income,[10] which reduces the advantage of incorporation relative to self-employment.[11] Compared with employment, there remains a substantial net saving for either form of small business activity, principally in the form of lower National Insurance contributions.

These National Insurance advantages apply generally for all small businesses. Other tax savings may be more significant for particular kinds of small businesses. Owners of small companies who plan to take much of the return on their investment in the form of a capital gain, by selling some or all of the shares in the firm to an outside investor, rather than in the form of

---

[9] The marginal tax rates shown for basic-rate taxpayers in Table 19.2 can be derived by increasing the value of output used in Table 19.1 from £400 per week to £401 per week and repeating the calculations. The marginal tax rates shown for higher-rate taxpayers can be obtained similarly, using the rates indicated in the note to Table 19.2.

[10] Each £1 of dividends received carries a tax credit of £0.11. For higher-rate taxpayers, the 'grossed-up' value of £1.11 is taxed at 32.5%, giving a tax liability of £0.36. The dividend tax credit is set against this liability, giving a tax payment of £0.25. For basic-rate taxpayers, the 'grossed-up' value of £1.11 is taxed at 10%, giving a tax liability of £0.11 before the credit, and hence no tax payment.

[11] The marginal tax rate of 41% for a higher-rate self-employed individual is simply the NIC rate of 1% plus the income tax rate of 40%. The marginal tax rate for a higher-rate small company proprietor taking additional income in the form of dividends is 40.75%, obtained as $0.21 + (1-0.21)\times0.25 = 0.4075$, where 21% is the small companies' rate of corporation tax and 25% is the effective tax rate on dividend income.

dividend income, may further benefit from preferential tax rates on capital gains. Owners who are eligible for 'entrepreneur's relief' are currently taxed at only 10% on qualifying capital gains, although nominal capital gains are taxed, with no allowance for general price inflation.[12] Investors in small companies that qualify for special tax treatments such as the Enterprise Investment Scheme, or investments channelled through tax-favoured Venture Capital Trusts, may benefit from very generous personal tax treatments of the returns on their investments—although schemes like these at least have the virtue of being targeted towards specific types of small businesses where arguably there are particular reasons for this fiscal support.

The difference between the rate of corporation tax charged on 'small profits'—21% in 2010–11—and the standard rate of corporation tax charged on higher profits—28% in 2010–11—has narrowed in recent years.[13] This gap is due to narrow further, with announced reductions in the standard rate to 23% by 2014–15 and in the small profits rate to 20% from 2011–12. As discussed in the introduction to this chapter, it is difficult to think of the problem to which a preferential tax rate for all small companies provides an appropriate solution. A further disadvantage of the UK approach is that by eliminating any benefit of the small profits rate for companies with annual profits above £1.5 million, the system imposes a higher marginal rate of corporation tax on companies with annual profits between £300,000 and £1.5 million. This form of support for small companies thus introduces a disincentive for companies below the threshold to expand, adding a fiscal barrier to growth in a way that appears very poorly designed if the intention is to offset other disadvantages faced by expanding small companies.

The rationales for taxing company profits are quite different in the case of large corporations and smaller companies. For big businesses, much of the impact of corporation tax is likely to be shifted onto domestic workers, as we discussed in Chapters 17 and 18. The main rationale for a source-based

---

[12] This treatment may result in capital gains being more attractive than dividend income for higher-rate taxpayers, who pay income tax on dividend income, though not for basic-rate taxpayers. Chapter 14 provides more discussion of capital gains taxation in the UK.

[13] The small profits rate applies to taxable profits below £300,000 per year. The standard rate applies to taxable profits above £1,500,000 per year. Between these two thresholds, a higher marginal rate of corporation tax applies, so that all benefit of the small profits rate is clawed back from firms with annual taxable profits above £1,500,000.

corporate income tax is then to tax location-specific economic rents, and the appropriate tax rate will depend on the mobility of rent-generating business activities and on corporate tax rates charged in other countries. For smaller companies, a more important rationale for corporation tax is to protect the personal tax base, and the key is then to align the combined level of taxation implied by taxes on company profits and taxes on personal dividend income (and, in some cases, on capital gains) with those on income from employment and income from self-employment. As we discuss further below, this alignment of tax treatments for income from different sources can be achieved without requiring a special, low rate of corporation tax for smaller companies.

19.2. PROMOTING ENTERPRISE OR TAX AVOIDANCE? A RECIPE FOR COMPLEXITY AND CONFUSION

The taxation of small businesses in the UK over the last decade indicates a tension between the desire of governments to stimulate certain activities associated with particular kinds of small businesses and the concern of governments to protect the personal tax base when large numbers of small businesses take advantage of poorly targeted tax breaks. This conflict was particularly transparent in the curious case of the zero starting rate of corporation tax, as described in Section 19.1. However, the same tension underlies a range of complex anti-avoidance legislation that has been introduced or extended in recent years, with the aim of preventing certain types of small companies benefiting from general features of the tax system. Leading examples include measures aimed at 'personal service companies' or 'managed service companies', where an individual who might otherwise be employed by a larger firm instead sets up a small company which sells the same service to a single client, thereby permitting a substantial saving in National Insurance contributions.

The root cause of this tension is the difference between the overall rates at which income from employment and income in the form of distributed profits from a small company are taxed. The potential saving from converting wages or salary into distributed profits has encouraged a shift of economic activity away from employment within large firms and towards contracting between large firms and small, owner-managed companies.

Whatever one thinks about the economic case for subsidizing particular kinds of small businesses—for example, those that are highly innovative or that have considerable growth potential—it is difficult to rationalize tax advantages on this scale for all small businesses. Evidently, this view underpins the growth of anti-avoidance legislation in the UK.[14] However, by tackling symptoms of the problem, rather than addressing the difference in the rates at which labour income and capital income are taxed, the result has been a dramatic increase in the complexity of the legislation covering these aspects of small business taxation, rather than a coherent solution.

The lessons we draw from this experience are that the overall tax rates applied to income from employment, self-employment, and distributed profits need to be aligned much more closely than they are now in the UK. Any case for fiscal support for particular activities undertaken by small businesses should be reflected in targeted tax advantages for verifiable expenditures that are closely related to those activities, not in preferential tax rates for all small businesses. This support could include, for example, more generous tax allowances for research and development (R&D) expenditures undertaken by small companies than by larger companies (if there is compelling evidence that R&D by smaller companies tends to generate greater spillover benefits, or would otherwise be inefficiently low as a result of high costs or limited availability of finance). Similarly, it could include a more generous corporate tax treatment of investment expenditures undertaken by smaller firms (again if there is compelling evidence of higher social returns than for investment by larger companies), or a more generous personal tax treatment of investments that finance the expansion of some kinds of smaller businesses. There are already examples in the UK tax system of such more sharply focused tax support for R&D and investment by small enterprises, which could be refined or extended in line with developments in the empirical evidence on which they are based. Reducing the bias against more risky investments implied by asymmetric treatment of taxable profits

---

[14] Crawford and Freedman (2010) provide a detailed discussion of various special measures that have been introduced in the UK to limit the extent to which particular types of small companies can exploit these savings.

and losses has considerable merit in its own right, and would also be particularly beneficial for smaller enterprises.

Innovative small businesses, and those with high growth potential, would continue to benefit from fiscal support of this kind. However, the systematic tendency to shift economic activity away from larger companies, and towards smaller businesses which may have no particular capacity or desire to innovate or expand, would then be greatly reduced. As a result, the need for complex anti-avoidance measures, to prevent small companies being established primarily to take advantage of tax savings, would be considerably reduced. The tax system would also be fairer in its treatment of individuals with different opportunities to convert their income into different forms.

In the remainder of this chapter, we set out a range of possible reforms that would reduce these differences in the tax treatment of income derived from employment, self-employment, or running a small company. We begin by discussing more modest proposals that involve only changes to tax rates, within the broad structure of the current UK tax system. However, we conclude that more radical reform, involving changes to the personal and corporate tax bases that we have outlined in Chapters 14 and 17, would be required to achieve complete alignment of the tax treatments of income from labour and capital across different legal forms. This discussion focuses on reforms to the current UK tax system, but these basic principles could be applied in many other contexts.

19.3. ALIGNING THE TAXATION OF LABOUR INCOME AND CAPITAL INCOME

Closer alignment of the taxation of income from employment and self-employment could be achieved by increasing the National Insurance contributions paid by self-employed individuals towards the combined level paid by both employers and employees in respect of income from employment. Any difference should reflect only the actuarial value of differences in entitlements to state social security benefits, and these entitlement differences should be limited to benefits where it would be administratively difficult to extend full coverage to the self-employed.[15] Alternatively, NICs could be integrated with the personal income tax in one of the ways discussed in Chapter 5, and residual elements of the 'contributory principle' for state social security benefits be replaced by different entitlement rules, with equal treatments of employed and self-employed individuals in so far as this is administratively feasible.

To align the tax treatment of distributed profits with the tax treatment of income from employment, a piecemeal approach would be to introduce a tax on dividends paid by firms and/or on dividend income received by individuals, broadly equivalent to the NICs paid by employers and employees on wages and salaries.[16] Imposing a tax on dividends paid by companies to non-resident shareholders would be constrained by bilateral tax treaties with other countries, while treating resident and non-resident shareholders differently would be constrained by EU Treaty obligations. These factors point to reform of the tax treatment of dividend income received by UK taxpayers as the more promising way of aligning the overall tax rates paid on labour income and distributed profits. This is consistent with the taxation of company profits on a source-country basis and the taxation of personal capital income on a residence-country basis.

In the current UK tax system, higher-rate taxpayers are liable for additional personal income tax on dividend income, which requires higher-rate taxpayers who receive dividends to declare this income on an annual tax return. Basic-rate taxpayers are not liable for additional personal income tax on dividend income, so most basic-rate taxpayers who receive dividends are not required to file annual tax returns. Taxing dividend income received by basic-rate individuals would certainly require more basic-rate taxpayers to file tax returns. However, this would not apply to dividends on shares held in Individual Savings Accounts (ISAs), and there could also be a *de minimis* exemption for annual dividend income under some small amount, below which the tax revenue at stake would not justify the additional administrative and compliance costs associated with completing a tax return. With these arrangements, the main group of basic-rate taxpayers affected

---

[15] For example, this may be difficult where the level of a benefit payment is related to past earnings.

[16] Our discussion here assumes that National Insurance contributions have not been fully integrated with the personal income tax.

would be proprietors of small companies. With no tax advantage to dividend income, many small business owners could avoid this requirement by choosing to take regular remuneration in the form of wages or salaries, rather than distributed profits.

There are, however, important reasons why simply increasing the personal taxation of dividend income may not be attractive, in the absence of more fundamental reforms to the personal and corporate tax bases. In isolation, increasing taxes on dividend income would raise the rate at which the normal return on equity-financed corporate investments would be taxed. The UK tax treatment of shareholder income is unlikely to have any significant impact on the investment decisions of large corporations, whose shares are traded internationally. However, an increase in the cost of capital for smaller, domestic companies that may be particularly reliant on issuing new equity as a source of investment finance—particularly those where managers and owners may be the same, or closely related, individuals— would be an undesirable side effect of simply aligning the tax rates applied to labour income and distributed profits with no reform of tax bases. Saving behaviour would also be affected, and there may be important equity concerns—for example, in relation to retired shareholders who have saved out of taxed income and would then be faced with additional taxation of their dividend income.

These considerations suggest that full alignment of the tax rates applied to labour income and capital income should be accompanied by significant reforms of the personal and corporate tax bases. The rate-of-return allowance (RRA), which we outlined and discussed in Chapters 13 and 14, would exempt the normal return on capital invested in company shares (outside ISAs) from personal taxation. The allowance for corporate equity (ACE), which we considered in Chapters 17 and 18, would exempt the normal return on equity-financed investments from corporate taxation. The presence of these allowances for financing costs would not affect the marginal tax rates that apply to additional company profits or personal dividend income, so at the margin they would not affect incentives to convert labour income into distributed profits. Importantly, this would allow the tax rates at which personal dividend income is taxed for both basic- and higher-rate individuals to be increased, so as to align the overall tax treatments of distributed profits and income from employment, while at the same time reducing the cost of equity capital for small, domestic firms, compared with the current tax system.[17]

The introduction of an RRA for dividend income and capital gains on company shares within the personal income tax has other advantages, as described in Chapters 13 and 14—notably, avoiding the lock-in effect of a standard capital gains tax, and avoiding the taxation of purely nominal increases in share prices, resulting from general price inflation. Similarly, the introduction of an ACE has other advantages, as described in Chapter 17— notably, eliminating the tax bias in favour of debt-financing of corporate investment, and equalizing the tax treatment of investments in different types of capital, without any need for tax depreciation allowances to closely approximate true depreciation schedules.

In order to align the tax treatment of investments in unincorporated businesses with the tax treatment of investments in companies, it would also be appropriate to allow the RRA within the personal income tax to cover business assets used by sole traders and partnerships. This could be implemented on an optional basis, so that self-employed individuals with few business assets could choose to forgo the RRA, in return for simpler tax reporting (i.e. they could choose to have all their income taxed as labour income, should they prefer this arrangement).

A reformed tax system of this type could eliminate most of the existing incentives for small businesses to adopt particular legal forms purely for tax reasons, and for owner-managers of small companies to take their remuneration in the form of distributed profits rather than wages or salaries. The combinations of tax rates that would be needed to achieve full alignment of the tax treatments of these forms of income would depend on the extent to which National Insurance contributions are integrated with the personal income tax. As an illustration, suppose that NICs were to be fully integrated with the personal income tax, resulting in marginal personal tax rates of around 40% for basic-rate taxpayers and 50% for higher-rate taxpayers. Suppose also that the small profits rate of corporation tax were to be

---

[17] Standard corporate income taxes tend to raise the cost of capital for equity-financed investments, as explained in Chapter 17. This effect is eliminated by the ACE allowance. In so far as company investment decisions are influenced by personal taxes, the cost of capital for investment financed by issuing new equity is further increased by standard dividend income taxes. This effect can also be shown to be eliminated by the RRA. See e.g. Sørensen (2005).

abolished, with all corporate profits taxed at the standard rate of 28%. In this case, full alignment of marginal tax rates on income from employment, self-employment, and distributed profits would require (effective) personal tax rates on dividend income of around 17% for basic-rate taxpayers and around 31% for higher-rate taxpayers.[18]

Dividend tax credits would play no role in this system, and could be eliminated. Capital gains (or losses) on company shares (held outside ISAs) would need to be taxed at the same rates as dividend income, to align the tax treatment of distributed profits and retained profits. The RRA would be available to set against both dividend income and capital gains, and any unused allowance (i.e. if the sum of dividend income plus capital gains is less than the RRA for the current period) would be carried forward for use in later periods, marked up using a risk-free nominal interest rate. The RRA itself would also be calculated with reference to a risk-free nominal interest rate. As explained in Chapters 13 and 14, a neutral treatment of capital gains and other sources of income from capital is then consistent with taxing nominal capital gains on realization.

Targeted tax advantages for particular types of small enterprises could then be introduced within this system. If, for example, the government wishes to lower the cost of investment for small companies, this objective can be achieved by providing more generous tax allowances for investment spending by small firms. One approach is illustrated by the Annual Investment Allowance, introduced in the UK in 2008–09. In 2010–11, this provides a 100% first-year allowance for the first £100,000 of investment in plant and machinery by all companies.[19] For small firms, this effectively permits all investment in plant and machinery to be deducted from taxable income in the year the expenditure is incurred. This approach could be

[18] In this example, taxing company profits in excess of the ACE at 28% and taxing dividend income in excess of the RRA at 17% for basic-rate taxpayers ensures that any reported profits above the risk-free rate of return that are paid out in the form of dividends are taxed at a combined rate t given by $(1-t) = (1-0.28) \times (1-0.17) = 0.6$, giving an overall tax rate of 40%, in line with the personal tax rate that would be applied to reported income from employment (and to income from self-employment in excess of the RRA on unincorporated business assets). The corresponding calculation for higher-rate taxpayers requires $(1-t) = (1-0.28) \times (1-0.31) = 0.5$.
[19] This will be reduced to only the first £25,000 of investment in plant and machinery from April 2012.

retained within a corporation tax with an ACE allowance. As we discussed in Chapter 17, this expensing treatment is no more generous in present-value terms than any other depreciation schedule when combined with the ACE allowance. Nevertheless, by reducing tax payments in the period when investment outlays are incurred, the up-front allowance could be more valuable to small firms experiencing difficulties in financing their investment. This approach could be extended to cover investment in a broader range of assets. One could go further and allow more than 100% of the first (for example) £100,000 of investment spending to be deducted from taxable income—this kind of 'super-deduction' is currently available for expenditure on R&D.

The reforms to the personal and corporate income taxes that we have outlined here would address almost all of the distortions to the choice of legal form for small businesses highlighted by Crawford and Freedman (2010). One exception is the incentive for couples that face different marginal tax rates to transfer income from the partner with the higher marginal tax rate to the partner with the lower marginal tax rate. While this applies to some extent to all forms of (taxed) capital income, effecting such transfers can be significantly easier if both parties are employed by, or jointly own, the same small company. The opportunity for tax savings here stems not from different tax treatments of labour income and capital income, but from the combination of independent taxation of couples and a progressive rate structure in the personal tax system.[20] If both these features are retained in the design of the tax system, either there will be opportunities for couples to reduce their combined tax liability, or specific anti-avoidance measures will be required to prevent this.

19.4. CONCLUSIONS

This chapter has highlighted differences in the combined rates of income tax and National Insurance that apply to wages, income from self-employment, and distributed profits in the UK tax system. These differences distort

---

[20] Chapter 3 provides further discussion of the cases for independent or joint taxation of couples.

choices between employment, self-employment, and running a small company. They provide an inducement for labour income to be converted into less heavily taxed forms of business income, and are inequitable because some people can exploit these opportunities more easily, and to a greater extent, than others. They have resulted in complex anti-avoidance legislation which addresses symptoms rather than underlying causes of problems. There may be powerful arguments in favour of tax advantages for some activities undertaken by some types of small enterprises. These should be addressed using targeted tax measures, not by lower tax rates for all profits of all small businesses.

Small business taxation is inherently complex, involving the boundaries between personal and corporate taxes and between the taxation of labour income and capital income. This is an area where it is essential to have an integrated view of the tax system as a whole, and where design flaws in particular components are readily exposed. We have shown that the combination of a personal income tax with a rate-of-return allowance and a corporate income tax with an allowance for corporate equity fares particularly well here. With suitable alignment of tax rates—which in essence requires lower personal tax rates on dividend income and capital gains on company shares than on other sources of income, recognizing the corporate tax paid on the underlying profits—this approach could eliminate tax incentives to convert labour income into capital income, and avoid tax distortions to the legal form in which small business activities are conducted. In our view, this design would have much to commend it.

20

Conclusions and Recommendations for Reform

The tax system plays a central role in all modern economies. Taxes account for between 30% and 50% of national income in most developed economies, with the UK lying somewhere in the middle of that band. The way in which these huge sums of money are raised matters enormously for economic efficiency and for fairness. As many countries look to address fiscal deficits by raising more money through their tax systems, the importance of getting the structure of taxes right can only increase.

The tax and benefit system should have a coherent structure based on clearly defined economic principles, such as those laid out in this volume. There should be a clear vision of the ideal system, in which the various elements fit properly together and from which unnecessary distortions have been eliminated. Making strides towards a coherent system such as this would be valuable at any time. It is likely to be even more valuable when the tax system needs to do more work.

We have looked at the major components of a modern tax system and, with a particular focus on the UK, we have developed a range of proposals for reform. In making these proposals, we have been guided by economic theory, by the evidence on the impact of taxes, and by knowledge about the distribution of incomes and the working of the economy.

In this, the 20th and final chapter of the book, we bring together the main lessons and conclusions of the whole review. We start by laying out the broad features of a good tax system. We move on to look at how the UK system stacks up against this ideal, before going through our main recommendations for reform. We end by bringing these recommendations together into a single reform narrative, with some particular consideration of priorities for reform, timing, and transition. Where possible, we come down in favour of particular proposals. Often the arguments are more finely balanced and we refer readers to the preceding chapters for a more complete picture of each of the specific reforms and their alternatives.

20.1. A GOOD TAX SYSTEM

It is inevitable that taxation will impose costs beyond the actual sums that are raised and can be used to fund public spending. There are administrative costs to government and taxpayers in running the system, and welfare losses as people change their behaviour to reduce the tax they pay. The challenge in this review has been to design a tax system that can raise the revenue that government needs to achieve its spending and distributional ambitions whilst minimizing economic and administrative inefficiency, keeping the system as simple and transparent as possible, and avoiding arbitrary tax differentiation across people and forms of economic activity. In this section, we draw together our discussions in the rest of the book to outline the overall properties of a good tax system.

The core—though not the entirety—of our proposal is for a progressive, neutral tax system. Each of the three key words of that formula— 'progressive', 'neutral', and 'system'—is important.

First, consider the system as a whole.

A good tax system should be structured to meet overall spending needs. Earmarking of revenues for particular purposes should be avoided. There is no reason for spending on particular items to be tied to receipts from particular taxes. And earmarking of revenues that does not impose a binding constraint on spending is empty rhetoric: 'an exercise in deceiving voters that their tax payments [control] government spending in a way which they simply will not, ... misleading taxpayers rather than expanding democracy'.[1]

---

[1] Institute for Fiscal Studies, 1993, 64–65.

More generally, not all taxes need to address all objectives. Not every tax needs to be 'greened' to tackle climate change as long as the system as a whole does so. And not all taxes need be progressive as long as the overall system is. In general, the right tools for achieving distributional objectives are direct personal taxes and benefits. Since the rates on these can be adjusted to achieve the desired degree of progressivity, other aspects of the tax system can be focused on achieving efficiency.

Second, seek neutrality.

A tax system that treats similar economic activities in similar ways for tax purposes will tend to be simpler, avoid unjustifiable discrimination between people and economic activities, and help to minimize economic distortions.

But neutrality does not always equate to minimizing economic distortions: it can sometimes be efficient to discriminate between different activities for tax purposes. Important examples are taxes on alcohol and tobacco and on activities that damage the environment. In such cases, there is a compelling case that people left to their own devices will behave in ways that harm themselves and others and which can be influenced by tax policy. Similar exceptions apply to pension saving and research & development (R&D), where society wishes to encourage beneficial behaviour. There are somewhat subtler arguments applying to goods associated with work (such as childcare), where there is a case for a more lenient tax treatment in order to offset the disincentive to work created by the tax system as a whole.

But such arguments must be treated with healthy caution. Even if a theoretically compelling case can be made, the advantages of departing from neutrality must be weighed against the disadvantages of complicating the system. Defining and policing boundaries between differently taxed activities is fraught with difficulty: it increases administrative and compliance costs, and creates perverse incentives to dress up one kind of activity as another. Hence, the hurdle for departing from neutrality should be high, requiring a strong and clear justification. This test is only likely to be passed by a handful of headline items such as environmentally harmful activities, 'sin taxes', pensions, R&D, educational investments, and childcare. This is a far narrower list than the exceptions that we observe in practice.

Third, achieve progressivity as efficiently as possible.

We have emphasized the primary role played by the rate schedule for personal taxes and benefits in achieving progressivity. There is an inevitable trade-off between redistribution and work incentives. One cannot tax the rich, or top up the incomes of the poor, without affecting behaviour. But one can design the system carefully to minimize the efficiency loss associated with achieving progressivity. This means having a rate schedule that reflects knowledge of the shape of the income distribution and the responsiveness of people to taxes and benefits at different income levels. It also implies taking decisions over both whether to work (including when to retire) and how much to work into account in addition to other responses such as tax avoidance and migration.

It also makes sense to design the rate schedule to take into account other observable characteristics that reflect labour supply incentives, potential earning power, or needs. For example, mothers of school-age children and people around retirement age are particularly responsive to work incentives. They should, therefore, face lower effective tax rates than others. There are, of course, limits to how tax and benefit payments might be conditioned on characteristics, with some constituting unfair and illegitimate discrimination. And being more generous to people with certain characteristics can create an undesirable incentive to acquire those characteristics. There is also some tension here with seeking neutrality. So the hurdle for such departures should, again, be high.

In designing a tax system to be progressive, we need to think hard about the kind of progressivity we want. Much discussion focuses on the effect of taxes on people's current incomes. Ideally, though, we should try to assess the progressivity of the tax system in terms of people's lifetime resources, not just as an annual snapshot. One way of getting closer to doing this is to consider the distribution of expenditure and not just the distribution of income. Lifetime income and lifetime expenditure will be very similar (the main difference being bequests made or received); but annual income and annual expenditure will differ much more as people borrow and save to reflect fluctuating incomes and varying needs over their life cycle. In the absence of perfect measures of lifetime resources, shorter-term measures of income and expenditure can therefore provide complementary indicators of lifetime resources and should be considered carefully in combination with each other. We must also remember, however, that some people are constrained in how much they can borrow, making a snapshot of current income more relevant for them.

What does a progressive, neutral tax system look like?

When it comes to income taxation, there is a strong case for keeping things simple: a single tax on income with an allowance and (say) two or three rates, combined with a single benefit to support those with low income and/or high needs. The design of the rate schedule should reflect the best available evidence on how responsive people at different income levels and with different demographic characteristics are.

Income from all sources should be taxed according to the same rate schedule. However, unlike a standard income tax, our approach would allow all costs of generating that income to be deducted, as we explain below. Applying different rates to different income sources complicates the system, unfairly favours those taxed more lightly, distorts economic activity towards lightly taxed forms, and facilitates tax avoidance. Taxing income from all sources equally does not just mean taxing fringe benefits in the same way as cash earnings. It also means applying that same rate schedule to, inter alia, self-employment income, property income, savings income, dividends, and capital gains.

It makes sense to tax most business income before it leaves the company, through corporation tax. But we should reduce the personal tax rates on corporate-source income (dividend income and capital gains on shares) by the same amount to reflect the corporation tax already paid. The *combined* rates of corporate and shareholder taxation should equal the tax rates levied on employment and other sources of income.

This single rate schedule should be applied to income after allowing deductions for the costs incurred in generating income, such as work-related expenses and inputs to production. Failing to allow these deductions distorts economic decisions, encouraging low-cost–low-revenue activities over equally valuable high-cost–high-revenue activities. Of course, it is not always easy to distinguish expenditure related to income generation from consumption expenditure. But the principle at least is clear.

The principle also applies to saving and investment. Generating future income requires sacrificing current consumption. In that sense, saving and investment are costs associated with generating future income. This can be recognized in one of two ways:

- Cash saved or invested can be treated as a deductible expense when it arises, as currently applied to personal saving in the case of pension contributions and to business investment in limited cases where 100% first-year allowances are available.

- A deduction could be given each year for the opportunity cost of capital previously saved/invested. This is the rate-of-return allowance (RRA) treatment of saving and the allowance for corporate equity (ACE) treatment of business investment, neither of which has ever been used in the UK although both are now used in other countries. For assets where only the risk-free ('normal') rate of return is likely to be earned, this approach can be simplified, and returns on such assets can just be tax free.

Timing aside, these two treatments are equivalent. With stable tax rates, the stream of allowances given each year under the second approach has the same present value as the up-front deduction given under the first approach. In both cases, the 'normal' rate of return to savings/investment is tax exempt. And, in both cases, any 'excess' returns above this will be taxed in full.

This approach helps to resolve a conundrum that policymakers around the world have struggled with for decades: the tension between preventing tax avoidance on the one hand and minimizing disincentives to save and invest on the other. Eager to encourage saving and investment, policymakers have sought to reduce tax rates on capital income; but wary of opening the door to widespread conversion of labour income into capital income, they have also sought to keep tax rates as closely aligned as possible. The result has usually been an awkward compromise, with capital income taxed at reduced rates (and often different forms of capital income taxed at different rates), leaving some disincentive effects and some scope for avoidance. Taxing capital income in full *while giving a full deduction for capital costs* addresses both problems.

Attempting to tax capital income without giving a deduction for capital expenditure causes a number of problems. In practice, capital gains can only be taxed when assets are sold, not when the increase in value occurs (giving rise to the inefficient 'lock-in' effect). Saving and investment will be discouraged more at some times than others unless full indexation for inflation can be achieved (something which has never been done). And investment in some assets will be discouraged more than in others unless deductions for depreciation match true economic depreciation (something which is impossible for legislation to achieve accurately). Not only do 'standard' capital taxes discourage saving and investment in general; they also (and perhaps more importantly) penalize different forms of saving and investment to different degrees, and therefore distort the form that saving and investment take.

While achieving neutrality between different forms of saving and investment is our general aim, there may be a good case for treating pension saving more generously. Behavioural evidence suggests that people tend not always to make decisions in far-sighted and rational ways. Individuals with inadequate retirement savings are also more likely to draw on costly state benefit programmes in retirement. Encouraging them to save in a pension when young makes this less likely.

A tax on income that exempts a 'normal' rate of return to capital, as we propose, is broadly equivalent to a tax on expenditure. Of course, there are other ways to implement a tax on expenditure, such as via a value added tax (VAT). Our starting point for VAT is the presumption that it be applied to all final consumption expenditure by households, but that expenditure on business inputs should be untaxed (which VAT achieves by allowing traders to reclaim VAT charged on their inputs). This means avoiding zero and reduced rates of tax on sales, and avoiding exemptions (which prevent deduction of input costs) as well. If it is difficult to impose VAT in the usual way on certain goods and services—notably financial services and housing— then economically equivalent taxes to substitute for VAT on these items should be sought. The tendency of government to adopt different tax rates across commodities frequently comes from failing to look at the tax system as a whole and to see that the rate schedule of personal income taxes and benefits is the instrument best suited to achieving redistributive ends.

Taxes levied on income without deducting the costs of generating that income, or levied on sales without deducting input costs, or levied directly on business expenditures, are in general grossly inefficient and have no place in a good tax system. This leads to a presumption against all kinds of transactions taxes, input taxes, and turnover taxes.

There are, however, some cases in which taxing all income (or expenditure) equally and deducting all costs is not the right approach.

Pure economic rents can, in principle, be taxed without creating an economic distortion. One example is the 'excess' return to capital; taxing such returns does not discourage saving and investment. In practice, it can be difficult to pinpoint rents, and so we are wary of attempting to tax them at higher rates than ordinary income. But where rents can be identified accurately, targeted taxes can be applied. In particular, there is a strong case for levying a land value tax, which is a tax on pure rent—if the practical difficulty of valuing land separately from the buildings on it can be overcome.

Taxes used to correct market failures can also justify a non-uniform rate structure. Raising the price of activities that cause harm can be an efficient way to discourage them because it ensures that reductions occur among those who find it easiest to make them. The major environmental problems that ought to be priced are carbon emissions and congestion. There is also a good case for taxing tobacco and alcohol because of the combination of harm to others and unforeseen harm to themselves that smokers and drinkers do.

As an alternative to taxing damaging goods, a 'cap-and-trade' system of issuing limited permits for the good and allowing the permits to be traded can achieve a similar result of raising the good's price and reducing its consumption by those who least need the good. It is important that such permits be auctioned rather than simply handed out, so that the revenue can be used to reduce other distortionary taxes (offsetting the work disincentives created by raising the price of the good in question). Whether taxation or a cap-and-trade system is used, however, it is vital to target the damaging activity precisely and to impose a consistent price across all sources of damage: neutrality between different sources of carbon, for example, is needed to ensure that climate change is tackled in the least costly way. Badly designed policies can easily dissipate the potential gains from discouraging damaging activities.

As noted above, the main difference between lifetime income and lifetime expenditure is gifts and bequests. There is a good case for taxing such transfers of wealth, particularly to the next generation. This has the potential to reduce the inequality of life chances between different children that arise by accident of birth, at a fairly low economic cost. To achieve this, we lean towards a tax on lifetime receipts. Efficiency and equity are best served if this is a tax on all receipts—all kinds of asset, whether transferred on death or during the donor's lifetime. There are, though, inevitable practical difficulties associated with trying to tax transfers. If these difficulties mean that much wealth that is transferred cannot be taxed, then a good tax system may be caught between two very much second-best situations—either leaving these transfers permanently untaxed, or trying to capture them by introducing limits to the tax exemption of normal returns to savings, with all the attendant problems with taxing capital income that we have highlighted.

This vision of a good tax system pulls together ideas from across all the chapters of this book. It is summarized in the left-hand column of Table 20.1 under five headings—taxes on earnings, indirect taxes, environmental taxes, taxation of savings and wealth, and business taxes. It will be clear by now that there are many aspects of the UK tax system that fail to live up to this ideal. They are detailed in the right-hand column of the table. A jumble of tax rates, a lack of a coherent vision of the tax base, and arbitrary

Table 20.1. A good tax system and the current UK tax system

A good tax system	The current UK tax system
Taxes on earnings	
A progressive income tax with a transparent and coherent rate structure	An opaque jumble of different effective rates as a result of tapered allowances and a separate National Insurance system
A single integrated benefit for those with low income and/or high needs	A highly complex array of benefits
A schedule of effective tax rates that reflects evidence on behavioural responses	A rate structure that reduces employment and earnings more than necessary
Indirect taxes	
A largely uniform VAT – with a small number of targeted exceptions on economic efficiency grounds – and with equivalent taxes on financial services and housing	A VAT with extensive zero-rating, reduced-rating, and exemption – financial services exempt; housing generally not subject to VAT but subject to a council tax not proportional to current property values
No transactions taxes	Stamp duties on transactions of property and of securities
Additional taxes on alcohol and tobacco	Additional taxes on alcohol and tobacco

(cont.)

discrimination across different types of economic activities are hallmarks of the current system. There are many examples in each category which we

Table 20.1. (*cont.*)

A good tax system	The current UK tax system
Environmental taxes	
Consistent price on carbon emissions	Arbitrary and inconsistent prices on emissions from different sources, set at zero for some
Well-targeted tax on road congestion	Ill-targeted tax on fuel consumption
Taxation of savings and wealth	
No tax on the normal return to savings – with some additional incentive for retirement saving	Normal return taxed on many, but not all, forms of savings – additional but poorly designed incentives for retirement saving
Standard income tax schedule applied to income from all sources after an allowance for the normal rate of return on savings – with lower personal tax rates on income from company shares to reflect corporation tax already paid	Income tax, National Insurance contributions, and capital gains tax together imply different rates of tax on different types of income—wages, profits, capital gains, etc. – some recognition of corporation tax in dividend taxation but not in capital gains tax
A lifetime wealth transfer tax	An ineffective inheritance tax capturing only some assets transferred at or near death
Business taxes	
Single rate of corporation tax with no tax on the normal return on investment	Corporation tax differentiated by company profits and with no allowance for equity financing costs
Equal treatment of income derived from employment, self-employment, and running a small company	Preferential treatment of self-employment and distributed profits
No tax on intermediate inputs – but land value tax at least for business and agricultural land	An input tax on buildings (business rates) – no land value taxes

have highlighted throughout the book. We now turn to discuss these deficiencies and make a set of concrete proposals which illustrate how the current system can be improved.

20.2. PROPOSALS FOR REFORM OF THE UK TAX SYSTEM

We have set out our vision of an effective tax system which eliminates many of the current distinctions between different activities, which incorporates what we know about responses to taxes to minimize undesirable impacts on behaviour, and which involves a consistent approach to taxing externalities. Our approach demands a coherent understanding of how incentives and progressivity operate across the tax and benefit system as a whole and across people's lifetimes.

In this section, we move from this high-level vision to compare the current UK system against some of these principles and to summarize some of our specific proposals. We illustrate the differences between our vision and the current UK system in two ways: first by setting out seven broad flaws of the current system and then by comparing specific features of a good system with the UK system.

Against the criteria set out in our vision, the seven major flaws in the UK tax system are:

1. Despite improvements for some groups in recent years, the current system of income taxes and welfare benefits creates serious disincentives to work for many with relatively low potential earning power. The benefit system in particular is far too complex.

2. Many unnecessary complexities and inconsistencies are created by the fact that the various parts of the tax system are poorly joined up. These range from a lack of integration between income taxes and National Insurance contributions (NICs) to a lack of coherence between personal and corporate taxes.

3. The present treatment of savings and wealth transfers is inconsistent and inequitable. There is no consistent tax base identified, saving is discouraged, and different forms of savings are taxed differently.

4. We remain some way short of having a coherent system of environmental taxes to address imperatives around climate change and congestion. The effective tax on carbon varies dramatically according to its source, and fuel duty is a poor substitute for road pricing.

5. The current system of corporate taxes discourages business investment and favours debt finance over equity finance. Its lack of integration with other parts of the tax system also leads to distortions over choice of legal form. Corporate taxes have also been subject to increasing international pressures.

6. Taxation of land and property is inefficient and inequitable. There is a tax on business property—a produced input—but not on land, which is a source of rents. Taxation of housing involves both a transactions tax and a tax based on 20-year-old valuations.

7. Distributional goals are pursued in inefficient and inconsistent ways. For example, zero and reduced rates of VAT help people with particular tastes rather than being targeted at those with low overall resources; and council tax is regressive for no obvious efficiency-improving reasons.

In the rest of this section, we go through our main specific proposals for reform, under each of the headings in Table 20.1. We cannot stress enough, though, that we divide the proposals up in this way largely for convenience of reading and understanding. As we have already emphasized, it is important to consider the proposals as an overall package. That package can be shaped to achieve different degrees of progressivity, depending on the precise parameters that are chosen for the income tax and benefit systems. But the efficiency of the tax system depends on how the different elements of the reform interact.

20.2.1. Earnings Taxation and Work Incentives

The personal tax and benefit system should be progressive, coherent, and designed to reflect what we know about the shape of the income distribution and how different groups respond to work incentives.

Coherence requires first that the income tax system itself be sensibly structured. We need to move away from pointless complexities such as that which sees the marginal rate rise from 40% to 60% at £100,000 of income before falling back to 40% at £112,950. More importantly, we need to move away from having separate systems of income tax and NICs, with different sets of rules and exemptions, pointlessly increasing administration and compliance costs and making the system less transparent. National Insurance is not a true social insurance scheme; it is just another tax on earnings, and the current system invites politicians to play games with NICs without acknowledging that these are essentially part of the taxation of labour income. The two systems need to be merged. Given our proposal to apply the same rate schedule to income from all sources, integration would be a good opportunity to, in effect, broaden the NICs base to cover self-employment and capital income in full. Since alignment of rates must include employer NICs, either employer NICs must be integrated along with employee NICs and income tax or else an equivalent tax would have to be levied on non-employment income—though we acknowledge that neither of these would be politically easy.

The second substantial change that we believe is a prerequisite for an effective tax and benefit system is a significant simplification and integration of the benefit system. The current structure of multiple benefits with an array of overlapping means tests leaves some people facing effective marginal tax rates of over 90%. It is complex, inequitable, and inefficient.

As well as reforms to the delivery of earnings taxation, we have considered reforms to the rate structure of personal taxes and benefits. We have examined the case for reducing effective tax rates for low earners (particularly in light of growing evidence that decisions over whether to work at all are more responsive to incentives than decisions over how much to work) and the question of the appropriate tax rate on the very highest incomes (bearing in mind evidence on the range of ways that high-income individuals can respond to taxation). Reforms in these areas could have major implications for employment, earnings, and tax revenues; but firm recommendations would require political value judgements that we are not in a position to make.

We have also looked at reforms that make better use of what we know about how behavioural responses to incentives vary by the ages of household members. We can more confidently make proposals in this area, since reforms can be designed that are neither progressive nor regressive overall, redistributing mainly across the life cycle so that people face stronger incentives at the times they are most responsive to them. Targeting incentives where they are most effective can improve welfare overall, and the specific reforms we have simulated would generate large increases in employment rates.

First, work incentives should be strengthened for families whose youngest child is of school age, reflecting the finding that the mothers of older children are more responsive to the incentives in the tax and benefit system than are mothers of younger children. To illustrate one way this could be done in the current UK tax and benefit system, we simulated a reform to Child Tax Credit that would make it more generous (and so means-testing more extensive) for families whose youngest child is aged under 5, and less generous (with less means-testing) for families whose youngest child is aged 5 or over. Although there is substantial uncertainty, we estimate that these reforms could lead to a net increase in employment of around 52,000 (or roughly 0.2% more workers) and an increase in aggregate annual earnings of around £0.8 billion. In a life-cycle sense, these reforms would have offsetting effects once in place, with families who receive Child Tax Credit gaining when children are younger and losing later. Effectively, resources are shifted towards families with pre-school children.

Second, work incentives should be strengthened for those in their later working life, aged 55 to 70—a group that is highly responsive to incentives. To illustrate one way this could be done within the existing tax and benefit system—obviously the available instruments would be different if our other proposals were implemented—we simulated the impact of reducing the age at which employee and self-employed NICs stop being payable from state pension age to age 55, reducing the age at which a higher tax-free personal allowance is available from 65 to 55, and increasing the age of eligibility for Pension Credit to 70. The simulations point to an increase in employment of about 157,000 (or 0.6% of the workforce) and an increase in aggregate annual earnings of just under £2 billion. As with our Child Tax Credit simulations, much of the distributional impact would consist of offsetting effects over the life cycle.

The current tax and benefit system is unnecessarily complicated and induces too many people not to work or to work too little. By creating a simpler and more rational system, minimizing disincentives where they matter most, the reforms we propose have the potential to deliver major economic gains.

20.2.2. Indirect Taxation

By applying zero rates, reduced rates, and exemptions to large swathes of spending, the current VAT system creates a combination of administrative complexity, arbitrary distortions between different kinds of consumption, and inequitable treatment of consumers with different tastes. Increases in VAT rates—from 17.5% to 20% in January 2011, for example—just make these problems bigger. There are good economic efficiency arguments for taxing time-saving goods less heavily, and goods that require leisure time more heavily, in order to offset the general disincentive to work that taxation creates; but, with a few exceptions (notably childcare), we think the potential gains from introducing such differentiation are outweighed by the practical disadvantages.

International experience shows that a narrow VAT base is not inevitable. The UK zero-rates far more goods than almost any other country: for example, the UK and Ireland are the only EU countries to apply a zero rate to most food, water, books, and children's clothes. New Zealand provides a working example of how it is possible to apply the standard rate of VAT to almost all goods and services. The costs of having such a narrow VAT base are large. Considering just the distortion to spending patterns—ignoring the costs of complexity—simulations suggest that, if uniformity were optimal, extending VAT at 17.5% to most zero-rated and reduced-rated items would (in principle) allow the government to make each household as well off as it is now and still have around £3 billion of revenue left over. The true figure could be higher or lower than this.

The situation in the UK persists largely because of a failure to consider the system as a whole. In a modern tax system, VAT is a poor choice of tax to use to achieve redistribution. VAT should therefore be extended to virtually all goods and services at the full rate, but this should be done in combination with an appropriate package of reforms to the personal tax and benefit system to address the distributional and work incentive effects of broadening the VAT base. We have shown how this is feasible. Our core reform proposal involves broadening the VAT base to include goods and services that are currently subject to a zero or reduced rate—mainly food, passenger transport, books and other reading matter, prescription drugs, children's clothing, and domestic fuel and power. Taken in isolation, this would raise around £24 billion with a VAT rate of 17.5%. But it would also hurt the worse off and have adverse effects on work incentives. To offset this, we have illustrated one possible package of cuts in income tax and increases in means-tested and non-means-tested benefits that would, in combination with VAT base broadening, create a revenue-neutral reform. On a snapshot measure, our overall package looks progressive when measured against people's expenditure, but slightly regressive when measured against income. It is likely to be approximately distributionally neutral on average across people's lifetimes—a good example of the limitations of looking at a snapshot of income and the importance of taking a lifetime perspective.

A novel and important feature of our proposals is the focus on work incentives and construction of a compensation package designed to avoid damaging them.

VAT cannot be extended so straightforwardly to all forms of consumption. Housing is not currently subject to VAT. But given where we start in the UK, it makes more sense to tax people's annual consumption of housing services than to levy VAT on new properties when they are built (or existing properties when they are next sold). Such a tax, proportional to the current consumption value of housing, would be a big improvement on the UK's current regime for taxing housing. Council tax is based on valuations that are 20 years out of date, it is highly regressive with respect to property values, and it gives a discount for sole occupancy—features that are unfair and encourage inefficient use of the housing stock. Stamp duty land tax, as a transactions tax, is highly inefficient, discouraging mobility and meaning that properties are not held by the people who value them most, and its 'slab' structure—with big cliff-edges in tax payable at certain thresholds—creates particularly perverse incentives. Replacing these two taxes on a revenue-neutral basis with a simple tax proportional to up-to-date consumption values of properties, essentially as a substitute for VAT, is a much-needed step forward.

VAT exemptions are especially damaging since they prevent firms from reclaiming VAT paid on their inputs, distorting the pattern of production.

We have focused on probably the most important of these exemptions—that for financial services. Exemption makes financial services too expensive for businesses and too cheap for households (so that it is too difficult for firms to obtain finance but too easy for households to borrow, for example). It creates a bias towards vertical integration and distorts international trade, as well as creating awkward boundaries between differently taxed activities. We do not set out in this book to solve the particular problems with the financial system exposed by the recent crisis—that is a matter for regulation at least as much as for taxes—but before imposing additional taxes on the financial sector, we should at least make sure that it is subject to the same taxes as other businesses. The way in which financial services are provided means that VAT could not be applied to them in the standard way, but there are several ways in which a tax economically equivalent to VAT could be applied. Finding the most practical way forward should be a priority.

As a purely practical matter, the practice of zero-rating exports creates a break in the VAT chain which makes VAT more vulnerable to tax evasion. Moving away from such zero-rating—imposing some VAT at borders, reclaimable by importers (so there is still no net tax levied but enforcement is made easier)—would be a worthwhile improvement.

We are not recommending an entirely uniform system of indirect taxes. More compelling are arguments for additional taxation of especially harmful activities. Taxes on alcohol and tobacco are good examples, and their continued use is important. The other major category of harmful activity is environmental damage, to which we now turn.

20.2.3. Environmental Taxes

The case for pricing environmental externalities through the tax system is a strong one. There have been a number of innovations in environmental taxes in the UK in recent years. But it remains the case that there are two overwhelming priorities for the application of environmental taxes: greenhouse gas emissions and congestion on roads. Unfortunately, the current systems of taxes on these two externalities remain a long way from being coherent.

With an EU Emissions Trading Scheme (ETS) of rather limited coverage existing alongside a complex array of different and inconsistent domestic policies, effective taxes on greenhouse gas emissions vary dramatically according to both the source of the emission (the type of fuel, for example) and the identity of the user (domestic or business, for example). Indeed, the reduced rate of VAT payable on domestic fuel consumption acts as an effective subsidy to the creation of carbon emissions. This situation would be improved by our proposals to broaden the VAT base more generally, but further increases are required. We urgently need to impose a consistent price on carbon emissions, encompassing both a reformed ETS and a simpler, more coherent system for taxing emissions not covered by the ETS.

The economic costs of not having a coherent system of motoring taxation are large. The government estimates that annual welfare benefits of up to 1% of national income are available from a road pricing scheme that varies charges by place and time of day to accurately reflect actual congestion levels and costs. Introducing such a scheme would be expensive and controversial, and smaller and less accurate schemes may need to be devised on the way to such a comprehensive system. But the scale of benefits suggests that moving to a national system of road pricing is a priority. The quid pro quo for introducing congestion charging should be a major reduction in fuel duties, the current rates of which would (in the presence of congestion charging) be far higher than could be justified by carbon emissions alone. Whilst there are, of course, major practical challenges associated with such a development, there is a premium on acting quickly. As cars become more fuel efficient, and eventually electric cars replace traditional vehicles—a change that may well have to happen if we are to meet targets for reducing carbon emissions—the current system of fuel taxation will become even less effective at limiting congestion. It will also raise less and less revenue from motorists (leaving less to offer 'in exchange' for congestion charging).

20.2.4. Taxation of Savings and Wealth

The taxation of savings should treat different forms of savings in broadly comparable ways, should not introduce important incentives for individuals to consume earlier rather than later in their lifetimes, and should not have effects that are unduly sensitive to the rate of inflation. Significant reforms are needed in the UK to reduce arbitrary differences in the tax treatment of different assets, to exempt from taxation, as far as possible, the normal return on savings, and to make the system inflation-proof. Getting the taxation of savings right is also important in ensuring that the personal and corporate tax systems line up.

These goals can be achieved by an approach that taxes only 'excess' returns, and which exempts from taxation the component of income and capital gains earned on savings that corresponds to a risk-free or 'normal' rate of return—for example, that paid on medium-term government bonds. Our main recommendations for reform would accomplish this by making interest on ordinary bank and building society accounts free from taxation, and by providing a 'rate-of-return allowance' (RRA) for substantial holdings of risky assets such as equities, which can provide higher returns. For simplicity, we would retain a tax-free treatment of the returns from smaller holdings of equities and mutual funds, along the lines of UK equity ISAs. As well as being more efficient than the current system, reducing tax distortions to the timing of consumption, we believe these proposals would also make it fairer. The current tax system treats most harshly those assets that are most important to individuals with smaller amounts of savings, particularly interest-bearing bank and building society accounts. More favourable tax treatments are provided for pension plans and owner-occupied housing.

The RRA would be calculated by applying a risk-free nominal interest rate to a cumulated stock of savings held in particular assets. No explicit indexation is required—the stock of savings here just corresponds to past purchases of these assets, net of past sales. Nominal income plus any nominal capital gains realized in the current year, in excess of the RRA, would then be taxed at the individual's marginal income tax rate. In cases where the RRA exceeds the return on these assets realized in a particular year, the difference would be carried forward to set against nominal returns in later years, marked up by the same nominal interest rate used to determine the RRA. Other than specifying this nominal interest rate, no more information is required to operate this system than is needed to tax capital gains on these assets in a conventional income tax. In most circumstances, the normal rate of return can be well approximated by a nominal interest rate on medium-term government bonds. A similar approach is used to tax dividends and capital gains on company shares in Norway.

As well as reducing the distortion in favour of current consumption over saving under a standard income tax, this RRA approach to the personal taxation of income from capital has important practical advantages. The taxation of capital gains raises major problems for a conventional income tax: taxing gains on realization rather than on accrual creates a 'lock-in' effect, encouraging people to delay the sale of assets whose value has risen; while taxing purely nominal gains makes effective tax rates highly sensitive to inflation. Piecemeal attempts to deal with the latter problem by taxing nominal capital gains at preferential rates invites tax avoidance, favouring the conversion of earned income into more lightly taxed capital gains where this is possible. The succession of wholly unsatisfactory reforms to capital gains taxation in the UK over the last 15 years bears witness to these problems. The RRA approach addresses all of them. It also operates coherently with corporate taxation, an important ingredient of any well-designed system of savings taxation. The rate of personal tax on excess returns from company dividends and capital gains on company shares would be reduced, relative to those on other assets, to reflect tax on the underlying profits that is paid at the corporate level. Indeed, the RRA in the personal income tax is a natural counterpart to the allowance for corporate equity, our preferred scheme for corporate taxation.

There are theoretically equivalent ways in which taxation of the normal return on savings could be eliminated. As a practical reform proposal, the RRA has potential advantages over the pure expenditure tax (EET) approach recommended in the Meade Report.[2] The RRA collects tax revenue up front and provides tax relief only as returns are realized, making the transition to it comparatively straightforward. It also mitigates the risk of loss of revenue occurring as a result of those who did the saving avoiding future tax liability by moving abroad before they draw down their savings. In the context of increased international migration, this is an important consideration.

That said, for pension saving the current expenditure tax treatment looks broadly right because alternatives have the potential to be highly complex.

---

[2] Meade, 1978.

Some tax advantage (above simple EET) is probably justified to encourage, or reward, the tying-up of savings in a form that restricts access for a long period. There is, though, a strong case for simplifying the current UK system of pension taxation, and changes should be made to eliminate the inconsistencies that make employer contributions substantially tax privileged relative to employee contributions. These latter anomalies result from the distinctions drawn between income tax and NICs, and between employer and employee NICs. So, if we could achieve our long-run vision of a system in which these are consolidated into a single tax on income, this issue would be avoided.

We do not have a single number to put on the costs of the distortions in the current system of savings taxation. However, work undertaken as part of this review[3] suggests that, even on a conservative reading of the economic literature, reducing taxation of the normal return to savings would have significant effects on the quantity and distribution of savings over the life cycle, thereby raising lifetime welfare.

For most people, our proposals on savings taxation would reduce the tax they pay on the returns to their savings. The main exceptions would be those who make large returns in the form of capital gains or who earn very high returns more generally.

Our proposals are driven by a view of savings as playing a crucial role in ensuring that the tax system is efficient and equitable over an individual's life cycle. But there is a case for thinking differently about wealth that is transferred between people—especially as an inheritance between generations. In our view, recent increases in wealth inequality, coupled with increases in housing wealth for particular groups, increase the case for taxing wealth transfers on both equity and efficiency grounds. The current UK inheritance tax is unfair in many ways—it fails to tax those who pass on gifts during their lifetime and benefits those who can arrange their affairs to escape taxation at death, while taxing more highly those (usually of more modest means) who cannot arrange their affairs so as to avoid taxation. It is inefficient because it creates many tax-driven behavioural changes and leads to some asset classes, such as agricultural and business assets, being tax

---

[3] Attanasio and Wakefield, 2010.

favoured for no clear reason except, presumably, the influence of the agricultural and family business lobbies. The different treatments of capital gains realized at death and those realized during working life also lack justification in the context of our broader proposals to reform savings taxation. We do not think that a tax on estates at death is the best way to approach these issues—there is a stronger case, in principle, for a tax on lifetime receipts, taxing transfers received on an ongoing and cumulative basis. There are important administrative and transition challenges to be addressed in bringing such a proposal to fruition. However, as a long-term proposition, the case for moving in this direction is persuasive.

20.2.5. Business Taxation

Our recommendations for business taxation have three main components.

First, we are proposing to abolish the current system of business rates and replace it with a system of land value taxation, thereby replacing one of the more distortionary taxes in the current system with a neutral and efficient tax. Business rates are not a good tax—they discriminate between different sorts of business and disincentivize development of business property.

Our second proposal concerns the treatment of small businesses and self-employment. The current system distorts choices over organizational form—the choice between employment and self-employment on the one hand, and the choice between running an unincorporated business or a small company on the other hand—as well as decisions over the form of remuneration—for example, whether the sole proprietor of a small company pays herself in the form of salary or dividends. These discrepancies are inequitable and lack any clear rationale. The difference between the corporation tax rates paid by firms with higher and lower profits also lacks a compelling justification.

Our recommendations would align the taxation of income from employment and self-employment, increasing the NICs paid by self-employed individuals to match those paid by employers and employees combined in relation to employment (preferably in the course of integrating NICs with the personal income tax). To align the tax treatment of distributed profits with the tax treatment of income from employment, a minimal approach would increase the taxation of dividend income received by individuals by an amount broadly equivalent to the NICs paid by employers and employees on wages and salaries. Again, this could be done as part of the integration of income tax and NICs. Capital invested by individuals both in business assets of sole traders and partnerships and in equity issued by companies would be eligible for the rate-of-return allowance described in Section 20.2.4. In both cases, this would remove the 'normal' returns on these investments from personal taxation.

Our third proposal on business taxation is the introduction of an allowance for corporate equity (ACE) within the corporate income tax. The ACE provides an explicit deduction for the cost of using equity finance, similar to the existing deduction for the cost of interest payments on debt finance. This levels the playing field between different sources of finance. Like the RRA, the ACE can be designed to eliminate the effect of the corporate tax on the required rate of return for all forms of corporate investment. Different assets that firms invest in are treated equally, with no sensitivity of tax liabilities to the rate of inflation. With this form of corporate tax base, investment projects that just earn the minimum required or 'normal' rate of return are effectively exempt from corporate taxation, and revenue is collected from those investments that earn above-normal rates of return, or economic rents.

Exempting the normal rate of return on capital from corporate taxation fits well with our proposal to exempt the normal rate of return on capital invested in the business sector from personal taxation—as would be achieved by a rate-of-return allowance for corporate equities and unincorporated business assets. Suitable alignment of tax rates on corporate profits, dividend income, capital gains on company shares, and other sources of personal income can then ensure that owner-managers of small firms have no tax incentive to pay themselves in the form of dividends rather than salaries, and achieve an equal tax treatment of income derived from employment, self-employment, or running a small company. Much complex anti-avoidance legislation would then become redundant.

Experience with the operation of an ACE-type allowance in Belgium and other countries suggests that this approach is both feasible and compatible with EU Treaty obligations. Some opportunities for international companies to shift taxable profits out of the UK would be reduced by the introduction of an ACE—notably the scope for using debt borrowed (and tax deductible) in the UK to equity-finance subsidiaries operating (and taxed) in other jurisdictions with lower corporate tax rates.[4] Other mechanisms through which multinational firms can reduce their UK corporate tax liabilities, such as the manipulation of transfer prices, would remain. However, at a given corporate tax rate, these opportunities would be no greater than under the current corporation tax base.

The introduction of an allowance reflecting the underlying cost of using equity finance would have a significant revenue cost. This could be recouped by raising the corporate tax rate, but in our view this would be a mistake. The appropriate rate at which to tax rents earned in the corporate sector must balance the advantages of taxing sources of rent that are largely immobile against the disadvantages of (attempting to) tax sources of rent that are highly mobile and that are likely to relocate to other jurisdictions should the UK tax rate become out of line. Inevitably, this depends on corporate tax rates in other countries, which have fallen over the last three decades and which may well fall further with increased economic integration. Increasing the corporate tax rate would also increase incentives for multinational firms to shift taxable profits out of the UK. If the current UK corporate tax rate is more or less appropriate, the implication is that by taxing the normal return on equity-financed investments, we are currently raising too much revenue from corporate taxation. Our recommendations are thus to introduce an ACE without increasing the corporate tax rate, to accept that less revenue will be collected from the corporate tax, and to rebalance the shares of revenue from corporate and other taxes as part of an overall package of reforms to the tax system as a whole.

In this context, it is particularly important to understand the issue of tax incidence and who bears the costs of distortions introduced by the tax system. By raising the cost of equity-financed investment, the corporate income tax also tends to reduce the overall level of corporate investment. In an open economy, the cost of this distortion will largely be borne by domestic workers. Owners of capital can invest elsewhere. Lower investment in the UK implies less capital per worker and lower labour productivity. In the long run, this will be reflected in lower real wages, making domestic

---

[4] Any purchase of equity in a subsidiary company would reduce the ACE available to the parent company.

workers poorer. Taxing wages directly would allow the same revenue to be collected with more capital per worker and hence more output per worker— a more efficient outcome that would also leave domestic workers better off, notwithstanding the higher tax rate on labour income.

As with other elements of our proposed reform package, it is possible to put at least some indicative scale on the value of reform. It has been estimated that a revenue-neutral reform package introducing an ACE with an offsetting increase in a broad-based tax on consumption would, for the UK, deliver long-run increases of 6.1% in investment, 1.7% in wages, 0.2% in employment, and 1.4% in GDP, leaving the representative consumer better off by an amount equivalent to 0.2% of GDP.[5] While these simulations are subject to wide margins of error, they do confirm in a rigorous empirical framework that eliminating the taxation of the normal return to equity-financed corporate investment could result in a significant increase in capital per worker. This in turn could produce worthwhile gains in wages, employment, output, and welfare. Crucially, this does depend on using another part of the tax system to recoup the revenue cost of the ACE. Offsetting the revenue loss by increasing the corporate tax rate would be much less attractive, inducing multinational firms to shift both real activity and taxable profits out of the country.

20.3. THE REFORM PACKAGE AND TRANSITION

Our main proposals are summarized in Table 20.2. Between them, they represent a radical set of reforms aimed at creating a much more efficient and effective tax system. They would take the UK tax system much of the way towards being a progressive, neutral system. The combination of excluding the normal rate of return to capital from tax, aligning tax rates on income from all sources, and significantly widening the VAT base would move a long way towards neutrality. We have shown how progressivity can

---

[5] See de Mooij and Devereux (2009, table B.4). Using a similar approach, Radulescu and Stimmelmayr (2007) estimated somewhat larger gains for Germany from a revenue-neutral introduction of an ACE combined with an increase in the rate of VAT.

be maintained—or changed if desired—through using the personal tax and benefit system. This is where the progressivity in the system as a whole should come from. It is important to combine this with reforms that simplify and rationalize the benefit system and that ensure that personal taxes and benefits are designed to take account of what we know about people's responsiveness to incentives. Where there is a strong case for deviating from neutrality—as where environmental externalities exist—such departures

Table 20.2. Main recommendations

Taxes on earnings
Merge income tax with employee (and ideally employer) NICs
End the opaque practice of tapering personal allowances and move to a transparent, coherent rate schedule
Introduce a single integrated benefit, getting rid of the very highest effective marginal tax rates (90% and more) faced by some low earners
Strengthen work incentives for those whose youngest child is of school age and for 55- to 70-year-olds relative to others

Indirect taxes
Remove nearly all the current zero and reduced rates and, where possible, exemptions from VAT. Introduce a comprehensive package compensating the less well-off on average whilst maintaining work incentives.
Retain a destination basis for VAT while ending the zero-rating of exports
Introduce a tax equivalent to VAT on financial services
Replace council tax and stamp duty land tax on housing with a tax proportional to the current value of domestic property, to stand in place of VAT on housing

Environmental taxes
Introduce a consistent price on carbon emissions, through a combination of extended coverage of the EU Emissions Trading Scheme and a consistent tax on other emission sources. This would include a tax on domestic gas consumption.
Replace much of the current tax on petrol and diesel with a national system of congestion charging

(cont.)

Table 20.2. (*cont.*)

Taxation of savings and wealth

Take interest on bank and building society accounts out of tax altogether

Introduce a rate-of-return allowance for substantial holdings of risky assets (e.g. equities held outside ISAs, unincorporated business assets, and rental property) so that only 'excess' returns are taxed

Tax capital income and capital gains above the rate-of-return allowance at the same rate schedule as earned income (including employee and employer NICs), with reduced rates for dividends and capital gains on shares to reflect corporation tax already paid

Maintain and simplify the current system of pensions taxation, ending the excessively generous treatment of employer contributions and replacing the tax-free lump sum with an incentive better targeted at the behaviour we want to encourage

At least remove the most obvious avoidance opportunities from inheritance tax and look to introduce a comprehensive lifetime wealth transfer tax

Business taxes

Introduce an allowance for corporate equity into the corporation tax to align treatment of debt and equity and ensure that only 'excess' returns to investment are taxed

Align tax treatment of employment, self-employment, and corporate-source income

Replace business rates and stamp duty land tax on business property with a land value tax for business and agricultural land, subject to confirming practical feasibility

need to be much better designed and more clearly focused on the externality created than at present. This should involve consistent pricing of carbon and charges for motorists that reflect the main externality they cause, i.e. congestion.

Whilst implementing all these changes would undoubtedly represent a revolution in tax policy, it is also possible to overstate the degree of change. We have looked to achieve our progressive, neutral system not with a single tax on expenditure or income, but through a mix of taxes very similar to those in place today—VAT, personal income tax, and corporation tax would remain, though the base for each would be different. From a practical point of view, maintaining a variety of taxes like this is likely to be important simply to diversify revenue sources. And, of course, maintaining a progressive personal tax and benefit system is necessary for effective redistribution.

That said, the range and scale of our proposals are such that we have set out a prospectus not for the next Budget or the one after that, but for a long-term programme of reform. Practical and political difficulties will need to be overcome before some of these proposals can be implemented. In some cases—some of the VAT proposals and some proposals on carbon pricing, for example—international agreements will need to be reached before implementation is possible.

It is fair to ask, then, what are our priorities—which of the recommendations are the most substantial, which can be implemented quickly, and which will require a longer period before implementation? Equally, there are several areas we have discussed where we have indicated that we are unsure of what is possible from a practical point of view or where we do not believe the evidence is yet clear enough to be sure of the appropriate reform agenda.

The most important of our recommendations are those that would end what are clear current distortions in the tax system and where we think the evidence is strongest that they could increase economic welfare. Among these we would certainly include applying VAT to a wider range of goods and services (including substitutes for VAT on housing and financial services), moving towards a system of congestion charging for motorists and consistent pricing of greenhouse gas emissions, and reforming the system of personal taxes and benefits to make it simpler and apply low effective tax rates to those groups known to be most responsive to incentives.

Just as far-reaching are our proposals to overhaul the taxation of savings and profits in a way that would exclude the normal rate of return from taxation and align the tax treatment of income from earnings, savings, self-employment, and companies. Extending NICs to self-employment and capital income would be the biggest step towards ending the incentive to convert labour income to capital income; this would fit naturally with integration of income tax and NICs, though integration must encompass employer (as well as employee) NICs or else an equivalent tax should be levied on non-employment income. The introduction of an ACE would also ensure that the damaging bias in favour of debt over equity finance for companies is eliminated. As we suggested earlier, we believe that our approach in this area has the potential to resolve the ongoing and almost universal tension between preventing tax avoidance on the one hand and minimizing disincentives to save and invest on the other. We can charge similar marginal rates of tax on all income whilst excluding normal returns to capital from taxation, thereby maintaining incentives to save and invest whilst minimizing opportunities for avoidance.

Importance, though, does not necessarily tell us much about the appropriate timing. Some changes may require considerable development and investment, time for consultation, or time for people to understand and adjust to them. Congestion charging is important, but the planning and investment required would not allow it to happen for several years—though that planning should start soon. We have outlined radical changes to savings and business taxation. In an ideal world, these changes would be announced quickly and in a way that would not allow people and companies to plan their affairs in anticipation of the transition. In practice, such an immediate change could not be consistent with good policymaking. Substantial planning and consultation would be required before measures could plausibly be implemented, with timescales measured in years rather than months.

There are other potentially important changes where we have not been able to say conclusively exactly how they could be made. The most important of these is probably finding a way to apply VAT or a surrogate to financial services, where we have outlined possible ways forward without having designed the definitive solution. We would also like to replace business rates with a land value tax, something that depends upon having a reliable means of valuing land separately from the buildings on it. We believe this might well be possible, but would certainly want to see more work done to confirm that. Meanwhile, our tentative proposals to introduce a form of lifetime accessions tax depend on solving a range of implementation problems, and we have, perhaps, less confidence these could be overcome.

But this is no counsel of despair. Preparations for most of this reform programme could, and indeed should, start in earnest very quickly. Many of the problems we face at present arise from a lack of long-term planning and strategy and a failure to address issues that require such planning. But there is also much that could be implemented in much shorter order. There is no reason why stamp duty land tax on housing and council tax should not be replaced with a tax on the consumption value of housing (standing in place of VAT) as soon as a hugely overdue revaluation exercise can take place. Extending VAT to most goods and services could be implemented quite quickly alongside a compensation package—though there may be a case for phasing this in gradually to dampen the effects on those who would lose out. Reforms to earnings taxation and the benefit system should also be feasible sooner rather than later. Getting rid of a number of specific problems, such as the tapering of allowances which creates such bizarre marginal rate structures, could be done virtually overnight. The same is true of ending the taxation of interest-bearing accounts, removing the most obvious inheritance tax loopholes, and making changes to how the benefit system accounts for age.

Of course, in such a major set of changes, there are difficulties that go well beyond the practicalities of reform. A system designed as we have suggested would affect people and businesses very differently from the system we have now. Even if we could gain general agreement that the system we envisage would be a good place to reach, we would not necessarily find it easy to get there. While a transfer of legal tax liabilities from companies to individuals would not change the ultimate incidence at all in the long run, it will certainly look like a simple tax increase to most people. While we may, rightly, be concerned primarily with tax burdens on individuals across their lifetimes, any change will come in while each individual is at a particular point in their life cycle—and they are bound to focus on its immediate impact.

All these things undoubtedly make change politically challenging. But there are changes that we have suggested that go beyond the politically challenging. They impose real costs on people, and costs that may vary systematically and in ways that some may not consider equitable. These are of three types.

First, there are many reforms we have proposed that, while distributionally neutral on average, undoubtedly hit some people in particular circumstances: those who prefer to spend their money on books and cakes rather than DVDs and biscuits, or those who are self-employed, for example. In one sense, there is no getting around this type of issue in any reform that makes anyone worse off. Intellectually, the right thing to do is consider which is the better equilibrium—one in which we are benefiting the self-employed at the expense of everyone else, or one with neutrality between those in different forms of work. Practically, the transition is a challenge.

Second, we have argued that, over the life cycle, many of our reforms even out. A rise in VAT and a fall in other taxes will hit people when their consumption is high relative to their income, and benefit them when income is high relative to consumption. An increase in benefits for families with young children and a cut in benefits for families with older children should, on average, cancel out over a lifetime. Again, the 'on average' is important— there will be winners and losers. But there is a different point as well. If I already have older children, the fact that the reform will even out for the next generation is of little comfort. I have missed the boat and I am simply left worse off. This effect can be obviated to some extent by phasing the reform in, and our discussion of this reform suggests how that could be done. It is more difficult to deal with the life-cycle effect of the VAT proposals. To the extent that older people have consumption high relative to their income, it is no comfort to the current generation of older people that they would have benefited from the new system when they were younger, had it been in place. But the reform package we illustrate does not, in fact, mean pensioners losing out on average.

Third, there is the issue of capitalization. Our proposed reforms— particularly reforms to capital taxation—will impact on the value of some assets, and therefore create windfall gains and losses for asset holders, in ways that some will consider unjust. For example, replacing council tax and stamp duty land tax with a tax proportional to current property values will reduce the value of some properties and increase the value of others. Our proposed reforms to inheritance tax will presumably reduce the value of agricultural land and of unquoted businesses.

These are important issues, and real costs will be imposed on people. Change will have to be managed carefully and often brought in gradually. In some cases, that might make the transition easier. In some cases, particularly where the issue is about hitting particular cohorts of individuals, it may be important to make the transition a gradual one. But many of the costs relative to the status quo are unavoidable. They need to be weighed in the political scales. Our view is clear, though: the long-term benefits of change far outweigh the transitional costs. We cannot forever succumb to the tyranny of the status quo.

That status quo involves complexity, unfairness, and significant economic costs. One consequence of it, on which we have already commented, is the amount of taxpayers' energy that goes into avoiding tax and governments' energy that goes into combating avoidance. The more complex and inconsistent the tax base, the more avoidance will be possible and the more legislation will be required, so the more effort is put into shoring up tax revenues rather than into following a coherent strategy. Certainly, one of the central problems of dealing with tax avoidance in the UK has been the propensity of governments to tackle the symptom—by enacting ever more anti-avoidance provisions aimed at the particular avoidance scheme—rather than addressing its underlying cause—often the lack of clarity or consistency in the tax base. Following our agenda should tackle some of the underlying inconsistencies and unnecessary dividing lines within the UK's tax system and hence should produce a system that is more robust against avoidance. If activities were taxed similarly, there would be no (or, at least, much less) incentive for taxpayers to dress up one form of activity as another—and there would correspondingly be little or no revenue loss to the Exchequer if they did so. We are not so naive as to believe that our proposals will banish avoidance to the outer limits of the tax system, and, given the exponential growth in anti-avoidance legislation in recent years, there may be a case for reconsidering the enactment of a statutory general anti-avoidance rule or principle (a 'statutory GAAR') as is found in Australia, Canada, and New Zealand, all of which share a common legal heritage with the UK. But the primary response should be to address the fundamental causes of avoidance rather than blindly resorting to anti-avoidance provisions, whether of a general or a specific nature. Simply demonizing tax avoiders and exhorting them to behave better is also a feeble stratagem. Lord Kaldor's dictum that 'the existence of widespread tax avoidance is evidence that the system, not the taxpayer, is in need of reform' is surely the right starting point.[6]

The need for reform is evident, as is the need for a clear and coherent strategic policy direction. That strategic direction needs to be set out and understood. Individual policy initiatives need to be assessed against it. There is an urgent need for government to set out and pursue a long-term agenda

---

[6] Kaldor, 1980.

of tax reform. The political benefits of doing so should have been well-enough signposted by the experience of the 1997–2010 Labour government, which went through a series of poorly-thought-out changes and reforms that were later reversed at considerable political cost. The introduction then abolition of a 10% income tax band, the introduction then abolition of a bizarre capital gains tax regime that rewarded people according to how long they held assets, and the introduction then abolition of a zero rate of corporation tax on low profits are just three of many policy mistakes arising from a lack of direction.

We hope our report can at least set the ground on which an effective long-term strategy can be built. At the very least, this should help avoid the cost and disruption of unplanned and incoherent change. We hope it could ensure a much better and more effective tax system going forward.

20.4. CONCLUSIONS

In recent years, nearly 40p in every pound earned in the UK has been taken in tax. And the growth in government to such levels was perhaps one of the most striking developments of 20th century history. Taxes at the level that we now see have a significant impact on all of us individually. They also affect the economy's aggregate performance and the ability of government to spend on essential public services. Whatever the total level of taxation and public spending, it is better if the government ensures that the tax system is designed to do least harm to the productive potential of the economy and to economic welfare more generally, and that the system is viewed as fair.

But governments find it difficult to carry out tax policy in a consistent way. Unlike the economic ideal that we have discussed throughout this volume, tax policy is created in a political process with much concern for how it plays on the evening news and ultimately at the ballot box. Given the potential for the distortion of policy through this, there are some genuinely encouraging aspects of tax policy over the past 30 years. The taxation of savings and of mortgages, and some elements of corporate taxation, have improved over time, and some work incentive issues have been improved through the expansion of in-work support for low earners, and indeed by cuts in the very high top rates of income tax that existed in the 1970s.

But the picture is not all good. Governments have frequently set about increasing taxes not where they are least economically damaging, but where they are least transparent or most transiently popular. This has led to mistakes which later required rectification (which itself created political tensions). Often, poor economics ultimately becomes poor politics.

Governments also, understandably, shy away from making tough decisions, postponing pain, which on occasion stores up much greater problems in future. The facts that we still pay a tax based on the value of our houses in 1991 and that we still have two separate systems of income taxation are both products of failure to tackle politically difficult anomalies in the tax system.

Government in a media-driven democracy is difficult and there is a need to work within the bounds of the politically feasible. But there is a better way to make tax policy. There are taxes that are fairer, less damaging, and simpler than those we have now. To implement them will take a government willing to be honest with the electorate, willing to understand and explain the arguments, willing to listen to and to consult experts and public alike, and willing to put long-term strategy ahead of short-term tactics.

And the costs of not doing so, while opaque, are very large. Our best estimates suggest that economic welfare could be improved by many billions of pounds annually if the taxation of income, expenditure, profits, environmental externalities, and savings were reformed in the ways we have suggested.

As readers of this book will have gleaned, some of the required changes are easily understood and perfectly simple. Others are rather less so. We hope we have made a contribution to the debate, to the search for clarity, and to the process of holding government to account. But this is a project for the long term. We, and we hope our readers, will continue to put pressure on government to rationalize taxes, to be honest with us when changes are made, and to be bold when boldness is required. It is time for government to grow up and map out a rational course for tax policy.

References

Adam, S. (2005), 'Measuring the Marginal Efficiency Cost of Redistribution in the UK', Institute for Fiscal Studies (IFS), Working Paper 05/14 (http://www.ifs.org.uk/publications/3399).

— and Brewer, M. (2010), *Couple Penalties and Premiums in the UK Tax and Benefit System*, IFS (Institute for Fiscal Studies) Briefing Note 102 (http://www.ifs.org.uk/publications/4856).

— and Browne, J. (2010), 'Redistribution, Work Incentives and Thirty Years of UK Tax and Benefit Reform', Institute for Fiscal Studies (IFS), Working Paper 10/24 (http://www.ifs.org.uk/publications/5367).

— — and Heady, C. (2010), 'Taxation in the UK', in J. Mirrlees, S. Adam, T. Besley, R. Blundell, S. Bond, R. Chote, M. Gammie, P. Johnson, G. Myles, and J. Poterba (eds), *Dimensions of Tax Design: The Mirrlees Review*, Oxford: Oxford University Press for Institute for Fiscal Studies.

— and Loutzenhiser, G. (2007), 'Integrating Income Tax and National Insurance: An Interim Report', Institute for Fiscal Studies (IFS), Working Paper 07/21 (http://www.ifs.org.uk/publications/4101).

Ainslie, G. (1975), 'Specious Reward: A Behavioral Theory of Impulsiveness and Impulse Control', *Psychological Bulletin*, **82**, 463–96.

Akerlof, G. (1978), 'The Economics of "Tagging" as Applied to the Optimal Income Tax, Welfare Programs, and Manpower Planning', *American Economic Review*, **68**, 8–19.

Alesina, A., Ichino, A., and Karabarbounis, L. (2007), 'Gender Based Taxation and the Division of Family Chores', National Bureau of Economic Research (NBER), Working Paper 13638 (http://www.nber.org/papers/w13638).

Alt, J., Preston, I., and Sibieta, L. (2010), 'The Political Economy of Tax Policy', in J. Mirrlees, S. Adam, T. Besley, R. Blundell, S. Bond, R. Chote, M. Gammie, P. Johnson, G. Myles, and J. Poterba (eds), *Dimensions of Tax Design: The Mirrlees Review*, Oxford: Oxford University Press for Institute for Fiscal Studies.

Altshuler, R., and Auerbach, A. (1990), 'The Significance of Tax Law Asymmetries: An Empirical Investigation', *Quarterly Journal of Economics*, **105**, 61–86.

Andelson, R. (2001), *Land-Value Taxation around the World*, Oxford: Blackwell Publishing.

Apps, P., and Rees, R. (2009), *Public Economics and the Household*, Cambridge: Cambridge University Press.

Arulampalam, W., Devereux, M., and Maffini, G. (2007), 'The Direct Incidence of Corporate Income Tax on Wages', Oxford University Centre for Business Taxation,

Working Paper WP07/07 (http://www.sbs.ox.ac.uk/centres/tax/papers/Pages/PaperWP0707.aspx).

Atkinson, A. (1995), *Public Economics in Action: The Basic Income / Flat Tax Proposal*, Oxford: Oxford University Press.

— and Piketty, T. (eds) (2007a), *Top Incomes over the Twentieth Century: A Contrast between Continental European and English-Speaking Countries*, Oxford: Oxford University Press.

— — (2007b), 'Towards a Unified Data Set on Top Incomes', in A. Atkinson and T. Piketty (eds), *Top Incomes over the Twentieth Century: A Contrast between Continental European and English-Speaking Countries*, Oxford: Oxford University Press.

— and Stiglitz, J. (1976), 'The Design of Tax Structure: Direct versus Indirect Taxation', *Journal of Public Economics*, **6**, 55–75.

— — (1980), *Lectures on Public Economics*, London: McGraw-Hill.

Attanasio, O., and Wakefield, M. (2010), 'The Effects on Consumption and Saving of Taxing Asset Returns', in J. Mirrlees, S. Adam, T. Besley, R. Blundell, S. Bond, R. Chote, M. Gammie, P. Johnson, G. Myles, and J. Poterba (eds), *Dimensions of Tax Design: The Mirrlees Review*, Oxford: Oxford University Press for Institute for Fiscal Studies.

— and Weber, G. (2010), 'Consumption and Saving: Models of Intertemporal Allocation and Their Implications for Public Policy', *Journal of Economic Literature*, **48**, 693–751.

Auerbach, A. (1985), 'The Theory of Excess Burden and Optimal Taxation', in A. Auerbach and M. Feldstein (eds), *Handbook of Public Economics*, Volume 1, Amsterdam: Elsevier.

— and Bradford, D. (2004), 'Generalized Cash-Flow Taxation', *Journal of Public Economics*, **88**, 957–80.

— Devereux, M., and Simpson, H. (2010), 'Taxing Corporate Income', in J. Mirrlees, S. Adam, T. Besley, R. Blundell, S. Bond, R. Chote, M. Gammie, P. Johnson, G. Myles, and J. Poterba (eds), *Dimensions of Tax Design: The Mirrlees Review*, Oxford: Oxford University Press for Institute for Fiscal Studies.

Aujean, M., Jenkins, P., and Poddar, S. (1999), 'A New Approach to Public Sector Bodies', *International VAT Monitor*, **10**, 144–9.

Autor, D., and Dorn, D. (2011), 'The Growth of Low Skill Service Jobs and the Polarization of the U. S. Labor Market', MIT, Department of Economics, Working Paper (http://econ-www.mit.edu/files/1474).

Banks, J., Blundell, R., and Tanner, S. (1998), 'Is There a Retirement-Savings Puzzle?', *American Economic Review*, **88**, 769–88.

— and Casanova, M. (2003), 'Work and Retirement', in M. Marmot, J. Banks, R. Blundell, C. Lessof, and J. Nazroo (eds), *Health, Wealth and Lifestyles of the Older*

Population in England: The 2002 English Longitudinal Study of Ageing, London: Institute for Fiscal Studies (http://www.ifs.org.uk/elsa/publications.php?publication _id=3088).

Banks, J. and Diamond, P. (2010), 'The Base for Direct Taxation', in J. Mirrlees, S. Adam, T. Besley, R. Blundell, S. Bond, R. Chote, M. Gammie, P. Johnson, G. Myles, and J. Poterba (eds), *Dimensions of Tax Design: The Mirrlees Review*, Oxford: Oxford University Press for Institute for Fiscal Studies.

— Emmerson, C., and Tetlow, G. (2007), 'Better Prepared for Retirement? Using Panel Data to Improve Wealth Estimates of ELSA Respondents', Institute for Fiscal Studies (IFS), Working Paper 07/12 (http://www.ifs.org.uk/publications/4007).

— Karlsen, S., and Oldfield, Z. (2003), 'Socio-Economic Position', in M. Marmot, J. Banks, R. Blundell, C. Lessof, and J. Nazroo (eds), *Health, Wealth and Lifestyles of the Older Population in England: The 2002 English Longitudinal Study of Ageing*, London: Institute for Fiscal Studies (http://www.ifs.org.uk/elsa/publications.php? publication_id=3088).

— and Oldfield, Z. (2006), 'Understanding Pensions: Cognitive Function, Numerical Ability and Retirement Saving', Institute for Fiscal Studies (IFS), Working Paper 06/05 (http://www.ifs.org.uk/publications/3586).

Barker, K. (2004), *Delivering Stability: Securing Our Future Housing Needs* (http://webarchive.nationalarchives.gov.uk/+/http://www.hm-treasury.gov.uk/ consultations_and_legislation/barker/consult_barker_index.cfm).

Becker, G. (1991), *A Treatise on the Family*, Cambridge, MA: Harvard University Press.

Bell, K., Brewer, M., and Phillips, D. (2007), *Lone Parents and 'Mini-Jobs'*, York: Joseph Rowntree Foundation (http://www.ifs.org.uk/publications/4052).

Bennett, F., Brewer, M., and Shaw, J. (2009), *Understanding the Compliance Costs of Benefits and Tax Credits*, IFS Report 70, London: Institute for Fiscal Studies (http:// www.ifs.org.uk/publications/4558).

Bentham, J. (1789), *An Introduction to the Principles of Morals and Legislation*.

Bentick, B. (1979), 'The Impact of Taxation and Valuation Practices on the Timing and Efficiency of Land Use', *Journal of Political Economy*, **87**, 859–68.

Bernheim, B. (2002), 'Taxation and Saving', in A. Auerbach and M. Feldstein (eds), *Handbook of Public Economics*, Amsterdam: Elsevier Science BV.

— and Rangel, A. (2005), 'Behavioral Public Economics: Welfare and Policy Analysis with Non-Standard Decision-Makers', National Bureau of Economic Research (NBER), Working Paper 11518 (http://www.nber.org/papers/w11518).

Bettinger, E., and Slonim, R. (2006), 'Using Experimental Economics to Measure the Effects of a Natural Educational Experiment on Altruism', *Journal of Public Economics*, **90**, 1625–48.

Bird, R. (2010), Commentary on I Crawford, M. Keen, and S. Smith, 'Value Added Tax and Excises', in J. Mirrlees, S. Adam, T. Besley, R. Blundell, S. Bond, R. Chote, M. Gammie, P. Johnson, G. Myles, and J. Poterba (eds), *Dimensions of Tax Design: The Mirrlees Review*, Oxford: Oxford University Press for Institute for Fiscal Studies.

— and Gendron, P.-P. (2007), *The VAT in Developing and Transitional Countries*, Cambridge: Cambridge University Press.

Blow, L., Hawkins, M., Klemm, A., McCrae, J., and Simpson, H. (2002), *Budget 2002: Business Taxation Measures*, IFS (Institute for Fiscal Studies) Briefing Note 24 (http://www.ifs.org.uk/publications/1774).

Blundell, R., Bozio, A., and Laroque, G. (2011), 'Labor Supply and the Extensive Margin', *American Economic Review*, **101**, 482–6.

— Emmerson, C., and Wakefield, M. (2006), 'The Importance of Incentives in Influencing Private Retirement Saving: Known Knowns and Known Unknowns', Institute for Fiscal Studies (IFS), Working Paper 06/09 (http://www.ifs.org.uk/publications/3593).

— and Hoynes, H. (2004), 'In-Work Benefit Reform and the Labour Market', in R. Blundell, D. Card, and R. Freeman (eds), *Seeking a Premier League Economy*, Chicago: University of Chicago Press.

— and MaCurdy, T. (1999), 'Labour Supply: A Review of Alternative Approaches', in O. Ashenfelter and D. Card (eds), *Handbook of Labour Economics*, Amsterdam: North-Holland.

— Meghir, C., and Smith, S. (2004), 'Pension Incentives and the Pattern of Retirement in the United Kingdom', in J. Gruber and D. Wise (eds), *Social Security Programs and Retirement around the World: Micro-Estimation*, Chicago, IL: University of Chicago Press.

— Pashardes, P., and Weber, G. (1993), 'What Do We Learn about Consumer Demand Patterns from Micro Data?', *American Economic Review*, **83**, 570–97.

— and Preston, I. (1998), 'Consumption Inequality and Income Uncertainty', *Quarterly Journal of Economics*, **113**, 603–40.

— and Shephard, A. (2011), 'Employment, Hours of Work and the Optimal Taxation of Low Income Families', Institute for the Study of Labor (IZA), Discussion Paper 5745. Forthcoming *Review of Economic Studies*.

Boadway, R., and Bruce, N. (1984), 'A General Proposition on the Design of a Neutral Business Tax', *Journal of Public Economics*, **24**, 231–9.

— Chamberlain, E., and Emmerson, C. (2010), 'Taxation of Wealth and Wealth Transfers', in J. Mirrlees, S. Adam, T. Besley, R. Blundell, S. Bond, R. Chote, M. Gammie, P. Johnson, G. Myles, and J. Poterba (eds), *Dimensions of Tax Design: The Mirrlees Review*, Oxford: Oxford University Press for Institute for Fiscal Studies.

Boadway, R. and Pestieau, P. (2003), 'Indirect Taxation and Redistribution: The Scope of the Atkinson–Stiglitz Theorem', in R. Arnott, B. Greenwald, R. Kanbur, and B. Nalebuff (eds), *Economics for an Imperfect World: Essays in Honor of Joseph E. Stiglitz*, Cambridge, MA: MIT Press.

Bond, S., and Devereux, M. (2003), 'Generalised R-Based and S-Based Taxes under Uncertainty', *Journal of Public Economics*, **87**, 1291–311.

— Hawkins, M., and Klemm, A. (2004), 'Stamp Duty on Shares and Its Effect on Share Prices', Institute for Fiscal Studies (IFS), Working Paper 04/11 (http://www.ifs.org.uk/publications/1847).

— and Xing, J. (2010), 'Corporate Taxation and Capital Accumulation', Oxford University Centre for Business Taxation, Working Paper WP10/15 (http://www.sbs.ox.ac.uk/centres/tax/papers/Pages/PaperWP1015.aspx).

Bovenberg, A., Hansen, M., and Sørensen, P. (2008), 'Individual Savings Accounts for Social Insurance: Rationale and Alternative Designs', *International Tax and Public Finance*, **15**, 67–86.

— and Sørensen, P. (2004), 'Improving the Equity-Efficiency Trade-Off: Mandatory Savings Accounts for Social Insurance', *International Tax and Public Finance*, **11**, 507–29.

Bradford, D. (1982), 'The Choice between Income and Consumption Taxes', *Tax Notes*, **16**, 715–23.

Brewer, M. (2006), 'Tax Credits: Fixed or Beyond Repair?', in R. Chote, C. Emmerson, R. Harrison, and D. Miles (eds), *The IFS Green Budget: January 2006*, Commentary 100, London: Institute for Fiscal Studies (http://www.ifs.org.uk/publications/3552).

— and Browne, J. (2009), *Can More Revenue Be Raised by Increasing Income Tax Rates for the Very Rich?*, IFS (Institute for Fiscal Studies) Briefing Note 84 (http://www.ifs.org.uk/publications/4486).

— — and Jin, W. (2011), *Universal Credit: A Preliminary Analysis*, IFS (Institute for Fiscal Studies) Briefing Note 116 (http://www.ifs.org.uk/publications/5415).

— Goodman, A., and Leicester, A. (2006), *Household Spending in Britain: What Can It Teach Us about Poverty?*, Bristol: Policy Press (http://www.ifs.org.uk/publications/3620).

— O'Dea, C., Paull, G., and Sibieta, L. (2009), *The Living Standards of Families with Children Reporting Low Incomes*, Department for Work and Pensions Research Report 577, Leeds: CDS (http://research.dwp.gov.uk/asd/asd5/rports2009-2010/rrep577.pdf).

— Ratcliffe, A., and Smith, S. (2010), 'Does Welfare Reform Affect Fertility? Evidence from the UK', *Journal of Population Economics*, online 16 September (http://dx.doi.org/10.1007/s00148-010-0332-x).

—, Saez, E., and Shephard, A. (2010), 'Means-Testing and Tax Rates on Earnings', in J. Mirrlees, S. Adam, T. Besley, R. Blundell, S. Bond, R. Chote, M. Gammie, P. Johnson, G. Myles, and J. Poterba (eds), *Dimensions of Tax Design: The Mirrlees Review*, Oxford: Oxford University Press for Institute for Fiscal Studies.

— and Shaw, J. (2006), *How Many Lone Parents Are Receiving Tax Credits?*, IFS (Institute for Fiscal Studies) Briefing Note 70 (http://www.ifs.org.uk/publications/3574).

— Sibieta, L., and Wren-Lewis, L. (2008), *Racing Away? Income Inequality and the Evolution of High Incomes*, IFS (Institute for Fiscal Studies) Briefing Note 76 (http://www.ifs.org.uk/publications/4108).

British Aggregates Association (2005), *An Analysis of Trends in Aggregates Markets since 1990 – and the Effects of the Landfill Tax and Aggregates Levy*, Bath.

Browne, J. and Phillips, D. (2010), box 2.1 in R. Chote, C. Emmerson, and J. Shaw (eds), *The IFS Green Budget: February 2010*, Commentary 112, London: Institute for Fiscal Studies (http://www.ifs.org.uk/publications/4732).

Browning, M., Bourguignon, F., Chiappori, P.-A., and Lechene, V. (1994), 'Income and Outcomes: A Structural Model of Intrahousehold Allocation', *Journal of Political Economy*, **102**, 1067–96.

Buchanan, J., and Musgrave, R. (1999), *Public Finance and Public Choice*, Cambridge, MA: MIT Press.

Carroll, R., and Hrung, W. (2005), 'What Does the Taxable Income Elasticity Say about Dynamic Responses to Tax Changes?', *American Economic Review*, **95**, 426–31.

Case, A., and Paxson, C. (2008), 'Stature and Status: Height, Ability, and Labor Market Outcomes', *Journal of Political Economy*, **116**, 499–532.

Cave, M. (2009), *Independent Review of Competition and Innovation in Water Markets: Final Report*, London: Department for Environment, Food and Rural Affairs (http://archive.defra.gov.uk/environment/quality/water/industry/cavereview/).

Centre for Social Justice (2009), *Dynamic Benefits*, London.

Chaloupka, F., and Wechsler, H. (1997), 'Price, Tobacco Control Policies and Smoking among Young Adults', *Journal of Health Economics*, **16**, 359–73.

Chetty, R. (2009), 'Bounds on Elasticities with Optimization Frictions: A Synthesis of Micro and Macro Evidence on Labor Supply', National Bureau of Economic Research (NBER), Working Paper 15616 (http://www.nber.org/papers/w15616).

Choi, J., Laibson, D., Madrian, B., and Metrick, A. (2004), 'For Better or for Worse: Default Effects and 401(k) Savings Behavior', in D. Wise (ed.), *Perspectives on the Economics of Aging*, Chicago, IL: University of Chicago Press.

Chung, W., Disney, R., Emmerson, C., and Wakefield, M. (2008), 'Public Policy and Retirement Saving Incentives in the UK', in R. Fenge, G. de Ménil, and P. Pestieau (eds), *Pension Strategies in Europe and the United States,* Cambridge, MA: MIT Press.

Committee on Climate Change (2008), *Building a Low Carbon Economy: The UK's Contribution to Tackling Climate Change,* First Report, London: TSO.

Convery, F., McDonnell, S., and Ferreira, S. (2007), 'The Most Popular Tax in Europe? Lessons from the Irish Plastic Bags Levy', *Environmental and Resource Economics,* **38**, 1–11.

Copenhagen Economics and KPMG (2011), *VAT in the Public Sector and Exemptions in the Public Interest* (http://ec.europa.eu/taxation_customs/resources/ documents/common/publications/studies/vat_public_sector.pdf).

Crawford, C., and Freedman, J. (2010), 'Small Business Taxation', in J. Mirrlees, S. Adam, T. Besley, R. Blundell, S. Bond, R. Chote, M. Gammie, P. Johnson, G. Myles, and J. Poterba (eds), *Dimensions of Tax Design: The Mirrlees Review,* Oxford: Oxford University Press for Institute for Fiscal Studies.

Crawford, I., Keen, M., and Smith, S. (2010), 'Value Added Tax and Excises', in J. Mirrlees, S. Adam, T. Besley, R. Blundell, S. Bond, R. Chote, M. Gammie, P. Johnson, G. Myles, and J. Poterba (eds), *Dimensions of Tax Design: The Mirrlees Review,* Oxford: Oxford University Press for Institute for Fiscal Studies.

Creedy, J., and Disney, R. (1985), *Social Insurance in Transition: An Economic Analysis,* Oxford: Oxford University Press.

Cremer, H., and Pestieau, P. (2006), 'Wealth Transfer Taxation: A Survey of the Theoretical Literature', in L.-A. Gérard-Varet, S.-C. Colm, and J. Mercier Ythier (eds), *Handbook of the Economics of Giving, Reciprocity and Altruism,* Volume 2, Amsterdam: North-Holland.

CSERGE (1993—Centre for Social and Economic Research on the Global Environment, University of East Anglia), *Externalities from Landfill and Incineration,* Department of the Environment, London: HMSO.

Cullen, J., and Gordon, R. (2007), 'Taxes and Entrepreneurial Risk-Taking: Theory and Evidence for the U.S.', *Journal of Public Economics,* **91**, 1479–505.

De Mooij, R., and Devereux, M. (2009), 'Alternative Systems of Business Tax in Europe: An Applied Analysis of ACE and CBIT Reforms', European Commission, DG Taxation and Customs Union, Taxation Paper 17.

Department for Environment, Food and Rural Affairs (2008), *Synthesis Report on the Findings from Defra's Pre-Feasibility Study into Personal Carbon Trading,* London (http://www.decc.gov.uk/assets/decc/what%20we%20do/global%20climate %20change%20and%20energy/tackling%20climate%20change/ind_com_action/per sonal/pct-synthesis-report.pdf).

Department for Transport (2004), *Feasibility Study of Road Pricing in the UK,* London (http://webarchive.nationalarchives.gov.uk/+/http://www.dft.gov.uk/pgr/

roads/introtoroads/roadcongestion/feasibilitystudy/studyreport/feasibilityfullreport
).

— (2006), *Transport Demand to 2025 & the Economic Case for Road Pricing and Investment*, London (http://webarchive.nationalarchives.gov.uk/+/http://www.dft. gov.uk/about/strategy/transportstrategy/eddingtonstudy/researchannexes/research annexesvolume3/transportdemand.pdf).

Department for Work and Pensions (2006), *Security in Retirement: Towards a New Pensions System*, Cm. 6841, London (http://www.dwp.gov.uk/policy/pensions-reform/security-in-retirement/white-paper/).

— (2010a), *Income Related Benefits: Estimates of Take-Up in 2008–09*, London (http://research.dwp.gov.uk/asd/income_analysis/jun_2010/0809_Publication.pdf).

— (2010b), *21st Century Welfare*, Cm. 7913, London (http://www.dwp.gov.uk/docs/ 21st-century-welfare.pdf).

— (2010c), *Fraud and Error in the Benefit System: October 2008 to September 2009* (http://research.dwp.gov.uk/asd/asd2/fem/fem_oct08_sep09.pdf).

— (2010d), *Universal Credit: Welfare that Works*, Cm. 7957, London (http://www. dwp.gov.uk/docs/universal-credit-full-document.pdf).

— (2010e), *Low-Income Dynamics 1991–2008 (Great Britain)*, London (http://statistics.dwp.gov.uk/asd/hbai/low_income/low_income_dynamics_1991-2008.pdf).

Department of Energy and Climate Change (2009a), *The UK Renewable Energy Strategy*, Cm. 7686, London (http://webarchive.nationalarchives.gov.uk/+/http:// www.decc.gov.uk/en/content/cms/what_we_do/uk_supply/energy_mix/renewable/ res/res.aspx).

— (2009b), *Carbon Appraisal in UK Policy Appraisal: A Revised Approach* (http:// www.decc.gov.uk/assets/decc/what%20we%20do/a%20low%20carbon%20uk/carbo n%20valuation/1_20090901160357_e_@@_carbonvaluesbriefguide.pdf).

— (2010), *Quarterly Energy Prices*, 25 March.

Devereux, M. (1989), 'Tax Asymmetries, the Cost of Capital and Investment: Some Evidence from United Kingdom Panel Data', *Economic Journal*, **99**, 103–12.

— and Griffith, R. (1998), 'Taxes and the Location of Production: Evidence from a Panel of US Multinationals', *Journal of Public Economics*, **68**, 335–67.

Diamond, P., and Mirrlees, J. (1971), 'Optimal Taxation and Public Production: Production Efficiency', *American Economic Review*, **61**, 8–27.

Dilnot, A., Kay, J., and Morris, C. (1984), *The Reform of Social Security*, Oxford: Oxford University Press.

Dresner, S., and Ekins, P. (2006), 'Economic Instruments to Improve UK Home Energy Efficiency without Negative Social Impacts', *Fiscal Studies*, **27**, 47–74.

Dupuit, J. (1844), 'On the Measurement of the Utility of Public Works', *Annales des Ponts et Chaussées*, **7**.

Dye, R., and England, R. (eds) (2009), *Land Value Taxation: Theory, Evidence and Practice*, Cambridge, MA: Lincoln Institute of Land Policy.

Ebrill, L., Keen, M., Bodin, J.-P., and Summers, V. (2001), *The Modern VAT*, Washington, DC: International Monetary Fund.

Eddington, R. (2006), *The Eddington Transport Study*, London: Department for Transport (http://webarchive.nationalarchives.gov.uk/+/http://www.dft.gov.uk/about/strategy/transportstrategy/eddingtonstudy/).

European Commission (1987), *Completion of the Internal Market: Approximation of Indirect Tax Rates and Harmonisation of Indirect Tax Structures*, COM(87) 320, Brussels.

— (1996), *A Common System of VAT: A Programme for the Single Market*, COM(328) 96, Brussels.

— (2004), *Report from the Commission to the Council and the European Parliament on the Use of Administrative Cooperation Arrangements in the Fight against VAT Fraud*, COM(2004) 260 final, Brussels (http://eur-lex.europa.eu/LexUriServ/LexUriServ.do?uri=COM:2004:0260:FIN:EN:PDF).

— (2008), 'Measures to Change the VAT System to Fight Fraud', SEC(2008) 249, Brussels.

— (2010a), 'Taxation of the Financial Sector', Communication from the Commission to the European Parliament, the Council, the European Economic and Social Committee, and the Committee of the Regions, COM(2010) 549/5, Brussels (http://ec.europa.eu/taxation_customs/resources/documents/taxation/com_2010_0549_en.pdf).

— (2010b), 'Financial Sector Taxation', Commission Staff Working Document, SEC(2010) 1166/3, Brussels (http://ec.europa.eu/taxation_customs/resources/documents/taxation/sec_2010_1166_en.pdf).

— (2010c), 'Commission Staff Working Document accompanying the Green Paper on the Future of VAT', SEC(2010) 1455 final, Brussels (http://ec.europa.eu/taxation_customs/resources/documents/common/consultations/tax/future_vat/sec%282010%291455_en.pdf).

Evans, C. (2003), 'Studying the Studies: An Overview of Recent Research into Taxation Operating Costs', *Journal of Tax Research*, 1, 64–92.

Fane, G. (1987), 'Neutral Taxation under Uncertainty', *Journal of Public Economics*, 33, 95–105.

Farhi, E., and Werning, I. (2007), 'Capital Taxation: Quantitative Explorations of the Inverse Euler Equation', Laboratory for Macroeconomic Analysis, Working Paper CAS_RN_2007_3.

— — (2010), 'Progressive Estate Taxation', *Quarterly Journal of Economics*, 125, 635–73.

Feldstein, M. (1999), 'Tax Avoidance and the Deadweight Loss of the Income Tax', *Review of Economics and Statistics*, **81**, 674–80.

Fiszbein, A., and Schady, N. (2009), *Conditional Cash Transfers: Reducing Present and Future Poverty*, Washington, DC: World Bank.

Freedman, J., and Chamberlain, E. (1997), 'Horizontal Equity and the Taxation of Employed and Self-Employed Workers', *Fiscal Studies*, **18**, 87–118.

Freud, D. (2007), *Reducing Dependency, Increasing Opportunity: Options for the Future of Welfare to Work*, independent report to the Department for Work and Pensions, Leeds: CDS (http://www.dwp.gov.uk/policy/welfare-reform/legislation-and-key-documents/freud-report/).

Friedman, M. (1962), *Capitalism and Freedom*, Chicago, IL: University of Chicago Press.

Fullerton, D., Leicester, A., and Smith, S. (2010), 'Environmental Taxes', in J. Mirrlees, S. Adam, T. Besley, R. Blundell, S. Bond, R. Chote, M. Gammie, P. Johnson, G. Myles, and J. Poterba (eds), *Dimensions of Tax Design: The Mirrlees Review*, Oxford: Oxford University Press for Institute for Fiscal Studies.

— and West, S. (2002), 'Can Taxes on Vehicles and on Gasoline Mimic an Unavailable Tax on Emissions?', *Journal of Environmental Economics and Management*, **43**, 135–57.

Gale, W., and Slemrod, J. (2001), 'Rethinking the Estate and Gift Tax: Overview', in W. Gale, J. Hines, and J. Slemrod (eds), *Rethinking Estate and Gift Taxation*, Washington, DC: Brookings Institution Press.

Gallagher, E. (2008), *The Gallagher Review of the Indirect Effects of Biofuels Production*, St Leonards-on-Sea: Renewable Fuels Agency (http://webarchive. nationalarchives.gov.uk/+/http://www.renewablefuelsagency.gov.uk/reportsandpub lications/reviewoftheindirecteffectsofbiofuels).

Gendron, P.-P. (2005), 'Value-Added Tax Treatment of Public Bodies and Non-Profit Organizations', *Bulletin for International Fiscal Documentation*, **59**, 514–25.

Genser, B., and Winker, P. (1997), 'Measuring the Fiscal Revenue Loss of VAT Exemption in Commercial Banking', *Finanzarchiv*, **54**, 565–85.

George, H. (1879), *Progress and Poverty*, London: J. M. Dent.

Golosov, M., and Tsyvinski, A. (2006), 'Designing Optimal Disability Insurance: A Case for Asset Testing', *Journal of Political Economy*, **114**, 257–79.

Goodman, A., Johnson, P., and Webb, S. (1997), *Inequality in the UK*, Oxford: Oxford University Press.

— and Oldfield, Z. (2004), *Permanent Differences? Income and Expenditure Inequality in the 1990s and 2000s*, IFS Report 66, London: Institute for Fiscal Studies (http://www.ifs.org.uk/publications/2117).

Gordon, R. (1986), 'Taxation of Investment and Savings in a World Economy', *American Economic Review*, **76**, 1086–102.

Gruber, J. (2003a), 'Smoking "Internalities"', *Regulation*, **25**, 52–7.

— (2003b), 'The New Economics of Smoking', *NBER Reporter* (http://www.nber.org/reporter/summer03/gruber.html).

— and Koszegi, B. (2001), 'Is Addiction "Rational"? Theory and Evidence', *Quarterly Journal of Economics*, **116**, 1261–303.

— and Wise, D. (eds) (1999), *Social Security and Retirement around the World*, Chicago, IL: University of Chicago Press.

— — (eds) (2004), *Social Security Programs and Retirement around the World: Micro Estimation*, Chicago, IL: University of Chicago Press.

Grubert, H., and Mackie, J. (1999), 'Must Financial Services Be Taxed under a Consumption Tax?', *National Tax Journal*, **53**, 23–40.

Hall, R. (2010), Commentary on J. Banks and P. Diamond, 'The Base for Direct Taxation', in J. Mirrlees, S. Adam, T. Besley, R. Blundell, S. Bond, R. Chote, M. Gammie, P. Johnson, G. Myles, and J. Poterba (eds), *Dimensions of Tax Design: The Mirrlees Review*, Oxford: Oxford University Press for Institute for Fiscal Studies.

— and Rabushka, A. (1995), *The Flat Tax*, Stanford, CA: Hoover Press.

Hammond, P. (1988), 'Altruism', in J. Eatwell, M. Milgate, and P. Newman (eds), *The New Palgrave: A Dictionary of Economics*, Basingstoke: Macmillan.

Hanly, M., Dargay, J., and Goodwin, P. (2002), *Review of Income and Price Elasticities and the Demand for Road Traffic*, London: Department for Transport, Local Government, and the Regions.

Harrington, W., Morgenstern, R., and Nelson, P. (1999), 'On the Accuracy of Regulatory Cost Estimates', Resources for the Future, Discussion Paper 99-18 (http://www.rff.org/rff/Documents/RFF-DP-99-18.pdf).

Hashimzade, N., Khodavaisi, H., and Myles, G. (2005), 'Tax Principles, Product Differentiation and the Nature of Competition', *International Tax and Public Finance*, **12**, 695–712.

— and Myles, G. (2007), 'Inequality and the Choice of the Personal Tax Base', *Research on Economic Inequality*, **15**, 73–97.

Hassett, K., and Hubbard, R. (2002), 'Tax Policy and Business Investment', in A. Auerbach and M. Feldstein (eds), *Handbook of Public Economics*, Volume 3, Amsterdam: Elsevier.

— and Mathur, A. (2006), 'Taxes and Wages', American Enterprise Institute, Working Paper 128 (http://www.aei.org/paper/24629).

Haufler, A., and Pflüger, M. (2004), 'International Commodity Taxation under Monopolistic Competition', *Journal of Public Economic Theory*, **6**, 445–70.

— Schjelderup, G., and Stahler, F. (2005), 'Barriers to Trade and Imperfect Competition: The Choice of Commodity Tax Base', *International Tax and Public Finance*, **12**, 281–300.

Heady, C. (1993), 'Optimal Taxation as a Guide to Tax Policy: A Survey', *Fiscal Studies*, **14**(1), 15–41.

Heckman, J. (2006), 'Skill Formation and the Economics of Investing in Disadvantaged Children', *Science*, **312**, 1900–02.

— Lochner, L., and Taber, C. (1999), 'General Equilibrium Cost Benefit Analysis of Education and Tax Policies', in G. Ranis and L. Raut (eds), *Trade Development and Growth: Essays in Honor of T. N. Srinivasan*, Amsterdam: Elsevier Publishers.

Hedges, A., and Bromley, C. (2001), *Public Attitudes towards Taxation: The Report of Research Conducted for the Fabian Commission on Taxation and Citizenship*, London: Fabian Society.

Helm, D. (2008), 'Climate-Change Policy: Why Has So Little Been Achieved?', *Oxford Review of Economic Policy*, **24**, 211–38.

Highfield, R. (2010), Commentary on J. Shaw, J. Slemrod, and J. Whiting, 'Administration and Compliance', in J. Mirrlees, S. Adam, T. Besley, R. Blundell, S. Bond, R. Chote, M. Gammie, P. Johnson, G. Myles, and J. Poterba (eds), *Dimensions of Tax Design: The Mirrlees Review*, Oxford: Oxford University Press for Institute for Fiscal Studies.

HM Revenue and Customs (2009), *Meeting Our Challenges: Departmental Autumn Performance Report 2009* (http://www.hmrc.gov.uk/about/autumn-report-2009.pdf).

— (2010a), *Child and Working Tax Credits: Error and Fraud Statistics 2008–09* (http://www.hmrc.gov.uk/stats/personal-tax-credits/cwtcredits-error0809.pdf).

— (2010b), *Child Benefit, Child Tax Credit and Working Tax Credit: Take-Up Rates 2007–08*, London (http://www.hmrc.gov.uk/stats/personal-tax-credits/cwtc-take-up2007-08.pdf).

— (2010c), *Improving the Operation of Pay As You Earn (PAYE)*, Discussion Document (http://customs.hmrc.gov.uk/channelsPortalWebApp/downloadFile?contentID=HMCE_PROD1_030623).

— (2010d), *Measuring Tax Gaps 2010*, London (http://www.hmrc.gov.uk/stats/measuring-tax-gaps-2010.htm.pdf).

— (2010e), *Improving the Operation of Pay As You Earn (PAYE): Collecting Real Time Information* (http://customs.hmrc.gov.uk/channelsPortalWebApp/downloadFile?contentID=HMCE_PROD1_030851).

— (2010f), *2009–10 Accounts*, HC 299, London: TSO (http://www.hmrc.gov.uk/about/hmrc-accs-0910.pdf).

HM Treasury (2007), *Income Tax and National Insurance Alignment: An Evidence-Based Assessment* (http://webarchive.nationalarchives.gov.uk/+/http://www.hm-treasury.gov.uk/media/B/B/pbr_csr07_incometax713.pdf).

HM Treasury (2008), 'Public Finances and the Cycle', Treasury Economic Working Paper 5 (http://webarchive.nationalarchives.gov.uk/+/http://www.hm-treasury.gov.uk/d/pbr08_publicfinances_444.pdf).

— (2009), *Pre-Budget Report 2009—Securing the Recovery: Growth and Opportunity* (http://webarchive.nationalarchives.gov.uk/+/http://www.hm-treasury.gov.uk/prebud_pbr09_index.htm).

— (2010a), *Budget 2010—Securing the Recovery*, March (http://webarchive.nationalarchives.gov.uk/+/http://www.hm-treasury.gov.uk/budget2010_documents.htm).

— (2010b), *Budget 2010*, June (http://www.hm-treasury.gov.uk/junebudget_documents.htm).

— (2011), *2011 Budget*, March (http://www.hm-treasury.gov.uk/2011budget_documents.htm).

— and Department for Education and Skills (2007), *Final Evaluation of the Saving Gateway 2 Pilot: Main Report*, Research Study conducted by Ipsos MORI and Institute for Fiscal Studies (http://webarchive.nationalarchives.gov.uk/+/http://www.hm-treasury.gov.uk/media/7/0/savings_gateway_evaluation_report.pdf).

— and HM Revenue and Customs (2010), *Impact Assessments*, London (http://cdn.hm-treasury.gov.uk/junebudget_impact_assessments.pdf).

Hoffman, L., Poddar, S., and Whalley, J. (1987), 'Taxation of Banking Services under a Consumption Type, Destination Basis VAT', *National Tax Journal*, **40**, 547–54.

Holtz-Eakin, D., Joulfaian, D., and Rosen, H. (1993), 'The Carnegie Conjecture: Some Empirical Evidence', *Quarterly Journal of Economics*, **108**, 413–35.

House of Commons Environmental Audit Committee (2006), *Pre–Budget 2005: Tax, Economic Analysis, and Climate Change*, London: The Stationery Office Limited.

House of Commons Treasury Committee (2007), *Private Equity*, Tenth Report of Session 2006–07, HC567 (http://www.publications.parliament.uk/pa/cm200607/cmselect/cmtreasy/567/56702.htm).

Hoynes, H. (2010), Commentary on M. Brewer, E. Saez, and A. Shephard, 'Means-Testing and Tax Rates on Earnings', in J. Mirrlees, S. Adam, T. Besley, R. Blundell, S. Bond, R. Chote, M. Gammie, P. Johnson, G. Myles, and J. Poterba (eds), *Dimensions of Tax Design: The Mirrlees Review*, Oxford: Oxford University Press for Institute for Fiscal Studies.

Huizinga, H. (2002), 'A European VAT on Financial Services?', *Economic Policy*, **17**, 499–534.

IFS Capital Taxes Group (1989), *Neutrality in the Taxation of Savings: An Extended Role for PEPs*, Commentary 17, London: Institute for Fiscal Studies.

— (1991), *Equity for Companies: A Corporation Tax for the 1990s*, Commentary 26, London: Institute for Fiscal Studies (http://www.ifs.org.uk/publications/1914).

Inland Revenue (1999), *Tax Credits Act 1999 and Accompanying Regulations: Regulatory Impact Assessment* (http://www.hmrc.gov.uk/ria/ria9.pdf).

Institute for Fiscal Studies (1993), *Options for 1994: The Green Budget*, Commentary 40, London: IFS (http://www.ifs.org.uk/publications/5613).

Intergovernmental Panel on Climate Change (2007), *Climate Change 2007: The Physical Science Basis—Contribution of Working Group I to the Fourth Assessment Report of the IPCC*, Cambridge: Cambridge University Press (http://www.ipcc-wg1.unibe.ch/publications/wg1-ar4/wg1-ar4.html).

International Monetary Fund (2010), *A Fair and Substantial Contribution by the Financial Sector: Final Report for the G-20* (http://www.imf.org/external/np/g20/pdf/062710b.pdf).

Jacobs, B., and Bovenberg, A. (2008), 'Optimal Taxation of Human Capital and the Earnings Function', CESifo, Working Paper 2250 (http://www.cesifo-group.de/portal/page/portal/ifoHome/b-publ/b3publwp/_wp_by_number?p_number=2250).

Johnson, P., Leicester, A., and Levell, P. (2010), *Environmental Policy since 1997*, IFS (Institute for Fiscal Studies) Briefing Note 94 (http://www.ifs.org.uk/publications/4829).

Joyce, M., Sorensen, S., and Weeken, O. (2008), 'Recent Advances in Extracting Policy-Relevant Information from Market Interest Rates', *Bank of England Quarterly Bulletin*, 2008 Q2, 157–66.

Kaldor, N. (1980), *Reports on Taxation, I*, London: Duckworth.

Kaplow, L. (1995), 'A Note on Subsidizing Gifts', *Journal of Public Economics*, **58**, 469–77.

— (1998), 'Tax Policy and Gifts', *American Economic Review: Papers and Proceedings*, **88**, 283–8.

— (2008), *The Theory of Taxation and Public Economics*, Princeton, NJ: Princeton University Press.

Kay, J. (2010), Commentary on J. Banks and P. Diamond, 'The Base for Direct Taxation', in J. Mirrlees, S. Adam, T. Besley, R. Blundell, S. Bond, R. Chote, M. Gammie, P. Johnson, G. Myles, and J. Poterba (eds), *Dimensions of Tax Design: The Mirrlees Review*, Oxford: Oxford University Press for Institute for Fiscal Studies.

— and King, M. (1990), *The British Tax System*, fifth edition, Oxford: Oxford University Press.

Keen, M., Krelove, R., and Norregaard, J. (2010), 'The Financial Activities Tax', in S. Claessens, M. Keen, and C. Pazarbasioglu (eds), *Financial Sector Taxation: The IMF's Report to the G-20 and Background Material*, Washington, DC: International Monetary Fund (http://www.imf.org/external/np/seminars/eng/2010/paris/pdf/090110.pdf).

Keen, M. and Lahiri, S. (1998), 'The Comparison between Destination and Origin Principles under Imperfect Competition', *Journal of International Economics*, **45**, 323–50.

— and Smith, S. (1996), 'The Future of Value-Added Tax in the European Union', *Economic Policy*, **23**, 375–411 and 419–20.

— — (2000), 'Viva VIVAT!', *International Tax and Public Finance*, **6**, 741–51.

— and Wildasin, D. (2004), 'Pareto-Efficient International Taxation', *American Economic Review*, **94**, 259–75.

Kenway, P. and Palmer, G. (2007), *Poverty among Ethnic Groups: How and Why Does It Differ?*, York: Joseph Rowntree Foundation (http://www.jrf.org.uk/sites/files/jrf/2042-ethnicity-relative-poverty.pdf).

Kerrigan, A. (2010), 'The Elusiveness of Neutrality: Why Is It So Difficult to Apply VAT to Financial Services?', *International VAT Monitor,* **21**, 103–12.

King, J. (2007), *The King Review of Low-Carbon Cars—Part I: The Potential for CO_2 Reduction* (http://webarchive.nationalarchives.gov.uk/+/http://www.hm-treasury.gov.uk/d/pbr_csr07_king840.pdf).

— (2008), *The King Review of Low-Carbon Cars—Part II: Recommendations for Action* (http://webarchive.nationalarchives.gov.uk/+/http://www.hm-treasury.gov.uk/d/bud08_king_1080.pdf).

Kirby, K., Winston, G., and Santiesteban, M. (2005), 'Impatience and Grades: Delay-Discount Rates Correlate Negatively with College GPA', *Learning and Individual Differences*, **15**, 213–22.

Kleven, H., Kreiner, C., and Saez, E. (2009a), 'Why Can Modern Governments Tax So Much? An Agency Model of Firms as Fiscal Intermediaries', National Bureau of Economic Research (NBER), Working Paper 15218 (http://www.nber.org/papers/w15218).

— — — (2009b), 'The Optimal Income Taxation of Couples', *Econometrica*, **77**, 537–60.

Kopczuk, W. (2005), 'Tax Bases, Tax Rates and the Elasticity of Reported Income', *Journal of Public Economics*, **89**, 2093–119.

— (2010), 'Economics of Estate Taxation: A Brief Review of Theory and Evidence', National Bureau of Economic Research (NBER), Working Paper 15741 (http://www.nber.org/papers/w15741).

— and Slemrod, J. (2001), 'The Impact of the Estate Tax on Wealth Accumulation and Avoidance Behaviour', in W. Gale, J. Hines, and J. Slemrod (eds), *Rethinking Estate and Gift Taxation*, Washington, DC: Brookings Institution Press.

KPMG (2006), *Administrative Burdens – HMRC Measurement Project—Report by Tax Area, Part 11: Employer Taxes* (http://www.hmrc.gov.uk/better-regulation/part11.pdf).

Laroque, G. (2005a), 'Indirect Taxation Is Superfluous under Separability and Taste Homogeneity: A Simple Proof', *Economics Letters*, **87**, 141–4.

— (2005b), 'Income Maintenance and Labour Force Participation', *Econometrica*, **73**, 341–76.

Leape, J. (2006), 'The London Congestion Charge', *Journal of Economic Perspectives*, **20**(4), 157–76.

Leicester, A. (2006), *The UK Tax System and the Environment*, IFS Report 68, London: Institute for Fiscal Studies (http://www.ifs.org.uk/publications/3774).

Lewis, M., and White, S. (2006), 'Inheritance Tax: What Do People Think? Evidence from Deliberative Workshops', in W. Paxton, S. White, and D. Maxwell (eds), *The Citizens' Stake: Exploring the Future of Universal Asset Policies*, Bristol: Policy Press.

Lockwood, B. (1993), 'Commodity Tax Competition under Destination and Origin Principles', *Journal of Public Economics*, **52**, 141–62.

— (2010), 'How Should Financial Intermediation Services Be Taxed?', CESifo Working Paper 3226 (http://www.cesifo-group.de/portal/pls/portal/docs/1/1185178.PDF).

— de Meza, D., and Myles, G. (1994), 'When Are Origin and Destination Regimes Equivalent?', *International Tax and Public Finance*, **1**, 5–24.

Loretz, S. (2008), 'Corporate Taxation in the OECD in a Wider Context', *Oxford Review of Economic Policy*, **24**, 639–60.

Lundberg, S., Pollack, R., and Wales, T. (1997), 'Do Husbands and Wives Pool Their Resources? Evidence from the United Kingdom Child Benefit', *Journal of Human Resources*, **32**, 463–80.

Lyons, M. (2007), *Lyons Inquiry into Local Government—Place-Shaping: A Shared Ambition for the Future of Local Government*, Final Report, London: TSO (http://www.lyonsinquiry.org.uk/index98b2.html).

Mace, B. (2010), Commentary on J. Shaw, J. Slemrod, and J. Whiting, 'Administration and Compliance', in J. Mirrlees, S. Adam, T. Besley, R. Blundell, S. Bond, R. Chote, M. Gammie, P. Johnson, G. Myles, and J. Poterba (eds), *Dimensions of Tax Design: The Mirrlees Review*, Oxford: Oxford University Press for Institute for Fiscal Studies.

Machin, S., and Van Reenen, J. (2008), 'Changes in Wage Inequality', in S. Durlauf and L. Blume (eds), *The New Palgrave Dictionary of Economics*, second edition, Basingstoke: Palgrave Macmillan.

Manning, A., and Goos, M. (2007), 'Lousy and Lovely Jobs: The Rising Polarization of Work in Britain', *Review of Economics and Statistics*, **89**, 118–33.

Martin, D. (2009), *Benefit Simplification: How, and Why, It Must Be Done*, London: Centre for Policy Studies.

McAlpine, C., and Thomas, A. (2008), *The Triggers and Barriers to the Take-Up of Working Tax Credit among Those without Dependent Children*, HMRC Research

Report 86, London: HM Revenue and Customs (http://www.hmrc.gov.uk/research/report86-full.pdf).

McLure, C. (1999), 'Protecting Dual VATs from Evasion on Cross-Border Trade: An Addendum to Bird and Gendron', mimeo, Hoover Institution.

— (2000), 'Implementing Subnational Value Added Taxes on Internal Trade: The Compensating VAT (CVAT)', *International Tax and Public Finance*, 7, 723–40.

Meade, J. (1978), *The Structure and Reform of Direct Taxation: Report of a Committee Chaired by Professor J. E. Meade for the Institute for Fiscal Studies*, London: George Allen & Unwin (http://www.ifs.org.uk/publications/3433).

Meghir, C., and Phillips, D. (2010), 'Labour Supply and Taxes', in J. Mirrlees, S. Adam, T. Besley, R. Blundell, S. Bond, R. Chote, M. Gammie, P. Johnson, G. Myles, and J. Poterba (eds), *Dimensions of Tax Design: The Mirrlees Review*, Oxford: Oxford University Press for Institute for Fiscal Studies.

Merrill, P., and Edwards, C. (1996), 'Cash-Flow Taxation of Financial Services', *National Tax Journal*, **49**, 487–500.

Meyer, B., and Sullivan, J. (2003), 'Measuring the Well-Being of the Poor Using Income and Consumption', *Journal of Human Resources*, **38** Supplement, 1180–220.

— — (2004), 'Consumption and the Poor: What We Know and What We Can Learn', ASPE-Initiated Workshop on Consumption among Low-Income Families.

Mirrlees, J. (1971), 'The Theory of Optimal Income Taxation', *Review of Economic Studies*, **38**, 175–208.

— Adam, S., Besley, T., Blundell, R., Bond, S., Chote, R., Gammie, M., Johnson, P., Myles, G., and Poterba, J. (eds) (2010), *Dimensions of Tax Design: The Mirrlees Review*, Oxford: Oxford University Press for Institute for Fiscal Studies.

Muellbauer, J. (2005), 'Property Taxation and the Economy', in D. Maxwell and A. Vigor (eds), *Time for Land Value Tax?*, London: Institute for Public Policy Research (IPPR).

Myles, G. (1995), *Public Economics*, Cambridge: Cambridge University Press.

Newbery, D. (2003), 'Sectoral Dimensions of Sustainable Development: Energy and Transport', in United Nations Economic Commission for Europe, *Economic Survey of Europe 2* (http://www.unece.org/ead/sem/sem2003/papers/newbery.pdf).

— (2005), 'Road User and Congestion Charges', in S. Cnossen (ed.), *Theory and Practice of Excise Taxation: Smoking, Drinking, Gambling, Polluting, and Driving*, Oxford: Oxford University Press.

— Santos, G. (1999), 'Road Taxes, Road User Charges and Earmarking', *Fiscal Studies*, **20**, 103–32.

Oates, W., and Schwab, R. (1997), 'The Impact of Urban Land Taxation: The Pittsburgh Experience', *National Tax Journal*, **50**, 1–21.

OECD (2006), *The Political Economy of Environmentally Related Taxes*, Paris: Organization for Economic Cooperation and Development.

— (2011), *Consumption Tax Trends 2010*, Paris: Organization for Economic Cooperation and Development.

Office for Budget Responsibility (2011), *Economic and Fiscal Outlook: March 2011*, Cm. 8036 (http://budgetresponsibility.independent.gov.uk/wordpress/docs/economic_and_fiscal_outlook_23032011.pdf).

Office for National Statistics (2009), *Wealth in Great Britain: Main Results from the Wealth and Assets Survey 2006/08* (http://www.statistics.gov.uk/downloads/theme_economy/wealth-assets-2006-2008/Wealth_in_GB_2006_2008.pdf).

Ofgem (2009), *Updated: Household Energy Bills Explained*, Factsheet 81, London: Office of the Gas and Electricity Markets (http://www.ofgem.gov.uk/Media/FactSheets/Documents1/updatedhouseholdbills09.pdf).

Parker, A., and Fischhoff, B. (2005), 'Decision-Making Competence: External Validation through an Individual-Differences Approach', *Journal of Behavioral Decision Making*, **18**, 1–27.

Parry, I., and Small, K. (2005), 'Does Britain or the United States Have the Right Gasoline Tax?', *American Economic Review*, **95**, 1276–89.

Pestieau, P. (2010), Commentary on J. Banks and P. Diamond, 'The Base for Direct Taxation', in J. Mirrlees, S. Adam, T. Besley, R. Blundell, S. Bond, R. Chote, M. Gammie, P. Johnson, G. Myles, and J. Poterba (eds), *Dimensions of Tax Design: The Mirrlees Review*, Oxford: Oxford University Press for Institute for Fiscal Studies.

Pigou, A. (1920), *The Economics of Welfare*, London: Macmillan.

Poddar, S. (2003), 'Consumption Taxes: The Role of the Value-Added Tax', in P. Honohan (ed.), *Taxation of Financial Intermediation: Theory and Practice for Emerging Economies*, Washington, DC: World Bank.

— (2007), 'VAT on Financial Services: Searching for a Workable Compromise', in R. Krever and D. White (eds), *GST in Retrospect and Prospect*, Wellington: Thomson Brookers.

— and English, M. (1997), 'Taxation of Financial Services under a Value-Added Tax: Applying the Cash-Flow Method', *National Tax Journal*, **50**, 89–111.

Poterba, J. (2002), 'Taxation, Risk-Taking, and Household Portfolio Behavior', in A. Auerbach and M. Feldstein (eds), *Handbook of Public Economics*, Volume 3, Amsterdam: Elsevier.

Prabhakar, R. (2008), 'Wealth Taxes: Stories, Metaphors and Public Attitudes', *Political Quarterly*, **79**, 172–8.

Radalj, K., and McAleer, M. (2005), 'Speculation and Destabilisation', *Mathematics and Computers in Simulation*, **69**, 151–61.

Radulescu, D., and Stimmelmayr, M. (2007), 'ACE versus CBIT: Which Is Better for Investment and Welfare?', *CESifo Economic Studies*, **53**, 294–328.

Reeves, R. (2007), *John Stuart Mill: Victorian Firebrand*, London: Atlantic Books.

Rhys Williams, J. (1943), *Something to Look Forward to: A Suggestion for a New Social Contract*, London: MacDonald.

Roberts, M., and Spence, M. (1976), 'Effluent Charges and Licenses under Uncertainty', *Journal of Public Economics*, **5**, 193–208.

Rosen, H. (1977), 'Is It Time to Abandon Joint Filing?', *National Tax Journal*, **30**, 423–8.

Rowlingson, K., and Mackay, S. (2005), *Attitudes to Inheritance in Britain*, Bristol: Policy Press.

Saez, E. (2002), 'Optimal Income Transfer Programs: Intensive versus Extensive Labor Supply Responses', *Quarterly Journal of Economics*, **117**, 1039–73.

Sainsbury, R., and Stanley, K. (2007), *One for All: Active Welfare and the Single Working-Age Benefit*, London: Institute for Public Policy Research (http://www.ippr.org/publications/55/1588/one-for-all-active-welfare-and-the-single-working-age-benefit).

Sandford, C., Godwin, M., and Hardwick, P. (1989), *Administrative and Compliance Costs of Taxation*, Bath: Fiscal Publications.

Sandmo, A. (1976), 'Direct versus Indirect Pigouvian Taxation', *European Economic Review*, **7**, 337–49.

Sansom, T., Nash, C., Mackie, P., Shires, J., and Watkiss, P. (2001), *Surface Transport Costs and Charges: Great Britain 1998*, Leeds: Institute for Transport Studies.

Schneider, F., and Enste, D. (2000), 'Shadow Economy: Size, Causes, and Consequences', *Journal of Economic Literature*, **38**, 77–114.

Select Committee on Work and Pensions (2007), *Seventh Report*, Session 2006–07, HC 463 (http://www.publications.parliament.uk/pa/cm200607/cmselect/cmworpen/463/46302.htm).

Shaw, J., Slemrod, J., and Whiting, J. (2010), 'Administration and Compliance', in J. Mirrlees, S. Adam, T. Besley, R. Blundell, S. Bond, R. Chote, M. Gammie, P. Johnson, G. Myles, and J. Poterba (eds), *Dimensions of Tax Design: The Mirrlees Review*, Oxford: Oxford University Press for Institute for Fiscal Studies.

Slemrod, J. (2004), 'Small Business and the Tax System', in H. Aaron and J. Slemrod (eds), *The Crisis in Tax Administration*, Washington, DC: Brookings Institution Press.

— (2006), 'Taxation and Big Brother: Information, Personalisation and Privacy in 21st Century Tax Policy', *Fiscal Studies*, **27**, 1–15.

— and Kopczuk, W. (2002), 'The Optimal Elasticity of Taxable Income', *Journal of Public Economics*, **84**, 91–112.

Society of Motor Manufacturers and Traders (2010), *New Car CO_2 Report 2010* (https://www.smmt.co.uk/shop/new-car-co2-report-2010-2/).

Sørensen, P. (2005), 'Neutral Taxation of Shareholder Income', *International Tax and Public Finance*, **12**, 777–801.

— (2007), 'The Theory of Optimal Taxation: What Is the Policy Relevance?', *International Tax and Public Finance*, **14**, 383–406.

— (2009), 'Dual Income Taxes: A Nordic Tax System', paper prepared for the conference on *New Zealand Tax Reform—Where to Next?*.

Stern, N. (2006), *Stern Review: The Economics of Climate Change*, Cambridge: Cambridge University Press.

— (2008), 'The Economics of Climate Change', *American Economic Review: Papers and Proceedings*, **98**, 1–37.

— (2009), *The Global Deal: Climate Change and the Creation of a New Era of Progress and Prosperity*, New York: Public Affairs.

Stiglitz, J. (1998), 'Using Tax Policy to Curb Speculative Short-Term Trading', *Journal of Financial Services Research*, **3**, 101–15.

Taylor, C., Denham, M., Baron, R., and Allum, A. (2010), *Welfare Reform in Tough Fiscal Times: Creating a Better and Cheaper Benefits System*, London: Taxpayers' Alliance (http://www.taxpayersalliance.com/welfarereform.pdf).

Thaler, R., and Shefrin, H. (1981), 'An Economic Theory of Self-Control', *Journal of Political Economy*, **89**, 392–406.

Tobin, J. (1970), 'On Limiting the Domain of Inequality', *Journal of Law and Economics*, **13**, 263–77.

— (1978), 'A Proposal for International Monetary Reform', *Eastern Economic Journal*, **4**, 153–9.

Tuomala, M. (1990), 'Optimal Income Taxation and Redistribution', Oxford: Clarendon Press.

Turley, C., and Thomas, A. (2006), *Housing Benefit and Council Tax Benefit as In-Work Benefits; Claimants' and Advisors' Knowledge, Attitudes and Experiences*, Department for Work and Pensions Research Report 383, Leeds: CDS (http://research.dwp.gov.uk/asd/asd5/rports2005-2006/rrep383.pdf).

US Department of the Treasury (1992), *Integration of the Individual and Corporate Tax Systems: Taxing Business Income Once*, Washington, DC: US Government Printing Office.

Valuation Office Agency (2009), *Property Market Report January 2009* (http://webarchive.nationalarchives.gov.uk/+/http://www.voa.gov.uk/publications/property_market_report/pmr-jan-09/index.htm).

— (2010), *Annual Report and Account 2009–10* (http://www.voa.gov.uk/corporate/_downloads/pdf/annualReport_2009_10.pdf).

Varsano, R. (2000), 'Sub-National Taxation and Treatment of Interstate Trade in Brazil: Problems and a Proposed Solution', in S. Burki, F. Eid, M. Freire, V. Vergara, and G. Perry (eds), *Decentralization and Accountability of the Public*

Sector, Proceedings of the Annual World Bank Conference on Development in Latin America and the Caribbean—1999, Washington, DC: World Bank.

Vickrey, W. (1999), 'Simplification, Progression, and a Level Playing Field', in K. Wenzer (ed.), *Land-Value Taxation: The Equitable and Efficient Source of Public Finance*, Armonk, NY: M. E. Sharpe.

Viscusi, W. (1995), 'Carcinogen Regulation: Risk Characteristics and the Synthetic Risk Bias', *American Economic Review*, **85**, 50–4.

Wakefield, M. (2009), 'How Much Do We Tax the Return to Saving?', IFS (Institute for Fiscal Studies) Briefing Note 82 (http://www.ifs.org.uk/publications/4467).

Watkiss, P., and Downing, T. (2008), 'The Social Cost of Carbon: Valuation Estimates and Their Use in UK Policy', *Integrated Assessment*, **8**, 85–105.

Weil, D. (1994), 'The Saving of the Elderly in Micro and Macro Data', *Quarterly Journal of Economics*, **109**, 55–81.

Weitzman, M. (1974), 'Prices versus Quantities', *Review of Economic Studies*, **41**, 477–91.

Zee, H. (2006), 'VAT Treatment of Financial Services: A Primer on Conceptual Issues and Country Practices', *Intertax*, **34**, 458–74.

Index

Printed and bound by CPI Group (UK) Ltd, Croydon, CR0 4YY